What Christian could bear to part with Paul's letter to the Ephesians? The church is indebted to this epistle for its stunning and captivating portrait of our Triune God and his saving love for his people. We may be grateful that Richard D. Phillips, a seasoned and skilled preacher of the Word of God, has gifted the church with this expository commentary on this precious letter. Phillips' exposition is faithful to the text, theologically astute, and full of application to the reader. Whether you have never read this letter or have read it dozens of times, Phillips' *Ephesians* will help you to see in new ways the riches and the depths of the gospel of Jesus Christ.

—Guy Prentiss Waters
James M. Baird, Jr. Professor of New Testament
Reformed Theological Seminary
Charlotte, North Carolina

By guiding readers through the wide range of issues covered in Ephesians, Richard Phillips has provided us with a mini-course in theology. Readers will benefit not only from the solid biblical exegesis, but also from the insightful and moving illustrations that bring each chapter to life. Here is a worthy resource to help readers mine the depths of God's Word in readable and practical fashion.

—Brandon D. Crowe
Associate Professor of New Testament
Westminster Theological Seminary
Philadelphia, Pennsylvania

Solidly orthodox and Reformed. Phillips gives theological arguments and devotional suggestions for the pastor presenting the great truths of Ephesians to a congregation. This commentary is a must if preaching or teaching through Ephesians. What a joy to read!

—Robert J. Cara
Provost and Chief Academic Officer, RTS System
Hugh and Sallie Reaves Professor of New Testament
Reformed Theological Seminary
Charlotte, North Carolina

A rich and insightful commentary on Paul's most theologically comprehensive letter. Dr. Phillips' books are self-recommendable; he has gained a reputation for accuracy of exegesis, profundity of thought, and a fluency of style that reflects a lifetime of expository preaching and application. With sureness of foot, and a steady hand, this book addresses culturally sensitive areas of modern life (marriage, family, work) with the finesse of a pastor-theologian. Easily rises to the top of recommendable books on Ephesians.

—Derek W. H. Thomas
Senior Minister, First Presbyterian Church, Columbia SC
Robert Strong Professor of Systematic and Practical Theology, RTS Atlanta

EPHESIANS

A MENTOR EXPOSITORY COMMENTARY

RICHARD D. PHILLIPS

MENTOR

Unless otherwise indicated Scripture quotations are taken from *The Holy Bible, English Standard Version*, copyright © 2001 by Crossway Bibles, a division of Good News Publishers. Used by permission. All rights reserved. ESV Text Edition: 2007.

Scripture quotations marked NIV are taken from *The Holy Bible, New International Version*®. NIV®. Copyright©1973, 1978, 1984 by International Bible Society. Used by permission of Zondervan. All rights reserved.

Scripture quotations marked NKJV are taken from *The New King James Version*. Copyright © 1982 by Thomas Nelson, Inc. Used by permission. All rights reserved.

Scripture quotations marked KJV are taken from *The King James Version*.

Richard D. Phillips graduated from Westminster Theological Seminary in Philadelphia, PA and was part of the pastoral staff of Tenth Presbyterian Church of Philadelphia, PA. There, Rick was mentored by the well-known Bible teacher, Dr. James Montgomery Boice, and began his calling as a weekly preacher of God's Word. After serving at Tenth Presbyterian from 1995-2002, Dr. Phillips accepted the call to be Senior Minister of First Presbyterian Church of Coral Springs, Florida. After five years there, he moved to Greenville to serve as Senior Minister at Second Presbyterian Church in Greenville, South Carolina in 2007.

Rick is married to Sharon and they have five children: Hannah, Matthew, Jonathan, Ellie and Lydia.

Copyright © Richard D. Phillips 2016

ISBN 978-1-78191-317-8

in the
Mentor Imprint
by
Christian Focus Publications
Geanies House, Fearn, Ross-shire
IV20 1TW, Scotland
www.christianfocus.com

Cover design by Daniel van Straaten
Printed by Bell and Bain, Glasgow

All rights reserved. No part of this publication may be reproduced, stored in a retrieval system, or transmitted, in any form, by any means, electronic, mechanical, photocopying, recording or otherwise without the prior permission of the publisher or a license permitting restricted copying. In the U.K. such licenses are issued by the Copyright Licensing Agency, Saffron House, 6-10 Kirby Street, London, EC1 8TS www.cla.co.uk.

Contents

1. Grace and Peace to You
   Ephesians 1:1–2   1

2. What Is a Christian?
   Ephesians 1:1   9

3. Blessing for Blessing
   Ephesians 1:3   17

4. Chosen in Christ
   Ephesians 1:4   23

5. Predestined as Sons
   Ephesians 1:5   29

6. To the Glory of His Grace
   Ephesians 1:6   37

7. Redemption in Christ
   Ephesians 1:7–8   43

8. Through His Blood
   Ephesians 1:7   51

9. The Salvation Mystery
   Ephesians 1:9–10   59

10. The Glorious Plan of God
    Ephesians 1:11–13   67

11. Marked with a Seal
    Ephesians 1:13   75

12. The Deposit of Our Inheritance
    Ephesians 1:14   83

13. Paul's Prayer for the Church
    Ephesians 1:15–17   91

14. Knowing God
    Ephesians 1:17   99

15. The Three 'What's'
    Ephesians 1:18–20   107

16. Christ Exalted
    Ephesians 1:20–23   115

17. Prayer and the Sovereignty of God
    Ephesians 1:15–23   123

18. Dead in Sin
    Ephesians 2:1–3   131

19. The World, the Flesh, & the Devil
    Ephesians 2:1–3   139

20. But God
    Ephesians 2:4   147

21. Spiritual Resurrection
    Ephesians 2:4–5   155

22. Together with Christ
    Ephesians 2:5–6   163

23 The Glory of God in Salvation
    Ephesians 2:7   171

24 By Grace, through Faith
    Ephesians 2:8–9   177

25 God's Workmanship
    Ephesians 2:10   185

26 Without Christ
    Ephesians 2:11–12   191

27 Brought Near to God
    Ephesians 2:13   197

28 Christ Our Peace
    Ephesians 2:14   203

29 The New Humanity
    Ephesians 2:14–16   211

30 Access to the Father
    Ephesians 2:17–18   219

31 Citizens and Children
    Ephesians 2:19   225

32 A Holy Temple
    Ephesians 2:20–22   233

33 A Prisoner of Christ
    Ephesians 3:1   241

34 A Mystery Revealed
    Ephesians 3:2–7   249

35 Unsearchable Riches
    Ephesians 3:7–9   257

36 The Manifold Wisdom of God
    Ephesians 3:9–13   265

37 Strengthened with Power
    Ephesians 3:14–16   273

38 Christ in You
    Ephesians 3:17   281

39 The Measure of Christ's Love
    Ephesians 3:17–19   287

40 The Fullness of God
    Ephesians 3:19   293

41 Far More Abundantly
    Ephesians 3:20–21   301

42 A Worthy Life
    Ephesians 4:1–2   307

43 Spiritual Unity
    Ephesians 4:3–4   315

44 One in the Lord
    Ephesians 4:5–6   321

45 Gifts from on High
    Ephesians 4:7–10   327

46 Building the Church
    Ephesians 4:11–12   333

47 Growth and Maturity
    Ephesians 4:13–15   339

48 Growing Up Together
    Ephesians 4:15–16   345

49 Darkened and Lost
    Ephesians 4:17–19   351

50 In the School of Christ
    Ephesians 4:20–29   357

51 Grieving the Holy Spirit
    Ephesians 4:30   363

52 Imitators of God
    Ephesians 4:31–5:2   369

53 Sexual Purity
    Ephesians 5:3–7   375

54 Children of Light
    Ephesians 5:8–14   383

Contents

55 Redeeming the Time
   Ephesians 5:15–17   389

56 True Spirituality
   Ephesians 5:18–21   395

57 Wives Submitting to Husbands
   Ephesians 5:22–24   401

58 Husbands Loving Wives
   Ephesians 5:25–35   409

59 In Discipline and Instruction
   Ephesians 6:1–4   417

60 Faith at Work
   Ephesians 6:5–9   423

61 Spiritual Warfare
   Ephesians 6:10–13   429

62 The Armor of God
   Ephesians 6:14–15   437

63 The Weaponry of Our Warfare
   Ephesians 6:16–17   443

64 Prayer: Our Secret Weapon
   Ephesians 6:18–20   449

65 Grace and Peace Be with You
   Ephesians 6:21–24   455

Endnotes   461

Subject Index   471

Scripture Index   485

To Philip Graham Ryken

in thanks for twenty years of friendship and shared ministry

and

to the Beloved,
in whom the Father has blessed us with every spiritual blessing
(Eph. 1:3-6).

1

Grace and Peace to You

Ephesians 1:1–2

Paul's Epistle to the Ephesians has been celebrated with the highest possible praise. Samuel Taylor Coleridge called it 'the divinest composition of man.'[1] It has likewise been described as 'the crown of St. Paul's writings' and 'the Queen of the Epistles.' John Mackay, former President of Princeton Theological Seminary, described Ephesians as the 'greatest,' the 'maturest,' and 'for our time the most relevant of all Paul's works. For here is the distilled essence of the Christian religion, the most authoritative and most consummate compendium of our holy Christian faith.' Recounting his own conversion through the reading of this letter, Mackay says, 'I saw a new world…everything was new…I had a new outlook, new experiences, new attitudes to other people. I loved God. Jesus Christ became the center of everything…I had been "quickened"; I was really alive.'[2] This aptly describes what Ephesians is all about.

Realizing the profundity of this book may make us apprehensive. We should realize, however, that though Ephesians is profound it is marked by a simple clarity. James Montgomery Boice wrote: 'If Ephesians *is* profound, it is so not for the mysterious nature of its unfathomable deep secrets, but for the clear way it presents the most basic Christian truths…What is the appeal of this book? In my judgment it is just this: it presents the basic doctrines of Christianity comprehensively, clearly, practically, and winsomely.'[3] What makes Ephesians so beloved and valuable is not its genius or complexity but its clear and thorough teaching of the doctrines of salvation, of the church, and of the Christian life.

Paul, an Apostle

Following the custom of his day, Paul began this letter with his name and office: 'Paul, an apostle of Christ Jesus.' Paul wrote thirteen biblical books, comprising just under one quarter of the New Testament. Apart from Jesus Christ, it is hard to think of anyone who left so great a mark on the history of the Christian church.

F. F. Bruce began his study of Paul's life by frankly admitting his love for the great apostle. He extolled Paul for 'the attractive warmth of his personality, his intellectual stature, the exhilarating release effected by his gospel of redeeming grace, the dynamism with which he propagated that gospel throughout the world.'[4] Paul is best known for the depth and coherence of his theological writings, yet he 'was first and foremost a missionary...who wrote letters to churches in order to sustain his converts in their newfound faith.'[5]

Paul describes himself simply as 'an apostle of Jesus Christ.' The word *apostle* means 'one who is sent,' or simply, 'messenger.' In the New Testament era, apostles were missionaries who traveled about preaching the gospel and forming churches. Most importantly—and surely Paul intends to emphasize this—apostles bore the authority of Christ in their teaching and rule, an authority granted them by the risen and exalted Lord Jesus himself. Martyn Lloyd-Jones defines an apostle as 'one chosen and sent with a special mission as the fully authorized representative of the sender.'[6] Peter O'Brien writes, 'As an apostle he has the authority to proclaim the gospel in both oral and written form, as well as to establish and build up churches.'[7]

The apostles include the original twelve disciples of Jesus, with Matthias added to replace the betrayer Judas Iscariot. Acts 1:22 establishes the qualification that an apostle must have been personally discipled by Jesus and personally witnessed the resurrection. Paul fulfilled these criteria by his conversion experience on the Damascus Road, when he was also commissioned by the Lord. He was not one of the original disciples, but in Galatians 2:1–10 Paul recounts being received by them and accepted as apostle to the Gentiles. What Jesus said to the twelve just before his ascension into heaven, equally applies to Paul, 'You will receive power...You will be my witnesses' (Acts 1:8). He asserts his authority as an apostle in all of his writings, presenting his credentials and drawing attention to the official character of his writing.

Paul adds that he is an apostle of Christ 'by the will of God.' This was not a job Paul had sought and worked toward on his own. He was called by God and equipped by God's grace. It is on this basis that his teaching is to be received, not because of his own native genius and persuasive power, but in submission to God's will and Christ's commission. This contrast between divine and human authority was important to Paul; the opening words of Galatians work this out even more clearly: 'Paul, an apostle—not from men nor through man, but through Jesus Christ and God the Father' (Gal. 1:1). This means that whatever we find taught in this letter—and there are some challenging truths in Ephesians—comes from God himself and must be accepted in obedience to him.

Verse 1 presents the first of four times in chapter 1 that Paul speaks of 'the will of God.' This directs us right from the start to one of the great themes that runs through this epistle: the sovereignty of God. Ephesians tells us from start to finish that the gospel and Christianity are under the sovereign control of God. God sovereignly accomplished our redemption through Jesus Christ; by his sovereign will he sent apostles to preach the gospel; he sovereignly chose us from before creation to be saved; and at the time of his choosing he will sovereignly consummate and complete his redemptive plan to the glory of his name. Salvation is all a matter of God's sovereignty; we encounter this truth in the first verse of the book, just as we will find it standing out in glory all through Ephesians.

AUTHORSHIP AND DESTINATION

Scholars have posed two questions that are important to our study of Ephesians. The first has to do with whether or not Paul actually wrote the letter. Indeed, it is surprising to find that the majority of biblical scholars today deny Paul's authorship, most of them arguing that some brilliant assistant wrote Ephesians many years after Paul died, falsely using his name for credibility.

Those who deny Paul's authorship point out the impersonal character of Ephesians, which seems odd in a letter written to a church he had led for two and a half years. This is explained when we realize that Ephesians was written as a theological tract for wider circulation. Scholars also cite a supposed difference in language and style between Ephesians and other known Pauline letters. Forty-one words appear only here and eighty-four more are found in the New Testament but not elsewhere in Paul. Yet other letters have their own distinctive style and vocabulary, and, as William Barclay observes, 'It would be ridiculous to demand that a man with a mind like Paul's should never add to his vocabulary and should always express himself in the same way.'[8] Others note the similarity between Colossians and Ephesians, arguing that the writer of Ephesians used this other Pauline letter as his model. It is hard to see, however, how this similarity argues against rather than for Paul as the author of Ephesians.

Most importantly, this letter in God's Word explicitly claims to come from the apostle Paul. For another writer to have used his name involves a great deal of fraud, especially since he asks for the readers to pray for his—Paul's—ministry. Such a situation is inconceivable within a biblical view of the divine inspiration of Scripture, and as Charles Hodge observed, Ephesians 'reveals itself as the work of the Holy Ghost as clearly as the stars declare their maker to be God.'[9] The early church vigorously excluded pseudonymous writings from the canon, punishing those who attempted to pass off their own writings as apostolic. Yet the early church universally accepted Ephesians as Pauline, and objections to the contrary speak more eloquently against the state of scholarship today than they do about the authorship of this great letter.[10]

The second issue has to do with the recipients of Ephesians. The problem is that many early manuscripts do not contain the words 'in Ephesus' in verse 1. This, combined with the impersonal style, argues that Paul did not write this letter specifically to the church in Ephesus. The best explanation is that Paul wrote Ephesians as a circular letter or tract, which he sent with Colossians for the general benefit of the churches in western Asia Minor. Since his messenger, Tychicus (see Eph. 6:21 and Col. 4:8), would travel through Ephesus and up the Lycus Valley, Paul wrote Ephesians for the benefit of the churches along the way. This also explains the similarity between Ephesians and Colossians.

Obviously, some mystery remains, but we can be sure that Paul the apostle wrote Ephesians, along with Colossians, for the benefit of churches in western Asia Minor, probably in the early 60's during his first imprisonment at Rome.

Peace from God

Paul concludes his greeting with words found at the beginning of almost all of his letters: 'Grace and peace to you from God our Father and the Lord Jesus Christ.' Paul always interjects theology into his greetings, and here he puts before us two main themes of this letter: grace and peace. This expression serves as a table of contents: chapters 1–3 extol the greatness of God's grace, while chapters 4–6 call us to the life of peace. Martyn Lloyd-Jones writes: 'Grace is the beginning of our faith; peace is the end of our faith. Grace is the fountain, the spring, the source…But what does the Christian life mean, what is it meant to produce? The answer is "peace."'[11]

Before looking at the meaning of grace, let us first consider the peace that comes from God and the Lord Jesus Christ. The first thing we need to understand is what the Bible means by peace versus how it is normally used today. For people today, peace is simply the absence of strife, of war, or of conflict. We sign peace treaties and the only effect is that the actual fighting comes to a halt. The hatred is still there, the causes of strife are unrelieved, and no sense of unity arises, much less actual love. Yet we celebrate such things as peace. The Bible, however, ridicules such an idea. The prophet cried, '"Peace, peace," they say, when there is no peace' (Jer. 6:14).

The biblical idea of peace is so very different. Here, the idea comes from the Hebrew word *shalom*, the state of blessedness and harmony. Leon Morris comments, 'Paul…is not saying here that he trusts that the Ephesian believers will not find themselves caught up in a war. He is speaking about the deep and abiding peace that comes when people are right with God.'[12] This is what Jesus meant when he told his disciples, 'Peace I leave with you, my peace I give unto you; not as the world gives do I give to you' (John 14:27).

Peace is the great need of mankind. Our problem is that there is no peace because of sin. This pertains first to our relationship with God. Paul writes in Romans 8:7 that 'the sinful mind is hostile to God. It does not submit to God's law, nor can it do so.' Paul begins Ephesians 2 by expounding this problem in detail, speaking of man's sinfully corrupt nature and unwitting service to the devil. Lloyd-Jones explains, 'Man by nature, as he is born into this world, is a hater of God…he fights God, he is an enemy…everything in him by nature is utterly opposed to God.'[13] This is the teaching of Ephesians. People will deny this; perhaps you do. But man in sin is always a rebel to God and his law.

The inevitable result of sin is that God is alienated from us in return. In Ephesians 2:3 Paul says that sinful men and women are 'by nature children of wrath.' The peace of the gospel reconciles such people to God through Jesus Christ. This is the great problem of the world—man is at enmity with God and under God's curse in return. The gospel solution provides peace with God and full restoration.

The bulk of Ephesians 1 is given to praising God for how he solves the problem of sin in granting us peace with himself. First is God's electing grace, by which he ordained our salvation in eternity past. Then God sent his Son, Jesus, to remove our sin and accomplish our forgiveness by dying in our place on the cross. Verse 5 adds that God adopts us as his children through Jesus Christ. This is real peace with God: not just the removal of conflict and not just a piece of paper saying there will be no fighting for a while, but a righteous and loving relationship with God. In Ephesians 1:2 Paul speaks of peace from 'God our Father and the Lord Jesus Christ.' Paul longs for his readers to know this peace through his gospel message, as believers are brought into God's family as beloved children and receive power to live in peace under the lordship of Jesus Christ.

The peace of salvation comes through faith in Jesus Christ: as Paul writes in Ephesians 2:14, 'He himself is our peace.' Do you know peace with God? Are you able to say you know his favor and love? Do you love him in return, longing to do his will? The only way you can enjoy this peace is by coming to God through faith in Christ, confessing your sin, and trusting Christ's death and resurrection life, all of which were given so that you might have peace with God.

But Paul's vision is not limited to peace between heaven and earth; he also sees peace reigning in the place of the turmoil of this world. What about peace among the nations—isn't this the very thing our age is clamoring for? The last decades of world history have revealed continual strife and deadly violence not only on the battlefield but in the streets of the Middle East, Africa, Europe, and even America. There is no peace upon the earth, and man's attempts to produce it have all failed. Think, too, about our own relationships: our families, our workplaces, our neighborhoods. Is there not division of every kind: racial, economic, ethnic, regional, and professional strife? What is the answer? The answer is not training, not compulsion, and not treaties; the problem is simply too deep for these solutions. Man does not love God, and neither does he love his neighbor. But the gospel declared in Ephesians declares peace *with* God and peace *from* God.

Watchman Nee tells of a Chinese Christian who had his rice field on a hill. Every day he had to hand-work a water wheel to lift water up from the irrigation stream at the base of the hill. His neighbor had two fields below his, and one night he made a hole in the wall that separated their property so that the Christian's water would all drain down into his fields. The Christian was understandably angry, but wanting to honor God he took the matter to his church. There, his fellow Christians reasoned that if he simply retaliated for this hostile act, he would miss a chance to bear testimony to the peace of Jesus Christ. Following their counsel, the next day the Christian went down to the water wheel and pumped water into his neighbor's two fields. Only then, working late into the day, did he fill his own fields. When he was done, his neighbor came out to ask why he would act in such kindness, which ultimately led to the man's conversion to faith in Christ.[14] The Christian had peace with God, and he extended that peace to his fellow sinful man; we need to do the same, and especially to live in peace with our brothers and sisters in the family of God.

Men and women are at war not just with God and with others, but also within themselves. Isaiah 57:20–21 says, 'The wicked are like the tossing sea, for it cannot be quiet, and its waters toss up mire and dirt. "There is no peace," says my God, "for the wicked."' Man in sin is pulled apart, with an internal conflict we ourselves cannot subdue. On the one hand, sin makes us slaves of the world, the devil, and the cravings of the flesh. On the other hand, man cannot escape his knowledge of God and need for him. Isaiah put it exactly right—we are caught between two great influences like the churning sea with the earth and the moon each pulling it—our flesh desiring sin and our consciences accusing us before God—with no peace of mind, no rest of spirit, and no satisfaction of heart. Like the ocean when it meets the shore, our waves churn up mire and muck.

Do you know something about this? We are made by God in such a way that we can only have peace within ourselves when we have peace with him. You will never have peace in rebellion against God, by doing things your own way. Peace comes through submission to the Almighty, by faith in the Savior who removes the hostility and sends God's Spirit of peace. This is why Paul is able to tell Christians, even in the midst of the greatest turmoil this life can bring, in the face of death and sorrow, that through faith in Christ they may have God's peace. This is why Christians can face the terrible news of a fatal disease, the loss of a job, or persecution from the world. Paul says, 'In everything, by prayer and supplication, with thanksgiving, let your requests be made known to God. And the peace of God, which surpasses all understanding, will guard your hearts and your minds in Christ Jesus' (Phil. 4:6–7).

Grace to You

How are we to have peace with God and thus enjoy the peace of God? The answer is by God's grace. Can we repair our broken relationship with God? Can we perform works to appease him? No! Nothing we can ever do removes the guilt of our past sins, and nothing we do now is free from sinful motives and corruption. In short, we cannot save ourselves and God must therefore save us. This is the true problem Paul sets before us in Ephesians. Chapter 2 explores our need, first drawing out the full extent of our problem in sin and then pointing to our only hope in the grace of God, 'who is rich in mercy' (Eph. 2:4, NIV).

Grace is, first, an *attribute* of God: he is gracious. A. W. Tozer writes: 'Grace is the good pleasure of God that inclines Him to bestow benefits upon the undeserving. It is a self-existent principle inherent in the divine nature and appears to us as a self-caused propensity to pity the wretched, spare the guilty, welcome the outcast, and bring into favor those who were before under just disapprobation.'[15]

Grace also describes God's *way* of salvation, often defined as God's unmerited favor. This expression is true, except it does not go far enough. Grace is God's favor to us when we have merited the opposite. We have earned his hatred, wrath, and condemnation. Yet he causes us to be forgiven and made his precious children, bringing us into his household and lavishing us with every good thing. God gives that which is most precious to himself—his only Son—that he might remove our guilt on the cross, and by his blood reconcile us to God. This is the measure of God's grace, as taught in Ephesians. Paul writes: 'I pray that you…may have power…to grasp how wide and long and high and deep is the love of Christ' (Eph. 3:16-18). We are saved by God's grace alone, he says in Ephesians 2:8, not by our works but by God's gift; not because we loved him, for we have not loved God, but because he loved us and sent his Son to bear our sins and be our peace. God's grace finds expression in an unstoppable plan for our salvation, which Paul explains in Ephesians chapter 1. God's grace ordains our salvation, his Son, Jesus, accomplishes our salvation, and the Holy Spirit applies salvation to us through the gift of faith. A Christian may utterly rely on God's grace, which is, as Paul sums up in verse 14, 'to the praise of his glory.'

Finally, grace is God's *power* working in us for newness of life. This, too, Paul greatly desires that we should learn in Ephesians. His prayer at the end of chapter 1 makes this clear. He prays that 'having the eyes of your hearts enlightened,…you may know…what is the immeasurable greatness of his power toward us who believe, according to the working of his great might that he worked in Christ when he raised him from the dead' (Eph. 1:18-20). God has graciously given resurrection power for us to live as children of light, a redeemed people living holy lives to the praise of his name. Does it sound impossible that you would live differently, that you would lead a holy life? Jesus said, 'with God all things are possible ' (Matt. 19:26), because of the power of his grace working in our lives.

The grace of God was famously exhibited in the salvation of John Newton, the eighteenth century pastor who wrote the hymn *Amazing Grace*. Newton was raised in a Christian home, but his parents died when he was only six and he was sent to live with a harsh, unbelieving relative. Fleeing abuse, Newton ran away to sea and as a sailor he fell into gross sin. After a while he deserted to live in one of the worst areas of Africa because there he could, as he recounts, 'sin his full.'

During one voyage home to Scotland, Newton's ship was struck by a storm and began to sink. Newton was sent down into the pitch blackness of the hold to work the pump with the slaves. For days on end he pumped, and in the darkness his mind recalled the Bible verses his mother had taught him as a child. They spoke of God's grace and the cross where the Savior died for his forgiveness. The memory of these verses began working in Newton's life until, after leaving the ship, he repented, found forgiveness through Jesus, and went on to be one of the most powerful gospel preachers of his generation.

His was a story of grace. Newton was a vile sinner, but he saw that God sent his Son to die for him and that by God's free grace he could be forgiven. He realized that all of his life was within the plan of God's grace for his salvation, and he came to know God's grace as a power to overcome his sin. The result was a peace that came from God, that worked through his life, and then went out for the blessing of many others by God's mighty grace. Writing of his own salvation, and that of countless others, Newton wrote:

> Amazing grace!—how sweet the sound—
>   that saved a wretch like me!
> I once was lost, but now am found,
>   was blind but now I see…
>
> 'Twas grace that taught my heart to fear,
>   and grace my fears relieved;
> How precious did that grace appear
>   the hour I first believed.[16]

2

What Is a Christian?

Ephesians 1:1

In 1738, John Wesley boarded a ship in the British colony of Georgia to return home to England after two years as a Christian missionary. During the long voyage home, he had plenty of time to reflect on his life. He looked back over his time at Oxford University, where he was ordained a priest in the Church of England and distinguished himself for leading a group known as 'The Holy Club.' These zealous young men met nightly to study the Bible and devoted themselves to good works. This was followed by arduous missionary work in the New World. With these credentials it is a surprise to read what Wesley wrote in his journal while sailing home:

> It is now two years and almost four months since I left my native country in order to teach the Georgian Indians the nature of Christianity; but what have I learned myself in the meantime? Why, what I least suspected, that I, who went to America to covert others, was myself never converted to God!

Wesley had come to realize that for all his religious attainments—his degrees, his associations, his morality, his works—he lacked a saving relationship with Jesus Christ. Though an eminent member of the church, he was not a Christian. Wesley began searching for true salvation, and it was not long before he found it in the gospel of God's grace and especially in the precious blood of Christ. Wesley records with joy his coming to true and saving faith:

> I felt my heart strangely warmed. I felt I did trust in Christ, Christ alone for salvation; and an assurance was given me that He had taken away my sins, even mine, and saved me from the law of sin and death.[17]

Wesley's experience is an important one for us to reflect on, because many people in the church today are in the situation he was in. They have read the Bible, they have given time, labor, and money to the cause of religion, but they have never ceased relying on their works, their supposed goodness, and as a result have never entered into the eternal life that comes through faith in Christ alone.

This matter would undoubtedly have interested the apostle Paul. I say this because of the great labor he exerts in Ephesians to describe what a Christian really is. Paul employs a great variety of descriptions in Ephesians of what it means to be a Christian. Christians are the body of Christ, the family of God, a holy nation, and a temple in which God lives. Christians are those who are chosen in God's love, adopted as his children, and forgiven by Christ's blood. The Christian is the 'new man,' part of the new society in the new creation of Christ's resurrection life. Paul wants us to know what it means to be a Christian. He wants us to enter into the glories, the resources, and the obligations involved in a saving relationship with Jesus Christ. The first consideration must be, therefore, the definition of a Christian—and Paul provides a convenient answer to that question in the very first verse: 'To the saints who are in Ephesus, and are faithful in Christ Jesus' (Eph. 1:1). These words will be the focus of our attention as we answer the question, 'What is a Christian?'

To the Saints

Few Bible words have a sadder history than the first word Paul uses to describe a Christian: 'To the *saints*.' Most people think of saints as super-spiritual people who are far removed from the mundane affairs of normal life. How common it is to hear Christians exclaim, 'I'm not a saint, after all!' But as Paul and the Bible use the word, you cannot be a Christian unless you are a saint. Being a Christian makes you a saint by definition.

We need to consider the Roman Catholic teaching here, because it exerts such an influence on most people's use of this word. Saints, they say, are those few whose great spiritual achievements cause them to be set before the church 'as models and intercessors.'[18] That last designation is important, because according to Rome, these saints pray for us in heaven. 'We can and should ask them to intercede for us,' says the current Roman Catholic catechism.[19] People select patron saints and give names of saints to their children; in this manner, says Rome, 'we are assured of [the saint's] intercession.'[20] 'They do not cease to intercede with the Father for us,' we are told, 'as they proffer the merits which they acquired on earth.'[21]

Under this teaching, saints are adored, venerated, and trusted for salvation. One commonly finds Roman Catholics praying to the saints instead of to God, seeking help from and offering praise to mere dead human beings. The idolatry of this practice lies on the very surface. Furthermore, the idea that anyone may come to God on his own merits—much less with excess merits, as Rome teaches—is offensive to the biblical teaching of sin and of justification through faith alone, and denies the sufficiency of Christ as our Savior and intercessor. It flies in the face of Paul's plain statement in 1 Timothy 2:5, 'There is one God, and there is one mediator between God and men, the man Christ Jesus.' Harry Ironside, in a letter to a Roman Catholic priest, insisted on Christ as the only intercessor we need:

> Those who have confided in him as their savior need no other mediator than himself, for he is ever available, his heart is as tender as when here on earth, his love ever flows out to all his own. We need no other intermediary, neither his mother after the flesh, nor any saint or angel to entreat him on our behalf. He himself abides forever…he is our great all-compassionate high priest with God, our advocate with the Father, our one mediator, excluding every other.[22]

Therefore we must not think of saints as superior Christians who offer their merits for us to God, but in Paul's use, *all* Christians are saints. He uses this expression many times in his letters and a glance through them will show that he means ordinary, regular, sinful, struggling Christians like you and me. First Corinthians presents a classic example, for Paul upbraids those Christians for gross immorality. Yet he addresses even this letter 'to the saints' (1:2).

The word *saint* comes from the Latin word *sanctus*, and means *holy one*. Holiness means set apart by and for God. In this sense we must realize that sainthood is a fact concerning every Christian, something that has happened to all who are in Christ. Leon Morris explains:

> The essential idea…is that of being set apart for God. A holy place, such as a temple, is a building not to be used for secular purposes; it is set apart for the worship of God. Holy vessels are withdrawn from all other use and are used only in the service of God. Similarly, 'saints' are people who belong to God.[23]

It is God who makes us saints, who separates us and calls us from the world. Thus all Christians are set apart for God, by God. *Saints* describes something that has happened to us. We have been set apart for God, becoming his property and his holy people. Peter writes in 1 Peter 2:10, 'Once you were not a people, but now you are God's people.' We are saints, we are holy unto God; that is what we are.

Sainthood is a fact concerning Christians, but also a calling and an obligation. Those who are separated to God are thereby called to live holy lives. By definition, a Christian is different from someone who is not a Christian. He or she is separated not from people but from sin, not from the world itself but from the principle of worldliness. If you do not want to be different, you cannot be a Christian. Martyn Lloyd-Jones writes, 'You cannot be a saint and a Christian without being separated in some radical sense from the world. You do not belong to it any longer, you are in it but you are not of it…There is a separation which has taken place in your mind, in your outlook, in your heart, in your conversation, in your behaviour. You are essentially a different person; the Christian is not a worldly person, he is not governed by the world and its mind and outlook.'[24]

This description should increasingly characterize our lives. Do you find that you no longer think and respond in the way you used to, and that you have new and godly pleasures, interests, and pursuits that mark you out as different from the world? Are you becoming more holy? Take heart if you are, for this shows that God has separated you to himself, making you a saint.

To the Faithful

Paul's second description of the Christian is *the faithful*. He does not mean those who are trustworthy, or who can be relied upon, but those who live and come to God by means of faith. The New Testament constantly stresses faith—the need to believe the gospel message and trust in God in order to be saved.

This description tells us that to be a Christian we must believe certain things. For this reason, much of the New Testament is devoted to asserting truth and opposing false teaching so that people may believe and become Christians. You are not a Christian if you are simply a charitable person, lead a certain lifestyle, or possess morality and idealism. You are a Christian if you believe specific and essential truths which center on the person and work of Jesus Christ.

Paul stresses the necessity of doctrinal belief in all his letters. A clear example comes in 1 Corinthians 15:1–2, where Paul says, 'Now, I would remind you, brothers, of the gospel I preached to you, which you received, in which you stand, if you hold fast to the word I preached to you—unless you believed in vain.' There are certain truths you must believe; believing otherwise will leave you unsaved. He goes on to give a short list: 'that Christ died for our sins… that he was buried, that he was raised on the third day…that he appeared to Cephas, then to the twelve' (vv. 3–5). People say, 'I am a Christian but I just don't believe in the resurrection'; Paul says you are not a Christian unless you do. Furthermore, we must believe not just facts but also the doctrine tied to these facts. Jesus did not simply die; he died 'for our sins,' not merely as a moral example or as a statement of God's love for us, but as a substitute, a sacrifice of atonement. The doctrine of substitutionary atonement is essential to Christianity; without believing it you are not a Christian.

What, then, does it mean to believe? Classically, there are three elements to saving faith, beginning with *knowledge*. It is not enough simply to mouth words, follow some liturgy or go through some religious motions. A man was asked what he believed. He replied, 'I believe what the church believes.' He then was asked, 'Well, what does the church believe?' 'The church believes what I believe.' 'Okay, then what do you and the church believe?' The man finally said, 'We believe the same thing!' This is not faith, for faith requires knowledge and understanding. This is why we must emphasize teaching in the church, to explain what sin means and what it means that Jesus died for our sins on the cross and other vital truths.

Next comes *belief* or *assent*. There are people who have knowledge and can explain Christian truth perfectly well, but they don't believe it. Many scholars are like this. They understand the theory of the virgin birth and incarnation, the atonement of Christ, the resurrection and the new birth, but do not accept these doctrines themselves. But faith requires belief.

Third, saving faith requires *personal commitment*. It is not enough to believe in sin; we must acknowledge that *we* are sinners. It is not enough to assent that Christ is a Savior; he must be *our* Savior. This is why John Wesley's ultimate conversion was so credible; he spoke of *my* sin, *my* salvation, *my* Savior, and so must we.

We must not merely assent to truth, we must embrace Jesus himself: trusting him, relying on God's promises, committing our hope and salvation into his pierced hands and onto his shed blood. The story is told of a dry, academic preacher who suddenly broke out in tears in the middle of his own sermon; one of the people exclaimed, 'The preacher converted himself!' And it was true! Saving faith involves personal commitment; it involves the heart as well as the head. Believing God's Word, we give ourselves to Christ and take him as our own. We commit ourselves and our souls to his eternal safe keeping.

Are you looking for something to believe in, for someone to trust? This is the great want of our time. A survey of teenagers asked, 'What do you wish for most in your life?' Do you know what the answer was? It wasn't money, it wasn't success, it wasn't pleasure. 'What do you most want?' they were asked. The number one answer was, 'Someone we can trust.'[25] The cultural tragedy of our time is no one to trust, but you may turn to Jesus Christ and trust him with your heart, your mind, your life, and your eternal soul. If you are looking for someone to trust, you are looking for him. Have you believed and trusted in Jesus? He said, 'I am the way, the truth, and the life' (John 14:6); he is the Savior who will never let you down, never let you go, and never fail your need. Trust him and you will be saved.

Faith does not save us; Jesus Christ saves us. For this reason, we should think of faith as being primarily *receptive*. Faith receives Christ and his saving work for us. The hymn *Rock of Ages* aptly describes how faith makes us Christians: 'Nothing in my hands I bring, simply to the cross I cling.' Faith trusts and receives, open-handedly grasping what is promised and offered by God in Jesus Christ. We are not saved *by* our faith, but we are saved *through* our faith as it brings us to the Savior, Jesus Christ. He saves us. Faith brings us to him and lays hold of him for salvation.

Once we are brought to Jesus, our faith becomes an *active* principle. Believing these truths we begin to act upon them; committing ourselves to Christ, we manifest that commitment in our choices and actions. We are called to be faithful to Christ, reliable in his service, ready to defend the truth, and obedient to what he commands. 'To the saints, the faithful,' Paul writes, meaning every Christian, as a description of what we are but also a high calling for our lives.

To Those in Christ Jesus

Christians are saints and believers, and most importantly, Paul says, they are 'in Christ Jesus' (Eph. 1:2). This is our third description of a Christian: one who by grace is in union with Christ.

Often, when Christians read Paul's little phrase, 'in Christ,' we think of believing in Jesus. Paul's meaning is better expanded as 'in union with Christ.' By grace and through faith, Christians enter into a saving relationship with Christ by which we receive all the benefits of his redeeming work. We become one with Christ, so that all that is his becomes ours. Christians enter into the same relationship with the Father that Jesus eternally enjoys. He told Mary Magdalene after his resurrection: 'I am ascending to my Father and your Father, to my God and your God' (John 20:17). This means that Christians do not enter into a *similar* relationship with God that Jesus enjoys, but into the *same* relationship as wholly justified saints and dearly beloved children. What the Father said of Jesus he now declares of us: 'This is my beloved Son, with whom I am well pleased' (Matt. 3:17). Christians are saved in that the benefits of all that Christ did for our salvation and all that Christ has become by means of his death and resurrection have become ours through union with him. John Calvin wrote: 'All things that belong to our salvation are accomplished in our Lord Jesus Christ.'[26] Salvation, then, becomes ours as we have union with Christ through the bond of faith.

Union with Christ is, first, a covenant relationship. Having come to him in faith, Christians gain Jesus Christ as our representative before God. What Jesus did for salvation he therefore did for us. He died for our sins and therefore we are forgiven. Jesus fulfilled all the demands of righteousness and therefore we are justified in him. He rose from the grave and thus in Christ we possess resurrection life.

The Old Testament shows this covenantal pattern. Genesis 15 records God making a covenant with Abraham for his salvation and for others who would join him. If you wanted to be saved in that time, you had to be *in Abraham*. You had to enter his tents, place yourself under Abraham's authority, receive the mark of circumcision if you were a male, and then serve and trust the God of Abraham. If you entered into the faith of Abraham, you were saved according to God's covenant with him. This passed on to his descendants, so that salvation was *in Abraham, in Isaac,* and then *in Jacob*. Jacob's sons became the twelve tribes of Israel. If you wanted to be right with God and receive his blessings, you had to join Israel in the exodus and go with Israel into the Promised Land. This was a legal relationship, a covenant relationship, and even a geographical relationship. Later, God entered into covenant with David and the tribe of Judah, and salvation became a royal relationship securing salvation for those who looked in faith to God's promises for the Davidic throne.

Finally, the long-awaited Messiah came in the person of Jesus Christ, who fulfilled all the promises attached to the prior covenants. The New Testament shows that being 'in Abraham' had always been merely a way of being 'in Christ.' Therefore Jesus offered 'the new covenant in my blood' (Luke 22:20). Through faith in Jesus' atoning death, we come to him and receive the fulfillment of the salvation God has promised throughout the Bible.

As a covenant relationship, union with Christ is objective. You are either in Christ or you are not. This raises objective questions. Whose lordship do you profess? Whose salvation do you trust? In whose righteousness do you stand before God? You are either in Christ or you are trusting in something else—trusting in yourself, in false Messiahs, or false hopes for your eternal destiny. Paul writes, 'The Lord knows those who are his' (2 Tim. 2:19), and they are all *in Christ*. So the question is 'Are you in Christ?'

Union with Christ is not only a covenant relationship, but it is a personal, spiritual relationship. We come to Jesus the way that Ruth came to her mother-in-law Naomi: 'Where you go I will go, and where you lodge I will lodge. Your people shall be my people, and your God my God' (Ruth 1:16). This shows that faith in Christ involves a personal commitment to him. It means swearing loyalty to his cause. It means receiving his love and offering our own devotion in response. We fly his banner from the flagpole of our lives, becoming his disciples and calling him 'Master.' In turn, Jesus pledges to uphold our eternal cause, granting us to eat from his table of salvation and have fellowship with him forever. He sends his Spirit to live with us, working within us so that we will be transformed into his image 'from one degree of glory to another' (2 Cor. 3:18). He is our saving Shepherd whose Spirit gives us life and power, leads us into truth, speaks peace in our hearts, and causes us to cry out as children to God our loving Father. In these ways, union with Christ is not only an objective, covenant relationship but is also a subjective, spiritual reality. Paul therefore could sum up the Christian experience, writing: 'I have been crucified with Christ. It is no longer I who live, but Christ who lives in me' (Gal. 2:20).

IN EPHESUS, IN CHRIST

The apostle writes to readers who are in two places. They are 'in Ephesus' and they are 'in Christ Jesus' (Eph. 1:1). They had a relationship to the world by birth and they had a relationship to Christ through faith. Consequently, they were *in* the world but not *of* the world. They had duties to Ephesus—its rulers and people—but they had salvation in Jesus Christ and their relationship with him determined their true identity and eternal destiny.

The same is true of you, as a believer in Jesus Christ. Outwardly, there is nothing special about you. You look and dress and act largely in the manner of the culture around you. You derive benefits and accept obligations from earthly society. But God has made you holy to himself, separating you by grace for salvation in Christ. You are no longer bound up with the fate of this passing, dying world that is under God's wrath. You are in Christ, by God's grace and through faith, so that what is his is now yours. You no longer belong to the world, partake of its ethos, or follow the world's cravings and rules. 'In Ephesus,' we had a sinful manner of life, which Paul describes as 'corrupt through deceitful desires' (Eph. 4:22). In Christ, we gain a 'new self, created after the likeness of God in true righteousness and holiness' (Eph. 4:24). We now live in the world as Christ's covenant people, representing Christ, serving Christ, trusting Christ, and waiting for Christ to return, when the only world left will be the one in Christ, to the praise of God the Father.

A Christian is to be like the man in John Bunyan's allegory, *Pilgrim's Progress*. Bunyan's hero was born and lived comfortably in the City of Destruction. But he read in the Bible that the city was doomed to be judged with fire. He met a man named Evangelist, who told him to begin a pilgrimage to the Celestial City to be saved. Though his family and friends thought Christian had lost his mind, he resolved to depart from the City of Destruction. They called out to him, but he put his fingers in his ears, crying, 'Life! Life! Eternal life!' and left without looking back. Friends caught him and spoke of all the pleasures and comforts he was giving up, but Christian answered that all he was forsaking 'is not worthy of being compared with what I am seeking to enjoy…an inheritance incorruptible, undefiled, that does not fade away…reserved and safe in heaven.' The rest of the book details various challenges and difficulties that Christian faced before arriving safe in the Celestial City. But his new life began, just as it must begin for us, by forsaking the world so as to gain eternal life.

Undoubtedly, as Paul begins his great letter to the Ephesians, he would have us reflect on these matters just as John Wesley did on his boat. Am I a Christian? he asked. Am I a saint? Am I saved through faith? Am I in Christ, no longer belonging to the world? If you cannot give a definite answer to these questions, you should turn to Jesus now. You should repent and give yourself to him, believing his gospel and putting all your hope in his salvation. In Christ Jesus, you will be holy through faith and you will know the salvation of your soul.

3

Blessing for Blessing

Ephesians 1:3

The apostle Paul's letters are marked by both an intensity of teaching and an exuberance of feeling. Some people want to separate the head from the heart, but for Paul such a disconnect was unthinkable. It was the thoughts, the doctrine, in his head that set his heart on fire. One writer says, 'Put a pen into his hand and it is like tapping a blast furnace; and out rushes a fiery stream at white heat.'[27]

If this is true of Paul's letters generally, it is especially true of Ephesians. This first chapter, we find, is as robust in its doctrine as it is soaring in its heights of passion. Paul's greeting gives way to a hymn of praise to God that is one of the most instructive and inspiring passages in all of Scripture. In the original Greek text, it is a single long sentence running from verses 3 to 14. One writer calls it 'a swirl of words with a storm of thought behind them.'[28] If you believe what Paul writes about here, it will revolutionize your life.

When Paul thinks about salvation, he emphasizes the combined operations of the Trinity: Father, Son, and Holy Spirit. He also follows a historical progression, considering our salvation from eternity past to eternity future. Verses 3–6 focus on God the Father ordaining salvation in the past councils of eternity. Verses 7–12 speak of God the Son coming into the world to accomplish our redemption from sin. Verses 13–14 tell of God the Spirit applying that salvation to individuals in the present age. At every stage, the Trinity is working together: God the Father ordaining; God the Son achieving; and God the Spirit applying.

Why does Paul think this matters to us? Two objectives leap off the page, first, that we as believers might know our blessings. Verse 3 speaks of 'every spiritual blessing,' and Paul goes to great length to spell these out. There are few things more important for a believer to know than the rich blessings that are ours in Jesus Christ: blessings in the past, blessings in the present, and blessings in the future, all securely provided by God. We need to know, Paul says, 'what is the hope to which he has called you' (v. 18).

Paul's second objective is that this knowledge would inspire us to a life of adoring praise to God. To this end, verse 3 begins Paul's hymn with a progression of ideas built around the word *bless*. '*Blessed* be God,' Paul begins, drawing our attention to God's worthiness to be praised. He then tells us why: 'Who has *blessed* us.' In what way? 'With every spiritual *blessing* in Christ.' Benjamin Warfield observes, 'When a man's lips can frame only this one word—'Blessing, blessing, blessing!' we know what is in his heart.'[29] Paul would have the same be said of us as we enter into our study of the fullness of God's saving blessing in Christ. 'Blessed be the God and Father of our Lord Jesus Christ,' he exclaims, and that is what we need to learn to do.

The Source of Our Blessing

Focusing on verse 3, Paul first tells us *the source of our blessing*. From where do these salvation blessings come? He answers that our blessings have their origin in God. Hugh Martin explains, 'They originate in the mere grace and good pleasure of God, his unfettered, undeserved sovereign love.'[30] We see this in verse 3, where we bless, or praise, God because 'he has blessed us.'

In this passage from verses 3 to 14, Paul tells us about God being the one who blesses us. He says that our salvation is 'according to the purpose of his will' (v. 5). It is God's will that we should have these blessings, all 'to the praise of his glorious grace' (v. 6). God has 'lavished' salvation on us (v. 8); this is 'according to his purpose' (v. 9). Paul could not have expressed more extravagantly the great truth stated simply in James 1:17, 'Every good gift and every perfect gift is from above, coming down from the Father of lights.'

Note the emphasis on God the Father. 'Blessed be the God and Father of our Lord Jesus Christ' (Eph. 1:3). This warns us against a grave error common to many people: to attribute salvation to God the Son—to Jesus Christ—while considering God the Father a reluctant participant. We think of Jesus pleading his merits for us in heaven, and we may wrongly conclude the thrice-holy Father must be ill-disposed towards us, watching for a slip-up, aching for an opportunity to chastise, or be distant in his affections for sinners like us.

But what a significant error this is! If God the Son took our sins on the cross it was because the Father sent him into the world to accomplish this task. Jesus prayed before his arrest, 'I glorified you on earth, having accomplished the work that you gave me to do' (John 17:4). John 3:16 says, 'For God so loved the world, that he gave his only Son, that whoever believes in him should not perish but have eternal life.' Our salvation originates in the love of God the Father for us.

What a difference this makes to our security in salvation. There is no debate raging within the Godhead concerning our salvation. There is no tension, no awkward silences or heated conversations. Rather there is a grand conspiracy of love originating in the eternal and sovereign grace of the Father.

Perhaps the most crippling tendency many of us have is to doubt God's love for us. We live in a world scarred by sin; our own lives are plagued by our own sin and folly. We do not feel lovely—and we are not; we do not think we are worthy of love—and we are not. But the Bible says that 'God is love' (1 John 4:8). Romans 5:8 says, 'God shows his love for us in that while we were still sinners, Christ died for us.' God sent his precious Son to die for your sins—that is the proof of his love for you. He says: 'I know the plans I have for you, plans for wholeness and not for evil, to give you a future and a hope' (Jer. 29:11). Our blessings come from God the Father, according to his plan of grace for us.

Knowing that God is my heavenly Father is a particular help to me because I happen to be a father. I know what it is like to have a father's love for my children. Deep within me, far deeper than I can see or touch, there is love for the five people who call me Father. They can make me angry. They can cause me to punish them or take things away. But they cannot make me stop loving them. I take delight in providing for them. There is nothing more wonderful to me than seeing them grow in grace and knowledge. I delight to share even silly things with them, because I am their father. If only I were able, I would secure a wonderful future for them and I pray for that fervently. But, of course, my love for my children is only a pale reflection of God's fatherly love for me. He is without sin; he is perfect in love. Furthermore, God is not limited in wisdom or strength. God's fatherly love therefore means that I will be blessed as I trust in him. In response, there is nothing wiser than for me to long to please him, to give myself into his keeping and offer myself to his service. He is my Father, and I can completely trust him.

Paul emphasizes that it is this fatherly love of God, working for our blessing in salvation, that brings special praise to God in heaven. What a source of joy it is, to know that it honors and glorifies God that I should be forgiven, accepted, adopted, renewed, sanctified and made an heir of glory! What wonder it is, Hugh Martin writes, 'that I should be called not only to receive freely an infinite, sovereign, undeserved love, but that my reception of it should be the means of throwing light, to the angelic beings, during the eternal ages, on the glorious character and perfections of God?'[31]

The Nature of Our Blessing

Having seen the source of our blessings, we consider *the nature of these blessings*. What kind of blessing does the apostle have in mind? Verse 3 tells us, 'every spiritual blessing.' Christians derive many worldly blessings from God. Jesus tells us in the Sermon on the Mount not to be anxious for anything because God carefully considers our every need (Matt. 6:25-32). But what causes Paul to ring forth with special praise to God is the spiritual blessing that belongs to every Christian. There is a double meaning to this. Paul means blessings that are spiritual in character; but these are also blessings that come through the Holy Spirit's work in our lives.

What are these spiritual blessings? Paul works this out in the verses to come. What a blessing it is to know that God has chosen you to be adopted into his household, that before the creation of the world he set his sovereign love on you. However much the world may revile us, Christians are told of God's free and saving love, forged in the eternal furnace of his changeless will. Think, for instance, of a young man who has to work hard for very little pay. But he knows that soon he will come into an inherited trust fund that will provide him with millions. Think of the peace and the comfort this knowledge gives him in the midst of present struggles. We have this knowledge on the grandest scale. Paul writes in Romans 8:16-17, 'If we are children of God, then we are heirs—heirs of God and fellow heirs with Christ.' We have the spiritual blessing of knowing our status as chosen children of God and heirs of eternal glory.

What a difference it makes to know that our sins are all forgiven. Psalm 32 says, 'Blessed is the one whose transgression is forgiven, whose sin is covered.' Here is peace of mind that money cannot buy, that no pleasure or fame can replace. There is no Christian who cannot revel in this spiritual blessing. Paul adds that God is 'making known to us the mystery of his will' (Eph. 1:9). What a great spiritual blessing comes to us through the knowledge of God's Word! Furthermore, having believed, we are 'sealed with the promised Holy Spirit, who is the guarantee of our inheritance' (Eph. 1:13-14). If we are in Christ we can know that the Holy Spirit is working in us with power for godliness. There is hope for change and a promise of perfection in glory. What a spiritual blessing this is, and we have it now!

Paul praises God for *every* spiritual blessing, all of which every believer may fully partake. There is no difference when it comes to these spiritual blessings; all of them are for all of us. This is *not* God's design with material blessings. God makes some people rich and others poor; some live in comfort and others in pain. But every believer may bless God for the whole of the spiritual blessings with which he has blessed all who are in Jesus Christ. You may be poor, you may be mistreated, you may be hated and reviled, but God's Word stands true: 'The house of the righteous contains great treasure' (Prov. 15:6).

Do you know these blessings? Do they sustain you in the trials of this life? Do they keep your heart from a sinful love of this world? God is spirit, and his chief blessings are in keeping with his nature. They are all available to us now by faith; Paul stresses not merely our future enjoyment of spiritual blessings but their present possession: 'God…has blessed us.'

The Location of Our Blessing

Third, Paul makes a definite statement regarding *the location of our blessings.* He says God has blessed us 'in the heavenly places.' Paul never spells out exactly what he means by this expression, but since he uses it several times in Ephesians we can piece it together well enough. In 1:20, Paul says that God raised Christ from the dead and 'seated him…in the heavenly places.' In 6:12 he says that our present struggle is not against flesh and blood but 'against the spiritual forces of evil in the heavenly places.' Paul has in mind, therefore, the spiritual realm that we do not see but that is real and vital to our lives. This is what Jesus was talking about when he said to Pilate, 'My kingdom is not of this world' (John 18:18). His kingdom is unseen and spiritual. It is of faith now, but will be made visible in the world to come when he returns. This is where our blessings are found, not in the realm of things you can touch and feel. But our spiritual blessings are real—more real, in fact, than the worldly blessings we can see.

Let's just take one blessing, our adoption as children of God, which Paul writes of in verse 5. Spiritually, in the heavenly realms, we are blessed with adoption as God's children. This is true of us now but it is not visibly manifest in this earthly sphere. No royal robes fall from our shoulders, no visible insignia marks us out as royal sons and daughters. Angels minister to our needs, yet no eye beholds them. No crowds gather to watch as we pass by, though we are chosen for an eternal inheritance with Christ. The newspapers do not follow the day-to-day progress of our pilgrimage to glory. How odd all this is from the perspective of the heavenly realm. To the minds of angels, this is what is happening in this world—rebels against God are being converted, are adopted as his children and are journeying to their home in glory! The world could not care less; indeed, it looks down on those who are God's children. How strange that is to angels in heavenly realms!

Likewise, our redemption in Christ makes little visible impression on our earthly lives. Wearily we battle temptation. Painfully we toil under diseases and afflictions which take no notice of our spiritual status. Ultimately, death will place its bony hands upon us just like everyone else; our spiritual blessings will not keep us from the grave. Yet all the while in the heavenly places we have treasures of riches and wholeness and life everlasting; they are spiritual, they are real, and they strengthen us in the trials of this life.

Since our spiritual blessings are located in the heavenly realm, no one on earth can take them away. This was the testimony of the early church father Justin Martyr during the times of Roman persecution. In his *First Apology* (c. 150), Justin challenged the Roman authorities to consider Christians fairly. One thing they should notice is the Christian testimony in the face of tyranny and injustice. 'For as for us,' Justin wrote, 'we reckon that no evil can be done us,…and you, you can kill, but not hurt us.'[32] The joy and peace of the persecuted believers showed that their spiritual blessings were safe in the heavenly realm, far from the reach of wicked men. Justin continued:

> And when you hear that we look for a kingdom, you suppose, without making any inquiry, that we speak of a human kingdom; whereas we speak of that which is with God…For if we looked for a human kingdom, we should also deny our Christ, that we might not be slain; and we should strive to escape detection, that we might obtain what we expect. But since our thoughts are not fixed on the present, we are not concerned when men cut us off.[33]

The value of having spiritual blessings safe in the heavenly realm is especially seen in the face of death. For unbelievers, death is an unmitigated disaster. Queen Elizabeth I spoke on her deathbed to her lady-in-waiting: 'It is over. I have come to the end of it—the end, the end. To have only one life, and to have done with it!'[34] The French philosopher Voltaire, who had so mocked Jesus during his life, faced death with panicked despair. His physician recorded his last words: 'I am abandoned by God and man! I will give you half of what I am worth if you will give me six months' life. Then I shall go to hell; and you will go with me. O Christ! O Jesus Christ!'[35]

Faith in Christ enables believers to face death far differently, knowing the spiritual blessings that are ours in the heavenly places. Paul stated, 'For me, to live is Christ, and to die is gain' (Phil. 1:21). Paul wrote to Timothy when he realized that the emperor Nero would soon put him to death, saying that 'the time of my departure has come' (2 Tim. 4:6). His attitude was one of joyful expectation: 'I have fought the good fight, I have finished the race, I have kept the faith. Henceforth there is laid up for me the crown of righteousness, which the Lord, the righteous judge, will award to me on that Day' (2 Tim. 4:7–8). What a difference it makes in life and especially in death to possess spiritual blessings from God in the heavenly places, where no tyrant can deny them, no thief can take them, and no corruption will mar them.

The world thinks life is about acquiring money, power, and prestige; having exciting experiences; and feeding the fleshly nature with pleasures and entertainment. But Christians nurture our souls with fruit from a different tree; we think success is an increased perception and reception of spiritual blessings found in the heavenly realm by faith. This is why we spend time in Bible studies, in prayer meetings, in personal devotion, and at church. Our life together as believers is about strengthening our faith amid the troubles of life, so that by faith we might increasingly take possession of these blessings that are ours in Christ. What is more, they are blessings we desire to share with others as we lead them to God through faith in Jesus Christ.

This is a connection Paul makes about our spiritual blessings: they are *in the heavenly places* and they are *in Christ*. Paul writes in Ephesians 1:20–22 that when God raised Jesus from the dead he seated him 'at his right hand *in the heavenly places*, far above all rule and authority and power and dominion…And he put all things under his feet and gave him as head over everything to the church.' Jesus Christ is now

Lord of the unseen realm; all the blessings that reside in the heavenly places are under his control for the sake of his people.

What this means is that we must go to Christ for these spiritual blessings. All our blessings are *from* God the Father and *in* Christ. We might use a business analogy, with God the Father as the producer of all these spiritual goods; out of his eternal council all our blessings are made. Jesus Christ is the sole distributor, licensed by the Father to dispense these blessings. 'I am the way, the truth, and the life,' he said (John 14:6), and God's blessings are found in him alone.

Obtaining God's Blessings

This leads us to an all-important question. How do you get these blessings for yourself? The answer is obvious from all we have said. If you want to be blessed in the heavenly realms with all the spiritual blessings God gives, you must go to Christ, through faith and prayer, confess to him your need of his redeeming work, and receive from him all the blessings of salvation, beginning with forgiveness of sin and ending with an eternity in glory. John 3:36 tells us, 'Whoever believes in the Son has eternal life; whoever does not obey the Son shall not see life, but the wrath of God remains on him.' Have you done this? Have you come to Christ for your salvation? God has made him the one way by which we can have cleansing and adoption, forgiveness and redemption from sin.

If you have come to Jesus, then you need to know what your blessings are and to feed on them spiritually through faith. Your faith needs to declare to your heart that these spiritual blessings are yours. Are you anxious for the future? God's Word promises that in Christ you are beloved as God's child and your Heavenly Father will provide for you, since before creation he purposed an inheritance of eternal riches for you. Are you weak in the face of trials and temptations to sin? God has blessed you with access to the Holy Spirit through faith and prayer, to give you spiritual strength from the heavenly realms. Are you burdened by guilt, by your sense of failure, by lack of hope? Look in faith to the heavenly realm, where Christ is seated at God's right hand. He died for your forgiveness, and he lives forever to save you to the uttermost. Paul therefore says, 'We do not lose heart. Though our outer nature is wasting away, our inner nature is being renewed day by day…We look not to the things that are seen but to the things that are unseen. For the things that are seen are transient, but the things that are unseen are eternal' (2 Cor. 4:16–18).

If you have not come to Jesus, acknowledging him as Lord and Savior, if you have not confessed your need for him to give you the blessings that he alone can give, then you need to understand what this verse plainly implies. It is true that you may find blessings from God apart from Jesus Christ, but they are worldly ones only. God is good towards the world in common grace; he makes rain to fall and the sun to shine on the unjust and on the just (Matt. 5:45). You may find in God's kind providence all the blessings this world has to give: wealth, love, power, pleasure—blessings that will perish with this passing world. But of these spiritual blessings you will know nothing unless you are in Christ through faith in him. 'For the kingdom of God is not a matter of eating and drinking,' Paul wrote, 'but of righteousness, peace and joy in the Holy Spirit' (Rom. 14:17). This and much more will be yours if you will come to Jesus Christ, receiving God's saving blessings from him who came, died, and rose again that we might have eternal life in him.

4

Chosen in Christ

Ephesians 1:4

When I was ministering in the city of Philadelphia, some very large construction projects took place there. As I passed by these sites I noticed how much work went on before anything could be seen at level ground. Particularly with very tall buildings, a great deal of labor and care must be given to the foundation. If you want a building to stand fast, particularly one that reaches high into the sky, then you must dig deep and plant a very firm foundation.

Paul shows a similar concern in Ephesians 1 as he begins constructing the edifice of Christian salvation. He intends us to see a work of the ages that is infinitely high, reaching up forever. This is where Paul is headed as he begins his hymn of praise for the blessings of God. So he begins by digging deep, setting the firmest foundation. God is leading us into eternity future, and so it is in eternity past that God sets the groundwork of our security. Paul writes, 'He chose us in [Christ] before the foundation of the world, that we should be holy and blameless before him.'

The Doctrine of Election

Ephesians 1:4 provides one of the clearest statements of what is known as *the doctrine of election*. This teaching gets its name from the Greek word *eklektos*, the verb form of which is translated here as 'chose.' This verse and its doctrine teach that all the blessings we enjoy as Christians are grounded in the sovereign choosing of God, which took place in eternity past, long before we were born. Here is the foundation on which the salvation of every believer rests: God's own free and gracious choice of us. This is the strongest, firmest foundation possible—God's own eternal purpose—and it is upon this that Paul would have us ground our hope for salvation.

Paul tells us that our election is 'in him,' that is, 'in Christ.' This means that when God decided our salvation, he did so through Christ's saving work for us. Peter speaks of Christ as the 'lamb without blemish or defect…foreknown before the foundation of the world' (1 Pet. 1:19-20). Revelation 13:8 calls Christ 'the Lamb that was slain from the creation of the world' (NIV). These descriptions show that even in eternity past God's will included the problem of sin and sinners. There is no conflict, therefore, between the doctrine of election and salvation by faith in Christ, for God elected that Christ would die for the sins of his people and that the elect would have faith in Christ and thus be saved.

The Bible teaches that there was a covenant, or agreement, in eternity past between God the Father and God the Son. Hebrews 13:20 refers to this as 'the eternal covenant.' Jesus mentioned it in his prayer on the night of his arrest: 'Father…I have glorified you on earth, having accomplished the work that you gave me to do' (John 17:4). This looks back on what theologians call *the covenant of redemption*. God the Father laid a charge on the Son which he accepted, to take up our cause and die for our sins. In return, the Father promised him the salvation of all the elect, those chosen in eternity to be his people and bride. We are therefore chosen 'in Christ'—that is, through Christ and his redeeming work for us.

The doctrine of election says that the cause of our individual salvation is God's choosing us in Christ. 'Why is anyone a Christian?' we ask. We answer, 'Because he believed the gospel.' But we go on and ask, 'Why did one believe while others did not?' Was it because something in the Christian is more spiritual, that enables him to believe while others hear the same message and do not? The Bible says, No! It is not because of anything in us, but because of God's sovereign choice, his eternal election of individuals to be his own people through faith in Jesus Christ. This is good news to all who believe, for here is the foundation of your salvation—not something in you, who are so weak and changing, so mixed in your affections, and so inconstant in faith—it is the foundation of God's own sovereign choice from eternity past. 'He chose us in Christ before the foundation of the world.'

The Bible's Teaching, Not Man's

Having stated the doctrine taught in Ephesians 1:4, we should emphasize that *election is the Bible's teaching and not man's*.

This is a necessary statement because so many people consider this doctrine to be a human invention. Many point to John Calvin, whose name is given to a theological position that strongly affirms this doctrine, namely, Calvinism. Yet how wrong it is to assign this teaching to this man! For one thing, the doctrine has a long theological lineage that goes back far before Calvin and the sixteenth century Reformation. Augustine, the fourth century theologian and bishop, emphasized God's sovereign election most fervently. Indeed, if you read Augustine on these matters you may conclude that he must be a Calvinist, until you realize that he lived over a millennium before Calvin. All through church history a great many teachers have not only embraced but insisted on this doctrine, and in many centuries it was the strong majority view.

Of course, what really matters is not what theologians have believed, although it is helpful to realize church history's strong endorsement. What matters is what the Bible teaches. As Christians we are bound and obliged before God to accept what is plainly taught in God's holy Word, and upon inspection we will find that Scripture clearly and forcefully sets forth the doctrine of election.

Ephesians 1:4 alone makes this point: Paul's meaning, if difficult to accept, is unavoidable. Salvation begins with God choosing believers in Christ before creation. In Romans 9:10, Paul uses the example of Jacob and Esau to show that before they were even born God chose one and rejected the other. On what principle? Romans 9:11 tells us it was because of 'God's purpose of election.'

Another clear example is found in Luke's teaching in Acts 13:48. He was recounting Paul's preaching at Psidian Antioch, and in passing he observed, 'And as many as were appointed to eternal life believed.' Likewise, Peter taught election, addressing his first epistle 'to those who are elect' (1 Pet. 1:1), and in his second epistle urging his readers to 'make your calling and election sure' (2 Pet. 1:10).

What about Jesus? Did he have anything to say about election? Yes, in John 15:16, Jesus made a plain statement of election, saying, 'You did not choose me, but I chose you.' If we think back to the disciples' selection, we find this was true. Jesus sovereignly picked them out, when he might easily have chosen others. It was his choosing that decided their discipleship. Later, Jesus spoke of the eternal security that goes with divine election: 'All that the Father gives me will come to me, and whoever comes to me I will never cast out…And this is the will of him who sent me, that I should lose nothing of all that he has given me, but raise it up on the last day' (John 6:37–39). Jesus went on, 'No one can come to me unless it is granted by the Father' (John 6:65). Jesus explicitly directs his mission not merely to the world at large, but to those who were chosen by the Father and given to him, who therefore come to him and are saved. He prayed in John 17:9, 'I am not praying for the world, but for those whom you have given me.'

God's sovereignty in salvation is not restricted to the New Testament. Isaiah 46:9-10 says, 'I am God, and there is none like me, declaring the end from the beginning and from ancient times things not yet done, saying, "My counsel shall stand, and I will accomplish all my purpose."' In the exodus, Moses explained God's election of Israel with the same emphasis that Paul places on free and sovereign grace: 'It was not because you were more in number than any other people that the LORD set his love on you and chose you, for you were the fewest of all peoples, but it is because the LORD loves you and is keeping the oath that he swore to your fathers' (Deut. 7:7-8).

If you are wrestling with this doctrine, your question should be: Is it taught by the Bible? The question is not yet whether you understand it or if you like it. The question is, Does God teach it in Scripture? If he does, and just this brief survey shows that he certainly does, then your obedience to him requires you to receive it, and through the obedience of your mind you can expect God to lead you into understanding and rejoicing for what is often hard at first to accept.

Sometimes people ask me what it means to be Reformed in matters of theology. I always answer that being Reformed means that I believe not what I think should be true and not what I wish was true, but what the Bible teaches is true. This is what the term *Reformed* means, namely, re-formed according to the Word of God. By that definition I am not Reformed because I believe election; rather, I believe in election because I am Reformed, that is, because I submit my own reasoning to the higher authority of Scripture.

HUMILITY, NOT PRIDE

Some may wonder what difference the doctrine of election makes in our real lives? I want to work out some ways this shapes our thinking and thus our living, beginning with the fact that *election promotes humility and not pride*.

People think the opposite is true, that if I believe I am chosen by God I must think I am somehow special and superior. But election ascribes salvation not to any merit in the Christian, but rather fully embraces the biblical teaching of our depravity. It says that unless salvation is wholly of God then I could not be saved, so great is my sin and opposition to the things of God. Arthur Pink explains, 'The truth of God's sovereignty… removes every ground for human boasting and instills the spirit of humility in its stead. It declares that salvation is of the Lord...And all this is most humbling to the heart of man, who wants to contribute something to the price of his redemption and do that which will afford ground for boasting and self-satisfaction.'[36]

How can we boast when we realize that our salvation is in spite of our unworthiness, and only because of God's sovereign and amazing grace? Indeed, this is our great need—to have our pride and self-reliance laid low. And it is precisely this doctrine of sovereign election that humbles the believer's heart. We were chosen—and what a wonderful thing that is, to be chosen—not because of something in us that was commendable to God, but because of God's sheer mercy and grace. Paul says in Titus 3:5, 'He saved us, not because of works done by us in righteousness, but according to his mercy.'

HOLINESS, NOT LICENSE

The second way election helps us is that it promotes holiness. People say the opposite, that if my salvation is caused by God's sovereign mercy, then why should I be motivated to do the difficult work of becoming holy? But the Bible says the opposite, that *election promotes holiness and not license*. Holiness is the goal of our salvation; we are saved *to holiness*. This is Paul's own emphasis in Ephesians 1:4: 'He chose us...that we should be holy and blameless before him.'

This allows me to make the categorical statement that if you are not bearing evidence of holiness, and if you do not even desire to be holy, you have no reason to think you are elect. When God elected sinners, he elected them *to holiness*, so that holiness is the particular mark of the elect. Paul writes elsewhere, 'This is the will of God, your sanctification' (1 Thess. 4:3).

The great priority of the Christian life is not happiness, but holiness. God did not choose you to be happy—not in a worldly sense—but to be holy. We want to do what will make us happy; God says he wants us to do what will make us holy. We want to fit into the materialistic society around us, finding joy in a self-centered lifestyle; God wants us to be different from the world, finding joy in our relationship to him. We want to be consumers, having everything our own way; God wants us to be disciples of a cross-bearing Christ, having things his way. We want to use our money, time, and talents for ourselves. God wants us to use them for him, for the gospel, for the work of the church, and for the blessing of others.

Martyn Lloyd-Jones explains, 'Because we have been chosen to holiness we must and will become holy...According to Paul we are not chosen with the possibility of holiness, but to the realization of holiness...Being "chosen" and being "holy" are inseparable...God, who has chosen you to holiness, will make you holy; and if the preaching of the gospel does not do so, God has other means and methods. He may strike you down with illness, He may ruin your business. God will make you holy because He has chosen you unto holiness.'[37] This means that if we do not willingly pursue holiness, God will do it for us. Hebrews 12:6 says, 'The Lord disciplines the one he loves, and chastises every son whom he receives.' You don't want to pray, so God will give you reasons to pray. You don't want to tithe, so God will teach you to live frugally by other means. You don't want to give up that cherished sin. So God will work its painful consequences out in your life until you ask him for grace to repent. Not every trial we face is God's chastisement. But if you are a Christian who is not interested in becoming more holy, God promises you chastisement. Hebrews 12:10 says, 'He disciplines us for our good, that we may share his holiness.'

Holiness is a good thing. God's commands are for our good, our blessing, our joy, and our satisfaction. The wise Christian longs to be more holy—to be less worldly and to have his sinful passions subdued and to be more like God. She wants to partake of God's joy. And the doctrine of election is a great help in the matter of personal holiness. How can someone like me become holy? Because God has purposed it in Christ! This says that if I have trusted in Christ, I have a new identity: I am a saint and God is going to bless me with holiness. He has chosen me to this. I will be holy! What an amazing thought! If I am in Christ I can be sure of it. Knowing that this is my destiny, I find courage to embrace it; I am emboldened to a more active faith.

Have you ever seen members of royalty on television and noticed the dignity with which they carry themselves? It is easy for princes to learn a royal bearing. There is no difficulty at all in getting a princess to walk with grace and charm. Once they have realized who and what they are, they catch on with very little training. So also with holiness for God's elect. Once we realize that God has chosen us for holiness, that ours is a destiny in the light of glory, then holiness becomes natural. In just this way, understanding election will help you in the cause of holiness.

Assurance, Not Presumption

Election is the Bible's teaching and not man's. It promotes humility and not pride, holiness and not license. Furthermore—and here is much of its value to us—*election promotes assurance of salvation but not presumption.*

The difference between a right assurance of salvation and a dangerous presumption is clearly explained in the Bible. The Bible says you are saved through faith in Jesus Christ. Thinking you are saved apart from faith—because of good works, religious observance, baptism, church membership, or an experience you had long ago at a revival—is sheer presumption. Election, like salvation, is only 'in Christ.'

Election deals not with becoming saved, but with assurance of salvation. Election tells us that if we can say to God that we trust in Jesus, then God tells us our faith is securely founded on the solid rock of his eternal decree. We are not saved by believing we are elect; rather we believe we are elect because we have faith in Christ. Election conveys assurance not to unbelief but to the weakness of our saving faith, and in this it is of the greatest value to a Christian.

How many Christians lack the joy that ought to be theirs because they struggle with assurance? How many stumble on in weakness, burdened with doubts that would be erased if only they knew their salvation rested not in themselves but in God? Election tells us that it was God who sought us and not we who sought him, that God called us to himself because he chose us long ago. This teaching changes everything in my struggle for assurance of salvation and therefore with peace about my eternal soul! Romans 8:30 says, 'Those whom he predestined he also called, and those whom he called he also justified, and those whom he justified he also glorified.' This means that if God has called me to himself through Jesus Christ, it was part of his predestined plan. If he called me, he justified me by the blood of Christ and he will bring me to glory forever in heaven.

If you have never repented of your sin and come to God through Jesus Christ, I want to appeal to you to do so now. If you do, you can know that God has called you—you weren't seeking him, he was seeking you—and therefore you are safe forever with a future in glory because of his sovereign will.

Whenever I think of assurance I think of a street we used to live on in Philadelphia when our oldest children were small. We didn't have a yard, so we had to take our children up the street to a park to play. This little journey involved crossing one of the most dangerous intersections in the city. You stood on the sidewalk with hunks of steel blazing past just feet in front of you.

My little children, of course, were always terrified, so they drew near to me and held tight to my hands. That is what we have to do in the dangerous world in which we live. We hold tight to God, trusting in him, and if we don't hold his hand we may be lost. But it wasn't just my children's hands holding mine that kept them safe; I was holding theirs too. With an iron grip! They weren't about to break away. They belonged to me and I loved them with a love deep inside, and I was holding them tight. So it is with God. You must hold to him and press on in the difficulties of life. But he chose you to be his holy people, and he is holding on to you. In all your trials, you may trust in him and rest assured in his sovereign grace.

GLORY TO GOD, NOT MAN

This brings us to a final point, that *election promotes glory to God alone and not to man.*

Why does the Bible teach this doctrine? So far I said that it helps us to be humble, promotes holiness, and gives us assurance of salvation. But the most important reason is so that we realize that our salvation is all of God. Paul said in Romans 11:36: 'For from him, and through him and to him are all things. To him alone be the glory. Amen.' God purposed our salvation; he planned it; he chose us and now he has saved us. All our spiritual blessings and an eternity in glory ahead are all because of his wonderful grace. As James Montgomery Boice wrote in a hymn about election: 'Since grace is the source of the life that is mine, and faith is a gift from on high / I'll boast in my Savior, all merit decline, and glorify God 'til I die.'[38]

We were made to glorify God alone and he has saved us for 'the praise of his own glorious grace' (Eph. 1:6). We must therefore rest our souls solely in him. And when we know we are fully secure, having been chosen in Christ before the foundation of the world, that is when our hearts are fully able to say, 'Yes. All the glory goes to God.' And glorifying him, our hearts are taught to sing:

> Loved with everlasting love,
>   drawn by grace that love to know,
> Spirit sent from Christ above,
>   thou dost witness it is so.
> O this full and precious peace
>   from his presence all divine;
> In a love that cannot cease,
>   I am his and he is mine.[39]

5

Predestined as Sons

Ephesians 1:5

When I was in my early thirties, my wife and I were wrestling with God's call to the gospel ministry. We had been involved as lay workers in an evangelistic ministry and God had blessed our efforts in surprising ways. For over a year we wrestled with the question of God's calling.

There are a number of factors to consider in determining a call to the ministry. First, you need soberly to assess your gifts as a teacher of God's Word. Second, you have to wrestle with God's inward call in your heart. Third, you need the confirmation of the church. After some time, my wife and I concluded that the first two of these were pointing us to the ministry. Nonetheless, I concluded that we should not go in that direction. I was at the time a major in the United States Army, a career that I loved and in which I was succeeding, and I pointed out that I had only seven years to go before I qualified for retirement. It seemed reasonable to play my military career out and then use the retirement income to resource seminary.

Not long after this decision was made, however, my wife and I were making a long drive. At one point, she said, 'Honey, I am delighted not to have to be a pastor's wife, but are you sure we are really doing God's will.' I don't know about you, but I find that long car rides tend to loosen my tongue. So I replied, 'The real reason I am not going to seminary is that I am terrified to lose my identity as an Army officer. My rank and my place in the system define who I am and I am afraid to walk away from that security.'

Once the cat is out of the bag it is impossible to get him back in, and armed with a true understanding of my reluctance to follow God's call, my wife and I the next day walked into the dean's office of Westminster Theological Seminary to enroll. My problem, we realized, was that I did not acknowledge my change of status in Christ. I had been a son of the Army, being the son of a soldier and having spent my whole professional life in the Army uniform. Through faith in Christ, however, God had given me a new status, with a new identity and a new security, as a son in his own family.

Predestined According to God's Will

This is Paul's point in Ephesians 1:5. In his love—his infinite, eternal, and omnipotent love—God 'predestined us for adoption through Jesus Christ.' This teaching involves two key ideas, the first of which is predestination.

Predestination means that God determined something in advance, in this case that we should be children and heirs in his family. This verse complements the one that precedes it, which spoke of God electing, or choosing, believers before the foundation of the world. Verse 5 gives the reason for our election, namely, God's predetermined purpose for our adoption in Christ. God chose us in Christ to be holy and blameless because he had predestined us to be his sons.

Many find the idea of predestination difficult to accept, but the apostle's teaching is clear: he states that our spiritual blessings originate in God's eternal election on the basis of divine predestination. This means that God foreordained the salvation of the elect, here expressed in terms of holiness and sonship.

One way people deny this teaching is to say that God merely predestined that there would be a holy people to be his children through faith in Christ, without predetermining who they would be. All that Paul means, they say, is that God pre-organized salvation so that believers are adopted, without actually deciding who they would be. The problem with this view is the language that Paul uses. Paul does not say that God chose that there would be *a* holy people in Christ, but that he chose *us* for this. Verse 5 does not say that God predestined the principle of adoption as the way of salvation, but that 'he predestined us' to be actually adopted into his family. God chose *us* to be his holy people; he predestined *us* to be his adopted sons.

One argument that is marshaled against predestination comes from Paul's language in Romans 8:29. There, Paul writes: 'For those whom he foreknew he also predestined to be conformed to the image of his Son.' Notice that predestination is preceded by foreknowledge.

Opponents assert that this means that God foresaw that certain people will believe and he then because of their faith predestined their salvation. What God foresaw or foreknew was our faith, according to this view, so that salvation ultimately rests on our act of believing, which causes or allows God to choose us. However, this approach nullifies the very idea of election: it renders pointless the teaching Paul is so clearly trying to convey, namely, that salvation rests on God's own character and purpose. It denies what Paul writes in Titus 3:5, 'He saved us, not because of works done by us in righteousness, but according to his own mercy.'

Paul's text rules out this view, which is associated with Arminian theology. First, the question is raised as to what is the principle on which predestination rests. Predestination is according to…what? Paul specifies, 'He predestined us…according to the purpose of his will' (Eph. 1:5). Predestination rests not on the foreseen faith of the elect but on the sovereign will of God in his eternal counsel. Predestination is sovereign and gracious, resting not on what the believer does but on God's 'purpose' and 'will.'

Furthermore, Paul's statement of predestination in Ephesians 1:5 is preceded in verse 4 by the words 'in love.' Romans 8:29 says God predestined us having foreknown us; Ephesians 1:4–5 says that God predestined us 'in love.' These go together, for God foreknew us in the biblical sense—he loved us. We might read our passage, 'Having fore-loved us, he predestined us.' Paul does not emphasize that God foresaw what we would do but he foresaw us as his beloved people. This is what Moses explained in Deuteronomy 7:7–8. Why did God choose you, he asked Israel? It was not because you were great or numerous, 'But it was because the Lord loved you.' Behind the mystery of divine election is the greater and majestic mystery of God's sovereign love for sinners. What a difference it makes, what peace and joy it brings, to realize that our salvation depends on God's love for us, since God's love is eternal, unchanging, and almighty. God having loved us in eternity, predestined us for adoption as his sons, choosing us to be holy in his sight, all in and through our Lord Jesus Christ.

Predestination and Human Responsibility

There are two main objections against predestination. The first argues that *predestination rules out human will and responsibility*. This makes sense, for if salvation is based on a decision God made before time then what people do today seems to be of no significance. Many people point out passages in the Bible that demand a response or a choice, and therefore declare that predestination is impossible. Did not Joshua say to Israel, 'Choose this day whom you will serve...But as for me and my house, we will serve the LORD' (Jos. 24:15)? Does that not prove that we are saved by what we decide, rather than by what God decides?

The answer is that the Bible teaches both divine predestination and full human responsibility. Our theology must be able to incorporate Ephesians 1:5 and Joshua 24:15—the many passages that speak of God's sovereignty in salvation and those that declare man's responsibility before God. Critics respond by demanding how we can believe two principles that seem to conflict—God's full sovereignty and man's full responsibility. A. W. Pink responds that 'the harmonizing of God's sovereignty with Man's Responsibility is the gordian knot of theology.'[40] It is not necessary for us to reconcile apparent mysteries that are revealed in God's Word. Our calling is to believe all that God has taught, in this case including both human responsibility and divine sovereignty.

But doesn't predestination reduce people to puppets, automatically doing what God has decided long in advance? The answer is found by considering the picture of man in the Bible. Ephesians 1:5, among other verses, teaches predestination, but the same Bible plainly represents men and women as exercising genuine choice. Take Judas Iscariot. His betrayal of our Lord was prophesied in the Book of Psalms (Ps. 41:9) and also by Jesus before it even happened. The Old Testament even predicted how many pieces of silver he would be paid (Zec. 11:12–13). But is he excused for betraying our Lord? Not at all; he is plainly condemned as responsible for his wicked deeds. Jesus plainly stated Judas' responsibility and condemnation: 'Woe to that man by whom the Son of Man is betrayed! It would have been better for that man if he had not been born' (Matt. 26:24). Yet Peter preached that Jesus' betrayal was 'according to the definite plan and foreknowledge of God' (Acts 2:23). So which was it? Did Judas betray Jesus, for which he was responsible, or did God predestine Judas' sin? The answer is *Yes*. Men and women are fully responsible for their actions and God is wholly sovereign over all things.

The most powerful biblical example is Jesus Christ himself. Here is One whose life was not merely predestined, but prerecorded in a great many of its details. Yet who will call God's Son a puppet, without will or responsibility? Divine sovereignty and human responsibility worked hand-in-hand in Jesus' life just as they stand side-by-side in Scripture. We do not have to reconcile them but accept that God's Word teaches both.

Far from rejecting the sovereignty of God in light of human will and responsibility, Christians should especially rejoice in it. It is only because

God is sovereign that we can have hope in a world governed by so much human evil. Joseph the son of Jacob suffered greatly at the hands of his wicked brothers, who unjustly sold him into slavery. Years later, they were all able to marvel at how God's sovereign goodness overruled human evil. Joseph stated: 'you meant evil against me, but God meant it for good' (Gen. 50:20).

Since predestination is not opposed to human will, it also does not argue against evangelism. People say, 'If God predestines people to salvation, then why bother to preach the gospel?' The answer is that God ordains not merely the ends but also the means. He predestines some to be saved and commands us to preach the gospel to that end. If we do not preach and teach the gospel then none will be saved. But God has ordained that they will be; he has chosen his people to be saved. So he has also ordained that we would preach and share the gospel and therefore we will, exercising our human responsibility in accordance with his sovereign will. James Montgomery Boice adds:

> Besides, it is only election that gives us any hope of success as we evangelize. If God cannot call people to faith effectively, how can we? We cannot persuade them. But if God is working, then he can work in us even if we are inept witnesses. We do not know who God's elect are, but we can find out who some of them are by telling them about Jesus…We can speak to them boldly because we know that God has promised to bless his Word.[41]

Is It Fair?

The second main objection to predestination has to do with fairness. People argue that if Christians are saved because of God's predestined will, then it is not fair to hold others accountable for their sin and unbelief. It is helpful to know that this objection is dealt with in the Bible itself. In Romans 9, Paul presents the example of Jacob and Esau, reminding us that 'though they were not yet born and had done nothing either good or bad… [their mother Rebecca] was told, "The older will serve the younger." As it is written: "Jacob I loved, but Esau I hated"' (Rom. 9:11–13). Paul uses this as an example of predestination, then presents the objection based on fairness: 'What then shall we say? Is God unjust?' Paul's reply is both powerful and informative: 'By no means! For he says to Moses, "I will have mercy on whom I have mercy, and I will have compassion on whom I have compassion"' (Rom. 9:14–15).

Paul's point is that when we consider the salvation of sinners, justice is simply the wrong category. Justice offers only condemnation, since 'all have sinned and fall short of the glory of God' (Rom. 3:23). Therefore, all who demand justice from God will be punished under his unyieldingly just wrath. It is not as if God looked down on a neutral humanity, deciding to make some believe and others reject him. Rather, he looked upon a humanity that was unified in sin and unbelief. This is why election is 'in Christ,' joined with God's plan to send his Son to die for our sins. God passes by some sinful rebels to be saved, allowing them to continue their hell-bound course to the praise of his justice. Others he saves to the glory of his mercy, for as Paul says in Romans 9:16, 'It depends not on human will or exertion, but on God, who has mercy.'

Predestination is not unjust, because everyone in hell is condemned for their own choice to sin and reject God. A.W. Tozer said, 'There will be only one text in hell, and it may be cut against the great walls of that terrible place—"True and righteous are thy judgments, O Lord!"'[42] Boice writes, 'It is not justice we want from God; it is grace. And grace cannot be commanded. It must flow to us from God's sovereign purposes decreed before the foundation of the world, or it must not come at all.'[43]

Adoption as Sons

Paul teaches predestination, so it is important for us to believe and understand it. But it is just as important for us to know what we are predestined to. I asked earlier, 'What is a Christian?' This question is one of Paul's emphases in Ephesians. Verse 1 said Christians are 'saints who are… faithful in Christ Jesus.' Here, we add that a Christian is a child of God: 'He predestined us for adoption.'

Paul's idea of salvation as adoption seems to be drawn from the example of Roman civil law. Adoption was not uncommon in Roman society, and adopted children enjoyed the same full rights as natural-born children. Adoption generally involved the taking of sons, often to carry on a family line as heir. We may rightly speak of Christians as sons and daughters in God's family, including both men and women. But when we speak of the doctrine of adoption there is a male distinction that includes heirship. Daughters did not inherit in the Roman world, so in respect to our adoption in Christ, all believers are sons. Just as all Christians are *brides* of Christ, male and female both, so also are all adopted as *sons* of God.

The Christian writer Lew Wallace wrote the story *Ben Hur* about a Jewish prince who was taken as a slave by the Romans. Later he saved the life of a Roman consul, ultimately being adopted as his son and receiving his signet ring of power and authority. That rise from slave to royal heir depicts our elevation from shameful sinners to those made holy in Christ and adopted as God's own sons.

Adoption involved an elaborate legal procedure, culminating with the father presenting his new son before the Roman magistrate. Roman adoption caused a change of status so radical that all past debts and obligations were wiped out, just as God separates us from the debt of our sin. Adoption totally severed old family ties and allegiances, and in the same way Christians are separated by adoption out from sin and from the world.

This change of status is what I needed to remember when I was struggling for faith to answer God's call to enter the ministry. I had come to Christ in faith, but my identity and my security were still found in my former life. I had courage to obey God's call only when I realized that God had not only cleansed me from my sin but had entered me into a new life as his own son, with a new identity that came not from worldly rank or position but from my relationship to him. The same is true for everyone. Why, after all, do people put so much money into the cars they drive and excessively luxurious houses? It is not usually because of practical needs, but because we gain our identity and status in these things. Yet what a bondage earthly status is! You have to keep it up. You have to bear the burden, while the standard of prestige keeps going higher and higher. But God tells all who come to him in Christ that he will give you a far better identity, one that he values even if the world despises it, that of his own beloved son. You may not know the world's favor, but you will know God's love. In Christ, you gain the security of having an Almighty, all-loving, all-wise, covenant-keeping God to care for your needs. Realizing this will free you to be what God wants you to be. Paul wants us to know and lay hold of the blessing of adoption, because he knows that only then will we live to the praise of God.

Adoption makes us full members of God's family, not second-class children. It provides us with all the privileges of sonship, as well as its obligations. Let me just list some privileges. First, we have a relationship with God as our Father, with open access to his presence. Second, we have God's care and provision, materially and especially spiritually. Third, we have the privilege of God's Fatherly discipline as he leads us out of sin and folly. Fourth, we become heirs of all our Father's treasures and even of his glory forever.

The final privilege we receive in adoption is acceptance as beloved brothers with Jesus Christ. By nature we were a disgrace before God, having nothing in common with God's natural-born Son. But in his love, God predestined us for adoption, and therefore Jesus took up our flesh to make us holy and without blemish (as Ephesians 1:4 says), to make us fit to be his brothers. He became like us—becoming a man to pay the debt of sinful humanity—so that we might become like him through the outpoured Holy Spirit, sons of God. He is our elder brother, the natural born Son in whom we are adopted into sonship, so that our adoption is, as Paul says, 'through Jesus Christ.'

If you are a Christian, you are a son of God by divine adoption. Our status is established forever, so now we experience the blessings of divine sonship. The rest of our lives are to be lived learning about God's love, taking possession of the spiritual blessings that belong to us as sons and heirs, and doing God's will as beloved children who long to please the Father. Sons go into the family business, and the chief reward of devoted children is the father's pleasure and praise. This is what eternity holds for us who are made sons of God through Jesus Christ, and it begins now: the joy of pleasing our perfect and heavenly Father and basking in the light of his approval and praise.

Love So Amazing

In a church where I formerly served, there was a Christian couple who had tried unsuccessfully for many years to give birth to a child. With much prayer they concluded that they should adopt. They were driven by a great love within themselves that longed for a child, and motivated by the picture of God's love presented in this verse. It was 'in love' that they pursued adoption; love was the fountain and source of all that would transpire in this child's adoption, just as it is in God's adoption of us into his family.

This couple decided to adopt a child from Russia, so they made the applications, satisfied the requirements, and finally received a picture of the little girl who would be their own. All they had was a photograph, but they poured their love into the child they only knew this way, giving her a name, praying for her, and starting to buy the things she would need as a baby in their home.

Here was this orphan child in a far-away land, without parents and totally oblivious to the great love moving in the hearts of these Christians. They were planning her adoption and storing up blessings. I watched them gazing with love into just a picture of their child, realizing how this only dimly reflects God's loving foreknowledge of us. God set his love on us from afar and predestined our adoption.

The time came when the husband and wife departed for Russia. There were problems with their travel, but finally they arrived in a strange land where they would spend ten days seeking their child. They met with medical officials who suggested frightening reports of problems with the baby's health and development. At one point they had to fend off another family's attempt to get their baby. After days of persisting and working through the system they finally came before a Russian court to plead their fitness to take this baby girl. So many obstacles, so much expense, so many difficulties and problems—what brought them through it all? It was their great love for this child, whom they had known from afar but had named and cherished, and for whom they had stored up rich blessings. Finally, love won through and with great joy that baby came home as their daughter, to be lavished with their favor and to enter into the joy of their home.

Think, then, of what it took for God's love to win through in your adoption. God faced a greater barrier than distance or bureaucracy; he faced the obstacle of your sin, against which stood his own holy justice. But what lengths he pursued that you might be beloved as his child! He sent his natural Son into this world to take up our sin and bear it on the cross. Peter writes, 'Christ died once for sins, the righteous for the unrighteous, that he might bring you to God' (1 Pet. 3:18). This is the price God's love will pay to take away your sin and make you his child, the precious blood of Jesus, 'the Lamb slain from the creation of the world' (Rev. 13:8, NIV).

This is the pursuing love of God that crosses oceans of time, and in almighty grace takes you as his precious child. 'In love he predestined us for adoption through Jesus Christ, according to the purpose of his will.' How else can we respond but to cry out to him with childlike love in return, calling him 'Father,' and taking our place with joy as the sons of God. The Scottish preacher Eric Alexander expressed in a hymn the joyful response of adopted Christians:

> Your saving love has triumphed Lord,
>   Your grace has conquered me.
> Now pardoned, cleansed, redeemed, restored,
> I lift my heart in worship, Lord,
>   Your yielded child to be.[44]

6

To the Glory of His Grace

Ephesians 1:6

As Paul advances his hymn of praise to God for the blessings of salvation, he lifts us to greater and greater heights. In verse 3, he extols our heavenly blessings in the spiritual realms with Christ. In verse 4, we learn that God chose us in Christ to be 'holy and blameless.' Verse 5 takes us higher still, saying that God has predestined believers to be adopted as his children. This is a privilege for which words are barely available: in Christ, we have entered the same relationship that Jesus enjoys with God the Father.

As if this were not enough, Ephesians 1:6 brings us to a higher purpose. Paul is taking us upward, first to holiness and then to adoption. But high above these great peaks looms a greater summit, namely God's purpose to manifest and display in us the 'praise of his glorious grace, with which he has blessed us in the Beloved.' By telling us that God will display the glories of his grace in us, Paul intends to lift our hearts and minds up from the things of earth to the glories of heaven. Paul writes similarly in Colossians 3:1: 'If then you have been raised with Christ, seek the things that are above, where Christ is seated at the right hand of God.'

Ephesians 1:6 concludes the first section of Paul's grand hymn of praise to God. Verses 4–6 tell us that salvation begins in the sovereign grace of the Father, concluding with praise to God for this grace. These are two great principles of the Protestant Reformation that go together inseparably: *sola gratia*, salvation by grace alone, and *soli deo gloria*, glory to God alone. In them the whole of the Christian religion is contained. Paul summed up these themes in the great doxology of Romans 11:36, 'For from him and through him and to him are all things. To him be the glory forever! Amen.'

Paul directs us to God's glory in salvation by making three points. First, he reminds us that God's grace is glorious. Second, he tells us that God's grace comes to us only in Jesus Christ, the Beloved One of God. Finally, he points out that salvation is directed toward the praise of this glorious grace that is in Christ.

Glorious Grace

Paul's first point is that *God's grace is glorious*. This seems like an obvious statement; after all, everything about God is glorious, such as his justice, power, and goodness. But Paul's point is that it is particularly God's grace, especially God's grace, that will glorify him at the end of the ages. How, we should ask, does grace glorify God?

First, *God's grace is glorious in what it reveals to us about him.* We think of great philanthropists who give millions to build hospitals or museums. They are praised in the media and future generations will know from the buildings that bear their names about their generous concern for mankind.

Some time ago, the computer software mogul Bill Gates was in the news for giving tens of billions of dollars for philanthropy. His picture was on the cover of a national magazine for this. Christians should be the first to respond with approval. This man worked hard, had a vision, and now was giving back vast sums of wealth for the betterment of mankind. He was glorified for his generosity, and rightly so.

But great as this is, it is nothing compared to the love that flows from the grace of God. Earthly tycoons give only a portion of their vast riches; they give away money they probably could never manage to spend. How much more glorious is God in his abounding grace! God gave not excess riches, but he gave his one and only Son for us. Furthermore, these worldly philanthropists gave to their fellow man, to those who by rights they ought to love and care for. But God gave his grace to those who were his enemies, who had sinned against him and victimized him with intentional malice. Paul wrote: 'God shows his love for us in that while we were still sinners, Christ died for us' (Rom. 5:8). Consider as well the boundless love of Jesus. 'For you know the grace of our Lord Jesus Christ,' Paul says, 'that though he was rich, yet for your sake he became poor, so that you by his poverty might become rich' (2 Cor. 8:9).

God's grace tells us about his mercy and glorifies him for his willingness to forgive. One great picture of grace comes from the prophet Hosea, who lived in a time of widespread sin. God told the prophet to love and marry a faithless woman to symbolize his own relationship with Israel. Hosea thus married the woman Gomer, had three children by her and gave her his heart, but then Gomer left him to chase after her lovers. God used this not only to show how Israel had forsaken him, but also to reveal his own great love for his people.

As Gomer ran off into adultery, God had Hosea provide for her needs, never failing in his love. Gomer was passed from lover to lover, until she finally was brought naked in the town square to be sold as a slave. Into that scene came her husband, Hosea. God said to him, 'Go again, love a woman who is loved by another man and is an adulteress, even as the LORD loves the children of Israel' (3:1). Hosea went forth and put down the purchase price for the wife who had betrayed and humiliated him, foreshadowing our ransom by the blood of Christ. 'And I said to her,' Hosea recounts, 'You must dwell as mine for many days. You shall not play the whore, or belong to another man, so will I also be to you' (3:3). Reflecting on this scene, God declares to us, 'I will betroth you to me forever. I will betroth you to me in righteousness and in justice, in steadfast love and in mercy' (Hosea 2:19).

What kind of love is that? It is the love of heaven, the love of God by which sinners like us can hope to be saved. It is a love that is glorious in abounding grace and draws us to God.

Christians are called to display this same grace before the world. Grace is what is most attractive about Christianity, what sets it apart from every other religion. Nothing is more unappealing and out-of-synch with biblical Christianity than shrill judgmentalism or bitter divisiveness. And nothing so glorifies God in this world as the grace and forgiveness displayed by Christians. It is natural for us to sue people who do us wrong, to return harsh words with a poisoned response, to respond in anger when our rights are trampled, or to condemn and reject those who hurt us, but it glorifies God's grace when instead we respond with his love.

Christianity is a religion of the grace that comes from God. God's grace is glorious in revealing God's love for mankind, even for sinners, and when displayed in our lives it makes us as lights shining in the darkness of the world.

Second, *God's grace is glorious in the difficulty of what it attempts and achieves.* Men or women are honored for doing something very difficult. In the Olympics, athletic champions are crowned with glory and honor, and some of them with great riches. This is true in other fields. Great inventors like Benjamin Franklin and Thomas Edison are held in esteem for overcoming gulfs in our ignorance. The same is true with great industrialists, like Henry Ford, who solved serious problems of organization and production. There are explorers who overcame great difficulties of danger and prowess. Neil Armstrong will ever be glorified for being the first man to step on the moon. Researchers are held in the highest esteem for overcoming dread diseases. Jonas Saulk is still revered for defeating polio, saving countless millions of lives. Imagine today the glory that would rightly go to any man or woman who discovered a cure for AIDS or cancer.

But against all these, God's grace blazes with an unsurpassable glory. In salvation God overcomes the greatest problem of all, namely, our sin. This could not be put more powerfully than the way Paul does in chapter 2 of this letter. 'You were dead in your transgressions and sins...we were by nature children of wrath.' This is our problem, a corruption in our very nature because of sin. In sin, only one kind of life is open to us, one that is bound by 'the cravings of our sinful nature' and leads to judgment and death. 'But,' Paul says, 'because of his great love for us, God, who is rich in mercy, made us alive with Christ even when we were dead in transgressions—it is by grace you have been saved' (Eph. 2:1-5). This 'you' of salvation describes people like us who were by nature opposed to God and were spiritually dead, but God by his grace brought us to new life. We will glorify someone who cures cancer or any number of other afflictions, but here is God's grace which cures our greatest source of misery and condemnation, which causes us who were dead in sin to be born again to a living faith and to eternal life.

But even this is not the greatest difficulty surmounted by God's grace. Greater yet is the problem within God himself that must be overcome for us to be saved. God overcomes the inflexible demands of his own perfect justice; God's changeless and holy character stands against the salvation of sinners, and God's grace is glorified in finding a way to satisfy his own judgment through the sacrifice of his sinless Son. Here is the wisdom, here is the victory, into which even angels long to look (1 Pet. 1:12), that God may remain just and yet justify sinners through faith in Jesus Christ.

Third, *God's grace is glorious in the effects it produces.* This is what history will reveal in the end. Isaiah prophesied: 'The wolf shall dwell with the lamb, and the leopard shall lie down with the young goat, the calf and the lion and the fattened calf together; and a little child shall lead them...They shall not harm or destroy in all my holy mountain, for the earth shall be full of the knowledge of the Lord as the waters cover the sea' (Isa. 11:6-9). The result of grace is peace, divine peace, peace like a river flowing from the glorious grace of God. God's grace is glorified even now by the peace it brings to troubled hearts through faith in Christ.

The transforming power of God's grace will be glorified in the end, by not only repairing what was broken in the Fall but advancing it to glory. History began with the splendor of Creation, but it fell into shame and ruin through the entry of mankind's sin. God's grace will transform this world into a realm of heavenly glory, the redeemed City of God, 'having the glory of God, its radiance like a most rare jewel, like a jasper, clear as crystal' (Rev. 21:11). What will be true of the church and the regenerated universe will be equally true of us as glorified individuals. Jesus said, 'Then the righteous will shine like the sun in the kingdom of their Father' (Matt. 13:43).

God's grace is glorious—glorious in revealing God's great love, glorious in the difficulty of what it attempts and attains, and glorious in the results it effects—to the praise of God the Father forever.

Grace in the Beloved

The passage that verse 6 concludes is focused on the grace of God the Father. Nonetheless, Paul emphasizes that *God's grace comes to us only in Jesus Christ*. We have seen Paul's Christ-centeredness all through this letter; we are only now in verse 6, but it contains the seventh explicit reference to Christ. Christians are 'saints and the faithful in Christ Jesus'; our spiritual blessings are all 'in Christ'; our election was 'in him,' and we are adopted 'through Jesus Christ.' Now, as he writes of the glory of God's grace, Paul is unwilling to allow the slightest confusion about the centrality of Christ. Here, he refers to Jesus as 'the Beloved.'

There is a play on words here that does not come through in the English versions. Paul employs the noun form and then the verb form of the word *grace*, *charis* and then *chariten*. We might replicate Paul's thought by saying, 'to the praise of his glorious *grace*, which he has *begraced* us in the Beloved.' Grace is something in God—there it is a noun—but it only happens—it becomes a verb—in and through Jesus Christ. By speaking of Jesus as 'the Beloved,' Paul emphasizes that since we are in Christ through faith, God's infinite love for his Son secures his equal Fatherly love for us and thus makes certain our salvation. John Calvin says, 'He names [Christ] *the Beloved*, to tell us that by Him the love of God is poured out to us.'[45] However unlovely we may be—and as sinners we all are spiritually unlovely—God looks on us with loving delight because we are in 'the Beloved.'

That God's grace is available to sinners in Jesus Christ—and only in him—is the very heart of the Christian message. Harry Ironside tells the story of a Dr. Usher, who was a medical missionary in Turkey around a century ago. The province in which he labored received a new governor who was a staunch Muslim. At the time there was a seldom-employed law that foreigners could only remain in Turkey longer than a year if they converted to Islam, and the governor seized this as an opportunity to strike a blow at the Christians.

Wanting to be fair, however, the governor called the missionaries to a banquet, intending to give them a chance to convert before he had them expelled. He began by asking one of them how he thought a man could enter paradise. The Christian replied that through the merits of Jesus Christ our sins are forgiven. But at this the governor only scoffed: 'I cannot believe that God is less righteous than I am, and I do not believe it would be righteous for God because of His friendship for another, to forgive a sinner and take him to paradise.' He added that he himself would never be corrupt enough to set aside justice just because a guilty man was the friend of a friend.

During all this, Dr. Usher was seated at the governor's left hand. The question next came to him: 'What would you say? How may a man be assured of entrance into paradise?' Usher replied by asking to take the situation just presented and change it slightly. 'Let us think of you not merely as the governor of this province, but as the king. You have one son, the prince, whom you love tenderly. Suppose that I am the man who is in debt to the government, owing a sum so vast that I could not pay one part out of a thousand. In accordance with the law, I am cast into prison. Unworthy as I am, your son is a friend of mine: he has a deep interest in me and a real love for me. He seeks you out and says, "My father, my friend is in prison for a debt which he owes and which he cannot pay. Will you permit me to pay it all for him in order that he may go free?" And you say to him, "My son, since you are so interested and willing to pay the debt yourself, I am willing that it should be so."'[46] The prince then went to the proper authorities, paid the debt in full on behalf of his friend, and then took the receipt to have him removed from the prison.

Ironside comments that even this illustration hardly does justice to what Jesus did for us. 'Our Lord saw us in our great need. He paid for us, and having settled the debt He has now brought us into the royal family, washed us from every stain of sin, robed us in garments of glory and beauty, and given us a seat at the table of the King. He has taken us into favor in the Beloved so that the Father's thoughts of Christ are His thoughts of love for us who trust in Christ.'[47]

When we speak of Jesus paying our debt, we refer of course to his sacrificial death on the cross. He paid for us not in money, but in the coin of his own precious blood. God's grace is always in Christ, and it is most fully revealed at the cross. Paul explains in 2 Corinthians 5:21, 'For our sake [God] made him to be sin who knew no sin, so that in him we might become the righteousness of God.'

To the Praise of His Glorious Grace

Paul tells us in this verse that God's grace is glorious and that it is in Christ. But his particular point of emphasis has to do with our salvation by grace in Christ. *The purpose*, he says, *for which we are saved is the praise of this glorious grace of God*. Our salvation which is by grace alone is also to God's glory alone. This is the highest end that anything possibly could serve.

Let me briefly draw out some implications of this teaching. This passage opens a window into what is happening in this world of woe. 'What is God doing?' people ask. The answer is here, that he is storing up praise to the glory of his grace in the salvation of sinners through his Son, Jesus Christ. Christians sometimes wonder, 'Why did God allow sin into the world in the first place?' That is a deeper mystery than we are going to resolve, but at least a partial answer is that in our redemption from sin he is glorified as would not otherwise be possible. Paul alludes to this great reality in Romans 11:32, the last verse before the great doxology that concludes the doctrinal portion of that letter. There, he writes, 'God has consigned all to disobedience, that he may have mercy on all.'

Furthermore, Ephesians 1:6 tells us how great is the matter of our salvation and how significant it is to God himself. How typical it is for us to think of salvation merely in terms of our own emotional and spiritual experience, or merely in terms of a certain lifestyle as an end in itself. But ultimately, we find here, our salvation is not about us; God saved us with a higher motive than just our blessing. Do you realize what a solid ground this is for assurance? If we are in Christ by faith, our ultimate salvation is as certain as is God's purpose to bring glory to himself through the praise of his marvelous grace! Not only that, but by means of the Fall into sin and our subsequent redemption in Christ, God has destined us, as John Stott explains, 'for a higher dignity than even creation would bestow on us. He intended to "adopt" us as his children.'[48] God has so arranged salvation as to bring us the highest possible blessing and himself the highest possible praise, both of which result only through the glory of his grace.

Demands My All

I want to conclude the story about Dr. Usher and his Turkish governor. He told the governor the story of the king's son who paid the prisoner's debt, as an illustration of Christ's saving work for us. But he went on and concluded that the man who was saved would surely live his whole life in gratitude to the prince. 'You paid my debt,' he would say, so 'it is a joy for me to do something to show my gratitude.'

The governor listened carefully and he thought for some time. Finally, a light shone in his eye. He exclaimed: 'Oh, then, Dr. Usher, is this the reason why you have a hospital here in Turkey? Is this why you establish these schools and why you missionaries are giving your lives for our people? You are not trying to earn your way into paradise?' 'No,' said Dr. Usher, 'our way into paradise is settled because Jesus paid the debt, and now we serve because we love Him.'[49]

Beginning with that occasion, the Turkish governor, so staunch a Muslim on his arrival, changed his attitude toward Christians. He did not force the missionaries to leave, and went on to show them such kindness that he ultimately was dismissed from his office because of his leniency toward Christians. The man so determined to be the Christians' enemy had been reached through the grace of God, previously unknown to him, and the missionaries had genuine hopes that he actually had been saved.

Our salvation is 'to the praise of [God's] glorious grace, with which he has blessed us in the Beloved.' The fact that we, as sinners, are saved, gives praise to the glory of God's grace. And then the grace we show others, flowing out from God's love as it comes to us in Christ, redounds to the praise of his grace. It is for this that we are saved, and it is for this that we now are called to live—for the glory of God's grace. And it is in this, the greatest glory in all the world, that you will find the true purpose of your life, if you will believe on Jesus Christ—to live *in* the glory of God's grace, and to live *for* the glory of God's grace.

What will that mean for you? It will certainly mean a more serious commitment to God's Word and to his work in this world. It will mean turning from sin and self-centeredness. It will include living out God's grace through compassion and mercy for others. Isaac Watts, one of the great hymn writers, answered it probably the best: having surveyed 'the wondrous cross on which the Prince of glory died,' he then sang: 'Love so amazing, so divine, demands my soul, my life, my all.'[50]

7

Redemption in Christ

Ephesians 1:7–8

There are times in our study of the New Testament when we will find ourselves face-to-face with the very heart of the gospel. This study is one of those occasions. We should not be surprised that this is so, for as we progress through this great hymn of praise with which Paul opens Ephesians, we now come to the point where he considers the work of Jesus Christ. Already we have considered God the Father as the source of our salvation. Now that we turn to God's Son and his work we focus on salvation itself, on what salvation is and how it happens.

Savior from Our Sin

As we pass into this new section of Paul's hymn of praise, we are advancing from eternity past into history. God chose us for holiness and predestined us for adoption before there even was time. Now we read of Christ coming into the world, and Paul tells us he came to be our Redeemer.

If you stopped people on the street and asked them about Jesus Christ, most would probably say he came as a great moral teacher and example. But the Gospels make it clear that Jesus came to save us from our sins. This was the point the angel made to Joseph: 'You are to give him the name Jesus, because he will save his people from their sins' (Matt. 1:21). Jesus explained, 'The Son of Man did not come to be served, but to serve, and to give his life as a ransom for many' (Matt. 20:28). Jesus was born *into* this world to die *for* the world; as Paul tells us here, Jesus came to give us 'redemption through his blood, the forgiveness of sins.'

This brings us back to a question I have been repeatedly asking, 'What is a Christian?' Here we have another answer—a crucial one—that a Christian is a sinner who has been redeemed by the blood of Jesus Christ. If you are offended to be called a sinner, if you think that because you dress well and have good manners and present a good appearance that you are therefore different from the common lot of fallen man, that you are free from the great problem gripping our world in misery and guilt, then this verse says that whatever else you may be, you are not a Christian. Unless you are willing to be identified as a sinner, as one of the morally diseased race for whom Jesus came as the Great Physician, and unless you agree that Jesus had to die for you to be saved, then you simply are not one of those for whom he came. Jesus came as a Redeemer. He offered his precious blood that we might be forgiven our sins and then have new life through him.

Sin is the great problem facing this world, especially as it makes us guilty before God. Psychologists may deny the idea of sin and guilt, saying that we cannot be held responsible because our actions are the result of our genes, our environment, our parents, or something else external to us. But the Bible flatly declares that God holds us responsible for our sins. Romans 6:23 says, 'The wages of sin is death.' Our great need today is not therapy, not stress management, not social reform, but salvation from our sins.

Notice how significant it is that sin appears where it does in Paul's presentation of Christian salvation. So far he has spoken of God having chosen a people for holiness, predestining us to be adopted as his sons. There is, however, a barrier standing in the way of God's purpose. This is what Paul deals with next, just as it is this barrier that God addressed by sending his Son into the world. Martyn Lloyd-Jones writes, 'The great obstacle…is the obstacle of sin; sin in general and sins in particular. It is our sins that have come between us and God…So before we can ever arrive at the predestined position which God has purposed for us, something has to be done about this problem of our sin and our sins. It was to perform this special and particular work that the Son of God came into this world.'[51]

Redemption from Sin

The way that Jesus dealt with the problem of sin is set forth in verse 7: 'redemption through his blood.' Redemption is one of the great words of our faith. It is not without reason that so many of our hymns praise our Lord for this. Redemption is something to sing about, both in terms of what it does for us and what it cost to him: 'O for a thousand tongues to sing my great Redeemer's praise'; 'All hail, Redeemer, hail, for thou hast died for me'; 'I will sing of my Redeemer, and his wondrous love for me: on the cruel cross he suffered, from the curse to set me free.'

Redemption is a term that is borrowed from the marketplace and involves the idea of buying something. It presupposes some kind of bondage or captivity, circumstances that afflict us but from which we are not able to free ourselves. It was the common practice in ancient warfare for conquerors to take captives to be used as slaves. However, when someone of great wealth or high station was captured he normally was not enslaved but instead was redeemed, that is, set free after a ransom was paid. Redemption takes us from slavery to freedom, from affliction to salvation.

Redemption was an important part of the Old Testament economy. To keep some Israelites from falling into permanent slavery or destitution, there was a provision whereby a kinsman redeemer was obliged to pay his relative's debts, to purchase him out from slavery, and to buy back family land that had been lost (Lev. 25:25–28). This idea of redemption was extended in the Bible to include the rescue and deliverance of God's people in captivity. Redemption was normally by purchase but it could also be by power. The greatest Old Testament example of redemption by saving power was God's deliverance of Israel from their bondage in Egypt in the exodus. God told Moses: 'I will free you from being slaves to them, and I will redeem you with an outstretched arm and with mighty acts of judgment' (Exod. 6:6–7).

Redemption, therefore, speaks of God saving us from a situation we could never get ourselves out of, just as the Israelites would have remained in Egypt forever if God had not come to their aid. The New Testament takes this concept and applies it to the problem of our sin. Sin is our great problem, but even worse, it is a problem that we cannot solve by ourselves. We think of sin as a small thing, indulgences that do us little harm, especially if nobody seems to be hurt and if we are able to get away with them. But the Bible says that the result of sin is slavery, bondage, and crushing affliction out of which we are totally unable to escape on our own.

James Boice observes 'a parallel between the ways in which a person could fall into slavery in antiquity and how a person is said to be bound by sin in the Bible.'[52] First, he explains, a person might be born into slavery, and in the same way the Bible speaks of all mankind since Adam being born into sin, inheriting from his sin a sinful nature. David acknowledged this, lamenting, 'Surely I was sinful at birth, sinful from the time my mother conceived me' (Ps. 51:5). Second, as we noted, a person might be enslaved as a result of military conquest. Similarly, we are mastered by sin's power over our flesh and enticed into sin by temptations. Third, one might have debts he could not pay and find himself sold into slavery. Likewise, our sin creates a debt before God's justice that we can never repay and that binds us under the curse of guilt. In all of these ways, our situation in sin is like that of a slave, including the miserable living condition experienced by slaves.

This is the bad news of our sin; as Jesus declared, 'Everyone who sins is a slave to sin' (John 8:34). As slaves, we cannot live free lives. Because of our sinful nature's corrupting influence on our choices and desires, we cannot meaningfully speak of having a free will. Yes, we make choices, but our will is in bondage to sin, which is why we keep on sinning. Furthermore, we cannot relate to God in the way he intended, as beloved children, since our sin excludes us from his holy fellowship. Sin is bondage, and having been born in sin, having been conquered by sin, having accrued a great debt of sin's guilt before God, there is nothing we can do on our own to escape this slavery and its ruin.

BOUGHT BY HIS BLOOD

This is why Paul praises God for the redemption we have in Jesus Christ. Jesus came to us as Moses came to Israel in Egypt, to deliver us from bondage. But there is a second component for us to consider in the biblical idea of redemption, namely, the payment of a ransom as the instrument of our freedom. Jesus redeemed us, Paul says, 'through his blood.'

This statement refers to Jesus' death on the cross, which the Bible identifies as a ransom to free us from our sins. Jesus himself said that he came 'to give his life as a ransom for many' (Matt. 20:28). John Murray explains that our redemption consisted in Jesus' 'substitutionary blood-shedding…with the end in view of thereby purchasing to himself the many on whose behalf he gave his life a ransom.'[53]

The question arises as to whom Christ paid this ransom. Many in the early church taught that he paid it to Satan, since the Bible speaks of our bondage to him. This is the view enshrined in C. S. Lewis' fantasy, *The Lion, the Witch, and the Wardrobe,* where the Christ-figure Aslan must pay his blood to the satanic White Witch for sinful Edmund to be redeemed. 'You know that every traitor belongs to me as my lawful prey,' the White Witch demands, 'and that for every treachery I have a right to a kill.'[54]

The Bible does not speak, however, of Christ buying off the Devil or paying a ransom to him. While sinners are Satan's captives, it is not because he has any lawful right to them as his prey. Rather, Hebrews 2:14 says that by his death Jesus destroyed the Devil and his power. Satan is overcome in redemption by the power of Christ, but Christ's ransom was paid to God's law, to release us from the law's penalty on sin. This is what Paul writes in Galatians 3:13: 'Christ redeemed us from the curse of the law by becoming a curse for us.' Likewise, Colossians 2:14 speaks of Christ dying so as to 'cancel the written code, with its regulations, that was against us and that stood opposed to us; he took it away, nailing it to the cross.' By taking our sins upon himself, paying with his own blood the debt we owed to God's holy justice, Jesus redeemed us from the law's condemnation. Thus he destroyed the devil's power, which relied on the curse of God's law.

Sin has two main effects, one external and the other internal, one of which has to do with the guilt our sin accrues and the other with its power over us and in us. This is what Augustus Toplady so rightly described in the beloved hymn *Rock of Ages*: 'Be of sin the double cure, cleanse me from its guilt and power.'[55] Sin's external and legal effect—its guilt—separates us from God and brings us under his wrath. Sin's internal and spiritual effect—its power—keeps us in misery and weakness, overcomes our will through temptation, and bars us from obeying God's commands. Christ redeems us from both these effects of sin, yet Paul's emphasis in this verse is especially on the forgiveness of sin's guilt: 'We have redemption through his blood, the forgiveness of sins.'

Forgiveness of our sin is always first and foremost in salvation. It is forgiveness that takes us from God's curse to his blessing, from rejection to acceptance. It is of the greatest importance, then, that we should understand our forgiveness in light of Christ's redeeming work.

The question may arise in your mind, for instance, as to how thorough is this forgiveness. Does it mean that *all* your sins are forgiven? And to what extent does God forgive you? Is he like us, in that while he may want to forgive us, the pain and horror of what we have done is simply too strong for him fully to put away? The Bible answers all these questions emphatically. Paul says, 'He forgave us all our sins' (Col. 2:13). God promises, 'I will forgive their wickedness and will remember their sins no more' (Heb. 8:12). The psalmist therefore exults, 'As far as the east is from the west, so far has he removed our transgressions from us' (Ps. 103:12). Christ's redeeming work completely removes all our sins forever from God's sight. John thus writes: 'the blood of Jesus [God's] Son cleanses us from all sin' (1 John 1:7).

Charles Colson tells of watching a television interview with Albert Speer, Hitler's confidant and industrialist, who after World War II was stricken with a great sense of guilt for the horrors he had assisted. Of all the war criminals tried at Nuremburg, Speer was the only one to admit his guilt, for which he served twenty years in Spandau prison. In one of his books Speer commented that his guilt never could nor should be forgiven and that he would forever be seeking to atone for his sins. Commenting on this, his interviewer pressed him as to whether it would ever be possible for him to be forgiven. Speer shook his head, replying, 'I don't think it will be possible.' Colson remarks on Speer's obvious desperation to have his guilt removed. 'I wanted to write Speer,' he recalls, 'to tell him about Jesus and his death on the cross, about God's forgiveness. But there wasn't time. [That] interview was his last public statement; he died shortly after.'[56]

The best way to be sure about your full, complete, and final forgiveness through faith in Christ is to consider the value of the ransom with which Jesus bought you from condemnation.

No doubt your sin is very great. Most of us could stand to have a healthier appreciation of the extent and cost of our sin, but some of us are weighed down with sins we have committed that seem beyond redemption. Then consider the price with which you were redeemed, the precious blood of the Son of God. What debt can you have that cannot be purchased by that? Jesus having paid the price and suffered the punishment for your sin, what is there left for you to endure? God has been paid and the debt to his justice is gone. All that is left is for you joyfully to embrace the free forgiveness of God, who out of his grace redeemed you through the blood of his own beloved Son.

Paul's intention is that realizing the completeness of our forgiveness and the inestimable price paid for us by Christ, we should respond by giving the whole of our hearts in praise to God. He tells us that our redemption is 'in accordance with the riches of God's grace.' This is the kind of redemption that is appropriate to a God whose grace is so glorious and rich. When it comes to our redemption, we need not bring one penny, for God is rich enough in his grace to pay all that we need, and it glorifies him to save us in this way. Charles Hodge writes, 'It is the overflowing abundance of unmerited love, inexhaustible in God, and freely accessible through Christ.'[57]

R. Kent Hughes urges us to make a distinction here between the idea of God redeeming us *out of* the riches of his grace (which he certainly does) and the nobler idea of God redeeming us *according to* the riches of his grace. He cites a picture of John D. Rockefeller, at the time the richest man in the world, dressed in a top hat and waistcoat, placing a dime into the hand of an impoverished little child. Rockefeller gave those ten cents *out of* his riches, but the gift was hardly *in accordance* with his great resources.[58] Not so with God; his gift lavishes us with the blessings of salvation *in accordance* with the riches of his grace. This infinite gift is worthy of God's infinite treasures of grace and it commends us to grateful awe in response. God's riches are the cause of our redemption; it is because of this wealth of grace in God that Christ paid so great a price for us. Likewise, our redemption is the display of God's grace and it demands the highest praise of which we are capable. The hymnist says, 'I bless the Christ of God; I rest on love divine, and with unfalt'ring lip and heart I call this Savior mine.'

WITH ALL WISDOM AND UNDERSTANDING

At this point Paul's thoughts begin to cascade, as they often do in this letter. The emotional drive with which he writes sometimes makes it hard to analyze his thought neatly, and the next statement is an example of this difficulty. He is extolling God's grace which, Paul says, 'he lavished upon us, in all wisdom and insight' (Eph. 1:8). This clause may be taken in one of two ways. It may describe Christ's redeeming work as an example of God's wisdom and insight. Or Paul may be adding the gifts of wisdom and insight to the forgiveness of sin as blessings we receive through Christ's redeeming work.

The language here suggests to me that Paul is commending the 'wisdom and insight' of God as they are displayed in our redemption. In verse 6 he extolled 'the *glory* of God's grace.' Already here he has praised 'the *riches* of God's grace.' Now, then, he writes of the *wisdom and insight* of God's grace, and this certainly is a fitting addition for a trilogy of praise. It is the wisdom of redemption that causes angels to marvel; Christ's death on the cross is the foolishness of God that is wiser than the wisdom of men (1 Cor. 1:25). Here is a self-sacrificing love that befuddles the world's conventional wisdom and causes us to marvel at this way of salvation that is so sublime and divine. Whenever we think of the blood of Jesus Christ, shed for us, we should be reminded with thanksgiving of what God declares in Isaiah 55:9: 'As the heavens are higher than the earth, so are my ways higher than your ways and my thoughts than your thoughts.'

But Paul may instead mean that redemption not only gives us forgiveness but also equips us with 'all wisdom and insight.' *Wisdom* deals with our broad awareness of spiritual truth and the word used for *insight* speaks of spiritual discernment for dealing with actual situations. This is in fact what happens to us when Christ redeems us and makes us his own. In the Gospels we see him walking with and instructing the disciples, and now he does the same for us by his Spirit and through the Bible. In Romans 12:2–3 Paul writes of the mind renewal that comes about through God's transforming Word. As a result of this, he says, Christians are able to 'discern what is the will of God, what is good and acceptable and perfect.'

This is the freedom Jesus intends for us when he redeems us from sin, and it is this we are to seek by studying and applying the teachings of the Bible. The Gospel of Luke tells us of a man who was possessed by a great multitude of demons. Luke describes him as alienated from other people, dwelling among tombs, a violent and destructive man (Luke 8:26–9). Mark adds that he cried out at night and tore his skin with stones (Mark 5:5). What a picture of the bondage of our sin! But Jesus cast out the demons and redeemed the man, freeing him from his torment. Luke writes that the people who came out later to see what happened found the man, 'sitting at the feet of Jesus, clothed and in his right mind' (Luke 8:35). What a true picture of salvation, of the freedom into which Jesus redeems us. Jesus brings us to himself, clothes us in his righteousness, and blesses us with 'wisdom and insight,' so that restored to our right mind we might go on to do his will.

Redeeming Love

In studying the previous verse I mentioned the story of the prophet Hosea as an example of the glory of God's grace as it reveals his great love. God had Hosea marry Gomer, a woman who proved to be unfaithful. Yet all the while, as she pursued her lovers and descended further into sin, he remained steadfast in his love for her. That story comes to its climax in a scene that illustrates Christ redeeming us from our sin.

Sin makes us slaves, and Gomer literally ended up on the auction block, probably because of debts. God told Hosea to buy her back to demonstrate his own faithful love for us. Slaves were typically sold in the town square, stripped naked for all to inspect. This is the same degradation into which sin seeks to drag us all.

The men gathered to place bids on the stripped body of Hosea's wife, now to become a slave. 'Twelve pieces of silver,' bid one. 'Thirteen,' called a voice from the back, a voice she may have dimly remembered. 'Fourteen,' came the reply. 'Fifteen,' said Hosea. 'Fifteen silver pieces and a bushel of barley.' Stepping forward and reaching out to his wife, Hosea spoke, 'Fifteen pieces of silver and a bushel and a half of barley.' Everyone realized he could not be outbid and so the other men began to walk away. She was rightly his already, but sin had torn her away. Now he has bought her back with everything he has and then he drapes her with his love. The conclusion of the story in Hosea 3 says, 'So I bought her for fifteen shekels of silver and about a homer and a lethech of barley. And I said to her, 'You must dwell as mine for many days. You shall not play the whore, or belong to another man; so will I also be to you" (Hosea 3:2–3).

If we are in Christ, this is our story as well. James Boice comments:

> We were created for intimate fellowship with God and for freedom, but we have disgraced ourselves by unfaithfulness. First we have flirted with and then committed adultery with this sinful world and its values. The world even bid for our soul, offering sex, money, fame, power, and all the other items in which it traffics. But Jesus, our faithful bridegroom and lover, entered the market place to buy us back. He bid his own blood. There is no higher bid than that. And we became his. He reclothed us, not in the wretched rags of our old unrighteousness, but in his new robes of righteousness. He has said to us, 'You must dwell as mine…you shall not belong to another…so will I also be to you.'[59]

You may have noticed that I have concluded many of these studies with excerpts from Christian hymns. That was not intentional at first, but realizing what I was doing I then recognized how fitting it is in considering the great themes of our salvation set before us. How can we not sing, with thoughts of a Savior like this? More importantly, how can we not give all our trust, all our hope, all our love to him, offering the whole of our lives in grateful praise? Horatius Bonar expressed our response in this way:

> I praise the God of grace;
>   I trust his truth and might;
> He calls me his, I call him mine,
>   my God, my joy, my light.
> 'Tis he who saveth me,
>   and freely pardon gives;
> I love because he loveth me,
>   I live because he lives.[60]

8

Through His Blood

Ephesians 1:7

In his magisterial study titled *The Cross of Christ*, John R. W. Stott observes that 'every religion and ideology has its visual symbol, which illustrates a significant feature of its history or beliefs.' He cites the lotus flower, which symbolizes Buddhism, 'because of its wheel shape that is thought to depict either the cycle of birth and death or the emergence of beauty and harmony out of the muddy waters of chaos.' Modern Judaism employs the Star of David, which recalls its hope for a Messiah out of this royal line. Islam employs a crescent, an ancient symbol of sovereignty picked up from Byzantium. Secular ideologies also employ symbols. The Marxist hammer and sickle represented the urban and rural proletariat; they are crossed to indicate the unity of industrial laborers with peasant farmers. The sinister, bent cross of the Nazi swastika evoked Germany's pagan past and the ideals of Aryan supremacy.[61]

An Awkward Symbol

Christians likewise have their symbols. In the early church's age of persecution, the fish symbol served as a surreptitious way of identifying oneself as a Christian. The Greek word for *fish* provided an acrostic that had meaning only for church members; the letters stood for 'Jesus Christ, Son of God, Savior.' When persecution died down and Christians were able to depict their faith openly, it was the cross that came to the fore. Stott comments on how striking this choice of a symbol was, first of all because of the horror with which the cross was looked upon in the ancient world. He writes, 'How could any sane person worship as a god a dead man who had been justly condemned as a criminal and subjected to the most humiliating form of execution? This combination of death, crime and shame put him beyond the pale of respect, let alone of worship.'[62]

The Roman orator, Cicero, condemned crucifixion as 'a most cruel and disgusting punishment.' 'There is no fitting word,' he revulsed, 'that can possibly describe so horrible a deed.'[63] The Jews felt the same way, informed by Deuteronomy 21:23 that 'anyone who is hung on a tree is under God's curse.' More recently, Nietzsche decried the cross as the most abominable decadence, because it offers salvation to the weak, who ought by rights to be destroyed. Other modern thinkers belittle the cross because its related doctrines of God's wrath, man's sin, and the atonement are, as one put it, 'intellectually contemptible and morally outrageous.'⁶⁴ Ghandi, the Indian leader, admitted to having once been attracted to Christianity until he considered the cross. 'I could accept Jesus as a martyr,' he wrote, 'an embodiment of sacrifice, and a divine teacher.' But when it came to the saving significance of Christ's death, this was another matter. Ghandi wrote, 'That there was anything like a mysterious or miraculous virtue in it, my heart could not accept.'⁶⁵

With all this going against it, the cross is hardly an advertiser's dream. If only we could get rid of the cross, some have thought, we could win great masses to Christianity. Yet the cross persists as the emblem of all that Christians hold dear, so that Jesus' followers insist that to remove the cross is to lose everything. What is the greatest scandal to the world, what is most hateful and unacceptable to many about the New Testament depiction of Jesus, is at the same time the most blessed, most cherished, most indispensable and transforming fact of history and theology, to which we cling as that which is most necessary for the salvation of our souls. As Paul put it, 'For the message of the cross is foolishness to those who are perishing, but to us who are being saved it is the power of God' (1 Cor. 1:18). Thus he wrote of himself and all the true church following him, 'We preach Christ crucified: a stumbling block to Jews and foolishness to Gentiles, but to those whom God has called, both Jews and Greeks, Christ the power of God and the wisdom of God' (1 Cor. 1:22–24).

Sacrificial Death

Perhaps what is most noteworthy in verse 7 is the off-hand manner in which Paul refers to Christ's blood. He writes, 'In him we have redemption through his blood, the forgiveness of sins.' The lack of explanation here suggests Paul's confidence in his readers' understanding at this point. We know from other letters, such as Romans, that the saving power of Christ's blood was a central feature of Paul's systematic theology. Here in Ephesus, it seems, Paul has freedom simply to mention Christ's blood without elaboration, a happy situation he seldom encountered and one that we certainly should not assume today. It was often necessary for Paul and other apostolic writers—the writer of Hebrews especially comes to mind—to dwell deliberately on the nature and significance of Christ's death, and it is necessary for us to do so today.

For instance, it is important for us to know that when Paul speaks of Christ's blood it is his death that he specifically has in mind. There are some who think the reference to blood speaks not of Christ's death but of his life. It is common today to read summaries of the gospel or the doctrine of justification that make no mention of the cross, only the resurrection. Leviticus 17:11 says, 'The life is in the blood,' and on that basis some have taught that by pouring out his blood Christ gave access to the power of his life. But the point of that verse is quite the opposite. Since 'the life is in the blood,' blood sacrifice takes the life and causes the sacrifice's death. 'The blood of Christ' therefore means 'the death of Christ.' Paul makes this connection clear in many places, writing: 'He was delivered over to death for our sins' (Rom. 4:25). 'We were reconciled to [God],' he says, 'through the death of his Son' (Rom. 5:10). By taking the cup which in the Lord's Supper signifies Christ's blood, Paul writes, 'You proclaim the Lord's death until he comes' (1 Cor. 11:26).

Yet, when we speak of Christ's blood, it is a certain kind of death we have in view. It is essential that Jesus did not die in bed of old age or infirmity; his was a sacrificial death, by which he represented his people before God and vicariously suffered in our place.

All this was prefigured in the Old Testament sacrifices. There were different kinds of sacrifices under the old covenant, but at the heart of them all were the sin and guilt offerings. The Book of Leviticus presents these with several common features. First of all, the animal to be sacrificed had to be without blemish or flaw. God's people were not permitted to offer the weakest and least desirable from their flocks, but only the best and strongest and most pure. This pointed forward to the sinlessness of Christ; himself unblemished by sin, he alone was able to offer himself for the sins of others.

Second, God graciously provided the animal as a substitute to bear the penalty the sinner deserved. The key theological terms here are *vicarious* and *substitutionary*. The substitute suffered vicariously, that is, on behalf of the sinner.

Third, the blood of this sacrifice was sprinkled on the altar before the Lord, so that having seen the proof of the sacrificial death, God would forgive the sinner who came trusting in it. In many cases, the blood was likewise sprinkled on the one who had sinned, to show the removal of guilt. This whole procedure was called the making of atonement; over and over Moses summarizes in Leviticus, 'In this way the priest will make atonement for the man's sin, and he will be forgiven' (4:20, 26, 31, 35; 5:13, 18; 6:7; 12:8; 14:31).

The Book of Hebrews makes explicit the connection between these Old Testament sacrifices and the death of Jesus Christ. Like those earlier types, Jesus' death was a vicarious, substitutionary atonement. He suffered the death others deserved, in their place and on their behalf, to make atonement for their sins. Hebrews 9:13–14 notes that the old animal sacrifices were able to cleanse people only outwardly and ceremonially.

'How much more, then, will the blood of Christ, who through the eternal Spirit offered himself unblemished to God, cleanse our consciences from acts that lead to death, so that we may serve the living God!' Unlike the blood of bulls and goats, Christ's blood is an effectual, spiritual sacrifice. Therefore, Jesus cried in his death, 'It is finished!' (John 19:30). Hebrews 9:26–28 argues that no other sacrifice than Christ's is needed: 'He has appeared once for all at the end of the ages to put away sin by the sacrifice of himself. And just as it is appointed for man to die once, and after that comes judgment, so Christ [was] offered once to bear the sins of many.'

All this was made vivid in the final week of Jesus' life, which coincided with the feast of Passover. While our Lord entered Jerusalem for what we call Palm Sunday, sacrificial lambs were being herded by the thousands into the city. This was God's way of saying, 'Here is your true sacrifice, what the lambs had all along merely symbolized!' Later, when Jesus was crucified, the hammer-strokes nailed his hands and feet to the cross as the Jews were slaying their Passover lambs. This is what John the Baptist, the final prophet of the old dispensation, was getting at when he spoke of Jesus, 'Behold, the Lamb of God who takes away the sin of the world!' (John 1:29).

All these themes are bound up in Paul's mention of the blood of Christ: Jesus' vicarious, substitutionary, sin-atoning death as the true and only means that sinners may be forgiven and reconciled to God.

Propitiation & Expiation

Every club, profession, or political body has its own specialized terminology, and Christianity is no different. People complain when a preacher uses technical theological terms, but in a time when people remember multiple ten-digit passwords and enough technical knowledge about their computers to fill a textbook, I am unashamed to do so when it comes to the most important fact of history, the death of Christ. Technical terms aid us by affording precision in our thinking, and that is no less the case when it comes to the significance of the blood of Christ.

The Bible presents Christ's death from a number of perspectives, such as the temple setting, the law-court, the marketplace, and the family. In each case, the core idea is that of vicarious substitution, and from each point of view Christ is presented as the mediator between God and man who solves the problem of our sin.

First, let us consider the perspective of the temple setting. The word *atonement* speaks of a sacrifice dealing with sin, and the Bible describes this in terms of two effects. The first of these, *propitiation*, is directed toward God, specifically to the problem of God's just wrath against sin. The Bible assures us that God is angry not merely at sin but at sinners, as the example of Sodom and Gomorrah so vividly demonstrates. But God's wrath is different from the impetuous, often sinful, anger of human beings. God's wrath is righteous. It is good, holy, and appropriate. As J. I. Packer notes, God's wrath 'is never the capricious, self-indulgent, irritable, morally ignoble thing that human anger so often is. It is, instead, a right and necessary reaction to objective moral evil.'[66] This being the case, we as sinners need to be saved *from God*. God is rightly angry with us and to propitiate this wrath Christ died for us. God poured out the infinite hell of his wrath upon his Son—who by the power of his infinite life could bear it—and thus God's wrath is turned aside from us, or propitiated, by the blood of Christ.

When we think of God requiring a blood sacrifice to propitiate his wrath, we need to remember the vital point in the gospel that God himself provides the propitiation we need in the gift of his Son. Paul says in Romans 3:24–25 that we 'are justified by his grace as a gift, through the redemption that is in Christ Jesus, whom God put forward as a propitiation by his blood, to be received by faith.' Therefore, Christians are saved *from God*—this is our great need, to escape his holy wrath. And we are saved *by God*, who sent his Son to propitiate his own righteous anger through the blood of his cross.

Christ's death has the God-ward effect of propitiation, symbolized by the sprinkling of blood before God on the altar. But it also has an effect on us, symbolized by the sprinkling of blood upon the sinner. This is called *expiation*, that is, the removal of our sin. John wrote of this in his first epistle: 'If we confess our sins, he is faithful and just to forgive us our sins and to cleanse us from all unrighteousness' (1 John 1:9). This is expiation—the cleansing of our sin.

Christ's blood does more than turn God's wrath from us; it actually makes us clean. How significant this is for sinners, who though forgiven often feel dirty before God and man. But if Christ has died for you, he has cleansed you with his blood! Your sin is taken away. This blessing was symbolized on the Old Testament Day of Atonement. Leviticus 16:10 tells us the High Priest laid his hands on a goat, transferring the peoples' sins onto this substitute. The scapegoat, as it was called, was then led into the wilderness, never to be seen again, just as our sins are taken away by the blood of Christ. The writer of Hebrews emphasized the importance of this cleansing for our personal communion with God. Christ, he notes, has opened the way to God by his blood and now serves before God as our interceding priest. 'Therefore,' he says, 'let us draw near [to God] with a true heart in full assurance of faith, with our hearts sprinkled clean from an evil conscience' (Heb. 10:19–22). This is something to sing about, and it is not morbid when Christians therefore sing, 'There is a fountain filled with blood, drawn from Emmanuel's veins. And sinners plunged beneath that flood lose all their guilty stains.'[67]

Justification, Redemption, & Reconciliation

Christ's death is presented from the perspective of the temple, in propitiation and expiation, but also from that of the law-court. Here, the sinner's need is to be justified before God's law. Paul speaks of this in Romans 3, first going out of his way to show that 'by works of the law no human being will be justified in [God's] sight' (Rom. 3:20). The reason is that 'all have sinned' (Rom. 3:23) by transgressing God's law. Our problem again is God, now expressed in terms of his unyielding law. Paul then declares the good news of Christianity, that 'a righteousness from God…has been made known' (Rom. 3:21). We have no righteousness to present in God's court, but must be condemned as guilty, but God has a righteousness to give us so that we might be justified through faith in Christ.

Here, the key term is *justification*, which means to be found acceptable in God's court. In its full sense, justification involves both the imputation of Christ's perfect righteousness and the forgiveness of our sins. Imputed righteousness results from what theologians refer to as Christ's *active obedience*, that is, the entirety of his perfect law-fulfilling life. Forgiveness results from Christ's *passive obedience*, that is, his suffering of God's wrath through his death on the cross. It is this aspect of justification that is connected directly to Christ's blood.

Paul writes that sinners 'are justified by [God's] grace] as a gift, through the redemption that is in Christ Jesus, whom God put forward as a propitiation by his blood, to be received by faith' (Rom. 3:24–25). Not only does propitiation turn aside God's wrath, but it requires a verdict of innocent in the courtroom of God's justice for all who trust in Christ's blood. 'There is therefore,' Paul exclaimed, 'now no condemnation for those who are in Christ Jesus' (Rom. 8:1). This, too, is something to sing about:

> Jesus, thy blood and righteousness,
>   my beauty are, my glorious dress;
> 'Midst flaming worlds in these arrayed,
>   with joy shall I lift up my head.
> Bold shall I stand in thy great day;
>   for who aught to my charge shall lay?
> Fully absolved through these I am
>   from sin and fear, from guilt and shame.[68]

In addition to describing Christ's blood in light of the temple and the law-court, the Bible also speaks of the atonement in terms of the marketplace. In a previous chapter we considered our '*redemption* through his blood'. By the ransom price of his own death, Jesus paid the penalty of believers' sins, purchasing his people out from the bondage of the guilt and power of sin.

Finally, we should think of the atonement in light of family relationships. Sin has sundered our relationship with God. Because of our sin, God is alienated from us, unwilling and unable in his holiness to have fellowship with soiled sinners. We, in turn, are alienated from God in the corruption and folly of our sin. Christ died to bridge this gulf. His blood causes God to forgive our sins, since the debt has been paid, the offense atoned for, and his righteous wrath averted. Likewise, Christ not only redeems us from sin but restores us to fellowship with God as dearly 'beloved children' (Eph. 5:1). The result is *reconciliation*, which Paul extols in one of the great statements of the New Testament:

> All this is from God, who through Christ reconciled us to himself and gave us the ministry of reconciliation; that is, in Christ God was reconciling the world to himself, not counting their trespasses against them…We implore you on behalf of Christ, be reconciled to God. For our sake he made him to be sin who knew no sin, so that in him we might become the righteousness of God (2 Cor. 5:18–21).

Propitiation, expiation, justification, redemption, and reconciliation—what a great gospel is contained in the atoning work of Jesus Christ through his shed blood for us. Putting it all together, we are saved *from God*—his wrath no longer turned against us, his curse no longer on us—we are saved *by God*—who sent his only Son to die in our place and for our salvation—and we are saved *to God*, who now calls sinners to repent and believe, so that all who will come may be fully restored to his love. The wonder of this grace through the blood of God's own Son never ceases to fill us with joyful praise, so that our hearts sing in delight to him: 'Amazing love! How can it be, that thou, my God, shouldst die for me?'[69]

BLOODY RELIGION

With all this said, Christians have to confess the truth of our critics' complaint, that ours is a 'bloody religion.' One such critic is the Episcopal bishop John Shelby Spong, who wrote a book titled *Why Christianity Must Change or Die*. At the heart of his objection to historic Christianity is this matter of Christ's shed blood. According to Spong, such bizarre and primitive religious views can only repulse the modern man and woman. 'I would choose to loathe,' he writes, 'rather than to worship a deity who required the sacrifice of his son.'[70] Spong, and others like him, think it is high time the Christian church dispensed with the ugly symbol of the cross, which he calls 'an image that has to go.'[71] Yet, to his dismay, Christians still 'cling to the old rugged cross;' they sing still, 'O precious is the flow that makes me white as snow; no other fount I know, nothing but the blood of Jesus.'

One thing is revealed in all of this: your view of everything is determined by your attitude toward the blood of Christ. P. T. Forsyth was right when he wrote, 'Christ is to us just what his cross is.'[72] If the cross is an offense, then a crucified Christ is also an offense. He must be gotten rid of, replaced with some other religious icon. If the cross is foolishness, as it was to the Greeks of Paul's day, then Christ must be shunned lest you be embarrassed in proper society. If the cross is a stumbling-block, as it was to the Jews, then Christ must be destroyed and his followers persecuted. But if you look to the cross as a guilty sinner and see there your only hope of salvation, then Christ is to you a Savior and you will cling with all of your might to his cross.

There is a reason the world hates the blood of Christ, for the cross condemns the world. It is, as Martyn Lloyd-Jones wrote:

> a standing condemnation of every view and philosophy which says that men and women by their own efforts can reconcile themselves to God, or that they can atone for their sin. To all such views, the answer of the cross is that no one can do this. The cross is the proclamation of the insufficiency of mankind, and people dislike it because of that, for they believe in themselves and in their own power.[73]

The blood of Christ insults the self-reliance of this world by proclaiming all the biblical doctrines of salvation. The cross reveals God's wrath against our sin. We like to think that sin amounts to little, that God is not perturbed, that forgiveness is automatic, and that God is sure to accept us. But Christ's blood says that even when his own Son bore the guilt of our sin, God poured out on him the fullness of his wrath. 'Why have you forsaken me,' cried the sin-bearing Christ to God (Matt. 27:46), and equally forsaken is everyone not covered through faith in his blood. People are likewise offended by the gospel's offer of salvation. God's grace declares that we are failures, we are guilty, we are damned. God has to come and save us; God's Son had to come to 'seek and to save those that were lost' (Luke 19:10). In all these ways the cross offends by declaring us sinners, saved only by the grace of God in Christ.

But what if we look to the cross and admit that we are not righteous, if we realize that God rightly punishes every sin? What if we admit that we are helpless to save ourselves, hopeless save for God's grace? If you can say that, if you gaze on the blood of Christ and cry for him to be your Savior, then what is contemptible to the world is precious in your sight. For Christ's blood tells us that a Savior *has* come. Christ *has* taken our sins onto himself. He *has* shed his blood in our place. He *has* propitiated God's wrath and expiated our sins; he *has* won forgiveness of our sins so that we might be justified before God; he *has* redeemed us from the power and guilt of sin; he *has* reconciled God to us and us to God, all through faith in his blood.

To all who believe, the cross of Christ, the blood of Christ, reveals something exceedingly precious: the love of God for sinners. It says, 'God so loved the world that he gave his one and only Son, that whoever believes in him should not perish but have eternal life' (John 3:16). The blood of the cross declares: 'God shows his own love for us in that while we were still sinners, Christ died for us' (Rom. 5:8).

You see, then, why Christians rejoice in the blood of Christ, why we claim no higher allegiance, no greater glory, no brighter hope, than that which is symbolized with the cross which declares, 'his banner over me is love' (S. of S. 2:4). If you understand this, if you come to God through the shed blood of Christ, then you will lift your praise to God, along with the apostle Paul. 'Blessed be the God and Father of our Lord Jesus Christ, who has blessed us with every spiritual blessing in the heavenly realms,' he wrote. 'For in Christ we have redemption through his blood, the forgiveness of sins, in accordance with the riches of God's grace' (Eph. 1:3, 8). As Paul stated in Galatians 6:14, 'Far be it from me to boast except in the cross of our Lord Jesus Christ.' May Christ therefore receive all the glory, all the praise, and all the love in our hearts.

9

The Salvation Mystery

Ephesians 1:9–10

There are two story lines written into the fabric of this world. The first and most familiar is tragedy, which is the story of our world apart from God's saving intervention. This is the story the Bible tells just after its beginning in the Fall of Adam. Adam and Eve disobeyed God's command by eating of the tree of the knowledge of good and evil. They fell under God's curse and were cast out from the Garden (Gen. 3). As sin worked in the generations that followed, this story of tragedy continued, with Cain's murder of Abel in Genesis 4 and the growth of his wicked line in chapter 5, on to the dispersing of the nations in God's judgment at the Tower of Babel in Genesis 11. These chapters begin the story of tragedy that is written into our sinful world, and its pattern is always the same: sin against God, followed by alienation, curse, failure and misery.

Two Stories: Tragedy and Salvation

Literary scholars tell us that there are certain requirements that must be met for a story to qualify as a true tragedy. First, there must be initial greatness and goodness, with hope for glory and blessing. The tragic hero is always a person of virtue and lofty potential, but who is overcome by a fatal flaw. This is how the Bible presents mankind. Created by God with goodness and the stamp of his own glorious image, man nonetheless fell into sin. Sin is the fatal flaw of our race, and it always proves to be our undoing. This is the story told by the pen of human history on a broad scale. Empires rise and thrive in glory only to decay, fall tragically and disappear into oblivion. Tragedy is also told on a smaller scale through our own individual experiences. Our own capacity for achievement is undermined by our sin. Many marriages begin brightly but are soon dimmed by conflict or unfaithfulness. Careers launch with great expectations, but lead to struggle and often to disappointments that embitter the soul. God's curse to the first sinner, Adam, still dominates our tragic reality: 'By the sweat of your brow you shall eat your bread, till you return to the ground...for dust you are and to dust you shall return' (Gen. 3:18–19).

William Shakespeare was the master of tragedy. One of his most famous tragic plays was *Macbeth*. This is the story of a Scottish nobleman, renowned for valor and faithfulness, who came under temptation's power and fell prey to sin. His moral failure and guilt-wracked conscience ultimately led him to ruin. This is the tragic story, told in epic terms, that is familiar to us all in our ordinary lives. This is why stories like this are so irresistible in movies and books; like it or not, we connect with it because it is our story. Macbeth's cynical lines speak in a way we all have felt:

> Life's but a walking shadow, a poor player
> That struts and frets his hour upon the stage
> And then is heard no more. It is a tale
> Told by an idiot, full of sound and fury
> Signifying nothing.[74]

I said that there are two story lines in this world. The first is tragedy and the second is salvation. Whereas tragedy is the story of failure, alienation, and curse, salvation tells of triumph, redemption, and blessing. Here is the voice of laughter heard beside the sobbing tears. We find this story line in Shakespeare's comedies, which so often end in wedding scenes, with all the characters rejoined in hope and joy. We also find it in fairy tales, which tell us that 'they lived happily ever after.' We may think of fairy tales and fantasies as unreal, but we still read them to our children generation after generation, our secret hopes connecting with the happy ending we long for.

These are the two stories of this world. There is tragedy, which we know from lived experience, from the microscope and telescope of historical observation. Then there is the comedy of salvation, the story that comes from God and relies on the revelation in his Word. This is what Christianity presents to a world that, though fallen and cursed, cannot forget its hope of glory and blessing—the claim that salvation will overthrow the Fall, that redemption will conquer alienation, and that God's blessing will undo the curse of sin. 'The wolf will live with the lamb,' Isaiah said, 'the leopard will lie down with the goat, the calf and the lion and the yearling together; and a little child will lead them' (Isa. 11:6). It is this salvation story that Paul refers to in our passage as 'the mystery of [God's] will' (Eph. 1:9) that is manifested in the appearing of our Lord Jesus Christ.

We can unfold Paul's meaning in this passage in three points. First, we note the historical nature of Christianity. Second, we learn the historical purpose of Christianity. Third, we consider the historical perspective of Christian faith.

THE HISTORICAL NATURE OF CHRSTIANITY

When I speak of these two stories, it is not really fiction that I have in mind, although here is an example where art follows reality. These are not merely two stories but two histories working side-by-side in this world. There is the history taught in secular textbooks, that starts with the record of prehistoric civilization and progresses through the Mesopotamian Empires to Greece and then Rome, the Dark Ages followed by the rise of Europe, the ascent of New World nations like America, and now the new global age. The most penetrating modern and postmodern thinkers look on this history and label it hopeless, meaningless, and cursed. For all the excitement, they categorize it under the heading of tragedy, rendering on it Macbeth's verdict: all sound and fury signifying nothing.

Yet, Paul says, there is another history that the world at large is not aware of. This is God's redemptive-history, that is working forward according to the very different story line of salvation. This story is what Paul has been tracing in this great doxology in Ephesians 1. Salvation history begins before records were kept and empires began leaving their traces, indeed, before creation itself. This history began in the mind of God, entering into time through the coming of

Christ. It is a history that has a predetermined, pre-recorded finale in the glorification of God's redeemed people in and through the exaltation of his Son. Redemptive history reflects God's plan of the ages, omnipotently and mysteriously pressing on toward the goal stated in Ephesians 1:10, 'To unite all things in [Christ], things in heaven and things on earth.'

Paul's assumption is that it is vitally important for Christians to know the historical nature of their faith and salvation. Christianity is a religion that relies on historical events, that is, on God's great redemptive works that have happened in our world and are revealed in Scripture. If someone asks you what is in the Bible, a good answer would be the record of God's great saving acts in history, together with the explanation of how they achieve salvation for those who believe. According to Paul, the knowledge of this saving history is one of the great gifts we receive in Jesus Christ. In Ephesians 1:7–8, Paul wrote of God lavishing his grace on believers through the saving work of Christ. In verse 9 he speaks of God revealing this to us, 'making known to us the mystery of his will according to his purpose.'

Here we encounter for the first time in Ephesians the word 'mystery.' When Paul speaks of God's revelation as a mystery he means something different than what we tend to mean by this word. Paul does not mean that we are given clues with the task of figuring out their secret, the way a mystery novel challenges us to discover if the butler or the cook committed the murder. For Paul, the mystery of God's will is a story that can only be known by revelation, and is only known fully as events ripen to maturity in God's timing. The mystery of salvation is something no one could ever figure out by reason alone, not because it is irrational but because it is marvelous. God's mystery involves a wisdom of grace not revealed by the common experience of life, much less by the conventional wisdom of this world. Paul uses *mystery* seven times in Ephesians, speaking of 'the mystery of God's will,' 'the mystery of the gospel,' and 'the mystery of Christ.' The mystery is the salvation story made known by God's revelation through the prophets and apostles and brought to full expression in God's timing through the person and work of Jesus Christ.

If we think about this we will realize what exciting news Paul brings. He is saying that God's will—which men and women can never know through their own efforts—is revealed in the gospel. The mind of God is revealed through the person and work of Christ. Christianity brings to the world not a therapeutic program for earthly happiness, not a political-action agenda, and not a power-grab by one ethnic or religious group against others. Christianity presents God's revelation concerning his otherwise secret plan for saving the fallen world.

In these verses, Paul emphasizes themes we have already encountered. First, God's is a sovereign will—it is 'the mystery of his will according to his purpose' (Eph. 1:9). God is not consulting us, nor is the gospel a product of human investigation or consideration. It is revelation, a disclosing of God's sovereign, almighty will. Furthermore, God's purpose is and always has been focused on his Son, Jesus Christ: 'According to his purpose, which he set forth in Christ' (Eph. 1:9). We worship God through Christ not merely because Jesus helps us or because we can relate to him, but because God's eternal purpose is centered on him and manifested through him. Paul adds, in verse 10, that this is 'a plan for the fullness of time,' or, as the *New International Version* puts it, it all has been 'put into effect when the times will have reached their fulfillment.' This tells us that God's redemptive work advances progressively and that the Bible's revelation likewise is historically progressive. God placed Adam and Eve in the Garden and gave the covenant of works by which mankind might be justified. Adam failed and we fell under the curse of sin. But God had prepared the intervention of his own Son through the covenant of grace, so that all salvation would be through and in Christ. God was not caught off-guard by the Fall; he immediately made great promises of an offspring who would suffer but would conquer for our salvation (Gen. 3:15).

God pressed forward with his redemptive plan through long generations. He called Abraham to go to Canaan and begin the series of events that created Israel as a nation and brought them into the Promised Land. God gave the Law to Moses to preserve the nation and teach the people to look for a Savior. Over long centuries, Israel lived before God, her religious institutions informing the world of his salvation, their very existence proving that God had not abandoned the sinful human race. But even the Jews fell into sin, breaking the covenant God gave through Moses. Yet God remained faithful, and even this served to point forward to a new covenant in a Savior who would fulfill all that Israel had failed to do.

Meanwhile, events outside of Israel were conspiring to prepare the way not merely for the coming of the Messiah but for the spread of his gospel throughout the world. Greek philosophy flowered, providing many thought categories the gospel would later employ, as well as a common language for the ancient world with which to learn of it. Roman power arose, providing peace so that people, commerce, and ideas could travel freely from region to region. In all these ways, God—not consulting our wisdom and not seeking our approval—prepared the world for his Son, that he might accomplish the works needed for our salvation and that we might hear it and believe. At just the right time, Jesus came and died for our sins, rose from the dead, and sent forth his apostles to make known this mystery of God's will, a salvation plan that continues even now through the gospel until its culmination in the gathering of all things under Christ.

The Historical Purpose of Christianity

In Ephesians 1:9, Paul asserts the historical nature of Christianity and in verse 10 he declares the historical purpose of Christianity. The gospel reveals the great redemptive events of God's saving history, but also his saving purpose in Christ. For this, verse 10 takes us into the future. The mystery of God's will is a salvation story that is still going on, and Paul wants us to know the end. It is a history that has not yet reached its goal, namely, 'to unite all things in [Christ], things in heaven and things on earth.'

The key expression is 'to unite all things,' which in the Greek is a single word, *anakephalaioo*. Paul uses the same word in Romans 13:9 to speak of the summing up of all the commandments under the heading of love. Here, his point is that history has a destination, a purpose and a climax, and that these are all contained in the gathering of all things together under the lordship of Jesus Christ.

This teaching runs against the grain of modern thought, which assures us that history has no purpose and no goal. It has become fashionable for skeptics to speak in the manner of liberal scholar G. N. Clark, who asserted: 'There is no secret and no plan in history to be discovered. I do not believe that any future consummation could make sense of all the irrationalities of preceding ages.'[75] The prominent atheist Richard Dawkins has said, 'The universe we observe has…, at bottom, no design, no purpose, no evil and no good, nothing but blind pitiless indifference.'[76] This kind of thinking is given as a justification for sensual, self-serving lives: why should we live by any higher code if life is all meaningless? As Paul once agreed, 'If the dead are not raised, "Let us eat and drink, for tomorrow we die"' (1 Cor. 15:32).

We ought to look with sympathy on such unbelieving people. The meaning of history is a dark mystery to them, partly because the only history they know—the tragic story of a sinful world—is in fact hopeless, and if we did not have the revelation of God we would no doubt think the same way. But theirs is also a culpable ignorance; their minds are willingly shut to the Word of God and its story of salvation. God's Word says there is a purpose to history and therefore to our lives. God has revealed that purpose, stating that he is uniting 'all things in [Christ], things in heaven and things on earth.'

Paul has been praising God for salvation, extolling Jesus as the *means* of our redemption, which is 'through his blood' (Eph. 1:7). But now he shows Jesus as the *end* of our salvation, so that we and the entire cosmos are redeemed under and into the headship of Jesus Christ, whom God has exalted in the highest. Peter O'Brien explains, 'Christ is the one *in whom* God chooses to sum up the cosmos, the one in whom he restores harmony to the universe. He is the focal point, not simply the means, the instrument…through whom all this occurs.'[77]

Remarkably, Paul says that 'all things' will be brought together under Christ, things 'in heaven and on earth.' He does not mean by this a universal salvation in which none are condemned, for that would involve a fatal inconsistency in his own thought and in the Bible. It is a universality within redemption, a bringing together all that has been saved and restored by, in, and unto the Lord Jesus Christ.

There are two ways we can properly understand this. Charles Hodge understands 'all things' as including only those believers now in heaven and those still on earth, since the context is one of salvation through Christ's blood, and these are the objects of his death. It is the whole company of the redeemed that is brought together under Christ, along with the holy angels who serve God and minister to them. Hodge says, 'The apostle refers to the union of all the people of God…in one body under Jesus Christ their head. They are to be constituted an everlasting kingdom.'[78]

Andrew Lincoln points out, however, that 'heaven and earth' was a common Jewish expression for the whole of created reality. Paul teaches elsewhere that the whole creation came under the curse of sin and looks forward to final deliverance through Christ. Romans 8:19–21 says, 'The creation waits with eager longing for the revealing of the sons of God…The creation itself will be set free from its bondage to decay and obtain the freedom of the glory of the children of God.' This, then, is the 'all things' of which Paul writes in our passage, that at the end of history the entire created order, now subjected to corruption in the Fall, will be restored to unity, harmony, order, and eternal glory under the lordship of Jesus Christ.[79]

It is significant that this Greek word, *anakephalaioo*, contains the prefix *ana*, which means *again*. It is a restoration, a bringing of things together *again* under Christ. This presupposes a prior disintegration, an alienation and separation resulting from sin. There was a perfect condition, it was lost, but now it will be restored through union with Christ. This shows how important the first chapters of Genesis are to the Christian worldview. There was a tragedy but now there is salvation. There was alienation but now there is redemption. There was separation but now there is reconciliation. There is a curse but blessing lies ahead. Therefore, if realism toward this world demands that we embrace tragedy and its story—and it does—there is a higher realism that Christians embrace, a realism towards God and his saving intervention. There is a real Fall, but a restoration that is more real still. Our story is now salvation in Christ, and we look forward to the bringing of all things together again under his headship.

Revelation 11:15 shows how complete this restoration will be in the end: 'The kingdom of the world has become the kingdom of our Lord and of his Christ, and he shall reign for ever and ever.' The prophet Isaiah foresaw this same restored world, rejoicing: 'They shall not hurt nor destroy in all my holy mountain; for the earth shall be full of the knowledge of the Lord as the waters cover the sea' (Isa. 11:9). First John 3:8 says, 'The reason the Son of God appeared was to destroy the works of the devil.' Thus redemption in Christ involves a whole restoration of the fallen creation, a total undoing of all the work of sin, and an advancing of creation into the harmonious glory originally intended by God. Our task in this present age is to participate in this work with Christ, serving as agents of his peace and especially as heralds of his gospel so that others will hear, believe, and be saved.

The Historical Perspective of Christian Faith

Most stories are ruined by knowing the end in advance, but not this one. This is because, even with Paul's revealing of the great salvation mystery, our minds can scarcely conceive of what it will be like when all is restored in the glory of Christ. God may safely tell us the ending without spoiling any of the excitement.

Indeed, we need to know the end so as to live in the present in light of that glorious triumph. The nature of Christianity is historical, and there is a historical purpose revealed in the Christian gospel. Therefore, the Christian faith takes on a historical perspective, what some have rightly called an eternal perspective on this present life.

For one thing, knowing the end helps us face the truth about the present world. It is not, it turns out, one big Disneyland where we may frolic safely, but rather a spiritual wasteland and battlefield. Life in sin *is* tragedy. Life *is* pointless without Christ. Christians should agree with the most miserable skeptics on this point. We agree that all the world's pomp and show really is nothing but 'sound and fury signifying nothing.' 'This world in its present form,' Paul says, 'is passing away' (1 Cor. 7:31). But, instead of leading us into despair this awareness frees us from the bondage of the world's idolatries.

For this reason, Christians are the greatest realists on earth. We recognize the tragedy of life for what it is; far from being made aloof from the struggles of this age, we like Jesus are men and women of sorrow and often of tears. But Jesus said, 'Blessed are they that mourn, for they shall be comforted' (Matt. 5:4), and we are comforted by the mystery that is revealed of God's saving plan. By faith in the gospel we are freed from living under the power of the world's despair.

Let me put this a little differently. The world lives from the present to the uncertain future, filled with anxiety and doubt. But the Christian lives from the certain future back to the present, and our lives are thereby made secure in the knowledge of God's sure salvation. We are delivered from despair to the peace and joy that are in Christ. Paul writes in Colossians 1:13-14, 'He has delivered us from the domain of darkness and transferred us to the kingdom of his beloved Son, in whom we have redemption, the forgiveness of sins.' Physically we are part of the old dying world, but spiritually we are part of the new world that even now is coming back to life. This is why the Christian life is filled with wonder; we see amidst this ruin of a world a grand restoration that is more real than any fairy tale magic.

Paul writes of our living *in* this world but being *of* another: 'Though our outer nature is wasting away, our inner nature is being renewed day by day. For this slight momentary affliction is preparing for us an eternal weight of glory beyond all comparison, as we look not to the things that are seen but to the things that are unseen. For the things that are seen are transient, but the things that are unseen are eternal' (2 Cor. 4:16-18). We are thus to live like Abraham, who dwelling in the tragic world as a tent-dwelling nomad saw by faith the salvation reality to which his own hopes were joined. He was, says the writer of Hebrews, 'looking forward to the city that has foundations, whose designer and builder is God' (11:10).

Let me conclude by applying this idea as directly as possible. If we live with an eternal perspective, realizing that the purpose of this world is to bring all things together under Christ, this knowledge will shape our approach to everything. Knowing the mystery of God's will, we will live for eternal things, not worldly things. We are glad to have money to buy things for this life, but we are just excited to use our money for the gospel cause that will endure forever. We have earthly ambitions for contributions and achievements in this life, but a greater ambition for serving the kingdom of Christ, the glory of which will never end. We are sorry to experience trials and hardship, but we see them in the light of God's purpose, knowing that he is training us for an inheritance in glory. We realize that the story we have entered in Christ is not tragedy but salvation, however difficult the present may be, and knowing this gives us courage to trust in God and do his will. Literally speaking, our story is a comedy, and thus like the Proverbs 31 woman, we 'laugh at the days to come' (Prov. 31:25).

Perhaps most significantly, knowing that God's purpose for history is 'to unite all things in [Christ], things in heaven and things on earth' (Eph. 1:10), we therefore want to know Jesus. Do you know him? He is the only Savior and the eternal Lord. We find salvation only by yielding to him the obedience of faith, believing his story and surrendering to his historical reign. We then count it our great blessing to open his Word and open our minds and hearts to his teaching. We count it a blessed privilege to approach the throne of grace in prayer through his name. And we desire above all else in this life to serve, please, and glorify our Savior, together with our loving Heavenly Father, who has purposed all things for us in Christ, according to the marvelous mystery of his sovereign and gracious will.

10

The Glorious Plan of God

Ephesians 1:11–13

One of the Bible's most striking descriptions of God is that of the potter with his clay. Jeremiah was told, 'Go down to the potter's house, and there I will let you hear my words' (Jer. 18:2). He found the potter shaping the clay on his wheel, working it as 'seemed good to [him] to do' (Jer. 18:4). God explained, 'O house of Israel, can I not do with you as this potter has done?…Like the clay in the potter's hand, so are you in my hand' (Jer. 18:6).

There are three parts to this illustration. First is the potter, a figure that speaks of God's sovereign authority over men and nations, as well as his interest and involvement with what he is making. G. Campbell Morgan observes, 'Looking at the potter as he sits at the wheel and places his hand upon the clay…I see his keen interest as the clay changes its form under his fingers…I see his close and unvarying attention to his work; his eye is never lifted from the clay while the wheel revolves and his hand is moulding…I also recognize his power…infinite so far as the clay is concerned.'[80]

Second is the clay, which is molded according to the potter's will and suitable for his purpose. Thus is man in his spiritual nature, able to reflect God's artistry and purpose. Third is the potter's wheel, which speaks of circumstances God employs as tools to mold his people, who are his workmanship. Isaiah says: 'We are the clay, and you are our potter; we are all the work of your hand' (Isa. 64:8).

God's Sovereign Plan

Jeremiah's image fits Paul's way of thinking in Ephesians. One of his chief themes here is the sovereignty of God, and in verse 11 he returns to it. He writes, 'In him we have…been predestined according to the purpose of him who works all things according to the counsel of his will, so that we who were the first to hope in Christ might be to the praise of his glory' (Eph. 1:11-12). God has a purpose in which he is utterly sovereign, according to which the salvation of Christians was predestined, all to the glory of his name. Here we have the potter, the vessels he is shaping, and also a plan by which he works all things so that his artistry is gloriously revealed.

It is a great comforting truth of Scripture that God is working according to a sovereign plan and that everything happens 'according to the counsel of his will.' Think of what this meant to the Jewish exiles in the time of Jeremiah. Jerusalem was under seige and many Jews had already been carted off into captivity. How distressing it was to see their whole way of life destroyed, foreign idols exalted, and pagan lords holding sway over the people of God. Yet God comforted his people with a message of his sovereignty: 'For I know the plans I have for you, declares the LORD, plans for wholeness and not for evil, to give you a future and a hope' (Jer. 29:11).

Christians rightly apply this verse to their own lives: God has a plan for his people and is working for their good. Thus we are assured that no trial we experience is outside of his control. Through faith we will arrive in a blessed place that God has planned and to which he is leading us, so that our trials, however great, are but the turns of the potter's wheel as God fashions our character for his glory.

It is this kind of sovereignty that Paul sets before us in verse 11. Looking at the terms he uses and the ideas he sets forth, we see the extent of sovereignty that he has in mind. He says we have been *predestined*, that is, our lives were foreordained, and our salvation was determined in advance by God. Some people try to water down the idea of predestination by saying it is according to God foreseeing our faith. This approach throws our assurance back onto us, so that God's choosing of us relies on our choosing him, with the result that the success of salvation ultimately relies on us and the glory of salvation belongs at least in part to us. Ephesians 1:11, however, perhaps more than any other verse in Scripture, refutes this teaching. Paul says we have been predestined. But according to what principle does God predestine those who are saved? Paul could not answer the question more emphatically, in a way that radically shuts out any ultimate reliance on human will or effort or activity. We are predestined, he says, 'according to God's counsel.'

This leads to another key term, God's *purpose*. God works out everything 'according to [his] purpose.' Salvation is directed to a goal that is God's idea and his sovereign choice. It is his will, not ours, that determines everything. Furthermore, God's plan has *oversight*: God 'works all things.' God works his plan. He who originated it and planned it also oversees its execution. He is working in history and in our circumstances, 'according to the counsel of his will.' God's plan has an *object* and *end*, namely, 'the praise of his glory.' You will not find a more complete statement of God's sovereignty in salvation, nor one as foolproof against denial. This statement of God's sovereignty follows the exact progression that Paul employs in the great doxology of Romans 11:36: 'For from him and through him and to him are all things.' So it is in our salvation. It is 'from him,' that is it originates from his purpose and will, and 'through him,' as he works it all out, and it is 'to him,' that is, to the praise of his glory alone. Thus Paul concluded: 'To him be glory forever. Amen' (Rom. 11:36).

One point that Paul clearly wants his readers to grasp is that our salvation is wholly directed to God's glory. Our forgiveness and redemption, together with our election and adoption, are not ends but means. There is a great end far above our salvation, namely, the glory of God. This emphasis on God's glory therefore should permeate our Christian lives. Lloyd-Jones writes, 'The essential proof of salvation…is that the supreme object and ambition of the Christian's life now is to live to the glory of God.'[81] The Christian is one who actively, willingly, and joyfully promotes God's glory. We are advancing in Christianity precisely to the extent that this can be said of us.

Heirs and God's Inheritance

In this passage, Paul emphasizes three things about God's plan as it deals with us. First, verse 11 begins, 'In him we have obtained an inheritance.' The Greek verb (*eklerothemen*) means being chosen by lot, with the idea of inheritance in mind. Since this is a passive verb it can be translated to say that we have 'been made an inheritance.' Thus Paul means either that we have become heirs of God or that we have become God's own inheritance. In verse 14, Paul speaks of the Holy Spirit as a guarantee of 'our inheritance,' which argues for the former view. But verse 13 says we are marked with a seal by the Spirit, which speaks of God's marking his own possession, which argues for the latter view. Therefore, it seems that the best way to handle Paul's use of this term is to consider both perspectives.

According to God's plan, Christians are heirs of God. This idea takes us back to the example of Old Testament Israel. Upon entering the Promised Land, all tribes and families received their allotted portion of land on which to live. Together they inherited the land of blessing and each had their own portion, distributed by lot. Likewise, Christians have a place in the eternal provision of heaven. Moreover, we remember the special status of the priestly tribe of Levi. Unlike the other tribes, the priests received no allotment of land. Rather, their inheritance was the Lord himself : 'The Lord is his inheritance' (Deut. 10:9). This idea carries over to Christians, who are a kingdom of priests (1 Pet. 2:9). Romans 8:17 says if we are 'children, then heirs—heirs of God and fellow heirs with Christ.' As co-heirs we will own everything with Jesus, indeed, we will 'share in God's glory' in mutual possession with Christ.

We are heirs of God and ultimately it is himself that God bequeaths to us. He is our inheritance. We possess God by knowing him, and we will have an ever-increasing possession of God for eternity, beginning now. We possess God as our own by loving him, trusting him, and praising him, and in all these ways he gives his own heart in return. Like the glory cloud dwelling within Israel, God lives in us, moving and empowering us to reflect and partake of his glory.

At the same time, we are God's inheritance. God said to Israel: 'The Lord has taken you and brought you out of the iron furnace, out of Egypt, to be a people of his own inheritance, as you are this day' (Deut. 4:20). Moses adds: 'The Lord's portion is his people, Jacob his allotted heritage' (Deut. 32:9).

These two ideas come together in the great promise of the new covenant in Christ: 'I will be their God, and they shall be my people' (Heb. 8:10). We are to know God and be known of him, to love God and to be loved by him in covenant marriage, to glorify God and share his glory as co-heirs with Jesus. This is our high destiny in Christ, our extraordinary privilege, and if we are aware of it we will make this relationship with God the chief pursuit of our lives.

In an extraordinary essay, *The Weight of Glory*, C.S. Lewis points to this calling as fulfilling our deepest longing. He says that we now possess a portion of God's glory through what we see in nature; for instance, the beauty of a sunrise is there for us to see if we only get up early enough. He then comments, 'But we want so much more...We do not want merely to see beauty, though, God knows, even that is bounty enough. We want something else which can hardly be put into words—to be united with the beauty we see, to pass into it, to receive it into ourselves, to bathe in it, to become part of it.' This is what God has planned for us. As Lewis summarizes, 'The leaves of the New Testament are rustling with the rumor [that we will put on] that greater glory of which Nature is only the first sketch.'[82] God's plan thus culminates with Christians being heirs of his glory and God's own inheritance forever.

Jews & Gentiles Reconciled in Christ

The second insight Paul provides regarding God's plan has to do with the fulfillment of his covenant purpose in Christ. This idea comes through in terms of the Jews and the Gentiles, each in succession becoming God's people through union with Jesus Christ. Neither of these is mentioned explicitly, but they are implicit in the way that Paul speaks of *we* and *you*. Speaking of Jews, he says that '*we who were the first to hope in Christ* might be to the praise of his glory' (Eph. 1:12, italics mine). Speaking of his Gentile readers he adds, 'In him *you also*, when you heard the word of truth..., were sealed with the promised Holy Spirit' (Eph. 1:13, italics mine).

Verse 12 thus speaks in a restrictive sense: it was Paul's *we*—believing Jews—who fulfilled the Old Testament statements of Israel as God's inheritance. God had promised that Israel would be his own portion, and in the gospel-believing Jews this purpose was fulfilled. Paul argues this way elsewhere, saying in Romans 11:1 that God did not abandon his promises to the Jews because many Christians like Paul himself were Jews: 'I ask, then, has God rejected his people? By no means! For I myself am an Israelite, a descendant of Abraham, a member of the tribe of Benjamin.'

Therefore, it is 'we who were the first to hope in Christ,' that is, Christian Jews, who fulfill God's purpose. But Paul is not proposing some Jewish superiority in the church, because this also became true of Gentile believers when they believed. The decisive issue is 'in him,' that is, 'in Christ.' Really, it is Christ who fulfills the promise of Old Testament Israel; it is Jesus who is the Father's portion. The believing Jews became God's inheritance in the same way the Gentiles did, namely, 'in him,' which is how verse 11 begins, that is, by believing in Jesus and his gospel. It is 'in Christ' that we become heirs of God and his own possession, for, as Paul elsewhere writes, 'all the promises of God find their Yes in him' (2 Cor. 1:20).

God's glorious plan first worked through the Jews as the original disciples hoped in Christ. God then used them—Jewish evangelists and apostles like Paul—to preach the gospel for the inclusion of the Gentiles. This fulfilled the great promise spoken to Abraham so long before: 'I will make of you a great nation, and I will bless you… in you all the families of the earth shall be blessed' (Gen. 12:2–3). This also introduces a theme Paul will expound in chapter 2, the reconciling of all the peoples into one new humanity in Christ. Charles Hodge explains:

> The purpose of God is to bring all the subjects of redemption into one harmonious body…This purpose is realized in the conversion of the Jewish Christians…and…the Gentile Christians, to whom his epistle is specially addressed, are comprehended in the same purpose…Both Jews and Gentiles are, by the mediation of Christ, and in union with him, brought to be partakers of the benefits of that plan of mercy which God had purposed in himself, and which he has now revealed for the salvation of men.'[83]

If both Jews and Gentiles enter into God's covenant plan for salvation through union with Christ, then we too will be saved only through discipleship with him. Moreover, one of God's chief aims in uniting us to Christ is to bring about the kind of peace that has so long eluded the powers of this world. God's plan brings salvation in Christ and in Christ believers, even the once hostile Jews and Gentiles, all become one. This is God's plan for cosmic reconciliation, with vast implications for the church. James Montgomery Boice comments:

> I am sorry for churches made up of one class of people, as many American churches are, for they lack opportunity to show this new unification of people effectively. Church growth specialists tell us that this is the best way for churches to grow, people being most attracted to those who are like themselves, and it may be so…But at what cost is this growth purchased! I would rather have less growth and more glory given to Christ. I would rather have small totals but a larger body in the sense of a larger number of the types and conditions of people who are included in it.[84]

By Grace, Through Faith

God's glorious plan brings him praise, first, by making us heirs of God and God's own inheritance, and second by bringing Jews and Gentiles together through union with Christ. Third, Paul notes that in God's plan salvation is received by the simple means of faith in the gospel of Jesus Christ. Paul states this principle about both Jews and Gentiles: the former 'were the first to hope in Christ,' and the latter were included in Christ when they 'heard' and 'believed' 'the word of truth, the gospel of your salvation' (Eph. 1:13). Paul makes no mention here of works or merits, but only faith in Christ.

If we think about Paul's teaching we will recognize the genius of this design. God's plan is directed to giving glory to God alone. God's way of salvation must therefore be able to incorporate us into Christ without detracting glory from God. This aim is accomplished by salvation through faith in Christ. Paul explains in Romans 4:16, 'That is why it depends on faith, in order that the promise may rest on grace.' Faith is something we do, and by it we are really joined to Christ, but faith is not a work that originates in our effort or merit. Faith is God's gift through the Holy Spirit, a point Paul makes in Ephesians 2:8–9, 'For by grace you have been saved through faith. And this is not your own doing; it is the gift of God, not a result of works, so that no one may boast.' By faith you are actively involved in your relationship to God, you are called 'to work out your own salvation with fear and trembling,' but only because 'it is God who works in you, both to will and to work for his good pleasure' (Phil. 2:12–13). Therefore, faith is a way for us to be joined to Jesus Christ for salvation in which God alone is glorified, because faith is the result of his grace at work in us.

Verse 13 offers a helpful definition of faith: 'In him you also, when you heard the word of truth, the gospel of your salvation, and believed in him.' The gospel is the good news of Jesus Christ, the proclamation of what Jesus did to save sinners. The gospel includes both historical fact and doctrine. The gospel teaches that Jesus died and by his death gained forgiveness of our sins. The gospel proclaims that Jesus rose from the dead as our Lord, God having accepted his sacrifice and appointed him the means of our salvation. Faith means believing the saving truth in Jesus Christ, receiving him as our Lord and Savior and committing ourselves to him.

When Paul says that God's plan offers salvation through faith in Jesus, this is true for every era in history after the Fall of Adam into sin. The Jews of old were saved through faith in the gospel of Christ, as he was presented in the types and ceremonies of the Old Testament. Paul thus stressed that Abraham was saved by faith in the gospel: 'Abraham believed God, and it was counted to him as righteousness…So then, those who are of faith are blessed along with Abraham, the man of faith' (Gal. 3:6, 9). In Paul's own day believing Jews were saved by faith, being 'the first to hope in Christ,' and then Gentiles were incorporated into Christ by means of faith in his gospel they had heard.

Salvation always coming through faith in Jesus, Christians must therefore proclaim the gospel! Our message is not self-help methods, not political agendas, but Christ crucified and raised from the dead. Paul said, 'For I delivered to you as of first importance what I also received: that Christ died for our sins in accordance with the Scriptures, that he was buried, that he was raised on the third day in accordance with the Scriptures' (1 Cor. 15:3–4). He stated, 'If you confess with your mouth that Jesus is Lord and believe in your heart that God raised him from the dead, you will be saved' (Rom. 10:9). Paul then defined the work of the church, saying:

> But how are they to call on him in whom they have not believed? And how are they to believe in him of whom they have never heard? And how are they to hear without someone preaching? And how are they to preach unless they are sent? As it is written, 'How beautiful are the feet of those who preach the good news!' (Rom. 10:14–15).

These are questions for the church to ponder today, in which so many other messages often crowd out the gospel of Christ's death and resurrection, by which alone men and women can be saved.

God has a plan for our salvation in which he is utterly sovereign, yet he has decreed the necessity of faith. Ephesians 1:11–13 thus shows the highest view of God's sovereignty fully at home with the need for evangelism. People say, 'If God is sovereign in salvation, then why bother preaching and witnessing?' Our answer is that we must evangelize because God's plan calls for belief in the gospel so that men and women may be saved. God brings people into Jesus Christ through faith in 'the word of truth, the gospel of your salvation' (Eph. 1:13). In fact, it is only through faith in Christ that our individual election is revealed. John Calvin explained:

> How do we know that God has elected us before the creation of the world? By believing in Jesus Christ… Whosoever then believes is thereby assured that God has worked in him, and faith is, as it were, the duplicate copy that God gives us of the original of our adoption. God has his eternal counsel, and he always reserves to himself the chief and original record of which he gives us a copy by faith.[85]

This means that you can be part of God's saving plan, you can know yourself as one of his cherished people, reconciled through Christ, whoever you are, wherever you come from, and whatever you have done, if you will believe that Jesus died for your sins and rose as your Lord and Savior. If you will trust in him you will be able to know that by God's eternal plan his saving love has been set on you.

The Potter's Hands

John Stott concludes his study of these verses by describing what he calls 'a clash of wills' whenever people first encounter the biblical teaching of God's total sovereignty in salvation. He says:

Such Christian talk comes into violent collision with the man-centredness and self-centredness of the world. Fallen man, imprisoned in his own little ego, has an almost boundless confidence in the power of his own will, and an almost insatiable appetite for the praise of his own glory. But the people of God have at least begun to be turned inside out. The new society has new values and new ideals. For God's people are God's possession who live by God's will and for God's glory.[86]

People sometimes dislike the Bible's imagery of God as the potter, fashioning and shaping us according to his purpose. They find it oppressive that God exercises such sovereignty over our destinies. But for those who know God and his love in Jesus Christ, the feel of the potter's hands upon the rim of our lives is not a cause for resentment but rather for joy. If you come to know God, our sovereign potter, through Jesus Christ, then you will come to trust him, love him, and delight in the hand of his providence as it shapes and moves your life. You will realize that in all things God is working for your good (Rom. 8:28), and that in his hands we 'are being transformed into [his] image from one degree of glory to another' (2 Cor. 3:18).

Put a bit differently, if you resent the hand of God shaping your life then let me encourage you to look at that hand. What you will see there is the mark of nails that pierced the flesh of Jesus Christ, the marks of God's love for you that took up the cross, dying in your place, 'the righteous for the unrighteous, that he might bring us to God' (1 Pet. 3:18). That hand is beckoning you to come, hear the gospel and believe, joining the throng of those in Christ who have become heirs of God and God's own precious possession, Jews and Gentiles of all kinds becoming one in Jesus, partaking of his glory and praising God forevermore.

11

Marked with a Seal

Ephesians 1:13

John Bunyan's classic allegory, *Pilgrim's Progress*, tells of Christian's journey from the City of Destruction to the Celestial City. After many difficulties and dangers, Christian finally arrives at the gates of heaven with the bells joyfully ringing. There, he presents the certificate he had earlier received and that promised him entry. The document is carried to the King, who inspects it for authenticity. After it is approved, Christian is allowed entry into the shining city for an eternity of happiness.[87]

This is a scenario envisioned by Paul in his letter to the Ephesians. In Ephesians 1:13 he says, 'When you heard the word of truth, the gospel of your salvation, and believed in him, [you] were sealed with the promised Holy Spirit.' The seal he mentions is the kind embossed on an official document to validate its authenticity, like that which we find on a passport or birth certificate today, and like the one Christian presented at the gate to the Celestial City. Without the seal the document cannot be accepted, but with the seal it must.

Paul turns to this idea at a point of transition in his three-part hymn of praise to God for his blessings in salvation. Already he has spoken of God the Father *ordaining* our salvation in sovereign grace. Next, he wrote of God the Son *accomplishing* the work of our salvation through his blood. Now he turns our thoughts to the work of God the Spirit, who *applies* to us what Christ has achieved, sealing us as God's own and cherished possession.

The Holy Spirit as Seal

Ephesians 1:11–12 summarizes all that Paul has said so far. He speaks of God's glorious plan in which we are saved by faith, becoming both God's cherished people and his heirs. Paul now continues with that thought, especially picking up the idea that we are God's own portion and possession. Since we belong to God, he marks us with a seal. In Paul's day, a prominent person would choose an emblem as his official seal. Using melted wax he affixed an imprint of this emblem to an object he wanted to identify as belonging to or coming from him. In this same way Paul speaks of God identifying all who belong to him by the sealing ministry of the Holy Spirit.

Scholars identify at least four purposes of a seal. First, a seal is used *to authenticate* or confirm something as genuine and true, as with the seal on a passport or other document. In this way the Holy Spirit authenticates professing Christians as genuine. Second, a seal *marks* an object as one's property. Today, we brand cattle and other livestock; in Paul's day, slaves were marked similarly to other kinds of possessions. Keith Warrington writes: 'The fact that a believer is sealed with the Holy Spirit indicates that the one who arranged for the sealing, namely Christ, owns him.'[88] Third, a seal *renders* something *secure*. A seal was placed on Jesus' tomb after his crucifixion to keep the body from being taken. Likewise, believers are protected by the seal of the Holy Spirit. Fourth, a seal was used to *complete* a business transaction. When 'the deal is sealed,' the purchase is final and the property changes hands. Thus when Jeremiah had bought the field at Anathoth, he 'took the sealed deed of purchase' (Jer. 32:11). Likewise, 'The moment the Spirit comes into the life of a believer, the process of salvation is not only commenced but, in a sense, it is also concluded.'[89] The presence of the Spirit shows that redemption has been accomplished and the believer's salvation cannot now be stopped. Through the Spirit, then, believers are *authenticated*; we are *marked* as belonging to Christ; and we are *secured* and protected from things that might separate us from God, and our redemption is *completed*, the ransom price having been paid and accepted by God.

There was good reason for this teaching on the Holy Spirit to have special meaning to the Ephesian church, as we learn in Acts chapter 19. When Paul first came to Ephesus he met some disciples and for some reason doubted their Christianity. He asked if they received the Holy Spirit when they believed. They replied that they knew nothing of the Spirit, so Paul inquired further. The men knew only John's baptism, that is, the testimony of John the Baptist that the awaited Messiah was soon to come. Paul taught them about Jesus, and they believed the gospel and were baptized. Acts 19:6 says, 'When Paul had laid his hands on them, the Holy Spirit came on them, and they began speaking in tongues and prophesying.' The point was not that believers must speak in tongues; the charismatic gifts were but a sign of the Spirit in that epochal age. The point was that in response to their faith in Christ, the men received the indwelling Holy Spirit. The coming of the Spirit validated their profession of faith as true and marked them as God's new covenant people.

In addition to noting the Spirit as God's seal, Paul makes two further points about the Spirit. First, he writes of 'the promised' Spirit. Not only was the Spirit promised in the Old Testament, but it is through the Spirit that the promises of salvation are fulfilled in Christ. On the day of Pentecost, when the ascended Lord Jesus poured out the Spirit on the church, Peter explained it as the fulfillment of Joel 2:28–32. The point of that prophecy was that when the Messiah came and accomplished his work, he would pour out the Spirit on his people. As a result, people would know God and be saved by calling on his name. This is indeed how the Spirit works, revealing God to our hearts and placing the cry of faith on our lips, both marking us and securing our salvation. Leon Morris thus says, the promised Spirit 'is the guarantee that all God's promises will be fulfilled in the believer.'[90]

Paul also calls the Spirit 'holy.' The construction of this verse seems to emphasize this point: literally, Paul writes of 'the Spirit of promise, the Holy One.' How do we know, then, that someone is indwelt by the Spirit and thus marked as belonging to God? Through holiness. Through godly character, actions, and habits. Through evidence of sanctification. Charles Hodge puts this all together, writing, 'This, then, is the great gift which Christ secures for his people, the indwelling of the Holy Spirit, as the source of truth, holiness, consolation and eternal life.'[91]

Distinguishing Marks of the Holy Spirit

Let's make this practical. Is it possible for us to know that we really are saved and that we will get into heaven when we die? Can we credibly, if not perfectly, identify others as true believers? Paul answers both of these questions in the affirmative, because God sends the Spirit to seal all who are his own, and the Spirit is identified by tangible, observable effects of his indwelling presence (John 3:8).

Understanding this truth is important when dealing with new converts. Someone professes faith in Christ. What is it that proves the reality of their profession? The answer is evidence of the Holy Spirit. This is especially key in times of revival and mass conversions, when God is bringing many people to faith, but also when false professions bring many unregenerate people into the church.

One person who was greatly concerned about this subject was Jonathan Edwards, when his church in Northhampton, Massachusetts experienced revival in 1734. Edwards realized that some people were coming under a general spiritual influence without truly being saved. He wanted to discern false conversions and defend true conversions against those who questioned the revival. He responded with an important book titled, *The Distinguishing Marks of a Work of the Spirit of God*. His theme verse was 1 John 4:1: 'Beloved, do not believe every spirit, but test the spirits to see whether they are from God.'

Edwards approached the subject from two perspectives. First, he pointed out signs that should not be confused with a real work of the Holy Spirit, since they may simply be a sign of psychological stress or even counterfeits of true conversion brought about by the Devil. Edwards spoke this way of physical or emotional excitement, which may accompany a true work of the Spirit but also happens when no real converting work has taken place. This was Edwards' concern about bodily effects in general, 'such as tears, trembling, groans, loud outcries, agonies of the body, or the failing of bodily strength.'[92] Edwards warned not to confuse external excitement with inward spiritual change. He would not consider someone to be converted simply because he raised his hand, walked down an aisle, or prayed a prayer as coached by a preacher, much less because he became over-wrought with emotion. These things often happen when someone is converted, but they are not proof of a genuine work of the Spirit. They themselves are not the mark with which God seals his own.

What, then, are the distinguishing marks of a true work of the Holy Spirit? Edwards listed five true signs of the Spirit's work, genuine evidences that show that we are sealed unto God. First is *the elevation of esteem in Jesus Christ* as the Son of God and Savior. This is the single surest sign of the true operation of the Holy Spirit. 'He will bear witness about me,' Jesus said of the Spirit (John 15:26); 'He will glorify me' (John 16:14). False spirituality is not really interested in Jesus but is focused on self and on the excitement of what is taking place. But a true work of the Spirit exalts Jesus Christ and leads us to faith and love for him. Second, a true work of the Spirit *opposes the reign of Satan and causes us to turn from sin*. Mere moralism does not prove the Spirit's work, but Christ-exalting sanctification is always a sign of his presence. Third, a true conversion brings *an increase of interest in God's Word*, a desire to know what the Bible teaches and to put it into practice. Fourth, is a *sound grasp of true doctrine and a zeal to defend it against error*. People who come to love sound teaching, rejecting worldly and secular humanistic tenets, are evidently under the influence of God's Holy Spirit. Fifth is *the mark of love*. Edwards writes, 'If the spirit that is at work among a people operates as a spirit of love to God and man, it is a sure sign that it is the Spirit of God.'[93]

An exaltation of Jesus Christ, repentance from sin, interest in God's Word, and a grasp of sound doctrine, all coupled with a new love for God and for others. These are proofs of the Holy Spirit, marking us as God's own. It is as he works in these ways, deepening our relationship with God, that the Spirit is called by Paul 'the Spirit of adoption as sons, by whom we cry, "*Abba*, Father"' (Rom. 8:15).

The Spirit of Assurance

We have seen that the Spirit is the seal of God that was promised for our holiness and we have explored the distinguishing marks of the Spirit in our lives. This teaching has the greatest application to our spiritual lives, three of which are most prominent: the role of the Spirit in providing us assurance of salvation, in our persevering in faith to the end, and in facing the threatened judgment of God.

First, Paul's teaching on the sealing of the Holy Spirit provides a biblical basis for Christian assurance, while correcting false views of salvation by grace. In particular, we are warned against the idea that forgiveness of sin may be separated from the beginning of a new life characterized by increasing holiness. Paul asked, 'What shall we say then? Are we to continue in sin that grace may abound?' He answered, 'By no means! How can we who died to sin still live in it?' (Rom. 6:1–2). Those who are joined to Christ through faith and thus are forgiven and justified also are all 'sealed with the promised Holy Spirit' (Eph. 1:13). Our assurance of salvation can never rightly exist apart from the marks of the Holy Spirit. Indeed, along with our confidence in the promises of God, the evidence of the Spirit's presence in our lives is the most valid source of our assurance in salvation. Indeed, as Jesus himself put it, a profession of salvation without the evidence of a changed life is simply invalid: 'depart from me, you workers of lawlessness' (Matt. 7:23).

But what if there is only imperfect evidence of these marks? We exalt Christ, but not nearly so much as we should. We hate sin, but we still do it. We love the Bible but often neglect it, and our sound doctrine bears too little influence on our lives. We love others, but still there is the old, familiar love of self. Does that mean we may not really have the Spirit, that we may not be saved? If you understand the Bible's view of man as spiritually dead in sin, then you realize that if we truly have any of these things—incompletely but genuinely—it can only be because of the Spirit's work. No Christian will be perfect in this life (see Phil. 3:12), but no non-Christian will bear these true marks of the Holy Spirit, especially when they are tested under trials.

Therefore, if we have trusted in Christ and can see imperfect but genuine evidence of the Spirit's work, we should not doubt our salvation. Indeed, it is precisely because we have cause for doubt that God places his seal upon us. In heaven we will not have this need, for then we will be perfect. It is because we have need of assurance now that God sends the Spirit to seal us; it is because we now are so weak and inconstant that we need the Spirit whom God so freely sends.

If you show sincere evidence of the Holy Spirit's work, bearing fruit through faith in Jesus Christ, you may be thus assured that you do belong to God and that his power is at work in you. This is important to Paul, who prays later in this chapter for us to know 'the hope to which he has called you' (Eph. 1:18). With clear evidence of the Spirit's presence in your life through faith in Christ, you may be assured of your safety as God's own and cherished one.

The Spirit of Perseverance

Paul's teaching on the Spirit gives us not only a proper assurance of salvation but with it a confidence that we will persevere in faith to the end. Notice how Paul links the sealing of the Spirit with our believing in Christ: 'when you heard the word of truth, the gospel of your salvation, and believed in him, [you] were sealed with the promised Holy Spirit' (Eph. 1:13). This says that the Holy Spirit's sealing work comes in tandem with our faith.

We know from Scripture that it is the Spirit's regenerating work that enables us to believe. Yet Paul evidently refers to the sealing of the Spirit as something further than our initial regeneration. John Calvin explains, 'Besides our receiving of faith at the hand of the Holy Spirit and besides his enlightening of us by his grace…God also secures us in such a way that we do not fall away.'[94] By the Spirit's regenerating work we are given the gift of faith so as to be saved, and then, having believed, we are further sealed by the Spirit and thus made secure in salvation.

The sealing ministry of the Spirit should encourage Christians that just as our initial coming to faith depended solely on God's power, so also the keeping of us in faith relies on God's power and not our own. Calvin shows his pastoral insight when he writes of the same Spirit who first brought us to faith also working alongside our faith to keep us in the way of salvation:

Let us notice how volatile men are. He that is best disposed to follow God will soon fall, for we are so frail that the devil will overcome us every minute of time, if God does not hold us up with a strong hand…For if he did not fight for us, alas, what would become of us? We should be absolutely confounded, and not by reason of one stroke only, but there would be an infinite number of falls… As soon as we were in the way of salvation, we should at once be turned out of it by our own frailty, lightness and inconstancy, if we were not restrained and if God did not so work in us that we might, by his Holy Spirit, overcome all the assaults of the devil and the world. [The] Spirit is pleased to abide in us and to give us perseverance, that we do not draw back in the midst of our way.[95]

Therefore, the presence of the Spirit not only gives us assurance of salvation but confidence of our persevering to the end. If you are discouraged by weakness and sin, this is a source for your confidence. In his first epistle, Peter says that 'by God's power [you] are being guarded through faith for a salvation ready to be revealed in the last time (1 Pet. 1:5). Paul likewise spoke of the Spirit, saying he is 'sure of this, that he who began a good work in you will bring it to completion at the day of Jesus Christ' (Phil. 1:6). We are certain of our ultimate salvation because of the Father's sovereign election, the Son's perfect accomplished work, and the Spirit's ministry of sealing us, so that what God began he is certain to finish as well.

The Spirit and Judgment

A final way we should think of the sealing of the Spirit pertains to the final judgment of God. During the first Passover on the eve of Israel's exodus, every godly house was marked with the lamb's blood so that the angel of death passed over. Ezekiel 9 presents a similar picture. God was planning judgment of wicked Jerusalem, but first he sent an angel to place a seal on the faithful: 'Pass through the city, through Jerusalem and put a mark on the foreheads of the men who sigh and groan over all the abominations that are committed in it' (Eze. 9:4). Everyone who lacked God's mark was slaughtered in the judgment. This is how it will be in the end. Those who are marked by the seal of the Holy Spirit will be known and received by Christ when he returns to judge the unbelieving world (Matt. 25:34).

The same mark, however, that saves believers from God's wrath creates the opposite effect in this present world. Being identified as belonging to Jesus will cause you to be hated and condemned by the world. Jesus said, 'A servant is not greater than his master. If they persecuted me, they will also persecute you' (John 15:20).

This reality comes through forcefully in Revelation 13:16, where we are told that the beast will coerce people to receive his mark, the Antichrist's seal of acceptance. Everyone who does not have the mark of the beast will be persecuted. Revelation 14:9–10 adds, 'If anyone worships the beast and its image and receives a mark on his forehead or on his hand, he also will drink the wine of God's wrath.' This teaching does not merely describe something that will happen just before Jesus returns but pertains to the entire church age. The point is that if we do not have God's mark of ownership, if we are not sealed by God's Holy Spirit, it is not as if we have no mark and are not owned by anyone. You may say you are your own man or woman, but if you do not have God's seal of ownership you are in fact owned and sealed by the world in rebellion to God. The world will accept you for it, but God will judge you. We are either marked by God and persecuted by the world, or marked for acceptance by the world but condemned to be judged by God on the last day.

This being the case, there is nothing more important than that we should be 'sealed for the day of redemption' (Eph. 4:30) by God's Spirit. We are either sealed by God, having believed on Christ and his gospel, or we are sealed by the world through sin and unbelief. Only those whose sins are cleansed by the blood of Christ and who are sealed by the Spirit will escape the wrath of God that is to come. Revelation 22:4 says of them: 'They will see his face, and his name will be on their foreheads.'

Sealed in Christ

The kind of confidence Paul writes about here is something we need if we are going to grow in faith and godliness. It is not easy to turn from our sins, and this teaching about the Holy Spirit helps us. Yet it is not ultimately the Spirit to whom we must look to gain security, nor to him that we turn for the seal of God's blessing. Paul writes, 'In him you…were sealed with the promised Holy Spirit' (Eph. 1:13), that is *in Jesus Christ*. In the Greek, the words 'in him,' begin this sentence, just as they began verse 11, forming a deliberate parallel: '*In him* we have obtained an inheritance …*In him* you also were sealed.'

This means that if you lack assurance, it is to Jesus Christ that you must turn, for it is in him that you are sealed for the final redemption. If you feel condemned for your sin, 'the blood of Jesus cleanses us from all sin' (1 John 1:7). If you seek to have your salvation validated, it is Jesus who says, 'Everyone who acknowledges me before men, I also will acknowledge before my Father who is in heaven' (Matt. 10:32). If you seek power in your weakness, Jesus promised, 'My grace is sufficient for you' (2 Cor. 12:9). He adds, in Hebrews 13:5–6, "'I will never leave you nor forsake you.' So we can confidently say, 'The Lord is my helper; I will not fear; what can man do to me?'"

In *Pilgrim's Progress,* John Bunyan's hero enters the Celestial City having presented his valid and sealed certificate of acceptance. But where did he get it? Bunyan gets it right, because he tells us Christian had been staggering along with a great burden on his back, the weight of his sin, when at last he came upon a cross. 'He ran until he came to a peak where a cross stood; a little below, in the bottom, was a tomb. When Christian reached the cross, his burden became loose, fell from his back, and tumbled into the tomb. I never saw the burden again.' That is what happens to everyone who comes in faith to the cross of Christ—the weight of your guilt falls away, having been paid by his precious blood. But something else happened as Christian stood there weeping at the cross. Bunyan tells us:

> Three Shining Ones approached and greeted him. 'Peace,' the first said, 'Your sins are forgiven' (Mark 2:5). The second removed his filthy rags and dressed him in rich clothing (Zech. 3:4). The third put a mark on his forehead (Eph. 1:13) and gave him a sealed roll. He told Christian to look at the roll as he ran and to leave it at the celestial gate.[96]

There is the complete salvation for all who come to Jesus Christ in faith. We are forgiven our sins, clothed in the righteous robes of Christ, and sealed for salvation by the promised Holy Spirit. All this can be yours if you will come to Jesus in faith. All this is already yours if you are in Christ, so that now you may live for him who gave himself for you.

12

THE DEPOSIT OF OUR INHERITANCE

Ephesians 1:14

According to author James R. White, the Trinity is the forgotten doctrine of Christianity:

> Most Christian people have forgotten the central place the doctrine is to hold in the Christian life. It is rarely the topic of sermons and Bible studies, rarely the object of adoration and worship…The doctrine is misunderstood as well as ignored… it does not hold the place it should in the proclamation of the Gospel message, nor in the life of the individual believer in prayer, worship, and service.[97]

This concern could not be stated about the apostle Paul, who structured his whole approach to Christian salvation around the Trinity. This great opening section of Ephesians offers praise to God for the blessings each divine Person of the Trinity contributes to our salvation, which therefore rests on an unshakeable foundation.

The Trinity is perhaps Christianity's highest and greatest mystery. The Bible presents the one God in three persons. As the *Westminster Larger Catechism* explains, they are 'the same in substance, equal in power and glory; although distinguished by their personal properties' (Q. 9). Understanding how the three Persons work together answers many of our concerns about the stability of our salvation. How can salvation fail us, when it was ordained by God the Father before there even was time? Before creation, before any of the circumstances that threaten us were even possible, God decreed that we should be saved as his holy children. The triumph of Christ's saving work as God the Son likewise gives us assurance. How can sin condemn us when Christ has paid its penalty? How will the flesh, the world, or the devil destroy us while Christ now reigns in power, interceding for us in heaven?

Yet still there is need for the work of God the Spirit. How am I included in this salvation? How can I know these things are not merely true in the abstract but true for *me*? The answer is in the work of God the Spirit, who enters us into Christ by faith, thus to receive the benefits of the Trinity's saving work. The Bible says a cord of three strands is not easily broken (Eccles. 4:12); in the Trinity we have an unbreakable redemption in which we may rest secure.

This is why James White began his book by writing, 'I love the Trinity'—speaking both of God and of the doctrine.[98] Paul loved the Trinity, too, and that is why this doxology focuses on the work of God in three Persons. The God revealed in Trinity is a God of unfathomable glory, who meets our every need. If anyone asks you how you consider your salvation to be secure, you may point to the Trinity. Our salvation rests on the *sovereign authority* of God the Father, on the *finished work* of God the Son, and on the *indwelling power* of God the Holy Spirit.

The Age of the Spirit

Ephesians 1:14 focuses on the Holy Spirit, who in at least one specific sense is the most important Person for us in the Godhead. I say this because the Spirit is the only divine person whose primary contribution to our salvation is expressed in the present tense. All three Persons of the Godhead are involved in every aspect of our salvation—past, present and future. But the decisive contributions made by God the Father and God the Son are in the past, even though their present and future work remains essential. The Father ordained us. Christ died and rose again. All this is done. But in the work of the Spirit we now turn from the past tense to the present. The Father *ordained*; the Son *accomplished*; but God the Spirit *applies* salvation. The Spirit was always involved in our redemption, but it is now that he steps to the fore, as it were, so that this present age between the first and second comings of Christ is rightly called *the Age of the Spirit.*

In our last study I mentioned Bunyan's *Pilgrim's Progress*, the allegory that follows Christian through his many dangers and difficulties until he arrives safe at the Celestial City. It is to the challenges of this present life that the Holy Spirit's work is especially directed. It is the Spirit, on behalf of the Father and the Son, who comes to lead us through the Slough of Despond, up the Hill of Difficulty, out of Vanity Fair and past Doubting Castle. It is the Spirit who empowers our perseverance and keeps us in the faith. In Ephesians 1:14, Paul adds that he 'is the guarantee of our inheritance until we acquire possession of it.'

From time to time in these studies of Ephesians I have asked, 'What is a Christian?' This, too, may be expressed in terms of the Trinity. Verse 5 tells us that a Christian is a child of God the Father, since 'he predestined us for adoption' as his sons. In verse 7 we learned that a Christian is a sinner who has been redeemed by the blood of God the Son. We now find that a Christian is one who has received the Holy Spirit, who seals us for salvation and guarantees our full redemption.

The Holy Spirit is not an add-on for upper-level Christians. Paul says that 'when you heard the word of truth, the gospel of your salvation, and believed in him, [you] were sealed with the promised Holy Spirit' (Eph. 1:13). He does not mean that first comes saving faith and then, sometime later and perhaps only for a special few, comes the Holy Spirit. Paul means, as Robert Reymond explains, 'Faith in Christ is the instrumental cause of the sealing. That is to say, the moment one trusts in Christ, *that same moment* the Holy Spirit seals him in Christ.'[99] Paul speaks of the *promised* Holy Spirit, recalling that the Old Testament looked forward to his outpouring in the day of the Messiah. Jeremiah predicted, 'They shall *all* know me, from the least of them to the greatest' (Jer. 31:34, italics mine). Since the Spirit is poured out on *all* those who belong to God, it is not possible to be a Christian without receiving the Holy Spirit.

Therefore the question is, 'Have you received the Holy Spirit?' In our last study we examined a number of marks of the Spirit, but now I want to narrow them down to the one great mark of the Holy Spirit: saving faith in Jesus Christ. Handley

Moule says of the Spirit, 'His theme, His burden, is Jesus Christ. [His work] is to take of the things of Christ, to deal with…the finished work and inexhaustible riches of Christ, and…to manifest them to the spirit of man. It is to bring man, by a divine but inscrutable operation, to believe in Christ and to possess Him.' The Spirit's presence in your life is shown not by a fascination with the Spirit himself or with spirituality as such, but a fascination with Jesus Christ, a reliance on his work and a passion for his kingdom. Moule concludes, 'The Spirit lies hidden as it were behind Christ Jesus,' so that the Spirit is most in evidence when Christ is most exalted.[100]

The Spirit as Guarantee

In verses 13 and 14 Paul describes the Holy Spirit's work in applying salvation to our souls. First is the Spirit's *sealing* work, as he identifies, authenticates, and protects those who belong to God. Now in verse 14, Paul expands our understanding, adding that the Spirit is 'the guarantee of our inheritance.' We belong to God, so he marks us. But we also possess him as heirs, and he therefore gives the Spirit as the deposit of all that someday will be ours.

Paul describes the Spirit here with the Greek word *arrabon*. This was the down-payment paid at the time of a purchase, guaranteeing that the full amount would follow. According to the *English Standard Version*, Paul writes of the coming day when we will 'acquire possession of it,' that is, our final salvation. But since Paul uses a form of the word *apolutrosis*, which means *redemption*, the *New King James Version* renders this better, saying that the Spirit is our guarantee 'until the redemption of the purchased possession.' Paul is pointing to the coming of Christ when all things, including our salvation, will be brought to consummation. In Luke 21:27–28, Jesus spoke of his future return, saying, 'Then they will see the Son of Man coming in a cloud with power and great glory. Now when these things begin to take place, straighten up and raise your heads, because *your redemption* is drawing near' (italics mine). Paul refers to our redemption in this same way, pointing to the full fruition of what has already been established and begun at the cross of Christ.

Those who have come to Christ belong to God. The fullness of that relationship is yet to come, but God has made the down-payment that secures the whole. If we have the Spirit, through faith in Christ, this guarantees that we will be in heaven. We will one day know the fullness of blessings that God intends for his own.

Paul uses this word for guarantee (*arrabon*) two other times in his letters. In 2 Corinthians 1:22, Paul speaks about the confidence we can have in present difficulties, since it is God who makes us stand firm. He explains, 'He…has put his seal on us and given us his Spirit in our hearts as a guarantee (*arrabon*).' Yes, the life of faith is hard. And yes, some who call themselves Christians will not make good on their profession. What, then, is our assurance, especially when we learn how little we can trust our own spiritual resources? Our assurance is the presence of the Holy Spirit, who marks us as God's own and guarantees our perseverance. Just as when we make a down-payment on a home, so that an advance on the full amount guarantees our ownership, God secures our full redemption by giving us his Holy Spirit. The Spirit's presence serves, as one writer puts is, as 'the indisputable proof of God's determination to honor all the obligations he has assumed towards us under the covenant of grace.'[101]

The other use of this term is in 2 Corinthians 5, where Paul is looking forward to the day when his own earthly form will be exchanged for a heavenly body. He tires of the burdens of earthly life and looks forward to the journey's end. Speaking of this future glory, he adds, 'He who has prepared us for this very thing is God, who has given us the Spirit as a guarantee (*arrabon*)' (2 Cor. 5:5). This means, as Donald Grey Barnhouse says, 'We are not only saved, we are also safe. Christ paid the price of our sins, and the Holy Spirit maintains us in our sure position as children of God.'[102]

The Spirit as Foretaste

An important feature of the *arrabon*, the down-payment, is that it is paid in kind. We are going to buy a house with money, so we write a check as the deposit, which secures the property with an advance of money. In the same way, the gift of the Spirit is a foretaste of what God will give us in immeasurably greater extent upon the completion of our salvation.

Verse 14 describes the Spirit as the deposit of our inheritance. We are heirs of God. Just as he possesses us, we are to possess him. 'I will be their God,' he says, 'and they will be my people.' By the Spirit we begin this mutual possession of love. We begin to enjoy our inheritance.

In his novel, *The Testament*, John Grisham tells of a multi-billionaire who kills himself moments after signing his final will. His worthless, loveless, and greedy children eagerly await the date when the will is to be read and executed. In the meantime they immediately start a spending-spree, buying fabulous houses and luxury cars. But to their shock, they find that the entire fortune was bequeathed to a half-sister no one had ever heard of, a Christian missionary living far off in a jungle, and as a result destitution stared them in the face.[103]

Christians are not like that when it comes to the riches of God's redemption. We are not waiting to see what riches will come to us. God has publicly ordained and declared what will be given to all his children and heirs in Jesus Christ in the age to come. Paul says, 'This perishable body must put on the imperishable, and this mortal body must put on immortality' (1 Cor. 15:53). He adds in 2 Corinthians 5:1, 'We have a building from God, a house not made with hands, eternal in the heavens.' The apostle John could scarcely imagine what this will all be like. But what he knew filled him with wonder: 'Beloved, we are God's children now, and what we will be has not yet appeared; but we know that when he appears we will be like him, because we shall see him as he is' (1 John 3:2). Revelation 22:3-5 vividly pictures the glory of which we now are heirs:

> No longer will there be anything accursed, but the throne of God and of the Lamb will be in it, and his servants will worship him. They will see his face, and his name will be on their foreheads. And night will be no more. They will need no light of lamp or sun, for the Lord God will be their light, and they will reign forever and ever.

These things are sure. They are not just a dim possibility if the will is found in our favor. No, the documents are all signed and sealed, they have been made public and are held in trust until the day of their execution, when the exalted Lord Jesus will step forward to open the seals and bring all things to consummation. We are heirs with our fortune held securely. And just as many such heirs receive a generous allowance from the vast sum held in trust for them, so we are given the Spirit, who is the foretaste and firstfruit of all that remains to come. John Owen writes, 'By the Holy Spirit, then, we get a foretaste of the fullness of that glory which God has prepared for those that love him and the more communion we have with the Holy Spirit as an 'earnest' the more we taste of that heavenly glory that awaits us.'[104]

This reality was symbolized in Old Testament Israel with the offering of the firstfruits. When the harvest first came in the people held a festival, rejoicing and thanking God for the fullness that soon would come. Paul uses this same expression regarding the resurrection of Jesus Christ. 'Christ has been raised from the dead, the *firstfruits* of those who have fallen asleep.' (1 Cor. 15:20). His resurrection is the beginning of our resurrection. In principle, since he is raised, we are raised with him, which is why Paul often refers to us in Ephesians as belonging 'in the heavenly realms.' We are joined to Christ through faith and thus to his resurrection, the firstfruits of which were given us through the Spirit. This guarantees our resurrection and glorification and provides us a portion of the life that then will be ours in full.

This tells us that Christians have great riches available to us now. Paul writes in 2 Corinthians 3:18, that we 'are being transformed into the same image from one degree of glory to another. For this comes from the Lord who is the Spirit.' A Christian is a person with divine power to lead a heavenly life on earth. Christians are not orphans but children and heirs (John 14:16–18), with a vast fortune held in trust from which we draw even now by faith, growing increasingly in the riches of grace and in the knowledge of God. Later in this chapter Paul prays that believers would know 'the immeasurable greatness of [God's] power toward us who believe' (Eph. 1:19). Because of this power, despite our weakness, sin, and opposition, 'We are more than conquerors through him who loved us' (Rom. 8:37). Christians have power through the Holy Spirit and are called to advance increasingly in godliness, especially as the Spirit applies God's Word, which is the special instrument of our growth and sanctification (John 17:17).

Knowing this encourages us in the struggles of the present. But if we turn this around we gain an even greater encouragement regarding the future. For if the indwelling Spirit is merely a down-payment on that which is yet to come, we can scarcely imagine how great is that which lies ahead. R. Kent Hughes rightly implores us:

> Imagine the sublimest, most treasured experiences of the Holy Spirit we have ever had and then realize they are only a foretaste, the tip of the tongue on the spoon, of what is to come. Remember the release in coming to Christ and knowing you were forgiven? Remember the time you followed the Spirit's leading and were wonderfully used? Remember the satisfaction of finding the fruits of the Spirit surprising you with goodness where you once responded wickedly? Think of all this and then multiply it a millionfold. Here on earth we have experienced the first dollar of a million celestial dollars—the earnest. We have the dawning of knowledge, but then we will have the midday sun. "No eye has seen, no ear has heard, no mind has conceived what God has prepared for those who love him—but God has revealed it to us by his Spirit' (1 Cor. 2:9–10).[105]

If we have experience of these things then we know *in kind* what awaits us in heaven, though *in magnitude* we cannot begin to imagine such a weight of glory. Do you know something of these things? Do you know the release of sins forgiven? Do you know the satisfaction of useful service to God? Do you know the fruit of the Spirit and a power that has enabled you to turn away from sin? If you know nothing of these things, if they truly are all alien to your experience, then you cannot have the Spirit and according to your own testimony you are not a Christian. You are in danger: the danger that you are like the rotten, rebellious children in Grisham's novel, vainly expecting an inheritance that has been given to others, God's true children who serve him in this world. While you live it up now you are piling up debts that will have to be paid, and soon the façade of your life will come crashing down. What you need is to go to Jesus, confess your sin and trust him for your redemption, to be washed, renewed, and restored to God, and receive the promised Holy Spirit.

But if you do know about these things, if your heart leapt at the mention of the forgiveness of your sin, if you have knowledge of God through the light of his Word, then just imagine what it will be like when these things are multiplied by the infinite power and goodness of God! 'Oh, how my heart yearns within me!' cried Job even in his sufferings, at the thought of what awaits him in the resurrection dawn (Job 19:27). Thoughts of the same will cause our hearts to burn with anticipation, to sing with love for our Redeemer, and to labor with zeal for the advance of his kingdom.

The Most Valued Praise

We see, therefore, the significance of the Spirit's work in this present age of grace. His presence gives us *assurance*, for the down-payment guarantees that all will be ours in due time. His lively working gives *enjoyment*, as we partake now in measure of blessings to come beyond our imagining. As a result, we ought to be all the more eager to live in this present age for the glory of our wonderful God. This is how Paul completes this verse, and with it this whole great hymn of praise to God. It is all 'to the praise of his glory.'

This is the third time Paul has used this expression. It first appeared with regard to God the Father in his work of ordaining our salvation: 'He chose us in him before the foundation of the world that we should be holy and blameless before him. In love he predestined us for adoption through Jesus Christ, according to the purpose of his will, *to the praise of his glorious grace*, with which he has blessed us in the Beloved' (Eph. 1:4–6, italics mine). The work of the Father in eternity past, his glorious plan upheld even now and extending to eternity future, brings praise to the glory of his grace. Verse 12 similarly says our inclusion in Christ through faith is 'for the praise of his glory.' Now, in verse 14, the giving of God's Spirit as the seal and deposit on our full redemption is also 'to the praise of his glory.'

Do you realize just who is going to glorify God on the day of your final redemption? When the Bible describes the crowd of acclamation that will be praising God for his wondrous salvation of sinners like you and me, it includes an amazing host. It includes angels in the heavens. Revelation 7 depicts multitudes of the redeemed gathered all in white, with angels and the four living creatures standing around God's throne: 'They fell on their faces before the throne and worshiped God, saying, 'Amen! Blessing and glory and wisdom and thanksgiving and honor and power and might be to our God forever and ever! Amen!" (Rev. 7:11–12).

Do you realize that in the end the devil and the demons and all who followed them in hating God will have to acknowledge the glory of his grace in the matter of your salvation? Philippians 2:10–11 tells us, 'At the name of Jesus every knee should bow, in heaven and on earth and under the earth, and every tongue confess that Jesus Christ is Lord, to the glory of God the Father.'

And do you realize that the created realm itself will break forth in praise at the redemption of God's children? Romans 8:19 says, 'The creation waits with eager longing for the revealing of the sons of God.' Then will be its own deliverance from the Fall in the regeneration of all things. Isaiah 55:12 tells us, 'The mountains and the hills before you shall break forth into singing, and all the trees of the field shall clap their hands.'

And yet, with all that praise, from every corner of the universe, in heaven above and hell below, there is one voice of praise most precious to the heart of God. I mentioned that the Greek word for deposit is *arrabon*, and it is an interesting fact that in the development of the Greek language this word came to be used for a wedding ring. This, too, is a way we should think about the indwelling of the Holy Spirit, as the ring God slips on our finger, betrothing us to himself, and pledging his devotion for the wedding that is yet to come.

As a minister, I perform many weddings, and I always enjoy the exchange of rings. I say to each party, 'Have you a token to give of your fidelity to this covenant?' God likewise enters into covenant with us in Jesus Christ. He promises our full redemption in the glory yet to be revealed, and he gives to us the Spirit as a token of his fidelity. Putting the ring on the finger of his bride, the groom says, 'I give you this ring as a symbol and pledge of my constant faith and abiding love.' So also is the presence of the Spirit in your life a symbol and pledge of God's constant faith and abiding love to you.

There is a wedding ahead for us, the Bride of Christ entering into mutual possession with her Lord forever. This is how the Bible depicts the end: 'I saw the holy city, new Jerusalem, coming down out of heaven from God, prepared as a bride adorned for her husband' (Rev. 21:2). If that is how the Bible portrays the consummation of all things, then let me ask you, Whose praise do you think God will most delight to receive? Yes, there will be angels and archangels and four living creatures. There will be the stopped tongues of all God's foes—demonic and human—in hell. The whole creation will be in witness, extolling the glory of God's redemption. But when the doors of history open and the bride finally strolls down the aisle, the eyes of the groom will rest only on her. For it is the adoration of the bride that most enthralls the heart of the groom.

What a privilege! What glory awaits us! This being the case, how much must God delight in our adoring praise now, as he will then, so that the praise we give him now for the glory of his grace in our redemption is the most wonderful sound in all the vast creation. Let us, then, praise indeed our glorious God 'who has blessed us in Christ with every spiritual blessing in the heavenly places' (Eph. 1:3), our loving husband and groom, our Savior and our Lord.

13

Paul's Prayer for the Church

Ephesians 1:15–17

Prayer is the loftiest and most spiritual exercise of which we are capable as Christians. Prayer is having an audience with God, worshiping him directly, asking of him, and receiving spiritual blessings in his presence. It is no surprise, therefore, that prayer is difficult. This is why so many Christians look on prayer as an irksome duty, a chore that we accept but only with reluctance. As a result, many of us think, 'How much time *must* I spend in prayer?' rather than, 'How much time *may* I spend in prayer?'

Private prayer is a great blessing, but it is especially prayer together with other believers that lifts us up into heaven, and gives us a heavenly-mindedness towards one another. For that reason it is important for Christians to pray for one another, but also with one another. Along with membership in a solid, Bible-preaching church, regular Bible study and private prayer, the importance of praying with other Christians should be stressed as vital to the Christian life.

Given all this, Christians should pay special attention to the prayers in the Bible. In Ephesians 1:15–17, we begin to study a great prayer from the apostle Paul, a most eminent Christian whose spirituality flowed from an intimate relationship with Jesus Christ. In Paul's writings we have the prayers of one who is seasoned by decades of ground-breaking missionary labor and whose writings in Scripture possess the sanctity of biblical inspiration. The prayers in the Bible—in the Psalms, in the Old Testament histories, the prophets, the Gospels, and in the epistles—are not merely the prayers of eminent believers but the prayers that God inspired and recorded through them for our benefit. Apart from our Lord's direct teaching on prayer, there can hardly be more beneficial material for our own prayer life than to study prayers from the mouths of prophets and apostles.

Paul as a Man of Prayer

The apostle Paul is particularly noteworthy in this regard because of the great wealth of prayers we find in his letters. The Pauline epistles are laced with prayer, which probably reflects the intensity of Paul's own spirituality, as well as the demands of his ministry. The first thing we learn about Paul after his conversion is the statement of Acts 9:11, where Ananias is told 'he is praying.' The King James Version eloquently puts it, 'Behold, he prayeth.' That is not a bad beginning to anyone's spiritual biography. 'It is as though,' wrote Arthur

Pink, 'that struck the keynote of his subsequent life, that he would, to a special degree, be marked as a man of prayer.'[106]

Paul's letters are filled with prayer no doubt because Paul's life was filled with prayer. If you follow his travels and log the intercessions he writes about in his letters, you get a glimpse at how far-flung were his concerns in prayer. He wrote to the Philippians, 'I thank my God in all my remembrance of you, always in every prayer' (Phil. 1:3), language that is echoed in our passage. Paul's practice seems to have been to pray for whomever he is thinking. Whenever he heard a bit of news or recalled a person or a church he turned to the Lord on their behalf, thanking God for them and interceding for their well-being. No wonder, then, that he describes himself as praying constantly. 'I thank God,' Paul wrote to Timothy, 'as I remember you constantly in my prayers night and day' (2 Tim. 1:3). The man who exhorted us to 'pray without ceasing' (1 Thess. 5:17) seems to have practiced what he preached. Even though chained to Roman guards, Paul's ministry ranged far and wide in prayer.

We find a similar zeal with practically every Christian who has been greatly used by the Lord. Martin Luther often prayed two or three hours a day, and his great moments of faith were all preceded by long and fervent prayer. Roman Catholic leaders once sent an agent to spy out Luther's weaknesses, and the spy came back lamenting, 'Who can overcome a man who prays like this?' John Calvin often rose at 4 a.m. for prayer. John Knox cried out to God, 'Give me Scotland, or I die!' The same is true of leaders God used to bring revival to America. Jonathan Edwards spent whole days in prayer, seeking blessings for his people as well as power for his preaching. We find the same to be true of great men and women in the Bible. Moses, David, and Solomon are known for their prayers. Hezekiah, Daniel, Esther, Nehemiah, and Ezra all are shown in prayer before the defining moments of their careers. Of course, the greatest example is our Lord Jesus, who regularly went off alone for long periods of prayer.

These examples show the value of prayer to the Christian life. People will pay great sums of money and go to great effort to gain an audience with a famous or powerful person. But Christians have access to God himself. Surely, this is our greatest dignity and privilege. Yes, we gain many benefits from prayer, temporal and eternal. But even apart from the benefit, we have in prayer an audience with the King of Kings, the Lord of Hosts, with Almighty God! What is all the world in comparison with that! We have fellowship with God. 'We read that Moses was upon the mountain forty days with God,' writes Jeremiah Burroughs, 'and when he came down his face so shone that the people were not able to bear it…Converse much with God, be often with God, be near to Him and that will make you shine as lights in the midst of a crooked and perverse generation.'[107] Indeed, these words spoken of Paul, 'Behold, he prays!' are the best argument for any of us that our spiritual life is sound and prospering.

Paul was a man of prayer because he was a man of God. But his writings also stand out for their emphasis on prayer because of the demands of his leadership role in the fledgling church. Paul was the apostle to the Gentiles, a missionary who had on-going relationships with a great many churches. He prayed for them as a shepherd cares for the sheep, just as pastors today are obliged to pray much for their congregation. Paul counted this as a duty, as well as a difficult burden. He wrote, 'Apart from other things, there is the daily pressure on me of my anxiety for all the churches' (2 Cor. 11:28), and therefore he prayed.

Since so many of Paul's converts were former pagans, he may have felt a special need to write about his prayers to set a model for them. Furthermore, these early Christians often disappointed Paul, and prayer no doubt helped him to maintain a gracious spirit towards them. Dietrich Bonhoeffer emphasized this aspect of intercessory prayer in his account of life in the underground seminary he supervised in Nazi Germany: 'A Christian fellowship lives and exists by the intercession of its members for one another…I can no longer condemn or hate a brother for whom I pray, no matter how much trouble he causes me. His face…is transformed in intercession into the countenance of a brother for whom Christ died, the face of a forgiven sinner.'[108] Likewise, Paul's life of prayer no doubt fueled his patience and love for the often wayward churches he oversaw.

The Necessity of Prayer

Turning to Paul's prayer in Ephesians 1, the first thing it shows is *the necessity of prayer* to any effective gospel ministry. Paul has just written some of the most inspiring theological statements ever penned (Eph. 1:3–14). Yet he obviously did not think it sufficient simply to set forth his teaching unless he combined it with fervent prayers for God's blessing. Arthur Pink explains, 'The preacher's obligations are not fully discharged when he leaves the pulpit, for he needs to water the seed he has sown… Paul mingled supplications with his instructions.' Speaking of ministers, he adds, 'It is our privilege and duty to retire to the secret place after we leave the pulpit and beg God to write His Word on the hearts of those who have listened to us, to prevent the enemy from snatching away the seed, to so bless our efforts that they may bear fruit to God's eternal praise.'[109] Likewise church members have a duty to pray for their ministers and for God's blessing on the preaching of his Word.

This points out a danger that arises from our high view of Scripture. We believe and proclaim the sufficiency of Scripture. We constantly trumpet that the Bible is all that we need for life and godliness, for the knowledge of God and for salvation. Yet that does not make the blessing of Scripture automatic. The doctrine of Scripture's sufficiency does not in any way lessen the need for prayer. God's Word is the primary instrument he has given for building up his church, but even it only 'works' as God causes it to work. Salvation requires not merely the preaching of God's Word but also the ministry of the Holy Spirit to regenerate the sinful heart and enlighten the darkened mind, and for this we are to pray.

It is remembered at Tenth Presbyterian Church in Philadelphia that its long-time pastor, Donald Grey Barnhouse, could often be found in the sanctuary on Saturdays kneeling beside each pew, thinking about the people who often sat there, and asking God to bless them with the following day's sermon. Indeed, every true minister knows what it is to feel his own weakness and to labor in prayer for the supply of God's power. Think of the example of Jesus when feeding the five thousand. Standing before the thousands with so little to give them, he prayed to the Father for supernatural blessing and then, having prayed, he was confident in distributing the few loaves and fishes that fed so great a multitude. Preachers today who desire supernatural blessing on their ministries will likewise pray in thanksgiving and faith.

Here in Ephesians, we see the apostle setting down his pen after the elevated teaching of chapter 1, beseeching God to enlighten his readers' hearts that they might come to know him. If that kind of prayer was necessary to Paul, it surely is necessary for us as well.

Thanks for Faith and Love

In verse 15 Paul explains his reason for praying. 'For this reason,' he begins, pointing back to the whole of what he had taught in verses 3-14. The emphasis of that teaching was on God's sovereign grace in salvation. Many people consider this theme to be a disincentive to prayer, but it is the reason Paul prays. Knowing that God is sovereign over salvation and having heard of their 'faith in the Lord Jesus and…love toward all the saints' (Eph. 1:15), Paul prays to give God thanks for them. Paul does not credit the Christians for their faith and love, but God. D. A. Carson explains, 'Apart from God's powerful transforming work, these people would never have been converted. Without God, they would never have begun to display the trust, faithfulness, and love now richly displayed in their lives. Therefore whatever Christian virtues characterize them become the occasion for heartfelt praise to God.'[110]

Notice not only that Paul prays to God because he is sovereign, but also notice the qualities that Paul thinks are praiseworthy in a church. 'For this reason,' he explains, 'because I have heard of your faith in the Lord Jesus and your love toward all the saints, I do not cease to give thanks for you, remembering you in my prayers' (Eph. 1:15-16). It is no exaggeration to say that what excites many church attenders today is far different from what excited Paul. We are thrilled to see worldly measures of success: when attendance is up, when the church acquires money and worldly power. These things are not bad in themselves, but far more important is what Paul prays for—'faith in the Lord Jesus and love toward all the saints.' James Montgomery Boice commented:

Faith really is the essential thing, not numbers or programs, not budgets or buildings. It is by faith that we 'demolish arguments and every pretension that sets itself up against the knowledge of God, and we take captive every thought to make it obedient to Christ' (2 Cor. 10:5). The apostle John said, 'This is the victory that has overcome the world, even our faith' (1 John 5:4).[111]

Without faith and love, the church fails in its mission, however many people attend or however much money or power we attain. But with faith and love, the church is often vibrant and effective in spiritual terms, even when we are numerically few, or when we are poor and downcast in the world. Today, ministers and church leaders are pressured to focus on priorities that do not have the effect of building faith and love, but that appeal to the social and worldly desires of people. In this way, churches are often successful in becoming impressive to the world. But they are of little use to Jesus because they have neglected God's Word and prayer, which are God's means for strengthening faith and love. What Paul constantly looked for in his churches, prayed for, and thanked God to see was faith and love.

If we compare Paul's prayers to different churches we will see just how consistent he was. He wrote to the Colossians, 'We always thank God, the Father of our Lord Jesus Christ, when we pray for you, since we heard of your faith in Christ Jesus and of the love that you have for all the saints' (Col. 1:3-4). To Philemon he wrote, 'I thank my God always when I remember you in my prayers, because I hear of your love and of the faith that you have toward the Lord Jesus and all the saints' (Phil. 4-5). In 2 Thessalonians 1:3, he prays, 'We ought always to give thanks to God for you, brothers, as is right, because your faith is growing abundantly, and the love of every one of you for one another is increasing.' There is a lesson for us in the priorities of Paul's prayers. If faith is what Paul values and prays for, and if, as Paul says in Romans 10:17, 'faith comes from hearing,' then we ought to make the preaching and teaching of the Bible our great priority, along with the ministry of prayer.

To understand Paul rightly, we must define what it means to have faith in the Lord. Faith is often spoken of in a general sort of way. But Paul would not be thankful that people maintained merely a religious outlook on life until they trusted the crucified and risen Christ for their salvation. Many people believe in the idea of God and may be fine moral people, yet they are not Christians. It is not enough to look on Jesus as a great moral figure or even as a teacher that we should emulate. We must look to him as the Son of God, the Savior of sinners through the blood of his cross, and as the resurrected and living Lord in order to be saved by the faith for which Paul gives thanks. The Philippian jailer asked Paul, 'What must I do to be saved?' Paul answered by defining faith in terms of the saving work of Jesus, saying, 'Believe in the Lord Jesus, and you will be saved' (Acts 16:30–31).

Just as striking in Paul's prayers is the emphasis he places on love, especially love for fellow believers. The clear implication is that without love our faith cannot be considered genuine and true. Our faith is validated not merely by doctrinal correctness but also by our love for others, especially other believers. Here is a proof for which the devil has no answer: the love of Christians that is ready to give for brothers and sisters; the tears of one saint for the trials of another; and the palpable joy in the Lord that marks true Christian fellowship. John writes, 'Beloved, if God so loved us, we also ought to love one another. No one has ever seen God; if we love one another, God abides in us and his love is perfected in us' (1 John 4:11–12).

Christianity must always be defined both doctrinally and in terms of a lifestyle. This is why Paul's letters are so regularly divided into two sections, one of which lays out doctrine and the other applies the doctrine in terms of our lives. Ephesians is a classic example of this pattern, the first three and a half chapters presenting truth and the last two and half chapters applying it practically. Christianity, Paul says, consists of faith and of love. Therefore, he said in Galatians 5:6 that what really matters is 'faith working through love.'

LOVE AS THE TEST AND WITNESS OF FAITH

The requirement to love one another often turns out to be quite a challenge, and our failure in this regard often mars the witness of the church. William Edgar recalls the situation of the small and struggling Protestant church in France. During the twentieth century this Christian body possessed two world-class theologians, both of whom were experts on John Calvin. The two were bitter enemies, despite their shared theology and loyalty to the same church. Most of their differences were over technical matters: for instance, had Calvin read the writings of Copernicus before writing his commentary on Genesis? Over such issues the two men waged relentless conflict all the way to the grave. Edgar notes that the church they loved 'remains small and ineffective to this day, and it cries out for solid teachers who can build up rather than destroy.'[112] As another example, Edgar notes two seminary professors who waged a heated battle in prominent journals. After many years a student asked one of them why things had become so bitter. The professor commented that the two of them had never sat down to talk about their differences, which the student found surprising since the professors taught at the same seminary.

Why is love so hard? The answer is our sin. But it is our union with Christ through faith that makes love possible for sinners and obligatory for Christians. The basis of our love is our shared allegiance to Christ, but even more important is the shared Holy Spirit who lives within us. The Puritan Richard Sibbes wrote, 'As we are knit to Christ by faith, so we must be knit to the communion of saints by love.'[113]

Anyone who underestimates the challenge of love within the church probably has not been a Christian very long. It is not easy to love people who are different even when they are Christians, and who in many cases have sinned against you or you against them. Love among Christians therefore requires that we be ready to repent of our own sins, that we be eager to forgive those who have sinned against us, and that we turn to the Lord in fresh faith and obedience, seeking his aid through the Holy Spirit. Repentance, forgiveness, and new obedience—all these are fruits of our faith that allow us to love.

The stakes could not be higher, for at risk is the spiritual health of the church as well as its witness before the world. Jesus said, 'As I have loved you, you also are to love one another. By this all people will know that you are my disciples, if you have love for one another' (John 13:34–35). Francis Schaeffer explained, 'Without true Christians loving one another, Christ says the world cannot be expected to listen, even when we give proper answers…After we have done our best to communicate to a lost world, still we must never forget that the final apologetic which Jesus gives is the observable love of true Christians for true Christians…if the world does not see this, it will not believe that Christ was sent by the Father.'[114]

No wonder Paul thanked God for the faith and love of the Ephesians! Indeed, whenever we see Christians living together in truth and love, it is a sure sign that the Holy Spirit is at work through faith in Jesus Christ. Truth without love is not Christian truth; love without truth is not Christian love. Either without the other falsely represents God before the world. It is only with truth and love held together, as the Holy Spirit works through our faith in Christ, that the true God of the Bible is revealed to the eyes of the watching world.

The 'Secret' of Prayer

Paul's great desire was that the Ephesians should not only reveal God to the world but that they themselves should come to know him better. This is the primary request that he adds to the thanksgiving of this prayer: 'That the God of our Lord Jesus Christ, the Father of glory, may give you a spirit of wisdom and of revelation in the knowledge of him' (Eph. 1:17).

Our next study will focus on knowing God, but we should observe in closing that it is primarily through the Bible that God's people come to know him, and it is through prayer that we come to rightly understand the Bible. Paul sets the example in this chapter, joining his teaching to fervent prayer. James Boice writes, 'If we are to know God, we must spend time with him in Bible study, prayer, and meditation. You cannot get to know a person without spending time with him or her. No more can you get to know God without spending time with him.'[115]

The famous evangelist Harry Ironside illustrates this with an incident from early in his ministry. He went to visit a godly old man who was soon to die. While listening to the man talk of God, he was amazed at the man's astonishing knowledge of Scripture and grasp of doctrine. Before long, tears were streaming down Ironside's cheeks and he asked, 'Where did you get these things? Can you tell me where I can find a book that will open them up to me? Did you get them in a seminary or college?' The old man replied, 'My dear young man, I learned these things on my knees on the mud floor of a little sod cottage in the north of Ireland. There with my Bible open before me, I used to kneel for hours at a time and ask the Spirit of God to reveal Christ to my soul and to open the Word to my heart, and he taught me more on my knees on that mud floor than I ever could have learned in all the seminaries or colleges in the world.'[116]

Prayer and the Word: there is the secret to knowing God, growing in faith, and learning to love other Christians. It is people who sit at Jesus' feet, who spend time with God in prayer and through the Word, who thereby come to know him better and then reveal him to the eyes of the world.

14

Knowing God

Ephesians 1:17

Imagine yourself receiving a note from a trusted Christian mentor or advisor—perhaps a parent or former teacher—someone who knows you and loves you. The note tells you that the person has been praying for you, and even informs you of the content of those prayers. Perhaps the note speaks of a prayer for you to have patience. This would suggest that in his or her view this is something you lack or otherwise need. Perhaps the prayers were for contentment or zeal for the Lord's work. Those prayers would suggest that you may suffer from discontentedness or laziness.

In Ephesians 1:17 we have Paul writing to tell the Ephesian Christians what he has been praying for them. This was a church Paul was close to, having planted it and tended its growth for two years. He knows them and loves them. At the same time, we have observed that this letter was likely sent as a circular treatise, not only to the church in Ephesus but to those in the area surrounding. This is therefore a general letter, written not only for particular errors or needs, but for the general edification of the church.

Paul has heard of their faith and love (Eph. 1:15), and has been thanking God and praying for them. In verse 17 we have Paul's primary request, which suggests his sense of their greatest need:

'that the God of our Lord Jesus Christ, the Father of glory, may give you a spirit of wisdom and of revelation in the knowledge of him.'

The Priority of Knowing God

If we were to make a list of the pressing needs of the church today it would not take much thought to add quite a few items. We live in a godless, unbelieving culture, so we have a great need for evangelism and apologetics. Furthermore, there is gross ignorance within the church, so we need sound Bible preaching and teaching. Because of the mounting worldliness evident in the church, we need more holiness. Furthermore, as pagan ideals impact the government and culture we need to get involved in civic life. Such things require money, so we need financial resources. All of these needs are real, and all would have been needed in Paul's day much as in our own.

But when Paul relates his primary desire for the church, the Christians' greatest need, he turns to none of these. He prays that our God and Father would send the Spirit of wisdom and revelation, for 'the knowledge of him,' or as the *New International Version* puts it, 'so that you may know him better.' What does Paul most desire? That they may know God and know him increasingly.

The importance of knowing God was proved when Jesus prayed for this on the night of his arrest. In John 17:3, Jesus gave a great definition of salvation, praying to the Father, 'And this is eternal life, that they know you the only true God, and Jesus Christ whom you have sent.' Eternal life is knowing God, and it is for this that Paul chiefly prays. This is the heart and the fulfillment of God's covenant purpose, as stated in Jeremiah's new covenant promise: 'I will be their God, and they shall be my people. And no longer shall each one teach his neighbor and each his brother, saying, "Know the Lord," for they shall all know me, from the least of them to the greatest, declares the Lord' (Jer. 31:33–34). Knowing God is always the greatest need of the church, for, as John Calvin writes, 'The final goal of the blessed life rests in the knowledge of God.'[117]

In his study of Paul's prayers, New Testament scholar D. A. Carson singles out the knowledge of God as 'the urgent need of the church.' Speaking of the other things I have listed, he writes, 'Clearly all of these things are important. I would not want anything I have said to be taken as disparagement of evangelism and worship, a diminishing of the importance of purity and integrity, a carelessness about disciplined Bible study. But there is a sense in which these urgent needs are merely symptomatic of a far more serious lack. The one thing we most urgently need in Western Christendom is a deeper knowledge of God. We need to know God better.' We need, he says, to be turned away from our own felt needs, away from happiness and fulfillment as we understand them in worldly terms, and turned towards the glories and excellences of God. 'We think rather little of what he is like,' Carson observes, 'what he expects of us, what he seeks in us. We are not captured by his holiness and his love; his thoughts and words capture too little of our imagination, too little of our discourse, too few of our priorities.'[118] The great need of the church today, therefore, as of the church in the apostle's time, is the knowledge of God.

When Paul writes about knowing God, he includes personal, experiential knowledge. But this knowledge of God starts with knowing *about* God. A doctrinal knowledge of God is essential. For this reason, few studies are more profitable than the attributes of God. On God's character, his unchanging attributes, we utterly depend for our salvation; knowing *about God* is essential to a relationship *with God*.

When we speak of God's attributes, we mean aspects of his character, descriptions of what God is like as taught by the Bible. They are not things God *has* or *possesses*, but ways that God *is*. The attributes are descriptions regarding God's being and character that lead us into a true knowledge of him. God is holy, good, just, and true—those are all affirmations made in the Scripture. In other respects, God can only be described negatively: he is infinite—that is, he cannot be contained or exhausted; he is immutable—he cannot change; he is immense—he cannot be measured.

As you read the Bible you should be thinking about what the text is teaching you about God. In the creation account we learn of God's eternal nature, wisdom, power, and especially his glory. 'The heavens declare the glory of God,' David sings (Ps. 19:1). Noah's flood and other judgments reveal to us that God is holy and just. In the exodus we learn that God is faithful, good, and also mighty to save. Through all these and other accounts God shows us what he is like, knowledge that is essential to our faith.

Consider three reasons why we should study the nature of God. The first is the excellence of the subject matter. Charles Spurgeon commented:

There is something exceedingly improving to the mind in a contemplation of the Divinity. It is a subject so vast, that all our thoughts are lost in its immensity; so deep, that our pride is drowned in its infinity...But while the subject humbles the mind, it also expands it. Nothing will so enlarge the intellect, nothing so magnify the whole soul of man, as a devout, earnest, continuing investigation of the great subject of the Deity.[119]

It is through the knowledge of God that we come truly to know ourselves and have our thoughts elevated by God's Word.

Second, by studying and coming to know God we find a ready comfort for our fears and are made bold for obedience. This is what makes the attributes of God such an important study for children. One of our daughters was able to overcome her fear of separation as a little girl because of what she learned about God in the children's catechism. One question she learned was, 'Can you see God?' The answer was: 'No, I cannot see God, but he can always see me.' Knowing about God gave her confidence when separated from her parents.

Christians are likewise comforted in trials to know that God is wise in all things, that he is sovereign, that he is holy, good, and loving. These things being true, we see why Romans 8:28 can tell us, 'For those who love God all things work together for good, for those who are called according to his purpose.' Knowing who and what God is, Paul reasons, 'If God is for us, who can be against us?' (Rom. 8:32). Because of who he is, 'nothing in all creation...will be able to separate us from the love of God that is in Christ Jesus our Lord' (Rom. 8:39).

The knowledge of God not only comforts us but also emboldens us for obedience. In Isaiah 6, the prophet saw a vision of the Lord in all his holy majesty. Isaiah 7 goes on to show how the prophet boldly confronted the king of Judah when he entered into idolatrous alliances. Where did Isaiah get the boldness of chapter 7? It came from the knowledge of God discovered in chapter 6. We should study God because of the elevating influence of the subject matter and to give us the comfort and boldness we so greatly need.

The third reason is that our beliefs regarding God profoundly shape our understanding of the salvation he gives. How we relate to God, what expectations we have of the Christian life, and what we hope for in the future all depend on the kind of God he is. Defective views of God always exert a corrupting influence on our views of salvation.

One important example today is called 'Open Theism.' This teaching denies that God exhaustively knows the future. God is, according to proponents of this view, deficient in his understanding and as such he occasionally makes mistakes and is overcome by events. While God is certainly resourceful, they say, he is neither able to predict future events nor to control them with certainty. This teaching denies God's foreknowledge and sovereignty, and ultimately compromises such attributes as God's infinity and wisdom and immutability. So opposed is this view to the picture of God in the Bible that it is alarming that prominent evangelical institutions—including publishing houses and leading magazines—have actively propagated this heresy.

Is this harmless speculation or is there real danger? I think Bruce Ware's assessment is correct. In his critique, subtitled, *The Diminished God of Open Theism*, Ware asks, 'Can our hope in God to fulfill his promises be founded without mental reservation or qualification? Can a believer know that God will triumph in the future just as he promised he will?'[120] The answers depend on the kind of God he is. Ware is right when he says the openness heresy undermines our confidence, hope and reliance on the Lord. He writes:

> To the extent that the openness model of God penetrates our churches, we can anticipate a greatly lessened confidence in God and a much greater temptation to trust in our own insights and abilities. We can anticipate weakened prayer lives and more confidence in our own accomplishments. God will be viewed increasingly as a pathetic sort of figure, possessing good motives but terribly faulty in his attempts to steer the direction of our lives and of human history.[121]

How can such a terrible denial of important divine attributes have spread so far through the supposedly Bible-believing world? The only explanation is that we have lost sight of God and forgotten him. This is how the problems began in Old Testament Israel. Judges 2:10, for instance, tells us, 'There arose another generation after them who did not know the LORD.' If we want to avoid damaging errors today, preserve the vigor of the Christian faith for future generations, know the blessings God offers, and have our names added to the roster of the faithful, then we must follow the desire of Paul's prayer and make it our business to know God.

God Revealed through Jesus Christ

The second point made by this verse is that God is most singularly known and revealed through his Son Jesus Christ. This is something Jesus himself boldly insisted. He said: 'No one knows the Son except the Father, and no one knows the Father except the Son and anyone to whom the Son chooses to reveal him' (Matt. 11:27). That explains why, in praying that we would know God, Paul refers to him as 'the God of our Lord Jesus Christ, the glorious Father.'

God's highest and best revelation of himself to mankind is through his Son Jesus Christ. In 1 Timothy 6:16, Paul tells us that God lives in 'unapproachable light.' God is himself, as a spirit, invisible. Therefore he reveals himself not by taking things off but by putting them on. To Moses he showed himself as a burning bush. To Israel he came as a pillar of fire and smoke. But ultimately, he revealed himself by taking on human form, entering into our world and walking among us. God's highest revelation of himself to us is through his Son, the man Jesus Christ. Therefore Paul writes in 2 Corinthians 4:6 that God shined in our hearts 'to give us the light of the knowledge of the glory of God in the face of Jesus Christ.' Jesus is, says Hebrews 1:3, 'the radiance of the glory of God and the exact imprint of his nature.' God reveals himself to us through the person and work of Jesus Christ, who is 'the image of the invisible God' (Col. 1:15).

This is why Paul prays that we will know 'the God of our Lord Jesus Christ, the Father of glory,' who is revealed through his Son. Yet we are not meant merely to know *about* the true God by means of Jesus. More than that, it is through the ministry of God's Son, in union with Jesus Christ through faith, that we come into a personal and loving relationship with the true God. Jesus has come not merely that we might know about God more accurately, but that we should be reconciled to him through Christ's blood and become God's children, knowing him as our Heavenly Father.

Jesus made this point to Mary Magdalene when she recognized him after his resurrection. Jesus told her to inform the disciples that he had risen, and then said, 'I am ascending to my Father and your Father, to my God and your God' (John 20:17). His point was that having accomplished his work on earth as our Savior, he now would return to heaven in order to complete our reconciliation. The God he had known in intimacy as the Son would now be a Father to us. 'I will be their God and they will be my people,' God so often promised in Scripture, and now in Christ all this is realized.

Having revealed himself through Jesus Christ, God invites you to know him in a personal way, to enter into his love as his own beloved child, coming to God through Christ's saving work. The apostle John wrote of Jesus, 'To all who did receive him, who believed in his name, he gave the right to become children of God' (John 1:12).

In Ephesians 3, Paul prays in a manner very similar to the prayer here in chapter one. There, he reminds us that it is especially through the cross that God is revealed to sinful mankind and invites us to come to him. 'I pray,' Paul writes, 'that you...may have strength to comprehend with all the saints what is the breadth and length and height and depth, and to know the love of Christ that surpasses knowledge, that you may be filled with all the fullness of God' (Eph. 3:17–19). This is ultimately what Paul means by knowing God through Jesus Christ, being filled with the abundant and eternal life God gives to sinners who are reconciled through the work of his Son.

Knowing God through the Spirit's Ministry

In the great doxology that began the Book of Ephesians, we noted the Trinitarian framework with which Paul presented the blessings of salvation. Now that we turn to the matter of knowing God it is no surprise that Paul keeps this emphasis. To this end, he now directs us to the Holy Spirit. He has stated the priority of knowing God through his Son. He now prays that God 'may give you a spirit of wisdom and revelation'. Our third point, therefore, is that God is known through the ministry of the Holy Spirit.

God sent the Spirit to inspire men in the writing of Scripture. The Bible is his revealed Word because, as Peter puts it, 'men spoke from God as they were carried along by the Holy Spirit' (2 Pet. 1:21). Yet the revelation process does not cease with the inspiring of Scripture. God also sends the Spirit to us so that we are given spiritual understanding of what the Bible says. To the Spirit's inspiring work, God adds the Spirit's illuminating work. He reveals to us not things left out of the Scripture and not mystic clues hidden in the Scripture, but rather the plain truths he inspired in the Bible which without his illumination would remain dark to our fallen minds.

There is debate about whether Paul is referring in this verse to God's Spirit—with a capital S, as the *New International Version* does—or merely to our human spirits—with a small s, as the *English Standard Version* and *New King James Version* do. Is he praying for God to send the Holy Spirit or merely to empower our spirituality? On the basis of Paul's Trinitarian approach, and because of his typical usage elsewhere, I think we rightly see this as a reference to the Holy Spirit. But even in the latter case, Paul implies the need for God's Spirit to work within us. F. F. Bruce explains, 'A "spirit of wisdom and revelation" can be imparted only through him who is the personal Spirit of wisdom and revelation...Only as God reveals by his Spirit can his people understand by that same Spirit.'[122]

The passage where Paul most clearly explains the necessity of the Holy Spirit's illuminating work is 1 Corinthians 2. Paul tells us there that because of our sinful, spiritually dead natures, it is necessary for the Spirit to work within us so that we comprehend and receive what God has said. Paul explains, 'The natural person does not accept the things of the Spirit of God, for they are folly to him, and he is not able to understand them because they are spiritually discerned' (1 Cor. 2:14). The reason sinful people *do not* accept God's Word, he says, is that they *cannot*: they are *not able*, being spiritually dead and blind. Augustine explained, 'Just as the sun is not seen by the blind, though they are clothed as it were with its rays, so is the light of truth not understood by the darkness of folly.'[123] This is what Jesus said to Nicodemus: 'Unless one is born again he cannot see the kingdom of God' (John 3:3). Apart from the enlivening, eye-opening work of God's Spirit, sinners not only cannot enter God's kingdom but cannot even see it in the light of God's Word.

No wonder, then, that Paul prays for God to send the Spirit to give us wisdom and revelation. These two terms, wisdom and revelation, speak not merely of the ability to receive God's Word but also to digest it, so that we are made, as Paul says to Timothy, 'wise for salvation through faith in Christ Jesus' (2 Tim. 3.15). Evidence of this work of the Spirit is seen in the faith and love that Paul commends in the Ephesians. But he prays, as we should, for more of this work so that we might know God better.

KNOWING GOD
THROUGH THE WORD AND PRAYER

Putting this all together, this is Paul's prayer—that his readers would know God—in terms of understanding and of a relationship—as Jesus Christ reveals him and brings us to the Father in faith, and as the Holy Spirit works in our hearts with his regenerating and illuminating work. This is an excellent prayer—one we ought to pray for ourselves and for others.

But, as always, the Christian life consists of more than asking God for things in prayer. Our prayers imply a final point, which is a question: How are we to pursue the knowledge of God?

The answer, I think, is found in Paul's example here. He wants his readers to know God, so he has written them with his teaching. As Paul will insist later in this letter (3:2–5), he writes not as a private person but as God's appointed ambassador, giving them authorized teaching on God's behalf. If we want to know God, then we must become students of this and other books in the Bible. Jesus once prayed for us, saying, 'Sanctify them by the truth; your Word is truth' (John 17:17). Search through the Bible to find those who really knew God and boldly did his will. You will find that they were people of God's Word, giving themselves to its study and learning in it to know and serve God. Search the annals of church history and you will find the same. We, too, therefore must be people of God's book.

Do you want to know God? Do you want to experience his presence in your life? Do you want to receive the fullness of his grace as you walk through this life with him? Then give yourself to his Word, the Bible, and he will meet with you there and show you his glory.

Paul also shows us that if we want to know God we must be people of prayer. Isn't this the combination we find in this chapter—Scripture and prayer together? In prayer we ask for the Spirit's illuminating work so that we will profit from the Bible, and we come into communion with the Father, through the access gained by the Son.

To some people this seems tedious and mundane. Ours is a mystical age in the church, and people do not want to have to study the Bible and think, or to order their lives to make room for prayer. They want to know God through some fool-proof method that fits into their busy lives.

Instead of walking step-by-step up the slopes of Mount Zion, they want to be flown directly to the top in a helicopter! I have noticed, in this regard, that many top-selling Christian books today tell ministers to stop laboring on their sermons and cease trying painstakingly to teach the Bible. Instead, they are to aim for the emotions with moving stories, seeking to produce stimulating experiences instead of the more demanding work of knowing God as he reveals himself in his Word.

In reading such material I am reminded of the experience of the prophet Elijah, who also wanted to hear from God and be encouraged by a direct encounter with divine power. Elijah went up Mount Horeb seeking God and there he learned a lesson we need to learn as well. Setting the prophet out on the mountain, God told Elijah to await his coming.

> Then a great and powerful wind tore the mountains apart and shattered the rocks before the Lord, but the Lord was not in the wind. After the wind, there was an earthquake, but the Lord was not in the earthquake. After the earthquake came a fire, but the Lord was not in the fire. And after the fire came a gentle whisper (1 Kings. 19:11–12).

It was in the whisper that God spoke to his prophet. Likewise, it is not in the experience of spiritual highs that we should seek the knowledge of God. Rather, it is as we sit quietly with the Bible on our laps, as we draw apart in prayer, as we come to church and sit before faithful preaching—it is in this way that we come to know God. We come to know him step-by-step as we walk through our lives as people of his Book and of prayer, looking to him in faith. We trust him in our need, we obey him in temptation, we serve him in the world, we look to him with tear-filled eyes in times of sorrow, we laugh with thanks in times of joy, and through his Word and in prayer we come to know God, as we trust and obey, through faith in Jesus Christ and by the power of the Holy Spirit that he sends.

> When we walk with the Lord
>   in the light of his Word,
>   what a glory he sheds on our way!
> While we do his good will,
>   he abides with us still,
>   and with all who will trust and obey.

15

The Three 'What's'

Ephesians 1:18–20

When Nebuchadnezzar had conquered Jerusalem, he brought Judah's king, Zedekiah, to his capital city of Babylon. There in the imperial center, Zedekiah might console himself on the sights of the world's greatest city. He might look upon grand halls and palaces, the hanging garden that was a wonder of the world, and the vast walls in lofty sentinel. But Zedekiah saw none of these things, since before his journey to Babylon his eyes had been put out. Instead of beholding beauty, wealth, and glory, all of which were there before him, he lived in grim and dreary darkness.

In this great prayer that concludes Ephesians 1, the apostle Paul is determined that this should not be the case with his Christian readers. He prays, 'that the eyes of your heart may be enlightened' (Eph. 1:18, NIV). Paul wants us to see what is truly before us, yet which because of our spiritual blindness we fail to perceive apart from the Spirit's enlightening work. The Bible says the natural man, because of the sinful condition of his heart and mind, is blind to the glories and beauties of God. Jesus said, 'Unless one is born again he cannot see the kingdom of God' (John 3:3). Paul is praying here for believers, those who have been born again by the Spirit through the Word to a saving faith in Jesus Christ. Yet we, too, require the on-going illumination of God's Spirit, who Paul has described in the prior verse as 'the Spirit of wisdom and revelation' (Eph. 1:17, NIV).

In his great allegory, *Pilgrim's Progress*, John Bunyan tells of his hero, Christian, who after climbing the Hill of Difficulty stayed for a rest at the Castle Beautiful. Before he resumed his journey to the Celestial City, the castle owners took him up on a hill to gaze ahead to where his destination could just be seen. There in the Delectable Mountains was the city he sought, and the sight of it emboldened him for the troubles yet ahead.

Paul wants the same for us, that eyes would be opened in our hearts so that we might gain a spiritual apprehension of the blessings that are ours in Christ. This vision, he knows, will embolden us for the trials of our pilgrimage toward heaven. Three things particularly are on his mind, the knowledge of which he says constitutes an enlightened view of life. These are expressed in terms of three *whats* that we should know: 'what is the hope to which he has called you, what are the riches of his glorious inheritance in the saints, and what is the immeasurable greatness of his power toward us who believe' (Eph. 1:18–19).

The Hope to Which He Has Called You

Paul first prays that we may know what is 'the hope to which he has called you,' or more literally, what is 'the hope of his calling.' For most people the word *hope* means little more than a feeble optimism or wishful thinking. We 'hope' for good news without any expectation of receiving it. But the hope that Paul mentions is a mighty certainty of things looked for though not yet experienced. Christian hope is made strong by our confidence in God, who calls us to follow and promises us great blessing.

When Paul speaks of our calling, he refers to the beginning of our Christian life in the mercy and grace of God. Consider Abraham, who was called by God while living in Ur of the Chaldees. Abraham had done nothing to earn God's favor and there is no evidence that he was seeking God in any way. Joshua 24:2 tells us that, like his father, Abraham worshiped other gods. But God came to him and called him out of the darkness of sin and condemnation to walk before him in faith. God gave him great promises. He said, 'Fear not, Abram, I am your shield; your reward shall be very great' (Gen. 15:1).

Abraham's calling is repeated in the experience of every believer. God comes to us in our sin, calling us to lead a new life that looks to God with hope for what he promises in the gospel. Theologians distinguish between the *general* call of the gospel, which goes out to everyone whether they believe or not, and the *effectual* call by which Christ gathers his people with divine power. The gospel is preached generally to all the world and, through it, Christ calls with saving power those who believe. Christ's effectual call gives power to this Word to open the heart and instill true faith. In Matthew 9:9, Jesus 'saw a man called Matthew sitting at the tax booth, and he said to him, 'Follow me.'' By the effectual call the tax collector 'rose and followed him.' What Jesus said to the twelve disciples is true of all believers: 'You did not choose me, but I chose you' (John 15:16). To be a Christian is to have been called by Christ with saving power through the gospel.

Paul's point is the great hope that arises from the effectual nature of God's calling. Knowing that our conversion was God's sovereign work, we are certain of receiving all that he has promised. Just as a building rests on its foundation, the Christian hope rests on the divine calling, knowing as Paul said in Romans 11:29 that 'the gifts and the calling of God are irrevocable.' If I have been called by God, then my hope is secure. God's covenant promises become, as Hebrews 6:19 states, 'a sure and steadfast anchor of the soul, a hope that enters into the inner place behind the curtain.' Like Abraham, our calling is followed by a lifetime of faith, with many trials and challenges. We know there will be many pains, but we have a greater hope of gain through the call of God. Charles Spurgeon wrote of the Christian:

> First, he hopes and believes that he shall be under divine protection for ever and ever, that he shall be the object of divine love time out of mind, and when time shall be no more...He expects a stormy voyage, but because Christ is at the helm he hopes to come to the fair havens at the last. He expects to be tempted, but he hopes to be upheld. He expects to be slandered, but he hopes to be cleared. He expects to be tried, but he hopes to triumph. Sustained by this hope he dreads no labors and fears no difficulties.[124]

Paul wants us to know what is the hope of our calling. This prompts us to ask what other hope we may find in this world? Are you hoping just to get along, to stay out of trouble, and to have a little fun along the way? Are you hoping to store up a rampart of money and power, fame and achievement, hoping that these will hold out life's storms and bring you the fullness you desire? Are you hoping in your own ability, in the success of the corporation or the country, in your degrees or your connections? All of these things, though valuable in some sense, will fail to sustain you or fulfill the longings of your soul.

The Christian hope can stand up to every trial and even to death, since our salvation is grounded in the promise of Christ to forgive our sins, raise us from the grave, and enter us into eternal life. Psalm 27 says, 'The Lord is my light and my salvation; whom shall I fear? The Lord is the stronghold of my life; of whom shall I be afraid?' (Ps. 27:1). Isaiah therefore says, 'Those who hope in the Lord will renew their strength. They will soar on wings like eagles; they will run and not grow weary, they will walk and not be faint' (Isa. 40:31, niv).

What a difference it makes to ground our hope on God's calling, rather than on a decision we made or a resolution we made. If our salvation originates from something in us, it will have to be sustained by something in us. But if our hope arises from the calling of God, from his purpose and promise and power, then this is a sure hope in which we may trust and rejoice even in times of trial.

The Riches of His Glorious Inheritance

Paul further wants to enlighten us as to 'what are the riches of his glorious inheritance in the saints' (Eph. 1:18). There is debate as to the meaning of this statement. One view is that Paul refers to the riches that God has in *his* inheritance in the saints. The roster of advocates of this view is impressive, including Peter O'Brien, Donald Carson, F. F. Bruce, Andrew Lincoln, and Charles Spurgeon. In this case Paul is referring to the riches of glory that God acquires for himself through our salvation. The Old Testament often spoke in this way. Psalm 33:12 says, 'Blessed is the nation whose God is the Lord, the people whom he has chosen as his heritage!' God has invested in us his love and wisdom, his workmanship and care, and especially the precious blood of his Son, and we should know the riches he gains in our final salvation. Ultimately, this is why we are saved, so that God may have 'the riches of his glorious inheritance in the saints.'

The second way of taking this statement is that Paul wants us to know the riches that *we* have in God, the glorious inheritance that God provides to the saints. This is the view taken by John Chrysostom, John Calvin, Charles Hodge, Martyn Lloyd-Jones, John Stott, and James Montgomery Boice. The Greek text allows equally for either reading, but I think there is good reason to favor the second interpretation. First of all, Paul has already mentioned 'our inheritance' in verse 14, as it is guaranteed by the Holy Spirit. It would be most likely that he is speaking of the same thing now in his prayer. Second, in his similar prayer at the beginning of Colossians (which in many ways parallels Ephesians), Paul writes that Christians 'share in the inheritance of the saints in light' (Col. 1:12).

Paul prays, then, for us to know the riches of the glory of the inheritance that God has for us in Christ. Having begun with reference to the beginning of our salvation—our calling—Paul now wants us to apprehend the riches that await us at the end.

Notice how excited Paul is getting, as he starts to pile up superlatives. First, our inheritance is so abundant that he refers to it as *riches*. God says in Proverbs 8:18, 'Riches and honor are with me, enduring wealth and righteousness.' Second, this inheritance is rich especially in *glory*. We shall see the glory of God and partake of it. Daniel 12:3 says, 'Those who are wise shall shine like the brightness of the sky above; and those who turn many to righteousness, like the stars forever and ever.' Paul writes in Romans 8:16–17, 'We are children of God, and if children, then heirs—heirs of God and fellow heirs with Christ, provided we suffer with him in order that we may also be glorified with him.' Third, as an *inheritance*, it is something that is secure. It is not earned but given. Once received it is held as a possession by right. Fourth, it is an inheritance *in the saints*, that is, held in communion with all the company of the redeemed. The joys we know now as we share in our gifts and graces, in worship and prayer, and in the fellowship of faith, will pale before the inheritance we have together in the riches of God's glory.

Since Paul so greatly wants our hearts to see these riches, we should dwell on what we have a right to expect at the end of our Christian journey. While we wait we are sustained by hope, but at the end hope will give way to full possession. And what will we then have?

Our inheritance includes a perfect justification in the day of God's final judgment. All of us will be present before the great white throne for a final division. To one side those who have not come to Christ will go to the condemnation their sins have deserved. To the other side will go the sheep who are saved by the Good Shepherd's blood, to be led by him to streams of living water. What a treasure it will be then to hear the words of Jesus in Matthew 25:34: 'Come, you who are blessed by my Father, inherit the kingdom prepared for you from the foundation of the world.'

If that is not enough, there is more. We will not only be acquitted of guilt but will be perfected in holiness. Christians are to anticipate the day when we will no longer contend with sinful motives, with an impure heart, with vile, angry, and selfish thoughts. Thomas Watson writes, 'Death smites a believer as the angel did Peter, and made his chains fall off (Acts 12:7). Believers at death are made perfect in holiness…Oh! what a blessed privilege is this, to be without spot or wrinkle; to be purer than the sunbeams; to be as free from sin as the angels!'[125] Hebrews 12:23 speaks of those in heaven as 'the spirits of the righteous made perfect,' and that is what we will be.

Martyn Lloyd-Jones tells a story about Philip Henry, the father of the great Bible commentator, Matthew Henry. He had fallen in love with a young lady who belonged to a much higher social class, but who was a fervent Christian. Her parents were unhappy about the match, and questioned her, 'This man Philip Henry, where has he come from?' Their daughter's reply was priceless: 'I don't know where he has come from, but I know where he is going.'[126] This is true of all who have come to God through faith in Jesus Christ. Wherever we are from, we are going to an inheritance in heaven the like of which our feeble minds can scarcely conceive.

We see, then, why Paul writes as he does— riches, glory, and inheritance! John Chrysostom exclaimed, 'What language shall be adequate to express that glory of which the saints shall then be partakers?' There is none, he concludes. [127] The apostle John was similarly overwhelmed. He writes, 'Beloved, we are God's children now, and what we will be has not yet appeared; but we know that when he appears we will be like him, because we shall see him as he is' (1 John 3:2). Our ultimate inheritance is God himself; he gives himself to us in Christ even as he takes us to himself. With renewed eyes we will see in heaven what now only the eyes of our hearts can see: the vision of God in his glory, infinite perfection extended to us in infinite love. Revelation 22 foretells, 'They will see his face, and his name will be on their foreheads. And night will be no more. They will need no light of lamp or sun, for the Lord God will be their light, and they will reign forever and ever' (vv. 4-5).

His Incomparably Great Power

Third, Paul wants us to realize 'what is the immeasurable greatness of his power toward us who believe' (Eph. 1:19). He first directed our attention to the beginning of our Christian life, our calling, then to the end, our inheritance as saints. Now he speaks of what we need in the present, power from God to conquer in faith.

The apostle Paul is well known for his doctrine of justification by faith apart from works. In Ephesians 2:8-9 he writes: 'by grace you have been saved through faith. And this is not your own doing; it is the gift of God, not a result of works, so that no one may boast.' Because of this, many people fail to appreciate the importance to Paul of good works and godly lives, to which we are saved. We find this in Ephesians 2:10: 'For we are his workmanship, created in Christ Jesus for good works, which God prepared beforehand, that we should walk in them.' D. A. Carson writes, 'Paul cannot be satisfied with a brand of Christianity that is orthodox but dead, rich in the theory of justification but powerless when it comes to transforming people's lives.'[128]

In describing the resources that God provides to enable good works, Paul practically falls over himself in a deluge of words. Verse 19 employs no fewer than four different terms for God's incomparably great and mighty power. The first is *dunamis*, from which we get *dynamite*, and which speaks of raw power to overcome obstacles. The second is *energeis*, from which we get *energy*, which speaks of God energizing his people for godliness (see Phil. 2:12-13). The third word, *kratos*, and the fourth, *isxuos*, both mean might or strength. Leon Morris summarizes, 'Paul is using a multiplicity of words denoting power to bring out the truth that…there is mighty power in God and it is a power directed towards the betterment of believers.'[129]

In case we thought Paul could say nothing greater about God's power that is available to Christians, he adds the supreme analogy, saying that the power God has for us is 'according to the working of his great might that he worked in Christ when he raised him from the dead' (Eph. 1:19-20). According to Paul, God's power for Christians is not merely *like* the power that raised Jesus from the grave but is the *very* power that raised Jesus from the grave. The resurrection power by which Christ conquered death is now at work in us to conquer sin. Benjamin B. Warfield writes that the Christian 'is a new man, recreated in Christ Jesus by the almighty power of the Holy Spirit.'[130] That same resurrection power continues to work in the believer's life towards the goal of Christ-like and God-honoring holiness.

In Romans 6:8-10, Paul makes the same point a bit differently. There, Paul tells us that if we look at the history of Jesus Christ in his death and resurrection, we are seeing our own spiritual biography in him: 'Now if we have died with Christ, we believe that we will also live with him' (Rom. 6:8). Jesus died for sin and rose again by God's power. We likewise were dead in sin but have now been spiritually resurrected in Christ.

'For the death he died he died to sin, once for all' Paul explains, 'but the life he lives he lives to God' (Rom. 6:10). We need to know, Paul is saying, that by our faith we are joined to Christ not only in his death to sin but also in his resurrection power for new life to God. Thus Paul writes in Galatians 2:20: 'I have been crucified with Christ. It is no longer I who live, but Christ who lives in me.' Because Christ lives within us by the Holy Spirit, Christians have power in order to believe and do good works.

One of the most common errors in our time is that Christians seek power for new living practically everywhere but from God in the resurrection life of Jesus Christ. For many believers, Christian music is the power by which they seek to conquer sin. Others are devoted to rituals, sacred talismans, or self-help schemes. The problem with these approaches is that the power of sin is greater than any earthly power or solution. We need a power that comes from heaven! So God would have us turn to him in prayer and through his Word for a supernatural power that transcends anything that we can achieve by our best efforts. Jesus taught that when we ask, our loving Heavenly Father 'gives the Holy Spirit to those who ask him' (Luke 11:13). In the resurrection power of the Spirit, Christians can now prayerfully resist temptation, put off hindrances and besetting sins, develop godly character, and bear spiritual fruit. There is a power from beyond this world that is greater than sin, the power of Almighty God working in the lives of those who seek it from him through Jesus Christ.

This is the Bible's answer to a vital question people want to know. I once spoke to a recent convert who had been reading in the Bible of the kind of life God wants him to live. He asked, bewildered, 'How am I supposed to do these things?' He was grateful to be forgiven through faith in Christ and he wanted to follow him in obedience, but what was the power to enable him? The answer is the resurrection power of Christ, which God provides to our faith through his Word and in prayer.

This is a matter relevant to us all. How are we, with our selfish hearts and our sinful minds ever going to follow in the way of Christ? The Bible tells us that true love must be 'patient and kind…It does not insist on its own way; it is not irritable or resentful' (1 Cor. 13:4-5). But this runs contrary to every instinct of our hearts. How are we to love like this? Or there is Philippians 2:4-5, which says that we should have Christ's attitude in seeking the interests of others ahead of our own. The problem is that our minds don't work that way, they are not filled with thoughts of others but immediately our minds demand that we look after ourselves. The list of these things goes on and on—how am I, still contending with my sinful flesh, to walk in the holiness and love of which I read in Scripture?

The answer is here. What is the power I need? It is 'the immeasurable greatness of his power toward us who believe, according to the working of his great might that he worked in Christ when he raised him from the dead and seated him at his right hand in the heavenly places' (Eph. 1:19-20). This is what happens as we walk with Jesus, with our Bibles open and our hearts turned upward in prayer, day-by-day and year-by-year, that by the Spirit he sends we 'are being transformed into the same image from one degree of glory to another' (2 Cor. 3:18). Paul therefore prays that the eyes of your heart may apprehend this power and that it may become real in your life as you trust in Jesus Christ.

A Thousand Sacred Sweets

I mentioned poor king Zedekiah, who was unable to look on the marvels of Babylon, with its hanging gardens and high parapets. But how much greater a tragedy if we should fail to see with the eyes of faith the incomparable vision of all that is ours in Christ! How tragic if we should walk through life without the hope that our calling provides? How impoverished must our lives be if we know nothing of the riches of his glorious inheritance that awaits us in the end? How frustrating it would be to struggle vainly with sin, not relying on God's power which comes to us through prayer and God's Word. When the eyes of our hearts are opened to see these wonderful truths, what a difference they make! It is no surprise that these themes have been among the favorites of great hymn writers. Isaac Watts had the eyes of his heart enlightened, and he wrote wonderfully of salvation:

> The men of grace have found,
> glory begun below;
> celestial fruit on earthly ground
> from faith and hope may grow.
>
> The hill of Zion yields
> a thousand sacred sweets,
> before we reach the heavenly fields
> or walk the golden streets.
>
> There shall we see His face
> and never, never sin;
> There from the rivers of His grace
> drink endless pleasures in.
>
> Then let our songs abound,
> and every tear be dry:
> We're marching through Immanuel's ground
> to fairer worlds on high.[131]

Doesn't this vision make the pleasures of sin seem dull and unworthy in comparison? Doesn't it amaze you that anyone would renounce these incomparable blessings for the fleeting pleasures of a dying world? God forbid that any of us should turn away from this salvation that is all of God and to the praise of God's glorious grace. May he instead open the eyes of our hearts that we may see, and that, seeing all that he has for us in Christ we might live for him who loves us so.

16

Christ Exalted

Ephesians 1:20-23

This study brings us to the end of the first chapter of Ephesians, which is a carefully organized introduction to the whole epistle. After the opening greeting, Paul presents two long sentences, the first of which is a great hymn of praise and the second is his prayer of thanks and petition to God for his readers. In this chapter Paul has deftly introduced the themes he is going to develop later. We have at points observed these themes: the sovereignty of God; the nature, blessing, and destiny of Christians; and the coordinated efforts of the divine Trinity for our salvation.

Given the importance of this opening chapter, the note Paul chooses to strike at its end is undoubtedly significant. Here we encounter the theme that rises above the others and in which they are tied together: the believer's union with the crucified, risen, and exalted Christ.

Christ Ascended and Exalted

Paul ends this chapter with the same theme on which the Gospel accounts end, the ascension and exaltation of Jesus. Forty days after his resurrection, Christ was taken up before the disciples, visibly rising into heaven as the Shekinah glory cloud enfolded him. Thus was his earthly ministry concluded and his heavenly reign begun.

The exaltation of Christ is God's ultimate vindication of our Lord. Remember the scene as Jesus was dying on the cross. The religious leaders mocked, 'He trusts in God; let God deliver him now, if he desires him. For he said, "I am the Son of God"' (Matt. 27:43). Here is God's reply. Christ's resurrection and ascension prove beyond a doubt that God accepted Christ's obedient life and especially his death as the sacrifice for our sins. The world despised him, but God exalted him to the highest place, proving that his claims were all true.

Paul presents Christ's exaltation in two terms, first in terms of his exalted *dignity*. He writes that God 'seated him at his right hand in the heavenly places, far above all rule and authority and power and dominion, and above every name that is named, not only in this age but also in the one to come' (vv. 20-21).

In his exalted dignity, Jesus is portrayed as seated at the place of honor in heaven. Christians have long understood this to signify his finished work as our Savior. Hebrews 1:3 says, 'After making purification for sins, he sat down at the right hand of the Majesty on high.' This contrasts with the Jewish priests who never sat down in the temple. Hebrews 10:11 says, 'And every priest stands daily at his service, offering repeatedly the same sacrifices, which can never take away sins.' But because Jesus' sacrificial death perfectly satisfied God's justice, God exalted him to sit in the heavenly sanctuary. Furthermore, sitting denotes the dignity that Jesus shares with God. All others stand in God's presence, but Jesus sits with him on the throne. The fact that he is sitting shows that his position and reign are firmly established. This is what Daniel saw in his vision, that 'with the clouds of heaven there came one like a son of man, and he came to the Ancient of Days and was presented before him. And to him was given dominion and glory and a kingdom, that all peoples, nations, and languages should serve him; his dominion is an everlasting dominion, which shall not pass away, and his kingdom one that shall not be destroyed' (Dan. 7:13–14).

Second, Jesus's ascension establishes his *exalted dominion*. It is not merely honor that Jesus has received but royal authority. We see this in that he is seated at God's right hand. Kings place someone at their right hand to grant honor and to show participation in their rule. This is the highest place that heaven itself can afford, and such a place is granted to our Lord Jesus Christ. We have here the fulfillment of Psalm 110:1, which the apostles often used as a proof of Christ's divinity and lordship: 'The Lord says to my Lord: "Sit at my right hand, until I make your enemies your footstool."'

The writer of Hebrews points out how this shows Christ's *supremacy to the angels*, writing that he became 'as much superior to angels as the name he has inherited is more excellent than theirs' (1:4). Paul makes this same point in verse 21, placing Jesus 'far above all rule and authority and power and dominion, and above every name that is named, not only in this age but also in the one to come.' These are designations for spiritual beings. Many commentators see these as different grades and ranks within an angelic hierarchy, although that really is not Paul's point. Paul writes here in the same way he earlier spoke of God's mighty power, piling on every conceivable designation. He brings forth every word that is in current usage for a spiritual power and he places Christ above them all.

Paul is probably reacting against a superstitious idea current in the area of Ephesus at that time, that angels and other semi-divine spirits have to be placated before we can get to God. This was an early form of what would later be called Gnosticism. Paul's letter to the Colossians, which he sent along with Ephesians, shows his concern about this false teaching (see Col. 1:16–20; 2:8–15). In Ephesians, Paul is pointing out that since Christ is exalted over all, any such ideas must fall away before his supremacy. Furthermore, Ephesus was a center of pagan magical activity, in which sorcerers evoked 'names' or 'titles' of various powers. But all these ideas are countered by the exaltation of Christ, to whom believers have access by simple faith. Whatever title or name one can think of, either now or in the future, it pales before the status and honor and privilege given to Christ. He is 'far above…every name that is named, not only in this age but also in the one to come' (Eph. 1:21).

Paul further emphasizes Christ's dominion in verse 22, 'And [God] placed all things under his feet.' All these rulers and authorities, powers and lords—many of which may have been thought threatening to the Christians in that pagan age—are not only inferior to Christ but they are subject to him. The imagery reminds us of Joshua's victory over the five Amorite kings. After their defeat, Joshua brought forth the five chieftains. Calling his generals, he said, 'Come near; put your feet on the necks of these kings' (Jos. 10:24). It was a sign of their complete subjugation to his power and was a prelude to their execution. That is the situation of every hostile power, circumstance, and danger to which we are exposed—they are under Christ's feet, all our enemies soon to be put away.

This is what Jesus declared before his ascension: 'All authority in heaven and on earth has been given to me' (Matt. 28:18). We need to remember this today, since many Christians associate Christ's reign only with his Second Coming. Too many Christians look only to the future for Jesus' reign on earth to begin. Certainly, Jesus' return in glory will put an end to all conflict against him. But even now, while the battle still rages, Jesus reigns over heaven and earth. He is glorified now; he wears the crown even as we serve him here, no less than he will in the day of his glorious return. And the divine power that raised him to heaven's throne, delivering him from the agony of the cross to the triumph of his exaltation in honor and dominion, is the same power he employs to lift us from our sins and from the power of this evil world so that we might follow Jesus and join him where he is.

Christ and His Church

Paul is directing our attention to the exalted station of Christ so that we will trust and honor him, but also to help us understand all that it means to be joined to him in faith. To this end, he adds that God 'gave him as head over all things to the church, which is his body, the fullness of him who fills all in all' (Eph. 1:22–23).

Paul uses several metaphors in Ephesians to describe the union between Christ and his church, including the metaphor of a family, a building, and the union of a husband and wife in marriage. The chief designation he employs is that of a head with its body. This metaphor points to the organic union between Christ and his church. A human being is not just a collection of parts but an integrated whole. Such is our spiritual union together with Christ. The head and the body are one, inseparable. Paul's teaching rules out any scheme in which a mere human is placed over the church as head, such as in the Roman Catholic Church and its pope. The church has only one head, who lives and reigns forever, Jesus Christ. Further, Paul's metaphor suggests that the head is the source of life and vitality for the body, just as the nervous system of the brain conveys energy and activity to the various body parts. Jesus taught this in his comparing the church to a branch that gains life only in union with the vine: 'Apart from me,' he explained, 'you can do nothing' (John 15:5).

This teaching has the most profound implications for the life and work of the church. It means that whatever the church is doing, Christ is doing. Realizing his holy dignity and glory ought to restrain the church from worldly or otherwise unworthy practices, especially in our worship services. In his seven letters to the churches of Revelation, Jesus commanded holiness among his people. 'Repent,' he commanded them, 'If not, I will come to you and remove your lampstand from its place, unless you repent' (Rev. 2:5).

Likewise, if we are in union with Christ he will rule us as the head rules the body. Christ reigns as the church preaches and obeys the Bible, making God's Word our charter and measuring stick. If our churches are instead taking their direction from secular techniques and church marketing consultants, whose prescriptions so often run directly contrary to the teaching of Christ's Word, it is hard to see how we can continue to consider ourselves in union with Christ.

Christ, as the head of his body, provides life to the church. This takes place through the ministry of the Holy Spirit. Jesus promised the first disciples: 'You will receive power when the Holy Spirit has come upon you, and you will be my witnesses' (Acts 1:8). It is by the Holy Spirit that we receive power for gospel witness. This being the case we should pray for the working of the Spirit, and we should keep in step with the Spirit as he calls us to walk in obedience to God's Word.

Christ Exalted for the Church

In this context Paul makes an amazing statement that shows why all this matters for us. Verse 22 says that God 'gave him as head over all things to the church.' This Jesus, exalted in his heavenly dignity and universal dominion, with all things under his feet and all glory attached to his throne, is given by God to us the church.

We often speak about God's gift to us at Christmas time. In the birth of the baby Jesus, God gave to us his only begotten Son. Or, we talk this way about Christ's death. God in his grace gave Jesus to die in our place. But we seldom speak this way about Jesus' ascension into heaven. And yet, Paul reminds us, this is the culminating gift, the enthronement of him who was born in the lowly manger to enter into our race, who died for us and rose again. In his ascension into heavenly glory and power Jesus' work was brought to triumphant fulfillment. No less than in the birth of Christ, and no less than in his death, God has given him to us. If his birth brings us joy, if his death brings us peace, then Christ's ascension, his taking up the throne for us, ought to give us a final confidence and hope that nothing can ever shake. It was because God gave the exalted Christ to us, as he gave the humble Christ to us, that Paul could write in Romans 8:39 that 'nothing will be able to separate us from the love of God in Christ Jesus our Lord.'

We should note three specific implications of God's gift to us of the exalted and enthroned Lord Jesus. They are that Christ's exaltation proves the assurance of our salvation, the power available to us in Christ, and the preeminence of the church as the body of Christ.

First, Christ's exaltation is a great proof of *the assurance of our salvation*. Jesus Christ is enthroned forever above all powers and dominions at the right hand of God. It is a man, a human being, who sits upon that throne. He is inseparably joined to us as the head to his body. Surely, then, our salvation is utterly assured. We are like Joseph's brothers, who came to Egypt only to find their long-lost brother enthroned over the mighty foreign land. This is what we shall find in heaven, that one of us, who offered himself for us, is seated in the place of honor and power. He sits enthroned in a human body marked by the wounds he suffered for us. This proves that our sins are put away forever and that we who trust in him will certainly find a place with him there.

Furthermore, our every foe has been conquered by the exalted Christ. In his death, resurrection and ascension Jesus has subdued all his foes and ours, including sin, the world, the devil, and death. We may now face all of these without fear. Yes, we must still contend with people and powers that tempt, afflict, and oppose us. But they are enemies he has already subdued. Our present conflict is with defeated foes. Instead of truly threatening our salvation, they are made by Christ to be instruments of our sanctification and growth, enemies Christ allows only to go far enough to do us good in our struggles as we learn to trust in him. 'In this world you will have tribulation,' he told the disciples, 'But take heart; I have overcome the world!' (John 16:33).

The second implication is to see what Paul was driving at when he spoke of *the power available to us* because Christ is exalted. God gave him as head over everything to the church. Therefore what aid could we need that is beyond his ability to give? What obstacle is so great that he cannot remove it? What calling have we received that he cannot supply the power to fulfill? What challenge must we endure, what temptation or trial do we face, with what sin are we burdened but that Christ cannot overcome it as he works in us with his almighty power?

Paul himself proves the power of Christ to call, convert, and commission his people. Who was the man who wrote this letter? Paul was by his own assessment the greatest sinner in all the world, the harshest critic, and most hateful persecutor of Christians. Yet how easy it was for Christ to turn this violent Pharisee into an apostle of grace, the man who did more to establish the early church than anyone else. Christ changed his mind, changed his heart, and changed his life. Jesus simply appeared to Paul on the Damascus Road and called him to be an apostle. On what basis, then, do you doubt that the exalted Christ can change your heart, deliver you from your sins, and make use of your life? He will certainly do so, according to his own particular plan and purpose for you, if you are joined to him by faith and if you seek to do his will.

Another example comes from Paul's plea in 2 Corinthians 12. Paul writes of receiving a thorn in his flesh, 'a messenger of Satan to harass me.' He couldn't stand it. He couldn't take it any longer, whatever it was. Three times he pleaded for the Lord to take it away. But God did not take it away. Instead, he gave Paul power to endure it cheerfully. He said, 'My grace is sufficient for you, for my power is made perfect in weakness' (2 Cor. 12:9). Paul, who earlier complained that it was unbearable, replied, 'Therefore I will boast all the more gladly about my weaknesses, so that the power of Christ may rest upon me' (2 Cor. 12:9). We think that Christ's power has let us down or is disproved if we have any troubles, temptations, or weaknesses that have not been done away with. But Jesus says that his power enables us to endure in them by faith so that he may be glorified in our weakness. Martyn Lloyd-Jones writes:

> As we contemplate life and all its difficulties, and as we are tempted by Satan to feel that all is impossible, and that we cannot go on because we are so weak and the difficulties so baffling, we must remind ourselves of this truth and say: I am a very small and unimportant member, but I am a member of the body of Christ; I am 'in him', and therefore, whatever may be true of me personally, the life of the Head is in me…I am in touch with Him, His vital energy is in me…As our eyes are opened to this truth we can take fresh courage, and take up our task again and say: In Christ I cannot fail, I must not fail, He will not allow me to fail.[132]

The third implication of Christ's enthronement is *the preeminence of the church*. People, even Christians, do not think much of the church. The church is someplace they go to get something for themselves, to get a lift, get some help, or make some friends. The world looks on the church as something insignificant and weak. The great things in this world deal with skyscrapers and stock markets, rising and falling empires. This was especially a danger for the fledging churches of Paul's day, who were viewed, and might have viewed themselves, as an insignificant cult among a sea of religious groups. But here we see that the church cannot be rightly understood apart from seeing the exalted Christ, who rules over every power and all of history, and its relationship to him. The church is the preeminent institution in all the world because it is the body of him who is seated at God's right hand in the heavenly realms. Only the church, among all institutions in this world, will endure forever, its accomplishments blazing forever when all else has passed away.

There is therefore no greater privilege than membership in the church. There is no greater calling than the Christian's calling to offer his gifts and talents, time and money to the work of the church. A Christian who gives all his energy to his job, who uses her talents only for personal gain, who spends his money all on himself, neglecting the work of the church which will last forever, is simply a fool. Such a person does not recognize that the church is the body, the temple, and the bride of him who is exalted on high. In the end it is what Christ has done through the church that will matter most, will most shine in glory, and will have been most worth the offering of our lives. A Christian who is not involved in a ministry of the church, who does not pray regularly for the church's work, who is taking but never giving to the church, should ask himself if he really understands what this life is about, if she really sees this Christ who is exalted, and if so what kind of response is appropriate to that realization.

The Church as the Fullness of Christ

Paul concludes with one of the most remarkable statements in the New Testament. He describes the church as 'the fullness of him who fills all in all' (v. 23).

There are two ways in which the church may be understood as 'the fullness' of Christ, and scholars are divided on the issue. The first and most accepted view is that Paul means the church is filled with and by Christ, 'who fills all in all.' The advantage of this view is that it fits with what we find elsewhere in the Bible. Andrew Lincoln explains, 'Everywhere else Christ is portrayed as actively filling believers rather than being filled by them…[otherwise] a deficiency in his person would be implied.'[133] Charles Hodge takes this view, explaining, 'As the body is filled or pervaded by the soul, so the church is filled by the Spirit of Christ; or, as God of old dwelt in the temple, and filled it with his glory, so Christ now dwells in his church and fills it with his presence.'[134]

All of that is true, but the second view better fits what Paul is particularly saying here. Paul's writing here is very bold, and we should not shrink from being equally bold; he frankly says that the church fills Christ, even as Christ is the One who fills all things in every way.

In what sense might we say that we are the fullness of Christ? It is of course true that, being God, the Lord Jesus is self-sufficient and does not need us or anything else. He is hardly an empty or half-empty vessel! Yet as our mediator and redeemer, Christ is joined to the church as the head to the body and in that sense he requires us in order to be complete. This is the straightforward meaning of Paul's words in this verse. First he names us the body to Christ's head and then designates the church as the fullness of him who fills all things. John Calvin writes:

> This is the highest honor of the Church, that, unless He is united to us, the Son of God reckons Himself in some measure imperfect. What an encouragement it is for us to hear, that, not until He has us as one with Himself, is He complete in all His parts, or does He wish to be regarded as whole![135]

This is the highest ground of our hope for

salvation. Arthur Pink says, 'There cannot be a Redeemer without redeemed, a Shepherd without sheep, a Bridegroom without a bride, a living Head without a living body. He is *her* fullness as the Lord of life and grace; she is *His* fullness since by means of the glory He has put upon her He will hereafter be magnified.'[136] This being the case, we see why Christ so loves his church and why he secures for us a place where he is and provides for us his own power. Even this filling of himself is his own work, his own filling of all things in every way to the praise of his glorious grace. He says, 'Because I live, you also will live' (John 14:19).

ALL THINGS TOGETHER IN CHRIST

Back in verse 10, Paul described God's ultimate purpose as 'to unite all things in [Christ], things in heaven and things on earth.' It is with this idea that he now wraps up the chapter, with Christ exalted over all, filling and being filled. This great theme ties in with all the other themes touched upon in this chapter. They are all brought together 'in Christ,' an expression Paul has used no fewer than eleven times in Ephesians 1.

First, we have considered in this chapter the incomparable blessings that belong to our salvation. These blessings are found in Christ. Their source is the exalted Christ, who is the head of the body, his church, and who sits enthroned at God's right hand above all other rule and authority, power and dominion. Paul said in verse 3 that God 'has blessed us in Christ with every spiritual blessing in the heavenly places.' We see now how that is, for the heavenly realms is where Christ is exalted in dignity and dominion.

Another theme Paul has emphasized is the sovereignty of God. God ordained our salvation 'according to the purpose of him who works all things according to the counsel of his will' (Eph. 1:11).

But the ultimate expression of God's sovereignty is the exaltation of Christ and of the church with him. Now it is Christ who wields that scepter for our sake. 'All our days,' writes D. A. Carson, 'fall within the sweep of the sovereignty of one who wears a human face, a thorn-shadowed face. All of God's sovereignty is mediated through one who was crucified on my behalf.'[137] The heavenly rule is exercised for our benefit and blessing. God's sovereignty can no longer be considered a dark and ominous threat, but is now a cause for the greatest gratitude and confidence and an incentive to the most expectant prayers.

Finally, we have often noted what this chapter says about the identity and nature of a Christian. What is a Christian? we have asked. Here is the ultimate answer. A Christian is one who is joined to Jesus Christ through faith, is redeemed by his blood on the cross, is a member of the church which is his body, and thus receives assurance and awesome power for salvation. With this in mind, the final verses of this chapter tell us that what matters above all else is how we stand with regard to Christ. The world rejected him. They spurned his grace, nailed him to the cross, and consigned him to the grave. But God

> raised him from the dead and seated him at his right hand in the heavenly places, far above all rule and authority and power and dominion, and above every name that is named, not only in this age but also in the one to come. And he put all things under his feet and gave him as head over all things to the church, which is his body, the fullness of him who fills all in all.

Therefore, the destiny of every individual is determined by how we stand in relation to Jesus Christ. If we stand in indifference or in opposition, we will be placed under his feet in defeated subjection, soon to be judged and condemned for our sins. But if we come to him in grateful faith, as the One who loved us and gave himself for us, he will be our Savior and our Lord, we will be his people, we will be blessed by him forever, filling and being filled, so that his exaltation might be completed in our exaltation and praise unto him.

17

Prayer and the Sovereignty of God

Ephesians 1:15–23

Our last study brought us to the end of Ephesians 1. Since Ephesians 1 is noted for its emphasis on the sovereignty of God and for Paul's great prayer in response to his teaching, before we depart this chapter we should look back and consider the relationship between prayer and the sovereignty of God.

There are two reasons to do this. The first is that many people have concerns over this matter. If God is as sovereign as Paul depicts him in this chapter, then the whole realm of human activity—especially prayer—seems to come into question. My second purpose is to use this discussion as a summary of this chapter, which presents a great salvation that rests secure on God's sovereign grace and leads us into a living relationship with him through faith in Jesus Christ.

Why Pray?

The question is, 'Do prayer and the sovereignty of God go together?' If God is sovereign in all things, if God has ordained everything in advance according to his predetermined plan, then what is the point of prayer? Why should we tell God our needs and cry to him from our hearts if he knows all things in advance? For some, this is a problem that calls the whole matter of God's sovereignty into question. 'We know God wants us to pray,' they argue, 'and the idea of a sovereign, predestinating God seems incompatible with prayer.'

One way to realize that prayer must be compatible with God's sovereignty is to consider the example of the apostle Paul. Throughout his many letters, Paul repeatedly and deliberately emphasizes God's sovereignty. This is what we have found in Ephesians 1. In verse 4, Paul says that God 'chose us…before the foundation of the world.' Verse 5 adds that he predestined us for adoption into his family. Verse 11 teaches that we were made heirs 'having been predestined according to the purpose of him who works all things according to the counsel of his will.' It is hard to imagine what stronger terminology Paul could possibly use to convey the idea that we are saved by God's sovereign grace. Indeed, Paul does not limit God's sovereignty to the sphere of salvation, but says in Acts 17:26, 'He made from one man every nation of mankind to live on all the face of the earth, having determined allotted periods and the boundaries of their dwelling place.' God's sovereignty is unrestrained in Paul's thinking, but is unequivocal and total.

As God said through Isaiah, 'I am God, and there is none like me, declaring the end from the beginning and from ancient times things not yet done, saying, 'My counsel shall stand, and I will accomplish all my purpose'' (Isa. 46:9-10). Like Isaiah in the Old Testament, it is Paul in the New Testament who is especially identified with the sovereignty of God.

The question therefore arises, 'Did Paul's belief in God's complete sovereignty cause him to lose interest in prayer? Because God is in control did Paul think little of the Christian's activity and responsibility?' If, as many say, prayer and the sovereignty of God are incompatible, we should expect to see this play out in Paul's example more than in any other. But, in fact, not only is Paul noted for his teaching of God's sovereignty, he is also eminent as a man of prayer. Not only Ephesians, but all his letters overflow with prayer like flowers blossoming in a garden. Furthermore, he often prays with direct reference to God's sovereignty. In 2 Thessalonians 2:13, he writes, 'We ought always to give thanks to God for you, brothers beloved by the Lord, because God chose you as the first fruits to be saved.'

We are confronted, then, with this situation: the apostle most noted for teaching the highest view of God's total sovereignty was not thereby discouraged from praying, just as his belief in predestination did not lessen his zeal for evangelistic outreach and preaching. Instead, while strongly emphasizing God's sovereign election, Paul was singular in zeal for evangelism and prayer. C. Samuel Storms is surely right when he concludes, 'That Paul should speak with perfect ease of both sovereign election and prayer…requires that we view them as theologically (and logically) compatible. Divine sovereignty does not preempt prayer, nor does prayer render God's choice contingent.'[138]

We will find the same situation if we turn to the greater example of our Lord Jesus Christ. Think, for instance, of Jesus prediction of Peter's denial. 'I tell you, Peter,' he said, 'the rooster will not crow this day, until you deny three times that you know me' (Luke 22:34). Jesus' espousal of divine sovereignty and foreknowledge is shown by his advance certainty of minute details such as the number of Peter's denials and crowing of the rooster. Jesus also knew that Peter would repent and be restored. And yet, none of this sovereign foreknowledge deterred him from prayer. Instead, Jesus responded: 'Simon, Simon…I have prayed for you' (Luke 22:31-32).

THE REASON FOR PRAYER

Paul's example gives us sufficient reason to view prayer and God's sovereignty as fully compatible. But this prayer that concludes Ephesians 1 offers us particularly keen insight into the relationship between the two. The passage from verses 15-23 specifically tells us three things about prayer and the sovereignty of God. It says that because God is sovereign, we have every *reason* to pray, we have every *need* to pray, and we have every *encouragement* to pray.

First is God's sovereignty as *a reason for prayer*. This is Paul's explicit statement in verses 15-16: '*For this reason*, because I have heard of your faith in the Lord Jesus and your love toward all the saints, I do not cease to give thanks for you, remembering you in my prayers.' 'For this reason' looks back on all that Paul had just taught, namely, God's sovereign grace in Christ. It is in light of this that it occurs to him to pray for his readers. He thinks of them, recalls their faith and love, and reflecting on God's sovereignty he exclaims, 'I do not cease to give thanks for you.'

So, if God is sovereign, why should we pray? First and foremost, we pray to thank him for the blessings of his sovereign grace. This is a vital reason for our prayer: to thank God for what he has done in our own lives, knowing it is all of him, and also for what he has done for others. Indeed, this recalls Paul's beginning to the whole letter, writing in verse 3: 'Praise be to the God and Father of our Lord Jesus Christ, who has blessed us in Christ with every spiritual blessing in the heavenly places.' That is what he does in prayer: he praises and thanks God for all that he has done for us in Christ.

It is precisely because God is sovereign, because the salvation of these people came from his pure choice, that God alone is praised for their salvation. Were salvation not based on God's sovereignty, but at least in part on our supposedly free wills, then the praise would not all go to God. But Paul does not praise and thank the Ephesians for their faith and love, nor does he credit their pastors or even himself. Since God's sovereign grace is the cause of their salvation, all the praise and thanks goes to him, and therefore Paul has a reason to pray to God.

Many people today reject Paul's doctrine of God's sovereignty, and one result is a diminishing emphasis on prayer in our churches. Towards the end of his ministry, James Montgomery Boice began to notice that in so many of the churches he visited less and less time in corporate worship was being given to prayer. What prayer there was was tacked onto the service and dealt almost exclusively with requests for people who were sick and other needs. Christians were not reflecting on God's attributes or God's works in their prayers, nor were they praising or thanking him. Reflecting on the great Reformation theme of *soli deo gloria*—to God alone be the glory—Boice wrote about those who deny God's sovereignty: 'They want to glorify God…but they cannot say "to God *alone* be glory," because they insist on mixing human will power or ability with…gospel grace.'[139]

As long as we believe that salvation results from man's sovereignty, from human choice and decision, denying the Bible's teaching that man contributes only his sin and that God saves us by his sovereign, almighty grace alone, we will continue to focus on what we are doing and ought to do, neglecting prayer and the giving of praise and thanks to God. If ultimately it is human will that decides salvation, then we will appeal to humans and seek to please them instead of God. In contrast to the man-centered spirit of our age, Paul's grand view of God's sovereignty supplies a compelling reason for us to pray, namely, to give praise and thanks to God for his grace.

The Need for Prayer

God's sovereignty also provides *the need for prayer*, as this passage shows. Paul asks, 'that the God of our Lord Jesus Christ, the Father of glory, may give you a spirit of wisdom and of revelation in the knowledge of him, having the eyes of your hearts enlightened' (Eph. 1:17–18).

Since God is sovereign, we must pray to him because salvation wholly depends on the spiritual resources we cannot create but which he is able to provide. Specifically, Paul realizes that we utterly depend on God giving his Holy Spirit to enliven and illuminate our hearts, to make us spiritually receptive, and to open blind eyes to the light that is shining. First Corinthians 2:14 says, 'The natural person does not accept the things of the Spirit of God, for they are folly to him, and he is not able to understand them because they are spiritually discerned.' This is why Paul so often prays both for the conversion of unbelievers and for the spiritual growth of believers, because the work of God's Spirit is necessary for both. Likewise, we must pray to the sovereign God for ourselves and for others, beseeching the Spirit's quickening and illuminating work.

This raises a question: 'Does prayer change God's will?' Is God's mind, attitude, or purpose altered by our prayers? To understand prayer rightly, and its relationship to God's sovereignty, we must realize that the answer to this question is No. Prayer does not change God's will.

There are people who insist that if prayer does not change God's mind or will, then there is no need to pray and the Bible's emphasis on prayer is a sham. But far from being outraged at the idea that prayer does not change God's will, Christians should be profoundly grateful. God is, after all, all-wise. What wisdom might we contribute to his thinking that would produce a superior understanding? Likewise, God is completely holy. Do we wish that we, being sinful and corrupt, could exert a moral influence on God's holiness? And what sort of influence do we think it might be? God's mind is informed by omniscience—perfect knowledge of all things, past, present and future. Do we wish him to change his mind based on our ignorance? For all these reasons, we should be glad that God is sovereign and that our prayers do not change his mind.

The Bible makes clear that God's will is not changed by prayer or anything else, having been firmly established in eternity. Isaiah 46:11 says, 'I have spoken, and I will bring it to pass; I have purposed, and I will do it.' In Ephesians 1:11, Paul tells us that God 'works all things according to the counsel of his will.' He asks, in Romans 11:34, 'who has known the mind of the Lord, or who has been his counselor?' The answer is no one. Christian leaders glibly talk of our prayers shaping God's policy today, but if God's purpose is an eternal one, as Paul insists, then his policy is *not* being shaped today.[140] Our folly does not dictate to God's wisdom. Our sinfulness does not direct his holiness. Our ignorance does not overrule his perfect knowledge. If our prayers changed God's will, then we would be sovereign, not he, and his will could no longer be described as Paul does in Romans 12:2 (NIV), 'his good, pleasing and perfect will.'

Prayer does not change God's will. Now let me ask the question a different way: 'Do our prayers change *things*?' Are there things that happen that would not have happened had we not prayed or if we had prayed for something different? Here the answer is Yes. Our prayers do change things, because God is sovereign and has ordained prayer as a means to the ends that he also has ordained. While prayer does not change God's will or plan, prayer is used by God within his will and plan. It is in this sense that he says to all his people, 'Pray to me, and I will hear you' (Jer. 29:12).

Even if prayer did not change circumstances it would still be worthwhile to pray, first simply to praise God, but also because prayer changes us. Prayer changes our attitude to circumstances that God may not wish to change. Paul says, 'in everything by prayer and supplication with thanksgiving let your requests be made known to God. And the peace of God, which surpasses all understanding, will guard your hearts and your minds in Christ Jesus' (Phil. 4:6–7). This alone is an important reason to pray. People who insist that prayer only matters if God grants our wishes fail to appreciate the importance of adoration and the value of the peace that God gives.

But prayer goes beyond changing us: it changes things, it changes events, it changes outcomes. Why? Because the God to whom we pray is sovereign—he is able to do all things—and he has ordained prayer as a means by which all he has ordained will come to pass. Therefore we should pray for all our needs, for help, for relief, for God's power to overcome dangers and temptations, and to help us in our witness and ministry, because it is through our prayers that God intends to provide these things. As Martin Luther said, 'Prayer is not overcoming God's reluctance, but laying hold of His willingness.'[141]

C. Samuel Storms offers an example of how prayer serves as a means God has provided to accomplish the ends he has ordained. Suppose, he writes, God decided that a man named Gary will be saved through faith in Christ on August 8. Suppose, also, that unbeknownst to me God wills to bring him to faith in response to my prayer for Gary on August 7. Storms asks,

> Does this mean that God's will for Gary's salvation on the eighth might fail should I forget or refuse to pray on the seventh? No. We must remember that God has decreed or willed my praying on the seventh for Gary's salvation, which he intends to effect on the eighth. God does not will the end, that is, Gary's salvation on the eighth, apart from the means, that is, my prayer on the seventh…From a human perspective, it may rightly be said that God's will for Gary is dependent upon me and my prayers, as long as it is understood that God, by an infallible decree, has secured and guaranteed my prayers as an instrument with no less certainty than he has secured and guaranteed Gary's faith as an end.[142]

Why, some then will ask, should I bother praying, if it is all decreed by God? The answer is that I do not know what God has ordained until it happens. Having Gary's salvation on my heart, what else should I do but pray and use every other opportunity to lead him to faith and salvation, trusting God to bless these means as he is so often glad to do?

Prayer does not change God, but it does change things, according to God's eternal counsel and sovereign will. Therefore, Paul sees an urgent need for prayer, and he prays that God will send the Holy Spirit to lead the Ephesians into a deeper knowledge of God and power for newness of life.

Encouragement to Prayer

God's sovereignty gives us every *reason* to pray, as well as every *need* to pray. Finally, we have every *encouragement* to pray, because Christ is exalted over all, exercising God's royal sovereignty for the church.

We utterly fail to grasp Paul's emphasis in this chapter unless we realize that God's sovereignty is exercised in Christ and through Christ for our salvation. This means that if you want to know that God has chosen you for salvation, you must come to Jesus Christ in faith. But it also means that if you belong to Christ then God's sovereignty is exercised by him for your benefit. This is why Paul ends the chapter by showing us Christ exalted: 'He raised him from the dead and seated him at his right hand in the heavenly places, far above all rule and authority and power and dominion, and above every name that is named, not only in this age but also in the one to come' (Eph. 1:20–21). God exalted Christ for a reason, namely, Paul continues, to be 'head over all things to the church, which is his body, the fullness of him who fills all in all' (Eph. 1:22–23).

When we bow our heads and lift our hearts to God in the name of Jesus, that is the name of the One who sits at God's right hand in glory and power. The Son of God is enthroned as a man, knowing all too well what it is to sorrow and suffer, to have need of God's help, of God's grace, of God's mercy, and of God's power in the Holy Spirit. Hebrews 4:15–16 reflects on this:

For we do not have a high priest who is unable to sympathize with our weaknesses, but one who in every respect has been tempted as we are, yet without sin. Let us then with confidence draw near to the throne of grace, that we may receive mercy and find grace to help in time of need.

Since God has exalted his Son, the man Jesus Christ, to the place of sovereignty, we are encouraged by his ability to understand our needs. Furthermore, since this is the same Lord Jesus who loved us and gave his life for our sins, we can be sure of his willingness to employ his divine power and authority for our sakes. Our prayers are received into hands that were pierced for us. What greater encouragement could we have about the welcome our prayers will receive in the courts of heaven? Paul reasons in Romans 5:10, 'If while we were enemies we were reconciled to God by the death of his Son, how much more, now that we are reconciled, shall we be saved by his life.'

The story is told of a Civil War soldier who went to the White House with a pressing need he thought only the President could help him with. To his dismay, he found a great number of people seeking an audience and a staff of assistants whose job it was to keep them out. Dejected, the soldier fell into a seat, where a young boy came up to him and asked him why he felt so sad. The man replied, 'I came a long way to see the President, but now I realize I won't be able to.' The little boy grabbed him by the hand and led him past the guards and the staff of assistants, through a number of doors and into the oval office where the President was working. 'Father,' the boy said, 'This soldier needs your help.' Abraham Lincoln put down his pen, looked up, and said, 'Certainly, my son. Now my friend, what can I do to help you?' That is what it means to us that God's Son, Jesus Christ, is there in heaven, exalted for us, so that we will always have access in prayer to the heavenly Father.

The Scepter Raised

If God is sovereign why should we pray? We have every *reason* to pray because of the thanks we owe to God for his sovereign grace. We have every *need* to pray because of our whole reliance on the work of his Holy Spirit. But above all this, we have every *encouragement* to pray because of our assurance of God's favor in Christ, his own Son and our Savior, who grants us unfailing access to the Father, and whom God has established as head over all for the sake of the church.

There is a story in the Bible that speaks of the great privilege of this access and favor. The story is that of Esther, the Jewish girl who became Queen of Persia. The Book of Esther deals with a plot by the evil official Haman to have the Jews persecuted. Godly Mordecai, Esther's uncle, appealed for Esther to use her influence to protect God's people. Esther was afraid to act, because one could only approach the king in his inner court if first summoned by him. Anyone who approached the king without being summoned was required by law to be put to death (Esther 4:11). The person could only be spared if the king, seeing him or her, extended his golden scepter, admitting the petitioner into his royal presence. After three days of prayer and fasting, Esther summoned the resolve to go forward. First she put on her royal robes, and only then did she go into the king's inner chamber and stand before him. Esther 5:2-3 tells us what happened:

> When the king saw Queen Esther standing in the court, she won favor in his sight, and he held out to Esther the golden scepter that was in his hand.

Then Esther approached and touched the tip of the scepter. And the king said to her, 'What is it, Queen Esther? What is your request? It shall be given you, even to the half of my kingdom.'

If that is the response of a pagan monarch towards his wife, how much more can we expect when we appear in Christ's name before the throne of our heavenly Father. Like Esther, we must be careful to come in the robe God has given us, the perfect righteousness of Jesus Christ, imputed to us through faith in his blood. So dressed, as Christ's own bride, we will surely be precious in his sight. And, with our Savior Jesus enthroned forever as Lord over all, we will find the scepter permanently raised for us. The wrath of God's law was put aside once for all at the cross, the veil removed that once kept us out from God's presence, and the scepter of access is now extended to us forever. As Paul writes later in this epistle, 'Through him,' that is, Christ, 'we have access to the Father' (Eph. 2:18).

Count Zinzendorff wrote, 'Jesus, thy blood and righteousness, my beauty are, my glorious dress; midst flaming worlds, in these arrayed, with joy shall I lift up my head.'[143] This will be true in the future at the final judgment, when we ourselves come to stand before God's throne in the righteousness of Christ. It is also true now, as our prayers come to him and are received into sovereign hands with love and care and joy. What an encouragement to come to God in the name of and through faith in the Lord Jesus Christ. To him be glory forever.

18

Dead in Sin

Ephesians 2:1–3

When the apostle Paul first arrived in Ephesus, the Christians he met had a deficient understanding of the gospel, knowing only the baptism of John the Baptist and having heard nothing of the Holy Spirit. Paul baptized them into the name of the Lord Jesus and then the Spirit fell on them in power (Acts 19:1–6). Perhaps it was because of this initial experience that Paul's letter to the Ephesians delivers such a clear and comprehensive exposition of the doctrine of salvation. Having begun this letter with a doctrinally rich hymn of praise to God in chapter 1, Paul follows in chapter 2 with what Klyne Snodgrass describes as 'one of the clearest, most expressive, and most loved descriptions of salvation in the New Testament.'[144]

What Is Sin?

We always want to be careful to begin our understanding of biblical doctrines where the Bible itself begins. This is especially important in this chapter, in which Paul begins his teaching on salvation by stating what kind of people we were before God came to us with saving grace. Paul begins:

And you were dead in the trespasses and sins in which you once walked, following the course of this world, following the prince of the power of the air, the spirit that is now at work in the sons of disobedience—among whom we all once lived in the passions of our flesh, carrying out the desires of the body and the mind, and were by nature children of wrath, like the rest of mankind.

Paul's purpose is to show us the spiritual condition of everyone apart from Christ, and especially to show that God's work of redemption begins with a recognition of our complete sinfulness.

When we begin to talk about sin it is important that we have a biblical understanding of what sin is. Paul supplies this by using two words which together summarize the Bible's teaching on sin. Paul says we were dead in 'trespasses and sins.' The first of these terms, trespasses (Greek, *paraptomasin*) indicates deviating from the right course, crossing a boundary, or breaking a command. This expresses our rebellion against God's rule. God has said, 'You shall not,' but we have. God has said, 'You shall,' but we have not. All of us are guilty of trespasses, for we have not perfectly kept God's law.

The second word, translated here simply as sins (Greek, *hamartiais*), means to fall short of the mark. It is used of an arrow that lands short of the target. It means failing to meet the required standard, in this case, God's perfect standard of holiness. In Romans 3:23, Paul says this applies to us all, writing that 'all have sinned and fall short of the glory of God.' We are not the people that God intended us to be.

Sin Causes Death

The Bible teaches that God made mankind good, without sin. Man's fall into sin is chronicled in Genesis 3. God had forbidden Adam and Eve to eat from the tree of the knowledge of good and evil, upon pain of the punishment of death (Gen. 2:17). When the devil tempted our first parents so that they broke this command and sinned for the first time, the curse of death fell upon our race. Paul explains in Romans 5:12 that 'sin came into the world through one man, and death through sin.'

This raises a vital question to which our passage gives an important answer: Just how sinful are we apart from Jesus Christ? Exactly what effect did the Fall have on mankind?

There have historically been three views about man in his relationship to sin. The first is the view of liberal theology, otherwise known as 'humanism.' According to this view, man, despite his occasional mistakes, is well. People are basically good and, left to themselves under normal circumstances they can be expected to do good things. So far as the Fall was concerned it was a fall upward. By experimenting with good and evil, by not allowing God's commands to hold him back, man is growing into his true divine potential.

The liberal Jewish rabbi, Harold Kushner, argues this position, stating that by breaking God's commands in the Garden, Adam and Eve expanded their horizons; this, he is so bold as to say, is what God was hoping our first parents would do. He sees sin causing not man's expulsion from paradise, 'but the story of the first human beings graduating' into a world of choices and liberation. 'I don't believe that eating from the Tree of Knowledge was sinful,' he writes, '[but] one of the bravest and most liberating events in the history of the human race.'[145]

According to the Bible, however, sin produced not liberation but separation from the holy rule of God to the cursed domination of Satan. Sin cast the human race out from the blessing of God's favor to the curse and death that is the life of sin. Perhaps the greatest condemnation of Kushner and others who espouse the liberal, upward view of the Fall is their agreement with the Serpent, that is, Satan, who assured Adam and Eve that by sin, 'You will not surely die,' but 'your eyes will be opened, and you will be like God' (Gen. 3:4–5). The liberal, secular view of man is literally the doctrine of the devil.

The second view, held by many evangelicals today, strongly contends against the liberal view by insisting that the Fall was not upward but downward. But this view sees that having fallen into sin, man is merely sick. This is the view of Arminianism, so named for the sixteenth century theologian, Jacob Arminius. He insisted that while man has certainly been corrupted by sin, his fallen condition is not so bad as to render him incapable of cooperation in salvation. Often the analogy will be made with a man who is on his deathbed. He is so weak that he cannot get out of bed, so he needs the doctor to bring the medicine that will heal him. His hand may be so weak that he cannot even hold the spoon. Nonetheless, if he is going to take the medicine, he must, by his own power and will, open his mouth to receive the saving fluid. The medicine is God's grace, without which the sick man cannot possibly be healed or even escape death. But he retains some small power, and he must exercise it if he is to be saved. This exercising of his own free will is the decisive key to his salvation.

The third view is that held by Reformed theology, also associated with the great ancient theologian, Augustine, and sometimes called Calvinism, for the Protestant Reformer, John Calvin. This view says that man in sin certainly is not well. But neither is he merely sick. His condition is far worse: he is, as Paul says in verse 1, 'dead in trespasses and sins.' What fallen man needs is not medicine but a resurrection. His salvation depends, as Paul wrote in Romans 9:16, 'not on human will or exertion, but on God, who has mercy.' The Reformed doctrine of sin is known as *total depravity*. We are not partially depraved, with our wills remaining free to choose Christ and believe the gospel. Rather, our nature is so entirely corrupted that we are unable to take any action for our own salvation until God's grace has imparted to us a new nature that is able to believe and be saved.

This is the Bible's teaching about men and women in sin. We are not well, not even sick, but spiritually dead. Paul does not mean that we lack biological life: we still walk and talk, eat, drink, and work. But doing all this in the realm of sin, we are dead to the things of God.

We know someone is dead because he no longer responds to stimuli. We talk to him but he does not answer. We touch him and he does not move. This is the way people who are spiritually dead respond to God and his Word: they have no comprehension, even when the Bible is taught; when the gospel offer is made, they do not respond.

Martyn Lloyd-Jones put this in practical terms:

The man who is not a Christian finds the Bible very boring, and expositions of the Bible very boring. He does not find films boring, he does not find the newspapers boring, he does not find the novels boring; but he finds these things boring. He does not enjoy conversations about the soul and about life and death and heaven and God and the Lord Jesus Christ. He cannot help it, but he just sees nothing in it and he is not interested. He is interested in men and their appearance, and in what they have done and in what they have said; the world and its affairs appeal to him tremendously. The position is perfectly simple; these other things are spiritual, they are God's thing, and that kind of man sees nothing in them. Why? Because he is 'dead' and has no spiritual life.[146]

A myth about the famous nineteenth century philosopher and father of utilitarianism, Jeremy Bentham, provides us with an illustration. When he died, he gave his great wealth to the University College Hospital of London, but according to legend, there was on one condition. His body was to be preserved, and at every meeting of the board of directors his corpse was to be dressed in a formal suit and seated at the boardroom table as a grisly reminder of his views and intellectual legacy. Bentham's body, now dead for over 180 years, was to be wheeled out for board meetings, with the chairman announcing, 'Jeremy Bentham, present but not voting.'[147]

Supposedly, Bentham is present, but there is nothing he can do, nothing he can contribute, nothing he can say. He hears nothing that is said. Though present, he is dead. That is a vivid picture of how he lived with respect to the things of God, and what we all are like until we are brought to spiritual life by Christ's resurrection power.

'All'—'By Nature'

You may be thinking, 'I can see how this applies to some people, but I doubt that it applies to most of us—and it certainly is not true of me!' But notice that Paul specifies in verse 2 that 'we all' were like this. According to Paul, this is the universal condition of mankind apart from the saving grace of God. You may pass as respectable in the sight of men, but in the sight of God all have sinned, all have trespassed, and apart from Christ all are dead in sin.

In verse 3, Paul tells us why all are dead in sin. He says that we were 'by nature children of wrath.' 'Children of wrath,' means that we deserve God's condemnation. But the key expression is that this is true of us by our nature. This is why we are all dead in trespasses, because since the Fall our whole beings are corrupted by sin. We are not sinners because we sin; we sin because we are by nature sinners.

When Adam and Eve disobeyed God, they did not immediately experience physical death, though ultimately their bodies did die. More importantly, they died spiritually. This is shown by the fact that they ran from God in the Garden and tried to cover their nakedness with fig leaves. As Augustine explained, the kind of death Adam experienced was 'God's desertion of the soul.'[148] He added, 'The punishment for that sin…was, to put it in a single word, more disobedience.'[149] Death entered into man's nature in the form of moral and spiritual corruption, so that Paul could write elsewhere of those in sin, 'Though living, they are dead' (1 Tim. 5:6).

Our problem is that this condition has been passed on to us: this is what is meant by the doctrine of *original sin*. Original sin is not the first sin itself committed by Adam and Eve. It is the consequence of that sin and the condition of depravity into which it cast our entire race. Original sin means that we are born with natures inclined to evil. John Calvin explains, 'For all of us tend to evil, and we are not only inclined to it, but we are, as it were, boiling hot with it.'[150]

This truth can be proved by the sinfulness of our children from the most tender age. King David said in Psalm 51:5, 'Behold, I was brought forth in iniquity, and in sin did my mother conceive me.' Anyone who has raised little children knows what he was talking about. J. C. Ryle, who loved children dearly, gives this realistic assessment:

The fairest babe, that has entered life this year and become the sunbeam of a family, is not, as its mother perhaps fondly calls it, a little 'angel', or a little 'innocent', but a little 'sinner'. Alas! As it lies smiling and crowing in its cradle, that little creature carries in its heart the seeds of every kind of wickedness! Only watch it carefully, as it grows in stature and its mind develops, and…you will see in it the buds and germs of deceit, evil temper, selfishness, self-will, obstinacy, greediness, envy, jealousy, passion, which, if indulged and let alone, will shoot up with painful rapidity. Who taught the child these things? Where did he learn them?[151]

The answer is that he did not learn them—transgression and sin come naturally to our race without instruction. This is why training in righteousness is so difficult, while children can learn the ways of sin at the first exposure. We are all 'by nature children of wrath.'

Sin is the great and universal problem of all mankind. Our problem is not mere ignorance or lack of education; however educated we become we never graduate beyond the problem of sin. Our problem is not a bad environment, however bad our situation may in fact be; being by nature spiritually dead sinners, we are the ones who ruin every good environment. Our problem is not lack of money, so that it can be fixed by winning the lottery or by advancement at work; nor is it lack of technique, so that the right self-help advice will set us all straight. Our great problem is this, as John MacArthur explains: 'Because [man] is dead to God, he is dead to spiritual life, truth, righteousness, inner peace and happiness, and ultimately to every other good thing.'[152] The leopard cannot change its spots and we cannot escape our guilty and corrupt nature. Thus we are hopeless unless we are saved by God.

SIN REDUCES US TO CRAVINGS

Paul continues in these verses to work out the implications of this spiritually dead condition. What does it mean to be dead in sin? Paul tells us, in verse 3, that *sin reduces us to cravings*. Men and women were made in the image of God, to reflect his glory and partake of his holiness. But, being dead in trespasses and sins, Paul tells his Christian readers, 'We all once lived in the passions of our flesh, carrying out the desires of the body and the mind' (Eph. 2:3).

There are several key words here, the first of which is translated *lived* (Greek, *anestrapemen*), and which really denotes a lifestyle. Paul says that sinfulness is characterized by a certain way of life. The second key word is translated *passions* (Greek, *epithumiais*). This could also be rendered as *lusts*. Man in sin lives according to the lusts of his flesh, that is, his sinful nature.

Surely this is an apt description of our culture. The American lifestyle is driven by sinful cravings. We immediately think of the sensuality which dominates our society. Almost anything can be sold with an ad featuring a scantily clad woman. The pornography industry is booming as never before; by far the largest amount of internet commerce involves men driven by their sexual lusts. We add to this other cravings—the lust for money, for narcotic highs, for drunken stupors, and our society demonstrates perfectly how sin reduces men and women to animal cravings.

Paul adds to this that we 'carry out the desires of the body and the mind' (Eph. 2:3). Literally, this reads, 'doing the will of the flesh and the mind.' By *mind*, Paul means our *thoughts*—in this case our evil thoughts. Secular people boast about their free will, and even many Christians insist that unbelievers have a free will. But Paul knows that their will is not free but is bound to their sinful nature and their wicked thoughts. They have a will, but it is governed always by their desires. Later in Ephesians, Paul explains, 'They are darkened in their understanding, alienated from the life of God because of the ignorance that is in them due to the hardness of their heart. They have become callous and have given themselves up to sensuality, greedy to practice every kind of impurity' (4:18–19). This perfectly describes the morass into which Western Civilization has sunk, just like the Roman world of Paul's day. It does not describe minds and wills that are free.

The apostle James chronicled this depravity in James 4:1–2: 'What causes quarrels and what causes fights among you?' he asks. 'Is it not this, that your passions are at war within you? You desire and do not have, so you murder. You covet and cannot obtain, so you fight and quarrel.' If you are merely bought into the covetousness of our consumer society, and especially if you drink from the entertainment trough of sensual sin, you are a vital part of this devastating reign of death. By sin, man, alienated from God, spiritually dead and enslaved, is reduced to the level of the beast, living in misery and perpetually unsatisfied desire.

SIN LEADS TO ETERNAL DEATH

The last thing Paul tells us about mankind being dead in sin is that *sin leads to our eternal destruction*: we 'were by nature children of wrath, like the rest of mankind' (Eph. 2:3).

The Bible teaches clearly that God judges both sin and the sinner. People say God hates the sin and loves the sinner. That is true, in that he offers salvation for sinners in Jesus Christ. But in the end, on the great day of God's final judgment, it will not merely be sins but sinners who are cast into the fiery chasm of hell.

God's holiness demands that his wrath be poured out on sin. He proved this at the cross, for even when it was his own perfect Son who bore our sins, God poured out the full furies of hell upon his soul. What will it be like, then, for those who bear their own sins into God's judgment, not having them forgiven through the blood of Jesus Christ? Paul says elsewhere that in his return as Judge, Jesus will come 'in flaming fire, inflicting vengeance on those who do not know God and on those who do not obey the gospel of our Lord Jesus. They will suffer the punishment of eternal destruction, away from the presence of the Lord and from the glory of his might' (2 Thess. 1:8–9). Therefore, to be dead in sins is ultimately to suffer eternal death; not annihilation, but eternal condemnation and judgment in the wrathful hands of a holy God.

Jesus Christ Is the Solution to Sin

I have learned as a preacher that people do not like to hear about sin. Not much, anyway. But, according to Paul, if we ignore or avoid the subject we cannot understand the salvation God offers us in Christ. Paul shows us that the only way to understand and receive salvation is to admit and confess our sin. The point of talking about sin is not to tear people down but to enter them onto God's saving path at his appointed place of entry. The Bible says, 'Humble yourself in the sight of the Lord, and he will lift you up' (James 4:10).

I can imagine going into a leper colony to preach, to find that people there don't much like to hear about leprosy, or to preach to blind people who don't want to always talk about the darkness they are suffering. Along those lines, I understand why sinners don't want to hear about sin; they have to deal with it enough and could use something cheerier. But what if you went into the leper colony, having the cure to their disease? Wouldn't it, then, be your duty to talk about it? So it is with sin in the church and in the Bible. It may seem good to have your mind relieved from the pain and anxiety of sin with some pulpit comedy or sentimental stories. But it is decisively better to have your sin conquered, overcome, and removed. That is why the Bible constantly talks about sin, why our worship must always bring us as sinners to the cross of Christ, and why faithful preaching does not shrink from pointing us to the problem of sin. You may go elsewhere to be entertained or to find an emotional lift. But the church of Jesus Christ is about salvation, and salvation requires that we face the facts about sin.

Sin is the great problem of the world, for which man has no solution. But here is good news; the light that has dawned in the land of the shadow of death. Jesus Christ has conquered sin by dying on the cross as an offering for us, and he offers salvation to all who will come, confess their need, and believe on him. He offers life to the dead, freedom for those in bondage, and heaven for those bound for hell.

This is something not only for non-Christians but also for believers in Christ to hear and remember. It was to Christians that Paul wrote this epistle. Christians need to hear about sin as a means to recalling the wonder of what God has done in our salvation and to make alive our love to God. If we want to realize how great is the salvation God has given us by his grace, then we must realize the depths to which we had sunk and the helplessness from which he saved us in Christ. We preach sin not to beat people down, but as the first step to lifting them up with the saving grace of God.

The glory of Christianity is that we not only can feel better for a while, but be made better forever. We can not only experience holy religious moments, but we can be holy in Christ. We can not only escape for a time the thoughts about ours and others' sins and the pain of a dying, cursed world, we can be cleansed of sin and made a part of the new and sinless resurrection world. We can be forgiven, born again, and enter a new life—not one that is governed by sinful cravings but by a holy passion for God; a life that leads not to eternal destruction in shame but to everlasting life in glory.

How does this happen? It happens by coming as sinners to the Savior, Jesus Christ. This first means confessing that you have been dead in trespasses, you have been reduced to cravings and to the bondage of a corrupt soul, and you have been worthy of eternal condemnation in the court of God's justice. It then means trusting Jesus to take your sins away by his death on the cross in your place, and then to send the Holy Spirit to make you spiritually alive forever.

Sin is death, Paul wrote in Romans 6:23, 'but the free gift of God is eternal life in Christ Jesus our Lord.' Sin is bondage to lusts and cravings. But Jesus said, 'If you abide in my word…you will know the truth, and the truth will set you free' (John 8:31–32). Sin leads to eternal death, but Jesus said, 'I am the resurrection and the life. Whoever believes in me, though he die, yet shall he live' (John 11:25–26). 'Truly, truly,' Jesus said, 'I say to you, whoever hears my word and believes him who sent me has eternal life. He does not come into judgment, but has passed from death to life' (John 5:24).

From death to life. From bondage to holy liberty. From wrath to resurrection. Believe on the Lord Jesus Christ, and you will be saved.

19

The World, the Flesh, & the Devil
Ephesians 2:1–3

In the opening words of Ephesians 2, Paul describes man apart from Christ as 'dead in trespasses and sins.' It may seem surprising that having described us this way he then goes on to talk about the way in which we have lived. We lived but were dead; we were dead but we lived. This is the second major point Paul makes about life in sin in these opening verses. He wanted us to know that man in sin is spiritually dead. But he also wants us to know what kind of life spiritually dead sinners live.

Paul considers it important for us to understand what sin is all about. The reason is that apart from an understanding of sin we cannot understand Christianity. Take, for instance, the doctrine of the incarnation. Why did the eternal Son of God take up flesh and live in this world? Because of the greatness of the problem of sin. Because man, whom God created for himself, was spiritually dead and in bondage to sin. People who say they don't want to talk about sin therefore don't want to know the purpose for Christ's coming into the world. 'You shall call his name Jesus,' the angel told Joseph, 'for he will save his people from their sins' (Matt. 1:21).

Take also the crucifixion of our Lord. What was it for? Peter tells us, 'Christ also suffered once for sins, the righteous for the unrighteous' (1 Pet. 3:18). Furthermore, take Christ's present work in heaven. Jesus is interceding for us with the Father in heaven. Why? To deal with our present sins. John writes, 'If anyone does sin, we have an advocate with the Father, Jesus Christ the righteous' (1 John 2:1). Even something as basic as the love of God cannot be grasped apart from sin. It is the greatness of our sin, for which God gave his own beloved Son, that measures the greatness of his love for us.

Not only can you not understand Jesus Christ and Christianity, but unless you face the biblical facts about sin you cannot understand the world as it is. Martyn Lloyd Jones writes, 'You cannot understand the whole of human history apart from this, with all its wars and its quarrels and its conquests, its calamities, and all that it records. I assert that there is no adequate explanation save in the biblical doctrine of sin.'[153]

Finally, unless you understand the Bible's doctrine of sin you cannot even understand yourself. Sin is the power that wants to control your life, and from which you must be delivered by Jesus the Savior.

In the last chapter we considered the results of sin: sin is death, sin reduces us to cravings, and leads to eternal destruction. Now we look back over these verses to see what the life in sin is like. Paul tells us that life in sin is bondage to three great powers: the world, the flesh, and the devil.

FOLLOWING THE COURSE OF THIS WORLD

What does it mean to live in sin? The first thing Paul tells us that it is *to live in conformity with the world*. He writes, 'You were dead in the trespasses and sins in which you once walked, following the course of this world' (vv. 1–2).

The Bible uses the term *world* in a variety of ways. John 3:16 says 'God so loved the world, that he gave his only begotten Son.' In that case, *world* speaks of the human race in its entirety. But more often, *world* speaks of the sinful world system in rebellion to God. In Galatians 1:4, Paul speaks of 'this present evil world.' The antithesis between God and the world is clearly stated in 1 John 2:15-16: 'Do not love the world or the things in the world…For all that is in the world—the desires of the flesh and the desires of the eyes and pride in possessions—is not from the Father but is from the world.'

This is what Paul has in mind when he speaks about living 'in conformity with the world.' He means the world in its values, in its materialism, in its unbelief and opposition to the rule of God. Leon Morris observes that Paul 'reminds the Ephesians that before they became Christians they not only were dead in their sinfulness, but their pattern of life was one dictated by the world in which they lived and not by any such motive as a pure desire to do the will of God…The world is always sensual and obviously given over to evil.'[154]

Much of Paul's desire is for his readers to walk not in the ways of the world, but rather to walk in good works (2:10), to walk worthily of their calling (4:1), to walk 'in love' (5:2), and as children of light (5:8). By speaking of a walk, Paul means our active approach to life, which should not be worldly but godly. As he famously put it in Romans 12:2, 'Do not be conformed to this world, but be transformed by the renewal of your mind.'

There is nothing easier to prove than that non-Christians are controlled by the world. One of the great lies of our time is the world's supposed commitment to tolerance. In reality, the world demands absolute conformity and will ostracize and ridicule you if you do not conform. We learn this from an early age and the result is that people's ideas are derived from the newspapers and magazines. The way people dress, how they talk, their hair styles, the music they listen to is utterly controlled by the latest fashion that is praised in the media and thus by other people. Undoubtedly, the most powerful influence of our time is the media. It is nothing less than astonishing to see how in a few generations, television and music have almost eradicated the Christian values that once formed the backbone of our nation and replaced them with other values once rejected as obviously immoral. How did this happen? Not by presenting fair and rational arguments, but by making sin seem attractive and pleasurable; living in a godly manner is not so much repudiated intellectually but made to seem narrow and stupid. For this reason the amount of television and internet you view is closely related to how worldly you are. It is not that television and movies are inherently evil; godly themes can also be conveyed by these mediums. But it is a thoughtless imbibing of unbelieving worldviews through shows and movies that leads so many 'in the course of this world.'

It is hard to overestimate today how important it is that Christians not live according to the values of the world. You used to hear about a category of people called 'carnal Christians'. This designated people who were saved but who lived in accordance with the world. I am glad not to hear that expression much anymore because it is utterly unbiblical. A professing Christian who lives in a consistently worldly manner is nothing more than a false professor of faith. In 1 Corinthians 6:9–10, Paul explains, 'Do not be deceived: neither the sexually immoral, nor idolaters, nor adulterers, nor men who practice homosexuality, nor thieves, nor the greedy, nor drunkards, nor revilers, nor swindlers will inherit the kingdom of God.'

One thing this means is that what we expose ourselves to matters. Worldliness happens subtly. If you want to be worldly, then just watch a lot of television, read all the best-sellers without discrimination, go to movies that glorify adultery and play video games or plug in to music that promotes lust and violence, hate and even death. You will become worldly all too quickly.

This applies especially to young people. They are under so much pressure to be 'with it', which often is just another way of saying 'worldly'. Therefore young Christians must be helped to understand that to follow Christ is to take up the cross. We can either 'follow the course of this world,' or we can follow Jesus Christ. We can either be followers of Christ along his narrow way that leads to life, or we can join the broad way that leads to death (cf. Luke 13:24). The apostle John warns us, 'The world is passing away along with its desires, but whoever does the will of God abides forever' (1 John 2:17).

It is not only young people, however, who are prone to conforming to worldly values. David McCullough tells of Abigail Adams' experience in the lavish culture of Paris when her husband John Adams served as America's ambassador to France. When Abigail first arrived from Puritan New England, she was horrified by the indecency of the French women and especially by the gross immodesty of the Parisian opera. Because of the beautiful music, however, Abigail continued to attend and found, as she wrote to her sister, 'my taste reconciling itself to habits, customs and fashions which at first disgusted me.'[155] So it is for all Christians, that by frequent exposure we become used to immorality and in this way are drawn into the likeness of the world.

If this is true of Christian individuals, surely the worst thing the church can do is pattern itself after the world. Yet churches are criticized today not for being too worldly but too holy. It is a mortal sin of church-growth to make anyone uncomfortable in the church. Yet to be truly used by God, to make a difference for Christ in our time, we must be willing to be different—not because we are trying to be stuffy or formal or high and mighty, but because we are trying to be faithful. It is when we are centered on God that the world notices that there is something different about us. Many will scoff, but others will come, pay attention and be saved. Lloyd-Jones summarized:

> The glory of the gospel is that when the Church is absolutely different from the world, she invariably attracts it. It is then that the world is made to listen to her message, though it may hate it at first… It should not be our ambition to be as much like everybody else as we can, though we happen to be Christian, but…our ambition should be to be like Christ, the more like Him the better, and the more like Him we become, the more we shall be unlike everybody who is not a Christian.[156]

Following the Prince of the Power of the Air

The first power governing people in sin is the world. Second, Paul directs our attention to a power that is much more sinister. To live in sin, he says, is *to live under the domination of the devil*. He says the man or woman in sin follows 'the prince of the power of the air, the spirit that is now at work in the sons of disobedience' (v. 2).

This may sound like a strange designation for the devil, but it is consistent with his portrayal all through the Bible. By 'air' Paul means the spirit realm. The devil, or Satan, is the ruler of the evil spiritual powers and his rebellious spirit energizes all the disobedience of mankind. In Ephesians 6:12, Paul writes, 'For we do not wrestle against flesh and blood, but against the rulers, against the authorities, against the cosmic powers over this present darkness, against the spiritual forces of evil in the heavenly places.' Jesus called Satan 'the ruler of this world' (John 12:31), and Paul called him 'the god of this world' (2 Cor. 4:4) who blinds the minds of unbelievers.

Satan is not, in fact, a god, but rather a fallen archangel. But he has usurped the place of God in the lives of men and women in sin. Augustine said that man is like a horse and can have only one rider at a time. Either the horse is ridden by God or it is ridden by Satan. Paul teaches here that those who are dead to God are under Satan's rule; indeed, they are realizing the devil's fondest ambitions by rebelling against God and destroying themselves in sin.

Furthermore, Paul tells us how this works. He says that Satan is 'the spirit that is now at work in the sons of disobedience.' The verb translated 'at work' is the Greek word *energeo*, from which we get the noun *energy* and the verb *energize*. Paul used this same verb in Ephesians 1:19-20, when he reminded the Christians about the 'greatness of [God's] power toward us who believe, according to the working [that is, energizing] of his great might that he worked [energized] in Christ when he raised him from the dead.' It is God by his Holy Spirit who energizes godliness, just as he energized Christ's resurrection, and it is the devil who by his evil spirit energizes all disobedience. Satan is the spirit of the age—this present, evil, condemned world in which we live.

It was the devil's influence that caused our first parents to plunge into sin. He is still at work, and his aim is the same as it always was—to insinuate that God is not really good, that his ways will hold us back, tempting us into believing that through sin we will find fulfillment. When we fall in sin Satan then accuses us so that we believe that God will never take us back. The devil rules a vast host of demons who operate unseen, carrying out his program of rebellion and sin.

Most significant to Paul's thought here is not the temptation that the devil or his minions might afflict directly on us. Rather, it is that as the ruler of this world, Satan controls the world and supplies it with its evil values. Surely you do not think it is by chance that a culture that turns from God always takes on the same characteristics! It is not by chance that a godless society always becomes sensual and violent, that families break down and moral absolutes are discarded, that poverty and ignorance and cruelty begin to reign. Yet all the while, rebels against God think they are charting their own original course, though it is always the same. Man in sin is not free, as he imagines, but under the vicious rule of Satan. The devil always rules when God's rule is denied, either individually or on a grand scale.

If you wonder why it is that the world's entertainment leaders keep pushing farther and farther into sin, this is why. If you wonder why the legislatures and courts advance into pagan ways of thinking, this is why. There is a spirit to this age, and Satan is energizing the rebellion of the world. This is why the fashion leaders and the best-sellers and trend-setters all take us in the same direction. James Boice comments, 'This tells how the devil enslaves men and women. It is not that he is personally present. He is only one creature and can only be present in one place at one time. It is rather through the evil spirit or outlook present in the world that he rules us.'[157] We may be from time to time under direct assault from unseen spiritual powers, although most of us have probably never directly encountered the devil himself. But we are under his control when we give ourselves to sin and follow the values that are popular in the world.

FOLLOWING THE WILL OF THE FLESH

Man in sin is governed by the world's expectations, and also by the devil. But there is a third force that drives everyone who lives in sin: the sinful nature, or the *flesh*, which rules us from within. To live in sin, Paul says, is *to be dominated by the lusts of the flesh*.

If you peruse Paul's letters you will see how deadly serious he is about the matter of not living in the lusts of our sinful nature. He writes in Romans 6:12–14:

> Let not sin therefore reign in your mortal bodies, to make you obey their passions. Do not present your members to sin as instruments for unrighteousness, but present yourselves to God as those who have been brought from death to life, and your members to God as instruments for righteousness. For sin will have no dominion over you, since you are not under law but under grace.

In Romans 13:13–14, Paul adds, 'Let us walk properly as in the daytime, not in orgies and drunkenness, not in sexual immorality and sensuality, not in quarreling and jealousy. But put on the Lord Jesus Christ, and make no provision for the flesh, to gratify its desires.'

The way to conquer the bondage of lusts, Paul says, is two-fold. First, we must 'make no provision for the flesh.' This means that we are not to subject ourselves to likely sources of temptation. In our day, we think first of all about sexual morality; it is essential that Christians be different at this point. But different people are susceptible to different temptations. Paul lists some of them in Galatians 5:19–21: 'Now the works of the flesh are evident: sexual immorality, impurity, sensuality, idolatry, sorcery, enmity, strife, jealousy, fits of anger, rivalries, dissensions, divisions, envy, drunkenness, orgies, and things like these. I warn you, as I warned you before, that those who do such things will not inherit the kingdom of God.' However we find ourselves driven by our sinful nature, we must come to God for forgiveness and for power in the Holy Spirit, and then we must proactively avoid sources of future temptation.

But it is not enough merely to strive against sin and avoid temptation. We must also, as Paul said, 'Put on the Lord Jesus Christ' (Rom. 13:14). In the long run, the only way to avoid being enslaved by sinful desires is to become more and more like Christ through his Word and through prayer. The apostle writes, 'You were taught in him, as the truth is in Jesus, to put off your old self, which belongs to your former manner of life and is corrupt through deceitful desires, and to be renewed in the spirit of your minds, and to put on the new self, created after the likeness of God in true righteousness and holiness' (Eph. 4:21-24).

One of the great tragedies of the nineteenth century was that of Oscar Wilde. His brilliant mind won him the highest academic honours. His literary genius won him accolades; his charm and kindness made him well liked. However, because he fell into fleshly temptation of various kinds, the most famous of which was homosexuality,

Wilde fell from his high perch, ending up in prison and disgrace. He wrote of all this:

> The gods had given me almost everything. But I let myself be lured into long spells of senseless and sensual ease…Tired of being on the heights I deliberately went to the depths in search of new sensation…I grew careless of the lives of others. I took pleasure where it pleased me, and passed on. I forgot that every little action of the common day makes or unmakes character, and that therefore what one has done in the secret chamber, one has some day to cry aloud from the house-top. I allowed pleasure to dominate me. I ended in horrible disgrace.[158]

This is something for us all to remember. When we dabble in sin, we are risking our character and the domination of the devil who rules through the sinful passions. Sin always takes us farther than we wanted to go, keeps us longer than we meant to stay, and demands far more than we ever wanted to pay, even the price of our souls.

The Devil's Banquet and the Feast of the Lord

Life in sin is life under the domination of the devil. It is a life spent following the course of the world, the spirit of which is controlled by Satan. It is a life driven by fleshly desires, which are the devil's whips to keep his slaves in line.

Therefore, the choice between righteousness and sin is nothing less than the choice between the rule of God—the holy, good, and loving Creator and Redeemer—and the rule of Satan—the lying, enslaving, accusing, destroying devil.

In a brilliant sermon, Charles Spurgeon depicts this choice as the choice between two banquet halls. There is the banquet of the devil and the feast of the Lord. Spurgeon takes as his theme verse a statement made at the wedding at Cana where Jesus turned the water into wine. The wine Jesus had miraculously made was presented to the master of the banquet, who exclaimed, 'Everyone serves the good wine first, and when people have drunk freely, then the poor wine. But you have kept the good wine until now' (John 2:10).

Spurgeon explains that this is the difference between the world, the flesh, and the devil on the one hand and the Lord Jesus Christ on the other. The devil's banquet gives all of its luscious pleasures up front; only afterward do things turn sour. Spurgeon considers the man of fleshly desire, to whom the devil first comes with the sparkling cup of pleasure. It intoxicates his senses, be it sexual pleasure or narcotic highs or gambling or any other fleshly lust. He thinks, 'What a fool I was, not to have tasted this before!' Spurgeon explains, 'He drinks again; this time he takes a deeper draught, and the wine is hot in his veins. Oh! How blest is he! What would he not say now in the praise of Bacchus or Venus, or whatever shape Beelzebub chooses to assume? He becomes a very orator in praise of sin.'[159]

But in time the first course is over, and devil brings out a different cup. This is not the cup of pleasure but of satiation. This is the poor wine that follows the good. It lacks the excitement the now dulled senses crave, but gives just enough to keep him drinking. It gives only disappointment to go along with addiction.

This second cup is followed by a third, the cup of wrath and damnation. '"Drink of that," says the devil, and the man sips it and starts back and shrieks, "O God! that ever I must come to this!" "You must drink, sir!" the devil replies…"Drink, though it be like fire down your throat!…He who rebels against the laws of God, must reap the harvest."'[160] This is the grim cup that never features in the advertisements for sin. The devil always sets forth the best wine, the pleasurable wine first, knowing that thereby he will someday put the cup of wrath to the lips of our souls.

How different is the feast of the Lord Jesus Christ. His practice is exactly opposite from that of the devil. The master of the wedding said to him: 'Everyone serves the good wine first, and when people have drunk freely, then the poor wine. But you have kept the good wine until now.'

At Jesus' table, the feast of salvation, the bitter and difficult things come first, and to those who press on in faith there are better things to come. In this life, Christ's people are often afflicted. Spurgeon writes, 'Jesus brings in the cup of poverty and affliction, and makes his own children drink of it…This is the way Christ begins. The worst wine is first.'[161] The same is also true in our reception of the gospel. We must first drink the bitter cup of conviction of sin, the very drink Paul is serving in these opening verses of Ephesians 2. He knew it well, having tasted it himself.

But then comes another cup. In it Jesus has mixed something better. Spurgeon writes, 'I have drank of [the cup of conviction] and I thought that Jesus was unkind, but, in a little while, he brought me forth a sweeter cup, the cup of his forgiving love, filled with the rich crimson of his precious blood.'[162] Jesus' second cup brings us consolation for all our trials and relief for our sense of guilt. As he drinks deeper and deeper from that cup of fellowship and love, the believer grows in communion with God, until at last he cries, 'The Lord is my chosen portion and my cup…The lines have fallen for me in pleasant places' (Ps. 16:5–6). Finally, Jesus brings the best cup last, the taste of which is incomprehensible in blessing to those of us who have yet to enter heaven. It is the cup of glory, the cup of resurrection life, the cup that makes us sing: 'You make known to me the path of life; in your presence there is fullness of joy; at your right hand are pleasures forevermore' (Ps. 16:11).

That is the promise of God for all who were dead in sin, following the course of the world, obeying the prince of the power of the air, and doing the will of the flesh, but who by faith in Christ are born again to a new life, are forgiven and cleansed from all their sins, and take their place at his banquet feast. All the others serve the good wine first, but then when the people are drunk, in comes the bad. But Jesus calls us now to join him at the cross, to the bitterness of confessing our sins and to the struggle against the world, the flesh and the devil. Yet he will lead us on to the crown of life, when only the best wine will be served and where joy abounds forever.

20

But God

Ephesians 2:4

A number of years ago, a society for the spread of atheism published a tract exposing the depravity of Bible heroes. One after another, the leaflet showed the villany of such men as Abraham, Jacob, Moses and David. Under the face of Abraham an inscription read that here was a coward who was willing to sacrifice the honor of his wife to save his own skin. It lists where the Bible admits this and then where the Bible calls him 'the friend of God'. 'What kind of God,' it asked, 'would befriend so dishonorable a man?' Under Jacob's picture was the Bible's description of him as a liar and a cheat, and also where God makes him the prince of his people. What does this say about the character of a God who would even call himself 'the God of Jacob'. Next came a reminder that Moses was a murderer, yet God picked Moses to bring his law into the world. David was worst of all. He seduced Bathsheba and then had her husband killed to cover it up. Yet this is 'the man after God's own heart,' the leaflet complained. What kind of God could find so much to praise in a man like this and why would anyone serve him?

How do we, as Christians and followers of the Bible's God, answer these complaints? The first thing we should say is that everything the atheist tract said is true. It is true—indeed a glorious truth—that the heroes of the Bible, excepting Jesus Christ, are all scoundrels and criminals, breakers of God's law and sinners to the core.

This, by the way, shows the Bible's honesty; no other religious tome dares to display the human weakness and sins of its heroes the way the Bible does, because the Bible is not trusting in man but in God.

Furthermore, it is true that God saves sinners, making them his own friends, children, and servants. God 'justifies the ungodly,' Paul writes (Rom. 4:5). So we agree on this with the atheists. The difference is that we see this as God's glory and not his shame. Since we are sinners like the people in the Bible, the fact that God saves sinners does not subject him to our disdain but commends him for our affection.

This glorious truth that God saves us in and despite our guilt and shame is taught by Paul in the two words that begin Ephesians 2:4. In the first three verses of Ephesians 2, Paul has labored to show the truth of what the world and the atheists say about us—that we are no better than anybody else, we were spiritually dead, captives to the world, the flesh and the devil, justly under the condemnation of God and man. Paul admits this—insists upon this—and then writes two words that change everything: 'But God.' Martyn Lloyd-Jones comments, 'These two words, in and of themselves, in a sense contain the whole of the gospel. The gospel tells of what God has done, God's intervention; it is something that comes entirely from outside us and displays to us that wondrous and astonishing work of God.'[163]

These two words declare that when man's resources and strength are gone, while sin has brought us into a hopeless situation, there is yet a great hope because God himself has intervened to save us. Before God's grace we were lifeless, enslaved, and bound for condemnation. But because of what God has done in Jesus Christ, believers are 'made alive with Christ' and raised with him to reign forever.

Having introduced these two words, 'But God,' I want not to consider them in terms of what they have to say about the Christian message, about the Christian's God, and about the Christian life.

The Christian Message

Sometimes, in order to understand a message correctly, you have first to be clear about what it does not say. This is a helpful exercise when it comes to Paul's presentation of the gospel in this chapter. We need especially to note that Paul is not calling us to take action. This may seem surprising, given all he has said about the terrible reality of sin. We might expect him now to say, 'Let's all take a firm stand against sin. Let's organize ourselves and straighten out our lives so that we will no longer be dead in sin.'

The reason he does not say this is because of what death means. Paul says, 'You were dead in trespasses and sins' (Eph. 2:1), and this means that for our part the struggle is over. We are like Jesus' friend Lazarus in John 11. He was dead and buried, and the one thing Jesus did not do was wait for Lazarus to act. Likewise, the Christian message to the world is not one of morality or spiritual exercises, or any other kind of human activity. Christianity does not offer you self-help techniques that promise to fix your life. It does not offer you stairs that you can ascend to God. Christianity tells the hard truth that in sin you are already dead, you are under God's wrath, and there is no hope in anything you can do.

Realizing this helps us to understand just what the Christian gospel is, and just what Paul says has happened for our salvation. He writes that God has intervened at the point of our hopelessness in order to save us. This is the proclamation he has been moving to since this chapter began. He began, 'You were dead in trespasses and sins,' and then he had to explain that: we were in slavery to the world, the devil and the flesh, and we were objects of God's wrath. Now, in verses 4–5, he arrives at the solution: 'But God…even when we were dead in our trespasses, made us alive together with Christ.' We were dead, but God has made us alive in Christ. As Jonah said in his prayer from the depths, 'Salvation is of the Lord' (Jonah 2:9).

The atheists complain about the sins of Abraham and Jacob, Moses and David. But perhaps the best example of sin and salvation comes from even earlier in the Bible. Adam and Eve were placed in the Garden with every blessing they could possibly hope for. God merely insisted that they acknowledge him as Lord, forbidding them to eat from just one tree, the tree of the knowledge of good and evil (Gen. 2:16–17). But, tempted by the devil, our first parents disobeyed that one prohibition and fell into sin. Lloyd Jones asks:

> What defence is there for Adam and Eve, made in the image of God, in Paradise, in absolute perfection

with the friendship and the companionship of God, with all the blessings that anybody could ever desire? What did they do? They deliberately rebelled against God; they disobeyed him and put their own wills before his. Is there any excuse for them? Can any plea be put forward?[164]

Adam and Eve had no excuse. They could not plead ignorance, for God had clearly revealed his will. They could not say they were not warned, because they were. 'Nothing can be said for them. They had no defence and deserved not only to be driven out of Paradise, but to be destroyed totally and eternally.'[165]

The same is true of us. We have no excuse for our sin. We cannot plead ignorance of God's law, which has been taught in the Bible and is stamped by God on our consciences. We have deliberately flouted our knowledge of right and wrong. God has created us, he has given us everything good, he has told us clearly what is our obligation before him and warned us of the penalty of death that resides on sin. Lloyd-Jones therefore concludes: 'We must realize that as members of the human race we deserve nothing but total destruction.'[166] We may blame God, as so many do, but the fact is that we are at fault.

Let's return to Adam and Eve. They had sinned and were under God's judgment. They were guilty and at fault. What now could they do? First, they tried to evade God's wrath, putting on fig leaves and running away. These are still our main strategies: to cover our sin with the false righteousness of supposedly good works, corrupted as they are by sin, or by seeking to forget or deny the reality of God. Adam and Eve failed to escape, because God is God; he saw them and he found them out. As Psalm 139 says, 'Where can I go from your Spirit? Where can I flee from your presence? If I ascend to heaven, you are there! If I make my bed in the grave, you are there!' (Ps. 139:7–8). Then they tried to blame God, but God knows all things and cannot be fooled. God is the judge and is not threatened by our petty complaints and accusations.

You see their predicament. When God came to Adam and Eve, they could do nothing to make themselves right with God. They could not remove their guilt. They could not erase their responsibility. They could not deny the corruption of sin in their hearts or keep sin from tainting any good works they might offer to assuage the wrath of God.

So what happened to our first parents? Were they eternally destroyed, as they might well have been? The answer is found in Paul's statement: 'But God'. Genesis 3:21 tells us what God did to save them, because for all their sin and guilt God loved them still: 'The Lord God made for Adam and for his wife garments of skins and clothed them.' God was under no obligation to save Adam and Eve, but he did. He did it by sacrificing an innocent animal in their place, transferring their guilt to the substitute which bore the penalty of death for them, and then clothing them in its innocent skin. This was a picture, of course, of what God was going to do through Jesus Christ, to save all of his people from their sin.

What was true of Adam and Eve is true of us. We are hopeless in our guilt and sin, without any way of making right all that was wrong. Isaiah wrote, 'All we like sheep have gone astray; we have turned every one to his own way.' So what will happen? But God! Isaiah states, 'But the Lord has laid on him the iniquity of us all' (Isa. 53:6).

These are the two greatest words in the Bible, on which we must rest for salvation: But God. When mankind was lost in sin, when you and I were lost, condemned, and without hope, God sent his Son to be the Lamb slain for us. Paul writes in

Romans 5:8, 'But God shows his love for us in that while we were still sinners, Christ died for us.' Paul says in our passage, 'You were dead in trespasses and sins…But God…made us alive together with Christ.' God sent his own Son to bear our sins on the cross, dying the death that our sins deserve, and in his resurrection power giving us eternal life.

This is the Christian message, and Augustus Toplady puts its story on our lips:

> Not the labours of my hands
>   can fulfill Thy law's demands
> Could my zeal no respite know,
>   could my tears forever flow
> All for sin could not atone;
>   Thou must save, and Thou alone.

Is that the message that you have believed for your salvation? Have you confessed that you are dead in sin apart from God's saving grace, and that because of his mercy and love you are saved by the work of Christ alone? Can you sing the remaining words of the hymn:

> Nothing in my hand I bring,
>   simply to thy cross I cling.
> Naked, come to thee for dress;
>   helpless look to thee for grace.
> Foul, I to the Fountain fly;
>   wash me, Savior, or I die.

The Christian's God

Paul's great teaching tells us not only about the Christian message, but also about the Christian's God. If we are to believe this message of salvation that is wholly of him, this tells us much about what we believe about God himself.

The first thing this shows is that *God is sovereign*. This is good news, because it is a sovereign God, a God who is in active control of events in the world that he made, who can intervene for our salvation. The words 'But God' go right along with Paul's teaching in chapter one on God's sovereignty in salvation: 'He chose us in [Christ] before the foundation of the world… in love, he predestined us for adoption through Jesus Christ, according to the purpose of his will' (Eph. 1:4–5). God's sovereignty is a comfort to his people, because it says the one on whom we utterly rely is able to accomplish all of his will.

The second thing the gospel shows is that *God is holy and just*. Verse 3 says that sinners are 'children of wrath.' People don't like to hear this, but because of God's holiness we must. God told Adam that if he sinned he would die, and that is exactly what happened (see Rom. 5:13). We experience physical death because of God's just punishment, and we are all born spiritually dead as the consequence of Adam's sin.

Even God's solution to the problem of our sin shows his holiness and justice. The great Puritan theologian, John Owen, explains:

> To see Christ…beloved of the Father, fear and tremble, bow and sweat, pray and die; to see him lifted up on the cross, the earth trembling beneath him as if unable to bear his weight; to see the heavens darkened over him…and to see that all this is because of our sins is to see clearly the holy justice and wrath of God against sin. Supremely in Christ do we learn this great truth that God hates sin and judges it with a dreadful and fearful punishment.[167]

Third, Paul's teaching tells us that *God is filled with mercy and love*. In verse 4 he says, 'But God, being rich in mercy, because of the great love with which he loved us.' This is the *why* of the Christian message. What can explain a gospel that is all of God, in which hopeless sinners find grace in the hands of the holy God they have offended? The answer is found in 1 John 4:8, 'God is love.' The answer is found in Exodus 34, after Moses had asked the Lord to see his glory. God hid him in a cleft of the rock, and passed by, saying, 'The Lord, the Lord, a God merciful and gracious, slow to anger, and abounding in steadfast love and faithfulness' (Exod. 34:6). This is how the gospel glorifies God instead of shames him; it shows what God is really like and makes him attractive to those who know him: God's love is great and he is rich in mercy.

The Scottish minister, Alexander Whyte, told of an evening when an older minister came to discuss some pastoral matters. When their business was completed, the old man seemed to linger and to want the conversation not to end. Finally, after discussing the situation of many other people, he asked, seemingly in jest, 'Now, sir, have you any word of comfort for an old sinner like me?' Whyte realized that behind the half-smile was a real seriousness and even a deep agony. He wrote later, 'It took my breath away. He was an old saint. But he did not know the peace of forgiveness.' Not exactly sure what to do, Whyte walked over and sat beside the older minister, opened his Bible to Micah 7:18, and read, 'He delights in showing mercy.'

'He delights in showing mercy.' You remember the atheist's tract complaining about how God could fellowship with scoundrels like those found in the Bible. This is the answer. Yes, Abraham was a coward and idolater. But God delights in showing mercy, so Abraham was called to walk with God and become our forerunner in faith. Jacob was a liar and a cheat. But God delights in showing mercy, so Jacob was made a man of integrity and the father of God's people. Moses was a man of violence. But God delights in mercy,

so Moses became, the Bible says, the meekest of all the men upon the earth (Num. 12:3). In this way, Moses was fitted to be God's ambassador and law-giver. David was an adulterer and murderer. But God, who is rich in mercy, enabled him to repent, just as he will allow you to repent and be forgiven. David prayed, 'Have mercy on me, O God, according to your steadfast love; according to your abundant mercy blot out my transgressions' (Ps. 51:1). God had mercy on David and restored him fully.

This was Dr. Whyte's answer to the suffering old minister: 'He delights to show mercy.' The next morning he received a letter in reply. It read:

> Dear friend, I will never doubt Him again. Guilt had hold of me. I was near the gates of Hell, but that word of God comforted me, and I will never doubt Him again. I will never despair again. If the devil casts my sin in my teeth, I will say, 'Yes, it is all true, and you cannot tell the half of it, but I have to deal with the One who delights in showing mercy.'[168]

This is the God revealed in Paul's teaching. As the Psalmist sang, 'Who is like the Lord our God, who is seated on high, who looks far down on the heavens and the earth? He raises the poor from the dust and lifts the needy from the ash heap, to make them sit with princes, with the princes of his people' (Ps. 113:5-8). Who is holy and just, but rich in mercy and abounding in love? 'There is none holy like the LORD,' sang Hannah in her song. 'There is no rock like our God' (1 Sam. 2:2).

THE CHRISTIAN LIFE

The two words, 'But God', describe not merely how we are saved at first but also how we live our whole lives as believers. Having defined the Christian message and the Christian's God, 'But

God' also defines the Christian life. It is by God's action, intervention, and prompting all through our lives, to which we respond in faith, that he leads us in a new life and ultimately brings us home to heaven.

The life of Abraham shows this clearly as well. Abraham was living as a pagan in Ur of the Chaldees. But God called him to journey into a distant land of promise. Abraham believed God and set out on his trip. Before he got to Canaan, however, Abraham settled down in Haran, only part way there. But God came back and prodded him forward. Abraham went to Canaan and then a famine struck, so he headed down to Egypt. It was there that he embarrassed himself by having his wife taken in by Pharaoh in order to save his own skin. Things were going badly, 'but the Lord afflicted Pharaoh and his house with great plagues because of Sarai' (Gen. 12:17). God was working in Abraham's life, and Pharaoh gave Abraham great riches to take his wife away. Abraham returned to Canaan, but grew disconsolate because God had promised to give the land to his descendants, and Abraham did not have a single son. But God came to him and showed him the stars in the sky, encouraging his faith with a promise that his offspring would be as numerous as the lights of heaven.

Abraham grew tired of waiting, so he took Sarah's maidservant and had a son with her. This tore his household in two, and Hagar and her son were unjustly sent out into the desert. But God found Hagar and preserved her from Abraham's folly. Abraham and Sarah despaired of bearing God's promised son, Abraham nearing 100 years old and Sarah being 90. But God sent his angel to renew the promise and to open Sarah's womb, so she gave birth to a child, Isaac.

After this great blessing, Abraham was in danger of becoming complacent, but God came to him with a new challenge. God directed him to take his son, Isaac, and offer him as a sacrifice. Abraham, by now, had learned to trust the Lord, so he obeyed. Upon Mount Moriah, at the spot where later Solomon would build the temple, Abraham raised the knife to kill his beloved son and heir. But God sent an angel, who called out, 'Abraham, Abraham, do not lay your hand on the boy,' and God provided a ram to be sacrificed in Isaac's place (Gen. 22:11–12). Finally, Abraham grew old and died. His body was placed in the grave and his life on earth came to an end. But God received his spirit and we know that Abraham entered into the paradise of God, where now he lives forever in glory.

Do you see what this shows?—that the whole Christian life is a glorious adventure, with God as our Savior and Lord, teacher and guide. God calls you to faith and you have no idea where God is leading you, you cannot imagine how the changes the Bible talks about could happen in your life. The answer is here—'But God'. The problems are not really yours but God's, and he is more than able to accomplish all his desire in your life.

You realize, for instance, that you can never become a man of spiritual stature, of solid faith, of self-control and godly dignity. But God can make you such a man. You know that you could never become a woman of inward, spiritual beauty, a bearer of virtue and a source of redeeming love for others. But God can make you such a woman as you trust in him and walk in his ways.

That is the whole Christian life, a journey of discovery into the workings and wonders of God. God intervenes and directs, coaxes and chastises, inspires and empowers. God challenges us and renews our weary souls. He provides the encouragement we need. He convicts our sin. He tests and strengthens our faith. And in the end he makes us vessels of his glory, so that we can say with Paul, 'We have this treasure in jars of clay, to show that the surpassing power belongs to God and not to us' (2 Cor. 4:7).

The point is that God is sufficient to meet our every need. Are we ignorant of God and his truth? The fact is that apart from God, we are. Paul writes, '"No eye has seen, no ear has heard, no mind has conceived what God has prepared for those who love him"—but God has revealed it to us by his Spirit' (1 Cor. 2:9–10, NIV).

Are we tempted? Certainly we are. 'Temptation…is common to man; but God is faithful, who will not allow you to be tempted beyond what you are able, but with the temptation will also make the way of escape, that you may be able to bear it.' (1 Cor. 10:13, NKJV).

Are we weak and foolish? Yes, we are. 'But God chose what is foolish in the world to shame the wise; God chose what is weak in the world to shame the strong; God chose what is low and despised in the world, even things that are not, to bring to nothing things that are, so that no human being might boast in the presence of God' (1 Cor. 1:27–29).

Are we, or will we be, victimized by the sins of other people? Yes, we can be sure of that happening some time or another. The Bible says, however, 'You intended to harm me, but God intended it for good to accomplish what is now being done' (Gen. 50:20).

James Montgomery Boice therefore concludes, 'May I put it quite simply? If you understand those two words—"but God"—they will save your soul. If you recall them daily and live by them, they will transform your life completely.'[169]

These two words also help us to realize that we may safely follow God's Word all the days of our lives. Let us, then, respond in faith to all that he does in and through our lives. Let us give all the glory to God, in whose sovereign grace we rest our hope. And let us live with the truth that the Psalmist wrote, 'My flesh and my heart may fail, but God is the strength of my heart and my portion forever' (Ps. 73:26).

21

SPIRITUAL RESURRECTION

Ephesians 2:4–5

If I were asked to summarize the apostle Paul's message in Ephesians, I would not hesitate to say that there is one major emphasis that comes through everything he says in this letter. Paul wants us to know that to become a Christian is to be fundamentally changed as a person. A Christian is fundamentally different from non-Christians and different from the person he or she was before coming to Christ in faith. The changes effected by Christ are not on the periphery of a person but at the very center, changing his basic identity, his nature, and what he is in his essence. This emphasis is seen elsewhere in Paul's writing, of course. He says in 2 Corinthians 5:17: 'If anyone is in Christ, he is a new creation. The old has passed away; behold, the new has come.' This is what Ephesians is all about.

Becoming a Christian is not like joining a country club or taking up a hobby or undertaking a career change. These things affect one area of your life but not the others. They are add-ons which do not define who you really are, activities to which you devote a certain amount of your life, whereas Christ is your life if you are in him. 'For me, to live is Christ,' Paul insists (Phil. 1:21).

Unfortunately, believers are all imperfectly committed to the Lord. But according to Paul's teaching, anyone who treats Christianity as just one compartment of his life, or whose essential person is unchanged by his faith, simply is not a Christian and is not saved. This is true not merely of some Christians—those who are especially devout or committed—but for all Christians. You are not a Christian at all unless an essential change has happened in the core of your person. Martyn Lloyd Jones writes:

> If [Christianity] is not controlling the whole of your life, then you are just not a Christian. Christians are not people of whom it can be said that their lives are identical with everybody else, but they have an extra something in addition…No, to be a Christian, says Paul, means that at the very centre, at the very core of your being and existence, this new something has come in and controls everything.[170]

LIFE FROM THE DEAD

In Ephesians 2:5, Paul defines what has happened to a Christian in the most radical terms possible: 'When we were dead in our trespasses, [God] made us alive together with Christ.' Paul says the change that happens to a Christian is as radical as life from the dead. We cannot imagine a more fundamental or comprehensive change.

According to Paul, conversion to Christ involves a spiritual resurrection. You were dead—dead in sins, dead to God, dead in condemnation—but God has given you life. What has happened to us spiritually is what happened when Jesus stood before the tomb and cried, 'Lazarus, come out' (John 11:43). Lazarus rose from the grave, and Jesus commanded that his grave clothes be removed. This has happened spiritually to all whom Jesus calls to his salvation.

Our spiritual rebirth is analogous to what happened in the creation of the world. It is a re-creation and follows the pattern of the first creation. Genesis 1 tells us that God created all things by his Word, and likewise Peter says to believers, 'You have been born again…through the living and abiding word of God' (1 Pet. 1:23). Furthermore, we are told that in the first creation 'the Spirit of God was hovering over the face of the waters' (Gen. 1:2). In the same manner, God's Spirit applies God's Word to our hearts and animates our spirits with a new principle of life.

The result of this regeneration is that we are made anew; we pass from death to life. We should think of conversion in two simultaneous ways, both judicially and spiritually. Judicially, that is, legally as we stand before God's throne of judgment, believers pass from condemnation to justification. Jesus said: 'Truly, truly, I say to you, whoever hears my word and believes him who sent me has eternal life. He does not come into judgment, but has passed from death to life' (John 5:25). Paul says in verse 4 that we were 'dead in our trespasses', and in verse 3, 'children of wrath.' Though we have merited death through our sins, Christ nailed our sins to his cross and granted us life through the gift of his perfect righteousness imputed to us through faith alone.

But Christianity involves more than a legal change of status; to be saved means far more than to be forgiven. We were legally under the curse of death, but our natures were also spiritually dead, unresponsive to God. Now we have been made spiritually alive to God in Christ. Lloyd-Jones, again, explains it well:

> Regeneration is an act of God by which a principle of new life is implanted in man, and the governing disposition of the soul is made holy…God by His mighty action puts a new disposition into my soul.[171]

The rebirth does not give us new faculties. We had a brain before; we have a brain now. We had souls, we had a will, we had a body, and all that remains true. We also had certain talents, abilities and experiences, and we retain them as Christians. But there is a new governing principle that is made alive at the very center of our being. Our spirits, which were dead to God, are regenerated and made alive to him. The old faculties and abilities are governed in a new way so that, while we remain ourselves, everything has changed. James Boice shows how this changes every aspect of our lives:

> When God breathes new spiritual life into us in the work known as regeneration, we become something we were not before. We have a new life. That life is responsive to the one who gave it. Before this, the Bible meant nothing to us when we read it or it was read in our hearing. Now the Bible is intensely alive and interesting. We hear the voice of God in it. Before this, we had no interest in God's people…Now they are our very best friends and co-workers. We love their company and cannot seem to get enough of it. Before this, coming to church was boring. Now we are alive to God's presence in the service. Our worship times are the

very best times of the week. Before this, service to others and witnessing to the lost seemed strange and senseless, even repulsive. Now they are our chief delight. What has made the difference? The difference is ourselves. God has changed us. We have become alive to him. We are new creatures.[172]

This transformation is not something optional for the front-line Christians. These are not things that are true merely for those who will rise to leadership positions in the church. Ultimately, there is no two-tier Christianity. This enlivening is something all Christians have experienced, and know they have experienced. Jesus said to Nicodemus, 'Unless one is born again he cannot see the kingdom of God' (John 3:3). Nicodemus was puzzled at the idea of entering his mother's womb a second time, but Jesus assured him that it was a spiritual rebirth. 'That which is born of the flesh is flesh, and that which is born of the Spirit is spirit,' Jesus replied. 'You must be born again' (John 3:6–7).

The new birth is necessary to salvation; you cannot be forgiven, you cannot be changed, and you cannot enter into heaven unless, as Paul says in Ephesians 2:5, you who were dead in trespasses are made alive together with Christ.

So how do you know you are born again, that you have passed from death to life? The most essential answer is that it is by the new birth that sinners repent and believe on Jesus Christ. It is by the Word and God's Spirit that anyone truly believes, so that those who trust in Christ are born again and enter a new life in which all the other blessings of salvation are certain to follow.

Dead to Sin, Alive to God

Just as we think of conversion in two ways—one legal and the other transformational—we should think of the life to which we have been born again in two ways. Those who are born again are *dead to sin* and *alive to God*. The end has come to our former sinful ways and a new life has begun.

Paul's clearest teaching on the theme that Christians are dead to sin is found in Romans 6. There, he challenges the idea that God's grace could lead to a life that continues in sin: 'Are we to continue in sin that grace may abound? By no means! How can we who died to sin still live in it?' Just as Jesus died on the cross for our sins, by union with him in faith we too have died to sin, 'in order that, just as Christ was raised from the dead by the glory of the Father, we too might walk in newness of life' (Romans 6:1–4).

The implication of the new birth is that *we must no longer live as we did before*. We are no longer what we were; our old life has ended, and therefore we must no longer try to live in the old manner. We can never go back to the old life—and let me say that if we try to live in the old way we only make a mockery of ourselves. God's Spirit lives in us now, so we cannot prosper in the ways of sin. An adult cannot become a child again, but he can disgrace himself with childish behavior. Likewise, as Christians, the only thing for us to do is renounce the old life of sin, the end of which was death, and embrace the reality that we are no longer to live as we formerly did. John Stott puts it this way:

> Our biography is written in two volumes. Volume one is the story of the old man, the old self, of me before my conversion. Volume two is the story of the new man, the new self, of me after I was made a new creation in Christ. Volume one of my biography ended with the judicial death of the old self. I was a sinner. I deserved to die. I did die. I received my deserts in my Substitute with whom I have become one. Volume two of my biography

opened with my resurrection. My old life having finished, a new life to God has begun.¹⁷³

This takes us directly to the second, positive reality involved in our having been brought from death to life by God. Christians are dead to sin and also *alive to God*. The rebirth is the beginning of the spiritual life of walking with God in righteousness and truth and love. Paul puts this together in Romans 6:11: 'So you also must consider yourselves dead to sin and alive to God in Christ Jesus.' We need to know this lest we should be tempted to return to the former ways of sin and death.

God has done for us what Hernando Cortez did for the Spanish explorers who landed in Mexico. As soon as they arrived in the New World, Cortez burned the ships that might take them back to their former life. With the ships burned, his army had nowhere to go but forward into victory and into the riches of their new life.

That is exactly what God has done for us in Christ. We cannot pretend not to have the Holy Spirit dwelling in us and convicting us of sin. We cannot deny or reject the authority of the God we have come to know. We cannot keep God's Word from stirring up our hearts and enlightening our minds. The life of spiritual death is behind us— and praise the Lord for that. We are alive to God and we are now to live for him. Paul therefore commands us: 'Let not sin therefore reign in your mortal bodies, to make you obey their passions. Do not present your members to sin as instruments for unrighteousness, but present yourselves to God as those who have been brought from death to life, and your members to God as instruments for righteousness. For sin will have no dominion over you, since you are not under law but under grace' (Rom. 6:12–14).

This means we are to offer our eyes to God, no longer sinning in lust or envy or otherwise watching sinful things, but using them to bring godly things into our minds. We are to offer our lips to God, making our speech a source of blessing and salvation, instead of, as James 3:8 puts it, the 'restless evil, filled with poison,' that used to characterize our speech. We are to offer our feet to God, so that they take us into places of worship and ministry rather than of sin and folly. We are to offer our hands to God, helping those in need and lifting up those who are fallen. This is the new life to which we have been saved; it could not be more practical.

Because of the new birth, Christians are dead to the old life of sin and must no longer live as we did before. How is it possible for us to live in such a radically new way? The answer is the spiritual resurrection by God's grace by which we are alive to God! We not only *must not* live as we did before but we *need not* live as we did before. Combined with a new obligation is a new ability. We are able in Christ to do what we never could before. Why? Because the power of God is now working in our lives. This is the point of Paul's analogy between our rebirth and the resurrection of Jesus. Our new life is energized by the same power that raised Jesus from the grave. Therefore things that are naturally beyond our power are now possible to us in the power of God. 'My grace is sufficient for you,' God says, 'for my power is made perfect in weakness' (2 Cor. 12:9). Therefore, Paul boasted, 'I can do all things through him who strengthens me' (Phil. 4:13).

Do you realize, if you have come to faith in Christ, that God's own power is available for your growth in grace and godliness? When you pray asking for strength to turn from sin or grow in godly character, God's power flows to you through the channel of your faith and by the work of his Holy Spirit. As Paul wrote, 'The kingdom of God does not consist in talk but in power' (1 Cor. 4:20). The availability of Christ's resurrection power is the cause of our boldness in the Christian life; this is why we can aspire to holiness and godly love. For as Paul wrote to young Timothy, 'God gave us a spirit not of fear but of power and love and self-control' (2 Tim. 1:7).

Jesus & Nicodemus

I mentioned Jesus' teaching to Nicodemus in John 3, one of the most important passages on the spiritual rebirth. Nicodemus came to Jesus at the beginning of our Lord's ministry, after Jesus had taught and performed miracles in Jerusalem. Nicodemus represented everything the world admires, everything in which a man might place his confidence for salvation. John 3:1 introduces him as 'a man of the Pharisees...a ruler of the Jews.' The Pharisees were those most admired by the people for their religious piety. No one performed more and better religious works than people like Nicodemus. Furthermore, he was 'a ruler of the Jews' (John 3:1). He was a member of the Sanhedrin, the highest ruling body among the Jews in that day. Moreover, we can be sure that Nicodemus was also a scholar. All Pharisees were devoted students of Scripture. Given his Greek name, Nicodemus must also have come from a family that studied the philosophers. What more could a man be than this? It is hard to pick a similar figure from our own time who combines all this: religious devotion, political power, ethical excellence and erudite scholarship.

This is the man who came to Jesus. John tells us he came by night, perhaps to avoid being seen consulting a mere carpenter turned rabbi like Jesus of Nazareth. But Nicodemus saw something he admired in Jesus; he said, 'Rabbi, we know that you are a teacher come from God, for no one can do these signs that you do unless God is with him' (John 3:2). It seems that Nicodemus was offering his considerable help to Jesus' ministry. If Jesus were just a human rabbi, I am sure he would have accepted; the partnership of such a man could mean access, recognition, political pull and financial support.

But Jesus was not just another human teacher, and he was not impressed by either Nicodemus or his assistance. Jesus replied, 'Truly, truly, I say to you, unless one is born again he cannot see the kingdom of God' (John 3:3). This was Jesus' message to a man like Nicodemus, just as it is his message to everyone who thinks to be saved by his pedigree or power, by popularity or good works or petty morality.

What are you bringing to Jesus for your salvation? Do you, like so many people, expect God to accept you as 'a basically good person.' If so, Jesus will convict you of the reality of your sin and demand that you confess your need of his grace. Do you offer the clean hands of supposedly good works? Then Jesus will point to the spots your eyes do not see. He will tell you to clean out the inside of your heart, where filthy things live and flourish. Whatever works or human merit you bring to God expecting to be commended and accepted in the holy courts of heaven, Jesus says to you as to Nicodemus, 'You must be born again,' even to see the kingdom of heaven.

This is something Paul had to learn. He once boasted in similar sources of self-righteousness, things he considered spiritual assets—his bloodline, his upbringing, his circumcision, his religious works and morality, his hatred of God's enemies. But when God opened his eyes, he realized, 'Whatever gain I had, I counted as loss for the sake of Christ. Indeed, I count...them as rubbish, in order that I may gain Christ and be found in him, not having a righteousness of my own that comes from the law, but that which comes through faith in Christ…that I may know him and the power of his resurrection' (Phil. 3:7-10). Just as Paul realized, and just as Jesus demanded of Nicodemus, whoever you are you must repent of your former life, of your claims to merit before God, laying hold instead to God's grace in Jesus Christ, by which you a sinner may be born again.

Saved by Grace

This is the statement Paul makes in completing verse 5: 'By grace you have been saved.' We hear a lot about grace, but here we find what it really means to be saved by grace alone.

To be saved by grace means that *you do not deserve what God has granted to you*. It is not something that happens because of what you are or what you have done—but in spite of what you are and what you have done. Grace is often defined as God's unmerited favor. That is true, but it does not go far enough. Grace is God's favor to those who have merited his wrath. Paul says, 'We were dead in our trespasses'; we were at war with God and under God's just condemnation. But by his sheer grace alone—not because of something in you but because of something in him, because, as verse 4 says, 'God is rich in mercy'—God saved you when you deserved to be condemned, when you were unable even to lift a finger to believe and come to God. As Paul wrote in Titus 3:5-6, 'He saved us, not because of works done by us in righteousness, but according to his own mercy, by the washing of regeneration and renewal of the Holy Spirit, whom he poured out on us richly through Jesus Christ our Savior.'

Grace also means that *you did not achieve salvation by any power within yourself* but by the resurrection power of God working in your life. 'God made us alive' when we were dead—this, too, is what it means to be saved by grace.

Having been saved by grace, we continue to live by grace. Christians do not grow through their own effort or their own inner strength, but through the grace of God that works mightily in our lives through God's Word and prayer. Therefore the Christian who wants to grow in his or her faith, to bear the spiritual fruit that is of God, will devote himself to the Bible and will regularly draw near to God in prayer.

Third, this passage tells us that *to be saved by grace is to be joined to the Lord Jesus Christ through faith*. It was 'together with Christ' that God made us alive. It is because Christ died for us and rose again for us that we die to our old lives and live anew to God, as Christ's redemptive power works through every area of our lives.

The Two 'Musts'

I think back to Jesus' teaching to Nicodemus that 'You must be born again.' But he made a second statement in John chapter 3 that also centers on the word *must*. When Nicodemus asked how this could be, Jesus replied, 'The Son of Man must be lifted up, that whoever believes in him may have eternal life' (John 3:14-15). When Jesus told Nicodemus of his need to be born again, he knew that for this to happen it was necessary for him to die on the cross for our sins.

Nicodemus did not understand this at first and he departed from our Lord. But he shows up again in John's Gospel. In John 7 we are told that he spoke up for Jesus before the Sanhedrin and was criticized for sympathizing with Jesus. He still stood apart from Christ, trusting his political and religious credentials, though God was calling in his heart and Nicodemus was starting to listen.

As often happens, the new birth did not take place without God working for some time in his life.

The day came, however, when what Jesus had spoken of actually happened: the Son of Man was lifted up on the cross. Nicodemus was there, and as he stood by and watched, he surely remembered Jesus' words: 'You must be born again…the Son of Man must be lifted up'. Finally, then, the scholar and politician and religious leader saw the kingdom of God. He saw Jesus upon the cross as the Savior of his own soul; he saw his own redemption by the shedding of Christ's precious blood; and by God's grace, through faith, he was born again.

John 19:38–39 tells us what happened. After Jesus' death, 'Joseph of Arimathea, who was a disciple of Jesus…asked Pilate that he might take away the body of Jesus, and Pilate gave him permission…Nicodemus also, who earlier had come to Jesus by night, came bringing a mixture of myrrh and aloes.' Finally, Nicodemus came out into the light with his commitment to Jesus. He cast aside his reputation among the religious, scholarly, and political elite. He turned his back on fame and wealth and the lifestyle they offered and turned in faith to the crucified Jesus Christ, willing to be his disciple, come what may. 'So it is,' Jesus had said to him on that fateful first night's meeting, 'with everyone who is born of the Spirit' (John 3:8).

The Son of Man must be lifted up on the cross, because you must be born again. It is by believing that Jesus died for your sins, and that he rose again to grant you eternal life, that you, like Nicodemus, 'even when you were dead in trespasses, are made alive together with Christ' (Eph. 2:5).

22

Together with Christ

Ephesians 2:5-6

One of the best summaries of Christianity comes from the nineteenth century Scotsman, Hugh Martin. Martin wrote that Christianity can be summed up in two expressions: 'Christ for Us', and 'We with Christ'. This perfectly sums up Paul's thought in Ephesians chapters one and two. Chapter one tells what God has done for us in Christ, apart from which we cannot be saved. The New Testament proclaims this over and over: Christ was made sin for us (2 Cor. 5:21); he was made a curse for us (Gal. 3:13); he died for us (Rom. 5:8); he rose from the grave for us (Rom. 8:34; 2 Cor. 5:15); and he ascended into heaven and rules in power for us (Eph. 1:22). Everything Jesus did, he did for us, that we might be saved: 'Christ for us.'

But, as Martin points out, 'Christ for us' must be joined to 'We with Christ.' We must receive Christ and trust him for our salvation and become his disciple. Therefore, the New Testament says, we were 'crucified with Christ' (Gal. 2:19). And as Paul says in Ephesians 2:5-6, 'we were made alive with Christ, and raised with Christ, and seated with Christ in heavenly places.' Martin explains, 'If he lived for us, we now live with him, for as he was, so are we in the world.'[174] Jesus' experience has become our experience. Just as he died for our sin, we now die to our sin with him. Just as he was resurrected to live with God forever, so we now also live a new life in service to God.

Union with Christ

This is the great doctrine of the believer's union with Jesus Christ. Arthur Pink wrote, 'The subject of spiritual union is the most important, the most profound, and yet the most blessed of any that is set forth in sacred Scripture.' But then he lamented, 'Sad to say, there is hardly any [subject] which is now more generally neglected. The very expression "spiritual union" is unknown in most professing Christian circles.'[175]

What then does it mean to be united with Christ? Paul explains it with three statements found in verses 5 and 6. He says in verse 5 that believers are 'made alive together with Christ.' He adds, in verse 6, that we were also 'raised up with him' and 'seated with him.' These three expressions sum up Paul's understanding of what it means to have union with Christ through faith.

It is helpful to know that Paul coined three new words in this description. The union with Christ of which he speaks was a new reality that had not previously been known, so there were no suitable words available to Paul. Just as people today come up with new words as needed, such as *internet* or *networking*, Paul too invented new words. His new words here each involve a combination using the Greek prefix *sun*, which means *together with*. For the first, he combines the verb for *to live* (Greek, *zoein*), with the verb for *to make* (Greek, *poiein*), and adds the prefix *with*. His new word is 'made alive together with.' The second and third words are simpler ones: Paul adds *with* to the word for *to raise up*, and also to the verb that means *to be seated*: made alive with, raised up with, and seated with.

With these three words, Paul expresses the believer's union with Christ. But what kind of union is it? Our union with Christ is obviously not a physical one; we were not physically dead and we have not physically been raised up to heaven.

The Bible speaks of our union with Christ in two senses. The first is a covenant union. It is often called 'federal headship'. When we receive Jesus as our Savior, we become the beneficiaries of all that he did; our sins are credited to him to be put away on the cross and his righteousness is credited to us. This is what the expression 'Christ for us' gets at—believers are joined to Christ in God's saving covenant so that we receive the benefit of what Jesus did. Jesus came into the world with a work to be done, and as he died upon the cross, he cried out in satisfaction, 'It is finished' (John 19:30).

But that is not the only kind of union of which the Bible speaks. There is also the believer's spiritual or experiential union with Christ. This is Paul's emphasis in these verses. He means that the experience of Jesus in his death, resurrection, ascension and heavenly reign sets the pattern for our experience on earth and then in heaven.

God's Son became like us so that we might become like him. This is what Paul meant when he wrote, 'I have been crucified with Christ. It is no longer I who live, but Christ who lives in me' (Gal. 2:19–20).

This defines a true Christian. A Christian is not merely someone who comes to church and assents to certain doctrines. A Christian is one in whom Christ is living, and whose life is increasingly taking on Christ's pattern of death, resurrection, ascension to heaven and eternal reign. Everything Paul speaks of in these verses is described in the past tense: having died with Christ, a believer is made alive with Christ, is raised up with Christ and is seated with him in the heavenly realm.

Verses 5 and 6 involve ideas that are difficult to understand, until we realize that Paul is contrasting our present experience with his description of our past in verses 1–3. There is a parallelism that unlocks the meaning of Paul's three invented words. Paul said we were 'dead in trespasses'; now he says we have been 'made alive together with Christ.' He said we were in bondage to the world, the flesh and the devil; now he says we have been raised up into a heavenly citizenship. He said we were 'by nature children of wrath.' But we are no longer under God's condemnation and have been seated with Christ in the heavenly realms.

Made Alive Together with Christ

The first of these terms describes what has happened to us in our conversion to Christ as a spiritual resurrection.[176] We were 'dead in trespasses,' but God has 'made us alive together with Christ.' We were uninterested in the things of God; now we find them exciting and important. We were unresponsive to God's promptings and repulsed by the Bible, but now we find ourselves being molded by God's Word and eager to learn more of the Bible's teaching. We never used to pray, except out of desperation; now we talk with God all the time. What has happened? Just as God raised Jesus from the dead, he has made us spiritually alive. We were living as if God did not exist, or, like Adam and Eve after their sin, we were trying to escape from God. But now we not only know that God is there, but we trust him as our Lord and Savior.

Martyn Lloyd-Jones uses the illustration of a flower that is closed up at night, its petals turned inward and its face closed to God. That is how our hearts and minds formerly were with respect to God. But the sun comes up in the morning and its rays strike the flower's petals. What happens? The petals open toward the sun and soak in its life-giving rays. That is what God has done with us.[177] Paul says in 2 Corinthians 4:6 that God 'has shone in our hearts to give the light of the knowledge of the glory of God in the face of Jesus Christ.' We are now alive to God and our lives are turned to him for light and salvation in Jesus Christ. This is what it means to be born again, to be made alive to God together with Christ.

Raised Up with Christ

According to Paul, the life that was dead in sin had two chief features. There were two sides to our problem: our guilt and our bondage in sin. Speaking of sin's bondage, he said we were 'following the course of this world, following the prince of the power of the air…in the passions of our flesh, carrying out the desires of the body and the mind' (Eph. 2:2–3). If the life in sin involves that kind of bondage, then salvation in Christ means deliverance and liberation. Paul refers to this in his second description of our union with Christ, writing in verse 6 that God 'raised us up with him.'

This refers to Jesus' ascension into heaven and its significance for believers. Jesus was taken out of this world and entered into his heavenly life. Likewise, we who are still physically in this world are no longer of it. We are no longer slaves to the thoughts and desires of the world. We are no longer in bondage to the prince of this present, evil age—that is, the devil. We are no longer powerless before the temptations of sinful desires. Just as Christ ascended into heaven, we, too, are no longer ruled by worldly powers but are under the authority of the kingdom of God.

In Philippians 3:18–21, Paul explained this principle by contrasting those who belong to this world and the Christian, whose citizenship is now in heaven. Of the worldly person, he wrote, 'Their end is destruction, their god is their belly, and they glory in their shame, with minds set on earthly things.' But of the Christian, he says, 'Our citizenship is in heaven, and from it we await a Savior, the Lord Jesus Christ, who will transform our lowly body to be like his glorious body, by the power that enables him even to subject all things to himself.'

This is the difference between a Christian and the man or woman of the world. The worldly man worships those things that satisfy his fleshly cravings. Furthermore, he glories in things that are shameful, having his mind set on earthly goods. That is a perfect description of the values and ideals of this present world, along with those who belong to it. But a Christian is one who has been spiritually taken out of the world. His citizenship is in heaven and the things he hopes for are there, safe and secure with Christ. He does not look forward to worldly riches, glory, fame, or pleasure, but has set his hope on a heavenly reward. Paul adds that he awaits the return of

Jesus Christ and the final resurrection; that is the salvation he seeks.

This union in Christ's heavenly life is something God has done to and for everyone who believes. This is not just a qualification for top Christians, but is the basic description of everyone who is truly joined to Christ and is saved. It is not optional, but fundamental to Christianity. For sure, the implications are still being worked out in our lives. In fact, this principle shows us what Christian growth and maturity look like, that we think less and less like the world around us and more like the ascended Christ. Worldly affairs and pleasures occupy less of our attention and we think more about Christ and heaven. We are like a person who has both his home address and his business address on his calling card. Heaven is our home; this present world is just our place of business for the time being. Our thoughts, desires, and affections are increasingly with Christ in heaven. We are in the world, but no longer of it. The apostle John expressed this same idea:

> Do not love the world or the things in the world. If anyone loves the world, the love of the Father is not in him. For all that is in the world—the desires of the flesh and the desires of the eyes and pride in possessions—is not from the Father but is from the world (1 John 2:15–16).

People complain about this kind of Christianity. You hear the expression, 'That person is too heavenly-minded to be of earthly good.' I have found that this complaint has it exactly backward. It is the heavenly-minded people who are the most earthly good, who are most merciful and who give sacrificially to others and to God's work. Instead, it is the earthly-minded person who is of little heavenly good! It is the man or woman whose heart is still attached to worldly status symbols and worldly entertainments, to worldly boasting and worldly ambitions, who has little or no time to serve the kingdom of God and sacrifice for the blessing of other people.

The true Christian, Paul says, 'has been raised up together with Christ.' There is no other way to serve and worship God. We cannot look up and down at the same time. We cannot serve both God and money (Matt. 6:24). We cannot live for this present life and also store up treasures in heaven. Jesus said, 'Where your treasure is, there your heart will be also' (Matt. 6:21). We can either live as if this present life is our ultimate destination, seeking to enrich and fill ourselves with everything we desire, as if there is no God and as if eternity is but a mirage. The Bible says to such a person, 'You fool!' (Luke 12:20). Or we can believe the Bible's teaching that this life is not our destination, but only preparation for eternity to come. The Christian's destination is in eternity, in heaven, and we must live now as those whose hopes have been raised there together with Christ.

Seated with Christ

Third, Paul says God 'seated us with him in the heavenly places in Christ Jesus' (Eph. 2:6). This refers to Christ's reign in power, seated in heaven at the right hand of God the Father. Believers partake of this and its effects become real in our present experience.

Following the contrast with verses 1–3, we see that this corresponds to our condemnation in sin as 'children of wrath.' In Christ, we are no longer condemned, but are seated with him in the presence of God. The opposite of condemnation and judgment is not just acquittal or forgiveness. We aspire to too little if we think that forgiveness is all we want from God. The opposite of condemnation is acceptance into God's inner circle, adoption into his family, and embrace close to his side, to be seated at his right hand together with Christ. God has 'seated us with him in the heavenly places in Christ Jesus.'

This idea would have been more familiar back in the days of kings and queens. A king would take someone into his favor and allow the man or woman to ride next to him while traveling. The favored person would have intimate fellowship with the king, sharing his thoughts and observations. He would be blessed with the king's attention and affection. This is what it means for us, who were condemned in our guilt, to be made alive with Christ, raised up with him, and then seated with him in the heavenly places.

A helpful example from medieval times is King Arthur's round table. There he gathered his loyal knights to his cause. They sat together for fellowship and council of war, profiting from Arthur's wisdom, and sharing with him his burdens and his triumphs. The Bible says that believers will 'reign with Christ' (2 Tim. 2:10); we will be his band of brothers, his mighty men and maidens, his trusted comrades in arms.

There is a scene early in J. R. R. Tolkien's *The Return of the King* that makes me think of Paul's teaching. The hero of the story, the mighty wizard, Gandalf, arrives at a great city just in time to help defend it from attack. With him is one of the hobbits, the small and insignificant people who play so important a role in the book. When Gandalf and the hobbit arrive, the reigning steward of the city is fascinated by the small creature, who in turn is awed by the ruler and the glory of his city. A bond between them is forged and the hobbit offers his fealty to the lord, who takes him into his service as his personal squire. He seats the hobbit beside him on his throne and during the day the ruler tells him the lore of the kingdom and recounts the great triumphs of his realm. The hobbit, meanwhile, shares with him the story of his adventures and sings songs from his native land.

This is a lovely picture of the great privilege that has been granted us by God as he takes us into his service and favor and even into his intimate presence. It reminds me of the apostle John seated next to the Lord Jesus at the Last Supper, resting his head upon Jesus' breast. When we celebrate the Lord's Supper, we should realize that we likewise have been seated at the table of Christ's fellowship, to partake of the glorious grace of God. C. Austin Miles expressed this wonderfully in a hymn:

> He walks with me, and he talks with me,
>   And he tells me that I am his own;
> And the joys we share as we tarry there,
>   None other has ever known.[178]

Do you know anything about that? Do you know what it is to be seated in the heavenly realms with Christ? When you read the Bible do you sometimes feel that God himself is disclosing parts of his glory to you? Have you felt the warmth of his interest and fellowship in prayer? This is the Christian life. God opens up his own heart to us and makes our cares his own.

Jesus' sitting down was not only a sign of his acceptance but also a sign of his total victory. The Bible says God seated Christ above every name and power and placed all his enemies beneath his feet. The same is true for us, being seated with him. As Paul says in Romans 6:14, 'Sin shall have no dominion over you.'

Christians sin, but no longer because we must. The world, the flesh and the devil may tempt you, but they can no longer rule you. Paul wrote in

Romans 8:2, 'The law of the Spirit of life has set you free in Christ Jesus from the law of sin and death.' Just as God raised our Lord Jesus into heaven and seated him at his right hand, so will God deliver you from the power and persecution and condemnation of this world. John wrote, 'The world is passing away along with its desires, but whoever does the will of God abides forever' (1 John 2:17).

Finally, being seated with Christ, Christians have full assurance of salvation. God receives us with the promise of his gospel: 'For I will forgive their iniquities, and I will remember their sins no more' (Heb. 8:12). Jesus adds, 'Come to me, all who labor and are heavy laden, and I will give you rest' (Matt. 11:28). God's Word asks us, seated as we are in Christ, 'Who shall bring any charge against God's elect? It is God who justifies. Who is to condemn? Christ Jesus is the one who died—more than that, who was raised—who is at the right hand of God, who indeed is interceding for us. Who shall separate us from the love of Christ?' (Rom. 8:33–35). Because we rest on Christ's finished work, safe and secure, Paul concludes, 'We are more than conquerors through him who loved us' (Rom. 8:37).

By Grace You Have Been Saved

Paul is describing true Christianity, something far more than mere attendance at church and knowledge of doctrine. This is an exalted life in total and fundamental contrast with the life we have known before. We were dead, but God has made us alive. We were slaves to sin, but God liberated us to live a heavenly life. We were condemned in our guilt, but God elevated us to the inner circle of his intimate fellowship, with rest and assurance of eternal blessing and life.

Many of us will have to admit that we know little or nothing of what Paul is saying. This is why we need to remember the exclamation he makes right in the middle of this carefully crafted teaching. You can always tell when Paul has something burdening his mind, because he simply cannot hold it in. Here, it slips out at the end of verse 5: 'By grace you have been saved.'

How important this is for us to remember. When Paul says that God made us alive together with Christ, raised us up with Christ, and seated us with Christ in the heavenly realms, he is not talking about something we have to do. He is not challenging us to get our acts together. He is talking about a gift that every Christian has received, yet how few realize the extent of God's grace for us in Christ. Paul's point is not to show you how you are failing and how disappointed God is with you, but rather to open your eyes to how dear you are to God and to know all that he has made available to you in Christ. This is all past tense. It is accomplished. If you are in Christ through a living faith, then you have been made alive with him, you have been raised up a citizen of heaven, and you have been seated with Christ in God's presence, clothed with forgiveness and favor and fellowship with God.

William Barclay tells of a Scottish woman who lived in squalor in the cellar of her large house. Shortly after George Matheson arrived as the new pastor of her church, a man stopped by to find that she now lived in the bedroom on the top floor and that all was neat and clean. He commented on the change, and she replied, 'Ay, you canna hear George Matheson preach and live in a cellar.'[179] So it is with Paul's teaching here. Are you living in the cellar of the salvation God has provided to you in Christ? Then move up into the rooms God has long since prepared for you and begin to live the life he has made possible for you in Jesus Christ.

If you are not a Christian, then this is what you are missing. You are dead in trespasses, alienated from God and his love, held fast in the bitter chains of a loveless, cruel and evil world. Even worse, whether you know it or not you stand condemned in the courts of God's eternal judgment. Here is good news, for if you will confess your sin and look to Jesus Christ for salvation, if you will cry to heaven, where he is seated with God, you will not only be completely forgiven but completely saved. You may be transformed and renewed, liberated from the bondage of your old, rotten life and granted a share in the eternal inheritance of glory.

If you are in Christ, if you have long since believed on Jesus and called upon his name, then start receiving by faith the riches that God proclaims to you from this text. You are no longer dead, so start living to God. You are no longer a slave to sin but a citizen of heaven. Start living for things that will never fade away. And you are nearer to the heart of God than you ever imagined, seated with him in Christ. Give him your heart and take his in return. Partake of his glory and then start reflecting his light into a world that is dead in sin, so that others might be saved by the same grace that gave this matchless gift to you.

23

The Glory of God in Salvation

Ephesians 2:7

One of the most challenging features of modern life is the sense of insignificance that so many people feel. What does it matter, they think, at least in the grand scheme of things, how they live or what they contribute in life?

In part, this outlook is fueled by our society's cult of celebrity. We think fame is what determines how significant a person is. Pop-artist Andy Warhol predicted that in the future 'everyone would be famous for fifteen minutes.' Since most of us will never be famous for even five minutes, we don't feel very important.

This insignificance is magnified by today's secular ideology, and especially by the theory of evolution, the whole point of which is that there is no God who either created or governs this world. As a result, there is no meaning to life. Harvard Professor Stephen Jay Gould sums up the implication of evolutionary atheism: 'We are here by accident…we have no intrinsic meaning.'[180] If this is true, then my job is just to make it through life, to have as many good times and as few bad times as possible, and to succeed in my selfish ambitions.

How does Christianity differ from this? Christianity says that there is a God and it is unto him that we live. Man, like all creation, was made by God and for God. As the first question of the *Westminster Shorter Catechism* so famously tells us, we do have a purpose: 'The chief end of man is to glorify God and enjoy him forever.'

The reality of God is bad news to unbelievers, because despite their unbelief, the eternal God is going to hold them to account. But the reality of God is wonderful good news to his people, because it means that even though we are ignored or despised by the world our intense longing for purpose and meaning, a longing that burns deep within our hearts, is fulfilled in the eternal glory of the God who loves us. Sinclair Ferguson says:

> The average man…has accepted the idea that life is without final purpose, and so he naturally devotes himself to whatever interests him at the moment. By contrast the Christian…walks on the path which God has laid; he enjoys the purpose for his life which God has ordained; he looks forward to the destiny which God has planned.[181]

God's Glory the Reason for Salvation

In Ephesians 2:7, Paul deals with this matter of meaning and purpose. He has been teaching about the glorious blessings that come to those who belong to Jesus Christ. He said that having been spiritually dead we have been made alive. Having been slaves to sin, we have been raised up into the liberty of a heavenly citizenship. Having been condemned in guilt, we are seated with God in loving fellowship. For many of us, this all seems too much to believe. Therefore, Paul tells us the reason for such an abundance of blessing for those who were once God's enemies. God did this, he says, 'so that in the coming ages he might show the immeasurable riches of his grace in kindness toward us in Christ Jesus.'

This tells us that *the reason for our salvation is the glory of God*. People hear the gospel and find it hard to believe that God would pardon and renew sinners by the sacrificial death of his Son. Why would God be willing to do this, they ask? The ultimate answer is that our salvation will serve to glorify God forever. Here is a great ground of assurance and hope to Christians who believe God's Word but feel so unworthy of salvation: it is precisely by saving people like us that God glorifies himself; it is precisely by loving his enemies and transforming us into loving children by his grace that God is glorified in our salvation.

In this sense, it is the greatest sinners who provide God the greatest glory, so that Paul could boast, 'Where sin increased, grace abounded all the more' (Rom. 5:20). This is not an incentive for us to sin, because salvation delivers us from sin. Instead, it is a demonstration of the power of God's grace. In the early days of Christianity, there was no greater enemy to the church than the man who later wrote this letter: Saul of Tarsus, who became the apostle Paul. Paul never tired of pointing out how much it glorified God to save a horrible man like him, making him a trophy of grace before the world (see 1 Tim. 1:15–16). It will be the same with you in your great sin, which is conquered by a grace that is greater still.

We need to realize that just as the chief end of man is to glorify God, so also the chief end of God is to glorify God. This is what God wants, for his glory to be displayed. When we talk about the glory of God, we mean the revealing of his perfections, the display of his glorious attributes. When we say that God desires his own glory, we mean that he wants to reveal who he is and what he is like. It is a sin for us to seek self-glory; indeed, self-glory is the fountain of so many of our sins. But God is the One being worthy above all to be glorified. For God to desire his own glory is not only good, it is the highest possible good. For him to be known is for glory to shine. As Paul wrote in Romans 11:36, 'For from him and through him and to him are all things. To him be glory forever.'

This tells us the purpose of creation: God created the universe to display his glory. 'The heavens declare the glory of God, and the sky above proclaims his handiwork,' says Psalm 19:1. Old Testament scholar E. J. Young writes, 'The entirety of creation…speaks with voices clear and positive of the glory of the Holy God. Wherever we turn our eyes, we see the marks of His majesty, and should lift our hearts in praise to Him who is holy. This is His world, the wide theater in which His perfect glory is displayed.'[182] The chief end of creation is to glorify God.

The same principle is true of redemption: in redemption, God achieves all his aims in creation. It was for the sake of God's glory that Jesus was born, lived, died and rose from the grave. On the night of Jesus' birth, the angels sang, 'Glory to God in the highest' (Luke 2:14). On the night of his arrest, Jesus began praying in the Garden of Gethsemane in the same fashion: 'Father…glorify your Son that the Son may glorify you' (John 17:1).

The same principle is also true when it comes to the Holy Spirit's work in our lives. Why are we born again? Why are we raised and seated together with Christ? So that God's glory may be seen forever through his grace in our lives.

God's Glory Displayed in Coming Ages

In great art galleries, like the Metropolitan Museum of Art in New York City, you will find collections of famous portraits. The men and women depicted on canvas lived long ago, when they were no doubt very important or at least beloved. But today, when crowds pass by admiring their portraits, it is not the men and women depicted who garner the praise, but the artist who painted them. We admire the skill, genius, and passion of the painter, which endures long after the subjects are no longer remembered.

This is similar to God's work in our salvation. God saved us and is doing his powerful work of transformation in our lives, so that in eternity to come his handiwork might be displayed in glory.

This is true in the present. People see the change that has come over us through our faith in Christ, and by our good works God is praised. But *it is especially in the ages to come that God will be glorified through our salvation.* Imagine the conversation of angels, millions of years from now, at the sight of a redeemed sinner resplendent in heavenly glory. 'Is that not one of those rebels,' the angel will marvel, 'a son of Adam, corrupted by sin, guilty of the gravest offenses to God's honor and rule? But look at him, now that God has finished his salvation? He is radiant in the righteous robes of Christ, beautiful in the holiness that has been perfected by God's Spirit, beloved of God the Father and one closest to his heart, his own child and heir of glory!'

It is especially in the future ages that we will praise God for the blessings now only begun but that then will be in full bloom. Yet even with the burdens of this present sinful world, with the pains and degradation of a mortal body, with the torments and struggles of contending with sin, we still have ample reason to praise and thank God. And in the age to come, with glorified bodies, with a nature that is cleansed from every residue of corruption, and with a routine joy that far exceeds the best we ever attain in this present life, think of the intensity and fervor with which our voices will give praise to God in heaven. We will be like Moses, who on the one side of the Red Sea, with Pharaoh's army bearing down, trembled and feared even though he trusted God. But once he had passed through the parted waters, had seen the destruction of Pharaoh's host, and was safe and secure on the other side, he sang with unrestrained joy of the glory of Almighty God. In heaven, we will sing Moses' hymn: 'The Lord is my strength and my song, and he has become my salvation; this is my God, and I will praise him' (Exod. 15:2).

In our present lives we are often afflicted, we stumble in sin, and the best of us are not very impressive when it comes to holiness and faith. It may be hard to believe, but everyone who is now joined to Christ in faith will one day be perfect in holiness and resplendent in the reflected glory of God. What an encouragement it is now to know what we will be then. Hugh Martin asks:

> Does not this constrain my wonder, joy, surprise, and praise...that I should be called not only to receive freely an infinite, sovereign, undeserved love, but that my reception of it should be the means of throwing light, to the angelic beings, during the eternal ages, on the glorious character and perfections of God?[183]

This is the very thing that God has promised in his Word. Daniel 12:3 says, 'Those who are wise shall shine like the brightness of the sky above; and those who turn many to righteousness, like the stars forever and ever.' Paul writes in Romans 8:18, 'I consider that the sufferings of this present time are not worth comparing with the glory that is to be revealed to us.' Therefore, however much we struggle in this pilgrim journey to heaven, those who walk with God are destined to display his glory in coming ages, to the eternal praise of his name.

God's Glory Displayed by His Grace

I have defined God's glory as the revealing of the perfections of his attributes. But Paul has something specific about God in mind when it comes to our salvation, namely, that it glorifies 'the immeasurable riches of his grace.' In creation, God displayed the glory of his power, wisdom, and beauty. But if his grace is to be displayed in glory, then God needed to exercise grace towards us. God glorifies his attributes by exercising them. He glorifies his sovereignty by reigning; he glorifies his justice by judging, and *he glorifies his grace by saving undeserving sinners like us.*

This helps us to answer in part the question of why God allowed sin to happen in the first place. God is not the author of sin (see 1 John 1:5), but since God is omnipotent and sovereign over all things (Rom. 11:36), the entry of sin was necessarily in accordance with his eternal decree. The question is Why? Paul gives one answer in Romans 11:32, 'For God has consigned all to disobedience, that he may have mercy on all.' Our verse gives us another clue, that God ordained our salvation from sin so that 'he might show the immeasurable riches of his grace' (Eph. 2:7).

Donald Grey Barnhouse told of a store window he saw in Paris. The shop was world-famous for making the finest, most intricate white lace. Some of the best specimens were on display in the store window, laid out on a background of the blackest velvet. Looking at the display, Barnhouse thought of how God uses the dark background of sin to display the marvels and intricacies and riches of his grace, about which we otherwise would never have any idea. John Owen concurs in this, explaining that our redemption from sin simultaneously increases the blessing to God's elect while magnifying his glory to a greater extent than did even the creation of the world:

> God's purpose was to raise sinners to an inconceivably better condition than they were in before sin entered the world. God now appears more glorious than ever he did before. Now he is seen to be a God who pardons iniquity and sin and who is infinitely rich in grace...To save sinners through believing will be seen to be a far more wonderful work than to create the world out of nothing.[184]

Paul writes that God glorifies 'the immeasurable riches of his grace' through our salvation. What are these riches? To remind ourselves we need only walk back through this letter to the Ephesians. In chapter 1, verse 3, Paul said that God 'blessed us with every spiritual blessing,' and then he went on to tell us what they are. Verse 4 says we were chosen by God before the foundation of the world to be holy in his sight. What is the value of that? What is it worth to be elected by God to receive the holiness without which you cannot get to heaven? Verse 5 says God predestined us to be adopted as his own sons in Christ. Verse 7 speaks of Christ's blood, shed for our forgiveness. Verse 9 speaks of the knowledge of the mystery of God's will, granted us through his Word. What do you possess that you would not give for these things?

When a jeweler wants to appraise a stone, he puts a special lens before his eye. Likewise, the riches of God's grace are seen only through the lens of faith. It is God's Word that reveals them to us, and faith in God's Word that makes these riches real to our lives.

If we have this faith and thereby see these riches, how can we be discontented in this present life? You say, 'But I am poor in this world.' But this life is short and you will soon have eternal riches beyond counting! 'But I am afflicted with temptations.' Yes, but those temptations will have less effect on you as you grow in grace, and in eternity you will be spotless and pure, untouched by any sin. 'But I am lonely.' Yes, but you can have fellowship now with the God of the universe, whose fatherly love is set on you forever. 'I am sick.' Yes, and hard though that is, what is mortal will soon be clothed in immortality, and what is corruptible with the incorruptible. So even through tears—and all of us will shed them—Christians can have joy because of the immeasurable riches of Gods' grace.

One of my favorite Bible stories that gets at this comes from the life of the prophet Jeremiah. The city of Jerusalem was besieged by the Babylonian army, and all the surrounding area had been trampled by enemy boots. God came to Jeremiah and told him to take his money and buy a plot of land in his hometown of Anathoth, which at that moment was occupied by the Babylonians. Jeremiah obeyed, buying land that no one else wanted, because to the eyes of sight it had no worth at all. By faith, he saw the future promised by God. He knew that the town would be rebuilt and would prosper in the hand of the Lord. He was buying low, and later he would sell high when God's promises were fulfilled (see Jer. 32:1–15).

The same is true for us today. When it comes to eternity, Christians are the ultimate inside traders. We know exactly where to put our money and which investments are certain to take off in the light of glory! Jesus said the kingdom of God is like a treasure a man found hidden in a field. The man who found it 'in his joy went and sold all that he had and bought that field' (Matt. 13:44). It is faith that enables us to see 'the immeasurable riches of God's grace.' If you are wise, then, instead of investing in this present, evil, passing world, you will invest your hopes, your time, your money, your sweat and tears and prayers in the kingdom of God, where, like Jeremiah's field, the riches of God's grace will yield dividends for an eternity in glory.

The riches of God's grace are revealed in his 'kindness toward us in Christ Jesus.' What is the value to God of the grace by which we are saved, but the price of his own beloved Son? What was the cost of this grace to Jesus Christ? Though he was the eternal, divine, and glorious Son of God, he set aside his glory to be born in poverty and undertake all the troubles of life in this world. He suffered the scorn and abuse of men and endured the terror of God's holy wrath on the cross, all to deliver into our hands this grace of God that truly is immeasurable in worth. This is the grace given to us to be shown in eternity, and only eternity will be big enough for the full display of the infinite riches of God's grace for us in Christ.

To God Be the Glory

I began by saying that many people today lack a sense of purpose or meaning. But Christians have been saved to a great purpose, for which we now live. The purpose of our salvation is not to take all our troubles away, but to give us the opportunity, in the midst of so many and great trials, to glorify God in this world. Jesus said, 'You are the light of the world…Let your light shine before men, so that they may see your good works and give glory to your Father who is in heaven' (Matt. 5:16). Just as our eyes cannot bare to stare into the sun, but only can stand to see its glorious rays reflected onto the nearby clouds, likewise unbelievers whose sinful natures recoil from contemplating God may look at the reality of his grace in our lives and discover God's glory for themselves.

So how do we glorify God? We glorify God, as Jesus said, by doing good works in his name (Matt. 5:16). We glorify God by telling others about his love and the free salvation that comes through faith in Christ. But most of all we glorify God through the holiness he desires in us, by cultivating the fruit of his Spirit in our hearts, by being no longer conformed to the world but transformed by the renewing of our minds through his Word (Rom. 12:2). God made us to bear his own image, and it is by the holiness that conforms to the character of Christ that we most glorify him in this world. Whatever else is different about individual Christians—and we are all very different in many ways—we are unified in this great purpose: to live for the glory of God in the beauty of holiness.

I want to go beyond even this and say that glorifying God is not only our purpose, but it is the great privilege of our lives. If you have ever met veterans of World War II, a war in which the issues of good and evil were clear and our soldiers knew themselves to be part of a noble crusade, you will find that they considered it the great privilege of their lives. Despite all the hardships they endured, some of them wounded and even bearing lifelong disabilities, they still would say, 'I am so honored to have been a part of it. And it was such a glory to be among such a great group of guys, a band of brothers and heroes!' This is how we should feel about our calling in Christ to bring glory to God. Martyn Lloyd-Jones writes:

> The privilege of being used of God in this way to vindicate His own eternal, glorious character! Why am I in this? Why did He ever look upon me?... Do we not all feel like saying that? Who am I, and what am I, that God should ever have looked upon me and chosen me to be part of His plan and His purpose...Christian people, think of yourselves like that, and go on to glory.[185]

Everyone, not just Christians, but everyone, will ultimately glorify God. Whether you are a believer or not, you will glorify God at the end of this age and forever after that. God's chief end is to glorify God, and being all-powerful, God will certainly achieve that end in each of our lives. But there are other things about him to glorify than his grace. God is just, holy, and almighty, and these he will glorify in the eternal condemnation of sinners who reject the offer of his gospel. James Montgomery Boice writes:

> Every person who has ever lived or will ever live must glorify God, either actively or passively, either willingly or unwillingly, either in heaven or in hell. You will glorify God. Either you will glorify him as the object of his mercy and glory, which will be seen in you. Or you will glorify him in your rebellion and unbelief by being made the object of his wrath and power at the final judgment.[186]

How much better for you to glorify God for his grace, exercised in his kindness to you in Jesus Christ, if you will turn from your sins, believe on the Lord Jesus Christ, and offer your life for the praise of the glory of the grace of our loving God.

24

By Grace, through Faith
Ephesians 2:8-9

There are some verses in the Bible that are so important to our understanding of the gospel that every Christian should know them by heart. John 3:16 is one of these: 'For God so loved the world, that he gave his only Son, that whoever believes in him should not perish but have eternal life.' Ephesians 2:8-9 falls into this same category, as Bible teaching essential to a sound grasp of Christianity. Here, the apostle Paul makes a definitive statement relating grace, faith and works in salvation: 'For by grace you have been saved through faith. And this is not your own doing; it is the gift of God, not a result of works, so that no one may boast.'

As we study these vitally important statements, Paul gives us three tasks. First, we must understand that salvation is by grace. Second, we must embrace faith as the God-given means of receiving this grace. Third, we must distinguish between faith and works so that our boasting will be only in God.

Salvation by Grace

In Ephesians 2:1-10, Paul's purpose is to explain how salvation comes to us as individuals. But he wants to do more than explain the doctrine of salvation: he wants to magnify the glory of God because of it. To that end, his key message is the one that opens verse 8: 'For by grace you have been saved.'

For Paul, this is the stupendous good news of the gospel, that God saves sinners by grace alone. Martyn Lloyd-Jones explains,

> It is in spite of us that God forgives us. We are Christian not because we are good people; we are Christian because, though we were bad people, God had mercy upon us and sent his Son to die for us. We are saved entirely by the grace of God; there is no human contribution whatsoever, and if you think there is, you are denying the central biblical doctrine.[187]

This is what Paul has been driving at in this whole section. This claim is why he began chapter 2 by saying that men and women in sin are spiritually dead, as unable to contribute something positive to their salvation as a dead man is able to rise from the grave. This is why in the midst of verses 4-6, which recount what salvation has done to us, Paul broke in and exclaimed, 'By grace you have been saved' (v. 5). This is why verse 7 gives as the reason for our salvation, 'so that in the coming

177

ages he might show the immeasurable riches of his grace.' Salvation is all of grace. This is the glory of Christianity, that God saves us who had no power to save ourselves, had nothing to commend ourselves to God, and had nothing to offer in payment. This is Paul's great assertion: 'For by grace you have been saved.'

There are two main ways in which the word *grace* may be taken. First, it denotes *an attitude within God*. God is gracious. A.W. Tozer writes, 'Grace is the good pleasure of God that inclines Him to bestow benefits upon the undeserving…A self-caused propensity to pity the wretched, spare the guilty, welcome the outcast, and bring into favor those who were before under just disapprobation.'[188] As the result of God's grace, Christians receive blessings we have not deserved and could never merit.

It is grace that causes a wealthy man to voluntarily pay the tuition of a poor student who otherwise could never go to college. It is by grace that a family takes in an orphan and adopts him or her into a loving home. But all these human examples, glorious as they are, pale before the grace of God. God responds to the guilt and rebellion of his creatures by offering his own Son to pay the debt of their sin and by renewing them with a new spirit to love and serve him and to enjoy blessings as his children. We are saved because of the gracious love in God that causes him to show such kindness to us in Jesus Christ.

No wonder that when Paul considers God's grace, he wants us to praise God. What a terrible pity that so many people hate and refuse God, not knowing his grace, which they so greatly need. This is what we need to tell people, that God has grace to forgive and bless them. This is what God wants: to be our God and be gracious to us.

The second way in which we should consider the term *grace* is as a system of disbursement.

God has blessings to give. God has eternal life to bestow on his creatures; he has fellowship with himself; he has participation in the blessed rule of his Son, Jesus Christ. The question is, How will he grant these blessings?

There are only two ways we can gain or receive something: either by earning it or by receiving it as a gift. Likewise, God may grant his blessings on the basis of merit or of grace. In Romans 4:4, Paul acknowledges these options: 'Now to the one who works, his wages are not counted as a gift but as his due.' These are the only two possibilities: as a gift or as our due. History shows that man prefers merit as the way of gaining God's blessings. This is what human religion always teaches unless corrected by God's Word. Man wants to stand on his own two feet and pay his own way. He wants to preserve his own dignity, even in the presence of God, and receive a salvation that will promote his own glory.

The problem is that man has merited not God's blessing but God's condemnation. This was Paul's point in verses 1–3: 'By nature, we are children of wrath.' Just by being born as members of the rebel human race, just by being the offspring of the sinners Adam and Eve, no man or woman can ever stand before God and demand blessing. Furthermore, as Paul writes in Romans 3:23, 'All have sinned and fall short of the glory of God.' Yes, merit is a way in which you might procure God's blessings, but it is a way that is no longer open to you or any other sinner. The prophet Isaiah knew this, lamenting that even our supposed good works 'are like a polluted garment' (Isa. 64:6), helplessly tainted by sin.

People say, 'All I want is for God to be just to me.' But you do not want God's justice; under God's justice you will be justly condemned to hell. But because God is gracious, and because he wants his grace to be glorified forever, God offers another way for you to be saved, by grace. God offers to satisfy his justice through the death of Jesus Christ in your place. God will then bless you with salvation—forgiveness and eternal life—as a gift. The result is, as verse 9 concludes, 'that no one may boast' before God. God wants to be God and he wants the worship of his people, not the boasting of self-righteous creatures. 'Humble yourselves before the Lord,' says the Bible, 'and he will exalt you' (James 4:10). God delights to save by grace, so that no one may boast before him.

SALVATION THROUGH FAITH

The Bible makes it plain that not everyone is or will be saved, so there has to be something that distinguishes those who have received God's grace and that brings it to them. Some people think this is nationality; Americans seem to think, for instance, that by virtue of our nationality God is on our side. Others think it is church membership or baptism; so long as they stay in the church and receive its approval, they will be all right. Others believe it is some intense emotional experience that ensures God's favor. But Paul tells us in verse 8 the one thing that provides us with God's grace and thus saves us: 'For by grace you have been saved through faith.' Salvation is *by grace* and *through faith*.

Faith is another word that requires definition. Norman Vincent Peale popularized a concept of faith that is widely held today. To him, faith was a general sort of optimism. His best-selling book, *The Power of Positive Thinking*, taught that if we believe all things are possible they will be. He wrote, 'According to your faith in yourself, according to your faith in your job, according to your faith in God, this far will you get and no further.'[189] Faith, according to this view, is a power that you need to exercise.

But this is not the Bible's teaching regarding faith. What matters about biblical faith is not the faith itself but faith's object. What matters is not just *that* you believe, but *what* you believe and *in whom* you believe. If what you believe in is not true and not saving, then your faith will be in vain. Christian faith is in God and in Jesus Christ, in the truths of God's Word and his promises for those who trust him. Faith is relying on God, receiving him and his Word for salvation. God has spoken and we are to believe his Word; God has acted for our salvation and we are to rely upon his saving work in Jesus Christ.

When we think of saving faith we should think of three necessary components. The first of these is *knowledge*. To have faith in something you must have knowledge and understanding of it. This is why the Bible is so important to Christian faith. We must know what God has revealed about himself, what he says about us and our situation, what he has done for us, and especially about Jesus Christ and his life, death, and resurrection for our salvation.

But knowledge alone is not enough. There are plenty of scholars who can explain all the doctrines of the Bible, but who do not believe they are true. Therefore, saving faith must include *belief* or *assent*. We must not only know what God has revealed, but we must believe in it.

But even assent is not enough to have saving faith. The apostle James pointed out that the demons know about God and believe that he is who he says he is. But they tremble! (James 2:19). Saving faith requires that we not only know and believe what the Bible says about God and Jesus Christ. It also requires *commitment*.

The first part of commitment is *trust*. Committing to God means trusting in him and in his Word and in the Savior Jesus Christ. Trust involves personal acceptance and reliance.

The Westminster Confession of Faith helpfully states that 'the principal acts of saving faith are accepting, receiving, and resting upon Christ alone for justification, sanctification, and eternal life' (XIV.2). Charles Spurgeon writes, 'The chief part of faith lies in…taking hold of it as being ours, and in the resting on it for salvation…It will not save me to know that Christ is *a* Saviour; but it will save me to *trust* him to be *my Saviour*.'[190]

Commitment also involves a *surrender* of ourselves to God. Arthur Pink explains that faith

> lies in the complete surrender of the heart and life to a divine Person. It consists in a throwing down of the weapons of our rebellion against Him. It is the total disowning of allegiance to the old master—Satan, sin, self, and a declaring 'we will not have this Man to reign over us' (Luke 19:14)…It is 'receiving Christ Jesus the Lord' (Col. 2:6), giving Him the throne of our hearts, turning over to Him the control and regulation of our lives.[191]

This is precisely what we find in the Bible when people came to saving faith in Jesus Christ. Doubting Thomas knew Jesus, but he held back from believing. Jesus appeared to him after the resurrection and offered to have Thomas place his fingers in his wounds. At that moment, Thomas came to a saving faith: he worshiped Jesus, saying, 'My Lord and my God!' (John 20:28).

Zacchaeus was a sinful tax collector who preyed upon the weak. When Jesus passed through Jericho, Zacchaeus was interested and so he climbed into the sycamore tree to see him. Jesus called Zacchaeus to himself, and we know from what happened that Zacchaeus committed himself to Jesus in saving faith. He replied, 'Lord, the half of my goods I give to the poor. And if I have defrauded anyone of anything, I restore it fourfold' (Luke 19:8).

Acts 16 tells us about Lydia, a successful businesswoman who Paul met in Philippi. God opened her heart and, having believed, she opened up her house and urged that Paul allow her to support his work. Believing, she gave herself wholly to Christ and his gospel.

The apostle Paul himself provides a prime example of saving faith. He was a violent hater of Christians, devoting himself to their torment and destruction. But when Jesus revealed himself to Paul and called him into his service, Paul offered the whole of his life to proclaiming the gospel. He who had wielded a harsh sword of hatred became the greatest teacher of the glory of God's grace.

These are examples of true saving faith, which always culminates in a commitment to Christ that involves personal trust and surrender. Saving faith involves what happens in a wedding ceremony. In the gospel, God's Son says to us, 'I will be your Savior and will take you as my bride.' In faith, we reply, 'I trust in you alone for my salvation, and I give myself into your service and rely upon you for all my blessing forever.' Jesus then gives us his own name. We were Sinner but now are Christian, and this denotes the change that is to characterize our lives.

The Gift of God

Faith is a subject that is often confused, which is why we need such careful teaching on it. We have already noted that faith is not merely a sort of optimism, but depends on its object. Furthermore, saving faith involves knowledge, belief, and commitment. But Paul says three things in verse 8 that we also need to appreciate. The first has to do with the word *through*, which Paul applies to faith. We are saved *by* grace and *through* faith.

The point is how faith functions in our salvation. Paul says that grace comes to us *through* faith. One way to think of this is of faith as a vessel in which grace is received. Think of a picnic on a hot day, in which there is a large container of lemonade. The soothing drink is available, but you still need a cup in which to pour it. If someone has no cup, they cannot have anything to drink. The cup is not a way of earning the lemonade, but is the means of receiving it. Likewise, faith does not merit us God's grace, but is the means whereby we receive salvation from God.[192]

Perhaps an even better way of understanding how we are saved through faith is to think of faith as the channel by which salvation flows to us. Grace flows through faith as water flows through a pipe. This keeps us from thinking that it is the strength or virtue of our faith that saves us, when, in fact, we are saved by the grace which comes through our faith. Salvation is *by grace*—that is, the ground or the basis for our salvation—and *through faith*—that is, the channel by which salvation comes to me.

Next, we must understand where faith comes from. Do you trust Christ because you are better or more spiritually motivated than people who don't? Is faith just the way we prove our worth and earn salvation? Many people in the church think this way, that faith is basically a work that God accepts because full obedience to the law is just too hard. Paul destroys such a theory in verse 8, writing, 'This is not your doing; it is the gift of God.'

There is dispute among scholars as to what Paul is saying here. Does *gift* point back to 'salvation' or to 'faith'? Is Paul saying that salvation is not our own doing or that faith is not our own doing, but is the gift of God? The answer is that it does not matter; Paul's point is the same in either case. If salvation is not of our own doing, and salvation comes through faith, then Paul's point must be that faith is God's gift and not something we produce or possess on our own.

This is why the salvation that comes through faith is by grace alone. Obviously, faith is something we do; we are actively involved in it. We have to believe and commit to God. But, since faith is something God works into us, something he gives out of his own sheer grace, salvation is not a result of our works. In Romans 4:16, Paul writes, 'That is why it depends on faith, in order that the promise may rest on grace.' Faith is the one way in which I may be personally entered into salvation, while that salvation remains the gift of Gods grace, with all glory going to him. Faith is not an achievement, but faith is a gift God graciously works into us by the power of his Holy Spirit. God promised this in Ezekiel 36:26, 'I will give you a new heart, and a new spirit I will put within you. And I will remove the heart of stone and give you a heart of flesh.'

Why is it that you believe on Jesus whereas your old friend does not? Both of you were, according to Paul, 'dead in your trespasses.' So why are you saved and not others? The answer is not because of something you did or something better in you, for there is nothing better in you. The answer is the free and sovereign grace of God, who gives faith to those whom he would save as the instrument of their receiving Jesus Christ and all the blessings that are in him.

For this reason, we should never trust in our faith—weak and inconstant as it is—but in God who showed his grace for us by giving us the faith that joins us to a strong Savior in Jesus Christ.

Paul makes this clear with the third statement he makes regarding faith. First he described it as the vessel or channel through which grace comes to us. Then he called faith God's gift. Finally, in verse 9, he contrasts faith with works. He says, 'By grace you have been saved through faith…Not a result of works, so that no one may boast.'

We contrasted grace with merit. Those are the two ways of salvation and, having sinned, we now can be saved only by grace. Similarly, faith and works are two opposing instruments of salvation. We merit salvation through works, but we receive grace through faith.

Another way of saying this is to observe that you must trust either in your own works or in the works of Jesus Christ. Someone's works must commend you to God, causing him to receive you as worthy and righteous. Most people today are trusting in their own works, even if they are religious ones. Why should you be allowed to enter into heaven? we ask. They reply in terms of their own works: I am a basically good person, I have attended church, I have given money, I have prayed, I have memorized verses in the Bible, I have not committed any serious crimes.

That is salvation through works! How appealing it is according to the spirit of our age. Self-justification is the way of man. Self-glory is the kind of salvation sinners want. But understand that God utterly rejects anyone who comes to him that way. Whatever you think of yourself, God cannot and will not get over the reality of your sin. You have exalted yourself against him and stained yourself with iniquity. 'The wages of sin is death,' he says (Rom. 6:23). Jesus said to such people who do not trust him as Savior, 'Unless you believe that I am he you will die in your sins' (John 8:24).

This was all dramatized at the beginning of the Bible when Cain and Abel, the two sons of Adam and Eve, approached God for acceptance. Cain offered his works, the fruit of the soil he had farmed. It seemed so impressive to him, but not to God. Abel came not with a symbol of his works but a symbol of his faith in God's promise to save. He brought a lamb, pointing forward to the cross of Jesus Christ. Cain by works was rejected while Abel through faith was blessed.

Abel put his faith not in his own works but in the work of Jesus Christ. So must we. Christians are saved by works—just not works that we do. We are saved by the work of Christ, fulfilling all righteousness in our place and dying for our sins on the cross. By faith, we repudiate our own works and receive his for our salvation. As Augustus Toplady put it in his hymn:

> Not the labors of my hands
>   can fulfill thy law's demands
> could my zeal no respite know,
>   could my tears forever flow
> all for sin could not atone;
>   thou must save, and thou alone.'[193]

'The wages of sin is death,' Paul wrote. That is our problem and our works cannot solve it. He therefore added the solution: 'But the free gift of God is eternal life in Christ Jesus our Lord' (Rom. 6:23). For this reason, salvation by grace alone, through faith alone, is salvation in Jesus Christ alone. It is coming to God as Abel did, looking in faith to the cross of Christ, where the grace of God brought forth a Savior to take away our sin and grant to us eternal life.

No Boasting?

Paul concludes this vital passage saying, 'So that no one may boast.' I want to conclude by saying that Paul really does not mean that. Paul does not mean that in reply to this salvation by grace, through faith, in Christ, we ought not to boast. What he means is that we must not boast in ourselves. But the very thing Paul wants is for us to boast in God, to glory in God, to extol before all the world this salvation that is by grace, through faith in Jesus Christ.

Indeed, this is the best way for you and me to make a difference in our generation. Ours is an age that delights in boasting in self. Ours is the time of the end-zone dance and the self-promoting political ad. Christians are to stand in contrast to the vain boasts of a spiritually dead, sin-enslaved, God-condemned world, by living humbly before God. By grace, we speak of a God whose mercy overwhelms our sin. Through faith, we testify to an all-sufficient salvation freely given from the hands of our loving God. This is our boast, given by the testimony of our lives: 'To God alone be the glory, for the riches of his grace and his kindness toward us in Christ Jesus.'

25

God's Workmanship

Ephesians 2:10

One of the areas of greatest confusion and controversy in Christian theology is the place of works in our salvation. Despite the clear Bible teaching on this matter, many Christians err on one side or the other.

One error is to makes works a prior condition of salvation. This is the error of the Roman Catholic Church, which teaches that we must be justified by a combination of faith and works. Their formula is faith + works = justification. They say that faith is like the band of a ring, and works are like the jewel it holds and which gives its value. The whole purpose of faith, therefore, is to present works for salvation.

The Protestant Reformation made its principal quarrel with Rome over this issue. The problem with justification by faith and works is that you can never know that your works are enough. Indeed, according to the apostle Paul, your works never *can* be good enough to justify you. 'No one does good,' he insists, 'no not one' (Rom. 3:12). Therefore, he taught in Ephesians 2:8-9, 'By grace you have been saved through faith…not as a result of works.' Faith is the ring, we proclaim, that presents not our works but the jewel of Christ and his work for us.

The error on the other side of works is held by many evangelicals. This is the error that says since salvation is not by works, then works don't matter at all. So long as I believe on Jesus, so long as I once made a decision for Christ or walked down an aisle at the minister's invitation, then whatever else I do has no impact on my salvation. This is called the *antinomian* view, *nomos* being the Greek word for law and *anti* meaning opposed to.

In recent years, some have insisted that so long as you profess faith in Christ, your salvation is assured even if you never bear any spiritual fruit and if you continue in a lifestyle of sin all the rest of your life.[194] Nothing could be more in conflict with the Bible's teaching. As Paul asked in Romans 6:1-2, 'Are we to continue in sin that grace may abound? By no means! How can we who died to sin still live in it!' Many who hold such a view, while filling our churches, will hear the dreadful words from our Lord when he returns: 'I never knew you; depart from me, you workers of lawlessness' (Matt. 6:23).

The Necessity of Works

The first thing Ephesians 2:10 teaches us is *the necessity of good works*. Works do not cause salvation, but salvation invariably causes good works. Having been saved from sin by grace through faith, we are saved to a life of good works as part of the on-going process of growth in holiness that we call sanctification. 'For we are [God's] workmanship, created in Christ Jesus for good works, which God prepared beforehand, that we should walk in them.'

Charles Spurgeon points out that if we were to auction off the pieces of salvation, the bidding for forgiveness would go very high but few would offer much for holiness. He writes, 'Suppose I took sanctification, the giving up of all sin, a thorough change of heart, leaving off drunkenness and swearing; many would say, "I don't want that; I should like to go to heaven, but I do not want that holiness." But God is not auctioning off mere portions of salvation; you must have all or none. You must have Christ as Savior and as Lord or not at all.' Spurgeon concludes, 'God will never divide the gospel. He will not give justification to that man, and sanctification to another—pardon to one, and holiness to another. No, it all goes together. Whom he calls, them he justifies; whom he justifies, them he sanctifies'[195] Just as light and heat are inseparably joined to the rays of the sun, likewise justification and sanctification are inseparable parts of the gospel. We are saved by faith alone, but saving faith never is alone. It always produces the good works that God desires.

This was Paul's teaching all through his many letters. In Titus 2:14 he wrote that Jesus died 'to redeem us from all lawlessness and to purify for himself a people for his own possession who are zealous for good works.' In 2 Corinthians 9:8, he wrote that God provides for all our needs, 'so that…you may abound in every good work.'

It is especially Jesus' teaching that we think of when it comes to the need for good works. In John 15:8, he taught, 'By this my Father is glorified, that you bear much fruit and so prove to be my disciples' (John 15:8). The fruit of good works does not make us disciples, but it glorifies God and proves that we are Christ's followers.

These passages prove that good works are necessary to salvation: necessary not as a *cause* but as a *consequence*. Without good works there is no reason to believe you are a disciple of Christ, and there is much reason to doubt that you are. First John 2:5–6 says, 'By this we may be sure that we are in [Christ]: whoever says he abides in him ought to walk the same way in which he walked.'

A good way to assess your spiritual state is how you respond to teaching like this. Do you resent being told that salvation involves good works and a changed life? Would you prefer a salvation that delivers you from the penalty of sin but not from sin itself? What is your attitude towards holiness? Do you want a purer, more godly, more loving heart, or are you happy with the one you have? The salvation that Jesus gives is one that involves a desire for a transformed life, and an increasing realization of that desire.

The Source of Works

Whenever the Bible talks about the necessity of good works, people begin to get nervous and uncertain about themselves. This is because Christians know all too well the power of our sin. But Paul reminds us in this verse not only of the necessity of good works but also their source. He says, 'We are God's workmanship, created in Christ Jesus for good works.' This means that the source of our good works is God's work in us. We are saved by grace and grace is the cause of our growth in holiness, so that our sanctification and works do not rely on our strength but on God's.

Earlier in this chapter, Paul said that God came to us when we were spiritually dead, when we had not the slightest desire to serve him, nor the smallest bit of spiritual life (Eph. 2:1-3). Paul described our salvation as a spiritual resurrection (Eph. 2:4-5). It was God who breathed spiritual life into our hearts in the first place, and it is God who will supply the strength we need to bear the fruit of good deeds.

I find that many Christians lack hope for godliness and strength for leading a changed life because they think they have to do so in their own power. But Paul says that we are God's workmanship. That means it is his work in us that will change us. Perhaps the best statement of this principle is found in Philippians 2:12-13. Paul writes, 'Work out your salvation with fear and trembling' (Phil. 2:12). This means that we are to apply our faith to every area of our lives, changing our approach to work, play, the way we treat people, sexuality, money, career ambitions, life goals, and daily habits. But, lest we despair of so difficult a task, Paul adds, 'For it is God who works in you, both to will and to work for his good pleasure' (Phil. 2:13). Yes, you have to work it out, but only as God is first working it into you. We change our approach because God changes our attitudes, changing our minds, hearts and desires to match his own.

This change happens especially through the ordinary means of grace God has provided: God's Word, prayer, and the sacraments. It is impossible to overstate the importance of coming to church each week, worshiping God, and hearing his Word faithfully taught. The same is true about personal Bible study and prayer. Paul writes in 2 Timothy 3:16-17, 'All Scripture is breathed out by God and profitable for teaching, for reproof, for correction, and for training in righteousness, that the man of God may be competent, equipped for every good work.'

Paul specifies that we were created for good works 'in Christ Jesus.' If you are born again and have a living faith, it was so that you would become more and more like Jesus, and so that Jesus himself would work in you powerfully through the Holy Spirit he sends.

This is what transforms our Christianity from a weak defeatism to a mighty boldness to do God's will. How can I dare to shine brightly for God? Because I was created anew in Christ for this very purpose and it is God's work in me to do this very thing! How can I ever leave behind former sins? Because God is giving me new pleasures that rise far above the old. How can I be willing to sacrifice for others and stop living for myself? Because I know a power working in me, a heavenly spring of life from which I am now able to drink, the cup of faith having been placed into my hand by God himself.

This is far more than merely asking, 'What Would Jesus Do?' as if he supplies only an example, leaving us to supply our own power. It is asking instead, 'What *will* Jesus do as I trust him, call upon him for strength, and renew my mind and heart through his Word?' Christianity is not merely a human effort to imitate Christ. Rather, it is 'Christ in you, the hope of glory' (Col. 1:27). As Paul says elsewhere, 'I no longer live, but Christ lives in me' (Gal. 2:20).

Jesus is sometimes depicted as a mountain guide who climbs up before us and then calls down commands for us to follow. This is true, so long as we realize that he also lets down a strong rope—which we might compare to his Holy Spirit—and for every feeble step we take upward he pulls mightily on that rope so that far sooner than we imagine we have climbed far higher than we ever thought we would. God's work, in Christ, by the Spirit, is the source of the new and glorious life we begin to lead as his cherished people.

A Plan for Good Works

The third thing Paul tells us in Ephesians 2:10 is the most amazing of all. He writes of the *necessity* of works, and the *source* of works, and then goes so far as to speak of a *plan* for works that God has for each of our lives.

Sometime ago I saw a bumper-sticker that read: 'God sent me into this world with work that I was to do. I'm so far behind that I will never die!' According to the apostle Paul, the second part of that may not be true, although it feels like it, but the first part most certainly is true. He describes our good works as those 'which God prepared beforehand, that we should walk in them.'

This means that God's plan for each of us includes specific good works that he has foreordained for us to do. This does not mean merely that God has designed that we would do good works in general. The Greek word means not merely to *intend* but to *prepare in advance*. Not only were we created for good works, but good works were created for us. Our job, Paul says, is to 'walk in them.' God has laid down a path of situations and good works for us, and we are to walk down that path seeking to do his will.

What good works has God ordained? First, God has revealed his law. Believers need to know and study the Ten Commandments; we will find that they provide us a path of life. David said in Psalm 19, 'The precepts of the Lord are right, rejoicing the heart; the commandment of the Lord is pure, enlightening the eyes' (Ps. 19:18).

In every situation, we are to obey God's law— worshiping him only, reverencing God's name, keeping holy the Sabbath, honoring those in authority, not doing violence but promoting others' well-being, guarding against lust, respecting others' property, speaking the truth in love, and cultivating godliness with contentment. The Ten Commandments are enormously practical. The shame is that so few believers even know what they are, much less use them as a guide for good works. As you go to work, as you start a day at school or in the home, you should say to God, 'I have hidden your word in my heart, that I might not sin against you' (Ps. 119:11).

Second, God has given each of us particular gifts, abilities and opportunities. We are to be faithful stewards of them, serving God's kingdom, promoting God's glory, imparting practical blessings. Some of us have the gift of teaching, so we are to teach. Others are empowered for exhortation and encouragement, others are gifted in helps, or in administration, or in comfort. Each of us is given a role to play and a way to serve, and it is important that we do our part as God predestined for us to do.

I find that a common problem in life is envy and discontentment. Everyone wants the gifts somebody else has, especially if they lead to praise and notoriety. Everyone wants to be in someone else's situation. People in the North dream of Florida; Southerners dream of snow. But you are where you are and who you are because God wanted you to be this way. He has good to be done in your life that no one else can do. He wants your life to provide a particular lens on his glory that none other can. You just have to be yourself in Christ, and do the good works God prepared in advance for you to do.

Third, there are good works that all Christians are to embrace as a willing duty. We are all different in many ways, but we are all called to pray, spread the gospel, worship with God's people and support God's work through generous giving. This is God's plan for us, and he has made full provision for our blessing through obedience.

If we will take these three categories seriously— obeying God's law, using our gifts, fulfilling the duties that Christians all share—our lives will be utterly transformed to the praise of God. We and others will see what Paul was so excited about in the teaching of this chapter. He began chapter 2 by describing a life, a walk, under the power of the world, the devil and the flesh. But now we walk in the power of God, leading a life that is energized by grace. What an exciting change!

One thing this means is that your life matters. There are things you can do that nobody else can do. Although you do not know what lies around the next corner, you know that, whatever it is, you can do God's will in it because God created it for you and you for it. G. Campbell Morgan wrote, 'If I can once accept this teaching and rest upon it I shall take my way into every new circumstance knowing these two things absolutely: first, God has prepared me in Christ Jesus for whatever the day has in store for me, and, secondly, all that to which I come, step by step as the veil recedes or the mists melt, though unknown to me, is not unknown to Him. Good works are afore prepared, afore ordained for us that we should walk in them.'[196]

Then, when it comes time for you to die, you can have the satisfaction of knowing that all your work is done. In the spring of 2000, the noted Bible teacher James Montgomery Boice learned that he had only weeks to live because of an aggressive cancer. He began working furiously, harnessing his rapidly fading strength to finish important projects and order the affairs of his far-flung ministries. I was often with him during those days, since he asked me to assist him in finishing his work. Before he got very far, however, it became clear that Dr. Boice simply did not have the stamina needed to continue. Was he frustrated? Angry? The answer is No. I will never forget the peace and the satisfied joy on his face when he realized his strength was gone and said to me, 'My work is now finished. I have done all I can, and therefore all that God intended for me to do in this life.' Not able to tie up all the loose ends, he simply put them into God's hand, as we prayed to the Lord together. Boice soon experienced what the voice from heaven stated in Revelation 14:13: 'Blessed are the dead who die in the Lord…They will rest from their labor, for their deeds will follow them.'

God's Workmanship

In the words that begin verse 10, Paul sums up all he has been teaching about salvation: 'We are his workmanship.' The Greek word is *poiema*, from which comes our word *poem*. It is a general term for a work of art. This means that our salvation is God's work and relies on his almighty power and sovereign will. It also means that of all God's great creations, the redeemed sinner who believes and lives for God is the greatest of all his masterworks.

'The heavens declare the glory of God,' says Psalm 19:1. Look out at night and see the splashing of lights from distant galaxies, and you know something of the grandeur of God's creation. Yet as marvelous as that is, the cosmos is not God's masterwork. Go find the most perfect shoreline. Watch as the sunset dances on the waters. Or stand beneath the purple mountains bathed in snow, pillars of granite thrusting skyward. The beauty of nature is overwhelming, yet these things are not God's highest work of art.

Psalm 8 reminds us that the tiny cry of a baby displays the glory of God. Surely this is the apex of the natural creation, a newborn baby, so complex and yet simple, eyes open, arms reaching for life. It is a physical marvel, its mind a dazzling computer recording everything it experiences. A baby's eyes focus light on the retina, simultaneously stimulating 125 million nerve endings. In a millisecond, that data is processed by the brain into a single image.[197] What a display of God's wisdom and power is the human body!

But there is something more magnificent than even that, says our verse. God's highest masterpiece is his spiritual transformation of the man or woman long dead in sin, who God raised from spiritual death, and now is saved to do good works in his name. God is spirit, and here is the great marvel of the spiritual realm, where Christ is enthroned. 'If anyone is in Christ,' Paul wrote, 'he is a new creation; the old has gone, the new has come!' (2 Cor. 5:17). This is God's master work of art, accomplished by the blood of Christ and the breath of the Holy Spirit.

This is the work taking place in your life if you are in Christ. It means that whatever God is calling you to do, he will ensure that you are able to do it. Knowing this, Paul said, 'I can do everything through him who gives me strength' (Phil. 4:13). It means that whatever trials or sufferings you are enduring, they have a purpose in God's plan for your life. You are his workmanship, and he is equipping you for good works to come. It means that what really matters is not where you are in God's plan for your life, but that you are in Christ, that you are born again, and that you therefore are a masterpiece of God's grace. And what God has begun by grace, he will complete and perfect in the day of Christ's return (Phil. 1:6).

Let me conclude with a few questions. Do you have any experience with what Paul is saying here? Are you aware of the gentle but unrelenting pressure of God's loving hands upon the clay of your life? Do you desire for more of God, more of his Word, more of his Spirit? Do you yearn for holiness? Are you doing works you never thought you would do, acting in ways that can only be accounted for by God?

If you know nothing of this, it is a warning that things are not well with your soul. Especially if you want only to be forgiven but not to be changed, then you completely misunderstand the salvation God is offering you. Martyn Lloyd-Jones rightly asserts: 'There is no value in a profession of Christianity unless it is accompanied by a desire to be like Christ, a desire to be rid of sin, a desire after positive holiness.'[198]

Until this has happened to you, then put aside all thoughts of work because you cannot do them. What you need is to be born again, to be saved by grace through faith. But if you have that desire not only to be forgiven but to be changed, to be rid of sin, and to be holy, then take heart. Rejoice! For that can only be because you are in Christ and God is working into you what he wants you to start working out. Press on to do good works in his power and to the glory of his name. 'For we are his workmanship, created in Christ Jesus for good works, which God prepared beforehand, that we should walk in them' (Eph. 2:10).

26

Without Christ

Ephesians 2:11–12

'Remember!' That has been the rallying cry of many a statesman and orator. 'Remember the Alamo!' was the motto that led Sam Houston's Texas Rangers in their war with Mexico. 'Never forget' is today emblazoned on t-shirts and bumper-stickers over photographs of the World Trade Center towers and the numbers 9–11–01.

'Remember' is also one of the most important commands in the Bible. Jesus spoke from heaven to the churches in the Book of Revelation, commanding, 'Remember, then, what you received and heard. Keep it, and repent' (Rev. 3:3).

When Israel entered into the Promised Land, remembering was given to them as the key to future faithfulness. The people had just come through the exodus—a great deliverance from bondage into freedom. Moses warned them, 'Take care, and keep your soul diligently, lest you forget the things that your eyes have seen, and lest they depart from your heart all the days of your life. Make them known to your children and your children's children' (Deut. 4:9). Remember! When the people failed to remember, the Book of Judges tells us that a generation grew up that fell into sin and judgment.

I know of a mother who sends her children out the door each morning, saying, 'Remember who you are, and whose you are!' That is what Paul has to say to us. Having given some of the clearest and most glorious teaching about salvation in Ephesians 2:1–10, he commands us in the next verse, 'Therefore remember!'

This is the very first command that Paul gives in Ephesians, which indicates its significance. Before he gets to any of the practical instruction that will follow, he first commands us, 'Remember!' This is how the Christian life is lived, by remembering what God has done for us and living in light of those truths.

Two Kinds of People

Ephesians 2:11 brings us to a point of transition in Paul's letter, and it would be wise now to review where we are. Chapter 2 presents Ephesians' theme of peace through grace in Jesus Christ. Verses 1–10 present the peace we have with God as he reconciles us to himself. We were objects of wrath but now are objects of his mercy. We were in bondage to the world, the flesh, and the devil, but now we are God's workmanship. The rest of the chapter, starting in verse 11, speaks of peace on earth as God reconciles believers one to another in Christ. At the end of the chapter 1,

Paul prayed that we might know the riches of our salvation; in chapter 2 he spells these out as peace with God and peace with one another, all by God's grace in Jesus Christ.

Paul begins this new section by recognizing the division among us. It is said that there are two kinds of people—those who think there are two kinds of people and those who don't! Paul is the kind of person who thinks there are two kinds of people. He wants us to remember what we were before and what we are now in Christ. He writes, 'Therefore remember that at one time you [were] Gentiles in the flesh, called 'the uncircumcision' by what is called the circumcision, which is made in the flesh by hands' (Eph. 2:11).

Whenever there is division there is always name-calling. Children learn this at school. Adults know this in politics, in our family squabbles, and sometimes even in the church. The ancient world knew about this as well, and Paul points to the chasm that most divided the ancient world, that between Jews and Gentiles. This division between them was highlighted by circumcision, the practice of removing the flesh of the male foreskin. Writing to the Ephesian Christians, people living in Asia Minor, Paul notes that by and large they were Gentiles, whom the Jews ridiculed as 'the uncircumcision'.

God gave circumcision to mark the Israelites as separate from the world and holy to God. The Israelites were to use their holiness to attract the pagan nations to the true God. Instead, the Jews used it as a mark of superiority and contempt for others. Far from caring for the spiritual state of the Gentiles, the Jews rejoiced in their belief that Gentiles were created only to stoke the fires of hell. They would not converse with Gentiles. They even passed a law forbidding a Jew to help a Gentile woman in childbirth, since that would bring another Gentile into the world.[199]

Sadly, some Christians look down on irreligious people in a similar way. They consider them more to be shunned than to be won by the grace of Christ. That spirit is as offensive now as was the Jews' attitude toward the Gentiles. By referring to Gentiles as 'the uncircumcision,' the Jews were rejoicing in their ignorance of God.

For their part, the Gentiles weren't wild about the Jews either. They threw the insult back, calling them, 'the circumcision.' Proud in their possession of Greek culture, the Gentiles looked down on everyone who did not participate in their way of life.

What mattered was not circumcision but the division, hatred, and warfare among men. Human beings will divide and fight over practically anything; for all our supposed progress in the centuries since Paul lived, the world has found no solution for this problem.

Without Christ

Notice what Paul says about circumcision, namely, that it was only something 'made in the flesh with hands.' Galatians 6:15 gave his clearest opinion, saying, 'Neither circumcision counts for anything, nor uncircumcision, but a new creation.' The same is true with all religious traditions and rituals today, that they have no value apart from their spiritual reality. In the case of the Jews, the physical circumcision was always meant to symbolize an inward devotion, not to serve as an outward source of pride. 'Circumcise therefore the foreskin of your heart,' Moses commanded them (cf. Deut. 10:16).

If the Jews lacked an inward correspondence to circumcision, the Gentiles' uncircumcision accurately depicted their spiritual state. Thus Paul wants the Christians to realize how impoverished was their former position: 'Remember that you were at that time separated from Christ, alienated from the commonwealth of Israel and strangers to the covenants of promise' (v. 12). That is more than ancient history; it also depicts people today who live apart from God.

First, Paul says, 'Remember that you were at that time separated from Christ.' His point is not merely that before becoming Christians they were without Jesus Christ; that much is obvious. But when speaking of Christ he means 'Messiah.' They lacked any savior.

This was true of the Greek religion and worldview, as it is true of secular humanism today. If you read the ancient Greeks you find that they had no hope for a savior. The Ephesians, for instance, lived in a city where the hideous goddess of fertility, Diana, or Artemis, was worshiped. If you purchased her favor, she supposedly might lend you the help of her power, but she offered no salvation from the great problems of life. Likewise, Greek philosophers had no idea of salvation. They viewed history as an endless cycle, with no purpose, no plan, and no destiny. In contrast, the Jews had a positive outlook on the future, despite their troubles. 'Even in their bitterest days the Jews never doubted that the Messiah would come,' says one writer.[200]

Sadly, the Gentile worldview has become dominant in our society; we need to realize that today's new thinking is anything but new. A worldview asks questions that shape reality for us: What and where am I? What is the problem? What is the solution? Today's secular worldview, imported directly from the pagan ancient world, says that we are products of chance living without purpose on a random orb in space. The problem is how to just get by with as much pleasure and as little pain as possible. The answer is to look out for yourself. What could be more bleak and ignoble than that? But what our society ignores is that this rampant individualism and selfishness is not working. This is why our cities are littered with the human refuse of an increasingly bankrupt society. This is why our most affluent suburbs are often scenes of the darkest despair and emptiness.

The Christian has a totally different worldview. He says, I am made in the image of God, placed in the world of his making, for his glory. The problem is sin, with its fruits of misery and death. But we have a real solution. We have a Savior, Jesus Christ, who has conquered sin and death on the cross. His resurrection is our victory and we live in the power of his triumph. Unbelievers have no Christ, no salvation, no victory. The best they can do is try to avoid reality. Christians have victory in Christ Jesus, our Savior.

Paul next points out that the Gentiles were 'alienated from the commonwealth of Israel.' In the time before Christ came and the gospel spread throughout the world, the little nation of Israel was alone the people of God. However great the Greeks and Romans might be, however much power or wealth, learning or glory they might acquire, they were still outside the circle of God's special love and care. Their days were numbered. To be saved, you had to be an Israelite in accordance with God's plan at that time in salvation history.

This reality is illustrated by the Old Testament story of Ruth and Naomi. Ruth was a foreigner who married into Naomi's Jewish family. After a famine killed all the men, Naomi decided to go back to Israel to live in God's care. Ruth apparently had learned much about Israel's God during her time of marriage. When Naomi prepared to depart, Ruth appealed to her: 'Do not urge me to leave you or to return from following you. For where you go I will go, and where you lodge I will lodge. Your people shall be my people, and your God my God' (Ruth 1:16).

Notice how Ruth put this. In order to say, 'Your God shall be my God,' she also had to say, 'Your people shall be my people.' She knew that she could not enter into God's salvation without entering into God's people.

Much has changed in light of the gospel, mainly that you do not have to be part of one nation or ethnic group. But you still cannot be saved without God's people becoming your people. Countless converts to Christ have learned that you cannot maintain all your old associations when you come to Christ and that you must enter into new ones. Above all if you find the church a dull, unappealing society for which you have little interest or affection, you should reconsider the reality of your salvation.

We are living in a time when the church is held in low esteem, even among Christians. This is, I think, in part an overreaction to the religious formalism of a prior generation, and due also to the worldliness of so many professing believers. Our society is individualistic and consumeristic, so people think of the church in those terms. Christians have no fear of belittling or dividing the church, even though it is the commonwealth of God's own people. Our low view of God's household is evidenced by our church shopping, church hopping, and, for many, church dropping.

But one of the greatest tragedies of being without Christ is being outside of his church. Martyn Lloyd-Jones writes:

> By being 'without Christ'...you are outside that circle in which God is peculiarly interested. You do not belong to the covenant people.... Today it is the Christian Church that corresponds to the commonwealth of Israel. The most terrible thing about a man who is not a Christian is that he is outside that circle and does not belong to the people of God.[201]

Third, Paul says the Gentiles were 'strangers to the covenants of promise.' At different times in history, God made covenants with his people: covenants made through Abraham, Moses, and David. But, interestingly, Paul mentions *promise* in the singular. There were many covenants, but one promise, one salvation, that God had always proclaimed. Geoffrey Wilson explains that the Gentiles 'were ignorant of the *one* promise of salvation which God had confirmed to Abraham and his seed in several covenants.'[202] That promise looked forward to and was fulfilled by the coming of Jesus Christ.

It is God's Word that records his covenants, but the Gentiles did not know or understand God's Word, just like people today who never come to church. That is why they were ignorant of God's promise. Lloyd-Jones points out that unbelievers today 'can read their Bible and it does not move them...They are strangers, they are like people from another country, they do not understand the language.'[203] Does that describe you? Are you a stranger to the promises of the Bible, so that it all means nothing and makes no sense? Then you need to cry out to God that by his Holy Spirit he would give you eyes to see and a heart to understand.

Without Hope and Without God

This, Paul says, is the kind of person the Gentiles were, as are their modern-day unbelieving counterparts. Christians are to remember that this is the kind of person we were before God's grace came to us. He wants Christians to realize what a blessing it is to be part of God's church and recipients of God's covenant promise of salvation in Christ.

Paul completes verse 12 by detailing the kind of life people lead apart from Christ. People may not mind being Gentiles or strangers to God, but the kind of life this produces is not so good. Paul memorably describes them as 'having no hope and without God in the world.'

Possessing no idea of a savior, the Greeks suffered an epidemic hopelessness. The same is true of today's secular culture, which is increasingly overwhelmed by despair. This lack of hope relates to our attitude regarding both life and death.

People today lack hope in life, which is why so many lead a mindless pursuit of pleasure and entertainment. Neil Postman aptly chronicled this in his book titled, 'Amusing Ourselves to Death.'[204] What is most depressing is that the few people who do think deeply are the most pessimistic people of all. Not all of these are highly educated. *Life* magazine ran an issue on the meaning of life. Jose Martinez, a taxi driver, offered this: 'We're here to die, just live and die…Life is a big fake. Nobody gives a damn. You're rich or you're poor. You're here, you're gone. You're like the wind. After you're gone, other people will come…We're gonna destroy ourselves, nothing we can do about it.'[205] For all our arrogant claims to achieving heaven on earth through materialistic progress, the reality is that, as Ravi Zacharias writes, 'never before in history has such hopelessness enshrouded so many people, as the heart's deepest longings remain unmet.[206]

If secular people have no hope about life, things get only worse when it comes to death. The Gentiles of Paul's day had no hope for life after death, expecting only to lie in the ground, as one of their philosophers wrote, 'bereft of life, voiceless as a stone.'[207] The same is true of people in every age. It is those who flout God most in life who most despair in the face of death. Napoleon cried out on his death bed, 'I die before my time, and my body will be given back to the earth…What an abyss between my deep misery and the eternal kingdom of Christ.' The famous unbelieving philosopher, Thomas Hobbes, died saying, 'If I had the whole world, I would give it to live one day.… I am about to take a leap into the dark.' Then there is the French writer, Voltaire. Teachers today love to have young students read his arrogant dismissal of Christianity. But they don't tell them about Voltaire's desperation in death. He cried out, 'I am abandoned by God and man! I will give you half of what I am worth if you will give me six months' life.'[208]

Compare that to the peace and joy Christians experience in death. One of the countless examples is Rowland Taylor, one of the English Reformers who could easily have avoided being burned at the stake if he had only been willing to deny his faith in Jesus. A few days before his martyrdom, Taylor wrote to his family:

> I believe that they are blessed which die in the Lord. God careth for sparrows, and for the hairs of our heads. I have ever found Him more faithful and favourable than is any father or husband. Trust ye, therefore, in Him by the means of our dear Saviour Christ's merits. Believe, love, fear, and obey Him: pray to Him, for He hath promised to help. Count me not dead, for I shall certainly live and never die.

That is hope! Taylor concluded the letter by citing Psalm 27: 'The Lord is my Light and my Salvation, whom then shall I fear?'[209]

Paul concludes his description of unbelieving people by telling us the reason they live and die without hope. Gentiles live, he said, 'without God in the world' (Eph. 2:12).

It was not strictly true that the Greeks had no religion and no gods. But you can be very religious and not have God. The Greeks had legions of gods, but none of them were true. None of them could save. None conveyed hope.

So it is today for all who trust the false god of success. Best-selling novelist, Jack Higgins, confessed, 'When you get to the top, there's nothing there.'[210] The same is true of those who trust the false god of money, which cannot buy joy, peace, or satisfaction; or the false god of beauty, which exacts a tyrannical service; or the false god of romance, which so often fades or betrays; or the false god of fame, fleeting and unfaithful. Only the true God, revealed in his Word, who saves us through Jesus Christ, can give the hope for which we long. Only he can be called 'my rock and my salvation, my fortress' (Ps. 62:2).

With Christ we have hope because we have the true and saving God, who entered the world to conquer sin and death. But, as Charles Spurgeon sums it up, 'Without Christ, though you be rich as Croesus, and famous as Alexander, and wise as Socrates, yet you are naked, and poor, and miserable, for you lack him by whom are all things, and for whom are all things, and who is himself all in all.'[211]

Never Forget

Paul reminds us of these truths because he wants believers to remember. 'Never forget!' he says, what you were before and what you have now in Christ. Because of God's grace you have a Savior, you are a blessed member of the people of God, with the Bible's promises signed and sealed for you. This appeal to remember yields at least three applications.

First, the reason for us to remember these blessings is to stir up our gratitude to God. Cicero rightly said that 'gratitude is the mother of every other virtue.' If you are thankful to God your heart will want to live for him. Remember what you were before God came to you in grace. Realize what you would be now and what would be your future destiny, were it not for God's gift in Jesus Christ. This is why Christians so greatly need the Bible's teaching on sin and judgment—not to put us down, but because if we do not realize what we were and what we deserved we will never praise God as we should.

Second, unlike the Jews in their contempt for the hopeless, godless Gentiles, we are to look with mercy on those without hope and without God. We are no better; we are objects of God's mercy. Therefore, let us devote ourselves to that greatest of all mercies: a living, speaking witness about the salvation God offers to everyone through faith in Jesus Christ.

Last, never give in to despair if you are a Christian. Never let resentment take hold of you when you suffer or have unfulfilled desires. Never let temptation be your master. Never forget the grace of God. Remember what God has done for you already and at what cost to himself. Never doubt his saving love. And therefore live with courage and resolve, with hope and joy, knowing that you are part of a grand design to glorify God and enjoy him forever. Remember who you are and whose you are. Remember, and do not forget.

27

Brought Near to God

Ephesians 2:13

As we study the Bible, we occasionally want to ask not only *what* the Scripture is saying but also *why*. This is especially true when it comes to a writer like the apostle Paul, the premier missionary and theologian of the apostolic church, and to a book like Ephesians, described by many as the crown of his writings. Surely the pastoral logic displayed here is significant for all believers.

The pastoral wisdom revealed by the apostle is different from the wisdom common in our day. If we were to ask people today, 'What do believers need to hear in order to grow spiritually and avoid the dangers of life?' most answers would be very different from those given by Paul. Most people today would emphasize techniques or behaviors that we as believers should do. Paul, in contrast, thinks we most need to know about God and what he has done for us in Christ. Paul's primary concern is always with theology: he believed that right theology produces clear thinking, which in turn leads to fruitful living.

The tragedy today is that so few Christians are interested in theology, which is another way of saying they are not interested in God. What people want to hear about is themselves, as well as about the personal life of the man in the pulpit. But notice how little attention the apostle pays to these things. He was God-centered in his thinking and living, and he wants his readers to be God-centered as well.

A Great Contrast

Paul's first exhortation in Ephesians urged us, 'Remember!' (Eph. 2:12). Remember what God has done for you. Remember what you were apart from Christ and what you now are and have in Christ. Ephesians 2:11–12 gives the negative side of this equation, what we were apart from Christ: aliens to God's people, strangers to the covenants of promise, without hope and without God in the world. In verse 13 he turns to the positive: 'But now in Christ Jesus you who once were far off have been brought near by the blood of Christ.' Realize, he says, what you were saved from, what you are saved to, and what it is that saves you.

Why does Paul want us to focus on theology? Because this is, explains Martyn Lloyd-Jones,

> the only way whereby we can ever understand the greatness of this salvation; and as we do so it will lead to joy and rejoicing, to praise and thanksgiving to an assurance and a confidence in Christ which nothing can shake. But in order to

come to that we have to realize two things. We have got to see what we were without Christ. Then we have to realize what is now true of us in the Lord Jesus Christ.'[212]

As Paul writes of those alienated from God and those brought near to God, he makes use of the illustration provided by the temple in Jerusalem. The temple consisted of a series of areas marked by increasingly restricted access. In the center was the inner sanctum, the Holy of Holies. Only the high priest could enter this room, and only one day of the year. Outside the veil was the Holy Place, where the priests served daily by keeping the candles lit, the incense burning, and the table of showbread fresh. Outside the temple was the priests' court, where the altar for the burnt sacrifices was kept fired. Here, also, only the priests could enter.

Around the temple building was a succession of courts. First was the Court of the Israelites, separated from the priestly area only by a low stone barrier. Ritually clean Israelite men could congregate here. Next, to the east, was the Women's Court, where Israelite women were free to come. Beyond this was the outer layer, the Court of the Gentiles, separated by a higher wall on which was posted a warning in both Greek and Latin forbidding any Gentile to pass, on pain of death. It seems likely that this is what Paul is referring to in verse 14 when he speaks about the dividing wall between the Jews and the Gentiles.

This tells us that the Gentiles' real problem was not their separation from the Israelites, but their separation from God. This is what the wall of division showed. This is also the problem with people outside of Christianity today. Like the Gentiles of Paul's day, they are alienated from the true and living God. They do not know him or his promises and they are not part of his people. This is why they have no solid basis for hope and no power to contend with sin and death. The best the Greeks could attain, like secular people today, was either a stoicism that embraced hopelessness or a hedonism that tried to avoid it. Paul's point to the Gentile Christians was that before they came to Christ they were godless in the true sense of the word, and so it is for unbelievers today. The answers to life's questions are found only in God; the solution to life's problems comes only from God; the purpose that gives value to life is the blessing and glory of God. To these things unbelievers are ignorant and blind, and so were we before coming to God in Christ.

This illustration of the temple and its courts also tells us that there is an absolute difference between believers and non-believers. Jews and Gentiles were alike in many ways, but there was this crucial, defining difference: the Gentiles were separated from God whereas the Jews were brought near. Some Jews may have been closer to God than others, but they all had access to God as his people. Some Gentiles may have been farther from God than others, but none of them could enter his presence. Here, then, is the difference that defines what Christianity is, and it is an absolute, objective difference. Christianity brings people past the barrier. In terms of the temple illustration we are brought through every barrier, even within the veil of the most holy place, to dwell in the light of God's presence and favor. All others are outside, beyond the wall that is God's law, far from God, aliens from God's commonwealth, strangers to the covenants of promise.

The key difference is not that Christians are better people or have improved themselves. This is an eventual by-product of Christianity, but not its defining reality. Many Christians are not better people, although God is working in them for righteousness. The difference is that union with

Jesus Christ through faith changes the status of those who were 'far from God' and makes them those 'brought near'. This radical change happens not because of what we have done but because of what Jesus has done for us, received by faith.

The whole purpose of the book of Ephesians is to make the point of what we have gained through Jesus Christ. Whereas as unbelievers we were 'separated from Christ' (Eph. 2:12), Ephesians 1:13 says that having 'heard the word of truth, the gospel of your salvation, and believed in him,' we now are 'in Christ.' We were 'alienated from the commonwealth of Israel,' but Ephesians 2:19 says we now 'are no longer strangers and aliens, but are fellow citizens with the saints.' We were 'strangers to the covenants of promise,' but now we are 'fellow heirs, members of the same body, and partakers of the promise in Christ Jesus through the gospel' (Eph. 3:6).

The contrast continues, with those apart from Christ described as 'without hope'. The Jews 'were the first to hope in Christ' but now the Gentiles, having also believed, 'were sealed with the promised Holy Spirit, who is the guarantee of our inheritance' (Eph. 1:12–14). Likewise, the Gentiles were 'without God'. But, Paul adds in 2:19, we are now 'members of the household of God.'

This is what Christianity is about! There are ultimately two kinds of people—and in the contrast we see just how great is the blessing that God is offering to all the world through Jesus Christ, and how great is the salvation we who have believed have received by God's grace. Remember this, Paul says, and it will change the way you live.

Brought Near

Paul's contrast is designed to make us grateful to God, but also to instill in us the confidence we need. In two key words, 'brought near,' Paul tells us the great privileges we now possess in Christ. We were saved from a life *without God* and we have been saved to a life of faith *with God*: 'But now in Christ Jesus you who once were afar off have been brought near' (Eph. 2:13).

According to this definition, salvation is foremost reconciliation to God. We were alienated from God but now we enter his household, becoming his children. A father is not responsible for every child in the world, but only for his own. He works to provide for all their needs, to give them a home, put food on the table, clothe and educate them. If you are a Christian, this is how things stand between you and God. You have been brought into his household, and God accepts responsibility to care for your soul. This does not mean that nothing bad will ever happen, but rather that you will find God a ready provider in every situation. He will discipline you, for he is also responsible for that. But he will not neglect the things you need, and he will secure your future, your growth, and your protection. People glibly talk about God being the Father of everyone, irrespective of faith or unbelief, but the Bible denies it. John 1:12 says, 'those who received [Jesus], who believed on his name, to them he gave the right to be called children of God.'

Paul's main idea here is access to God. Children have access to their father, and Christians have open access to heaven's throne. Even the Old Testament priests were separated from direct contact with God's presence by the veil that separated the Holy of Holies. But the simplest Christian has greater access than they, because the veil is removed in Jesus Christ. In Christ we have permanent and open access to God in prayer, certain of his gracious reception because we who were far off have been brought near through the superior priesthood of Christ.

Best of all, having been brought near to God in Christ, we begin a relationship with God. We come to know God—who he is and what he is like. We learn not merely things about him, but we grow in a relationship with him. This is the chief of God's covenant promises: 'I will be their God and they will be my people…They will all know me' (Heb. 8:10–11). To be sure, our realization of God in this life is incomplete and partial. But Revelation 21:3–4 shows the fullness of our communion with God that will unfold in eternity:

> He will dwell with them, and they will be his people, and God himself will be with them as their God. He will wipe away every tear from their eyes, and death shall be no more, neither shall there be mourning nor crying nor pain anymore, for the former things have passed away.

By His Blood

Most importantly, Paul tells us what has produced this great change, enabling us who were far from God to be brought into such blessing: 'Now in Christ Jesus you who once were far off have been brought near by the blood of Christ' (Eph. 2:13).

Reconciliation is needed when there has been a breach between two parties. The breach between us and God is our sin. God has a cause for offense with us; there is an issue that must be resolved before we can be restored to his fellowship and blessing. God is holy, and the reality of our sin stands between us and him. Even in human relationships, if there is a real and deep-seated problem between two people, they will not be able to get together—not really, not whole-heartedly, not permanently—until the matter is resolved. One writer says, 'If God and man are to be reconciled, it cannot be by the simple expedient of ignoring sin, but only by overcoming it.'[213]

How, then, did God resolve the problem of our sin and thus reconcile us to himself? Paul answers, 'by the blood of Christ.' There has been an atonement. A sacrifice for sin has been offered that is acceptable to God; indeed, it was the sacrifice of God's own appointing, for which he sent his Son into the world. Paul writes in 2 Corinthians 5:19 that 'in Christ God was reconciling the world to himself, not counting their trespasses against them.' He explains, '[God] made him to be sin who knew no sin, so that in him we might become the righteousness of God.' Therefore, he says, 'We implore you on behalf of Christ, be reconciled to God' (2 Cor. 5:20–21).

Matthew 27:51 says that when Jesus died on the cross, the veil in the temple was torn from top to bottom. That was the most holy of all barriers, the one that kept even the priests from direct contact with God. Its falling declares that now all may come to God through faith in the blood of Christ, that is, in Christ's death for our sin.

This is the good news for everyone, regardless of who and what you are. By his blood, Christ has opened wide the way to God. But notice that this is the one and only way by which you may come to God. Paul does not say we may come to God simply by virtue of being made in his image, for mankind is marred and shamed by sin. He does not say that you may come to God by being a good person. This is what people mainly think today and it is a fatal tragedy. In God's eyes you are not a good person, and it is only our self-serving, sin-stained perspective that allows us to think this about ourselves. 'There is no one good,' God says, 'No, not one' (Rom. 3:12). Paul does not say you may draw near to God through religion, by being a devout person, by partaking in rituals or by the sacraments alone. No mystical experience, however spiritual it may make you feel, will overcome the barrier of your sin. Only the blood of Christ can reconcile you to God and bring you near. Jesus reconciles us to God and brings us near to him not by good intentions, not simply by telling us that God is love and not by preaching the Sermon on the Mount, but by dying in our place as an atonement for our sin.

Jesus made this vividly clear in a parable about two men who came into the temple to pray. One was a Pharisee, the religious elite of Judaism, and the other was a tax collector, the spiritual scum of the nation. Jesus tells us the Pharisee stood before God, saying, 'God, I thank you that I am not like other men, extortioners, unjust, adulterers, or even like this tax collector.' Having boasted about who he was he proceeded to boast about what he did: 'I fast twice a week; I give tithes of all that I get.' He was confident that because of his pedigree, his morality, and his religion, God was certain to receive him. The tax collector's approach to God was altogether different. 'But the tax collector, standing far off, would not even lift up his eyes to heaven, but beat his breast, saying, "God, be merciful to me, a sinner!"' (Luke 18:10–13). The expression 'be merciful' has explicit reference to the sacrifices offered in the temple; literally, it is, 'be mercy-seated to me', the mercy-seat being the place where the atoning blood was offered to God.

In whose shoes would you rather be? Who was more likely of being received by God? Was it the moral and religious man, the man from the good family and the right connections, who came forward on the basis of these? Or was it the sinful man who admitted he was a failure, who could only beat his breast and ask God to forgive his sins through atoning blood? Jesus concluded: 'I tell you, this man'—the tax collector—'went home justified rather than the other.' The reason for this is that, being sinners, we are brought near only 'by the blood of Christ.'

This is the great reality that applies to everyone, as Paul explained in Romans 3:23–25:

> There is no distinction: for all have sinned and fall short of the glory of God, and are justified by his grace as a gift, through the redemption that is in Christ Jesus, whom God put forward as a propitiation by his blood, to be received by faith.

Jesus died as a propitiation, by his own blood turning away God's wrath from all who trust in him. People believe in many things but only one saves us; only one brings us near to God and restores us to his love. That is faith in Christ's blood, in his atoning death for our forgiveness and reconciliation to God. If you trust only in the death of God's Son to bring you to the Father, then you who were far away, without hope and without God, are now brought near as one of God's beloved children. You may not be the person you should be and you may be weighed down with your sense of unworthiness. But in Christ, God's blessing and love are yours and will remain yours not because you earned them but because Christ earned them for you. They were purchased in advance, as the apostle Peter wrote, 'not with perishable things such as silver or gold, but with the precious blood of Christ' (1 Pet. 1:18–19). Therefore, you may stop trying to win your place in God's favor, and stop fretting about your salvation but rest secure, knowing that though you were far away Christ's blood has brought you who were far away near to God.

Walls of Invitation

Paul's teaching in this verse begs a question, and nothing else matters compared to it. Are you separated from Christ in unbelief or are you in Christ and with Christ through faith in his blood? This is literally a life or death matter, with everlasting consequences. With or without Christ is what makes all the difference eternally.

I often think of the scene at Jesus' death, his cross standing between that of two other men. The two men crucified with Jesus represent all of humanity, and like all of us they had one thing in common. They were guilty men ripe for just condemnation. 'There is no difference,' Paul says, 'for all have sinned' (Rom. 3:23). But there was one difference between them, a difference that divides humanity in its two basic groups: one of the criminals cried out to Jesus for salvation. He was not a good person, and he was unable to do any good works or earn salvation in any way. He was already affixed to a cross. But by faith alone he cried out to Jesus. Jesus told him, 'Truly, I say to you, today you will be with me in Paradise' (Luke 23:43). Likewise, today, every sinner who calls in faith to the sin-bearing Savior gains immediate forgiveness and is reconciled to God. The other thief rejected Jesus, mocked him, and perished in his sins, to receive on his own soul the eternal punishment which he and all those like him deserve. Those are the two kinds of people in this world. Which kind are you?

This is the contrast Paul speaks of. If you are a Christian, it does not mean all your troubles are gone. But it does mean you are no longer far from God: condemned, estranged, and barred from his blessings. You have been brought near in Christ. Now, in your weakness, though you are prone to failure and sin, you may rely on Christ's blood for your relationship with God. Through Christ's blood you have access to God's grace so that you will grow stronger as you walk in faith. In Christ, you will gain power against sin as you turn to God in prayer, as God's Word transforms your mind, and as you worship with God's people.

Paul reminds these Gentile Christians of the wall that once separated them from God. The Bible ends with a picture of the heavenly city to come, and it, too, is surrounded by a wall. The apostle John writes in Revelation of the city that is to come: 'I saw no temple in the city, for its temple is the Lord God the Almighty and the Lamb. And the city has no need of sun or moon to shine on it, for the glory of God gives it light, and its lamp is the Lamb' (Rev. 21:22–23). This is the destination of all those now brought near to God in Christ. Of these things we may now partake spiritually through God's Word, prayer, and through our worship of God together.

But, as I said, it is a city with a wall. So how do you get in? How do you come to God? The Bible's last chapter tells us: 'Blessed are those who wash their robes, so that they may have the right to the tree of life and that they may enter the city by the gates' (Rev. 22:14). Only those, but all of those, washed clean in the blood of Christ may enter, drawing near to God and his blessings forever.

I mentioned that the walls around Israel's temple were marked with warnings for the Gentiles to stay out on pain of death. But the walls of this city, the city in which shines the light of Jesus Christ forever, are marked not with a warning but with an invitation for all to come by faith in his gospel. Jesus himself, who died to bring us near by his blood, gives the invitation to all. 'Come,' he says. 'Whoever is thirsty, let him come; and whoever wishes, let him take the free gift of the water of life' (Rev. 22:17).

Jesus invites you now to come near to God through faith in his blood, though you have been far away in sin and unbelief. If you will come, you will be reconciled to God, forgiven of your sins, and received with love as God's precious child, to live forever near to him.

28

Christ Our Peace

Ephesians 2:14

If there is one thing our world needs, it is peace. In political elections, platforms are dedicated to 'peace and prosperity'. Prosperity flows from peace, so a leader who can bring about peace, however temporary, is bound to be popular and successful.

One strategy for making peace is the use of the sword. This was the way of the ancient Roman Empire. Augustus Caesar, returning from his conquest of Western Europe, dedicated a great temple of peace in his own name, placing it on the Field of Mars, the Roman god of war. The point was that war is the way to peace. It was, however, peace for some and the sword for others. The ancient historian Tacitus commented of Rome: 'To plunder, butcher, steal, these things they misname Empire; they make a desolation and call it peace.'[214] Those who live by the sword die by the sword. The day finally came when the sword fell on Rome, and the statue Augustus had erected to himself as peacemaker was torn down; all that remains of it now is a broken-off little finger.

Another approach to peace is diplomacy. This may be a more virtuous strategy than war, but it is hardly any more successful. This is vividly displayed by the ceaseless round of peace treaties signed in recent years, none of which makes the slightest dent in the never-ending violence. Without changing the hatred, what they call peace is really a truce in which both sides reload for the next round of war. Most symbolic of the diplomatic approach was the statement of British Prime Minister Neville Chamberlain after his meeting with Adolf Hitler in 1938. While German factories were pouring out tanks and bombers, Chamberlain boasted, 'We have achieved peace in our time.' Soon those tanks and bombers were unleashed and his era of 'peace' was bathed in sorrow and blood.

Neither war nor diplomacy can ever achieve a true and lasting peace, which is why mankind has made absolutely no progress in this matter. Jeremiah complained of the false prophets, '"Peace, peace," they say, when there is no peace' (Jer. 6:14). So it is today. But whereas mankind has failed, Jesus Christ proclaimed on the eve of his death a victory over sin that yields true and lasting peace. 'Peace I leave with you,' Jesus claimed. 'My peace I give to you. Not as the world gives do I give to you' (John 14:27).

The most profound teaching in the Bible on how Jesus Christ gives peace is found in Ephesians 2:14–18, which begins with the great statement: 'For he himself is our peace.'

Sin Results in Conflict

According to the Bible, conflict is the result of sin. The reason we lack and so greatly need peace is because of sin and its effects.

We lack peace because sin is a violation of God's law and therefore of the way that God ordered the world for blessing. This reminds us that God's Law—the Ten Commandments, for instance—is not just an arbitrary set of rules made to keep us from having fun. Rather, God was setting down what is wrong and harmful in the world he has made. The second tablet of the Ten Commandments deal with things that cause conflict and harm. 'Honor your father and mother…You shall not murder…You shall not commit adultery…You shall not steal…You shall not lie…You shall not covet' (Exod. 20:12–17). When these commandments are broken—when we sin—the result is conflict and pain.

Another reason sin causes conflict is that at the heart of sin is selfishness. Sin says to gain for yourself at the expense of others. The apostle James said: 'What causes quarrels and what causes fights among you? Is it not this, that your passions are at war within you? You desire and do not have, so you murder. You covet and cannot obtain, so you fight and quarrel' (James 4:1–2).

Yet another reason sin causes conflict is that God curses sin. The first sin took place in Genesis 3, when Adam and Eve disobeyed God and ate of the tree of the knowledge of good and evil. God responded with curses that promised conflict. He promised enmity between the seed of the serpent and the seed of the woman, that is, between the unbelieving world and God's people (Gen. 3:15). He promised conflict between the man and woman in their marital union (Gen. 3:16) and even conflict between mankind and the created world: 'Cursed is the ground because of you,' he told Adam. 'In pain you shall eat of it all the days of your life' (Gen. 3:17).

Conflict and misery because of sin is the story of the generations that followed. Genesis 4 tells that because of jealousy and resentment, the first son born into the human race, Cain, murdered his younger brother, Abel. Cain's descendants were makers of war; the first human song ever recorded (Gen. 4:23) was written by Lamech to celebrate his killing of a man who started a fight with him. Genesis 11 takes us forward into history, when all of mankind united in a sinful desire to build the Tower of Babel in rebellion to God. God rewarded their sin with even more division, confusing their languages as a punishment.

There are three basic levels in which sin destroys peace. The first and most important is between man and God. This was vividly depicted when Adam and Eve responded to the first sin by fleeing from God (Gen. 3:8). Paul began his gospel teaching in the Book of Romans with this stark reality: 'The wrath of God is revealed from heaven against all ungodliness and unrighteousness of men' (Rom. 1:18).

Second, sin destroys peace within ourselves. Isaiah 57:21 says, 'There is no peace, says my God, for the wicked.' The prophet elaborated in vivid language: 'The wicked are like the tossing sea; for it cannot be quiet, and its waters toss up mire and dirt.' The sea is never at rest because it is pulled by the magnetic force of two contrary powers, the earth and the moon. Sin does the same to us: it is a power that gets hold of us and pulls us. Yet however we may want him to, God never goes away. However much man may reject God or disbelieve in God, we are still made in his image, with the reality of his moral order to contend with. Therefore the voice of conscience speaks against the pull of sin, and we are gripped by a restless inner turmoil.

Finally, sin destroys peace in our relationships with others. Prior to their sin our first parents lived in harmony and love: 'They were naked and had no shame' (Gen. 2:25). But as soon as they sinned they not only felt shame and put on fig leaves, but they immediately entered into conflict. When God confronted Adam for eating the forbidden fruit, he became the first in a long line of male blame-shifters. Using both hands God had given him—one to point at Eve and the other at God—he replied, 'The woman whom you gave to be with me, she gave me fruit of the tree, and I ate' (Gen. 3:12). Adam was thus alienated both from God and from his wife, Eve.

At the root of all our conflict is sin. James Montgomery Boice explains:

> The enemy of peace is not a lack of negotiations but the fundamental alienation that exists between every individual and God. It is because we are at enmity with God—that is the true meaning of sin—that we are also inevitably at enmity with ourselves, one another, and in a certain sense, with all the world.[215]

Salvation Brings Peace

The Bible teaches that redemption remedies the Fall; salvation repairs what is ruined by sin. This means that if sin brings conflict, then salvation restores peace.

When the Bible speaks of peace it means not just the absence of conflict, but the enjoyment of harmony and blessing. The idea is fully expressed by the Old Testament word *shalom*. *Shalom* is the peace that comes from God. It is what the Levitical priests spoke of in their benediction:

> The Lord bless you and keep you;
> The Lord make his face to shine upon you
> and be gracious to you;
> The Lord lift up his countenance upon you
> and give you peace (Num. 6:24–26).

This peace *from* God is only possible when we have peace *with* God. The barrier between us and God is our sin. Salvation brings the cure to sin. It gives us forgiveness so that we are justified in God's sight, and it overthrows the power of sin in our hearts so that our hostility to God is replaced with faith and love. Paul says, 'Since we have been justified by faith, we have peace with God through our Lord Jesus Christ' (Rom. 5:1).

The theological term for this is *reconciliation*. Paul says in 2 Corinthians 5:18–21 that God sent Christ into the world to reconcile lost sinners to himself: 'In Christ God was reconciling the world to himself, not counting their trespasses against them...For our sake he made him to be sin who knew no sin, so that in him we might become the righteousness of God.' Philip Ryken reminds us:

> Reconciliation teaches something remarkable about the character of God. He befriends his enemies. He loves those who hate him. He offers peace to those who have waged war against him. Although he is the one who has been wronged, he is the one who makes things right. He does all this while the battle still rages. 'When we were God's enemies, we were reconciled to him through the death of his Son' (Rom. 5:10).[216]

A good example of how peace *with* God gives us peace *from* God is found in the life of the Old Testament patriarch, Jacob. His name meant *Grasper*, and Jacob's whole life was spent grasping for things his sinful heart wanted. He sought generally good things, but he sought them in the wrong ways and with wrong motives. As a result he got no blessing and no peace. Jacob gained his father's covenant blessing by lying and cheating his elder brother, Esau; he gained his riches by tricking his father-in-law to take possession of the strongest animals in his herds. Along with his new possessions he gained resentment and conflict. God came to him one night when Jacob's enemies were closing in on him. God wrestled with Jacob, bringing his heart into submission. Finally Jacob, having spent his whole life trying to place his hands on the blessings he wanted, instead put them onto God. He cried out to God, 'I will not let you go unless you bless me' (Gen. 32:26). That was what God wanted: for Jacob to put his faith in him. God changed his heart and from that time forward Jacob knew a peace and blessing he never had before. God does the same for everyone who gains peace with him through faith in Christ.

Salvation gives us peace with God, peace in our hearts, and, finally, peace with other people. I mentioned that God came to Jacob at a time when Jacob was lonely and defeated. His father-in-law was chasing him from behind, and as Jacob returned to his homeland, his brother Esau was waiting for him with superior forces. Jacob tried to bribe Esau with the sheep and goats and cattle he had acquired from his wife's father, but he knew that these could not overcome Esau's hatred. He was outnumbered militarily and diplomacy was not going to work. But after Jacob had wrestled with God and come to peace with him, he was able to admit his faults and come to his brother asking forgiveness. God put his own love into Esau's heart and the brothers, long estranged, were united in peace (see Gen. 32–33).

Peace is only possible where sin is overcome and removed. Salvation means being justified with God through faith in Christ, and thereby we have peace with him. His righteousness works in our lives, so harmony and wholeness begin to replace conflict and brokenness. When we are able to repent and forgive, we have peace with one another. The apostle John explained, 'If we walk in the light, as he is in the light, we have fellowship with one another, and the blood of Jesus his Son cleanses us from all sin' (1 John 1:7).

HE HIMSELF IS OUR PEACE

Paul brings all these ideas together with the powerful statement of Ephesians 1:14. Speaking of our Lord Jesus Christ, he says, 'He himself is our peace.' It is because of Christ's work for us and our relationship with him that we receive peace and have peace to give.

When Paul says of Christ that 'he himself is our peace,' he is remembering one of the great prophesies of Jesus' birth: 'For to us a child is born, to us a son is given; and the government shall be upon his shoulder, and his name shall be called Wonderful Counselor, Mighty God, Everlasting Father, Prince of Peace. Of the increase of his government and of peace there will be no end' (Isa. 9:6–7). It was with this promise in mind that the angels sang on the night of Jesus' birth, 'Glory to God in the highest, and on earth peace among those with whom he is pleased!' (Luke 2:14).

Less well known is the prophecy that Paul quotes in Ephesians 2:14, from Micah chapter 5. That passage begins with a prophecy regarding the town of Bethlehem: 'You, O Bethlehem Ephrathah, who are too little to be among the clans of Judah, from you shall come forth for me one who is to be ruler in Israel, whose origin is from of old, from ancient days' (Micah 5:2). The prophet had foretold a day when the Jews would be conquered as God's judgment for their sin. But he promised that a ruler would rise up in a humble place, one who would be a divine savior. Looking forward with amazing specificity to the coming of Jesus Christ, Micah says that 'he shall stand and shepherd his flock in the strength of the Lord, in the majesty of the name of the Lord his God. And they shall dwell secure, for now he shall be great to the ends of the earth. And he shall be their peace' (Micah 5:4-5).

This is what it means to come to Christ in faith: to have him lead you through life as a faithful shepherd, who died for the sheep, so that even in a world without peace we can live securely, knowing that our eternal destiny is assured and our present life held in the hands of a loving God. Jesus himself is our peace. John Calvin says, 'This is a beautiful title of Christ: the Peace between God and men. Let no one doubt that God is favourable to him if he remains in Christ.'[217]

Paul has depicted man's relationship with God in terms of the Old Testament temple, with its series of barriers separating sinners from God's holy presence. Most important was the thick veil separating everyone—even the priests—from God's inner chamber. But where the veil once barred us from God, Jesus now stands inviting us into God's blessing. He is the mediator who brings peace, the veil having fallen at the moment when Jesus made atonement for our sins by his death (Matt. 27:51). He is also the mediator in our hearts, standing between us and the turmoil caused by our sin. And he stands between us and other people, giving us grace to forgive, serve, and love—to make peace by the power of Jesus Christ. In all these ways, as Psalm 29:11 tells us, 'The Lord blesses his people with peace' (NIV).

Living the Peace of Christ

So here is the question: do you have this peace? Are you experiencing and making peace? It is Christ who gives us peace and is our peace.

It is Christ who brings peace and love to marriages. Sin brought conflict between Adam and Eve, just as it does to couples today. The Bible tells wives to submit to their husbands, to respect them and to minister for their blessing. But women say, 'You don't know my husband. He isn't worthy of respect. He doesn't do what he is supposed to do.' Therefore there is conflict, hostility, resentment. But Christ is our peace. Because of their relationship to Christ and by the power he sends, wives can build up their husbands with respect and encouragement, because they want to honor Jesus and they trust God to bless what he has commanded. Husbands are told to love their wives as Christ loved the church, to sacrifice for their well-being, to cherish them and minister to the needs of their hearts. But men say, 'You don't know my wife. We're not compatible. We don't get along.' So let Christ be your peace. Remember his love for you and give it to your wife in his name. Forgive as the Lord forgave you. Pray with and for your wife because Christ died for you and God brought you together in marriage. Let Jesus stand within your marriage, bringing you together in love and mutual ministry because Christ is your peace.

The same is true in the workplace, neighborhoods, and families. Our lives are filled with conflict and embittered by resentment and hostility. If someone sins against you, let Christ be your peace. Forgive them and do them good. Peter wrote:

> For to this you have been called, because Christ also suffered for you, leaving you an example, so that you might follow in his steps. He committed no sin, neither was deceit found in his mouth. When he was reviled, he did not revile in return; when he suffered, he did not threaten, but continued entrusting himself to him who judges justly' (1 Pet. 2:21-23).

The same is true with circumstances. Bad news comes. Disaster strikes. Our hearts start filling with anxiety and turmoil. Let Christ be your peace. Remember that he who stilled the winds and the waves reigns on high for you. Remember that your loving God is sovereign over all things. Turn to Christ, trust in him, and hear his voice in your heart, 'Peace, be still' (Mark 4:39).

Christ is our peace, especially as we turn to him in prayer—when faced with conflict or anxiety, when tempted to sin or when sinned against. Paul writes, 'Do not be anxious about anything, but in everything by prayer and supplication with thanksgiving let your requests be made known to God. And the peace of God, which surpasses all understanding, will guard your hearts and your minds in Christ Jesus' (Phil. 4:6–7).

But the most important question is this: Do you have peace with God? Without peace *with* God you can never know the peace *of* God, the peace God gives. Even if you should cruise through life without major problems, if you are not right with God eternity will hold no peace for you. We enter this world as members of a race at war with God. Whether we acknowledge it or not, in our sin we have taken up arms against the Most High. Until we have peace with God we are living on the fault-line of a great earthquake that shakes us even now and will soon break apart in the final judgment.

But Christ is our peace with God. He does what man can never do, what no sword can impose and no treaty can enforce. Christ has removed the cause of conflict and hostility, and he is undoing the effects of sin in the lives of those who trust him. Jesus fulfilled for us the law we have broken. He has removed the veil and every barrier that stands between us and the light of God. He sends the Spirit to work the love of God into our hearts. He is the sacrifice who atoned for our sins and the priest who takes us by the hand and brings us as children into God's family and worshipers into God's presence. Christ is our peace with God, and therefore within ourselves, and thereby with other people and with the changing circumstances of life.

The Song of Peace

An obvious application is to ask you where there is a need for peace in your life. Are husband and wife strained by wear, tear, and conflict? Then come together in renewed forgiveness, repentance, and a commitment to Christ's peace. Recommit your relationship on the altar of prayer to God and renew the peace of Christ in your home. Is there a need for peace between parent and child, between family members or former friends? Christians have all the resources at our disposal to enjoy the blessing of peace in this life, and especially among fellow Christians. Jesus said, 'Peace I leave with you; my peace I give to you' (John 14:27).

We enjoy Christ's peace when we live according to Christ's Word. For instance, Matthew 18 tells us what to do when we have conflict with another Christian: 'If your brother sins against you, go and tell him his fault, between you and him alone' (Matt. 18:15). But how difficult it is to get Christians to practice this teaching. Instead, they gossip, spread complaints to everyone but the person they are criticizing, treat the person with passive-aggressive hostility, or demand elaborate counseling schemes, none of which can replace Jesus' simple prescription for peace. Jesus calls us to repent of our own sin, forgive others their sins, and rejoin in a bond of Christian peace through a shared commitment to his Word.

There are, of course, many situations in which we do not enjoy peace because the other side will not lay down the weapons of conflict. There are demands that cannot be fulfilled or grudges that others will not let go. In those cases, Paul urges us to do all that we can in the cause of peace, saying, 'If possible, so far as it depends on you, live peaceably with all' (Rom. 12:18). Sometimes all we can do is pray for forgiveness, for change, or for God's help in bearing with the conflict that we are not able to bring to an end. Paul's ultimate counsel is this: 'Do not be overcome by evil, but overcome evil with good' (Rom. 12:21). Because of the peace we have in Christ, the Bible gives one counsel of peace after another to Christians:

'Seek peace and pursue it' (Ps. 34:14);

'Let the peace of Christ rule in your hearts' (Col. 3:15);

'Strive for peace with everyone, and for the holiness without which no one will see the Lord' (Heb. 12:14);

'Blessed are the peacemakers, for they shall be called sons of God' (Matt. 5:9);

'Grace to you and peace' (Eph. 1:2).

I mentioned earlier the song of the angels when Jesus was born, heralding peace on earth through Christ. Earlier Zechariah, the father of John the Baptist, anticipated the Savior by praising God for his peace. Because of 'the tender mercy of God,' Jesus Christ was coming, 'to give light to those who sit in darkness and in the shadow of death, to guide our feet into the way of peace' (Luke 2: 78–79).

That song can be yours if you will come in faith to Christ and receive the gift of peace that God has offered us through him. If you will be his disciple, trusting him and making his Word the rule for your life, you will have found the path to peace. He will give you peace. He will be your peace. And he will use you to bring peace to a hurting, dying world.

29

The New Humanity

Ephesians 2:14–16

Genesis 11 records one of the great culminating moments in human history. Adam and Eve had fallen into sin, and the result was the violence depicted in the early chapters of Genesis. In chapter 11, mankind is united once more, joined in rebellion against God in an attempt to usurp his glory.

Genesis 11 begins, 'Now the whole earth had one language and the same words…They said, "Come, let us build ourselves a city and a tower with its top in the heavens, and let us make a name for ourselves"' (Gen. 11:1, 4). This was all part of the devil's subtle plan and an imitation of his own failed attempt to overthrow God's rule. God, stooping down to this puny venture, confused their language, and 'from there the Lord dispersed them over the face of all the earth' (Gen. 11:9). This was how the human race became scattered across the globe, divided into cultures, peoples, and nations at war.

So it was with the human race from the Tower of Babel until the coming of Jesus Christ. Jesus came to undo the effects of sin, including the Tower of Babel. As John stated, 'The reason the Son of God appeared was to destroy the works of the devil' (1 John 3:8). Therefore, if Genesis 11 is the culmination of the effects of sin, we should expect to see its reversal with Jesus' coming into the world.

This is the very thing we discover in the Book of Acts. On the day of Pentecost, just weeks after the resurrection of Christ and days after his ascension into heaven, the Holy Spirit was poured out by Christ upon his church. In that Pentecost gathering were men from all the nations and languages created in judgment at Babel, now brought together by the Spirit of God. When the apostle Peter began preaching and the tongues of fire fell upon them, 'They were amazed and astonished, saying…"How is it that we hear, each of us in his own native language?"…And all were amazed and perplexed, saying to one another, "What does this mean?"' (Acts 2:7–12).

What did it mean? It meant the coming of peace in Jesus Christ to the scattered tribes of men. Paul's readers were Gentiles living in Asia Minor. They had been, verse 12 says, 'separated from Christ, alienated from the commonwealth of Israel and strangers to the covenants of promise, having no hope and without God in the world.' Now, in Christ, they have been 'brought near by the blood of Christ' (v. 13), reconciled to God by the cross. But there is something more for them to know and experience, namely, that the never-ending war brought on by sin has now been won. We are at peace with God, yes, but we can also have peace with men. Ephesians 2:16 states that Christ reconciled us to God in such a way that he brought us together 'in one body through the cross, thus killing the hostility.' Here, Paul proclaims good news of peace: peace made possible through Christ's death, peace made real through Christ's resurrection, and peace experienced in the new humanity that is the body of Christ.

Peace Made Possible through Christ's Death

We know that Christ's death reconciles believers to God. Paul emphasized this in Ephesians 2:13: 'You who once were far off have been brought near by the blood of Christ.' But as his teaching continues, he points out that Christ's death also makes peace possible within the human race.

Verse 14 gives the reason. Paul speaks of the fundamental division within humanity, that between Jews and Gentiles. This was an outworking of the division created by God back in Genesis 3:15. God cursed the serpent, saying, 'I will put enmity between you and the woman, and between your offspring and her offspring.' Gentiles were all the various non-Jewish people. The separation of Jews was a provision of mercy and of protection for God's people. Without this enmity, godly families would be absorbed into the sinful world and its rebellion to God. Their preservation, and thus of the holy seed who would be their Savior, required that there be hostility between the people of God and the world. In the time of the New Testament, this division was defined as between the Jews and the Gentiles as mandated by the Old Testament legal code.

Paul refers to 'the dividing wall of hostility', created by 'the law of commandments and ordinances.' In a previous study we recalled the physical wall that kept Gentiles out of the temple courts, with warnings that threatened death to any who crossed. This wall seems to be in Paul's mind as a symbol for the whole system of rules designed to keep Jews separate from Gentiles. They could not sit down to a meal with Gentiles or even eat the same foods. They dressed differently. They could not intermarry or enter into real friendships. To the Gentiles, this made the Jews seem strange and aloof. The Jews came to regard the Gentiles as unclean and inferior.

Paul says that Jesus abolished all this and broke down the wall 'in his flesh'. This refers to his atoning death on the cross. Prior to Jesus' coming the system of the Old Testament law was the means by which the Jewish people entered into and expressed their relationship to God. No one else could come near to God. But, as Paul explains in Galatians 3:23–29, all this was a temporary measure to preserve the integrity of the covenant people until the Messiah should come. Jesus' coming abolished the administration of the Mosaic Covenant and offered everyone access to God through his death. Here is how Paul explained it in Galatians:

> The law was our guardian until Christ came, in order that we might be justified by faith. But now that faith has come, we are no longer under a guardian, for in Christ Jesus you are all sons of God, through faith…There is neither Jew nor Greek, there is neither slave nor free, there is neither male nor female, for you are all one in Christ Jesus (Gal. 3:24–28).

Christianity was able quickly to become a worldwide religion, as God intended, in part because cultural barriers could be overcome by the grace and truth of the gospel. Once the apostles understood that Christianity is to transcend every human division, they vigorously opposed every attempt to force Jewish cultural practices on Gentile converts. Anyone could become a child of God, just as they are, through a living faith that turned from false gods to the true God through Jesus Christ.

Jesus himself foreshadowed this new situation in John 4 when he sat down on a well next to a Samaritan woman. She was amazed because no Jewish man would ever sit and talk with a Gentile woman, much less ask her to give him a drink as Jesus did. Jesus spoke to her about the living water he offers to all who believe. In response to her puzzlement, Jesus said, 'The hour is coming, and is now here, when the true worshipers will worship the Father in spirit and truth, for the Father is seeking such people to worship him' (John 4:23). That woman became an evangelist to the Samaritans; people heard about Jesus and came to him, crying, 'We know that this is indeed the Savior of the world' (John 4:42).

When Paul says Jesus abolished the law, he does not mean the moral law, such as the Ten Commandments, which expresses God's unchangeable character. Jesus said, 'Do not think that I have come to abolish the Law or the Prophets; I have not come to abolish them but to fulfill them' (Matt. 5:17). Likewise, God's people today are to obey God's moral law. But we are no longer to uphold those temporary regulations that separated Jews from Gentiles and protected God's people from contact with unbelievers.

This is a vital matter today, when too many Christians think holiness is about checking out of the culture. Many Christians think they are being holy if they have no non-Christian friends, if they enjoy only Christian entertainment, if they have nothing to do with their neighbors or treat their unbelieving co-workers as unclean. But Christ's death has freed God's people from the juvenile bonds of such legalism; we now are to go out into the world, being in the world but not of it, as the salt that preserves it from death and the light that shines in the darkness. Jesus treated the woman by the well as a person of dignity and worth; though she was a Samaritan, he asked her to do a service for him (John 4:7). Though he was the very kind of person she had learned to hate, she was drawn to him because of his combination of grace and truth. In this, Jesus sets an important example for Christians today, who find themselves in a difficult situation in America and in Europe. There are increasing ways in which we cannot participate in secular society because of its sin. This re-erects the barrier between believers and unbelievers. In this respect, the worst effect of the advance of pagan morality, in the form of sexual perversion, drunkenness, foul speech, and radical selfishness, is in the hostility it has caused between Christians and non-Christians. The Christian in the workplace or in the dorm will often not be able to join the group and run with the crowd because of its ungodliness. While believers in Christ cannot always do away with this hostility, in the way that we treat non-Christians as people, with love, kindness, and dignity, we can bridge the divide one person at a time, showing them in person the grace of Jesus Christ which they encounter nowhere else in the world.

Christ's death has made peace possible within this world, through the gospel of his salvation. We are now his ambassadors, not of judgment and wrath but of reconciliation. As Paul said, so we say today, 'We are ambassadors for Christ, God making his appeal through us. We implore you on behalf of Christ, be reconciled to God' (2 Cor. 5:20).

Salvation Realized through Christ's Resurrection

Christ's death makes peace possible not only between man and God, but also among men. For this, Jesus did not merely die but also rose from the grave. It is Christ's resurrection that actually creates peace among men. This is why we must hold the cross and the open tomb together. Christ's death removes God's barriers to our acceptance, but it is the spiritual resurrection that takes place within us, as an out-working of Christ's resurrection, that changes us and brings us to God. It is by the Holy Spirit that we are 'made alive together with Christ' (Eph. 2:4). Now, Paul adds that Christ, by the power of his resurrection, has created 'in himself one new man in the place of the two, so making peace' (Eph. 2:15).

Paul says that in making us his disciples, Jesus created a new humanity and made us part of it. We are the people of his resurrection life, partaking of his power and joining the family of God. Jesus does not make peace by persuading two different types of people to get along for a while. He does not say to the Gentiles that they must be kind to Jews and vice versa. He says, 'You are no longer what you were. Do not think of yourself as a Jew any longer or as a Gentile any longer. Think of yourself as a Christian, a new kind of person. This is especially important today: we are no longer white or black, rich or poor, Northern or Southern—we are Christians. While we may still relate to these earthly categories, they are subordinated to our higher identity in Christ. Christianity is not a band aid on the old humanity, with all its conflict and division. Christianity is a new humanity in Christ, in his resurrection, a humanity that has passed through the death of the cross and through the open tomb of the resurrection to receive eternal life.

What is it that makes us members of this new humanity? The answer is, of course, the new birth, which is what happens when someone believes in Jesus. Paul said in 2 Corinthians 5:17, 'If anyone is in Christ, he is a new creation. The old has passed away; behold, the new has come.' In Christ we are something new; Christ died and rose again that he 'might reconcile us both to God in one body through the cross, thereby killing the hostility' (Eph. 2:16). Jesus brings us to God in such a way that he also brings us to one another. He gives us a new life and a new identity which now we share with our brothers and sisters in him.

This is the most radical way of making peace, by actually making us one. The closest analogy we have to this is to be part of a natural family. We say that blood is thicker than water. Family members stick together and help one another, even when they don't get along. According to Jesus, the bond of the Spirit is no less potent than that of blood, so that our spiritual family should be at least as close-knit as our natural family. He said: 'whoever does the will of my Father in heaven is my brother and sister and mother' (Matt. 12:50). Jesus makes us one by giving each of us the same Spirit, bringing all of us into God's family and making us brothers and sisters for all eternity. This is the true basis for Christian unity: our mutual relationship to God, our mutual love for Christ, and our mutual indwelling by the same Holy Spirit so that we experience a spiritual oneness in Christ.

Peace Experienced in the Church

This teaching informs us what the church is: one new man in Jesus Christ, the new humanity that will live forever and partake in Christ's glory throughout all ages. This is why reflecting upon Paul's message in Ephesians will remind us of the significance of the Christian church. There is nothing else like it, nothing else more important, and nothing else more worthy of our commitment, sacrifice and contribution. We are not a social club, not a self-help society. We are the new creation brought about by the Spirit of God through the resurrection of Christ, the holy society of heaven living in this present evil world.

Do you see why it is so important that we should love the church? Do you see why it is so vital that we pursue holiness with a passion? The church is the bride of Christ, the new humanity of the resurrection! Angels gaze upon us even now in wonder. Do you see why it is so important to be a part of the church? Only the church can know the peace of God, because it is in the church that Christ is making peace, through faith in him.

God sent Jesus to reconcile sinners to himself 'in one body through the cross, thereby killing the hostility' (Eph. 2:16). So if you want to be part of this new humanity, you must come to the cross. This is Paul's logic in the second half of Ephesians 2: 'But now in Christ Jesus you who were far off have been brought near by the blood of Christ…that he might create one new man in the place of the two, so making peace' (vv. 13–15). Verse 15 challenges the radical individualism so common today. To be part of Christ's church you must enter through the cross, but having come to the cross you must enter into Christ's church, the resurrection humanity where Christ reigns in peace. Salvation involves our personal reconciliation to God in Christ but then our reconciliation to others in the church of Christ.

One of the great signs of assurance of salvation is to experience this unity and peace. Have you ever encountered someone with whom you would have no natural reason for friendship? But he or she is a Christian. You begin to talk about our Savior. God's Word enters your conversation and your hearts are drawn together. This love is a strong sign of God's Spirit dwelling in your life. And it causes the world to marvel that in Christ we transcend every division the world knows and which the world cannot overcome—racial, national, economic, or occupational. In Christ, we enjoy a spiritual union bathed in love.

Paul's description of the church has the most profound implications for our approach to ministry. We are told today that people like to be with others just like themselves. Church marketing experts tell us that if we pick out one kind of person and focus on their preferences they will flock to the church and others who are like them will follow.[218] The result is one church for hip young white people, another for black people, another for Hispanics; one for the intellectuals, another for the emotionally needy; one for the outgoing and another for the reserved. According to this advice, the church today has become a sort of multiplex movie theatre. Many churches even divide their own congregation with one service that is liturgical, another that is traditional, and another that is rock-n-roll. It is a brilliantly successfully approach—if numbers are all that really matters.

But Paul says the church is to be one new man in Christ. Christ wants to bring together otherwise hostile groups into one new body. Christ is not glorified when people get together on the basis of human divisions or preferences. The world does that. What glorifies Christ is to find all different kinds of people together because of their spiritual bond in Christ. We want young and old, single and married, hip and square, rich and poor together, from every tribe and race. How is this possible? Only by the Spirit of God, uniting in Christ people who would otherwise have nothing to do with each other.

To a certain extent a particular church is bound to have a particular cultural feel, simply because it has a history and location. But there is a Christian culture that transcends all that. Worship should not be determined by cultural tradition, but should be shaped by the Bible as much as possible. We should mainly do things that Christians of all generations would recognize as distinctively Christian: confessing our sin and hearing God's pardon, proclaiming the creeds, reading Scripture, praying, singing psalms, hymns, and spiritual songs (Col. 3:16), preaching the Word, receiving the sacraments. As we mature as believers we love more and more those things that are biblical and care less for those things of our cultural background. We are people of the new in Christ, and not of the old of the world.

United in Christ

I want to conclude with three observations that flow from this text. The first has to do with the kind of peace God is making in this world. It is an inward peace, a peace of love, harmony, and fellowship. It is not merely the cessation of fighting or arguing, and Christians should never settle for that.

So do you know the kind of peace Paul is talking about? Is it found in your home, in your relationships at work, in your marriage? It is not always possible for us to enjoy the kind of peace we desire when it comes to non-Christians. Paul says in Romans 12:18, 'So far as it depends on you, live peaceably with all.' But in our relationships with Christians, and especially in our church and homes, we should experience this peace. This happens as we walk with God by the power of his Spirit and under the authority of his Word. Paul exhorts us in Colossians 3:15–16, 'Let the peace of Christ rule in your hearts, to which indeed you were called in one body. And be thankful. Let the word of Christ dwell in you richly.'

So why do many Christians know so little of this peace? I think it is because we do not realize all that is possible in the normal Christian life. I think it is because we do not know how willing and how able God is to answer our prayers with a supernatural work in our lives. Many Christians live as close to the world as they can and are under its influence, instead of living close to God and under his influence. We are to be in the world, but not of it. We lack peace because we lack holiness, that is, the renewing work of the Holy Spirit that turns our hearts to God. We thus do not take seriously the words of our Lord, 'Peace I leave with you; my peace I give to you' (John 14:27).

Second, this passage should transform our idea of what the church is. The church is not just a building or an institution. The church is a new human race, the eternal family of God's people whose work will endure long after every merely human achievement has fallen into dust. It is in the church that God is displaying his glory (Eph. 3:10), so God calls his people to serve for the up-building of the church (Eph. 4:12). You are called to use your gifts, contribute your time and money, your prayers and your tears, for the blessing and growth of the church, the new humanity in Christ.

Since Jesus bought the church with his blood in order to make peace, we should all loathe to disturb this peace and to bring division or conflict into the church. Apart from false teaching, nothing hurts a church more than division and conflict. So if we are part of a faithful, biblical church, we should do everything possible to seek its purity and peace. God forbid that any of us should disturb the peace of Christ's church, which he purchased with his precious blood!

Last, this teaching gives us a whole new perspective on the glory of Christ's saving work. We tend to think only about what Jesus does for us as individuals. But here we see a vast and grand panorama. Christ has overthrown the devil's work in the world. He has formed a new people for himself: a new race that transcends all the old conflicts; a new kingdom that overwhelms former allegiances and hostilities. Christ has not merely made some repairs on the old broken-down humanity. He has made something glorious and new in its place, using the raw materials of the fallen creation, cleansing us from sin and breathing into us the new life of his resurrection, thus making peace. This is where God's plan for history is heading, the fallen creation redeemed and restored in Christ: 'The wolf shall dwell with the lamb, and the leopard shall lie down with the young goat, and the calf and the lion and the fattened calf together…They shall not hurt or destroy in all my holy mountain; for the earth shall be full of the knowledge of the Lord as the waters cover the sea' (Isa. 11:6, 9).

This is our reality in Christ, and it is our future in Christ. As we trust in him and seek his peace, this resurrection reality will be our present experience in increasing measure, to our great blessing and to the glory of the grace of God.

30

Access to the Father

Ephesians 2:17–18

All through Ephesians, Paul addresses questions that are at the heart of his message: What makes someone a Christian? How does this happen? And in what does it result?

The first and most basic answer came in Ephesians 1:1, where Paul says a Christian is a 'saint', that is a 'holy one', through faith in Christ Jesus. By the time chapter 1 concluded, we learned that a Christian is beloved of God the Father (1:5), forgiven through the blood of Christ (1:7), and indwelt by the Holy Spirit (1:13). In chapter 2, Paul adds that a Christian is a sinner saved by grace, through faith, for the display of God's glory. As we continue in chapter 2, we find another answer to the question, 'What is a Christian?' Here, we find that a Christian is a person who has peace with God through the atoning blood of Jesus Christ, and experiences the peace of God that Jesus works into our hearts. For, as Paul exclaims, 'he himself is our peace' (Eph. 2:14).

He Preached Peace

As Paul explains it, the peace that believers have with God results from the saving work of Christ. Starting in verse 13, Paul explained that Jesus died in our place to give us peace with God through the forgiveness of our sins. He then rose from the grave and ascended into heaven to pour his peace into our hearts through the Holy Spirit. Now, in verse 17, he notes one more thing Jesus has done to give us peace: 'He came and preached peace to you who were far off and peace to those who were near.'

This is a remarkable statement, especially when we consider it in the order where Paul puts it. We might think that when Paul speaks of Jesus preaching peace he is referring to Jesus' earthly ministry, when he went about teaching and healing. But it is clear from the placement in Paul's teaching that he does not mean this. Jesus first died, then rose from the grave, and then preached peace. Also, we note that Jesus preached peace to those who were both far off and near, meaning to both Gentiles and Jews. The Gospels reveal that this did not happen during the three years of his earthly ministry.

Paul is therefore speaking of the time of the apostles, when the gospel went out to the Gentiles, when the Holy Spirit inspired the writing of the New Testament books, and when men like Paul went about preaching good news. This was, he says, the continued work of Jesus Christ as he proclaimed peace through his apostles.

This comes across in Acts 1:8, where Jesus spoke to his disciples just before he ascended into heaven. 'You will receive power when the Holy Spirit has come upon you,' he said, 'and you will be my witnesses in Jerusalem and in all Judea and Samaria, and to the end of the earth.' This means that when the apostles preached, Jesus was preaching through them. When they wrote the New Testament, Jesus was writing to us through them. This is true even today when a minister faithfully preaches Christ's gospel or when a faithful Christian shares the good news from God's Word, Jesus preaches, offering peace to sinners who are alienated from God, peace to the broken-hearted and fearful, and peace from God to a world gripped in conflict.

With the same love that bore our sins on the cross, Jesus speaks today through his Word. The love in his heart for the lost and the needy has not burned out. No less than when he cleansed the leper or forgave the woman caught in adultery, no less than when he multiplied a few pieces of fish and bread to feed the crowds, Jesus looks upon you with compassion, mercy, and the great love of God. He preaches good news of peace to you: peace with God, peace in your own heart, and peace on earth through the gospel of his grace. It is a peace he can offer because he purchased it with his blood; a peace he can give because he sends the Holy Spirit to all who believe; and a peace he preaches to you because mercy and grace still beats within his heart as he reigns in heaven and prepares his return. In all these senses, 'He came and preached peace to you who were far off and peace to those who were near' (Eph. 2:17).

Access to the Father

A second thing that stands out in these two verses is the clear evidence that Paul wants Christians to understand salvation and our relationship to God in terms of the doctrine of the Trinity. This is something that is distinctive to Christians: we do not relate merely to God in the abstract but to the three Persons of the Godhead. When we speak of having a 'personal relationship with God' it is because of what the Bible reveals about the Persons of the Trinity. Few passages in the New Testament present this as clearly as Ephesians 2:18: 'For through him [that is, Christ] we both have access in one Spirit to the Father.'

The doctrine of the Trinity is not just something for scholars to wrack their brains on. Trinity is who God is. So if we are to know God and relate to God, we must think about God as Trinity. We are living in a time when the Trinity is forgotten by many Christians. Some Christians think about Jesus only. Their worship is directed only to God the Son, and their salvation is founded only on what he does and gives. That is not what Jesus intends. Other Christians focus all their attention on 'plugging into' the Spirit and his power. But the New Testament emphasizes our relationship to the whole Trinity: Father, Son, and Holy Spirit.

This Trinitarian emphasis is important to Paul. In Ephesians 1:3–14, he worked out the blessings of salvation in terms of the Trinity. If we want to know and have all the blessings Christianity offers, then we must know all three Persons of the Godhead. Now in Ephesians 2:18 he applies this to our relationship to God. Our salvation involves and depends on all three members of the Trinity.

In this way, Paul wraps up his teaching on the peace made available to us through Jesus Christ. First, he makes the great statement that through Christ 'we have access to the Father.' This means that Jesus came into this world and died on the cross, not merely to bring us into relationship with himself, but most specifically to bring us into a relationship of love with God the Father.

This comes through in many places, but perhaps best in Jesus' prayer to the Father on the night of his arrest. In John 17:4, Jesus prays, 'I glorified you on earth, having accomplished the work that you gave me to do.' As Jesus goes on to say, that work was to reveal the Father and bring his people into a saving relationship with the Father. Similarly, when Jesus said in John 14:6, 'I am the way, the truth and the life,' it was in answer to Thomas' question about how they could know God the Father and enter into his blessing.

Therefore, Christianity's aim is that people who have been separated from God's love would now come to the Heavenly Father and enter into the light of his presence as beloved children. We are adopted into the family of God the Father, through the saving work of God the Son, by the ministry of God the Holy Spirit.

This makes a point of vast importance to our lives. So many people, even Christians, feel good about Jesus but think of God as a threatening, disapproving, and hostile force lurking in the background. The result is that they never enjoy the peace that Jesus came to give. God—God the Father—is seen as an angry judge who reveals that you have not lived up to his demands. God the Father is holy and perfect, and you are not holy and perfect. You do not pray like you should. You have not broken away from your sins the way you should. So you feel distant from God. You wonder if the promises of the Bible are really for you, because you don't measure up to the Father's unapproachable expectations.

If you feel this way, the gospel Christ preaches has two things to say to you. The first is that Jesus does not cajole a reluctant, grumpy, or unwilling Father to look on you in love. Rather, it was the Father who sent Jesus into the world because of his love for you. John 3:16 says, 'For God so loved the world that he gave his only Son.' Paul said in Ephesians 1:5, 'In love [God] predestined us for adoption through Jesus Christ.' If you trust in Christ, you can know that the heavenly Father loved you before you were even born, before the worlds came into existence. He knew you by name and wanted your heart to know his love. This is why Jesus came into the world—not to persuade a reluctant, angry God about you, but to serve a God of love by taking away your sin and making you a child of the Father.

But what about your unworthiness? What about the truth that you don't pray like you should, that you forget about God much of the time, and that you don't measure up to him? How can a holy God love you? The answer is the gospel Jesus came and preached. The gospel says that everything that needs to happen to open the way for the holy Father to pour his love on you was accomplished by Jesus Christ. You need to be righteous to stand in God's presence, and Jesus fulfilled the Law for you and grants to you by faith an imputed righteousness that is perfect in God's sight (see 2 Cor. 5:21).

But, you say, 'My sin and guilt makes me unclean before God and I feel nervous thinking about him.' The gospel replies that Jesus shed his blood to cleanse you once and for all before God. Ephesians 2:13 says, 'Now in Christ Jesus you who once were far off have been brought near by the blood of Christ.' The apostle John adds, 'If we confess our sins, he is faithful and just to forgive us our sins and to cleanse us from all unrighteousness' (1 John 1:9).

But you don't know where your heart will be tomorrow. Who knows if you will remain faithful to God? Yet Hebrews reminds you that Jesus lives and reigns in heaven, praying for you, ensuring the Holy Spirit's ministry in your life: 'Consequently, he is able to save to the uttermost those who draw near to God through him, since he always lives to make intercession for them' (Heb. 7:25).

Understanding Christ's work for you to achieve God the Father's purpose of love will change your life. It will cast away darkness with light. Martyn Lloyd-Jones described it:

> I am no longer filled with a craven fear of God. He is no longer to me some tyrant waiting to pounce on me and to damn me and to hurl me to hell. He is my loving Father who loved me with an everlasting love, with such a love as to send His only Son to die on the Cross for me. And the moment I realize that, I am at peace with Him.[219]

What Jesus wants, the reason he died and the cause for which he presently reigns, is for us to draw near to God the Father through him. He wants us to know the Father's love, which fulfills the deepest needs of our hearts. What do we gain from a father? We gain our identity and our name from our father. God will grant these to you. He will take you as his own child. We gain acceptance from our earthly fathers, and God wants to give his acceptance to you. Fathers grant provision, protection, and security, and God the Father wants to give you a destiny and an inheritance in glory. He will take care of you. These are the things that a father gives, and God the Father will give them to you through Jesus Christ.

Not a few people have a hard time turning to God as Father because of the painful experiences they have had with their earthly fathers. They were not accepted but were rejected. They received not care but abuse. Their father's discipline tore them down instead of building them up. But if you were let down by your earthly father in those ways or others, do not turn away from God the Father. Turn to him. He is the good and perfect Father. All that you ever longed for, and which earthly fathers sometimes fail to give, God the Father wants to give for the blessing of your heart.

Paul says that through Jesus all Christians, both Jews and Gentiles, have 'access to the Father.' The idea is more than that God is available to us, but that God invites us into his love. God delights to see his children because we are forgiven in Christ and clothed in his perfect righteousness. We should never fear to draw near to God, because through Jesus Christ we have access.

Back in the days when young men came to call at young ladies' homes, and the courting took place in the parlor, it was the women who initiated the relationship. Without an invitation it was considered rude for the man to show up at her home or to initiate personal contact. Without an invitation he would be turned away.

This is the way it is with God. If you show up at heaven without an invitation, you will be turned away. God is holy and his heaven is holy, and those stained by sin—even 'respectable' sins—will be turned away. So God sent his Son into the world to grant an invitation—to give access—to those who believe in him. And if you are in Christ then you have a permanent invitation into God's affections. He sees you clothed in perfect white, with all your stains removed by Christ's precious blood, and you are welcome with him.

Jesus wants you to have this relationship with the Father, and the Spirit's work is to empower you for this. We have 'access by one Spirit with the Father'. This is what makes us one in Christ, that we all have equal access by the same Spirit. The Spirit does not want us focusing on himself. 'He will glorify me,' Jesus said (John 16:14), and Jesus is glorified when sinners come to the Father in faith.

Thus our salvation is woven tightly in the combined work of the three Persons of the Trinity. You are saved because God the Father loves you, because God the Son gained your access on the cross, and because God the Spirit is working in your heart to bring you to God through faith. This is the pattern and structure of our whole salvation: we are saved to the Father, through the Son, by the Holy Spirit.

Praying to the Father

I want to apply this Trinitarian pattern directly to the matter of prayer. Ephesians 2:18 is one of the most important verses in the Bible when it comes to prayer. It tells us how prayer 'works.'

Most of us struggle with prayer because we do not understand what Paul teaches here. Our approach is what I like to call *The Wizard of Oz* model of prayer. This is the story of a girl from Kansas named Dorothy who is transported to the magical land of Oz. She wants to go home and is told to seek out the great and powerful Wizard of Oz, who lives in the Emerald City. As she travels there she is joined by the scarecrow, who wants a brain, the tin woodsman, who needs a heart, and the cowardly lion, who is ashamed of his fear.

After some adventures the little band arrives at the Emerald City and asks to see the wizard. They are told what many of us expect to be told about God: he is too busy for puny people like them; they have no right to intrude upon the great and powerful Oz. But, with daring and resourcefulness, Dorothy manages to get into the chamber to see the wizard. He is ominous and scary; his face is wreathed in flames and smoke. Fearfully, she makes her requests, but the wizard refuses to grant them. She must first complete a quest to prove her worth. It is only after she succeeds and returns with the broomstick of the Wicked Witch of the West that the wizard is willing to help, after which we learn that he is not really so great and powerful after all.

This is how many of us think about prayer. God is too busy and our prayers are a bother. If we even get his attention, we face a daunting, unwilling deity. If God does answer our prayers, it is only because we have first done something for him or otherwise won his favor, so that we are pretty much on our own. With all that, why bother to pray?

But what Paul writes here changes our view of God and of prayer. God is great and powerful, but he also knows and loves you. His eye is on you for every step of your journey. He did not wait in his distant chamber for you to come, but sent his Son into your world. It is true that your sins stand against you and that the devil opposes you, the way the wicked witch tried to stop Dorothy. But God's Son removed your sin and defeated the devil on the cross. He presents his achievement for you to the Father, who is glad to receive you and happy to care for you, who responds to your prayers with his love and grants you his peace (Phil. 4:7, 19). The scarecrow wanted a brain, and God will give you a right mind and a knowledge of truth; the tin woodsman wanted a heart, and God will plant a new heart within you, one that longs to do his will; the cowardly lion wanted courage, and God will strengthen you against fear. Dorothy wanted to go home, and God has prepared a home for you and will strengthen you as you journey through this life.

Returning to verse 18, we ask, 'Why will God answer our prayers?' The answer is because we have 'access to the Father.' Jesus is in heaven, hand-delivering all our prayers with hands that were pierced by nails for you. This is why we pray, 'in Jesus' name.' We are asking Jesus to be the mailman who delivers our prayers to God, and we are thereby certain they will arrive and be received with loving care.

But how can people like us actually pray and talk to God in a right way? Paul says it is 'by the Spirit.' In Romans 8:26, Paul says of prayer, 'The Spirit helps us in our weakness.' He enters into our prayers and sorts them out before God. Paul adds, 'The Spirit intercedes for the saints according to the will of God' (Rom. 8:27).

It makes a tremendous difference to understand how the three Persons of the Trinity work together to enable us to pray. But most importantly, Paul reminds us that we have a Heavenly Father who invites us to pray. Philip Ryken says, 'A real father is a man who has a passionate love for his family. Because of the warmth of his affection… his children have confidence to ask him for what they need.'[220] Surely that is why when his disciples asked, Jesus told them to come to God in prayer, saying, 'Our Father, who art in heaven.'

To Publish Peace

Let me conclude with three observations. The first is for those who have never trusted in Christ. This is what you are missing if your heart is closed to Jesus. The good news that Paul writes of in this chapter is the best you possibly could hear. It is good news for your eternal destiny and for your life on this earth, if you will believe. Jesus came to bring sinners near to God through his blood (Eph. 2:13). He came to be our peace (Eph. 2:14). He gives us access into the love of the Heavenly Father through his blood and by the ministry of the Holy Spirit. Why will you stand far off from that? Paul says in verse 17 that even as you hear this, it is Jesus himself, with all the love of God in his heart, who preaches good news of peace to you. As Paul elsewhere said, 'In Christ God was reconciling the world to himself, not counting their trespasses against them, and entrusting to us the message of reconciliation. Therefore, we are ambassadors for Christ, God making his appeal through us. We implore you on behalf of Christ, be reconciled to God' (2 Cor. 5:19–20). You can call upon God right now through faith in Jesus Christ, and you will be saved.

Second, if you have believed in Christ, then realize all that he has achieved for you according to God's own plan. You have access to God the Father, a permanent invitation into his love and a place in his heart forever. If that is true, then live in the light of God's love. Do not let feelings of guilt or inadequacy keep you from God, but let them remind you how precious is the blood of Christ and how amazing is the grace that draws you near. Martyn Lloyd-Jones wrote:

> The moment you see that you are made righteous by Christ and clothed in His righteousness, you can go to God with confidence. He is your Father, He is waiting to receive you and you can pray as you have never prayed before. The way is clear, it is a new and a living way that has been opened. You are at peace with God and at peace within; you have found rest for your soul.[221]

Finally, if we believe this and know it in our lives, surely we will tell others. Paul says that Jesus came and preached good news of peace; we know that Jesus wants us to go and do the same (Matt. 28:18–20). Once you know the reality of God's love for you, he will give you love for others and cause you to preach good news so that they, too, might have access to the Father, through the Son, by the Spirit. And then what Isaiah said about Jesus will be true of you also: 'How beautiful upon the mountains are the feet of him who brings good news, who publishes peace' (Isa. 52:7).

31

CITIZENS AND CHILDREN

Ephesians 2:19

In 1962, William Edgar arrived as a 17-year-old freshman at Harvard University. As he tells it, his life was focused around a trinity that consisted of soccer, French existential philosophy, and jazz piano. As he recounts in *Finding God at Harvard*, Edgar's freshman year was humbling: he found others who were better at soccer and piano and few who cared about his philosophy. By his sophomore year he was starting to adjust, when he took a survey course in Western literature. As often happens in universities, this class had one large lecture with the professor and then smaller discussion classes with teaching assistants. Edgar's teaching assistant was an articulate Christian named Harold O.J. Brown, who would go on to be one of the great theology professors of our time. Through Brown's Christian critique of literature and personal discussions outside of class, Edgar was introduced to a new Trinity: Father, Son and Holy Spirit. On his teacher's advice, he spent his sophomore summer at the Swiss Christian community, L'Abri, with the renowned apologist, Francis Schaeffer. When Edgar returned to Harvard for his junior year it was as a committed Christian.

Edgar's return to Harvard involved considerable change for him. He mainly remembered that everything seemed new and alive because he was alive to God. He abandoned his unbelieving philosophy. He regained his love for soccer, no longer needing to be the best but only to do his best. His music was especially impacted, and he sought out the Christian spirituality beneath much of the jazz music he loved. As many college-age converts have found, perhaps the most challenging changes were social. 'Some of my friends thought I had become a little strange!' he remembers. 'Though they did not exactly abandon me, I felt they were studying me. More challenging still, in my newfound faith I felt obliged to seek out other Christians.'[222]

ALIENS NO MORE

What Edgar experienced is consistent with Paul's explanation of Christian salvation in Ephesians 2. Ephesians 2:1–10 says we begin as sinners who are saved in a spiritual resurrection by God's grace, through faith in Christ. The second half of chapter 2 looks at salvation from a more corporate perspective. Starting in verse 12, Paul reminds us that apart from Christ we were aliens to God's people and covenant, and therefore 'without hope and without God in the world.'

When we trust in Christ and are saved, we not only become new individuals but enter into new relationships. These relationships are identified in verses 19 and 20: we become citizens of God's kingdom together with the saints, children in God's household together with brothers and sisters, and we become part of a building, a living temple, in which God lives by the Spirit. All of these are relationships we enter through Jesus Christ together with all fellow believers.

In this study we are going to look at the first two of these new relationships brought about by Christ, starting with *citizenship in God's kingdom*. Paul writes, 'So then you are no longer strangers and aliens, but you are fellow citizens with the saints' (Eph. 2:19). God rules over an eternal kingdom, and having come to God through faith in Christ we are no longer aliens to it but we have become citizens of it.

Paul uses two words to describe our former condition, the first of which is *strangers*, people who belong somewhere else but are traveling through. The second word, *aliens*, describes resident foreigners. These are people living among us who hold their citizenship elsewhere.

We all know what it is like to be an outsider, not to fit in or understand the place where we are. Often this comes to us when we are traveling in a different country. We do not know the language or the culture. The food is strange and the people act in ways we do not understand. Furthermore, strangers are treated with suspicion; aliens are not made to feel welcome because their loyalties are different. They do not belong and their presence makes people feel uncomfortable. Undoubtedly, this is how many foreign residents feel about living in the United States. Their status is insecure and much that they experience is unfamiliar and threatening. Strangers and aliens long for home, for acceptance and for belonging.

Like it or not, this is what Paul says was true about his Gentile readers before they came to faith in Christ. They were not part of God's kingdom. He used these very terms in verse 12, saying that they were 'alienated from the commonwealth of Israel and strangers to the covenants of promise.' God was in the world and he had a people, but they were not part of that. The fellowship of God and his people was strange and unfamiliar and they had no right to claim a place within it. Unsaved people are the same today. Even when Christians try to be friendly, unbelievers often do not feel comfortable at church. Their hearts were made to worship God but they do not know how. They may long for truth but they find God's Word strange. They need God in their lives but they do not know how to pray.

This is how it was for Paul's Gentile readers before he came to Ephesus with the gospel. Prior to that time, they groped around in pagan idolatry trying in futility to relate to God. So God sent his own Son into the world to make peace with men by dying on the cross. Through Jesus' resurrection, God sent new life into the world and through the apostles Christ preached his peace. The result was a great change for those who heard and believed; through faith in Christ they became 'fellow citizens with the saints.'

In our day, citizenship means sharing in the cause of your country and being allowed to vote. This is similar to what happens to us when we join the church; we take up its cause and have a right to participate in ministry. In Paul's time a bit more was involved in citizenship; citizens had a right to protection that non-citizens did not have. Once, when a mob rose against him in Jerusalem and the Roman commander was going to have him beaten, Paul revealed that he was a Roman citizen. Immediately, the whips were put away and the soldiers protected him. His citizenship granted him the right to appeal to Caesar for justice; in fact, it was while he was waiting for this audience in Rome that Paul wrote his letter to the Ephesians.

Likewise, being a citizen allows us to benefit from God's kingdom. The Romans enjoyed provision, protection, fair government and justice. In America, our citizenship secures for us freedom from unlawful seizure and freedom to make a living. What, then, are the benefits of citizenship in God's kingdom? Our main benefits are spelled out in the new covenant promise, found in Jeremiah 31:31-34 and in Hebrews 8:8-12. God says, 'I will put my laws into their minds and write them on their hearts, and I will be their God and they shall be my people...I will be merciful toward their iniquities and remember their sins no more.' We might think of these in terms of the three tenses of our salvation: the past tense—justification; the present tense—sanctification; and the future tense—glorification. These are rights that believers gain as citizens of God's kingdom.

In the Sermon on the Mount, Jesus spoke of his Father watching over every hair on our heads, so that citizenship in God's kingdom gives us freedom from anxiety. Our citizenship means that we have the Good Shepherd, Jesus Christ, to rule in us by his love. *The Westminster Shorter Catechism* says that Jesus executes his office of king 'in subduing us to himself, in ruling and defending us, and in restraining and conquering all his and our enemies' (A. 26). The Bible often describes God's kingdom in terms of a great city state, so we can rejoice at Psalm 46's description of the gospel flowing through that city, giving life and joy to all who drink from its waters: 'There is a river whose streams make glad the city of God...God is in her, she shall not be moved' (Ps. 46:4–5).

With these privileges come obligations. The Shorter Catechism addresses this simply. In answer to the question, 'What is the duty which God requires of man?' it says, 'The duty which God requires of man, is obedience to his revealed will' (Q.39). We are to trust God, love God, and serve God, all of which find expression through obedience to the Word of God in the Bible.

When Paul writes of our citizenship in God's kingdom we should remember where he was at that moment. Paul was in Rome, either in prison or in house arrest. All around him were the great buildings that were a monument to empire. Roman citizenship was the most prized possession one could have. If one did not receive it by birth—and only a few did—then it could only be purchased at great cost. Paul was a Roman citizen, having been raised in the Roman city of Tarsus. But that was not his glory. That was not his source of pride, hope, or confidence. 'Our citizenship is in heaven,' he boasted (Phil. 3:20). And as he writes from Rome to these Ephesian Christians, he wants heavenly citizenship to be their glory as well.

Imagine Paul saying this to the average Roman of his day. To a Roman, immortality was gained through participation in the greatness of Rome. Yet here was Paul throwing away all that Rome offered for the kingdom of a Galilean Messiah. To be a Christian always involves a clash of kingdoms, the kingdoms of this world and the kingdom of God and of Christ. This came through most vividly at Jesus' trial. Pontius Pilate scoffed at the idea of Jesus being a king. Jesus didn't have any of the accoutrements. He had no army, no treasury, no badge of office. 'So you are a king?' he scoffed. Jesus replied, 'My kingdom is not of this world' (John 18:36–37).

Jesus' kingdom is heavenly and not earthly. This distinction does not make his kingdom inferior, but superior. Above all the kingdoms of earth is Christ's heavenly kingdom. While the Caesars rule over the body, Jesus rules over the soul; while worldly kings may rule affairs in this life, Christ rules over eternity. This is why Paul was no longer impressed by the glory of Rome, and why he gloried only in the kingdom of God in which he held citizenship through faith in Christ.

Verse 19 shows one of the differences between worldly kingdoms and Christ's kingdom. Paul says, 'You are fellow citizens with the saints.' This speaks of the character of God's kingdom in which we are made citizens, in comparison with that of the world. God's kingdom is one of peace, love, and harmony. It is a holy kingdom, in which everyone who joins becomes one with the saints. This refers not to a few super-spiritual giants, but to all the people of God, those made holy by the blood of Christ. Ours is a kingdom of holy union, holy love, and holy purpose. James Montgomery Boice observes the difference between God's kingdom and the Roman Empire that held Paul captive:

> When Paul wrote these words the kingdom of Rome was at the height of its territorial expansion and glory. Rome dominated the world. Roman armies kept peace and dispensed justice. Roman roads linked the far-flung reaches of the Empire. Rome had stood for hundreds of years and was thought to be able to stand for thousands of years more. But Paul looked at Rome and saw it, not as one great united Kingdom, but as a force imposed on mutually antagonistic factions: rich and poor, free man and slave, man and woman, Jew and Gentile. And in its place he saw this new humanity, created by God himself, transcending these boundaries. This kingdom was destined to grow and permeate all nations, drawing from all peoples. It is a kingdom that cannot be shaken or destroyed.[223]

Where is the Roman Empire today? Where are the many empires that have risen and fallen since Paul's time? What is the destiny of every worldly kingdom, but to come and go as God desires? The apostle John wrote, 'The world is passing away along with its desires, but whoever does the will of God abides forever' (1 John 2:17).

Paul realized this as he wrote from his prison cell in Rome. If he would only renounce Christ, or even back off of the gospel, just fitting into the world as it was, he could have kept all that his Roman citizenship offered him. But he saw with a keener vision the realities of faith. He wrote in 2 Corinthians 4:17, 'This slight momentary affliction is preparing for us an eternal weight of glory beyond all comparison.'

Members of God's Household

Citizenship in God's kingdom is one result of our salvation in Christ. But Paul goes on to speak of another relationship that is more personal. We may be all members of the same country but not members of the same family, so Paul is bringing us closer in when he adds, 'and members of the household of God' (Eph. 2:19). Here is a relationship, and a unity with others, that is intimate and intense. Here we have gone from the legal relationship to a spiritual relationship. Just as blood unites a family, God's Spirit unites all believers as *fellow members of his household*.

One thing this means is that this relationship is only for those who are born again in Christ Jesus. Jesus said, 'You must be born again to even see the kingdom of God' (John 3:3). That is because God's kingdom is also a family, and just as a family is defined by blood relations, God's household is bound by an inner, spiritual unity. People may talk about God being everyone's Father, but the Bible says he is a Father only to those who are his children in Jesus Christ. John 1:12–13 says, 'To all who did receive him, who believed in his name, he gave the right to become children of God, who were born, not of blood nor of the will of the flesh nor of the will of man, but of God.'

That God should make us members of his own household speaks volumes about his amazing love. It would be enough to praise God through all eternity if he simply refrained from condemning us as sinners. We deserve hell, and God forgives us through Jesus Christ. This alone is more than we could have ever imagined. Martyn Lloyd-Jones writes: 'It would have been a wonderful thing if God had merely decided not to leave us in that state and not to punish us. But God's way of salvation does not stop at that. He elevates us to this dignity of children, He adopts us into His own family.'[224]

Imagine appearing before an uncompromising judge for a crime you most certainly did commit. All the evidence condemns you and you have no defense. But just when your sentence is to be read, the judge tells you that he loves you and that his own son has agreed to serve your sentence, and that, furthermore, he wants you to come home with him, to take his name and be his child, that he will teach you to sin no more and that you will enter into fellowship with others who are beneficiaries of that same love. What would you say to that? You would marvel at his grace and give all the love in your heart to such a man as that. This is what God does in his love, and through the sacrifice of his Son believers are members of the household of God.

This is the love Jesus presented in his parable of the prodigal son. The son had fallen into sin and squandered his father's estate in immoral living. But when he repented and started home in disgrace, his father saw him coming from a long way off. Jesus tells what happened:

> While he was still a long way off, his father saw him and felt compassion, and ran and embraced him and kissed him. And the son said to him, 'Father, I have sinned against heaven and before you. I am no longer worthy to be called your son.' But the father said to his servants, 'Bring quickly the best robe, and put it on him, and put a ring on his hand, and shoes on his feet. And bring the fattened calf and kill it, and let us eat and celebrate. For this my son was dead, and is alive again; he was lost, and is found.' And they began to celebrate (Luke 15:20–24).

If you have never come to God the Father through faith in Jesus Christ his Son, this is the love you are missing. This is the celebration that awaits every lost sinner who is a stranger and alien to the grace and salvation of God. God's people are a family that celebrates with great joy every sinner who is saved, and who are preparing now for an eternity together in the light of God's love.

If being a citizen of God's kingdom gives many benefits, how much greater are the benefits that flow from this more intimate relationship. A king must provide for his people, but how much more is a father concerned for his children. As children of God, we have the right to come to God in prayer and have him care for our needs. Jesus said, 'Your father in heaven knows what you need before you even ask him' (Matt. 7:8). 'If you who are evil know how to give good gifts to your children, how much more will your Father who is in heaven give good things to those who ask him!' (Matt. 7:11).

Wonderful as is God's Fatherly care in this life, it is far surpassed by what awaits all his children in the life to come. In Romans 8:17, Paul writes that we are 'if children, then heirs—heirs of God and fellow heirs with Christ, provided we suffer with him in order that we may also be glorified with him.'

A CHILD OF THE KING

If you put these two together, Paul's teaching that in Christ we are citizens of God's kingdom and children in God's family, then we are rightly described by the hymn that says:

> I once was an outcast stranger on earth,
>   a sinner by choice, and an alien by birth!
> But I've been adopted, my name's written down,
>   an heir to a mansion, a robe, and a crown
> I'm a child of the King, a child of the King!
>   With Jesus, my Savior, I'm a child of the King.[225]

These lines express the great reality for everyone who trusts in Jesus Christ. We were strangers and aliens. We did not fit in and we had no place in God's kingdom or his family. We had no real answer for the great problems of life, much less of eternity. Man in sin is estranged from God and from God's blessings. So God in his love sent Jesus Christ to be our peace, to reconcile us to God by suffering the punishment in our place and to bring us into a real community with peace and love. If you are not a Christian, these are blessings that God offers you through his Son, Jesus Christ.

If you are a Christian, God wants you to know these privileges and blessings that are your calling. The trouble with so many of our lives is that we do not understand the implications of what it means to be a Christian. We do not realize our position. From the perspective of heaven, during the eternity that is to come, we will be baffled by the attitude we so often now take, by our fixation on the things of earth, our doubting of God's faithful affection, and our lack of concern for the well-being of our brothers and sisters.

So often people think about what they have to give up if they become Christians. It certainly is true that following Christ will involve leaving off former habits and relationships and it certainly means turning away from sins we have loved. William Edgar discovered that when he came to Christ as a Harvard student. But he also learned that God was not narrowing his scope but vastly increasing it; God was making him a member of his glorious kingdom. God was not stripping him away from relationships where he belonged but was entering him into his true home, introducing him to those who would truly love him and with whom he had real spiritual unity. Years later, when his class returned to Harvard for their 25th reunion, Edgar had the privilege of preaching in the chapel about the blessings that flow from the death and resurrection of Christ, inviting his classmates to enter God's eternal kingdom for the salvation of their souls. In one of his books, he said of the gospel, 'To believe this message is to come home. Like the prodigal in Jesus' parable, we are homeless, lost in an alien land, until we come back home to the Father.'[226]

Man was made by God and for God. We each have a God-shaped hole in our hearts that can only be filled by returning to him, by entering God's kingdom and joining his household as children. Until we do, we are restless, hungry and thirsty for meaning and a place to belong. Through faith in Christ, God offers us nothing less than the fulfillment of these, our greatest and deepest needs. God sent his Son to save us from our sin. But forgiveness is just the beginning, not the end. Jesus Christ saves us to heavenly citizenship and to membership in a family where we belong. Edgar observed, 'Much of our contemporary culture is alienated from God. The gospel calls it to come home.'[227]

Only God, through Jesus Christ, can make life sacred, can give eternal meaning to our labor, and can offer us a home where we belong forever. When Christians realize that this is what we have, that this is what we are—royal children, princes and princesses in the kingdom and household of God—we will not have to be taught how to live. God simply calls us to be what he has made us in Christ, to serve faithfully in his kingdom and to love one another as brothers and sisters who share in his love.

32

A Holy Temple

Ephesians 2:20–22

There is a billboard that I have seen from time to time that always makes me smile and think about our Lord Jesus. The billboard says, We Buy Ugly Houses. I suppose that means that if your house is in bad shape and no one will buy it, these people will take it off your hands, fix it up, and sell it at a profit. It is probably a good business and one that may actually help people.

What makes me think about Jesus is that he does pretty much the same thing with us. Jesus is not like a prospective home-buyer who travels around with an agent looking for the most attractive, most luxurious house, already all put together, for the least cost to himself. Instead, his motto might be the one on the billboard: I Buy Ugly Houses. Not only is this true, but Jesus pays not the lowest cost possible but the highest price imaginable. The apostle Paul says to believers, 'You were bought with a price' (1 Cor. 6:20), and Peter tells us, 'You were ransomed…not with perishable things such as silver or gold, but with the precious blood of Christ' (1 Pet. 1: 18–19).

Jesus bought us not because we were so attractive or intelligent or good. What Paul wrote to the Corinthians is true of us, 'Not many of you were wise according to worldly standards, not many were powerful, not many were of noble birth' (1 Cor. 1:26). In fact, like ugly houses, Jesus bought us when we were covered in the guilt and the filth of our sin. Romans 5:6–8 says, 'While we were still weak, at the right time Christ died for the ungodly…God shows his love for us in that while we were still sinners, Christ died for us.' This is the good news of Christianity. We are not saved because we are so attractive or worthy. We are saved because of the compassion and grace of a loving God in Jesus Christ. And the best news of all is not only that Jesus buys ugly houses, but that he fixes them up, and then fills them with his Spirit so that God himself can come to live.

This is the teaching of the apostle Paul in this final passage of Ephesians 2. In Christ, he says, we are 'a holy temple in the Lord…a dwelling place for God' (Eph. 2:21–22). This is both Paul's conclusion to his doctrine of salvation and the bridge he builds to his teaching on the church and the Christian life in the following chapters, which shows us that the church is the outworking of Christ's saving work in individuals. Here, Paul tells us that the Christian church is built as the temple in which God will live forever; he describes the all-important foundation for the church; and he points to Christ himself as the cornerstone on which this temple rests.

A Holy Temple

Paul's main point is that the Christian church is built as a holy temple in which God will dwell. Unlike other buildings that are put together by bricks and mortar, this building is made up of God's people themselves and bound together by the Spirit of God. The apostle Peter said, 'As you come to him [that is, Christ], a living stone rejected by men but in the sight of God chosen and precious, you yourselves like living stones are being built up as a spiritual house, to be a holy priesthood.' (1 Pet. 2:4–5).

All through the latter half of Ephesians 2, Paul has had in mind the Jewish temple as a way of depicting the peace that Christ gives. There was a veil that separated sinful man from God and Christ removed it by his death. There was a wall of division between Jew and Gentile, and that, too, is now gone.

Paul must have thought about the temple as he traveled throughout the ancient world preaching and starting churches. Paul had many difficulties and disappointments, but his heart must have been thrilled to know that just as the stonesmiths in Solomon's day worked hard to fashion the great blocks to build that temple, he, too, was working hard for a temple that would shine in glory forever.

The Bible's teaching on the temple begins with God's promise to David that his son would build God's house: 'I will raise up your offspring after you, who shall come from your body, and I will establish his kingdom. He shall build a house for my name, and I will establish the throne of his kingdom forever' (2 Sam. 7:12–13). David realized that the Lord was speaking not merely of David's son and immediate heir, Solomon, but also of his future descendant, who would be both son of David and Son of God, the Lord Jesus Christ.

David's son, Solomon, did build God's temple in Jerusalem, and when the ark of the covenant was brought within its walls the glory of the Lord filled the place: 'A cloud filled the house of the Lord…for the glory of the Lord filled the house of the Lord' (1 Kings 8:10–11). All of this was symbolic of the true and spiritual fulfillment that would come through Jesus Christ. Some people complain about a spiritual fulfillment of Old Testament prophecies, but here we see that the spiritual fulfillment is the true fulfillment, as the Holy Spirit enters into the forms and symbols of the old covenant, bringing God's transforming presence with grace and power. The true temple is the spiritual house that is Christ's church, which even now is 'being joined together…into a holy temple in the Lord.' Just as the glory cloud filled Solomon's temple, God wants to fill your life and his church with the Holy Spirit. This is true and saving Christianity, to have God's Spirit live in you and change you to be holy as a fitting dwelling place for God.

This comparison with the Jewish temple tells us a number of things about the Christian church and about Christian people. The first is that we are saved and the church exists for the sake of God's glory. This is what made the temple in Jerusalem special, that God's presence filled the place with glory.

This leads me to ask, What is it that impresses us about a church or a person? Is it the kind of worldly glory that so attracts the natural man? God's glory is displayed not by sheer numbers or by wealth or by fleshly excitement, but by a people who reverence his Word, who worship in spirit and in truth, who display the fruits of God's Spirit, who adorn their lives with good works, and who wave Christ's banner of love.

This is the message God gave through the prophet Zechariah for the Jews who had returned to Jerusalem after the Babylonian exile. The original temple of Solomon's was gone, and the people were now building one far less glorious to take its place. Ezra tells us that while the crowd cheered when its foundation was laid, the old men, who had seen the original temple in their youth, were weeping because of the lesser glory of this second temple (Ez. 3:12). But God declared through his prophet Zechariah: 'I will be to her a wall of fire all around, declares the Lord, and I will be the glory in her midst' (Zech. 2:5). T. V. Moore comments:

> We learn here the true glory of the Church. It is not in any external pomp or power, of any kind; not in frowning battlements, either of temporal or spiritual pretensions; not in rites and ceremonies, however moss-grown and venerable; not in splendid cathedrals and gorgeous vestments, and the swell of music, and the glitter of eloquence, but in the indwelling glory of the invisible God.[228]

This principle applies to us as individuals as to the church. The prophet Jeremiah sums this up, saying, 'Let not the wise man boast of his wisdom or the strong man boast of his strength or the rich man boast of his riches, but let him who boasts boast about this: that he understands and knows me, that I am the LORD' (Jer. 9:23–24).

The church is, first, for the display of God's glory and, second, it is holy. The temple was a holy building, that is, it was set apart for the worship of God. Inside were holy vessels, used only for God's service, and holy people, the priests, who were set apart to worship God and serve his people. In the same way, the church is now set apart. We are not to be worldly. There is to be a noticeable difference between us and the world. This of course pertains to sin; as individuals and as a church we are to be marked by a freedom from sin and by obedience to God's Word. But it goes beyond this to an active desire to know God and live for him.

This holiness will be reflected in our attitude and our methods of ministry. A generation ago, A.W. Tozer spoke words that have been sadly unheeded by evangelical churches. He wrote, 'One of the most popular current errors, and the one out of which springs most of the noisy, blustering religious activity in evangelical circles, is the notion that as times change the church must change with them. That mentality which mistakes Hollywood for the Holy City is…gravely astray.'[229] Christians are set apart to lead holy lives to the glory and service of God in accordance with God's unchanging Word. Paul explained such a life in practical terms:

> Present your bodies as a living sacrifice, holy and acceptable to God, which is your spiritual worship. Do not be conformed to this world, but be transformed by the renewal of your mind, that by testing you may discern what is the will of God, what is good and acceptable and perfect (Rom. 12:1–2).

Whenever you talk about living for God's glory, about being holy, and about serving God with your life, people begin to think dreary thoughts about Christianity and the church. But in reality, a life devoted to God is exciting. Is there anything more wonderful than to realize that my life amounts to more than just occupying space and time, than just getting by and trying to have a decent time? I am made to bear God's image and in Christ I have been born again so that God himself might live in me and shine forth from me. After everything in this world is gone, I will still be a member of this church that is God's living temple, which Revelation 21:11 says will shine forever 'with the glory of God,' with a brilliance 'like that of a very precious jewel.' Realizing this destiny makes me excited about what it means to be a Christian and what it means to be part of Christ's glorious church, the construction of which is the greatest building project in all eternity.

A Firm Foundation

In introducing his teaching on the church, Paul directs our attention to the all-important matter of the church's foundation. When erecting a building, nothing is more important than laying a solid and true foundation. Paul therefore says that the church is 'built on the foundation of the apostles and prophets, Christ Jesus himself being the cornerstone' (Eph. 2:20).

In any building project, the foundation is laid only once. You do not build by laying a foundation over and over. You build one foundation and then build upward from it. Paul applies this principle to 'the apostles and prophets,' whose once-for-all work laid the foundation for Christians and the church.

You sometimes hear today of new apostles. But biblically this is impossible. The apostles were the earthly disciples of Jesus, who after witnessing the resurrection bore his authority in the world and were direct agents of his revelation. By definition, there can be no apostles today, both because no one can fulfill these requirements (Acts 1:21–22) and because a builder only lays a foundation once. The Roman Catholic Church claims that the pope sits in Peter's office, with his apostolic authority, giving him the right to interpret and even contradict Scripture. But this is impossible, because the apostles' task was to lay the foundation; we now are building upon that foundation and the apostles' work need not and cannot be repeated.

What did the apostles do in building the church's foundation? In part, they built the foundation by founding the first churches in accordance with God's will. But most significantly, the apostles wrote down for us the completed revelation of God's Word in the New Testament. As one hymn puts it, 'How firm a foundation, ye saints of the Lord, is laid for your faith in his excellent Word!'[230]

Paul speaks of 'the foundation of the apostles and prophets' (Eph. 2:20). There is some question as to whether this refers to the Old Testament prophets. I think this is not likely because in the Greek text these two are grouped together with only one definite article and also because Paul lists the apostles before the prophets, whereas the Old Testament prophets came before the apostles. Paul is probably referring to people who possessed the gift of prophecy spoken of in 1 Corinthians 12 and 13. We need to remember that during the first decades of the church the New Testament was just being written and it was many years before the various books were collected and disseminated. The early churches received God's Word through the apostles, but when the apostles moved on there were prophets who God used to continue giving his Word to the people of that generation. Charismatic churches today believe that the gift of prophecy still exists in the church, but Paul tells us here that like the apostles the New Testament prophets belonged to the foundation-laying apostolic age. Once the Bible was completed, their function, like that of the apostles, no longer existed.

What this means for us today is that our foundation as a church must be the apostolic teaching in the Bible. This does not restrict us to the New Testament, since the apostles based their own preaching on the Old Testament. Of the almost 8,000 verses in the New Testament, it is estimated that more than 2,500 quote or refer to the Old Testament.[231] The whole Bible must be the basis for all that we do. Just as a foundation bears the weight of a building and sets the pattern for its growth, so the Bible is the foundation for Christ's church. If we are to build safely, strongly, and faithfully then we must make God's Word the only infallible rule for our faith and practice. The Book of Acts tells us that the church in its earliest days was 'devoted to the apostles' teaching' (Acts 2:42), and so must we be today if we are to build upon their foundation.

Christ Jesus the Cornerstone

A building is not made secure by only the foundation, but every foundation requires and relies upon its cornerstone. In the building of great stone structures, the first thing you do is place the cornerstone, on which everything else rests and depends. In God's living temple that is the church this cornerstone is none other than, Paul says, 'Christ Jesus himself' (Eph. 2:20). As the famous hymn puts it:

> The church's one foundation
>   is Jesus Christ her Lord.
> She is the new creation,
>   by water and the Word.
> From heaven he came and sought her
>   to be his holy bride.
> With his own blood he bought her
>   and for her life he died.[232]

These verses tell us much about Jesus as the cornerstone of the church and correspond perfectly with everything Paul has taught in Ephesians 2. The church consists of those people redeemed and purchased by Jesus with his own precious blood. Ephesians 2:13 says we who were far away were 'brought near by the blood of Christ.' Therefore the cornerstone of the church consists of Christ's atoning death for sin, by which sinners who believe are forgiven and cleansed.

Jesus also created the church through the power of his resurrection. He has created 'in himself one new man,' says verse 14, in the place of all the divisions of the world and by the power of his Holy Spirit. Finally, Christ is the cornerstone because he is today a living Lord over and for the church. Ephesians 1:22-23 said that God 'gave him as head over all things to the church, which is his body.'

This statement tells us about the relationship between Christ and the apostles. Christ is the cornerstone from which the foundation extends. You sometimes hear today that we do not really know what Jesus himself taught, since we only have the information the apostles wanted us to hear. But this idea directly contradicts the Bible's teaching. On the night of his arrest, Jesus told the disciples that his Holy Spirit would come and 'guide you into all truth…He will take what is mine and declare it to you' (John 16:13-14). Before ascending into glory, Jesus breathed the Spirit upon them, saying, 'You will be my witnesses' (Acts 1:8). Paul himself was commissioned as an apostle by Jesus himself on the Damascus Road. Jesus said to him, 'I have appeared to you for this purpose, to appoint you as a servant and witness' (Acts 26:16).

Just as the foundation is the extension of the cornerstone, following its lines and anchored by its strength, so the apostles were Christ's own extension into the world. The apostles and their teaching derive their authority from Jesus and we are to treat their words in the Bible as his own Word to us. In a derivative way, the same is true of ministers set apart to teach the Bible today and of all Christians in our witness to the world. We are to follow Christ's example, we are to serve Christ by the Spirit that he sends, and we are to make God's Word our source of spiritual authority as we serve him in the church and represent him in the world.

The Church Door

According to Paul, Jesus Christ is in the house-building business. Speaking of gospel faith, Jesus promised, 'On this rock I will build my church' (Matt. 16:16). Like a magnificent cathedral, Christ's church continues to be built, not one brick but one believer at a time.

Just as the billboard says, Jesus starts by buying ugly houses. But he does not just patch them up and sell them. He fills them with glory by his own Spirit. He works a new creation. It begins in our rebirth and continues all through our lives. We are being spiritually renovated with divine power. He gives us a new heart, renews our minds, and fills our souls with the light of God. He is the master builder and he is himself the cornerstone.

But there is one more thing about Jesus and the church. He is also its door. Jesus is the only way you can enter this spiritual house, the only way you can be built into this living temple that is filled with God's glory. Jesus said, 'I am the door. If anyone enters by me, he will be saved' (John 10:9).

This truth is illustrated by the story of a young woman who came to church with a friend and soon realized that there was something seriously different about it. People talked about having a personal relationship with Jesus Christ. Someone asked her a jarring question: 'If you were to die tonight and stand before God, and if he were to ask you, "Why should I let you into my heaven?" what would you say?' She answered that she had received the sacraments and that though not perfect she was a basically good person. She then was invited to ask the question back, and the Christian answered in a very different way. He said his only hope was that Jesus Christ had died on the cross for his sins and risen from the grave to him eternal life as the gift of God's grace. When the conversation was over, the woman turned to her friend and said, 'Wow, those answers were completely different!' The church's pastor later remembered: 'Even though she was not yet a Christian, she could see that there was an eternity of difference between asking God to accept her on her own merits and asking him to let what Jesus did count for her. Not long afterwards the Holy Spirit brought her to saving faith in Jesus Christ.'[233]

This is the key point for anyone who is not part of God's great and spiritual house, who is not God's child, and who does not know what it means to be a citizen in God's kingdom. The only way you can be saved from your sins and enter into the blessings of God is through faith in Jesus Christ. He is the door, and if you will believe in him you will be saved. Then you will become part of his glorious church, the temple he is building for the dwelling of God forever.

Let me complete the woman's story for the sake of those who already believe. Some time later, the woman reflected on what had happened and lamented that in all the years she had attended church no one had ever given her the gospel. No one explained the cross and the free gift of salvation through faith alone. She had thought it was just up to her to be good enough for God. Do you see why it is important that we build the church in the right way—upon the gospel foundation of the apostles and on the cornerstone that is Christ, with Jesus himself as the door? Jesus said, 'If anyone enters by me, he will be saved' (John 10:9). If we bring people into the church through any other door than Christ himself as he is proclaimed in God's Word—through entertaining music, social programs, or emotional manipulations—then we do not bring them to salvation. They may be happy here, they may have felt needs met, but they will not be saved.

We can bring people in through all sorts of different doors, literally and figuratively. But they will only be saved and they will only be a part of God's spiritual house if they enter through Christ, trusting in his life, death, and resurrection for their salvation.

I praise the Lord that woman had a church near her where she could come, to which a caring Christian invited her, and where the gospel was not only preached from the pulpit but shared by a whole church of living witnesses. This is the kind of church God is calling us to be, and if we are faithful to our Lord we are promised that by the Spirit he will build us up together 'into a holy temple in the Lord…into a dwelling place for God by the Spirit' (Eph. 2:21–22).

33

A Prisoner of Christ

Ephesians 3:1

I was thirty years old when I was converted to Jesus Christ. I was raised in an exemplary moral and religious home, but had not been born again. After I went to college I ceased attending church almost completely and became absorbed into the sinful social scene around me. Having spent my twenties pursuing my career as a combat officer in the U.S. Army, I was sent to graduate school to prepare for the next phase of my career. My mother suggested that during this more relaxed period I try to round out my life, perhaps finding a wife and getting back involved in religion. As a result, I visited the nearest Presbyterian church (since I was raised Presbyterian), where I encountered for the first time a minister of God's Word who preached the gospel with boldness and authority. During my first worship service at the church, an evening service, I was convicted of my sin and turned to Jesus Christ for forgiveness and salvation.

During those two years of graduate school, a lot changed in my life. Formerly, I had devoted myself to the study of military history and strategy. Now, I found myself reading the Bible and studying theology with a passion. But that was not all that changed in my life. It wasn't long before I found it necessary to change some of my habits, especially those having to do with my social life. That had an effect on my friendships. I well remember attending the church singles' group on Friday nights instead of going out to the bars, and coming home to find mocking messages from my friends on my answering machine. After a while, I was no longer accepted by those supposed friends, especially when I tried to explain the changes in my life and my faith in Jesus Christ. Having lost my secular friends, I got more involved with Christians, whose example strengthened and inspired me, and after a while I began dating a woman who had lived all of her life as a Christian, and before long we were engaged to be married.

That two year period, which I will always remember as one of the most special times in my life, finally ended, and I reported back to the Army. My assignment was to the faculty of the United States Military Academy at West Point. Shortly after arriving and introducing myself to the Christian community there, I was asked to lead an evangelistic Bible study among the cadets. This led to writing Bible expositions for their devotions, and then to speaking at Christian gatherings. All this time, I had every intention of continuing my career as a combat commander. I was the son of a tank colonel and the grandson of one of George Patton's World War II generals, and I was raised with the assumption that I too would become a general and command in our nation's wars. This is what I wanted to do and what my whole life, so I thought, had prepared me to do. You can imagine how shocked I was when the Lord made it clear to me and my wife that he wanted me to leave all that and become a preacher of the gospel. It was only after almost two years of resisting God's call that I resigned my commission, entered seminary, and became a pastor at the church where I had been converted. Within a few years, I was a regular preacher in that church, expounding God's Word to the very pew in which I first came to know the Lord.

I share this information for a reason. I want to explain why I am always so amazed when I hear Christians, many of them preachers, complain that theology does not matter, or even is harmful to us spiritually. They say that if you get serious not merely about reading God's Word but also about understanding it and laying hold of the great doctrines taught in it, then you will become dry and academic, your heart will become cold, and your fascination with theology will keep you from living for God. I can only say that this has not been my experience. In fact, if someone had told me at the start all that was going to happen to me through my study of God's Word and reading of Christian books, I would not have had the courage to begin! God's Word is powerful, and the more we understand it, the deeper it penetrates our minds and our hearts, the more we are changed by God.

'For This Reason'

I am not the only person to give this testimony. Another is a far greater Christian, namely, the apostle Paul. He wrote in Romans 12:2 that we are to be 'transformed by the renewing of our minds.'

For two chapters in Ephesians Paul has expounded the most lofty and intense theology. In chapter 1, he laid out the blessings that flow to Christians through the three persons of the Trinity. God the Father chose us before creation to be his holy children. God the Son came into the world and died on the cross for our sins. God the Spirit sealed us individually to God through faith. As Paul completed chapter 1, he prayed to God that we might know the hope to which God has called us, the riches of our inheritance as his people, and the resurrection power available to us in Christ, who now reigns in heaven for our sakes.

That was just chapter 1. In chapter two he displayed the glory of our salvation through Jesus Christ. We were dead in sin but have now been 'made alive together with Christ' (v. 5). Salvation is a gift of God's grace, Paul wrote, received through faith alone, and that it always results in a life of good works. We are now 'God's workmanship, created in Christ Jesus for good works' (Eph. 2:10). In the second half of chapter 2, Paul said that his Gentile readers, having started 'without God and without hope in the world' (v. 12), were 'brought near by the blood of Christ' (v. 13). Christ has given us peace with God. Christians are a new humanity in Christ, 'fellow citizens,' 'members together in God's household,' and 'a holy temple…a dwelling place for God by the Spirit' (vv. 19–22).

So here we are at the beginning of chapter 3. We have learned so many interesting things! Now we have things to talk about with our church friends. But is that all? I hear it said that the things Paul has talked about are irrelevant, boring and impractical. But what could be more relevant and exciting than the knowledge of God and his salvation for us in Christ? What could be more practical than to have God's power working in my heart through the knowledge of the truth? Can it be that to get God's Word into our minds and our hearts, and to be gripped by it, will have no practical benefit for our lives?

I can only say that it is not what happened to the apostle Paul. He begins chapter 3 by saying, 'For this reason.' 'Because of all I have just taught, because I have this knowledge and it has been impressed not just in my head but also on my heart,' Paul writes, 'I have become a prisoner for Christ Jesus' (Eph. 3:1). That is what happens when God's Word gets into us, when we begin to understand what salvation is all about and what God is doing in this world. We become not detached intellects but 'prisoners for Jesus Christ.' This may be the best definition of what faith is all about and the best answer to the question, 'What is a Christian?' 'I am, because of this gospel,' says Paul, 'a prisoner for Christ Jesus.' Let us explore this claim in terms of the two parts of Paul's statement, that he is a prisoner 'for Christ Jesus' and also a prisoner 'on behalf of you Gentiles.'

The Prisoner of Christ Jesus

Paul begins Ephesians 3 with a thought he is not able to finish. What he meant to say finally gets out in verse 14: 'For this reason I bow my knees before the Father.' That is what Paul was planning to say. But as he began to think about praying for the Gentiles because of his knowledge of God's plan for their salvation, his heart overcame his mind and he blurted out the fact that as part of that very plan he became a prisoner of Christ.

This was literally true, for Paul was writing from his confinement in Rome. This reminds us of something that is true about this great book of Ephesians, as with the other books of the Bible. This is not a dry academic tome. It is a pastoral letter written by a real, flesh and blood man who was driven to suffer for the gospel and the salvation of his readers. Scholars sometimes criticize Paul's literary style because of passages like this. 'It is not polished,' they say, but Paul could not have cared less. He was not writing for future style critics, but for the simple believers in Ephesus whom he loved. His mind was gripped by his heart and what came out was passionate truth.

The truth about Paul was just this: he was a prisoner of Christ Jesus. It is remarkable that he puts it this way. He might well have said, 'I am a prisoner of the Emperor Nero,' which he was. But he did not believe he was in jail because of Nero. He might have said, 'I am in jail because of the opposition of the Jewish people, who rioted when I went to the temple,' since that was what brought him into custody in the first place. But he did not say that. If Paul was in prison it was because of Jesus Christ.

Why, then, was Paul suffering? His answer was because of Christ Jesus. Paul would not have been in prison, would not have suffered as he did, were he not a Christian. Formerly he was a Pharisee, a man respected by the world, a man with power and status in the religious order. If he had remained that he would still be free. He would probably have led a much more comfortable and carefree life. The reason he faced such difficulties and was now in prison was because of what happened to him when he met Christ on the Road to Damascus.

It is interesting that this man who now was in prison for his faith in Christ was once the man who put so many others in prison for that same faith. The Book of Acts tells us, 'Saul was ravaging the church, and entering house after house, he dragged off men and women and committed them to prison' (Acts 8:3). He was traveling to Damascus to do there what he had done in Jerusalem. On the way, the exalted Jesus appeared to him, saying, 'Saul, Saul, why are you persecuting me?' (Acts 9:4). Jesus converted him, changed his name to Paul, and sent him into Damascus to prepare for his ministry as an apostle. Jesus summoned a believer in Damascus to go help Paul, and said, 'I will show him how much he must suffer for the sake of my name' (Acts 9:16).

This is why Paul was in prison. Verse 1 may refer to his conversion, because he says, 'I, Paul,' perhaps reminding us of how his name got changed. It was because of his conversion that he was in prison. It was not because God was paying him back for all the bad things he had done, but because being an apostle involved this kind of suffering for and with Jesus Christ. Indeed, church history records that of the twelve apostles, plus Jesus' brother James and Paul, all but one were put to death for their testimony. Only the apostle John died of natural causes, and that was after a lifetime of trial and persecution.

To be an apostle of Christ meant sharing in Christ's sufferings, for that is the way the gospel goes forth. For this reason, Paul was imprisoned, beaten, stoned, shipwrecked, and placed in constant danger (see 2 Cor. 11:24–27). All of this could have been avoided by rejecting Christ or even just by backing off in his witness. Writing later to encourage his disciple Timothy, Paul explained his situation: 'I was appointed a preacher and apostle and teacher, which is why I suffer as I do. But I am not ashamed, for I know whom I have believed, and I am convinced that he is able to guard until that Day what has been entrusted to me' (2 Tim. 1:11–12).

That is fine for apostles, but what about you and me? Are we included in all this? The Bible makes clear that we are. While suffering was magnified in the lives of the apostles, Paul wrote, 'all who desire to live a godly life in Christ Jesus will be persecuted' (2 Tim. 3:12). Jesus said, 'If the world hates you, know that it has hated me before it hated you. If you were of the world, the world would love you as its own; but because you are not of the world, but I chose you out of the world, therefore the world hates you' (John 15:18–19).

The first reason that Christians will suffer the way Paul did—injustice, cruelty, hatred, ridicule—is simply because the world hates him. But why would anyone hate Jesus Christ, a man who went around teaching peace and healing the sick? The answer is that Jesus presents a clear challenge to this world and its system. His meekness offends its pride; his holiness exposes our sin. Especially, the cross of Christ offends the world. To the Jews it is a stumbling block, Paul said, and folly to the Greeks. The cross condemns the world, because it says that the only way for man to be made right with God was for God's own Son to come down and pay the penalty for our sins. Martyn Lloyd-Jones writes:

> The offence of the cross is this—that I am so condemned and so lost and so hopeless that if He, Jesus Christ, had not died for me, I would never know God, and I could never be forgiven. And that hurts; that annoys; that tells me I am hopeless, that I am vile, that I am useless; and as a natural man I do not like it.[234]

The cross offers salvation to all who confess their sins and believe on Jesus. But those who will not confess always want to get rid of Jesus, and Christians are bound to Christ in his offense before the world.

Second, God has ordained the cross as the way in which Christians fellowship with our Lord, and in this we are prisoners with Christ. Paul wrote in Philippians 1:29, 'For it has been granted to you that for the sake of Christ you should not only believe in him but also suffer for his sake.' Jesus said, 'If anyone would come after me, let him deny himself and take up his cross daily and follow me' (Luke 9:23). To be a disciple, then, is to be a prisoner with Christ.

The cross means that we must die to self-centeredness and self-ambition so that Christ might live in us. Paul said, 'I have been crucified with Christ. It is no longer I who live, but Christ who lives in me' (Gal. 2:19–20). For most of us, that requires difficulties and hardship. We have to know what it is to be afraid so that we lean on Jesus. We have to struggle with temptations, to commit ourselves to willing sacrifice, and to endure scorn from the world, all of which we could avoid by renouncing Christ, so as to draw near to him in faith.

Third, Christians endure the kind of hardship Paul did in order to know God's power in our lives. Paul wrote, 'I want to know Christ and the power of his resurrection and the fellowship of sharing in his sufferings' (Phil. 3:10). When Paul suffered the thorn in his flesh, God said, 'My grace is sufficient for you, for my power is made perfect in weakness.' Paul replied, 'Therefore I will boast all the more gladly of my weaknesses, so that the power of Christ may rest upon me.'

One man who knew about this was the Chinese evangelist, Watchman Nee. Raised to study the philosophy of Confucius, Nee attended a college run by Christian missionaries. He resented the 'Western religion' they tried to teach. It was with a hardened heart that he began listening to an evangelist who spoke about the death of Christ for sinners. Nee recalled, 'I broke down in tears and confessed my sins, and asked the Lord to forgive me. I accepted him, and because of his great love promised that I would serve him all my life.'[235]

Nee immediately began studying the Bible and what he learned began to reshape his life; in this he was just like Paul, whose knowledge of the gospel made him a prisoner for Christ. Nee gave up his career ambitions and became a preacher. In those impoverished times, he often had only a scrap of bread to eat and no place to lay his head. Nee was a prisoner of Christ, bound to leave his former life behind and to offer all that he had to the Lord. God blessed his ministry and used him in a powerful way in his generation.

When the Communists took over in China, many people begged Nee to leave the country to avoid arrest. He refused to do so, and in 1952 was imprisoned as a threat to the regime and sentenced to fifteen years. He served the whole sentence, and then was told he could only be released if he denied his faith. Two thugs were placed in his cell to beat him ceaselessly until he repudiated Christ, but he never did. Therefore he was sent to a hard-labor camp in a desolate mountain region. If he had only denied Christ he could have returned to his beloved wife, but instead she died without him. His own health collapsed. Finally, in May 1972, his heart gave out and Watchman Nee died on a tractor that was taking him to a hospital. The Communists spread the news that Nee had renounced Jesus Christ. But hidden under his pillow was a note that read simply, 'Christ is the Son of God. He died as the Redeemer for the sins of humankind, and was raised up from the dead after three days. This is the most important fact in the world. I shall die believing in Christ. Watchman Nee.' When family members later visited the camp, the commandant showed them the note and one of the prisoners told them about the way God had powerfully used Nee's witness among the prisoners.[236]

A Prisoner for the Gentiles

Paul says he was a prisoner for Christ Jesus, but also a prisoner 'on behalf of you Gentiles.' This was literally true. It was because Paul was known among the Jews for his ministry to the Gentiles that his presence in the temple sparked a riot (Acts 21:27 ff.). We should likewise hand ourselves over to Christ, to be used for the salvation of others. So many Christians are unwilling even to risk mild social discomfort, whereas Paul was willing to be chained in prison for the salvation of others. But all believers are called to be prisoners on behalf of those who do not yet know Christ.

Paul thought of his imprisonment as just one more way of preaching the gospel. His letter to the Philippians, written around the same time, concludes with the words: 'All the saints greet you, especially those of Caesar's household' (Phil. 4:22). This probably refers to his own guards whom he had led to Christ. Later, he wrote to Timothy, admitted that because of the gospel he was 'chained like a criminal.' But, he concluded, 'God's word is not chained' (2 Tim. 2:9).

Just as Paul suffered prison for the gospel, Christians can expect hardship as part of our witness. Like Paul, we rejoice to show the peace and joy that a believer has in Christ, and in that way to witness to unbelievers and inspire our fellow believers. Paul wrote to the Philippians: 'Now I want you to know, brothers, that what has happened to me has really served to advance the gospel…Because of my chains, most of the brothers in the Lord have been encouraged to speak the word of God more courageously and fearlessly' (Phil. 1:12–14).

But so often, we wonder, 'Does it really matter?' If I show faith in the face of sickness, if I use my loss of a job to show others that my faith is real, will it make a difference? When I lose a loved one, will people notice Christ's love in my life? If I demonstrate the power to turn from my old sins, will it really help someone else to see Jesus? If I talk to people about Jesus, will any be saved? On the one hand, all of these things are worthwhile simply for the sake of our Lord. But, we ask, will it make a difference to others?

Watchman Nee must have wondered that during his long years in prison. At the time of his arrest there were about 1 million Christians in China. Shortly after his arrest, all the churches were closed and the persecuted remnant of believers went completely underground. Most people did not expect the church in China even to survive. But today there are an estimated one hundred million openly professing Christians in China. How did this happen? One observer points to Christians like Watchman Nee, whose witness and whose prayers as prisoners for Christ reached so much farther than they themselves ever knew: 'It was out of the crucible of persecution and severe testing of a handful of men and women of faith that God did a deep heart-work that laid the groundwork for the revival to come…Walking the way of the cross they entered deeply into the fellowship of Christ's sufferings and emerged quietly triumphant.'[237]

All that You Are; All that He Has

As Western Christians study God's Word in a safe and comfortable setting, we must realize that our knowledge is not meant only for ourselves and for its blessing in our lives. If our hearts lay hold of God's Word and are truly gripped by the gospel, then we, too, will be prisoners of Christ and prisoners for the sake of those who do not yet know him.

Paul concluded his letter to the Colossians, which was a companion to Ephesians, saying:

'Remember my chains' (Col. 4:8). We, too, should remember Paul's chains, and realize that we no longer belong to ourselves. We have been bought with a price. If you want to retain control over your life, if you want to use all of your time, all of your money, and your talents for yourself, if you are not willing to take the risk of witnessing for Christ, then you have not been laid hold of by Christ the way Paul was, and the way Jesus wants you to be. But if you have, then all that you are and all that you have belong to Jesus. The good news is that if all that you have belongs to Jesus, then all that he has belongs to you. These riches include his spotless righteousness, a place in God's love, eternal life, and all the riches of heaven. All these are received through faith alone—not by works or even by witnessing. But that living faith makes us prisoners of Christ and his love. If we are joined to Christ in faith, Paul says, 'then we are heirs—heirs of God and co-heirs with Christ, if indeed we share in his sufferings in order that we may also share in his glory' (Rom. 8:17).

34

A Mystery Revealed

Ephesians 3:2–7

One of the glories of Christianity is the way it connects us with other people. Perhaps the best example of this is the apostle Paul. From the start of his Christian life on the Damascus Road, he lived to serve people and relied upon their love for him. In Ephesians 3:1, Paul said he was a prisoner 'for Christ Jesus' and 'on behalf of you Gentiles.' That shows how our relationship with Christ creates and shapes our relationship with one another.

This connectedness is vividly displayed all through Ephesians 3. Verse 13 shows that Paul was concerned that his arrest might discourage the Ephesians and cause some to doubt God's care. This section therefore appears in the Bible because of Paul's love and concern for his flock, because what happens to one Christian has such an impact on all. This reminds us that ministry is never just about truth in the abstract, but involves a passion for people and their spiritual well-being.

This is a much-neglected portion of Scripture, a passage seldom preached. But 2 Timothy 3:16 says that 'All Scripture is breathed out by God and profitable.' If we will pay careful attention, we will find this a very profitable passage, telling us much about the way God saves us into relationships and calls us to serve one another.

The Administration of God's Grace

Verse 2 elaborates on Paul's statement in verse 1 that he was a prisoner on behalf of the Gentiles: 'Assuming that you have heard of the stewardship of God's grace that was given to me for you.'

The first thing Paul notes is that his ministry was God's provision for the salvation of the Gentiles. He writes of the stewardship of God's grace for them. The word translated *stewardship* often has the meaning of *administration* or *plan*. The same word is used in Ephesians 1:10, where Paul writes that God has 'a plan for the fullness of time.' The reason these Gentiles were saved was because God had made provision for them to hear and believe the gospel. Paul was a key part of that plan, as Jesus made explicit when he converted him on the Damascus Road and called him to be an apostle especially to the Gentiles (see Acts 26:16–18).

The word also does mean *stewardship*, and this describes Paul's role in God's plan for the Gentiles. A steward is one entrusted with resources. He is given a task and will be held to account for his faithfulness. Paul received the apostolic gifts, chief of which was the revelation of the gospel. His task was to preach that gospel, especially to the Gentiles. As he put it elsewhere, 'Necessity is laid upon me. Woe to me if I do not preach the gospel!' (1 Cor. 9:16).

According to Jesus, all believers are likewise stewards of God's grace. God has a plan for the salvation of people in our world, as in Paul's, and we are each part of that plan. He has given all of us the gospel and each of us has particular spiritual gifts, of which we are stewards. Notice how Paul puts it in verse 2: the administration of God's grace was given 'to me for you.' This is God's way of ministry and of spreading the gospel. What he gives *to us* is *for others*, and we are called to share the gospel and to use the gifts God has given us in ministry to others, especially for the cause of their salvation.

Paul knew that he would be held to account for his stewardship. In 1 Corinthians 4:2, he wrote, 'It is required of stewards that they be found trustworthy.' Paul's salvation, like ours, was by grace alone and through faith alone; he was not earning his salvation. But just as parents not only love and accept their children, but also place demands on them, God requires us to be faithful servants and stewards of his grace.

Jesus taught this principle in his parable of the talents. A master was preparing to go on a journey but first called in his servants. 'To one he gave five talents, to another two, to another one, to each according to his ability' (Matt. 25:15). We all have different gifts from the Lord and in different measure; what matters is our faithfulness to the stewardship we are given. Jesus said that the one who received five talents put it to work and gained five more. So also with the one who had two talents; he gained two talents more. The master said to them upon his return, 'Well done, good and faithful servant. You have been faithful over a little; I will set you over much. Enter into the joy of your master' (Matt. 25:21).

This parable teaches that we will be rewarded for our faithful service when Christ returns. The reward is not our salvation; that is already given to us as a gift through faith in Christ. The reward is an increased scope for more service: 'You have been faithful over a little; I will set you over much.' The reward is also entering 'into the joy' of the Lord. Some of the greatest joys of eternity will be learning how God used us in others' lives: how our testimony or example contributed to their conversion, perhaps in ways we never knew; how our exhortation kept them from deadly sin; how our compassion encouraged them; and how God used our prayers to help and save others.

But there was one servant in that parable who was not faithful to the stewardship given by the Lord. He buried his talent in the ground and did nothing with it. Jesus said to him, 'You wicked and slothful servant!' and ordered him to be cast outside. It is not that the person lost his salvation because he did not serve the Lord. Rather, his unfaithfulness revealed that he was not a true servant at all, but a false and wicked one. Likewise, we are to demonstrate and prove our faith by good works (see James 2:18–26) as faithful stewards.

People sometimes think of ministry as a tiresome obligation. But Paul called it the 'stewardship of God's grace.' Paul's message was one of grace. Grace means God's favor extended to those who deserve condemnation. We are sinners and could never save ourselves, but God loves us and saves us by the free gift of Jesus Christ, received through faith alone.

Paul's particular point here is that the ministry is itself a gift of God's grace. It meant grace for the

Gentiles. They were without Christ and therefore 'without hope and without God in the world' (Eph. 2:12). How wonderful that God had a plan for their salvation, just as he does for people today to be rescued from sin, to be redeemed and forgiven, and to live in his presence in glory forever. It is all about grace!

Not only was this grace to the Gentiles, but Paul's ministry was also God's grace to him. He had been a violent man, bent on destruction and driven by hatred. By grace alone, Jesus called him, converted him, gave him a gospel and sent him forth into the world with power to preach. There, we know, Paul suffered greatly. But it was grace to him to burn as a torch for Christ, a light piercing the darkness. His sense of privilege and wonder comes through clearly in verse 7: 'Of this gospel I was made a minister to the gift of God's grace, which was given me by the working of his power.'

Whatever ministry God has given each of us—and we all have the gospel to share, along with particular gifts and opportunities to serve—it is likewise God's grace to us. What better way to live than as a servant and vessel of God's grace, given to us for others. If we will serve faithfully in Christ's name, it is we who will most be blessed.

A Mystery Revealed

If verse 2 elaborates on Paul's statement in verse 1, then verses 3–5 elaborate on verse 2's statement about Paul's stewardship from God. He explains, 'How the mystery was made known to me by revelation, as I have written briefly. When you read this, you can perceive my insight into the mystery of Christ, which was not made known to the sons of men in other generations as it has now been revealed to his holy apostles and prophets by the Spirit.'

Three times in this passage Paul uses the word *mystery*. This is an important word that he uses in other letters as well (Col. 1:26, 27; 2 Th. 2:7; 1 Tim. 3:9, 16). But Paul does not use this word in the way that we do. For us, a mystery is a set of clues that we use to figure out something unknown. We think of mystery novels, where the challenge is to figure out if the butler or the cook committed the murder. That is not what Paul means. Nor does Paul indicate here that Christianity is a vague religion in which truths are hard to define, something mystical or mysterious. That is the exact opposite from the point Paul makes here.

When Paul speaks of mystery, he means something that can only be known by revelation. He does not mean things that are inherently incomprehensible, but that God's purpose can only be known as God tells us in his Word. In his day, pagan 'mystery religions' abounded. When someone was initiated into one of these mystery cults, they were taught secret words. College fraternities mimic this today, with initiates having to learn arcane phrases and secret handshakes. Christianity is like this in one sense, in that we have knowledge nobody else has, namely, God's plan for salvation. The difference is that we want everybody to know our secrets.

The work of the apostles was to reveal the mystery of the gospel to the world. Paul says it 'was not made known to the sons of men in other generations as it is has now been revealed to his holy apostles and prophets by the Spirit.' Does this mean that the New Testament has a different message from the Old? The answer is No. But the gospel did not come into full flower until the coming of Christ and the apostolic teaching in the New Testament. The Old Testament is all about Christ, with prophecies and promises and pictures of him all through it (see Luke 24:27). But this was mysterious and unclear until Christ came. It was in the apostles' teaching, supported by others with the prophetic gift, that the mysterious came forth in clear revelation.

Most importantly, these verses tell us how God speaks to the world. The key word is *revelation*. The writings of the prophets and apostles in the Bible are not merely the collected thoughts of spiritual men. Not one of them says, 'I have been thinking about this and I have some ideas for you…' Instead, they all proclaim, 'The Word of the Lord came to me.' The Bible is truth revealed from God. This is Paul's constant testimony. He says in verse 3, 'The mystery was made known to me by revelation.' This is not his word; it is God's Word revealed to and through him.

Notice how Paul puts this. First, God provided revelation directly to him: 'The mystery was made known to me by revelation.' As a result, says verse 4, Paul had 'insight into the mystery of Christ.' Paul was not merely a pen used by God for dictation. Instead, God's revelation gave him insight into the gospel. He then wrote it down so that others would know what God had revealed to him. He says, 'When you read this, you can perceive my insight into the mystery of Christ.' This is vital, since it is Paul's written teaching that gives us access today to God's revelation. By reading Paul's letter, as with the other books of the Bible, we can receive and grasp the truth revealed by God to him. It is because of this that Martin Luther could say, 'Let the man who would hear God speak, read Holy Scripture.'[238] God's purpose is that we would have insight into his own thoughts and plans.

What a treasure we have in the Bible! This is reflected in the coronation service for a king or queen of England. Part of the ritual is for the moderator of the Church of Scotland to present the new monarch with a Bible, saying, 'The most precious thing this world affords, the most precious thing that the world knows, God's living Word.'[239]

At the end of verse 5, Paul mentions the role of the Holy Spirit. He says the mystery of salvation 'has now been revealed to his holy apostles and prophets by the Spirit.' This tells us how the revelation of God's Word actually happens. 2 Peter 1:20 tells us that 'No prophecy was ever produced by the will of man, but men spoke from God as they were carried along by the Holy Spirit.' By 'prophecy' Peter means the whole of the Bible's revelation. He says it does not originate in the will of men, as if it were their own ideas. It was men who spoke and wrote, but it was the Holy Spirit moving them so that God was revealing his own Word through them. The true author of the Bible, therefore, is the Holy Spirit, through whom men like Paul wrote God's Word. This is what we mean by the *inspiration* of Scripture: not that the writers were inspired in themselves but that the Holy Spirit worked in them and through them to speak from God.

According to the Bible, the Holy Spirit is also the one who enables us to believe and understand God's Word. Paul explains in 1 Corinthians 2:12 that 'we have received…the Spirit who is from God, that we might understand the things freely given us by God.' The same Holy Spirit who inspired the writing of Scripture spiritually illuminates God's Word to us so that instead of rejecting it as folly we receive it in faith.

This means that God's Word can be understood by any believer who reads the Bible, because the Holy Spirit illuminates God's Word to God's people. A tendency among scholars and many pastors is to emphasize the need for specialized learning even to understand the Bible. God has provided teachers to the church and scholarship is of great value, much as God has ordained preachers to teach his Word in the church. Yet

Paul insists that when the Ephesians read his letter—and many of them must have been quite uneducated—they could 'perceive my insight into the mystery of Christ' (v. 4). The same is true for you, and therefore you are to be a student of God's Word, learning for yourselves from the Bible itself, and not ultimately depending on any preacher or teacher except God the Holy Spirit speaking to you from the Word of God which he inspired in the Bible.

TOGETHER, TOGETHER, TOGETHER!

In verse 6, Paul spells out the particular mystery he has in mind: 'This mystery is that the 'Gentiles are fellow heirs, members of the same body, and partakers of the promise in Christ Jesus through the gospel.'

This speaks about the full partnership of Gentiles with Jews in the church. The Old Testament contained hints of this. God told Abraham in Genesis 12:3, 'In you all the families of the earth shall be blessed.' We think, as well, of Jonah's missionary visit to Nineveh, which resulted in the conversion of that great and wicked city. But on the whole, it never entered into the minds of the Old Testament saints that the Gentiles around them, who were such a threat to them, would be incorporated into their spiritual legacy. When the Roman army destroyed Jerusalem in 70AD, for instance, little did either the Romans or the Jews conceive that within 250 years, the Roman Empire would officially bend the knee to the Jewish rabbi, Jesus of Nazareth, whom Roman soldiers had crucified at the behest of the Jews.

Today we little appreciate the mystery involved in this. Ours is a church almost wholly comprised of Gentiles; only a small number of Jews are in most churches today. But in the early church there was a real danger of prejudice against the Gentiles. For Paul's original readers, it was scarcely imaginable that the rigid divisions in their world could be transcended by a shared love for Jesus Christ.

To make this point, Paul uses three words, each of which contains the prefix *together*. The first is fellow heirs, or, 'heirs together'. His point is that Jews and Gentiles in Christ are on equal footing, equally sharing in Christ's inheritance of glory. All Christians are all equally justified before God; we are all equal partakers of the Holy Spirit; we will all equally share in the glory of heaven. The particular emphasis of this word is not that we will all get a piece of the pie, but that we all share the whole together. This is how it is to be even now in the church.

Second, Paul says that Jews and Gentiles are 'members together' of the same body. This means that what benefits one benefits all, and what hurts one hurts all. We have a spiritual unity that involves the same kind of interconnectedness as the various parts of our body. Since Christ is our head (see Eph. 1:22), we work together in harmony as each of us receives our direction from him.

Third, Paul says we are 'partakers together of the promise in Christ Jesus.' The Bible is filled with promises and we grow strong by knowing them, relying on them, and partaking of them together. So much of the weakness of our faith is caused because we do not know what God has promised: about help in weakness, about God's readiness to forgive all who repent and believe, about God's power to change our hearts and make us holy, 'about strength for duty, comfort in trouble, guidance in perplexity, help in sickness, consolation in death, support under bereavement, happiness beyond the grave, reward in glory— about all these things there is an abundant supply of promises in the Word.'[240] We should study the Bible with a special interest in the promises of God, which make us strong in the faith.

Paul says here that we are partakers together of *the* promise, in the singular. He undoubtedly means the great promise of salvation for all who trust in Jesus Christ. Charles Hodge explains, 'The promise is the promise of redemption; the promise made to our first parents, repeated to Abraham, and which forms the burden of all the Old Testament predictions.'[241]

Notice what it is that brings this togetherness. Paul concludes verse 6 with the words, 'in Christ Jesus through the gospel.' A false unity, one that does not stand up to trials, can be manufactured through a working up of enthusiasm or through programs and services offered by the church. But true spiritual unity, as characterized here, comes only in Christ and through the gospel. That is why while other things may build religious empires, the gospel alone builds Christ's church and gives this unity: *heirs together, members together* in a spiritual body, and *partakers together* in the promise of salvation.

How Do You Fit In?

Taken together, these verses emphasize the interconnectedness that is distinctive to Christianity. This letter exists because of Paul's care for and unity with the Christians at Ephesus. He reminded them of his stewardship as part of God's plan for their salvation. Because of his ministry, they could know God's Word by reading it, receiving grace from God for spiritual life. Here, Paul describes the 'mystery of Christ,' namely, that God not only saved individuals but makes us part of a great union: heirs together, members together, and partakers together in the promise of salvation.

The question is, where do you fit into this? First, you have the same stewardship of the gospel that every other believer has, and God wants you to share the good news with others who don't know him. You also have your own particular gifts and you bring a particular ministry to the church that no one else has in quite the same way. You are simply to offer what you are and what God has given you. Paul says God's grace was given 'to me for you,' and likewise grace was given to you for others.

But you may say, 'I don't have much to offer.' Perhaps you are not even sure that you believe. If that is true, then you need to get into God's Word. God has given his revelation to us through the apostles, so you must read it, search it, and mine it, asking God the Holy Spirit to reveal God's truth to you. In that way you will receive the gift of faith, because 'everyone who calls upon the name of the Lord will be saved' (Rom. 10:13), and since faith comes through the Word of God. If you already believe, you will find God's Word 'profitable for teaching, for reproof, for correction, and for training in righteousness, that the man of God may be competent, equipped for every good work' (2 Tim. 3:16–17).

We have this three-fold mystery, that we are heirs-together, members-together, and partakers-together of salvation. This is not a unity we create, but a unity we are to embrace and serve. We are called to recognize the eternal value and destiny of every fellow believer. We are heirs together of God's glory! If there is a weaker Christian or one less mature than you, perhaps one you find annoying and difficult, realize that he or she is nonetheless bound for the same glory that awaits you. We are members together in a profound and spiritual union. The church as a whole can only grow spiritually as each member serves and grows. Therefore, let us encourage one another with the promise we partake together: that for all our weakness and sin and failures, God has promised to do a work of glory among us, if we will only turn to Christ and preach the gospel.

Paul thought of these things as a great and wonderful mystery. I wonder if we do—if we realize the greatness of what God is doing even now in our midst. But someday we will. The apostle John saw in the Book of Revelation:

> Behold, a great multitude that no one could number, from every nation, from all tribes and peoples and languages, standing before the throne and before the Lamb, clothed in white robes, with palm branches in their hands, and crying out with a loud voice, 'Salvation belongs to our God who sits on the throne, and to the Lamb!' (Rev. 7:9–10).

Will you be there? You can know that you will by faith 'in Christ through the gospel' (v. 6). If you will be there, then realize that what we do now is part of what will be then and for all eternity. We are all stewards of God's grace, joined together for an inheritance in glory, promised to us in Christ, a mystery now revealed in God's Word but also through us, to the praise of God's glory forever.

35

Unsearchable Riches

Ephesians 3:7–9

One of the lessons of church history is that there is always a relationship between the church's view of the gospel ministry and its view of the gospel itself. To some, being a minister is just one of many career options. A young man might be a doctor or a lawyer, he might go into business, or perhaps he might enter the ministry. He chooses based on the kind of lifestyle each offers, what kind of work he wants to do, how much money he might make and what sort of prestige is attached to each career. Preaching the gospel is considered a job not ultimately unlike any other and its success is determined by all the usual measures. Under this view, the gospel is just another commodity, something bought and sold. Christianity becomes a lifestyle choice or even something like a hobby that has to fit in alongside so many other pastimes.

This is something we are increasingly seeing today. A gospel minister is placed essentially in the category of an entertainer. His value is assessed by his dynamic personality. Ministry is becoming a business in which the bottom line is mainly numerical and financial. Just as in every other line of work, you need to get the best and the brightest people and because of their ability you will get the best results.

As we study Ephesians 3, we find that the apostle Paul had a very different idea of ministry, and therefore of the gospel and of Christianity. His ministry was not a job but a divine calling. His success depended not on his skill or the strength of his personality, but on divine power. His message was not about himself, not stirring stories, and not a therapeutic message designed to excite his listeners, but 'the unsearchable riches of Christ' (Eph. 3:8). He pursued not a career but a mission given him by God. That is why two millennia later, we remember Paul and why God is still using his labor. He offered not marketable goods and services but a divine gospel, good news from God that brings a supernatural salvation into this world.

The Minister's Calling

Paul's concern in this section of Ephesians is that his readers should not be discouraged by his imprisonment and that they should recognize the treasure they have in the gospel of Jesus Christ. In verse 6 he pointed out that it is 'in Christ Jesus through the gospel' that his readers have been made heirs together of God's eternal riches, members together in a spiritual body, and partakers together in the promise of salvation. These are not the kinds of things you can pick up at the shopping mall or even gain through a lifetime of labor. They are supernatural blessings from God that are received by simple faith in the gospel of Jesus Christ.

For this reason Paul wants us to have the highest possible view of the gospel. This comes through in all of his letters. In Romans 1:16, Paul wrote, 'I am not ashamed of the gospel, for it is the power of God for salvation to everyone who believes.' The gospel is not just an interesting theory or a mental trick that will give you more confidence. It is God's message of salvation through the death and resurrection of his Son, carrying divine power to save all who believe.

Paul put it the way he did—that he was 'not ashamed'—because the gospel is something the world despises. People either think it nonsense, because the gospel does not fit in with conventional ideas of human effort and progress, or they are offended by it, since it tells them they are not right with God. The gospel says they need Jesus to have died for them to be forgiven and avoid the fires of hell. This is why the gospel never has been and never will be popular with the world at large. Yet the gospel, so despised by sinful people, alone has power from God to save their souls.

Paul says, in verse 7, 'Of this gospel I was made a minister.' His calling was to preach the gospel. This is what he said in the opening verse of Romans: 'Paul, a servant of Christ Jesus, called to be an apostle, set apart for the gospel of God' (Rom. 1:1). The gospel is good news, the proclamation that while this world and the people in it are alienated from God because of sin, God has sent his Son into the world to die for our sin and to reconcile us to the heavenly Father. God offers us eternal life through a personal relationship with himself by faith in his Son, Jesus Christ. Peoples' problem today is not merely the challenge of getting on in life until death, but, as God reveals in the Bible, that beyond death is a judgment upon all our sin and a hell in which the wrath of God will be eternally afflicted upon all who are not forgiven in this world. What the gospel offers is the forgiveness we need, graciously extended by God at the cost of his own Son's precious blood shed for us.

The calling of the minister is therefore to proclaim this gospel into a world that has turned from God. The gospel is a message the world doesn't want to hear, but which it must hear if it is to be saved. The gospel minister is like a doctor to whom a prescription for medicine is entrusted. He has it written on a piece of paper. All around him people are dying of the disease for which he has the cure. But for most of them the symptoms are not bad enough to have yet gotten their attention. They do not believe they are sick, though in fact they are dying, some slowly and others more rapidly. Moreover, the medicine has an aroma that makes people think it will taste very bad. This is precisely what Paul says about the gospel. 'To those who are perishing,' he says in 2 Corinthians 2:15, it is 'a fragrance of death.' Therefore, by nature, people do not want the medicine the gospel minister has. But he knows that if only they would taste it, they would know how good it is; if only they would take the medicine, it would save them from their deadly disease.

What, therefore, is the calling of the minister? To preach the gospel. To proclaim to those dying of the disease of sin that God has written down the prescription for their salvation, that if they will trust in Jesus Christ and submit their lives to God—the very thing people do not want to do—they will be saved and will have eternal life. In fact, while this illustration of the gospel as medicine helpfully shows that people perish for refusing the salvation offered to them, the situation is actually far worse. As Paul taught in Ephesians 2:1, the gospel minister preaches salvation to those who are already spiritually dead. But he preaches knowing that the gospel has resurrection power to bring sinners to life through faith in Christ.

Paul's point is that God has not only given the gospel to the world, but he also calls ministers and makes them the gospel's heralds. Paul says, 'I was made a minister according to the gift of God's grace' (v. 7). He did not choose to be a minister. He did not decide upon a career choice that led him in this direction. God chose him to be an apostle and made him a minister by the calling of his grace. Paul thinks of it as a glorious privilege and a divine calling. He writes, 'To me… this grace was given, to preach to the Gentiles the unsearchable riches of Christ' (Eph. 3:8).

The same is true today. To choose the gospel ministry is an enormous presumption; being a preacher is not something we choose but something to which we are called by God. Charles Spurgeon was famous for advocating that no man should preach unless practically forced against his will. A man should enter the gospel ministry only under divine compulsion, the way that Paul said, 'Woe to me if I do no preach the gospel!' (1 Cor. 9:16). John MacArthur writes:

> Any person in the ministry of the church whom God has not appointed is a usurper. No matter how seemingly good his intentions, he can do nothing but harm to the work of the Lord and to the Lord's people…No man should enter the ministry unless he is absolutely certain of the Lord's calling.[242]

A man should enter the ministry and undertake to preach only if driven by a call from God that he cannot suppress and that is confirmed by the approval of the church. We refer to these as the internal call and the external call to ministry, both of which are necessary. When Jesus called Paul, he also appeared to a man named Ananias to confirm Paul's calling and assist Paul as he prepared to preach (Acts 9:13–16). That is why we have the ordination process today, so that through the church the Holy Spirit can confirm and prepare men who believe themselves called to preach.

Why is this important? I can think of two reasons. The first is that true gospel preaching requires God's power, and therefore it must be in response to God's call. The second reason is that I do not believe a man can endure the discouragements that accompany the faithful preaching of the gospel without a certain knowledge of God's call. Without awareness of God's calling to preach the gospel, the incentives to preach something else or to quit are just too strong.

The Minister's Power

This brings us to another matter on Paul's mind, the minister's power in preaching the gospel. He says the ministry of the gospel 'was given me by the working of his power' (Eph. 3:7).

Here, we remember Paul's conversion, in which his salvation resulted from the calling of Christ. He must have heard the gospel many times during his days as a persecutor in Jerusalem. But his heart was hard and cold toward it. But when Christ appeared to him, Paul was converted by an effectual calling. What Paul says here of his ministry is true of salvation for us all: it is 'the gift of God's grace, given by the working of God's power.' R. C. Sproul compares God's effectual calling with the outward and general call of the gospel:

> The unregenerate experience the outward call of the gospel. This outward call will not effect

salvation unless the call is heard and embraced in faith. Effectual calling refers to the work of the Holy Spirit in regeneration. Here the call is within. The regenerate are called inwardly. Everyone who receives the inward call of regeneration responds in faith.[243]

If this was true of Paul in his conversion, and if it is true in all of our conversions—that God the Holy Spirit must give us new life by regeneration—then the power of the gospel ministry lies in the power of God's Holy Spirit.

Charles Spurgeon, the nineteenth century English preacher, often spoke about the necessity of a minister relying on God's power rather than his own. As he mounted the steps to his pulpit he would pray, 'I believe in the Holy Spirit,' reminding himself that if he preached God's Word in faith he could count on God's own power to work through the message. Knowing that sinners are converted only by God's power, he relied on and prayed for the Holy Spirit to make his ministry effective.

I have to say that this is the only thing that gives me any confidence in preaching. If I believed I had to win over the consciences of rebellious sinners or to impress human hearts long trained to worldly tastes, I would despair of ever seeing any fruit from my preaching. But Paul shows that the power to convince and convert comes from God as his Spirit attends the simple and direct preaching of his Word. My job is faithfully to preach the Bible and proclaim the good news of Jesus Christ, knowing that the Word of God has 'divine power to destroy strongholds' (2 Cor. 10:4).

The same is true for you in your witness to the gospel. While you want clearly to present the gospel, the burden to persuade and convert rests not on you but on God, who gives abundant grace for the salvation of sinners. 'Faith comes from hearing…the Word of Christ,' Paul says in Romans 10:17. Our calling is to proclaim the good news of the Savior Jesus Christ and to pray, knowing that by his own power God uses our witness to call sinners to himself.

Earlier I used the illustration of a doctor who has a prescription to cure a great disease by which people all around him are dying. A prescription is just words on a piece of paper, just as we have in the Bible. But there is power in those words. In the case of the prescription, when people read it and act upon it, it tells them how to be healed. This is what the Bible does for our eternal souls and this is where its power lies. The gospel tells the sinner how to be saved from the wrath and judgment of a holy God. The gospel prescription says, 'Believe on the Lord Jesus Christ and you will be saved!' (Acts 16:31). It promises that 'the blood of Jesus, [God's] Son cleanses us from all sin' (1 John 1:7). If you will take this prescription and believe, you will be saved, your sins will be forgiven, and you will enter into God's love forever. The gospel is God's own power for the salvation of everyone who believes (Rom. 1:16).

Ravi Zaccharius tells the story of traveling through Lebanon with a bold missionary friend during the days of the Syrian occupation. Their van was loaded with boxes of Bibles and they pulled up to a Syrian army checkpoint. The soldier stuck his rifle in their face and asked what was in the boxes. The evangelist playfully replied, 'Dynamite.' Right when Zaccharius was sure they were going to be shot, his friend pulled out a Bible and placed it into the soldier's hand.

That is the very view Paul has of God's Word. Verse 7 speaks of the 'working of God's power.' Two great words are used there: *energies*, from which we get energy, and *dunamis*, which gives us dynamite. Paul knew that God himself was energizing his ministry of the gospel and doing a work of dynamic power; if we will follow his example we can know the same. God promised through the prophet Isaiah that his Word 'shall accomplish that which I purpose, and shall succeed in the thing for which I sent it' (Isa. 55:10).

THE MINISTER'S MESSAGE

Paul has informed us about the minister's calling and the minister's power. He also tells us what is the minister of the gospel's message, namely, 'the unsearchable riches of Christ' (Eph. 3:8).

What a great way to describe the Christian message: the unsearchable riches of Christ! Paul tells us that the Christian minister's message is not the details of his own life, not current events, not moral exhortation, but the unsearchable riches of Christ.

What is the gospel? The first thing Paul turns to is Christ himself. The gospel we preach is the person of Jesus Christ. This is what Jesus had in mind when he said in John 17:3, 'Now this is eternal life, that they may know you, the only true God, and Jesus Christ whom you have sent.' To know Jesus is to know God. To gaze upon his character is to know the character of God. To know Jesus and trust him, to walk in fellowship with him through this life and to belong to him for all eternity as a bride to her groom—this is the great, unfathomable treasure that is our salvation. To belong to Jesus is to be a sheep tended by the Good Shepherd, who laid down his life for us. To follow Jesus is to walk in the light, for he is the 'light of the world' (John 8:12). To come to him is to find rest for your souls, to receive living water welling up unto eternal life. 'I am the way, the truth, and the life,' Jesus said (John 14:6). Our gospel is nothing less than Jesus and his love, his glory, the beauty of his spirit, his precious redeeming blood, and the power of his resurrection life.

In addition to Christ himself, the unsearchable riches of the gospel also include all the blessings of salvation he gives to those who come to him in faith. These blessings are the things Paul has been teaching in chapters 1 and 2, and which we must know if we are to share the gospel message. God the Father has given us 'every spiritual blessing in Christ' (Eph. 1:3), and Paul has spelled them out. In Christ we are chosen by God for holiness and accepted into God's own family in the Beloved (1:4-6). Through the shedding of Christ's blood, 'we have redemption, the forgiveness of our sins' (1:7). To come to Christ in faith is to have him pour out the Holy Spirit into your life, as a deposit and firstfruit of what eternity holds in store for you (1:13-14). To trust Jesus is to experience a spiritual resurrection (2:5). It is to be saved by grace, through faith, to be God's workmanship, created in Christ Jesus for good works that God himself has appointed for you (2:8-10). It is to be a born again member of the new humanity in Christ, who gives us peace with God and peace in our lives (2:13-16).

Paul calls these riches 'unsearchable'. He does not mean that they are unknowable, but that we will never exhaust them, will never plumb the depths of the riches of Christ. If you take the most glorious moment of your communion with Christ—the joy of release when you first knew yourself forgiven, your times of closest communion in prayer, those Lord's Days when the Word of God thrilled your heart—then realize that you will spend eternity searching them out, discovering in new ways and in ever greater intensity 'the light of the knowledge of the glory of God in the face of Jesus Christ' (2 Cor. 4:6). Long after our careers are over and the money we stockpiled has been spent by others, we will be still searching out the riches of Christ. This is the highest calling for which every believer was created and redeemed. It will be the work of eternity and it is the primary work of our present lives.

Furthermore, what Paul knows of these unsearchable riches humbles his soul before God rather than making him proud. He realizes what a great privilege it is for someone like him, once an enemy of God and persecutor of the church, to serve a Savior like this: 'To me, though I am the very least of all the saints, this grace was given, to preach to the Gentiles the unsearchable riches of Christ' (Eph. 3:8).

Three times in his letters Paul gives a description of himself and they follow a notable progression. The first one comes in 1 Corinthians, which we believe to be one of Paul's earliest letters: 'For I am the least of the apostles, unworthy to be called an apostle, because I persecuted the church of God' (15:9). There, Paul says, 'Yes, I am an apostle, but in my mind I am the least of the apostles.' The next occasion is in our passage: 'I am the very least of all the saints.' Finally, he says, in one of his last letters, 'Christ Jesus came into the world to save sinners, of whom I am the foremost' (1 Tim. 1:15). This is the progression, what Paul's own growth as a Christian looked like: least of the apostles, least of the saints, the chief of sinners. This tells us that as we mature and grow in Christ, we do not think more of ourselves but less. Christian growth means a greater awareness of our sin, of our unworthiness before the holy God, but also a greater joy at the salvation God has given us by grace and a higher appreciation of 'the unsearchable riches of Christ.' Because of that, Paul thought it not a burden but a great privilege to preach the gospel.

The Minister's Mission

Our passage has shown the minister's calling, the minister's power, the minister's message, and finally, we have the minister's mission. Paul writes in verse 9: 'And to bring to light for everyone what is the plan of the mystery hidden for ages in God who created all things.' Paul's mission was to take the unsearchable riches of Christ to the world, bringing the gospel to light for everyone.

This is where this passage especially connects with us. You may have asked, 'What does this have to do with me? Paul is writing about ministers, and I am not a minister.' On the one hand, you are part of the church, so you need to know the Bible's teaching on the ministry of the gospel. But also you are involved, because just as God gave Paul the specific mission of preaching the gospel to the Gentiles, God has given you a mission and has placed you in the world. We have been given the truth as a stewardship: it is not for us to keep but for us to teach and proclaim to others who do not know it. We have been given unsearchable riches and we are to share them with a world that is so poor in the things of God. John Stott writes:

> Here then was the double obligation Paul felt, first to share God's truth and secondly to share Christ's riches. So what is needed today for a recovery of evangelistic zeal in the church is the same apostolic conviction about the gospel. Once we are sure that the gospel is both truth from God and riches for mankind, nobody will be able to silence us.[244]

We are men and women on a mission. God has placed us in a particular place, among particular people, all of us with the same gospel to live and proclaim. Some of you are mothers at home, perhaps homeschooling, perhaps involved in your children's class, or the team mom on a soccer team. God has placed you in the lives of people. You are given the mission of telling your children about Jesus, praying for their salvation and leading them to the unsearchable riches of Christ. This is a work of eternal consequences for them and for others whom God will reach through them. Devote yourself to it, knowing it is your mission from God. As you get to know unbelievers, pray for opportunities to share the truth and to give away the riches you have in Christ, and God will use you as he used Paul 'by the working of his power' (Eph. 3:7).

Others of us are placed in businesses and other workplaces. We have relationships with clients, with bosses, with peers and subordinates. These are all people who have lives, who have to face the reality of death, who live in ignorance of God and in poverty of spirit. God has given you truth and spiritual riches, with the mission of sharing it with them. This doesn't require you to be confrontational. But if you will pray for openings to share the gospel, God will give them to you. And if you pray for his power to simply attend his Word, you will be amazed at the barriers he will break down. Often, people who appear hardened to the gospel and committed to a life of sin are secretly thinking about God and life and death and eternity. If you live a consistent, loving Christian life such people will seek you out, especially when a loved one becomes sick or their job is threatened.

God has placed each of us in this world with a mission, with a message, with his own power to overthrow the strongholds of unbelief, and with a particular calling to which we all are simply to be faithful. Jesus said, 'You are the light of the world. A city set on a hill cannot be hidden…So let your light shine before others' (Matt. 5:14, 16). If we will be faithful to shine the light of the gospel in places where God has put us, we can be certain that he will supply the power, and then he will receive all the praise for the unsearchable riches in Christ he offers to all the world.

36

The Manifold Wisdom of God

Ephesians 3:9–13

When I lived in Philadelphia, the walk from the train station to my church took me past a grand old Baptist Church that had been founded over 300 years earlier. Over the years the church had fallen into decay. It had lost its doctrine and with that its spiritual influence, shining forth with neither moral clarity nor saving light. As one might expect, the church's design was attested to by the building's dingy and dark-stained stones.

About a year before I left the city, however, the church was designated as a national historical monument and government dollars were given to spruce up its outward appearance. For months, scaffolding covered its exterior as workers cleaned the stones. When finally the wooden frames were removed, the church shone once more and at least its outward glory was revealed. What happened to that building reminded me of a greater work God someday will do for his whole church. In this world Christians are not very impressive; we are stained by the elements and marred by wear and tear. But in the end, God will restore us in beauty so as to reflect fully his own glory.

A Revelation to Angels

In Ephesians chapter 3, Paul has been talking about the mystery God is revealing through the gospel. He has already used this term *mystery* three times in the chapter, speaking of the 'mystery made known by revelation' (3:3), the 'mystery of Christ' (3:4), and the mystery of the union of Jews and Gentiles in the church (3:6). The word *mystery* indicates things that could only be known by revelation; not things that we can figure out if we have enough clues, but rather things that would never occur to us unless revealed by God. According to Leon Morris, the gospel reveals a mystery because, 'There is a union between Christ and his people…The church is not a group of like-minded people who gather to pursue their mutual interests. It is a group of people united with Christ.'

In verse 9, Paul uses the word *mystery* a fourth time. He says his mission as an apostle was 'to bring to light for everyone what is the plan of the mystery hidden for ages in God who created all things.' Hidden in human history is a plan for revealing this mystery of God. The purpose of this plan is 'that through the church the manifold wisdom of God might now be made known' (3:10). Paul here refers to the revelation of God's wisdom in terms of those to whom this mystery is revealed, how the church reveals God's wisdom, and, finally, in what this says about the meaning of history and of life.

Handling the first of these issues, we should take special notice of the audience of this revelation, those to whom God's wisdom is made known. These are 'the rulers and authorities in the heavenly places' (Eph. 3:10), that is, the angels. Lloyd-Jones explains:

> The apostle is asserting that what is happening in the Church is so stupendous, so glorious, that even the bright angelic beings who have spent their entire existence in the presence of God, even they are staggered and amazed at what they see in and through the Church. These angels, created by God, have always been immediately in the presence of God; but according to the Apostle, what takes place in the Church is something that even they had never thought of or imagined. It surpasses even their knowledge, their comprehension, and even their imagination.[245]

It is to the 'rulers and authorities in the heavenly places' that God is revealing his wisdom through the Church.

Consider how much the angels already know about the wisdom of God. The angels were vastly informed on this subject before the coming of Christ. They were, for instance, in a wonderful position to observe God's wisdom in creating the world. On the macro-scale, the angels measured the galaxies and marveled in the great laws that govern planets, solar systems and nebulae. On the micro-scale they marveled at God's great wisdom as he crafted molecules, atoms, and sub-atomic particles, things about which science still has far more ignorance than knowledge. Creation reveals a magnificent complexity, but also a simplicity that marks the most accomplished genius imaginable. Think of the wisdom revealed in the flow of the seasons, in the growth of a flower, in the construction of the eye or the ear or the hand. All of this and more was laid before the eyes of angels from the beginning. Job 38:7 thus says the angels shouted for joy 'when the morning stars sang together.'

As time passed through decades and centuries, the angels' knowledge of God's wisdom only increased all the more. God's wisdom is shown not only in creation but also in history. The flood in Noah's time revealed God's judgment of sin, as did his triumph over the rebel ambitions of those who sought to build the Towel of Babel. The angels watched God's handling of all the nations in the Old Testament. In Daniel 2, the prophet's vision showed that while the great empires rise up they are thwarted in their pride, replaced by others God erects in their place. Ultimately all human kingdoms will be overthrown by the kingdom of God as sin leads to evil and evil to judgment. In this way, even secular history shows the wisdom of God.

Especially by following the history of Israel the angels learned so much of the wisdom of God. God took the pagan man Abraham with nothing to commend him, and promised him a multitude of offspring through a wife past child-bearing age. They watched as God himself bore the smoking fire pot through the animal pieces, entering into an eternal covenant of salvation. What kind of wisdom was that? Imagine how the angels wondered about God's wisdom while the Israelites were suffering so long under Pharoah's lash in Egypt, only to marvel at God's deliverance under Moses, when God's people marched out with the treasures of the Nile in their baggage. All the history of Israel reveals the wisdom of God in grace and truth.

Creation, secular history, and Old Testament history reveal the wisdom of God. But the manifold wisdom of God—and by *manifold* Paul means the great variety, like the colors in a prism—is displayed in the New Testament revelation given through the apostles. It is through the Christian church that the angels see new shades and hues in God's wisdom that never before had come to light.

How the Church Reveals God's Wisdom

Paul's premise is that the church is the lens through which God's manifold wisdom is best seen. We might put it this way, that if you really want to see something spectacular, if you want to go on a tour and see the magnificent sights, then you would do better to go to church than to the Grand Canyon or the Amazon River or the grand cities of Europe. These are dwarfed in terms of their display of the wisdom of God by the church of Jesus Christ.

How, then, does the church reveal the wisdom of God? Mainly, as *God's solution to the problem of sin*. Sin is a problem because of the character of God. The Bible reveals God as a God of both love and justice. The problem of sin is that these two attributes of God are on opposing sides when it comes to his dealings with sinful humanity.

Here is the problem—if God's love simply forgives sinners, then he transgresses the demands of his holy justice. But if God's justice simply takes its vengeance, then God's love is left unsatisfied. How can this be reconciled? What wisdom can untie this knot, making justice and mercy kiss? The gospel's answer reveals the wisdom of God in the heavenly realms. What never occurred to even the angels was that God's love is so great that he would offer his own divine Son to be punished in the place of sinners, and that his justice is so demanding that when even Jesus Christ, the sinless Savior, bore our sins, God poured out his wrath to the full.

Think of how astonished the angels must have been as this played out. Peter said, 'Even angels long to look into these things' (1 Pet. 1:12). Imagine, for instance, the astonishment of the angel sent to bear the news to the Virgin Mary: 'The Holy Spirit will come upon you, and the power of the Most High will overshadow you; therefore the child to be born will be called holy—the Son of God' (Luke 1:35). Imagine the angels' marvel as they watched God's Son laboring in a carpenter's shop, seeing Jesus sitting in the back row of the synagogue, too poor and unworthy to be allowed to sit closer—there, the King of Glory, the Incarnate God! What kind of wisdom is this!

Yet all that pales compared to the events of the cross. To all appearances, God was failing, dying, and suffering before the wickedness of men and at the hands of the Evil One. Imagine the legions of angels, awaiting the divine call from Jesus that would send them sweeping upon Calvary in fury and might. But that call never came. Jesus told Peter, when the disciple tried to defend him with a sword on the night of his arrest: 'Do you think that I cannot appeal to my Father, and he will at once send more than twelve legions of angels? But how then should the Scriptures be fulfilled, that it must be so?' (Matt. 26:53–54).

We can only imagine that there were serious, though reverent, questions in the minds of the angels when Jesus, the source of living water, called out, 'I thirst!' How much more dismayed must they have been to have heard the beloved Son of God lament, 'Father, Father, why have you forsaken me?' What a shock it must have been to angel ears to hear Jesus cry, 'It is finished,' and what questions they must have asked when their eyes watched Jesus actually die. The gospel is the answer to these angel questions, the answer that caused their holy minds to marvel at a greater wisdom in God than even they had suspected. They came to realize that what appeared to be defeat was in fact a grand triumph by Christ over his enemies. Rebellious humanity, guided by Satan's hand, wanted to do away with the Son of God, yet God was confounding them with a folly that was wisest of all. Christ's death was God's way of justly forgiving sinners; now that Jesus has died for you, God's justice demands your forgiveness. The cross was in this way, God's amazingly wise plan for using the devil's greatest triumph to secure his total and final defeat. Here is a wisdom hitherto unknown, as Charles Wesley extolled:

> Tis mystery all! The Immortal dies!
>   Who can explore His strange design?
> In vain the first-born seraph tries
>   to sound the depths of love divine!
> Tis mercy all! Let earth adore,
>   let angel minds inquire no more.

Imagine the thoughts of the angel who sat upon the rolled-away stone and told the women, 'He is not here, for he has risen, as he said. Come, see the place where he lay' (Matt. 28:6). The angels beheld the wisdom of the resurrection, the new creation in the crucified Christ. Here is where the church fits in, revealing the manifold wisdom of God. The church is the temple of the new creation, Jews and Gentiles together in Christ, the new humanity in which God himself will dwell by the Spirit. Back when Adam and Eve fell into sin, who could have imagined a more glorious end and a more wonderful blessing, secured by such wisdom and grace from God!

Paul writes of the manifold, the many-colored, wisdom of God. This is what the church displays in the amazing variety of our stories of salvation. Every one of us is needed to complete the picture; all our voices are needed to create the harmony that fully glorifies God. Some, like Lydia, find their hearts opened suddenly; others, like Nicodemus, must brood over time; others yet, like Peter, are restored from betraying their Lord, and then there is Paul, the chief of sinners and persecutor of the church, struck to the ground by the saving grace of Christ. In all of these, in all the church, what Jesus said is true: 'There is joy before the angels of God over one sinner who repents' (Luke 15:10). Because of us, the angels marvel at the glory of the manifold wisdom of God. It is because of what God reveals in all our salvation stories that Paul says, in the great doxology of Romans 11:

> Oh, the depth of the riches and wisdom and knowledge of God! How unsearchable are his judgments and how inscrutable his ways! 'For who has known the mind of the Lord, or who has been his counselor?' 'Or who has given a gift to him that he might be repaid?' For from him and through him and to him are all things. To him be glory forever. Amen. (Rom. 11:33–6).

That is the song of angels on the lips of men.

What the Gospel Reveals about History

When Paul speaks of 'the rulers and authorities in the heavenly places' (Eph. 3:10), he means not only the elect angels, but also the fallen angels. Far from glorifying God's wisdom, the devil and his demons have specifically rebelled against the wisdom of God's rule. We do not know exactly why the fallen angels, led by Satan, rebelled against God. It seems from what happened in the Garden, however, that they were offended by the wisdom of God's intention to create mankind in his own image. They were offended that a lesser creature would be crowned with such glory, so they opposed God's work. What we find all through the Bible is that the devil and the demons hate and oppose God's blessing on his church. They further rebelled against God's wisdom in forgiving our sin; they believe that God's way is not the right way but is folly and an offense.

But God reveals his wisdom not only in how he saves us but also in how he overthrows the devil's rebellion. James Boice writes:

> When Satan rebelled against God and carried the host of fallen angels, now demons, with him into eternal ruin, God could have crushed the rebellion and annihilated Satan and his hosts forever. That would have been just and reasonable. It might even have been merciful; for if God had gone on to create Adam and Eve, as he had no doubt determined to do beforehand, Satan would not have been there to tempt them, the pair would not have fallen, and sin and death would not have passed upon the race.
>
> But this would not have shown God's 'manifold wisdom'…It would not have shown that God's way, the way of truth and righteousness, is the only really good way and the only sure path to happiness.[246]

It is in the church that God shows the wisdom of his way. All the while Satan is tempting and turning humans against God, the Lord is working to redeem a new people who will do his will, on whose hearts he writes his law, who thus serve him in adversity, glory in weakness, and count suffering gain for the sake of Christ. God even allows the persecution of his people, so that as we praise him in trials we display the glory of the wisdom of his way. Show me a higher wisdom than Paul and Silas singing in a jail (Acts 16:25)! When Christians know a joy that the richest, most powerful, and most famous people cannot attain apart from Christ, this glorifies the manifold wisdom of God.

Do you realize that this is the purpose of our lives, to display this wisdom of God? Do you realize that when God shows that he can hold our allegiance even amidst flames, despite the heaviest attacks our enemies can deliver, that we bring glory to the only wise God? Do you realize that this is what history is about? Not the rising and falling of empires; not the advance of science; not the accumulation of personal fortunes and power. History is for the display of God's wisdom in the church, not to mention his power, mercy, and grace, and he will display his wisdom either in your condemnation or in your salvation.

This is Paul's emphasis in this chapter. He is in prison, and he does not want the believers in Ephesus to lose heart. Instead, he wants them to see that through such sufferings God displays his wisdom. None of it makes sense to unbelievers. But to our eyes, seeing, as Paul puts it in verse 11, 'the eternal purpose that [God] has realized in Christ Jesus our Lord,' we see an opportunity to display God's glory. If God's wisdom is revealed in the suffering of Christ on the cross, and if God's wisdom is revealed in the weakness of his church, then should we not expect it to work that same way in our lives? Paul therefore says his suffering 'is your glory' (Eph. 3:13).

In verse 12, Paul says that knowing this gives us boldness. We have confidence about our access to God in prayer, because we realize that we are doing his will and glorifying his name by standing firm against the flesh, the world, and the devil. This boldness comes only 'through our faith in him,' which is why there is nothing more important than for us to believe God's promises, to strengthen our faith with God's Word, and to empower our faith by prayer. Our faith is the greatest wonder in all the world, Paul says. And the sight of us trusting in God and doing his will in a world like this causes angels to exalt God's wisdom in saving us by his grace.

I want to point out one word in verse 10 that drives home this message to us. The word is *now*. Paul writes, 'So that through the church the manifold wisdom of God might *now* be made known to the rulers and authorities in the heavenly places.' This word 'now' tells us the drama is still going on. What Paul described as the display of God's wisdom to the elect angels—exulting in their joy—and to fallen angels—despairing in their rebellion against God—is something still going on. And it is going on in the church. Boice concludes,

> Now you and I are the players in this drama. Satan is attacking, and the angels are straining forward to look on. Are they seeing the 'manifold wisdom of God' in you as you go through your part and speak your lines? They must see it, for it can be seen in you alone. It is there—where you work and play and think and speak—that the meaning and end of history is found.[247]

This is what the church is all about. The church is not a building, and not just a collection of flawed people. It is the lens by which the multi-colored wisdom of God is glorified in Christ. What angels now realize we see with the eyes of faith, but the day comes soon when all creation will be filled with the knowledge of the glory and wisdom of God, as the waters cover the sea.

The Scaffolding Removed

In 1994, a celebration was held at Westminster Abbey in London to celebrate the 350th anniversary of the *Westminster Confession of Faith*. One of the speakers was Eric Alexander. He spoke about Paul and the early Christians as they faced such persecution and difficulty. He pointed out that their knowledge of what God was doing in history and for their own salvation 'injected a certainty into their tentative, weak, poor faith. It gave many of them a security in a desperately insecure world. Were we more heavenly-minded in our living, it would do the same for us.'[248]

Alexander went on to ask a series of pointed questions to make us think about our own lives. He asked:

> What is the really important thing that is happening in the world in our generation? Where are the really significant events taking place? What is the most important thing? Where do you need to look in the modern world to see the most significant event from a divine perspective? Where is the focus of God's activity in history?

How would you answer those questions? What would you identify as the great marvel of our time, the most interesting thing that demands our attention today? Alexander gave his answer:

> The most significant thing happening in history is the calling, redeeming, and perfecting of the people of God. God is building the church of Jesus Christ. The rest of history is simply a stage God erects for that purpose. He is calling out a people. He is perfecting them. He is changing them. History's great climax comes when God brings down the curtain on this bankrupt world and the Lord Jesus Christ arrives in his infinite glory. The rest of history is simply the scaffolding for the real work.[249]

Alexander finished with a story much like the one with which I began today. He said that the last time he had been in London, Westminster Abbey had been covered in scaffolding as workers were cleaning and beautifying it. 'One could not see its true beauty,' he noted, 'but one was aware that something of great significance was happening behind that scaffolding. Something of majestic beauty was to be revealed.' Drawing upon that, he applied it to our lives and to the church:

> There will come a day, when God will pull down the scaffolding of world history. Do you know what he will be pointing to when he says to the whole creation, 'There is my masterpiece?' He will be pointing to the church of Jesus Christ. In the forefront of it all will be the Lord Jesus himself who will come and say, 'Here am I, and the children you have given me, perfected in the beauty of holiness.'
>
> That is the day for which we are laboring. In that day, we shall be resurrected...We need to live for that day—the day when God will manifest his glory in his people. If we live for that day, it will change our living and it will change our serving. God grant it, as we say, 'even so, come Lord Jesus.'[250]

37

Strengthened with Power

Ephesians 3:14–16

There is one respect in which the church today most markedly differs from the early church and especially from the example of the apostles. The difference is not that the early church was devoted to the Bible and we are not. It certainly is true that biblical literacy is shockingly low among professing believers today and that few churches think it worthwhile to teach the Bible thoroughly. But it is also the case that a great deal of Bible study takes place today and that a great wealth of biblical study materials are available. The difference also is not a lack of focus on evangelism. We certainly need more effort in this direction and to equip more Christians to share the gospel. But I do not think it true that there is a general absence of evangelism in our churches. Furthermore, while the early church certainly shone more brightly in terms of community and brotherly love than we do today, it would be wrong to deny that real loving community exists within our churches. In these three areas, I find that it is generally easy to get Christians motivated and involved.

The area in which I think the church today most differs from the apostolic church is prayer. Whereas the Bible is literally filled with prayers, and the example of the apostles is one of constant and fervent prayer, most of us today look on prayer as a dreary and mainly unfruitful chore. This is the Achilles Heel of our churches today: a lack of commitment to prayer. This weakness undermines all our strengths; because we do not pray, everything else we are doing lacks the power that can only be had through prayer.

People do not pray today, or not much, in part because they are discouraged by the apparent lack of success. They have not received what they prayed for, so they stopped praying. In large part, this is because we are uninstructed in what we should be praying for and what we should expect from prayer. Other Christians doubt the value of prayer because of their belief in God's sovereignty. If God is in control, they wonder, why bother to pray? But none of us has a higher appreciation for God's sovereignty than the apostle Paul, yet he is noted as a man of constant and bold prayer.

In Ephesians chapter 3, we come to the second of Paul's prayers in this letter. Since his last prayer in chapter 1, Paul has set before us the whole doctrine of salvation, both as it applies to individuals and as it brings us together as one in the church. In Paul's mind, the proper response to this teaching is that we ought to bow our knees before the Father and pray.

Paul's Attitude to Prayer

Paul begins by telling us *how* he prayed: 'For this reason, I bow my knees before the Father.' It is not entirely clear to what he refers when he says, 'For this reason.' The best explanation is that he is looking back on chapter 2, which concluded with a great statement of what the church is intended to be. In Ephesians 3:1, Paul started this prayer, saying, 'For this reason,' but he interrupted his thought with the explanation of his suffering (Eph. 3:1–13). Now he gets to that prayer, which has the point of asking God to give the believers the resources they need to live up to their high calling in Christ.

Paul's attitude toward prayer provides a valuable model for us. First, we see how highly he valued prayer. Later on in the letter Paul is going to exhort the believers themselves. But the first thing he thinks to do is to pray to God for them. What a difference it would make in our lives and relationships if we first prayed and then spoke or acted! Instead of relying on our own influence and persuasion, we can often accomplish more by appealing to God for his influence and persuasion. Charles Spurgeon wrote, 'Prayer is the ship which bringeth home the richest freight. It is the soil which yields the most abundant harvest.'[251] Paul especially sets an example for ministers and other church leaders, that God would have us pray for the blessing and strengthening of our flock. Along with preaching, prayer is the chief work of a minister. The same principle applies to the believer's spiritual growth. Whenever you read the Bible, you ought to pray for God to do in your life what you are reading about in Scripture.

Second, in addition to seeing how much Paul valued prayer, he also specifies to whom he prays: the Father. This is in keeping with the pattern laid out in Ephesians 2:18, that we pray *to* the Father *through* the Son *by* the Spirit. When Paul speaks of praying to the Father, he has in mind the access we have as God's children. Hirelings may be forced to wait outside, but children have permanent access to the Father's heart.

Verse 15 describes the Father as the one 'from whom every family in heaven and on earth is named.' This can be taken one of two ways. Paul could be saying that every kind of family has its origin in God. This is suggested by a word-play in the Greek that does not come through in English. The word for father is *pater*, and 'every family' translates *pasa patria*. Paul's point with this word play may be that while we have all kinds of ideas of fatherhood and family, they all derive from his Fatherhood, which is the ultimate expression of the ideal. This helps with a point I often make to those who struggle with the idea of God as Father because of their disappointing or even abusive experience with their earthly father. This should not cause them to hold back from God the Father or fear a lack of love from him, because he is the ultimate expression of what fatherhood was always meant to be.

While that is true, Paul's point here is likely the other way of taking this verse, that God is the Father of the whole family of believers, including those who are already in heaven and those who are still on earth. This means that God is not only the perfect realization of fatherhood, but he is actually *our* Father. It is one thing to admire a man as an ideal father when you have no right to approach him as his own child. It is something far better to look to the perfect father and say, 'Daddy' to him. This is our privilege and it energized Paul's approach to prayer. He knew he had access to the Father because he was joined in faith to God's Son. Likewise, in Christ, we are objects of God's special, Fatherly love and he delights to hear our prayers.

Third, in addition to the value Paul puts on prayer and the person to whom Paul prays, verse 14 shows the reverent attitude he has in prayer: 'I bow my knees before the Father.' Children rightly respect their fathers, and our access into God's love does not change the reverence he is due. In most of the biblical examples of prayer the people are standing before the Lord (see Gen. 18:22; Mark 11:25; Luke 18:11, 13). But in times of great stress and need we often see God's people praying on their knees. One example is that of our Lord Jesus in the Garden of Gethsemane (Luke 22:41). Other examples include Daniel's prayers from Babylon (Dan. 6:1) and Stephen's prayer for the forgiveness of those who were stoning him to death (Acts 7:60). Perhaps the Ephesians would remember Paul's departure from them, when he knelt with their elders to pray for God's protection over their church. Our posture in prayer may vary depending on the situation, but our prayer should always be reverent.

Reverence, however, does not demand a lack of boldness in prayer. Paul's prayer reveals a heavy dose of both. Humility and boldness go together, since both arise from a biblical awareness of who God is. Especially when asking for things God has promised or that we know that God desires, we should pray with a holy boldness.

I do not always know whether or not it is God's will to grant the thing for which I am praying. I know that when people are sick or dying that God wants me to pray for them. But I do not know if it is God's will for them to get better. I know that I am to pray for those out of work, but I do not know that God intends to grant a particular job. Thus I often will pray, 'If it is your will.'

But we have the right—even the duty—to be bolder when it comes to things God has promised or that he has told us that he desires. I am talking about things like faith and holiness and the fruit of the Spirit in our lives. We should not say, 'If it be your will' for these things. God has told us that they are his will! We should pray boldly for the grace to repent of specific sins and to develop biblical character traits, for love and mercy and humility, for courage to witness, and for a desire to study God's Word and pray. These are the kinds of things Paul wants for the Ephesians—for them to be strengthened inwardly, for Christ to dwell in their hearts, for them to comprehend the love of God in Christ—and he does not beat around the bush with God, but prays for them boldly.

Paul prays with a confidence that believes God is willing and able to answer his prayers. He prays 'according to the riches of his glory' (Eph. 3:16). God's glory is all that he is: he is holy and true, merciful and loving, almighty and just. Many a wealthy man gives *out of* his riches, giving what may seem like large amounts to us but that are little to him. But God gives *according to* his riches. An earthly king is glorified when his subjects expect great things from him; this is all the more true when it comes to God. He gives in a measure that is appropriate and glorious to one so rich as he. God is not miserly or reluctant in answering our prayers and we dishonor him by praying with low expectations and dim hopes. Paul prayed with confidence, saying in Philippians 4:19, 'My God will supply every need of yours according to his riches in glory in Christ Jesus.'

How greatly we are hindered in our prayers because we forget the 'riches of his glory.' We do not pray for the salvation of flagrant unbelievers, because we think their conversion is too hard. Yet if we will pray according to God's riches we will realize that he is almighty to save the vilest of sinners. We pray feebly against our sins, not realizing that God is willing and able to deliver us from evil. We ask God merely to tolerate our presence rather than to fill us with his love, because we forget the abundance of his mercy and the extravagance of his grace. Because of the riches of God's glory, the apostle John wrote, 'This is the confidence that we have toward him, that if we ask anything according to his will he hears us' (1 John 5:14).

Martin Luther was an example of boldness in prayer. He once received a letter from a valued assistant, Friedrich Myconius, informing Luther that he was ill and soon would die. Luther immediately wrote back:

> I command thee in the name of God to live because I still have need of thee in the work of reforming the church…The Lord will never let me hear that thou art dead, but will permit thee to live. For this I am praying, this is my will, and may my will be done, because I seek only to glorify the name of God.

Now that is boldness in prayer! When Luther's letter arrived, Myconius was so near death that he could no longer even speak. But he miraculously recovered and lived six more years, dying only shortly after Luther himself had died.[252]

Praying for Power

I mentioned that Christians today differ from the early believers in terms of our lack of prayer. But in one respect we are exactly like them, namely, in our need for divine power so as to live for God as we ought. Having seen *how* Paul prayed, we now consider *what* he prayed for: that God 'may grant you to be strengthened with power through his Spirit' (Eph. 3:16).

Power is an important theme in Ephesians. Some scholars think this is in part due to the large occult presence in Ephesus, but I think it also reflects Paul's understanding of the Christian life. In his first prayer, he asked for them to be enlightened as to 'the immeasurable greatness of [God's] power toward us who believe' (Eph. 1:19), which he said is the very power God used to raise Jesus from the grave. Through union with Christ we have resurrection power for godliness. In Ephesians 3:7, he tells us that his own ministry was given him 'by the working of [God's] power.' At the end of this chapter, he says that God is 'able to do far more abundantly than all that we ask or think, according to his power at work within us' (Eph. 3:20).

The kind of power Paul has in mind is spiritual power. He prays that God 'may grant you to be strengthened with power through his Spirit' (Eph. 3:16). Spiritual concerns occupy little of our prayer space. We ask for physical strength, for increased intelligence, for athletic ability or powers of persuasion, for fitter and healthier bodies, and for better relationships. It may or may not please God to grant such requests. But we can be certain of God's desire to give us spiritual power for doing his will.

As Paul understands it, the Christian life is energized spiritually by the power of the Holy Spirit. By means of his power we are to seek the transformation of every part of our lives. Paul put it perhaps best in Philippians, when he wrote: 'Work out your own salvation with fear and trembling, for it is God who works in you, both to will and to work for his good pleasure' (Phil. 3:12–13). We are to 'work out' our Christianity into every area of our lives. But we can only do that because God's power is at work within us so that we are able to do his will. Without God's power we would never be able to stand up to the assaults of the flesh, the world, and the devil; but with God's power we can be spiritually strong so that every area of our lives is characterized by godliness. Morris observes:

It is a depressing fact of life that in every age people have found it much easier to go along with the low standards of the society in which they live than to accept the divine standards and put their energies into the service of God…Paul does not want them to be content with the low standards and poor achievements that the worldly-minded accept as the norm.[253]

Paul wants us to live out a salvation that is 'according to the riches of God's glory,' so he prays for God's power to energize our lives.

The best examples of what this looks like come from the Book of Acts. Jesus told the disciples, 'You will receive power when the Holy Spirit has come upon you' (Acts 1:8). We usually think of this power in terms of the miracles of the apostles, but it was equally important with regard to the spiritual power Jesus provides all believers.

Acts 2:42–47 tells us that the believers 'devoted themselves to the apostles' teaching…All who believed were together and had all things in common…They received their food with glad and generous hearts, praising God and having favor with all the people.' The church's devotion and unity and love were the result of God's power.

In Acts 4:29, the apostle prayed for boldness to proclaim the gospel in the face of persecution. God answered that prayer in Acts 5:41, when Peter and John responded to persecution by 'rejoicing that they were counted worthy to suffer dishonor for the name.' I mentioned Stephen praying on his knees for the forgiveness of the men who stoned him to death. Only God's power enables us to love and forgive even those who hate us. One of the men for whom he prayed was Saul of Tarsus, who became the apostle Paul, no doubt partly in answer to Stephen's prayer.

One of my favorite scenes from Paul's life is found in Acts 16. Paul and Silas were arrested in Philippi, beaten with rods, and thrown into jail. What happened next is a perfect picture of the power available to a Christian: 'About midnight Paul and Silas were praying and singing hymns to God, and the prisoners were listening to them, and suddenly there was a great earthquake, so that the foundations of the prison were shaken. And immediately all the doors were opened, and everyone's bonds were unfastened' (Acts 16:25–26). What a picture of the power of God working in the hearts of his people, who praise him in affliction and pray so that God works mightily to set them free! As a result, the man who supervised their jail was brought to faith. Seeing God's power working through Paul, he asked, 'What must I do to be saved?' Paul replied, 'Believe in the Lord Jesus, and you will be saved, you and your household' (Acts 16:30–31). It is by God's power that we believe and receive eternal life.

You see why Paul prayed for God to strengthen the Ephesians with power. He did not want them to lead a poor and weak Christian life that neither expects nor receives great things from God. He knew firsthand about the power of God, which enables us to repent and believe, to love and serve, to overcome the devil and walk in the light, to be freed from the chains of our fleshly existence and to partake of Christ's victory in a holy resurrection life.

Strengthened Within

We have considered *how* Paul prayed and *what* he prayed for. He concludes verse 16 by telling us *where* he prays for us to be strengthened with power: 'in your inner being.' This contrasts with the kinds of outward power we normally find so attractive. We are impressed with outward displays of power, but Paul prioritized God's work within us—not in the outward man but in the inner man.

There is nothing wrong with praying for help in the outward circumstances of life. But God's primary intention is to work within us. We ought therefore to focus our prayers more on the inner spiritual matters than on our outward, worldly concerns.

In 2 Corinthians 12, we read of Paul suffering from an unspecified 'thorn in the flesh,' for which he prayed to God. Paul was clearly worked up over this: 'Three times I pleaded with the Lord about this, that it should leave me' (2 Cor. 12:8). But it did not please God to change Paul's circumstances. Instead, he 'strengthened him with power in his inner being.' Paul tells us: 'He said to me, "My grace is sufficient for you, for my power is made perfect in weakness."' In response, Paul did not complain that God 'only' worked within him, instead of relieving his difficult trial. Instead, Paul rejoiced in the inestimable blessing of God's power working within. He wrote, 'Therefore I will boast all the more gladly of my weaknesses, so that the power of Christ may rest upon me' (2 Cor. 12:10).

The phrase 'may rest upon me' is the Greek form of the word that means 'tabernacle.' Literally, Paul says, 'so that the power of Christ may *entabernacle* me.' This is a word picture for what happened in Israel during its journey through the wilderness to the Promised Land. God's people were traveling through a dangerous, difficult land, with no food or water except what God miraculously provided. But when they stopped in the desert, the glory cloud of God would rest upon the tabernacle in their midst. His power was within them. This assured them of provision, safety, and far more significantly, fellowship with the God of glory and might. This was a picture of what Paul wanted for himself, and he rejoiced to be inwardly strengthened with God's might as the Sprit dwelt in him as in the tabernacle of old.

This is the kind of people God wants us to be: men and women who flourish spiritually even in barren circumstances. God glorifies himself especially by roses that bloom in the desert. He showed his power by feeding Israel with manna in the wilderness and making water spring from a rock. Likewise, it most glorifies God not to change our outward circumstances but, as Paul prays, 'to strengthen us with power through his Spirit in the inner being' (Eph. 3:16) and thus entabernacle us with his glory.

Paul made this prayer in a jail cell where he was a living embodiment of his aspiration for us. Not even chains could keep his spirit from soaring free and no Roman oppression could stop his ministry of prayer. God will do the same in and through our lives. When he strengthens us within and works his power through our lives—through our ministry and our love, our service and our testimony—he causes ripples to flow outward to others, impacting even future generations and bearing an everlasting fruit.

Praying with Power

Let me conclude by making three points about how knowing this should shape our attitude towards prayer. First, we need to learn from Paul how important prayer is. We need to think less about what our own efforts can accomplish and more about what God will do by his might in answer to our prayers. We should see prayer as an investment we make for things of eternal significance and glory. Can we not give a significant place in our lives and on our schedules for prayer, realizing its importance and power?

Second, this teaching ought to influence the content of our prayers. I would never discourage people from making requests about their needs and troubles. But we should spend more time just praising God for his blessings and asking him to glorify himself through our prayers. Jesus began the Lord's Prayer: 'Our Father in Heaven, hallowed be thy name' (Matt. 6:9). Jesus' first prayer concern was for God to glorify himself. Then, we should pray more for the affairs of the inner man—for faith and holiness, zeal and endurance, patience and humility, love and faithfulness. These are the fields in which our prayers are most likely and most quickly to bear an abundant harvest.

Third, we need to become serious about interceding for others in prayer. We lament that loved ones do not believe. Are we laboring for them in prayer? We see our nation sinking into a morass of evil. Do we pray for revival? We know people who are weak in faith, who are tempted by the world, who are discouraged by hardship. Are we praying for them to be 'strengthened with power in the inner being?' We want our church to be blessed and to be a blessing to others. Do we pray for the Holy Spirit to enliven God's Word among us and melt our hearts in obedience and love? If not, we should not expect these things to happen. Writ large over our weakness and failure is the diagnosis of James 4:2, 'You do not have, because you do not ask.' The believers of the early church were weak and vulnerable in the world, yet they set an example for us by praying to God, who filled them with a holy, spiritual might that changed history.

I mentioned a prayer in Acts 4, where the believers asked God for boldness and power. That passage ends on this theme, and it is an appeal for us to realize what we are missing if we do not pray: 'And when they had prayed, the place in which they were gathered together was shaken, and they were all filled with the Holy Spirit and continued to speak the word of God with boldness' (Acts 4:31).

'I bow my knees before the Father,' Paul writes. I wonder if he was thinking even about us who read his letter today, 'that according to the riches of his glory he may grant you to be strengthened with power through his Spirit in your inner being' (Eph. 3:16). May God cause us to enter into that prayer, and may he answer it by enlightening our minds and hearts, by molding our wills and desires, and granting us a zeal to do his holy will, all to the praise of his glorious name.

38

Christ in You

Ephesians 3:17

Paul's letter to the Ephesians is widely considered the loftiest of his writings. This is partly because Paul does not seem to have had to address any controversy here; Ephesians directs itself not to correcting error but to presenting the most concentrated exposition of Christian doctrine in perhaps all of Scripture.

Ephesians is also noted for the greatness of Paul's prayers, especially the one that concludes chapter 1 and this prayer at the end of chapter 3. In the first of these, Paul prays for God to enlighten our hearts with regard to God's work *for us*. Now, having completed his teaching on how God saves us and what God intends in our salvation, Paul prays for God's work to be completed *in us*.

This prayer of Ephesians 3 is rightly considered one of the great passages in Paul's writings. It is worthy of our most careful study and of being committed to memory. Here we have the distilled essence of the Christian experience; what Paul prays for in these verses is a summary of all that God intends for us in Christ. It is a catalogue of mighty works by which we are to be 'filled with all the fullness of God' (v. 19).

Like all of Paul's great statements regarding salvation, this prayer is structured in a deliberately Trinitarian fashion. Paul wants believers to relate not merely to Jesus but to all three persons of the Godhead. Here, he prays to God the Father to send God the Spirit to cause God the Son to reside in our hearts. Just as God's work for us was a combined effort of the Father, Son and Spirit, so also does God's work in us draw upon all the resources of the Trinity.

Christ Dwelling Within

In verse 16, Paul began his prayer by asking the Father 'to grant you to be strengthened with power through his Spirit in your inner being.' Verse 17 expands upon this, telling us what is the effect of this spiritual strengthening: 'so that Christ may dwell in your hearts through faith.'

This is Paul's main idea of the Christian experience, to have Christ dwelling within us. In Colossians 1:27, Paul summarized God's gift as 'Christ in you, the hope of glory.' Paul described his own life in Galatians 2:20, saying, 'I have been crucified with Christ. It is no longer I who live, but Christ who lives in me.'

How can Christ live in us? After all, the Bible says that after his resurrection Jesus ascended into heaven. How can he live in me, if he lives in heaven and is seated at the right hand of God?

That answer is that Jesus lives in us through the work of the Holy Spirit. This is Paul's point in this prayer, that the Spirit would strengthen us with power so that Christ would dwell in us. The Spirit takes the things of Christ and works them into us: Christ's love, Christ's holiness, Christ's compassion and mercy, Christ's forgiving heart and Christ's desire to do the will of God the Father. Christ lives in us by the Spirit he sends, who takes the things of Christ and works them into our hearts.

It is important to know that when Paul prays for Christ to 'dwell' within us, he uses a particular word with a specific emphasis. There are two words Paul might have used, both of which are based on the word *oikeo*, which means to dwell. The more common word is *paroikeo*, which means to visit. This was used of Abraham as a sojourner or pilgrim in the promised land. This is not the word Paul uses for Christ dwelling in our hearts. Here, he uses a word that only occurs three times in Paul, *katoikeo*. It means to take up a permanent residence.

It is clear that Paul is not talking about conversion, since he is praying for people who are already believers. Christ has already come to them. What he prays for now is that Christ may take up a permanent residence in their hearts, that Christ may come to rule over every part of who they are.

One way to understand this idea is given by Robert Munger in his booklet *My Heart Christ's Home*. He pictures the Christian life as a house, with Jesus going through it room by room. Jesus goes into the library, which may be compared to the mind. And he finds there all kinds of falsehood and trash. He wants to toss it all out and replace it with the truth of his Word. He goes into the dining room of the appetite and finds there all sorts of sinful desires. He wants to replace pride and greed and lust with godly desires like humility, meekness and love. He goes into the living room and finds that worldly company has been let into the heart and he wants to replace them with godly fellowship. Into the closet he peers, to find secret and cherished sins, which have to be brought out into the light and shown to the door.[254]

Jesus intends to live in our hearts, so they must be made fitting for him. John MacArthur writes, 'Jesus enters the house of our hearts the moment he saves us, but He cannot live there in comfort and satisfaction until it is cleansed of sin and filled with His will…He cannot be fully at home until He is allowed to dwell in our hearts through the continuing faith that trusts Him to exercise His lordship over every aspect of our lives.'[255] Jesus said, 'If anyone loves me, he will keep my word, and my Father will love him, and we will come to him and make our home with him' (John 14:23).

Most of us have moved into a new house, often one that needed quite a bit of fixing up. We may not like the wallpaper in the bedroom. The roof leaks in places and the kitchen isn't laid out right. Generally, when we move in we address the major items. Then as the months and years go by the house comes more and more to reflect our tastes. At first we are not all that comfortable, but after a while we begin to feel at home as our fingerprints are seen in more places. After a lifetime in the house it is so dear to us that we can scarcely think of living anywhere else.

This is how the Christian life works. When Jesus sends the Spirit into the believer's heart, he finds all sorts of problems. There is trash piled in the corners and so much of the décor does not fit his tastes. So he gets to work, and as we respond to his working in faith, he becomes more at home in our hearts and his influence is seen in more and more places. In the end, our heart will be a dear and beloved home of God and his Son. But between now and then there is work to be done. D. A. Carson observes:

> Make no mistake: When Christ first moves into our lives, he finds us in very bad repair. It takes a great deal of power to change us; and that is why Paul prays for power. He asks that God may so strengthen us by his power in our inner being that Christ may genuinely take up residence within us, transforming us into a house that pervasively reflects his own character.[256]

This is the very thing we should want to happen in our lives, and realizing that this is what Jesus is doing ought to motivate our faith. Christ wants to live in you, with the result that his glory will shine more and more in your heart and his love for you will become more evident. We ought therefore to pray for an increase of the Spirit's power and a more settled presence by Jesus Christ. Our prayer ought to be that of the hymn:

> Make my life a bright outshining,
>   Of thy life, that all may see
> Thine own resurrection power,
>   Mightily put forth in me.
> Ever let my heart become,
>   Yet more consciously Thy home.[257]

The Spirit's Work: To Reveal & Manifest Christ

You hear a lot today about 'spirituality' or 'being spiritual'. Here is the Bible's depiction of true spirituality, that Jesus Christ should increasingly dwell and rule in your heart. You may take it as a rule of thumb that whenever someone is talking much about the Holy Spirit, the Holy Spirit himself is not present. The reason is that the Spirit's work, the Spirit's desire, is for Christ to be exalted and enthroned. Jesus said of the Spirit, 'He will glorify me, for he will take what is mine and declare it to you' (John 16:14). G. Campbell Morgan explains:

> Christian people constantly pray for the coming of the Holy Spirit, and wait for His coming. In their minds there seems to be the idea that when the Spirit comes to them in fullness they will be conscious of the Spirit. There is no evidence of any such teaching in Scripture. If the Spirit come to us in fullness, He will make us conscious, not of Himself, but of Christ…The Spirit comes to reveal Jesus only. He has no other message, no other work than the unveiling of the face of Christ, in which we see the unveiling of the face of God.[258]

Should we, then, pray for the Spirit? Certainly. That is the very thing Paul is praying for in this passage: 'I bow my knees before the Father…that he may grant you to be strengthened with power through his Spirit in your inner being.' We need and should pray for the Spirit to work in us with power. But how will we know when the Spirit comes? Paul tells us, 'So that Christ may dwell in your hearts through faith.' We are experiencing the power of the Spirit as we are being more conformed to Christ, as he is more comfortable in more places of our hearts—in our minds, in our desires, in our wills, in our pleasures. The yielding of these to the rule of Christ is the goal of the Spirit's mighty working, and since we lack the power for this on our own we should pray specifically for the Spirit's power to be applied to places in our lives where Christ's rule is resisted by our sinful nature.

Are you unable to forgive as Christ forgave you? Then pray for the Father to strengthen you with the Spirit's power so that Christ's forgiveness will reign in you. Are you unable to let go a cherished sin? Pray for the Spirit to unclench the fingers of your hands from that sin. Have you been made aware of a characteristic that is un-Christ-like? Do you need humility or meekness or honesty, gentleness or a self-sacrificing spirit? Ask the Father to send the Spirit to apply his power to mold your character, so that Christ will take up residence there.

Rooted and Grounded in Love

What, then, is the effect of having Christ permanently take up residence in your heart, renovating you to suit his holy desires, and the Lord Jesus become more and more at home in you? Paul tells us in the end of verse 17 that if Christ dwells in you by faith you will be increasingly 'rooted and grounded in love.'

This is a famous example of Paul's supposedly poor literary style, a classic instance of a mixed metaphor. Paul speaks simultaneously in botanical and construction terms. Paul does not care about such criticism, however, since his concern is theological and pastoral.

This statement advances Paul's prayer one more step. He first prayed for strengthening by the Spirit. Then he prayed that the Spirit's power would enable Christ to settle down for an eternal stay in our hearts. But even this is not an end in itself. Our relationship with Jesus Christ has the goal of prompting and empowering a life of love. As Paul wrote to Timothy, the aim of our ministry 'is love that issues from a pure heart and a good conscience and a sincere faith.' Jesus said, 'Abide in my love. If you keep my commandments, you will abide in my love' (John 15:9–10).

It is essential for Christians to know that Christ loves us. The proof of this is the cross, where Jesus died for us. 'Greater love has no one than this, that someone lays down his life for his friends' (John 15:13). This is why the Christian life always starts at the cross. If you want to know yourself loved by Jesus Christ and his Father in heaven, then you need only confess your sin and trust in the cross of Christ, where he died to forgive you and enter you into a new life.

We are to be rooted in Christ's love the way a tree is rooted in good soil. Christ's love then flows through us as the power by which we love others. Likewise, using Paul's second metaphor, we are to be like a building grounded on the love of Christ. That is our solid rock, and his love is the pattern we follow in love for other people. As John Stott says of believers, 'Love is to be the soil in which their life is to be rooted; love is to be the foundation on which their life is built.'[259]

But notice that this does not just happen. There is a reason why so many Christians do not feel themselves to be rooted and grounded on Christ's love. That reason is that Christ has not been given a place of residence and rule in their hearts. They have resisted his renovation of their desires. They have neglected his enlightenment of their minds. They have refused to let him cast out unwholesome company and clean out the closet of their secret sins. Instead of praying for the help of the Spirit in their battle, they have avoided prayer, avoided worship, and avoided fellowship with God's people. Then they wonder why they feel no love and experience no power to love others. They complain that God has disappointed them, when they are merely experiencing the necessary results of a heart that is not yielded to the dwelling of Jesus Christ.

Let me apply, as an example, to the matter of marriage. How are we to love one another in marriage? The world says the key is compatibility. The problem is that no sinner is really compatible with another sinner. The world says that marriage works when we are happy. But we often do not make one another happy, because we do not know how to and do not particularly care really to love one another.

For these reasons, the key to marriage is not for your husband or wife to change in order to make you happier. What marriage demands is that we love one another, that we minister to and serve one another, and yield our hearts one to another in love. This is the love our passage is talking about. Not erotic love or emotional love—*eros* or *phileos*; these alone will never grow a strong marriage. It requires *agape* love, the love that comes from the will and is active, which our passage is talking about. But this love has to come from somewhere, and it is not going to come from our sinful nature. By our sinful nature, we love ourselves and want to use other people. Marriage does not change that but only concentrates it. Where does agape love come from? If we can answer that then we can have the key to marriage (as well as the key to friendship and to harmony at work and love in our families).

The key to marriage, the key to love, is what Paul writes about here: to have Christ take up permanent residence in every area of our hearts. James wrote, 'What causes quarrels and what causes fights among you? Is it not this, that your passions are at war within you? You desire and do not have, so you murder. You covet and cannot obtain, so you fight and quarrel' (James 4:1-2). This, then, is what we need—for Jesus to come within us, throw out our warring passions, and replace them with peaceable ones. Jesus wants to get rid of covetousness and replace it with contentment. If we will pray to the Father to send the Spirit to do the renovations Jesus is interested in, things will be different. James notes about this, however, 'You have not because you ask not' (James 4:2).

If you are not able to love, it is because there is at least one key place in our heart that you will not yield to Christ. Deceived by sin, you will not seek the Spirit's power from the Father to break that stronghold. It is your love of that sin, your idolatrous desire that is keeping Christ at bay, that accounts for your inability to love. If your marriage is to be saved and renewed, if your children are to grow up with the love they need, if God is going to use you in other peoples' lives as he wants to, you must give Christ access to the whole of your heart. There is no other way to love than to yield all to Christ's rule. Only then are we 'rooted and grounded in love' and therefore have love to share and enjoy.

How? Through Faith

This leads us to the final question, 'How do we do it? How do we have Christ dwell within us so that we are rooted and grounded in love?' Paul's answer is 'through faith'.

The Bible speaks of faith both as passive and as active. In our justification, in our original receiving of Christ as Lord and Savior, our faith is passive. This means that faith simply receives salvation as a gift. 'The gift of God is eternal life in Christ Jesus our Lord' (Rom. 6:23). If you do not have eternal life, you need only to receive it by believing on Christ. But once we have been saved, our faith is to express itself actively. It is in this sense that Paul speaks of Christ dwelling in our hearts 'through faith'. He might have said, 'Through the activity of faith.'

Faith becomes active as we 'keep in step with the Spirit' (Gal. 5:25). When I was in the Army we would march in formations. The sergeant would call out the cadence and what we had to do was keep in step. It is this way with the Spirit. Paul adds in Philippians 2:12-13, 'Work out your salvation with fear and trembling.' How? 'For it is God who works in you, both to will and to work according to his good pleasure.' God is working it in; we are to work it out with an active faith.

There are certain things that all Christians will do if they are acting by faith in response to God's Spirit and in obedience to Christ. First, they will commit themselves to the Word of God. Paul says in Romans 12:2, 'Do not be conformed any longer to this world, but be transformed by the renewal of your mind.' Jesus wants to take the folly and the falsehood out of your mind to replace it with truth and light and beauty. His instrument for this is God's Word. 'Sanctify them by the truth,' he prayed. 'Your Word is truth' (John 17:17). If you want Christ to live in you, then you must become a disciple through his Word, and you must devote yourself to the study of the Bible and the practice of its teachings. This is why Sunday School attendance and home Bible studies will always be one indicator of a strong church.

Furthermore, an active faith will cause a Christian to cooperate with Jesus in the cleansing of the heart. This takes place most powerfully through prayer. Our supplications should not mainly focus on our circumstances or even on the needs of others (important as those are), but should largely deal with God's work in our hearts, for which we seek the Spirit to work with power in specific areas of resistance and sin so that we are fitted for Christ's dwelling.

Third, Christians whose minds are being transformed by God's Word and whose desires are being remolded by God's Spirit in response to prayer, will then exercise their wills in obedience to God. You don't start with the will: you start with a renewed mind and changed desires, through the Word and prayer. But these changes are to be expressed through the will, through choices and through behaviors. There are things that are incompatible with Christ in the heart. 'What partnership has righteousness with lawlessness?' Paul asks. 'Or what fellowship has light with darkness?' (2 Cor. 6:14). So we must act. As Paul later says in Ephesians, 'Put off your old self, which belongs to your former manner of life and is corrupt through deceitful desires, and be renewed in the spirit of your minds, and put on the new self, created after the likeness of God in true righteousness and holiness' (Eph. 4:22–24).

The result of this life is Christ dwelling joyfully in our hearts and filling us with his love. Does the Christian life really, then, seem so unappealing? To know love and be rooted in love so that it flows through you, to be established on love so that it is your life's pattern? It starts with submitting your mind to God's Word so that you see the love of Christ. To this we add prayer to the Father for the work of the Spirit in our hearts. The result is Christ in you, filling your life with the things of God: with beauty and peace and joy, and especially love. 'God is love' (1 John 4:7). May God therefore strengthen you for Christ to take up his residence in your hearts, so that abiding in him and he in you, you may abound in the love of God.

39

The Measure of Christ's Love

Ephesians 3:17–19

The apostle Paul's chief motivation in writing Ephesians was the spiritual maturity of his readers. As a good pastor, he desired not merely for them to be born again as spiritual infants but also for them to grow up into spiritual adults. That is specifically the purpose of his prayer, which concludes with a request 'that you may be filled with all the fullness of God' (Eph. 3:19).

It is instructive that Paul did not advocate a perpetual childishness, as we tend to do today. One popular approach for churches is to aim for the level of the children, so their parents will be able to get them to come to church. The problem is that the whole church remains immature. Others think everything in the church should be aimed at the conversion of unbelievers. But for all of Paul's zeal for evangelism, his ministry was geared not only for this. As we will see in chapter 4, Paul believed that God calls a pastor to aim for the maturity of his people, so that they in turn will be evangelists.

What did Paul think would cause his readers to mature? Again, it is helpful to consider some of the options presented today. Some would have us undertake spiritual disciplines in order to mature, and there certainly is a place for that. Others seek a constant round of experiences that will induce a spiritual high. Others still would have us all take seminary-level courses in theology. What, then, did Paul think we need in order to mature? Our passage tells us he wants us to know and comprehend the love of Christ. All other things may be fine in their place, but you may have them without growing spiritually. Even knowledge of the Bible profits little without knowing Christ's love. The same is true of spiritual experiences. Spiritual disciplines without Christ's love offer only a fruitless ritualism. But to grow in your knowledge of the love of Christ is necessarily to grow in your faith and to have Christ's presence grow in your heart.

Paul believed in the power of love. This was his first priority in the path of our spiritual growth. Paul assumes that while his readers are saved and thus have known Christ's love, they do not adequately appreciate it and rely upon it. He thus prays for God to empower them to grasp this love 'that surpasses knowledge.' The love of Christ is greater than we can know. But Paul thinks it vital that we comprehend something of the greatness of the measure of Christ's love.

If you want to see the power of love, then you should get to know Christians who are involved in the foster care of children. New Testament scholar D. A. Carson writes about Christian friends who took in twin eighteen-month-old boys who were going to stay, they thought, for just a few weeks until they could be placed in a more permanent setting. The first night the little boys were crying in their cribs, as you would expect, only they were not making the slightest sound. It turned out that they had been beaten for crying at one of the nine homes in which they had lived during the year and a half of their little lives. An expert who was sent out to evaluate them concluded that the twins were hopelessly damaged emotionally and intellectually. As a result, the Christian couple decided to keep the boys until a good adoptive family could be found. Two years later, when another expert evaluated them prior to their adoption, no evidence of emotional damage could be found. What had cured the little children's hearts? The answer is love. Tender, careful love.[260]

Love literally works miracles. This is true not merely for emotionally scarred children, but for all of us who are crippled and twisted by sin—our own and others'. God takes us into his family as spiritual infants, and it is by comprehending his love that we are filled with his fullness.

The Measure of Christ's Love

How, then, do you know love? When one of my sons was six years old, he loved his kindergarten teacher, Mrs Wolfe. He made a box for Valentine's Day covered with red crepe paper and wrote all over it, 'I love you,' to his teacher. She may not have gotten the message when she saw that box, one of many in her class. But if she had seen the intense care he poured into making it, then she would have learned about his love for her.

Carson tells of being hospitalized as a boy with a life-threatening illness. He woke up one afternoon during his recovery to find his mother sitting beside his bed crying. He knew that his parents loved him before this, but seeing her tears at his sickbed, he better appreciated the reality of his mother's love.[261]

Philip Yancey thought he had missed out on a father's love because his father died of polio when he was just a baby. But years later he ran across a picture of himself as an infant that his mother had kept. The picture was crumpled and torn; he knew she had better ones and asked why she had kept it. His mother told him that she had wedged that photo into his father's iron lung, and that he had spent his dying months gazing upon his son, praying for and delighting in just a picture of his child. Yancey writes, 'Someone I have no memory of…spent all day every day thinking of me, devoting himself to me, loving me as well as he could.'[262] Thus he knew his father's love.

How do we know Christ's love for us? In verse 18, Paul makes a statement that has inspired many about the love of Christ for us. He asks God to show us 'what is the breadth and length and height and depth' of Christ's love 'that surpasses knowledge.' His point is that Christ's love for us is so great and so divine that we will never have full knowledge of it. But we should nonetheless learn to appreciate Christ's love by the measures of it that are provided in God's Word.

How are we to conceive of the *breadth*, that is, the width, of Christ's love? One answer is the one provided by Paul when he spoke of Christ bringing together Jews and Gentiles through the cross (Eph. 2:14–15). The point is that now in Christ every kind of person may come: that is the breadth of Christ's love. When we see Jesus' arms spread on the cross, we should see an open invitation for all the world. The same is true for every category today. Young and old, white and black and brown, rich and poor, educated and uneducated, churched and unchurched—Christ's love is wide enough to embrace them all. Paul wrote, 'Now in Christ Jesus you who once were far off have been brought near by the blood of Christ' (Eph. 2:13). That means that there is a place for you, whoever you are, whatever your sins, in the love of Jesus Christ.

Next, Paul speaks of the *length* of Christ's love. Christ loved us in eternity past, when we were 'chosen in him before the foundation of the world' (Eph. 1:4). Christ's love extends into eternity future, when we will be 'heirs together with him in glory' (Rom. 8:17).

The length of Christ's love may also be conceived in terms of the extent of our forgiveness. Psalm 103:12 says, 'As far as the east is from the west, so far does he remove our transgressions from us.' Alexander Maclaren therefore writes, 'The length of the love of Christ is the length of eternity, and out-measures all human sin.'[263]

What about the *height* of Christ's love? We think of Jesus lifted up high upon the cross. Jesus said, 'The Son of Man must be lifted up, that whoever believes in him may have eternal life' (John 3:15). The height of Christ's love rises higher still, up into heaven, raising sinners up to dwell with him in heavenly places with every spiritual blessing (Eph. 1:3).

This leaves the last of Paul's descriptions, the *depth* of Christ's love. There is no depth of sin but that Christ will not descend to redeem it by his blood. We naturally think of Jesus' death and burial, his descent into hell for us. Maclaren writes, 'My sins are deep, my helpless miseries are deep, but they are shallow as compared with the love that goes down beneath all sin…How deep is the love of Christ!…The depths of Christ's love go down beneath all human necessity, sorrow, suffering, and sin.'[264]

When Napoleon's soldiers conquered Spain they broke into the prisons of the Spanish Inquisition. In one dungeon cell they found the skeleton of a prisoner who still was chained to his wall. There they saw a cross etched into the rock. Above the cross was written, *height*; below it was written *depth*; on one arm was *length* and on the other *breadth*. As the poor believer starved to death he seemed to have been contemplating the wonder of Christ's love that bore the cross for his salvation.[265] These measures of love are worthy of contemplation, giving hope to everyone who believes. John Stott says, 'The love of Christ is 'broad' enough to encompass all mankind, 'long' enough to last for eternity, 'deep' enough to reach the most degraded sinner, and 'high' enough to exalt him to heaven.'[266]

It is not by chance that most believers read Paul's description and think of the cross, though the apostle does not explicitly make this connection. The reason is that 'the measure of love is how much it gives, and the measure of the love of God is the gift of His only Son to be made man, and to die for sins, and so to become the one mediator who can bring us to God.'[267]

Does Jesus love you? If not, it is hard to explain why he left the glory of heaven to take up flesh and enter into this world of sorrow and woe to be our Savior. The height and depth of Christ's love is the distance between heaven and the manger of Bethlehem, the difference between the eternal riches he left and the poverty he undertook in order to make us rich. Jesus humbled himself by coming into this world like us, and in this he shows his love.

Does Jesus love you? He said, 'Greater love has no one than that he lay down his life for his friends' (John 15:13). 'The cross,' says St. Augustine, 'was a pulpit, in which Christ preached his love to the world.'[268] Jesus showed his love by suffering in atonement for our sin. How can you doubt the love of Jesus Christ, when he has already died for you? Paul writes in Galatians 2:20, 'The life I live in the flesh, I live by faith in the Son of God, who loved me and gave himself for me.'

Jesus further proves his love to us in his ascension and exaltation into heaven by devoting himself in ministry for our salvation. 'Never will I leave you, never will I forsake you,' he says. 'Because I live, you also will live.' In his humiliation, in his crucifixion, and in his exaltation, Jesus proves his love for us through his self-giving ministry of salvation.

Comprehending Christ's Love

Paul intends us to possess more than an intellectual knowledge of Christ's love. I say this for two reasons, the first of which is that he prays that we might *comprehend* Christ's love. It is one thing for me to *apprehend* Christ's love, that is, to lay my hands upon it in the faith that saves my soul. But Paul wants more, for us to *comprehend* Christ's love and get our arms around it so that we can draw Christ's love near to our hearts. Secondly, Paul speaks of knowing Christ's love 'that surpasses knowledge'. Clearly, Paul has in mind a knowledge of personal experience and participation. Charles Spurgeon writes,

> An ungodly man may know something about Christ's love; he may believe in the fact of it; he may perceive something of the theory of it… But to know the love itself, to taste its sweets, to realize personally, experimentally, and vitally, the love of Christ as shed abroad in our hearts by the Holy Ghost, is the privilege of the child of God, and of the child of God alone.[269]

The first way believers come to comprehend Christ's love is through the believing study of Scripture. The children's song is right: 'Jesus loves me, this I know, for the Bible tells me so.' Christ's love is the most important thing for us to learn in God's Word. Like D. A. Carson opening his eyes to see his mother crying by his hospital bed, open your eyes to see Jesus praying in the Garden to receive the cup of wrath for you. Read his prayer to the Father for you in John 17. See Jesus suffering on the cross. 'Father, forgive them,' he prayed for you (Luke 23:34). Now risen and ascended, he has sent and empowered his witnesses for your sake. Jesus has sent the Holy Spirit to give you the gift of faith out of the love in his heart for you. Everything Jesus did in this world was to show his love to you, saving you at so great a cost to himself. We should therefore pray that in our study of Scripture we might know and experience the love of Christ for sinners who believe.

Second, we learn of Christ's love as we live in obedience to him. Jesus said, 'As the Father has loved me, so have I loved you. Abide in my love. If you keep my commandments, you will abide in my love' (John 15:9–10). Paul is explicitly getting at this in the progression of this prayer. He prayed that 'Christ may dwell in your hearts in faith' as the first step in knowing Christ's love. As Christ lives in us and reigns in every area of our lives, with the result that we obey him, we are empowered to know and comprehend his love.

I want to say this directly: obedience is necessary to a life of Christian blessing and to any depth of knowledge of Christ's love for you. It is disciples who follow Christ and take up their cross who know his love. It is as you strive against sin that you feel his loving strength. It is as you give to others in service that you feel more powerfully his love for you. When you trust Christ for your financial stewardship, you find that what he provides is better than what you could have hoarded. It is as you shine his light into the world, witnessing and living for Jesus, that the truth of his gospel shines with divine love in your own heart. Without doubt, the greatest encouragements I have received in ministry are those that came unplanned and unforeseen as Christ's way of showing me his love. I find that as I trust his way and minister according to his Word that he helps me by his unseen but almighty power. Those who live for themselves know little of Christ's love, but those who live for Christ abide in his love.

Third, we come to comprehend Christ's love in the trials and sufferings of life. Elizabeth Prentiss was a woman who grew in the knowledge of Christ's love through her many and intense sorrows. She struggled with ill health and grieved the death of a dear child. Instead of doubting Christ's love for her, she took her grief in prayer to the Savior who had himself embraced sorrow and suffering, and she offered herself to minister to the needs of other broken hearts. Writing later to a woman who also lost a child, Prentiss wrote, 'My dear friend, don't let this great tragedy of sorrow fail to do everything for you...The intent of sorrow is to toss us onto God's promises.'[270]

In sorrow, fear, and need, we learn more about Christ's love for us. God brings us to a place where the only person who can relate to our pain is Jesus, and he comforts us. As we prayerfully lay our head upon his chest, we feel the love for us beating in his heart. Jesus understands what we are going through: he was despised, hated, and unjustly reviled; he was betrayed by close friends; he sorrowed in the loss of those he loved; he faced the agony of suffering and death. He did all this out of love for us, so we might face our similar trials as 'more than conquerors through him who loved us' (Rom. 8:37).

Finally, Paul writes that it is 'together with all the saints' that we comprehend the magnitude of Christ's love for us. Paul is probably emphasizing our ability to learn of Christ's love through the experience of our brothers and sisters in the church. We understand God's Word as it is taught to us in the church and as others share their insights and experience. We better comprehend Christ's love by praying for others. When you have poured out your heart for a sick or sorrowing family or child in the church, your heart is naturally drawn toward them and you experience Christ's love through them. Seeing a friend overcome a besetting sin or grow stronger in faith or be sustained in a dark trial encourages us about what Christ will do for us as he has done it for them. It is in the church, as we live together as the flock of the Lord, that we together learn about the greatness of Christ's love for us.

Relying on Christ's Love

Why is it so important for us to know Christ's love? The answer is that it is only as we rely on the love of Christ that we have confidence to draw near to God and receive from him the blessings that are necessary to the life of faith. The only Christians who become spiritually fruitful, beautiful, and strong are those who can say with the apostle John that 'we know and rely upon the love that God has for us' (1 John 4:16, NIV).

This means that if you have not repented and turned to God in faith for your salvation, you should not be afraid to do so because of Christ's love for you. The whole motive behind Jesus' ministry in this world was love for the lost and sinful. 'The Son of Man came to seek and to save the lost,' Jesus said (Luke 19:10). He 'did not come to be served, but to serve, and to give his life as a ransom for many' (Matt. 28:20). That is Christ's love for you, and his call for you to follow him. His demand for you to repent and believe is an easy thing once you recognize how much he loves you. If you think coming to Jesus means losing out on life, realize that the Savior who loved you on the cross now reigns in heaven with power. To all who call on his name, he sends the Spirit, who gives new life and power for 'righteousness, peace, and joy in the Holy Spirit' (Rom. 14:17). 'Whoever believes in me,' Jesus taught, 'Out of his heart will flow rivers of living water' (John 7:38).

Those who have never believed need to see Christ's great love and to turn to him in faith for salvation. But Paul's point in this passage is for believers to comprehend God's love. This is our supreme need, for believer and unbeliever alike.

Knowing Christ's love is the key to sanctification, that is, the life-long process of growing in godliness and grace. John writes, 'In this is love, not that we have loved God but that he loved us and sent his Son to be the propitiation for our sins. Beloved, if God so loved us, we also ought to love one another…We love because he first loved us' (1 John 4:10–11, 19).

Therefore, knowing Christ's love, causes our hearts to grow into maturity. God's love makes us want to read the Bible, which feeds us. God's love makes us want to worship him in church, which strengthens our souls. It is love that draws us near to him in prayer and inspires us to serve in his name and causes us to seek the salvation of the lost around us.

I noted earlier that Paul believed in the power of love. I used the example of two children whose hearts were healed from abuse by the love of Christian foster parents. This is what Jesus will do for you, abused and wounded as your heart may be in this world, if you turn to him in faith. He will love you by enlightening your mind with truth, casting out the darkness of error and folly. Jesus will love you by sending his Spirit into your heart to soften hard places and bind up wounds. In fact, your wounds and broken places are the entryway for Christ's love into your heart. So present them to him for his loving ministry of grace. 'God's love has been poured into our hearts through the Holy Spirit,' writes Paul (Rom. 5:5). Jesus will love you by guiding your path and providing the loving correction that gains a harvest of righteousness from your life (Heb. 12:11).

Do you know Christ's love for you? When you feel unworthy and distant, do you see his arms stretched wide on the cross? When you feel cast down by sin or discouraged by life in a broken world, do you remember that Jesus came down from heaven to seek and to save the lost like you? When you feel that life has no meaning, do you see how high are Christ's plans for you, a destiny in glory with him? If you will comprehend the love of Christ—its breadth and length, its height and depth—through the Bible, in a life of obedience, amidst trials and sorrows, and together with all the saints—Christ's love will give you a future and a hope, with strength, peace, and joy in the Lord that no one can take away.

And when the time comes for you to leave the foster care of this present life for your permanent adoption into the heavenly dwelling of God, you will not merely have been healed and strengthened, but you will have been sanctified by love for the never-ending exploration of God's love that makes up the worship and work of eternity. Knowing this now, let the motto of your life be similar to that of the great Reformer John Calvin. He pledged, 'My heart I offer to you Lord, promptly and sincerely.' Paul's motto is given in Galatians 2:20, words fit for every heart that knows Jesus Christ: 'He loved me and gave himself for me. So the life I live in the flesh, I live by faith in the Son of God.'

40

The Fullness of God

Ephesians 3:19

One of the biggest problems of the early church, as is evident from the New Testament epistles, was the reluctance of some believers to press on to spiritual maturity. Paul dealt with this problem in 1 Corinthians, in which he reproved the church for their worldliness and sin. He reminded them that Christians have liberty not to flirt with sin but to draw near to God in holiness. Paul's concern was similar to that of the writer of Hebrews, who complained that long after they should have been eating meat, his readers were still drinking milk like spiritual infants. 'Therefore,' he urged them, 'let us…go on to maturity' (Heb. 6:1). We see this same emphasis in Ephesians. Here, we have a church that seems to have been at least relatively stable. But Paul needs to tell them about his prayer for their spiritual growth into maturity.

The New Testament warns us that this problem of perpetual immaturity is one we always have to confront. Paul concludes this prayer on this note, giving us a soaring description of Christian maturity: 'that you may be filled with all the fullness of God' (Eph. 3:19).

Filled with God's Fullness

Here we have one of the many statements by the apostle Paul that stops us in our tracks. Its boldness is nothing short of stunning. Paul defines Christian maturity, toward which we all should be striving, as nothing less that being 'filled with all the fullness of God.'

The first thing we need to do when we encounter a statement like this is to protect ourselves from error. This is the kind of verse that people run off with into the most excessive teachings, not constraining it by the whole counsel of God in Scripture. Some people take this kind of statement to mean that we are going to become divine, or will be incorporated into God, like a drop of water returning to the sea. This is the view of many Eastern pagan religions, that our individuality is ultimately lost in God, our personality absorbed and merged into the Eternal or Absolute. Another error is that of pantheism. 'Pan' is the Greek word for 'all'; pantheism is the belief that God is all and all is God. Here it is God who loses his personality, as he is merged into the creation. Both of these excesses are corrected by the Bible, which always insists on an essential distinction between the Creator and the creation, between God and man. We do not become gods and neither does God become us.

What, then, do we make of this remarkable description from Paul? Here is where a distinction made by the theologians can be helpful. Theologians speak of the attributes of God, those characteristics that describe what God is like. The attributes are divided into two categories. The first is God's *incommunicable* attributes, those attributes of God that are inseparable from deity and which cannot be imparted to finite creatures. Among these are God's immutability (that is, the unchangeableness of God's nature), infinity, omnipotence, omnipresence, and omniscience. God is all-powerful, he is present everywhere and knows everything. These are things about God that cannot be imparted to us. When Paul speaks of us being 'filled with all the fullness of God,' he cannot mean that we receive attributes that are proper only to God.

With that understood, we may now turn to the other category of God's attributes, his *communicable* attributes. These God can and does give to his people. First, we think of holiness. First Peter 1:16 says, 'Be holy, for he is holy,' so God communicates holiness to us. The same is true of God's goodness, love, mercy, faithfulness and more. These are things that Paul speaks about in Galatians 5:22 as 'fruits of the Spirit': 'love, joy, peace, patience, kindness, goodness, faithfulness, gentleness, self-control.'

Now we can understand Paul's definition of Christian maturity: 'that you may be filled with all the fullness of God.' He is speaking about God's communicable attributes. While remaining men and women, and while God remains God, we are to become like him in character. Another way of putting this, as Paul does in Romans 8:29, is that the goal of our salvation is that we are 'to be conformed to the image of [God's] Son.' We are to become like Jesus Christ. Christian maturity is defined, therefore, as Christ-like godliness.

We can compare this with statements Paul makes elsewhere in this very letter. In Ephesians 4:15 he speaks of maturity by saying 'we are to grow up in every way into him who is the head, even Christ.' He elaborates in 4:24, telling us 'to put on the new self, created after the likeness of God in true righteousness and holiness.' Christian maturity consists of Christ-like godliness.

Here, then, is the Bible's definition of the spiritual maturity to which all of us should be striving. It is not defined in terms of positions in the church hierarchy. You do not become more mature by becoming a minister, an elder, or a deacon (although such leaders ought certainly to be spiritually mature). Spiritual maturity is related to Bible knowledge, but one may have Bible knowledge without being mature. The same is true for spiritual experiences. Moreover, spiritual maturity does not consist of a single personality type; the out-going and the shy may be equally spiritually mature or immature. Spiritual maturity is defined in terms of Christ-likeness, as the attributes of God's character mold us into increasingly godly people.

A Heart Filled with God

All through this prayer, Paul is asking God to deal with our inner being. He asked that God 'may grant you to be strengthened with power through his Spirit in your inner being' (v. 16). Verse 17 says that Christ is to dwell 'in your hearts through faith.' Now, Paul speaks of us being 'filled will all the fullness of God.' The obvious idea is that of the Triune God living and moving within us.

It is important that we approach this from a practical standpoint and not leave this in the realm of mysticism. So we ask, What does the Bible mean by the heart? What does the 'inner being' consist of? There are three categories that we should think of, each of which the Bible relates to the 'heart'. These three are the mind, the emotions, and the will. When we ask, 'How is the heart filled with the fullness of God?' the answer is that this happens when God rules and shapes the heart. Where God's kingdom reigns, he fills with blessings. What we need, then, to be filled with the fullness of God, is to yield our minds, our emotions, and our wills to the sovereign rule of God.

Our first priority if we want to be filled with God is to yield our minds to the teaching of his Word. That Paul considers this to be of first importance is seen by the structure of this letter. First, he gives doctrinal instruction. Then he prays for Christ's love to mold our emotions, in this prayer. Then, starting in chapter 4 he exhorts us to exercise our wills in obedience to God. The mind, the emotions, and then the will—that is Paul's order.

This all begins with the mind. In Romans 12:2, Paul says, 'Do not be conformed to this world, but be transformed by the renewal of your mind' (Rom. 12:2). This same priority is seen in the ministry of Jesus Christ. When the crowds swarmed with people wanting to be healed, Jesus pulled away to go elsewhere. When Peter protested, Jesus replied, 'Let us go on to the next towns, that I may preach there also, for that is why I came' (Mark 1:38). Jesus' approach to Christian maturity and sanctification is best seen in his great prayer in John 17, where he asks the Father, 'Sanctify them by the truth; your Word is truth' (v. 17). Donald Grey Barnhouse applies this, saying,

> There is only one way to find righteousness and true holiness, and that is through the Word of God, and the application of its principles to the life by the Holy Spirit…It is through the sanctifying power of the Word of God that spiritual life is communicated to the believer. It will never be given in any other way than through the truth of the Scripture…I go so far as to say that no man has ever been saved apart from some definite truth out of the Bible and that there is no possible growth in Christian life apart from the deepening knowledge of this Book…The basis of spiritual growth is through the promises of God.[271]

Some may protest, saying that we need to maintain a free and open mind. But there is no such thing. The mind is always under the control of some master. Apart from Christ, our minds are under the three-fold rule of the world, the sinful flesh, and the devil. Our only choice is not whether or not to have a free mind, but which master to serve with our minds. Our minds can be ruled by error or by truth, by darkness or by light, by sin or by righteousness, by the devil or by God. Sin came into the world when Adam and Eve believed a lie of the devil. Second Corinthians 4:4–6 says that Satan 'has blinded the minds of unbelievers, to keep them from seeing the light of the gospel of the glory of Christ.' But into the hearts of believers, by his great grace, God has shined the light of his Word, 'to give the light of the knowledge of the glory of God in the face of Jesus Christ.'

If we want to be filled with the fullness of God, it is absolutely necessary that we decide to have God's Word rule our thinking. You will not and cannot grow into the spiritual maturity spoken of in the Bible unless and until you submit your mind to God's Word, determining with Romans 3:4, 'Let God be true and every man a liar' (NKJV). This means spending time prayerfully reading the Bible. It means making a place in your schedule for regular worship under faithful preaching and perhaps a group Bible study. But more than this, it means yielding your mind to what you are taught by God's Word. If you would mature as a Christian and be 'filled with God's fullness,' then you must accept what God says in the Bible. Proverbs 23:7 says, 'As [a man] thinks in his heart, so he is.' It does not matter if you are rich or poor, educated or uneducated, smart or dull-witted. You must submit your mind to the rule of God's Word or you will be ruled by sin and folly, unable to grow spiritually into Christ-like godliness. It starts with the mind.

Secondly, we must yield our emotions to be formed and molded by God's own heart. Anyone who believes that Christian maturity can be had simply through the mind had better stop reading Ephesians before he gets to this prayer in chapter 3. Paul wants us 'to comprehend…the love of Christ that surpasses knowledge' (Eph. 3:17–19). Comprehending Christ's love goes beyond the mind, the thinking of the heart, and penetrates into the feelings of the heart.

Jesus said, 'Abide in my love…Love one another as I have loved you' (John 15:9,12). His love is the power that is to shape our emotions. Paul faced this when as a Pharisee he oversaw the execution of the deacon Stephen. Looking on Paul and the other murderous men with the love and compassion of Christ, Stephen prayed, 'Lord, do not hold this sin against them' (Acts 7:60). Paul must never have forgotten that. He became a man whose heart was also filled with the love of Christ: with mercy for sinners, compassion for the weak and afflicted, sorrow for sin, and zeal for righteousness.

However great our knowledge of the Bible may be, if our emotions are not molded by the love of Christ then we have not learned rightly of God's Word. 'If I have…all knowledge,' Paul wrote in 1 Corinthians 13:2, 'but have not love, I am nothing.'

Third, we must have God ruling over our wills if we are to be filled with all his fullness. Just as true knowledge must be confirmed by love, true love is confirmed by godly choices. 'If you love me,' Jesus said, 'you will obey my commandments' (John 14:15). If we have Christ's love for others, that love will express itself in Christ-like actions that flow from an obedient will.

Jesus said, in John 6:38, 'I have come down from heaven, not to do my own will but the will of him who sent me.' Paul prayed in verse 17 that Christ might dwell in our hearts through faith. This reigning of Christ within us must involve an increasing obedience to God's will. This is why when Jesus taught his disciples to pray, he began, 'Our Father in heaven, hallowed be your name. Your kingdom come, your will be done, on earth as it is in heaven' (Matt. 6:9–10). For those whose minds and emotions are ruled by God, the first concern is God's glory, God's kingdom, and God's will. This is what it means to be 'filled with all the fullness of God.'

Paul's message is reproduced in a hymn, written by Frances Havergal. She begins:

> Take my life, and let it be
>   consecrated, Lord, to thee

This is what Paul is talking about. Later in the hymn, she adds:

> Take my intellect, and use,
>   every power as thou shalt choose

Then she brings it altogether:

> Take my will, and make it thine;
>   it shall be no longer mine.
> Take my heart, it is thine own;
>   it shall be thy royal throne

Each of us should make that prayer our own. As it is realized in our lives we will grow spiritually mature, being 'filled with all the fullness of God.'

Seeking after God

Let me wrap up this great prayer with a few observations. The first is that in light of Paul's request to God our aspirations for life are probably too low. Our goals are far below what God desires for us.

Is it not true that all most of us really want is a little happiness? And this happiness is defined in worldly terms: financial security, respect and prestige in the world, the opportunity to have pleasurable experiences and protection against at least some of life's unpleasantness. How staggering it is to us to read what Paul prays for believers: that we may be 'filled with all the fullness of God.'

Paul tells us that a Christian's experience is not merely about simply passing through the stages of life or climbing up the career ladder. This is how many of us think of life. We think of moving from childhood to adulthood, with marriage, child-raising, sending the kids off, starting over in the empty nest, growing old and then just dying. We think in terms of getting our education, starting our first job, building our career, attaining to success, and then enjoying that success in retirement until we are too old or are struck down.

But is that life? Is that growth? Is that maturity? The problem with our attitude toward life is that it doesn't deal with us as people, with our hearts, with who we are. Do we really think of life as moving forward when we just remain the same person, unimproved, untransformed—or as often happens, much worse at the end than at the beginning?

This prayer tells us to think of our lives differently. What is my life about? It is about gaining strength from God's Holy Spirit so that Christ may rule more and more in my heart, so that the Son of God may have a more settled residence in me. It is about being more rooted in his love and to have more of his love flowing through me, and that I may more and more be 'filled with all the fullness of God.'

This is what life is really about: knowing God and growing into his likeness; learning to love and learning to trust in God and bear his image. This is exciting. This is something we should be seeking apart from our circumstances. If we are having success, let that success serve this process of maturity. Are we afflicted with trials and failure and difficulty? Let them serve our growth into Christ-like, godly maturity, so that more of God will be in us.

Second, we should note that true Christ-like maturity always involves a harmony of God's attributes. We all naturally have some good characteristics. But the mark of the Spirit's work is a supernatural combination that produces a harmony of God's attributes. We can be either bold or humble in the flesh, but can we be both bold and humble? We can have truth without love naturally, or love without truth. Neither is a mark of Christian maturity, but truth with love comes only through God's Spirit. Jesus is described simultaneously as the Lion and the Lamb, two opposites together, and we are likewise to seek and realize all the fruits of God's Spirit, all the communicable attributes of God, 'all the fullness of God,' and this requires the indwelling of Christ by the Holy Spirit.

Third, I want to address non-Christians about the challenge found in this prayer. It is necessarily the case that you have no real understanding of what Paul is talking about. 'The natural man does not accept the things of the Spirit of God, for they are folly to him,' Paul says, 'and he is not able to understand them because they are spiritually discerned' (1 Cor. 2:14). But I want you to recognize the wonder of what is said in this prayer. Paul is telling believers they can have Jesus Christ living within them, and through him an indwelling of supernatural love that surpasses knowledge. While you are just killing time and living for yourself, there are the people in this world who possess the blessing of God. Jesus Christ offers this to you if you will believe on him, if you will bend the knee and call to him as Lord and Savior. Speaking of the pleasures of this world, Jesus said, 'Everyone who drinks of this water will be thirsty again.' Isn't this right? Sin and worldly pleasure leave you still thirsting. 'But whoever drinks of the water that I will give him will never be thirsty again' (John 4:13–14). 'I am the bread of life,' he added, 'whoever comes to me shall not hunger, and whoever believes in me shall never thirst…For this is the will of my Father, that everyone who looks on the Son and believes in him should have eternal life, and I will raise him up on the last day' (John 6:35, 40). This is God's message to you, and if you will believe on Jesus now, you will be saved from your sins. And as you walk with him, you will be satisfied and filled.

Last, Paul's prayer challenges all believers in Christ. Martyn Lloyd-Jones makes the observation that for most church members and professing Christians, their relationship to Christ is something just in the background of their lives. They think little about the Bible or Christ or God or their own spiritual condition, and they draw from very little of the power for godliness that is available to them in Christ. He compares our Christianity to our ability to dial 911 on the telephone. For the vast majority, Christianity is little more than the knowledge that we can make an emergency call when needed. He asks, 'Is Christian truth something you like to have, and to know that it is there if you are taken desperately ill, or some loved one is taken ill, or if you are suddenly confronted by the loss of your income, or when some disaster takes place, or when you are on your death bed?'[272]

If that is all Christianity is to you, what a challenge you have here from the apostle Paul. He is urging you to seek for so much more: to seek for God himself and all the fullness only he can give to your life. Are you seeking to be strengthened with power by the Spirit in your inner being? Are you opening doors in your heart for Christ to come there and reign? Are you growing in your comprehension of Christ's love so that his love for others is yours? Are you being filled with all the fullness of God? What a pity if you are not, for this is the only way to the spiritual blessings God has for us in Christ.

Jesus said, 'Blessed are the poor in spirit, for theirs is the kingdom of God.' Do you recognize your spiritual poverty and are you seeking for Christ to reign in you? He said, 'Blessed are those who mourn, for they shall be comforted.' Instead of the giddy, foolish laughter of the world, do you look around you with the love of Christ, mourning for and with a dying world? 'Blessed are the meek,' he said, 'for they shall inherit the earth.' Meekness does not describe a wimpy pushover, but the man or woman whose will is in submission to God. And Jesus said, 'Blessed are those who hunger and thirst for righteousness.' Is this you? Do you hunger and thirst for the things of God? Are you seeking to be filled with God's Spirit? 'Blessed are those…,' Jesus said, 'for they shall be filled' (Matt. 5:3–6).

God calls you to grow into Christian maturity, that you may be filled with him. This is what your life is about—not doing things, not gaining things, not buying and using things. Your life is measured before God by your growth into Christ-like godliness. God will accomplish this if you will seek it from him. 'They shall be filled,' Jesus says. Look at the life of anyone who ever did great things for God and you will find that he or she first sought to be filled with God. Talk to someone who lives a life of great spiritual blessing—of righteousness, peace, and joy in the Holy Spirit (Rom. 14:17), and you will find that her heart is filled with Christ and thus with the Spirit's power.

What should you do? Submit your mind, your emotions, and your will to God's gracious, loving, saving rule, and be filled with all the fullness of God. Then your life will no longer be barren, but will be fruitful of the things of eternity and of God and of love and of blessing, and they will never perish. 'The world is passing away along with its desires,' says 1 John 2:17, 'but whoever does the will of God abides forever.'

41

Far More Abundantly

Ephesians 3:20-21

In our study of Ephesians we have noted the richness of Paul's prayers and the important role they play in his letters. Another hallmark of the apostle is the doxologies with which he ends great doctrinal sections. A doxology is an exclamation of praise, and Paul writes them because the true goal of his teaching is that God should be glorified. Here at the end of Ephesians 3, which concludes the main doctrinal portion of this letter, Paul writes a most appropriate word of praise to God: 'Now to him who is able to do far more abundantly than all that we ask or think, according to the power at work within us, to him be glory in the church and in Christ Jesus throughout all generations, forever and ever. Amen.'

Paul's doxologies focus on some attribute of God that his teaching is highlighting. The Book of Romans unfolds the saving logic of the gospel, so Paul's doxology extols, 'Oh, the depth of the riches and wisdom and knowledge of God!' (Rom. 11:33). In 1 Timothy Paul is concerned for holiness, and so he praises 'the blessed and only Sovereign, the King of kings and Lord of lords, who alone has immortality, who dwells in unapproachable light, whom no one has ever seen or can see' (1 Tim. 6:15-16).

What does this doxology in Ephesians 3 tell us about Paul's concern in this letter? Here, he praises God for his incredible power in salvation, which is the special subject of Paul's teaching in this letter.

God's Incredible Power: An Antidote to Doubt

The doxology of Ephesians 3:20-21 is connected to the prayer that precedes it. Paul has been praying for amazing things, culminating in verse 19 with the request that 'you may be filled with all the fullness of God.' The problem is that most of us really doubt that such a thing is possible, at least for us. It may be possible for the really great believers—people like Moses and David, Peter and Paul, Martin Luther and John Calvin. But we do not believe it is possible for ourselves, and that doubt stands in the way of Paul's prayer. Therefore, he reproves our doubt and encourages our faith by praising God for being 'able to do far more abundantly than all we ask or think.'

This has been Paul's point all through this letter. In his first prayer, he asked God to enlighten the eyes of our hearts, 'that you may know...what is the immeasurable greatness of his power toward us who believe.' God's great might was proved by raising Jesus from the dead, and Paul tells us that this is the very power God intends to use in our lives for salvation (Eph. 1:18–20).

This truth is something we learn from our study of the Bible. When Moses and the Israelites were backed up against the Red Sea with Pharaoh's army bearing down upon them the people thought they were lost. But God parted the Red Sea by his great might. When Sennacherib's vast army camped outside Jerusalem and his herald mocked Israel's God, the people quaked in fear. But the prophet Isaiah told King Hezekiah to humble himself and turn to God in prayer. When he did the angel of the Lord stuck down 185,000 enemy soldiers in a night.

So it is for us. Our doubt tells us that we are in a hopeless situation, that our lives cannot be turned around, that what threatens us is just too strong, but from the Bible our faith learns that God is almighty to save those who believe. That is what he demands from us—faith in him—and Paul's doxology is designed to overcome our doubt with a reminder of God's incredible power.

Here we have one of the many times when Paul piles on terms to make his point. Our translations struggle to give the full effect. The *English Standard Version* renders it, 'Now to him who is able to do far more abundantly.' The *New International Version* says, 'Now to him who is able to do immeasurably more.' The *King James Version* says, 'Now unto him that is able to do exceeding abundantly above.'

None of them quite does justice to Paul's Greek, which adds layer on layer to extol the greatness of God's power. First he says, 'Now to him who is able to do.' Our God is able to do things. But he adds, 'Now to him who is able to do abundantly.' When God works it is abundant. Then he adds a prefix, 'Now to him who is able to do more abundantly.' Finally, not content with that, he adds, 'Now to him who is able to do far more abundantly.' Such is Paul's enthusiasm for conveying the might and infinite ability of God.

Paul adds to this two important statements. He says that God is able to do far more abundantly 'than all we ask.' God's power to give is greater than our power to ask. We cannot out-ask God. We cannot present requests to him that he cannot answer. It certainly is true that we often pray in a worldly or even sinful way, and we should not expect God's cooperation when we do. James 4:3 says, 'You ask and do not receive, because you ask wrongly, to spend it on your passions.' It is also true that God's answers to our prayers are governed by his wisdom and his sovereign plan for all things. But God calls upon us to pray and to make requests of him, and we should never doubt God's ability to answer our boldest prayers.

Most of us are guilty of limiting God by doubting what he is capable of doing. For instance, we don't pray for the conversion of a particularly stubborn unbeliever or bother to share the gospel with him, because we doubt that such a person can be saved. But we forget the power of God, which can overcome any hardened heart. Paul himself was the single most hateful opponent of Christianity in his day, and God made him the chief apostle of his grace.

The father of the modern missionary movement was William Carey. Born in 1761, he was a shoemaker by trade, but was converted and became a Baptist preacher. Carey was not well-educated and was not a particularly successful minister. But while reading the journal of Captain Cook's travels through the world, he was convicted of the need to take the gospel to 'the heathens.' God laid this upon Carey's heart and like Isaiah, he responded, 'Here am I; send me!'

Carey had some formidable obstacles. He had so little money he was practically starving. He lacked a good education, although he was gifted in languages. When he first proposed his plans, other ministers scoffed at him. One famously replied, 'Young man, sit down: when God pleases to convert the heathen, He will do it without your aid or mine.' Carey's wife refused to accompany him to India, his intended destination. Moreover, the government offered him no support and he was not even guaranteed permission to enter the country when he arrived.

But Carey believed God was calling him to take the gospel to India, and therefore that God would make a way. He knew that God was able to do far more abundantly than all he asked. At the first meeting of the missionary society he formed, Carey preached, 'Expect great things from God. Attempt great things for God.' That became the motto of the missionary movement God launched through his faith. In 1793 he arrived in India and by 1834, he had overseen the translation of the Bible into forty languages, had founded a college, had seen legions of missionaries join him and through what he started millions and millions have trusted in Christ and been saved.

Let us never limit God by doubting him and failing to ask great things of him. James 4:2 says, 'You do not have, because you do not ask.' God can miraculously heal the sick. He can restore the most hopelessly broken marriage. He can turn the heart of a wayward child. He can convert the chief of sinners. Let us not doubt and limit God by our lack of prayer. How often God must have said of us, 'If only they had believed and asked.' As Isaac Newton wrote:

> Thou art coming to a King,
>   large petitions with thee bring;
> For His grace and power are such,
>   none can ever ask too much.[273]

Paul adds also that God is able to do far more abundantly 'than all we think.' This is related to the former statement. But I would point out that this is the very thing God intends for us—to do far more abundantly than all we think. In 1 Corinthians 2:9, Paul says, 'What no eye has seen, nor ear heard nor the heart of man imagined, God has prepared for those who love him.'

This, too, is something we learn from studying the Bible. Abraham wanted to have a son to inherit from him (Gen. 15:2), but God intended not only for the number of his descendants to outnumber the stars in the sky but through him to bring the Messiah, who would bring salvation to all the world. Moses stood before the burning bush, asking God to deliver his people from slavery in Egypt. He scarcely imagined that God was going to use him to lead Israel into the Promised Land, and to give through him the Ten Commandments and the first five books of the Bible. We could go on to David and his desire to build a temple, not imaging that God intended a spiritual dwelling for all eternity, or Paul himself, who tried to start churches in the Roman empire but ended up laying the foundation for a worldwide church that will last forever.

Let's apply this to you. What will God do if you walk with him by faith? What will he make of your life? It is far abundantly more than you can ask or imagine. What if you will place God at the center of your life and no longer on the periphery? What if you will follow through on the thing God has laid upon your heart? What can happen if you fathers commit to the spiritual leadership of your home, to regular attendance at church, to involvement in a Bible study or Sunday School, to family devotions and prayers in your kitchen? What will God do if you start praying for the salvation of others, talking to them about the Bible or just inviting them to church? God will use what you give him to do far more abundantly than you could ask or think, and the long-term effects will be truly phenomenal.

God's Purpose in Our Salvation

Everything we have said about God's power is especially true when it comes to Paul's special concern in the Book of Ephesians, namely, God's transforming work in our lives. That is why Paul specifies, 'Now to him who is able to do far more abundantly than all that we ask or think, according to the power at work within us.'

What exactly is God able to do in the life of every single believer who trusts in his grace and power? That is what Paul has been teaching in chapters 2 and 3. In Ephesians 2:1-10, Paul tells us that God is able to deliver us from the bondage and condemnation of sin. Ephesians 2:1-3 says we 'were dead in trespasses and sins…following the course of this world, following the prince of the power of the air…by nature children of wrath.' We cannot imagine a more desperate situation than being spiritually dead and morally enslaved. But God has power to make us 'alive together with Christ' (Eph. 2:5). 'For by grace you have been saved through faith,' Paul says (Eph. 2:8). As a result, we who once were unable to obey God and know his blessing are now, 'God's workmanship, created in Christ Jesus for good works' (Eph. 2:10). God has power to deliver you from sin.

Paul goes on to talk about the problem of conflict and strife in the world. In his day, this was exemplified by the conflict between Jews and Gentiles. In 2:11-22, Paul tells us that God has power to bring peace and unity for all kinds of people in Christ Jesus. 'For he himself is our peace' (Eph. 2:14).

In chapter 3, Paul turns his thought to his own circumstances. He is concerned that the Ephesians should be discouraged by his imprisonment. Paul reminds them that God turns hardship into blessing, just as he was doing in Paul's own life. Paul ends his letter to the Philippians by sending greetings from some of the prison guards he has converted to faith in Christ. God has power to make flowers bloom in the desert, and to make us conquerors over affliction.

Finally, Paul concluded chapter 3 with his great prayer for a complete transformation of our spiritual lives. He asks that God would send the Holy Spirit to empower us to have Christ living in our hearts, reigning in us with power for righteousness, then for us to live more and more in the love of Christ and then to be filled with all that God has for us. If you will trust God and make yourself a man or woman of God's Word, a Christian who is devoted to prayer, and a disciple of Christ who walks with him in obedience and faith, God has power to do in your life far more abundantly than all you ask or think. How? 'According to his power at work within us.'

God's Glory in the Church

This raises a question that many people have: 'Why would God do this? Why would he work his power for my salvation? The answer is given in verse 21, 'To him be glory in the church and in Christ Jesus.'

Psalm 19:1 says, 'The heavens declare the glory of God, and the sky above proclaims his handiwork.' How much more is this true of the church, which, Paul says, displays 'the manifold wisdom of God' (Eph. 3:10). The Grand Canyon is one thing, Niagara Falls is another, the Milky Way something even greater. But they all pale compared to what God wants to do in your life and the glory it will bring to his grace and power. God wants to deliver you from sin's guilt and power, give you peace and the ability really to love, to turn life's hardships into opportunities for grace, and to transform your inner person so that you are 'filled with all the fullness of God' (Eph. 3:19). Martyn Lloyd-Jones writes,

> Nothing gives such glory to God as the Christian Church. God manifested His power when He created the world out of nothing; when He said, 'Let there be light' and there was light! The mountains, the rivers and the raging sea, lightning and thunder, all proclaim His glory…But there is nothing that so proclaims the glory of God as the Christian Church…Nothing is so wonderful as the fact that men and women, such as you and I are, men and women who were steeped and lost and dead in sin, should have become members of the body of Christ.[274]

Lest we forget, God's glory in the church is always 'in Christ Jesus.' This is how God saves us: by trusting Jesus Christ, by following Jesus as his disciples, by coming to God through the shed blood of his own Son, which cleanses us from sin, and by living in the power of his resurrection by means of his Word and of prayer. The Father ultimately glorifies his Son by receiving those Jesus brings into his presence and working in us saving power to restore us to his image.

This is why Paul prays that God would be glorified 'in the church and in Christ Jesus throughout all generations, forever and ever.' When every other glory has faded, when no one cares any longer how much money you made, how much fun you had, what house you lived in, what car you drove, and what vacations you took, the work that God is doing in you now will be reflecting glory to him forever and ever. It is God's transforming work in our hearts now, together in the church, in Christ Jesus, that will last 'throughout all generations, forever and ever.'

Many years ago now, I arrived in college as a freshman, wearing my high school letter jacket, covered with badges, stars, and patches from my high school glories. It was not long before I learned that no one cared about these in college, and I soon stopped wearing the jacket. What they cared about were college things, and those who had a leg-up were those who were doing college things in high school. It turns out that many high school heroes go on to accomplish little in their later life. Likewise, many who shine as stars in this brief present life will spend the long years of eternity covered in shame. They do not have any of the things of value in the life to come—righteousness, holiness, good works for the sake of Christ's kingdom, and a relationship with Jesus. But many who have lived now for the sake of eternity, despite having little in this present world, will, as Jesus said, 'shine like the sun in the kingdom of their Father' (Matt. 13:43).

What this means, if you are not a Christian, is that the most glorious thing you can do or have in this world, apart from Jesus Christ, is short-lived and vain. As John wrote, 'The world is passing away along with its desires, but whoever does the will of God abides forever' (1 John 2:17). You need to prepare for eternity by trusting in Jesus Christ and yielding to God's work in your life.

If you are a Christian, this means that you need to think biblically about your life. How often we complain about God for prayers unanswered that were about worldly things—about money and jobs, possessions and fleshly desires. All the while, God has given us the most matchless gift at so great a cost to himself—eternal life in Jesus Christ—and even now wants to work with supernatural power in our hearts for things that will last forever. Alexander Maclaren compares our salvation to a gift that is given us in the night. 'Like some gift given in the dark, its true preciousness is not discerned when it is first received. The gleam of the gold does not strike our eye all at once.'[275] But in the bright light of eternity we shall look back on our present lives and say about the blessings that every believer already has, even now, that God did 'far more abundantly than all that we could ask or imagine.' And we will wonder why we did not esteem it more, and praise him more, and live more fully for him in this life.

Our Response: 'Amen!'

What response should we make to this great doxology? Paul's eloquent summation occurs in the very last word: 'Amen.' That is a Hebrew word that comes over into our English and it means, 'Yes, it is so,' or 'Yes, let it be so.'

Looking back on Paul's whole teaching on salvation in Ephesians, can you say 'Amen' to God's offer to deliver you from guilt and from sin so that you are born again and given power to do his will? The world says sin is not all that bad and that no one can help it. Your 'Amen' comes through confessing your need of Christ's cleansing blood, trusting him and now living in obedience through his power.

Can you say 'Amen' to Paul's teaching that Christ is our peace? The world strives vainly for any kind of peace: peace in the heart, peace in the family, peace in the world. Your 'Amen' means finding your peace in Christ, living in peace within God's family that is the church, and bringing peace to others through your testimony to Jesus.

Can you say 'Amen' to Paul's testimony that God will take your trials and difficulties and use them to show the world God's power? The unbelieving world says that what matters most is having good circumstances and avoiding bad ones. Your 'Amen' means glorifying God and trusting in him when out of work, when facing sickness or even death, when persecuted for your faith, showing as Paul did that a prisoner for Christ is freest of all.

And can you say 'Amen' to God's desire to work in your inner being with power, so that Christ will dwell in your heart through faith? The world says that no one ever can really change; we just have to cope with life the way it is. But if you say 'Amen' to God, then you will commit yourself to his Word, to obedience, and to fellowship with God in prayer, knowing that God is working with power to change you into his image day-by-day and year-by-year.

That is our response to this whole glorious gospel: 'Amen, Lord, Amen.' And this, then, will be the motto and the motive of your whole life: 'To him be glory, in the church, which I serve, in Christ Jesus, whom I love and trust and follow, and in my own life, which I offer to God for this cause that is greater than any other: to him be glory right now, throughout all generations, and forever and ever, through his power that is able to do in me far more abundantly even than what I ever could ask or imagine. Amen.

42

A Worthy Life

Ephesians 4:1–2

With the beginning of chapter 4, we transition from Paul's main doctrinal teaching to the practical instruction in Ephesians. Such a transition will often create one of two responses from us. Some of us will be disappointed, because what they are really excited about is doctrine instead of life. Others will be relieved, since they consider the practical teaching to be of more value than the doctrine. Both of these responses have serious defects.

Those who feel disappointed to move from the doctrinal to the practical show that they really don't understand the point of doctrine. True Christian teaching is not intended to produce knowledge only. The whole point of doctrine is to create a faith that responds in action. This is why Paul did not end his letter after chapter 3.

But those who are relieved to be done with doctrine are also in danger of a mistaken view of Christianity. It is obvious that Paul considered it essential for us to know and understand the truth about God, ourselves, and salvation. Christianity is not simply a recipe of things you are to do. It is a relationship that demands knowledge, understanding, and faith. That Paul spends his first three chapters teaching doctrine indicates that the only proper foundation for Christian action is Christian truth.

Paul begins his practical teaching with an exhortation that is a model of pastoral leadership. He does not berate or even command his readers, though as an apostle he might have done so. Instead, he writes, 'I therefore, as a prisoner for the Lord, urge you.' Paul beseeches them in love, as one who is himself paying the price and setting them a sacrificial example of godliness.

He begins, 'Therefore.' This word always indicates that we must respond to the truth we have received. Since we believe this, therefore we must live this way. Verses 1 and 2 give us Paul's introductory statement on the Christian life, describing it as a 'walk,' focusing on four vital graces that make up Christian character, and giving us the key principle that we should live worthily of our calling in Christ.

The Christian 'Walk'

You can tell much about a person by the way he or she walks. A proud man will walk with his chin held high. A busy person will move briskly. A woman trying to get attention will sway. Paul urges his Christian readers to consider the manner of their walk, that it would be 'worthy of the calling to which you have been called' (Eph. 4:1).

It is characteristic of Paul to describe the Christian life as a 'walk,' and this alone tells us quite a lot. It says, first, that Christianity is not something that just takes up a certain corner of our lives. Instead, it involves the whole manner by which we live. This is what Paul emphasizes by speaking of walking worthily. There is, he indicates, a Christian lifestyle. There is a manner in which Christians are to live and in which they find blessings and commend the gospel to the world. It is a lifestyle that says 'Yes' to some things and 'No' to other things, because of the truths we believe and that govern our walk.

Various Bible writers speak in this way. First John 1:7 speaks of 'walking in the light,' referring to integrity and purity. John also says we must 'walk in the truth,' which means to hold fast to the Bible's teaching (2 John 1:4; 3 John 1:3, 4). Paul often contrasts different modes of walking. Second Corinthians 5:7 says, 'We walk by faith, not by sight.' In Romans 8:4, Paul says we must 'walk not according to the flesh but according to the Spirit.' Ephesians 5:2 says to 'walk in love,' following Jesus' example of self-sacrificing ministry. Ephesians 5:8 speaks of our moral conduct, saying, 'At one time you were in darkness, but now you are light in the Lord. Walk as children of light.' In all these ways, the term 'walk' signifies our whole manner of living; it is to be holy, believing, obedient, and loving.

The second observation we can make from the term 'walk' is that the Christian life involves continuous progress. None of us have arrived at our destination; we always have need for growth in maturity. Paul said this of himself: 'Not that I have already obtained this or am already perfect, but I press on…Forgetting what lies behind and straining forward to what lies ahead, I press on toward the goal for the prize of the upward call of God in Christ Jesus' (Phil. 3:12–14). God's call to us is upward into ever-increasing knowledge of him and an ever-increasing holiness. I cannot think of anything more exciting. We are all far too prone to arrive at some spiritual plateau and become comfortable there. But the Christian life is a ever-forward walk, leading us to so much more than we presently have and are.

Third, Paul speaks of the Christian life as a 'walk' because it requires effort on our part. We will not increase in godliness and grace without applying ourselves to our Christian life. We receive salvation as a free gift, through no works of our own, but we then grow in that salvation by 'working it out,' as Paul says, as God works it into us (Phil. 2:12–13). I am not going to grow without giving myself to the study and meditation of God's Word, without spending time in prayer, without participating in the life of the church and without regularly attending worship.

The Christian life is a walk, and Paul says we are to compare our walk to the teaching of God's Word. 'Is this worthy of my calling as a Christian?' I am to ask. Where it is not, I am to apply myself to repentance and new obedience in the power God gives.

Four Vital Graces

In verse 2, Paul becomes specific about where we are to apply our effort. What happens here is enormously significant. When Paul tells us to get practical, he does not first tell us to *do* things but rather to *be* things. The first priority in our practical Christian lives is to embrace the character change God desires in us. Verse 2 gives four vital graces essential to our Christian walk:

'with all humility and gentleness, with patience, bearing with one another in love.'

This is not just Paul's emphasis. This is also what we find in Jesus' teaching. The Sermon on the Mount, his main ethical statement, demands a great deal of action. But it begins with the Beatitudes, a statement of the kind of character Christians must have, which bears a close resemblance to what Paul writes here. Terry Johnson writes of Jesus' teaching, 'Formulas, programs, "three steps," "five stages," and "ten secrets" are not the key to Christian discipleship. "Success" in marriage, family, child-rearing, finances, work, Christian mission, and everything else flows from character. If the heart is right, everything else eventually falls into place. If the heart is not right, nothing else can become or remain right.'[276] This is Paul's emphasis as he lists these four vital graces.

The first is *humility*. *Webster's New World Dictionary* defines humility as 'having a consciousness of one's defects,' and being 'lowly' and 'unpretentious.' The ancient Greek and Roman world had nothing but contempt for humility. It was, to them, a slave-like quality unbecoming a man or woman of dignity. That is how our world thinks today. But Jesus showed us that humility is the first step in godliness. This was, in fact, the first of his Beatitudes: 'Blessed are the poor in spirit, for theirs is the kingdom of heaven' (Matt. 5:3). In Philippians 2:3-8, Paul explicitly cites Jesus' humility in urging us to follow his example:

> Do nothing from rivalry or conceit, but in humility count others more significant than yourselves… Have this mind among yourselves, which is yours in Christ Jesus, who, though he was in the form of God…made himself nothing, taking the form of a servant. And being found in human form, he humbled himself by becoming obedient to the point of death, even death on a cross (Phil. 2:3-8).

That tells us much about humility. Humility is opposed to rivalry and conceit; it has us think more highly of other people than ourselves. Jesus is our model, the one human being who ever had the right to self-glory. But he gladly took up the lowliest servanthood, and so should each of us.

The opposite of humility is pride. C. S. Lewis wrote, 'The essential vice, the utmost evil, is Pride. Unchastity, anger, greed, drunkenness, and all that, are mere fleabites in comparison: it was through Pride that the devil became the devil: Pride leads to every other vice: it is the complete anti-God state of mind.'[277] Lewis points out that pride is not happy just having something, but only by having more of it than others. Pride loves power and self-glory. This is why it is so opposed to God. Lewis sums up, 'Pride always means enmity—it is enmity. And not only enmity between man and man, but enmity to God.'[278]

The great biblical example of pride is Nebuchadnezzar, the Babylonian emperor whom God permitted to conquer Jerusalem. Looking out from his palace roof upon his great city, he boasted, 'Is not this great Babylon, which I have built by my mighty power as a royal residence and for the glory of my majesty?' The Bible tells us that 'While the words were still in the king's mouth,' God judged him by taking away his kingdom, inflicting him with insanity, and driving him out to live among the beasts (Dan. 4:28-33). That was not a random judgment; it was God's way of saying that a puny creature like man must be crazy to be proud and boastful before God. Proverbs 15:25 says, 'The Lord tears down the house of the proud.' Proverbs 16:18 adds, 'Pride goes before destruction, and a haughty spirit before a fall.'

Boice echoes Paul's appeal for Christian humility:

> We must humble ourselves. The reason for this is obvious. If pride is the original sin and the source of all other sins, as it is, and if humility is the opposite of pride, as we know it to be, then the cure will begin not at the periphery but at the very core of the problem. We must begin with humility, which means that we must begin with the confession that we are not adequate for the problems that confront us and must seek help from God.[279]

It is not possible even to be a Christian without humility. The proud man will not admit his sin and thus will not seek the cross as his only remedy. But the humble confess their guilt and their need of mercy. They love Jesus and his cross because he is their only salvation. They sing, 'Foul, I, to the fountain fly; wash me, Savior, or I die.'[280] Pride is the greatest cause of unbelief. Faith in Christ demands a humble confession of sin, and the proud people of the human race would rather perish than bend the knee.

Humility not only brings us to the cross to be saved, but it also brings us before God for his daily blessing. In Isaiah 57:15, God says, 'I dwell in the high and holy place, and also with him who is of a contrite and lowly spirit.' James 4:10 tells us, 'Humble yourselves before the Lord, and he will exalt you.'

This is where the grace of God begins in our lives. A life that is worthy of the gospel is first and foremost humble. While pride makes us want to exalt ourselves, humility makes us want to improve ourselves, and thus it leads us in pursuit of God's mercy and grace.

How do proud sinners, then, become humble? Humility comes from a true knowledge of ourselves, which is found in the Bible. If you want to be humbled, then read and believe what the Bible says about you: 'None is righteous, no, not one' (Rom. 3:10); 'We all like sheep have gone astray' (Isa. 53:6); 'All have sinned and fall short of the glory of God' (Rom. 3:23); 'The heart is deceitful above all things, and desperately sick' (Jer. 17:9).

Most of us are not humble because we compare ourselves to people we think are worse than we are. We can all look down on somebody for something. Instead, we should compare ourselves to Jesus and to his teaching and to God's moral law. This is the first purpose of the Ten Commandments, which serve as a mirror in which we can see our defects. If we read the Bible's moral teaching, the Sermon on the Mount or the parables of our Lord Jesus, and feel that we are doing all right, then we are deceived. What we need is humility. God's perfect law will humble us in his sight. Biblical truth will make us seek his mercy and grace, not boasting before God but seeking forgiveness at the cross, and not living in our own strength but in the power he gives to the humble.

Secondly, Paul calls us to *gentleness* or, as this is better rendered, *meekness*. Jesus, like Paul, followed humility with this grace, saying, 'Blessed are the meek, for they shall inherit the earth' (Matt. 5:5). People today think of meekness as being mousy and weak, but that is not the Bible's idea. The Greek word was used for animals that were domesticated and trained. Meekness therefore has the idea of a will that is rightly governed. The Bible calls Moses the meekest man in all his generation, yet here was a man who stood before Pharaoh and demanded, 'Let my people go!' Moses was meek because he was committed not to his own will but to God's. Jesus was one even more humble and meek than Moses. He used this same word of himself when he called the weary and heavy-laden to find their rest in him: 'For I am gentle and lowly of heart' (Matt. 11:29).

Matthew Henry points out that the hearts of men and women are by nature unruly like that of a wild donkey. 'But the grace of meekness,' he says, 'when that gets dominion in the soul, alters the temper of it, brings it to hand, submits it to management; and now the wolf dwells with the lamb and the leopard lies down with the kid, and a little child may lead them.' He says meekness is first directed toward God; it 'is the easy and quiet submission of the soul to his whole will.' We then are meek toward our fellow men, which is what is meant by translating this word as 'gentleness.'[281]

An example of meekness comes from the life of Charles Simeon, a great preacher in Oxford, England. Late in his career, in 1808, Simeon fell ill and had to go away for a lengthy convalescence. His younger assistant thus took up his preaching duties, for which everyone thought him poorly qualified. It turned out that the younger man displayed an astonishing gift for preaching so that people soon were excited and enthusiastic. Simeon's biographer tells us, 'Simeon, totally free from any suggestions of professional jealousy, greatly rejoiced. He quoted the Scripture, "He must increase; but I must decrease," and told a friend, "Now I see why I have been laid aside. I bless God for it."'[282] This is the hallmark of a humble and meek Christian heart: he not only thought little of himself compared to others but he was glad to see another advance in his place for the sake of God's kingdom. These graces give us freedom to rejoice instead of smouldering in envy and pride.

Paul goes on to list a third vital grace, *patience*. This has to do with our ability to endure hardship and persevere over a length time without anger or frustration, and it is essential to the fruitful Christian life. Patience requires us to accept our circumstances as from God's own hand and to wait calmly in faith for God's deliverance.

Paul's word for *patience* can also be translated *long-suffering*. R. C. Sproul pictures this by pointing out that everyone's personality may be compared to a minefield, with sensitive points where they are easily provoked and can be caused to flare up. Some people, he says, have only one or two mines per acre of personality, and they are therefore easy to get along with. Others have mines scattered everywhere beneath the surface, with what seems like wall-to-wall explosives, and it takes little to set them off.[283] As Christians we are to bring our hearts to God to have mines removed, so that we may suffer trials more graciously.

How do we become patient or long-suffering? A man came to his preacher and asked him to pray for him to have patience. The minister responded, 'Lord, please send great tribulation into this brother's life.' The man stopped and said, 'You must not have heard me rightly. I didn't ask you to pray for tribulation. I asked you to pray that I might have patience.' 'Oh, I heard what you said,' the preacher replied. Then he pointed out to him Romans 5:3, which reads, 'We rejoice in our sufferings, knowing that suffering produces endurance [or patience].'[284]

Most of us don't have to pray for sufferings. Instead, we should simply use the trials we already have to become, by God's grace, long-suffering and patient. Paul's teaching in Romans goes on to show how valuable it is: 'And endurance produces character, and character produces hope' (Rom. 5:4).

Last, Paul mentions *bearing with one another in love*. If patience has to do with enduring circumstances graciously, forebearance means dealing with people graciously. Once again, Paul uses the word *agape* for love. This is distinguished from *philia* love, the kind of love we have for people and things we like. *Philia* is based on receiving, *agape* is based on giving. *Agape* love is the love of God which we extend even to people we don't really like, who we find it hard to be around, and who may do things differently than we do. This is a love we have to cultivate as part of our worship to God.

As we will see in our further study, Paul's particular concern in Ephesians chapter 4 is Christian unity. We can see, then, why he focuses on these four graces. Humility is essential to unity, because pride is the source of most conflict. Meekness means governing our will so that we put God and others first. Patience is needed, because things don't always go our way within the church. Forebearance in love sums up what Jesus has done and daily does for us, and if we are to have unity and peace together we must bear with one another's faults because of the love we have from God.

There could hardly be a more valuable teaching today, when one of our chief problems is discord in the church. It is one thing for the church to be divided over important doctrinal matters. But many churches are in upheaval over matters of preference and pride, because of conflicts that could be easily resolved with mutual humility, meekness, patience and forebearance in God-given love. According to Paul, whatever else we may do, however morally upright we may be, however much we may serve the church and reach out to the lost, if we are not cultivating these four vital graces then we are not responding in a practical way to the gospel of God's grace.

The Calling of Christ

I want to conclude by returning to the great principle Paul set forth in verse 1: 'I urge you to walk in a manner worthy of the calling to which you have been called.' The key to the Christian life is to realize that you have been called by God in Jesus Christ, and that his calling changes everything for you. It changes your destiny, and it changes your path, your walk, as well. God's call means that you have God's power to do his will. But it also means you no longer belong to yourself. You have been bought with a price through the precious blood of Christ, and now you must live as befits a man or woman who bears his name in the world.

God called Abraham to leave his home and go to live in the Promised Land. 'Walk before me, and be blameless,' he said (Gen. 17:1). He calls all his people to leave behind their former way of life, by the same faith Abraham had to walk with him. Jesus called Peter and John to leave their fishing boats and follow him. He promised, 'I will make you fishers of men' (Luke 5:10), and he did. He called Matthew from a tax collector's booth, and he gave him power to leave behind a life of greed (Matt. 9:9). Christ called Paul to go forth as an apostle of his grace and when Paul found his burdens too great, Jesus said, 'My grace is sufficient for you, for my power is made perfect in weakness' (2 Cor. 12:9). Now he calls you to follow him. Every one of us has our own calling and they are different to a certain degree. But we all have this in common: we are called to be disciples of Christ who walk as he did by the power that he gives. He said, 'I am the light of the world. Whoever follows me will not walk in darkness, but will have the light of life' (John 8:12).

If you are not a Christian, then you may find these virtues unattractive. Who wants to be humble instead of proud, meek instead of self-promoting, patient instead of demanding, forebearing instead of domineering? But if you will look at the life of Jesus Christ you will find that he is the most perfect man ever to have lived, and these characteristics are most perfectly revealed in him. This is because Jesus is not merely a man but the very Son of God. And he calls you now by the preaching of his gospel to repent of your sins, believe, and follow him. Jesus will cleanse you of your guilt and then he will grant you a life of grace, peace, and divine love. He humbly said, 'The Son of Man came not to be served but to serve, and to give his life as a ransom for many' (Matt. 20:28). If you will trust him for your salvation he will teach you how to live as he lived because of the love he will pour into your heart. 'For,' as Psalm 149:4 says, 'the Lord takes pleasure in his people; he adorns the humble with salvation.'

43

Spiritual Unity

Ephesians 4:3–4

In his commentary on Ephesians, Harry Ironside tells of a train ride he took in the early twentieth century. The first morning he began his day as always by reading from his Bible. A German lady came by and asked him what he was doing. When he told her, she said, 'Wait, I go get my Bible and we have it together.' Some-time later, a Scandinavian man saw them. 'Reading the Bible?' he asked. 'Well, I think I'll get mine, too.' Soon, pretty much everyone in their car took part in the Bible study, which gathered every day during the long train ride. Before long, the conductor advertised it to all the cars, hymns and prayers were added, and Ironside would preach. When they finally arrived and the passengers debarked, the German lady who started it all came to Ironside and asked 'What denomination are you?' He answered, 'I belong to the same denomination that David did.' 'What was that?' she asked. 'I didn't know that David belonged to any.' Ironside replied, 'I am a companion of all them that fear Thee and keep Thy precepts.' The lady replied, 'Yah, yah, that is a good church to belong to.'[285]

Ironside's is the very attitude the apostle Paul wants to cultivate among his Ephesian readers. Having just begun Paul's practical instruction in this letter, we find that it divides into two main sections. First is an appeal to Christian unity in chapter 4. Second is an exhortation to moral purity. These are the two characteristics of God's people, the twin effects of the salvation Jesus purchased with his blood: that we should be one and that we should be holy. John Stott writes:

> Because God's people are called to be one people, they must manifest their unity, and because they are called to be a holy people, they must manifest their purity. Unity and purity are two fundamental features of a life worthy of the church's divine calling.[286]

Spiritual Unity

Ephesians 4 focuses on the first of these characteristics, Christian unity. Paul writes in verse 3 that we must be 'eager to maintain the unity of the Spirit in the bond of peace.' The chapter begins with two verses focused on: humility, meekness, patience, and forebearing love. But to what end are these to be directed? Paul tells us in verse 3 that Christian godliness is aimed towards oneness and peace.

Notice that Paul does not tell us to create this unity. Instead, we are to 'maintain' it. This is a vital point today, when so many people are clamoring for us to solve the 'problem of Christian division.' They usually point to the presence of so many denominations, many of whom are in sharp disagreement, and lament that the Christian church is not united.

What would Paul have to say to this assessment? Based on this passage, his first response would be to deny the problem, at least as it is often understood. The Christian church, he says, is not divided but is one. He says this in verse 4: 'There is one body.' Not that there *ought to be* one body, but there *is* one body, one unified church. Our problem is not that we lack unity, but that we don't manifest our unity in Christ.

We tend to view the church from an outward and organizational perspective whereas Paul's view is spiritual. The unity Paul is interested in is not one where we all come under the same organizational structure and all answer to one human chain-of-command. The unity he talks about is 'the unity of the Spirit.'

This is important because so many people are passionate about what is called the ecumenical movement, trying to get the different branches of Christianity to come together. It can be a good thing to lessen hostility and to get denominations talking. But what often happens is that matters of truth are pushed aside just to make an agreement. Matters of great importance are sacrificed just to get along: things like the authority of Scripture, the atoning work of Christ, and salvation by faith alone. We may have unity, but it is increasingly not Christian unity but worldly unity. People are seeking for Christians to be joined under a common church hierarchy. But let me suggest that the days when the church had the most outward unity, and the most political power, were the worst periods of church history. The Middle Ages show this. The church's true unity is a spiritual one and therefore is a unity based on the revealed truth of God's Word.

The union Paul is talking about is one created by the unifying presence of God's Holy Spirit. It cannot be legislated or brought about by human organization. But this does not mean we should not exert effort for the sake of unity. Paul would not have us try to create unity where it does not exist, but rather to realize the unity all true Christians already have. We are to labor 'to maintain' that unity, to manifest it in our relationships. The purpose of Christ's work is 'to create in himself one new humanity' in the place of prior divisions (Eph. 2:15). He prayed to the Father, 'That they may become perfectly one' (John 17:23). This being the case, unless we are actively guarding unity, we are opposing the Spirit's work and the peace Christ died to give. We must each strive to maintain unity, willing to suffer practically any inconvenience rather than to mar that unity, and protecting the peace of the church like the precious thing that it is.

INTERPRETING EPHESIANS 4:4–6

In verses 4–6, Paul lays out the basis of Christian unity. This is a somewhat enigmatic but also a powerful passage.

It will help to make some preliminary observations about these verses. Paul notes seven 'ones': one body, one Spirit, one hope, one Lord, one faith, one baptism, and one God. The number seven probably has significance: in the Bible it is often the number of completeness or fullness. On the seventh day God completed his creation, and the Book of Revelation speaks of the sevenfold Spirit of God, referring to the completeness of the Holy Spirit (Rev. 4:5). The purpose of these verses is to proclaim the complete unity that characterizes God and his work and which thus demands unity among God's people.

Another observation is that Paul organizes these seven 'ones' around the three Persons of the Trinity, in keeping with his Trinitarian emphasis all through Ephesians. Verse 4 speaks of our unity in the Spirit; verse 5 speaks of unity in the Lord Jesus; and verse 6 unites us in terms of the 'one God and Father of all'.

The order in which these appear is unusual, so Paul probably has a reason for listing the Spirit first, then the Son, and then the Father. Since Paul is speaking of the church, he is dealing with the end-point of salvation and working back to the source. Martyn Lloyd-Jones says, 'The church is a fellowship of the Spirit. We are what we are because of the work of the Spirit; but the Spirit would never have come, would never have been sent and given, were it not for the Son and what He has done. And the Son would never have come were it not that "God so loved the world that he gave his only-begotten Son."'[287]

One Body: A Call to Unity

Verse 4 works out the spiritual unity that comes from the presence of the Holy Spirit. 'There is, one body and one Spirit—just as you were called to the one hope that belongs to your call.'

In his writings, Paul describes the church in a number of ways. He calls us God's house and temple, as well as the bride of Christ. But his favorite description of the church is 'the body of Christ.' He especially uses this as a basis for his call to unity: you are one body, so work together. This is his point in 1 Corinthians 12:13, 'For in one Spirit we were all baptized into one body.'

This presents the organic union of the church. We are not a collection of parts that have been thrown together. Instead, the church grows organically as a living body. Because each of us is indwelt by the same Spirit, we have an essential unity. Therefore where one has pain we all suffer; where one has joy we all rejoice. Where sin infects one, the whole body is infected with sin. Wherever holiness flourishes, the whole body is strengthened.

This means that we have unity, but not uniformity. The human body has great variety. Some parts are strong and others are vulnerable. Some parts of our body have one function and others have different functions. Paul especially deals with this in 1 Corinthians 12, because of the great problem of division in that church:

> For the body does not consist of one member but of many. If the foot should say, 'Because I am not a hand, I do not belong to the body,' that would not make it any less a part of the body. And if the ear should say, 'Because I am not an eye, I do not belong to the body,' that would not make it any less a part of the body. If the whole body were an eye, where would be the sense of hearing? (1 Cor. 12:14–17).

Paul goes on there to say that even parts 'that seem to be weaker are indispensable' (1 Cor. 14:22), and that is true. Even those parts of the human body that we consider dishonorable are important and of value, Paul says. Likewise, we need all kinds of personalities and traits in the church.

For this reason, it is a great mistake for churches to insist on or pursue uniformity. People feel pressured to dress the same, to make the identical education choices for their children, to listen to exactly the same music. But God's kingdom is not a factory, pressing out carbon-copies. Instead, we are all individuals, but indwelt by the same Spirit, possessing the same life within, walking together along the same path to the same destination. This unity with diversity brings beauty and glorifies God.

We should not therefore expect everyone in the church to be exactly the same. People will respond differently in worship, for instance. Some are very quiet and even still, whereas others are more emotional. Different people will want to serve in different ways, according to their gifts and experiences. While we all are called to shared duties, such as prayer, evangelism, and financial giving, we may show particular interest in different aspects of Christian service.

The same is true in our families. What a mistake it is to expect each child to be the same. It is an especially great tragedy to belittle a child for being different from the others. A family is one, but it is filled with individuals. Parents should have the same aspirations, the same standards, and the same love for each child. But they should each be treated individually, because they are all different.

A final point made by Paul's statement that we are 'one body' is that while we are each a little different we are all interdependent. Emotional people should not separate from intellectuals, and vice versa; they each need the other. Paul says this about the hand and the foot and the eye and the ear. Every part of the body must be used or the whole body suffers and fails.

This means the church needs you. People don't think they are important if they don't have more public gifts, such as teaching or leadership. But we need followers and workers. We need you to be regular in coming to church; a good attendance encourages the preacher and the whole church. We need people who are sympathetic, people who are discerning, people who can handle problems, and people who can make others feel welcome. We are all to cultivate godly virtues: humility, meekness, patience, and love. But each of us is able to make particular contributions and God brings each of us into the church because we all are needed.

Paul says we are one body and must therefore strive for harmony and peace. We must go out of our way not to hurt anyone in the church, because we hurt the whole body. Even a splinter in one of our fingers is terribly distracting; so also is any conflict in the church or any one person who is prone to discord. Christians often fail woefully in this regard. We do not realize what damage we do to God's work when we speak ill of other people in the church, when we are insensitive or selfish, or when we complain or gossip. These are the things that ruin many churches. This is why Paul makes this his very first point of business in our practical response to the gospel. When we hurt a fellow Christian we hurt the church. And when we hurt the church we hurt Christ, since he has joined himself to us by the Spirit and is the head of the body that is the church.

ONE SPIRIT: THE SOURCE OF UNITY

Paul says, 'There is one body,' and also 'one Spirit.' The reason and the way we are joined together in a body is our union with the Holy Spirit. Charles Hodge explains, 'The body of Christ is one because it is pervaded by one and the same Spirit, who dwelling in all is a common principle of life. All sins against unity are, therefore, sins against the Holy Ghost.'[288]

Because of our faith in Christ, the Holy Spirit is working in each of our lives in the same way. There is diversity because we all are different and have different issues. But it is all cut from the same cloth. There is the same general pattern, the same general work and process, and the same outcome. To be a Christian, every one of us has to have been convicted of sin, and we are all being shown our sin by the Holy Spirit. Every one of us is brought to the cross of Christ for cleansing and is made his disciple to follow in obedience to his Word. We all have to study the Bible, pray, gather together for worship, and participate in fellowship if we are to flourish and grow. We are of different races, different backgrounds, different professions, and different personalities. Why would we come together, why would we become such fast friends, why would we sacrifice for each other and have such love? Because of the one Spirit dwelling in us all.

There is hardly a matter of more confusion among Christians today than the Holy Spirit. Many Christians have practically no idea of the Spirit and no sense of their need of his presence and power. Other Christians think of the Spirit mainly as some impersonal force for them to tap into to get an emotional high. Paul teaches that God's Spirit, the third Person of the Godhead, is the One who gives us power to live for God. He brings God's Word to life as it is heard and read. He comes to us when we pray. He lives in us and leads us as we seek to obey Jesus Christ. We know the Spirit is present not necessarily when we have some excitement, not when we are filled with self-satisfaction, but when we forget about ourselves and are absorbed with the glory of Christ, when we long to be more holy, and not the least when we are promoting unity and peace in the church.

This means that if we want unity we must seek the presence and power of the Spirit, since our unity is through him. We seek the Spirit through God's Word, which the Spirit inspired, and by praying to the Father to send the Spirit. Jesus concluded one of his parables on prayer by saying that if even sinful human fathers are willing to grant their children's requests, 'how much more will the heavenly Father give the Holy Spirit to those who ask him!' (Luke 11:13).

One Hope: A Cause for Unity

Paul concludes verse 4 with 'the one hope' to which each of us has been called. Here, too, is a basis for our unity: if we have believed in Jesus Christ, then he has not only paid the debt of our sins but has secured for us a place in eternal glory. Paul says, 'Through him we have obtained access by faith into this grace in which we stand, and we rejoice in the hope of the glory of God' (Rom. 5:2). Whatever our present trials, whatever our present differences, we believers are united by a certain future that we will share in glory, a hope that is ours together in Christ. The presence of the Spirit now is the guarantee and foretaste of all that will be ours (Eph. 1:13–14).

Imagine a group of high school students gathering at the end of their senior year. They are aware of relationships they have had and in certain respects are trying to hold onto what soon will be gone. They feel a reluctance for the change that will come to their lives. But then an announcement is made that tables are being set up according to the different colleges the students will attend in the fall. Suddenly there is a rearranging. People who had been joined together in high school go separate ways. Those who will share the same future have a new bond of unity. They talk in excited voices and make plans for where they will live, what classes they will take, how they will share rides and exchange tips for success. It turns out that they are wearing the same logos on their shirts and the same colors. Those with whom they previously shared school colors are now wearing different ones.

This is what it is like to be a Christian. We all come from different places and it is hard for our hearts to stop thinking in the old ways. But we are united by our shared future in eternity. Whether or not we would otherwise have anything in common we share the most important things of all: our faith in Christ, our union in the Spirit, and the hope of glory to which we have been called. We are no longer to think in old ways; we are especially to wean our hearts from sinful and worldly things. Indeed, we all need to talk less about things we have in common with worldly people and more about the heavenly hope we share with believers. People may ask us, 'Why are you so joined together in love?' We answer that we are travelers on the same path and journey together, partaking of the same spiritual food, trusting and obeying the same saving Lord, and looking forward to the sure hope of glory that lies just ahead, the 'city that has foundations, whose designer and builder is God' (Heb.11:10).

Do you realize this about every believer with you in church? Do you realize that for all their flaws and problems, for all that may annoy you or that you don't understand about them, they like you are destined in Christ to be perfected in glory and to serve in God's presence forever with joy unspeakable? These are your people, because this is our destiny together in Christ. Our purpose now is to offer that same hope to people living in darkness and despair, and our spiritual unity is essential to our witness of the gospel.

Are you perishing apart from Christ? Have you confessed your need of his cleansing blood and professed him as your Lord? If not, then the past and the present are all you have. No wonder you cling to them like passengers to the planks of a sinking ship. But Jesus Christ is calling you to a certain hope of eternal glory with him; he is the ark that will carry you safe to the shores of eternal life. You need only believe in him and be saved. And God will enter you into the body of his church in which we together rejoice in the hope of the glory of God.

The Bond of Peace

This is why it is so important that we believers exert ourselves—the word translated in verse 3 as *eager* has the idea of a great sense of passion and urgency—'to maintain the unity of the Spirit in the bond of peace.' To do this we need to go back to verse 2 and commit ourselves anew to humility, which causes gentleness, which helps us to be patient and forbearing in love. John MacArthur writes, 'These virtues and the supernatural unity to which they testify are probably the most powerful testimony the church can have…No program or method, no matter how carefully planned and executed, can open the door to the gospel in the way individual believers can do when they are genuinely humble, meek, patient, forbearing in love, and demonstrate peaceful unity in the Holy Spirit.'[289]

Verse 3 tells us to be 'eager to maintain the unity of the Spirit in the bond of peace.' What is the bond of peace? Paul said in Colossians 3:14, 'And above all these put on love, which binds everything together in perfect harmony.' The bond of peace is love. Indeed, there is a parallelism in the Greek text that is not apparent in the English, but which seems to be intentional. The Greek word for *bond* in verse 3 is a cognate of the same word used in verse 1 for *prisoner*. Paul says, 'I am a prisoner for the Lord,' and now he asks, 'Are you willing to be a prisoner of love?' Are you willing to yield unreservedly to Jesus Christ and commit yourself to love, so that together we may be bound in the blessings of peace?

44

One in the Lord

Ephesians 4:5–6

Few matters present so great a challenge as our calling to Christian unity. It is a challenge that comes from two directions and that therefore demands careful biblical discernment. On the one hand, we are required to have spiritual unity with all true believers. On the other hand, our Lord Jesus commanded us to be on the watch for false Christs and for wolves in sheeps' clothing.

A failure in spiritual unity is described by J. Dwight Pentecost. A church split so violently that lawsuits were filed, contrary to biblical teaching. The civil court rejected it, so it went to a church court. One side was awarded the church property, so the other side built their own church nearby. During the trial, it was revealed that the conflict started at a church dinner when one elder received a slice of ham that he deemed too small.[290] This is an extreme example of a common problem. We lack unity because we lack the virtues Paul cites in verse 2: humility and gentleness, patience and forebearing love.

The opposite error is that of a false unity, such as the situation described by Peter Jones at the Parliament of World Religions. He describes seeing 'a liberal Presbyterian professor in his long black robe; a Buddhist priest in his orange one; a Catholic cardinal in his royal purple splendor; the high priestess of the goddess Isis in her white robe and pointed headdress—all stood together in celebration of their spiritual unity.' As he watched, they 'held hands and danced around the room to the sound of a Native American Indian shaman's drum.'[291] This is the very opposite of the Christian unity to which Paul calls us.

Ephesians 4 is about true unity among Christians. In verse 4, Paul described this as a unity in the Holy Spirit, since believers are together in one spiritual body and share one hope. In verses 5–6, he completes his argument by turning to our unity in Jesus Christ the Lord and then in the one God and Father of all who believe.

One Lord

Verse 5 grounds our unity in our shared relationship with Jesus Christ. Paul designates Jesus with the title 'Lord,' as he often does, thus identifying him with the Old Testament name 'Jehovah' or 'Yahweh.' This reminds us that Jesus is sovereign over the kingdom into which we are saved. This follows from the statement in verse 4 that we are 'one body.' Jesus is the head of the body and Lord of the church. Therefore, we all are one in him and must practice unity.

This emphasizes that being a Christian is all about a personal relationship with Jesus Christ. Many are drawn to the church by a dynamic preacher or because they find something attractive about the congregation. But neither of these will make you a Christian. You are saved—brought to God for acceptance and eternal life—only through personal faith in Jesus Christ. A faithful and able minister may help you in many ways, and a good church is a joy. But Christianity involves salvation not merely from loneliness or lack of guidance. Christianity involves your standing before the holy God. It is about dealing with the problem of your sins and the coming judgment that threatens you with hell. It is about having a new life with power from God so that you stop sinning and live for him a hope of eternal glory in heaven. All of those things may be had as a free gift from God through faith in Jesus Christ, but only through faith in him.

This is the problem Paul dealt with in 1 Corinthians. He writes at the beginning of that letter, 'It has been reported to me by Chloe's people that there is quarreling among you, my brothers. What I mean is that each one of you says, "I follow Paul," or "I follow Apollos," or "I follow Cephas," or "I follow Christ." Is Christ divided? Was Paul crucified for you? Or were you baptized in the name of Paul?' (1:11–13).

You see what was happening. Each faction had the apostle it favored and despised the others. Perhaps they had been saved as a result of Paul's or Apollos' or Peter's ministry. But all of this was sinful division. We should never allow human loyalties or the particularities of our past experience to overshadow the fundamental and essential unity that everyone has who has believed the gospel of Jesus Christ. Isn't that an error we often commit? We want to make our past experience definitive for all Christians—they all have to have had the same experience we had—and so do not accept others who are true believers in Christ but whose experience is somehow different.

We remember how Jesus responded to the bickering of his twelve disciples as each sought to be greater than the others. On one occasion, Jesus set a little child before them, saying, 'Whoever humbles himself like this child is the greatest in the kingdom of heaven' (Matt. 18:4). The way to be a good and faithful disciple is not to take charge by force but by making oneself a servant of others in the church (Mark 9:35).

One thing that is true of every good leader is that he or she cultivates cohesion and unity among followers. Not surprisingly, Jesus emphasized this very thing. It is impossible for the church to be strong and effective if there is constant in-fighting. Our duty to him as Lord is to work harmoniously with all his other servants, especially within a given congregation but also within the broader church. If we put on the uniform of Christ, then we must serve his kingdom faithfully.

It is easy to respond to this by thinking how others have wrongfully advanced themselves or their agendas in the church. But the proper application is to see how often you have damaged Christ's church and his work by selfish ambition, by sinful striving, and by petty bickering. Indeed, so prone are each of us to disunity and selfish conflict that we must actively commit ourselves to humility and selfless service.

This was the lesson Jesus taught on his last night with the disciples. He took up a towel, knelt before each of them, and washed their feet. 'Do you understand what I have done to you?' he asked. 'If I then, your Lord and Teacher, have washed your feet, you also ought to wash one another's feet. For I have given you an example, that you also should do just as I have done to you' (John 13:12–14). The only way to be like Jesus, of course, is to focus our hearts on Jesus himself. It all flows from our personal relationship with Jesus. For us to be humble, peaceful servants, we have to be able to say with Paul, 'For me, to live is Christ' (Phil. 1:21).

During the Protestant Reformation, one of the most useful groups was known as the Moravians. These gentle believers generally got along with all the other Protestants and were greatly loved. While the Moravians were sound in the gospel, they had numerous errors in secondary matters of theology. But their ethos was summed up by their leader, Count Zinzendorf, who said, 'I have one passion, it is He, and He alone.'[292] How well that attitude compensates for many secondary errors and mistakes. If we all were focused on our one Lord—Jesus Christ himself—not on our vision of church success or on spiritual experiences or on this preference or that—but Christ first and always—then we would have a unity and the loving peace he alone can give, and most of our problems would pale into insignificance.

One Faith

When it comes to Christian unity, the most common approach today is first to remove every possible doctrinal division, giving importance only to the most general truths on which we can agree. Some people will see that as the way to do what I just emphasized—to focus on Jesus. The problem is that this does not follow the biblical and apostolic example, indeed, the example of our Lord Jesus himself, who treated matters of doctrine as of first importance. We are not focused on Jesus, for instance, if we do not believe the Bible's essential teaching on his person and work. Following his example and the Bible's teaching, we should never downplay truth in the interest of unity.

Some years ago, I saw an article in *Chrisitanity Today* magazine that asked what beliefs are essential to being an evangelical Christian. To my astonishment, only four items made the list. They included a general belief in the Bible as God's Word, a basic belief in God as transcendent and personal, some experience of conversion and a desire to share this experience with others.[293] It was about as minimal a creed as one could possibly have. It left out the deity of Jesus Christ, his death on the cross as an atonement for sin, his bodily resurrection, and his Second Coming, just to list the most important items.

This approach promotes the idea that so long as we have some belief in Jesus, we have unity despite radically differing beliefs. R. C. Sproul has observed, 'The culture would like to say, "One Lord, many faiths." But this is not the unity to which Paul refers. People say that truth divides, and Sproul responds,

> Yes, truth divides: it divides the sheep from the goats; it divides the gospel from heresy; it divides the Christ from the antichrist…Our culture preaches the doctrine of justification by a contentless faith. That is not Christianity; that is not biblical faith.[294]

Paul writes that there is 'one Lord, one faith.' He does not mean merely that all people with some kind of faith are one. Many people believe fervently, sincerely, but falsely, and they are not Christians. We hear today that so long as we are sincere in whatever we believe about Jesus, God will accept us. Nothing could be more alien to Paul's thought. Instead, true believers are united by the one faith that was revealed by God through his Word, which Jude 3 says was 'once for all entrusted to the saints' and for which we are likewise to contend.

The question arises, 'Who then is going to decide the non-negotiables of true and saving faith?' The answer is the Bible. Does the New Testament provide us with clear statements of what we absolutely must believe to be saved and thus to be Christians? The answer is Yes. What, then, are these necessary truths?

I first think of Matthew 16, where Jesus himself laid out the essentials of saving faith. He asked the disciples, 'Who do you say that I am?' Peter replied, 'You are the Christ, the Son of the living God.' Jesus responded with joy, saying of this profession of faith, 'On this rock I will build my church' (Matt. 16:15–18). Obviously, this presents the essential core of Christian truth.

First, Peter professed faith in the *person* of Jesus, saying, 'You are…the Son of the living God.' We cannot be saved without believing in the full deity of Jesus Christ, the very Son of God the Father. By extension, this makes the doctrine of the Trinity non-negotiable for true faith. The whole point of denying the Trinity is to dispute Jesus' claim to full deity and his relationship within the Godhead as Son to the Heavenly Father. Alarmingly, it has become fashionable in many evangelical circles to deny the Trinity and thus to refuse Jesus the faith he demanded. According to John, 'This is the antichrist, he who denies the Father and the Son' (1 John 2:22).

Second, Peter believed in Jesus' *saving work*. 'You are the Christ,' he said. 'Christ,' the Greek word for the Hebrew 'Messiah,' means 'anointed one.' In the Messiah to come the Jews looked for the Savior. We must trust in Jesus' saving work. John wrote at the end of his Gospel, 'These are written so that you may believe that Jesus is the Christ, the Son of God, and that by believing you may have life in his name' (John 20:31).

Paul expounds upon this in two important passages. First is 1 Corinthians 15:1–11. He begins by saying, 'Now I would remind you, brothers, of the gospel I preached to you, which you received, in which you stand, and by which you are being saved, if you hold fast to the word I preached to you—unless you believed in vain' (1 Cor. 15:1–2). Those are sober words; Paul says there are certain things we must hold to in faith to be saved. He then spells it out: 'For I delivered to you as of first importance what I also received: that Christ died for our sins in accordance with the Scriptures, that he was buried, that he was raised on the third day in accordance with the Scriptures, and that he appeared to Cephas, then to the twelve. Then he appeared to more then five hundred brothers at one time' (1 Cor. 15:3–6).

Here we have truths that by Paul's own teaching are 'of first importance.' These are primary matters of faith. What are they? First is that Jesus died, and that he did so as an atonement 'for our sins.' If we say that Jesus died not as a sin-offering but simply as an example of love, as many liberals do, then we are not Christians. Furthermore, Jesus did not merely appear to have died, but 'he was buried.' Next, we must believe that he was raised from the dead in accordance with the Scriptures and as proved by his subsequent appearances. So-called Christians who deny the reality of Christ's bodily resurrection are not Christians and are not to be treated as such by true believers.

To this we must add Paul's teaching in the Book of Galatians. The purpose of this book is to defend the doctrine of justification by faith alone against the heresy that says works are included in justification. Galatians 2:16 says, 'We know that a person is not justified by works of the law but through faith in Jesus Christ.' How important is this doctrine? Paul answers in Galatians 1:8, 'If we or an angel from heaven should preach to you a gospel contrary to the one we preached to you, let him be accursed.'

Including works in justification, that is, as the ground of our acceptance by God, is often and rightly associated with the Roman Catholic Church. But we are mistaken if we fail to realize how often it occurs in Protestant circles and even among those who claim to teach Reformed theology. It is always the desire of the sinful flesh to seek a justification by works, but we must come to God through faith alone in Christ if we hope to be saved. We must uphold justification by faith alone as a doctrine that is primary and necessary to Christianity.

These are the doctrines that, according to the New Testament itself, are non-negotiable to true and saving Christianity: the deity of Jesus, and by extension the Trinity, Christ's death as an atonement for our sins, his bodily resurrection from the grave, and justification by faith alone for our acceptance as righteous before God. We are not to claim Christian unity with those who deny these, but with those who do we are in fact one. This is the Bible's own standard of faith, from which we have no right to subtract or to add.

One Baptism

Next, Paul reminds us that there is not only 'one Lord,' and 'one faith,' but also, 'one baptism.' This is a remarkable inclusion, since our differing views on baptism have caused Christians to do everything but unite.

Paul's point in listing baptism seems to be that, just as faith enters us into the Christian life, baptism is the rite of entry into the church. The important thing about baptism is not how it is done—whether it is by immersion or by sprinkling—but that it publicly declares the death and resurrection of Jesus Christ for the forgiveness of our sins and for our spiritual cleansing. James Montgomery Boice puts it well:

> Paul is not concerned here with modes of baptism, but with what baptism signifies, namely, identification with Christ. That is the unifying thing. Have you been baptized into Christ? I do not care how you were baptized. I do not care whether it was in a baptistery or a stream, whether it was with a little bit of water or in a lot of water. Have you been publicly identified with Jesus Christ? That is the issue. And if that is the issue, then before the world we are identified together with Jesus Christ and must stand together for him.[295]

One God and Father of All

Lastly, Paul turns to the first person of the Godhead, writing in verse 6, 'One God and Father of all, who is over all and through all and in all.'

This statement that there is only one God repudiates the religious pluralism of our age. I earlier noted Peter Jones' description of the World Parliament of Religions, with supposed Christians gathering together with Buddhists and shamans, declaring that everyone's notion of God is equally true. Jones argues that this is the first lie of neo-paganism, that 'All is one and one is all.' This is the view taught by Disney movies like *The Lion King*, which replaces the idea of a Creator God with 'the circle of life.' The *Star Wars* movies likewise teach about 'the Force', which, according to Obiwan Kenobi, 'surrounds us and penetrates us; it binds the galaxy together…it is all powerful [and] controls everything.'

When Paul wrote that there is 'one God… who is over all and through all and in all,' he had something very different in mind. This is the personal, sovereign God revealed in the Bible, not an impersonal 'Force' or cycle of nature. By saying that God is 'Father of all,' Paul is speaking about God's people, who are his children through faith in Jesus Christ. Peter Jones reminds us, 'The starting point of Gospel truth is that God the Creator…is the one and only God, and that all which is not God was created by Him.'[296]

Paul warns us against false and pagan views of spiritual unity, views that would have us worship the creation instead of the Creator. But his emphasis here is that God is the Father of all believers, so there is one unified Christian family. John Stott says, 'Is there only one God? Then he has only one church. Is the unity of God inviolable? Then so is the unity of the church…. It is no more possible to split the church than it is possible to split the Godhead.'[297]

This one God and Father is 'over all.' What does this mean but that God has a sovereign purpose for the universe and for his people. Ephesians 1:10 spoke of God's 'plan for the fullness of time, to unite all things in [Christ], things in heaven and things on earth.' It is for this reason that the church began with Pentecost, when believers from all the human races and tongues, which the Book of Genesis tells us had been scattered and confused as God's judgment on sin (Gen. 11:7-8), were united and enabled to understand one another. This event was a symbol of God's intention to bring together in Christ 'one new man…so making peace' (Eph. 2:15). This is God's purpose and plan. Therefore, if God is over us, and if we are to serve God faithfully, we will cherish this unity God has granted us in Christ. If you want to do God's will, then be a person who brings people together in Jesus Christ.

Paul also says that God is 'through all'. This means that we are the 'instruments or agents through whom he works.'[298] Therefore, if we want to be used of God then we must commit ourselves to 'the unity of the Spirit in the bond of peace' among true believers in Christ (Eph. 4:3). 'Blessed are the peacemakers,' Jesus taught, 'for they shall be called sons of God' (Matt. 5:9).

Finally, Paul concludes this great statement of Christian unity by saying that the one God and Father is 'in all'. Paul said at the end of his teaching on salvation in chapter 2 that we are 'being joined together…into a holy temple in the Lord…a dwelling place for God by the Spirit' (Eph. 2:21-22).

If we understand that, we will not have a problem with Christian unity. If we realize that our gathering in the church is for the glory and pleasure of God, then we will forget about ourselves and determine to do everything possible to exalt our great saving God. God the Spirit has brought us into one body. God the Son has baptized us into one faith. And God the Father has made us one family. He has made us his instruments for reconciliation and love. And he has granted us this matchless privilege and glory, that he has come to dwell in us, forever to make us his own holy habitation.

Compared to that, what is the point of your or my petty ambitions? For the sake of that, are we not eager to set aside our grievances against one another? On the one hand, may God forbid that we would seek this kind of union with those who are alien to Christ. But on the other hand may God even more forbid that we should fail to do everything possible among believers, by his power, 'to maintain the unity of the Spirit in the bond of peace.' So unity starts in our own hearts: humility, meekness, long-suffering, and forebearing in love. It is essential to our worship and our service to God. And very few things will be more important to our usefulness to him and our own enjoyment of the blessings God has for us in this life, together in Christ.

45

Gifts from on High

Ephesians 4:7–10

In its teaching about the church, the Bible employs organic rather than machine metaphors. This is true, for instance, about church growth. We live in a machine world and are therefore impatient. We expect that if we have the right inputs lined up, then we will be able to press a button and the desired outputs will immediately appear. But the Bible speaks of church growth in agricultural terms. Writing to Timothy, Paul describes the gospel minister as a 'hard-working farmer.' A farmer first clears the terrain, plows the ground, plants the seeds, waters, tends, and protects the plants, waiting and praying often for quite a while. But at the right time he receives a harvest of great abundance. This ought to warn us against quick-and-easy church growth schemes that produce rapid results, but little eternal fruit. If we use the world's methods, we get the world's results, often quickly. If we use God's methods, things are often much slower, but they are the results God wants and they last forever.

Another difference between a machine view of the church and a spiritual view of the church has to do with our definition of Christian unity. Paul has been writing in Ephesians 4 about church unity, but what he has in mind is quite different from uniformity. John Stott writes, 'We are not to imagine that every Christian is an exact replica of every other, as if we had all been mass-produced in some celestial factory. On the contrary, the unity of the church, far from being boringly monotonous, is exciting in its diversity.'[299]

Grace Apportioned

It is to emphasize this diversity that Paul writes in verse 7, 'But grace was given to each one of us according to the measure of Christ's gift.' We have so many things in common as believers in Christ: one Spirit, one body, one hope; one Lord, one faith, one baptism; one God and Father (vv. 4–6). We have all admitted our sins, trusted in Christ's saving work and been born again of the same Spirit. But we are not plastic copies cut from a mold; our unity is spiritual and it allows for great variety, like flowers in a garden, each one similar but each unique. We have different personalities and backgrounds. Especially, Christ's work in our lives shows variety in the different spiritual gifts that he grants us by the Holy Spirit.

The teaching on spiritual gifts is important to the New Testament. The usual word for them is *charismata*, from the Greek word for 'grace,' which is *charis*. This is what Paul means in verse 7 when he says 'grace was given to each one of us.' The relationship between spiritual gifts and God's grace is important: they are not things we have earned and they are not based on our ability. Instead, they are sovereignly granted 'according to the measure of Christ's gift.'

The New Testament provides five different lists of spiritual gifts, each of which is somewhat different, speaking of nineteen in all (Rom. 12:6-9, 1 Cor. 12:8-10, 28-30, Eph. 4:11, and 1 Pet. 4:11). They include things that belonged only to the apostolic age—gifts of healing, prophesy and tongues—and gifts important to the church today, like teaching, service, exhortation, helps, and leadership. The important thing is, as James Boice writes, 'Every Christian has at least one gift, like the people who received talents in Christ's parable. Moreover, since these are given by God, they are to be used for his glory and according to his plans rather than to enhance our own glory or further our plans.'[300] We are not intended all to have the same gifts, though all of our gifts are important. Furthermore, according to Romans 12:5, we are 'individually members one of another.' That means that the spiritual gifts Christ has given us do not belong to us but to the body, so that we must use our gifts in the church and the church relies on us doing so. Christ's gifts are not like those we often receive at weddings or on Christmas, many of which we really cannot use. The gifts Christ gives are exactly suited to the work he wants us to do and which his church needs if it is to be built up.

He Gave Gifts

This matter is so important that the question arises, 'How is it that Christ is able to bestow these gifts for the building of his church?' That is the question Paul addresses in verses 8-10.

He quotes here from Psalm 68, which celebrates God's triumph as revealed in the history of Israel. The psalm culminates in a description of the procession of the ark of the covenant as it was brought by David up to Mount Zion. In verse 18, he compares this to God's dwelling on Mount Sinai during the exodus. Speaking of that great victory, he writes, 'You ascended on high, leading a host of captives in your train and receiving gifts among men.' By quoting this verse in Ephesians 4, Paul says this is ultimately fulfilled in the ascension of Jesus Christ to heaven after his victory on earth. Like a military conqueror who returns in triumph, with his captives dragged before him and laden with treasures he has received and which he now bestows upon his loyal supporters, likewise did Christ return to heaven from the earth. Indeed, Paul argues that Psalm 68 is only truly fulfilled in Jesus Christ, because, 'In saying, "He ascended," what does it mean but that he had also descended?' (Eph. 4:9). In order to ascend one must first descend, and the only time God descended was in the coming of Jesus Christ.

This has been a difficult passage for many interpreters over the years, starting with Paul's statement in verse 9 that Jesus 'descended into the lower regions of the earth?' The first question is, What is 'the lower regions' of the earth? Some have thought this refers to Mary's womb in the incarnation. Others point to the grave in which Jesus was buried. One strand of interpretation dating to the early church sees this as what is called 'the harrowing of hell.' This describes Jesus' supposed visit to hell after his death and before his resurrection, to which Peter may be referring in 1 Peter 3:19-20.

However, a careful study of Scripture will show that the descent Paul has in mind is simply Jesus' descent from heaven to earth in his incarnation, so that 'the lower regions' is a way of speaking about our world in a way that emphasizes its distance from heaven. In John 8:23, Jesus says, 'I am from above, you are from below. You are of this world; I am not of this world' (see also Acts 2:19). All through the New Testament, the matching piece to Jesus' ascent into heaven is his coming to earth as a man. Paul's point here is simply that Christ ascended to heaven because he first descended to earth.

The second question is, Who are the captives of verse 8? According to the idea that 'the lower regions' refers to hades, these captives are the souls of dead saints who Christ broke out of the realm of death and took with him back to heaven. The problem with this view is that it does not fit the imagery of Psalm 68, which Paul is citing here. In the scenario of a military triumph, the captives are those enemies who have been defeated and now are led in subjugation. This best represents Christ's spiritual victories over his enemies while on earth.

The third issue has to do with the fact that Paul does not precisely cite the verse from Psalm 68. In verse 8, he says, 'When he ascended on high he led a host of captives, and he gave gifts to men.' The problem is that Psalm 68:18 says that 'he received gifts from men.' How do we explain what some claim to be an error or misuse of Scripture?

The first thing to realize is that Paul is an apostle who has the authority to give us divinely-inspired interpretations of the Old Testament. His point is not to twist or change the Scripture, but to apply it rightly to our situation. Psalm 68 shows the conquering God ascending with treasures he has earned; Paul's point is that the purpose of this was to bestow gifts upon his people. In his study of Psalm 68, Derek Kidner explains that Paul's rendering 'summarizes rather than contradicts the psalm.'[301] Perhaps the best commentary on this is Peter's Pentecost sermon, preached on the very day that what Paul describes happened. Peter explained: 'Jesus…being therefore exalted at the right hand of God, and having received from the Father the promise of the Holy Spirit, he has poured out this that you yourselves are seeing and hearing' (Acts 2:33).

It is probably noteworthy, therefore, that Psalm 68 was sung in the synagogues during the feast of Pentecost, which celebrated the giving of the Law at Mount Sinai. Paul may be using this Psalm to deliberately make the connection between God's gift of the Law to Israel on Mount Sinai, depicted in Psalm 68:18, and Christ's gift of the Holy Spirit to the church at Pentecost. John Stott explains, 'As Moses received the law and gave it to Israel, so Christ received the Spirit and gave him to his people in order to write God's law in their hearts.'[302] This may also suggest the difference between the law and the gospel: the law, through Moses, demands obedience that God receives from us; the gospel, through Christ, gives salvation to us on the basis of what he has given to God, namely, perfect obedience on our behalf.

It is important that we do not lose sight of the big picture on account of these details. Ephesians 4:8–10 is making a point that is vital to the drama of our redemption. We seldom think about Christ's ascension into glory, but it is essential to the work of our salvation in his first coming. Indeed, it may be said that Jesus died and rose again so that he could ascend to heaven and bestow salvation upon us through the Holy Spirit, which includes our spiritual gifts.

Indeed, if you have never heard, this is the story of all stories. The great God of heaven descended into our lowly earth, born of a virgin and thus taking up our mortal existence. He became man in every respect, only without sin. Jesus' life on earth was one of warfare, and he conquered on our behalf. Lloyd-Jones writes, 'Our Lord conquered the last enemy. Every enemy that has ever enslaved man, and kept him in bondage, has been routed and defeated. Thus, having completed the work, He rose and ascended from earth to heaven.'[303]

Who are these captives, defeated and led in humiliation? They are, first, the world, which hated Jesus because of his perfect holiness. He says now to us, 'In the world you will have tribulation. But take heart; I have overcome the world' (John 16:33). They include sin, which ruins our lives, wrecking our relationships and marring all our achievements, making us miserable and ultimately casting us into hell. Sin assailed Jesus with all the temptations common to man and rested upon his shoulders as he bore God's wrath for us on the cross. But by dying in our place he overcame the power of sin. He took away our guilt and now he sends the holy Spirit to overcome the sin that lives within us. Jesus' captives include death. Hebrews 2:14–15 says, 'He himself likewise partook of [flesh and blood], that through death he might…deliver all those who through fear of death were subject to lifelong slavery.' Through faith in Christ, death is no longer our enemy but is the gateway into heaven.

Finally, Jesus conquered the devil. Hebrews 2:14 says that he destroyed 'the one who has the power of death, that is, the devil.' This fulfilled the first prophesy of the Bible, after Satan engineered man's fall into sin. In Genesis 3:15, God spoke to him of an offspring of the woman who would come: 'he shall bruise your head, and you shall bruise his heel.' Satan did indeed bruise Christ's heel, inflicting suffering on him at the cross. But by taking away the guilt of our sin, Christ crushed his very head, overthrowing Satan's kingdom completely. These are the captives Christ leads before him in utter defeat, our greatest enemies overthrown by his saving work. It is probably best presented in song:

> Bruised is the serpent's head,
>   Hell is vanquished, death is dead;
> And to Christ gone up on high,
>   Captive is captivity.
> All his work and warfare done,
>   He into his heaven is gone;
> And beside his Father's throne,
>   Now is pleading for his own.[304]

Do you rejoice in that? Have you turned to this Christ in faith? Have you admitted that you are defeated by these enemies—by the world, by sin, by the prospect of death, and by the devil in his evil schemes? If you will confess your sin and need and trust in Christ, then Jesus will be your Savior, and from on high where now he reigns he will bestow on you grace for salvation and service to him.

Christ ascended into heaven, Paul says at the end of verse 10, 'that he might fill all things.' This completes the drama of redemption. Jesus is in heaven that he might now fulfill all the promises and predictions of Scripture. He sends the Holy Spirit to fill us with his power and presence. He also works through us by the gifts that he gives—and this seems to be Paul's particular point—so that he might fulfill his plan of history in the building of his church.

The Ascension of Christ

The ascension of our Lord Jesus is an important truth and one that is much neglected in our thinking. We think of Jesus in the past tense, having died and been raised from the dead, and we think of him in the future as coming again in glory and might. But too few of us relate to

Jesus in the present tense, as one who is alive and reigning on high and who is our present Savior and Lord.

I want to conclude with some reflections about Christ's ascension, beginning with it as a proclamation of Jesus' deity. This is especially noteworthy about Paul's citation of Psalm 68 with reference to Jesus' ascension. There is no question that the psalmist, King David, was speaking of the Lord in that Psalm. In the verses immediately after the one Paul quotes, David says, 'Our God is a God of salvation' (Ps. 68:20). That is what the name 'Jesus' means—'The Lord saves.' In applying David's words to Jesus Christ, Paul is making the explicit connection that Jesus is the Lord of the Old Testament; his ascension is the one celebrated by David in Psalm 68.

When Jesus was at the nadir of his humiliation, dying in shame on the cross, the chief priests mocked him, saying, 'He trusts in God; let God deliver him now, if he desires him. For he said, "I am the Son of God"' (Matt. 27:43). That was the challenge, and the ascension was God's bold reply. Paul spells it out in Philippians 2:8-10:

> He humbled himself by becoming obedient to the point of death, even death on a cross. Therefore God has highly exalted him and bestowed upon him the name that is above every name, so that at the name of Jesus every knee should bow, in heaven and on earth and under the earth, and every tongue confess that Jesus Christ is Lord, to the glory of God the Father.

The ascension proclaims Christ's enthronement as divine king.

Second, the ascension of Christ informs us about the Christian's hope. Since Jesus has left this world, our hope is not here. Charles Spurgeon writes, 'From the hour when our Lord left it, this world has lost all charms to us…The flower is gone from the garden, the first ripe fruit is gathered. Earth's crown has lost its brightest jewel …No, earth, my treasure is not here with thee, neither shall my heart be detained by thee.'[305]

Christ has gone to heaven and by faith we are seated there with him, so our hopes are found there, too. Paul therefore wrote in Colossians 3:1-2, 'If then you have been raised with Christ, seek the things that are above, where Christ is, seated at the right hand of God. Set your minds on things that are above, not on things that are on earth.'

Third, we realize the spiritual resources available to us now because Jesus has ascended into heaven and sits enthroned at God's right hand. Jesus has spiritual resources to give that we greatly need: power to believe, strength to overcome temptation, grace to love and to serve. This was the point of his discussion with the disciples on the night of his arrest. He was talking about going away and they were troubled. Jesus told them, 'It is to your advantage that I go away, for if I do not go away, the Helper will not come to you. But if I go, I will send him to you' (John 16:7). Jesus was, of course, talking about the Holy Spirit. When Jesus was in the world he walked with the Twelve disciples, teaching and instructing them. But now that he has ascended and has sent the Spirit, Jesus lives in his disciples—millions of us—and he is not merely speaking words into our ears but by the Spirit's power is transforming us into his image (2 Cor. 3:18). The ascension of Christ made all the difference in Peter's life; with the Spirit's power he was no longer a man of sin and doubt but a man of faith and holiness. That is the power available to all of us because of the Spirit whom Christ sends to us from heaven and for whom we should pray.

Since Christ has ascended in triumph, as Paul emphasizes in these verses, the Christian life has a supernatural character. We do not rely on techniques and mere human effort, but on power that comes through obedience to God's Word. This is Paul's emphasis all through Ephesians; the power of Christ is the key to the Christian life.

Christ has a role for each of us to play in the work of his church, and this, too, is supernatural. This is Paul's point with regard to spiritual gifts. Christians often want to know what God is calling them to do, and the answer is found here. He has given us grace 'according to the measure of Christ's gift' (Eph. 4:7). What gifts has he given you? You are to use them in service to his kingdom and for building his church. This is God's calling on your life. Edmund Clowney writes, 'Every gift you have received, then, is a calling of the Spirit. You dare not ignore your gifts, neglect them, or wrap them in a napkin to be presented unused to Christ on his return (Luke 19:20)…When he gives, he calls; when he calls, he gives.'[306]

How do you discern your spiritual gift or gifts? The answer is that spiritual gifts are revealed during and through service to Christ. You should respond to needs in the church that you are able to meet. As you serve, you should pray for discernment about your gifts and ask others in the church to tell you what they see. Mainly, though, your gifts will be revealed by Christ's blessing to you and to others. When you are using your gifts you are not burdened with the ministry but filled with joy, and usually you encounter results that indicate the Spirit's power. So do not wait for a mystical revelation of your gifts. Begin serving Christ, eager for him to reveal the gifts and calling he has graciously appointed for you.

Last, if you have not yet become part of Christ's church by believing on Jesus and his saving work, then his ascension speaks a word to you as well. Because Jesus ascended into heaven, he now sends the Spirit with power into the hearts of sinful men and women, *bringing them to spiritual life and granting them power to believe.* The ascended Christ sends forth his living Word even as it is preached by his ministers and shared by simple believers. By that Word he is calling you to believe, and by believing to be forgiven of your sins and receive eternal life. Jesus did not ascend as a conqueror to add you to the list of his defeated enemies, but to win you and to save you.

In his parable of the talents, Jesus spoke of the gifts he has given believers. He said he will come back and demand an account. To those who have served faithfully, Jesus will say, 'Well done, good servant!' and reward us with far more than we ever could imagine (Luke 19:17). But in that same parable, Jesus also spoke of those who rejected him as lord. They hated him and said, 'We do not want this man to reign over us' (Luke 19:14). That is the voice of unbelief, then as well as now; the problem is not intellectual but is one of moral rebellion against God. When he returns, Jesus will act like the conquering Lord Paul depicts in our passage. Jesus foretold what he will say when he returns: 'As for these enemies of mine, who did not want me to reign over them, bring them here and slaughter them before me' (Luke 19:27).

If you reject Jesus Christ now, your condemnation then will be just and it will be terrible. Turn to him now and be saved, and then someday soon you will ascend along with all the people of God to the place of glory and triumph where Christ has gone before us, and from which he bestows so many blessings and gifts to those who trust in him.

46

Building the Church
Ephesians 4:11–12

In Ephesians 4:5, Paul says we are united in 'one faith.' This is the faith Peter first declared in Mathew 16:16. Jesus had asked, 'Who do you say that I am?' Peter replied, 'You are the Christ, the Son of the living God.' This is called the 'Great Confession' and Jesus responded to it with a great promise: 'I tell you, you are Peter, and on this rock I will build my church' (Matt. 16:18). Jesus was not promising to build a church out of Peter himself. Just a few verses later, Peter spoke in unbelief and Jesus compared him to the devil (Matt. 16:23). It is Peter's confession of faith that is the rock on which Christ will build his church.

The Teaching Gifts and Offices

Given that Christ promises to build on the faith that is revealed by God the Father, we should not be surprised that in Ephesians 4:11 Paul emphasizes the teaching gifts and offices in the church. In verse 7, he introduced the topic of spiritual gifts, which the ascended Lord Jesus distributes to his people 'according to the measure of [his] gift.' That means each and every believer has at least one spiritual gift that he or she is to use for service to Christ. Now, in verse 11, Paul focuses on one of these gifts—the teaching gift—and the offices in the church that go with it. In discussing this topic Paul provides us a biblical philosophy of ministry for building the church.

Verse 11 says, 'And he gave the apostles, the prophets, the evangelists, the pastors and teachers.' Paul highlights these teaching offices not because teaching is the only gift that matters, but because there is a priority given to it in building the church. It is the ministry of the Word that empowers and energizes the whole people of God with their various gifts, which they use for service as biblically guided.

First, Paul mentions the apostles. These are those select men, called personally by Jesus, who were eye-witnesses of Christ's resurrection. They were equipped not only with miraculous powers but especially with divinely inspired and authoritative revelation from God. Their task, as Paul discusses in Ephesians 2:20, was to lay the foundation on which the church was to be built throughout history, both by bringing the first churches into existence and by providing us the written record of the gospel in the New Testament. By definition there are and can be no successors to the apostles; their office and function was once-for-all in the founding of the Christian church.

The prophets are related to the apostles. These are not the Old Testament prophets, since they came before and not after Christ's ascension. Rather, this was a provisional office in the early church for that period before the New Testament was written and collected. The apostles came and moved on, but the churches needed the kind of teaching eventually recorded in the Gospels and epistles. These prophets were temporary, like the apostles, and once the New Testament was written there was no longer a need nor a place for them in the church. It is noteworthy, I think, that in Paul's pastoral letters, written late in his ministry, where he provides for the ordering of the churches, he makes no mention of the prophetic office, which seems already to have passed away.

Does that mean, however, that our Lord made no on-going provision for the ministry of the Word? The answer is No, because there are two permanent offices that Christ gave, namely, the evangelists and the pastor/teachers. The evangelists are those who spread the gospel to new places. Today, these are mainly our missionaries. But this includes those called and gifted by God to itinerant ministries directed mainly toward the unbelieving world around us here at home.

The evangelists include some of the greatest men in the history of the church, men like George Whitefield, who were used to spur great revivals that changed history. Charles Spurgeon said, 'These are they who preach the gospel in divers places, and find it the power of God unto salvation; they are founders of churches, breakers of new soil, men of a missionary spirit, who build not on other men's foundations, but dig out for themselves…I scarcely know of any greater blessing to the church than the sending forth of earnest, indefatigable, anointed men of God, taught of the Lord to be winners of souls.'[307]

Finally, there are the pastor/teachers. These two functions are included in one office. This is made clear by the fact that Paul uses the definite article for them both together: he speaks of the apostles, the prophets, the evangelists, but then the pastors and teachers.

The word for pastor is really the word shepherd, and this tells us what a pastor's work is about: to tend and watch and lead and feed the flock of Christ. Peter exhorted pastors to 'shepherd the flock of God that is among you, exercising oversight, not under compulsion, but willingly…being examples to the flock' (1 Pet. 5:2-3). Spurgeon says of pastors, 'These are sent to feed the flock; they abide in one place, and instruct converts which have been gathered… What would the church be without her pastors? Let those who have tried to do without them be a warning to you.'[308]

The Priority of Teaching

The fact that the pastor is also called a teacher tells us that the minister's most important function is to feed God's flock with the bread of his Word. This needs to be emphasized today because of increasingly secular views of the ordained ministry. Some today have taken corporate titles—calling themselves CEO's—and acting more as entrepreneurs than as pastor/teachers. Sometimes people have expectations of ministers that no one ever could meet. Philip Ryken tells of a job description he saw for 'The Perfect Pastor':

> He condemns sins, but never upsets anyone. He works from 8:00 a.m. until midnight and is also the janitor. He makes $60.00 a week…and gives about $50.00 a week to the poor. He is 28 years old and has been preaching for 30 years…The Perfect Pastor smiles all the time with a straight face

because he has a sense of humor that keeps him seriously dedicated to his work…He spends all his time evangelizing the unchurched and is always in his office when needed.[309]

When people want their pastor to do everything, the result is pastors who do not do well that one thing for which they are specifically provided, the faithful and clear and serious teaching of God's Word. But Paul's philosophy of ministry indicates that urgent priority must be placed on Bible teaching. This is a full-time calling, to which the pastor must be set apart and for which he must be supplied with time and with prayers. John Stott explains, 'Nothing is more necessary for the building up of God's church in every age than an ample supply of God-gifted teachers.'[310]

This means that those called to serve as pastors must devote themselves first and foremost to the teaching of God's Word, which also means devoting themselves to prayer and study. Ministers are valued today more for their personality than for faithfulness in teaching the Bible; this preference for entertainment over enlightenment is largely the cause of our spiritual anemia. Christ builds his church through pastors devoted to teaching God's Word and through congregations who desire faithful Bible teaching above all else.

This tells us, by the way, what content is to make up our sermons, namely, the teaching of the Bible. God's flock is not well fed on endless amusing stories or on anecdotes from the minister's life. These are entertaining and usually popular. But the pastor is called to teach God's Word. Neither is the pulpit to be given over to current topics or to some social, moral, or political cause that has the minister's attention. There are any number of cultural issues that we might address—abortion, homosexual marriage, legal challenges to Christian symbols, corporate cheating, institutionalized racism, or school prayer. Who can argue against Christians speaking out on issues like these?

Some might point to great Christian social reformers: men like William Wilberforce, whose efforts ended slavery in England in the early 1800's, or Martin Luther King, whose civil rights campaigns produced such change in late twentieth century America. I would applaud those men and many others. Then I would point out that they were not pastors—or had given up the pastoral calling to pursue their social efforts.

The question is this: what is the work to which God has called the pastor? The clear answer of the Bible is that the pastors are to teach God's Word, so that the people of God are equipped for every good work, some of whom will be called to engage the culture on moral and political issues. Whenever pastors turn from their calling to teach the Bible, the church is weakened along with its impact on society and our message to the world is confused. Our message is the good news of a crucified and risen Savior and the new life he gives. To be sure, faithful expository preaching will touch on a wide range of topics, including those of social concern, but the agenda will be that of the Holy Spirit speaking in the Word rather than some worldly concern.

The best way for the church to influence society is for her pastors to preach the whole counsel of God and for the people of God to become more holy. It is the light of the gospel shining out through godly lives that will bring true transformation to society, one convert at a time. These new Christians then speak out and share and vote according to the truths of the Bible, which they know because they were taught them in church.

The single thing the church most needs is the Word of God. Without the Word, there will be no converts, since as Peter says, 'You have been born again…through the living and abiding word of God' (1 Pet. 1:23); there will be no Christian growth or sanctification, since Jesus prayed to the Father, 'Sanctify them by the truth; your Word is truth' (John 17:17). Without the faithful, serious teaching of the Bible, there will be no wisdom for godly decision-making, since Psalm 119:105 says, 'Your word is a lamp to my feet and a light to my path'; and there will be little true spiritual blessing, since Psalm 19:8 says, 'The precepts of the Lord are right, rejoicing the heart.'

This is the emphasis found all through the New Testament. Early in Jesus' ministry he was drawing large crowds because of his ability to heal. Instead of capitalizing on the attention, Jesus pulled away and went elsewhere, much to the surprise of his disciples, when his teaching ministry was being distracted. 'Let us go on to the next towns,' Jesus said, 'that I may preach there also, for that is why I came' (Mark 1:38).

We see the same emphasis in the Book of Acts. Some needs among the widows were causing disputes, but Peter refused to be the one who solved the problem. Instead, he formed the first deacons to deal with such things. He said of himself and the other apostles, 'It is not right that we should give up preaching the Word of God to serve tables…We will devote ourselves to prayer and to the ministry of the Word' (Acts 6:2, 4).

This was Paul's instruction to Timothy for the challenges he would face. Problems would occur in the church—every kind of godlessness, falsehood, and sin—but Paul exhorted Timothy to stick to the ministry of the Word. He wrote: 'All Scripture is breathed out by God and profitable for teaching, for reproof, for correction, and for training in righteousness, that the man of God may be competent, equipped for every good work' (2 Tim. 3:16–17). Therefore, he charged Timothy, 'Preach the word; be ready in season and out of season; reprove, rebuke, and exhort, with complete patience and teaching' (2 Tim. 4:1–2).

The Bible calls for pastors to be teachers, and also for teachers to be pastors. Teaching is not to be done by aloof academicians, but by pastors who work among the people. Pastoring is valuable to sermon preparation; the Bible is best understood and taught within the context of pastoral ministry. With this combination of pastoral care and faithful Bible teaching the church is well led and well fed.

A Questionable Comma

This tells us about the calling and the work of the ordained ministers. But what about lay people? How does a biblical philosophy of ministry relate regular Christians to their pastors? The answer is found in verse 12. Christ appointed pastor/teachers 'to equip the saints for the work of ministry, for building up the body of Christ.'

There is controversy in the interpretation of this verse, one that stems from a comma placed in the *King James Version* between the phrases 'equip the saints,' and 'for the work of ministry.' The issue is this: Is Paul teaching that the pastor/teachers have three callings, each separated by a comma: equipping the saints, doing the ministry, and building the church? Or do the pastor/teachers equip the saints so that they will do ministry and thus build the church, in which case the questionable comma should be deleted? According to the first view, the only person who really matters is the minister. Everyone else just sits in the pews and writes the checks. The pastor equips the saints, does all the ministry, and builds the church.

There are two reasons why the first interpretation is wrong, and why the comma is rightly removed (the Greek text, of course, had no punctuation marks). The first reason is that Paul's point here is that Christ gave all kinds of gifts to the church. While there is priority given to teaching it is not the only gift that matters. Other gifts have their role to play in ministry and building the church. The second reason for removing the comma is grammatical. Paul does not use the same preposition between these three phrases, as he would if they were a series in the same list. The first preposition, *pros,* indicates a simple relationship: 'He gave…pastors and teachers *to* equip the saints.' The next two phrases are joined by the preposition *eis,* which indicates an ultimate purpose and which here tells us what the saints are to be prepared for: the work of ministry and building the church.

This is important because the church is often plagued by errors with regard to the relationship between the ordained ministers and regular Christians. The first error is called *clericalism.* This is the view promoted by the mistaken comma in this text, that performing all the ministry and building up the church are what the ministers do. 'In this view the work of the church is to be done by those paid to do it, and the role of the normal member of the church is to follow docilely.'[311] Historically, it is best represented by the priests of the Roman Catholic Church, although it is found among Protestants as well. Many ministers promote this view by wanting to be in charge of everything and sometimes by holding their church in tyranny. An example in the Bible is that of Diotrephes, who the apostle John said 'likes to put himself first, [and] does not acknowledge our authority' (3 John 9). The church is impoverished under this view, because while Christ has distributed gifts to all the believers, only a small few of them have the opportunity to exercise them. In his first epistle, Peter warned pastors to be 'not domineering over those in your charge' (1 Pet. 5:3), which is the case under clericalism

The second error runs to the other extreme. It is called *anticlericalism,* and it is a reaction against what I just described. Here, the church strips ministers of their power or even does away with them, and thus does not benefit from Christ's provision of those called to teach and exercise spiritual authority. The Book of Acts shows that Paul appointed elders in each of his churches and entrusted these men to train and lead the flock (Acts 14:23; 20:17). The pastoral epistles specifically command the appointment of leaders, whose qualifications are clearly laid out (1 Tim. 3:1–13; Titus 1:5–9). Furthermore, Paul specifically calls for gifted teachers to be set aside for full-time teaching and pastoral work (1 Cor. 9:4–14; 1 Tim. 5:17).

The true model for ministry is neither clericalism nor anticlericalism, but the approach set forth by Paul in our passage. John Stott called it a *dual* approach to ministry.[312] Ministry starts with the teaching of God's Word by faithful and gifted pastors. This does not replace other ministries in the church but inspires them and provides the biblical understanding and motivation the people need. Through public and personal teaching of God's Word, the pastors 'equip the saints for the work of ministry, for building up the body of Christ.' Stott sees this well portrayed by a church bulletin he once saw. It was an Anglican church, so the bulletin listed the Rector and then gave his name. Next came the Associate Rector and then the Assistant Rector with their names. But finally came the following: 'Ministers: the entire congregation.'[313] That is Paul's teaching and Christ's design for the building of his church.

Every Member Ministry

Our passage's priority on the teaching of God's Word means that whatever your gift is, your usefulness to Jesus Christ starts with learning the Bible. To be useful to Christ you must develop a godly character. This happens, Paul says in Romans 12:2, as we are no longer 'conformed to this world' with its sinful ways of thinking, but are 'transformed by the renewal of your mind.' Our Lord Jesus has provided the teaching of the Bible in the church through its pastors, and to grow you must be regular and serious in your attendance upon the preaching of God's Word.

Being equipped by God's Word, you are then to actively engage in 'the work of ministry.' Some of this involves lay teaching for those so gifted. We need Sunday School teachers for children and adults, and leaders for Bible study circles. God calls us to be a caring church, and that means people must be willing to greet visitors, to take their turn in the nursery, to bake dinners for the sick, to listen patiently to a grieving heart, and to help out with visiting the homebound or with providing help to the elderly and the poor.

Christ has given you a spiritual gift and you are to use it in ministry for his glory. I once met a man who refused to start serving because he feared where it would lead him. He told me, 'If I start using my gifts, I will end up as a missionary in Africa!' But the choice is not between what will make God happy and what will make you happy. Those who are most blessed are those who most serve in Christ's name, even in faraway places. Indeed, there are few things more satisfying than to exercise the spiritual gift Christ has given to you. I find that the truly unhappy people are those who are unwilling to trust God and who do little for other people. They think only about themselves. The really happy people are those who serve God and others, because as they do the Spirit of God flows through them as 'a spring of living water' (John 4:14). I think that what is perhaps most exciting about ministry is to know that God is using you for things of eternal significance, and even to build up the body in which God himself will come to live forever. What could be better than that?

Are you willing to spend your life on things that will last forever? If not, what are you living for? If you are not a Christian, the only thing you have to live for are things that will never last and which even now fail to satisfy. But the Bible says that Jesus' kingdom is for ever and ever; it will shine in glory when all else has passed away. If you will trust in Christ, your sins will be forgiven by his blood, shed on the cross for you, he will enroll your name in the assembly of heaven, and he will equip you for ministry that will have eternal and glorious consequences to the praise of God the Father, Son and Holy Spirit. Daniel 12:3 says that those who trust God and serve him 'shall shine like the brightness of the sky above; and those who turn many to righteousness, like the stars, forever and ever.'

The Bible presents us with a simple and profound model for building the church. The pastor is to teach God's Word faithfully. That Word will equip the saints, and as they minister in Christ's power, with all the variety of their spiritual gifts, our Lord Jesus will build his church. And when every mere human and worldly glory has passed away, long after all our earthly trophies have crumbled into dust, Jesus Christ will be there to say to us, 'Well done, good and faithful servant. You have been faithful over a little; I will set you over much. Enter into the joy of your master' (Matt. 25:21).

47

Growth and Maturity

Ephesians 4:13–15

We are told today that every church needs a vision. This is an import from the business world, and an idea that has merit. It is always a good idea to look ahead with an idea of where you are going. The problem with most church visions, however, is that they are secular in nature: they involve worldly criteria and measurements—numbers, programs, size of budget, or buildings. There is nothing wrong with such thinking in a corporation—its purpose is secular. But there is something terribly wrong with such thinking in the church, the purpose of which is spiritual. Numbers are not bad and effective ministries are a blessing, and all of that requires money and often a large building. But such things should never comprise our vision for the church. It has often struck me that Paul never tells us the size of the church in Ephesus or the amount of money in its budget—how are we supposed to know if the church was any good or not? The reason Paul does not dwell on such things is that his thinking is spiritual, his aims are spiritual, and thus his vision for the church is a spiritual vision.

In Ephesians 4, Paul has presented a powerful model of ministry for the church. He began by speaking of unity: all believers are to 'be eager to maintain the unity of the Spirit in the bond of peace' (v. 3). He then added the importance of our spiritual gifts, highlighting the gift and office of teaching. The church is to be empowered by the teaching of the Word of God, which equips all the members for ministry to build up the body of Christ. All of this is directed towards a goal or vision, which is what Paul supplies in verse 13.

A Vision of Maturity

Paul's vision for the church is one of spiritual maturity in Jesus Christ. He writes, 'Until we all attain to the unity of the faith and of the knowledge of the Son of God, to mature manhood, to the measure of the stature of the fullness of Christ' (Eph. 4:13). Here Paul advances his line of thinking in this chapter. Having begun with an emphasis on unity, he now includes the goal of spiritual maturity.

What is spiritual maturity? Paul defines it, first, as attaining to 'mature manhood.' 'Mature' is sometimes translated as 'perfect'; the Greek word is a form of *telos*, which means the end or completion. The idea is that we should aim to come to the completion of the process begun in our salvation; we should become spiritual adults.

Paul further defines maturity as 'the measure of the stature of Christ.' He is speaking not of height, but of moral and spiritual stature. Our character is to be conformed to that of Jesus Christ. He gets at this again in verse 15, writing that 'we are to grow up in every way into him who is the head, into Christ.' Paul is thinking of the church corporately. Christ is the head, and the church which is his body is to become spiritually mature so as to be a fitting counterpart to him.

This is the New Testament's teaching about our lives as individual Christians and together as a church. In Romans 8:29, Paul says we are 'to be conformed to the image of his Son in order that he might be the firstborn among many brothers.' We are saved to holiness, which is measured in terms of our conformity to Jesus Christ.

Prior to becoming a minister I worked for a while as a management consultant, helping organizations work out their vision for the future. One technique I used was to ask executives to write an imaginary newspaper article that they would like to see written about them a certain number of years in the future. One person might say, 'I'd like to read that we produce the most creative products in our field.' Another might answer, 'I want to read that we have the finest craftsmanship.' Yet another might respond, 'Ours is the most courteous and helpful customer service staff.'

Christians do not need to imagine a newspaper article; we already have the Gospels, which show us the life and character of Jesus. Jesus was morally pure. Relationally, he showed sacrificial love: Jesus came 'not to be served, but to serve' (Matt. 20:28), and we are to be like that. Spiritually, Jesus delighted in prayer and loved God's Word. He said, 'Man shall not live by bread alone, but by every word that comes from the mouth of God' (Matt. 4:4). Jesus was obedient to God the Father, and he told us to pray, 'Your kingdom come, your will be done, on earth as it is in heaven' (Matt. 6:10). We are increasingly to be like that, both individually and as a church. The 'fruit of the Spirit' (Gal. 5:22) is a depiction of his character; the Sermon on the Mount, and especially its opening section, called 'The Beatitudes', describes what Jesus was like and provides the Bible's vision for us.

If the question is, 'What is our vision for the church?' our answer must be 'to be like Jesus—morally, spiritually, in our relationship with others and especially in our relationship to the Heavenly Father.

The question naturally arises as to whether we can attain to ultimate maturity in this life. Some people teach 'Christian perfectionism,' that a believer may become morally and spiritually perfect in this life, without any sin or spiritual flaw. This is thought of as a gift of God, usually through some supernatural experience. Can we attain to perfection in this life? The Bible's answer is No. Paul certainly did not consider himself to have arrived. He wrote in Philippians 3:12, 'Not that I have already obtained this or am already perfect, but I press on.' The apostle John wrote, 'If we say we have no sin, we deceive ourselves, and the truth is not in us' (1 John 1:8). It is not until after death that a Christian is fully complete and perfected in glory. John says of heaven, 'What we will be has not yet appeared; but we know that when he appears we will be like him, because we shall see him as he is' (1 John 3:2).

While we will never be perfect in this life, every Christian is entered on a life-long process of growth in holiness. This is called 'sanctification'. Verse 15 tells us we should 'no longer be children.' No matter how accomplished we are in life, when we are born again through faith in Jesus, we begin as spiritual babes and need to grow up. Jesus told us to have a *child-like* faith, one that trusts him completely, but not a *childish* faith, one that remains ignorant and weak in the things of God. This is why the idea that a church should aim its worship and teaching at the level of the most immature people is contrary to Scripture; we are to grow up as a church, not remain children.

This is a matter of vital importance to many Christians. They are stagnant, not growing in holiness and love. So many believers are like the tribes of Israel when they settled into the Promised Land of Canaan. They had conquered their major enemies, but there were still pockets of enemies all around. Instead of pressing forward with the conquest as God commanded, they settled in and took it easy. Before long, they were interacting with the pagans and then intermarrying with them. Within just years of the exodus and the conquest of the Promised Land, Israel was defiled through idolatry and other sins and ultimately came under God's judgment.

That is what happens when we settle onto a moral and spiritual plateau, accommodating our remaining sins and character flaws, not pressing onward to greater godliness. When later we fall into unthinkable sins that lead to ruin and misery, it will have been due to our failure to press on now to more and greater maturity. We never stand still; we always move either forward or backward. Our calling is to press on to this vision of maturity according to the stature of Christ.

A Plan for Growth

It is not enough, however, for a church, or other organization, to have a vision. There must also be a plan, a road map for getting there. This is what Paul provides in the opening lines of verse 13: 'Until we all attain to the unity of the faith and of the knowledge of the Son of God.' Here, unity, which was Paul's initial emphasis in this chapter, is joined to maturity; it is through increasing maturity that our unity becomes more durable and real. Paul says our growth comes through 'the unity of the faith and of the knowledge of the Son of God' (v. 13).

By 'the unity of the faith' Paul seems to mean our attainment of sound doctrine. He speaks of 'the faith'—not the act of faith but the content of our faith—which fits the immediate context and Paul's emphasis on the teaching office. This is contrary to conventional wisdom, which says that the way to cultivate unity is to avoid doctrine. But Paul's teaching is the very opposite; the only unity he knows is in the faith. Yes, doctrine divides; it divides light from darkness, the sheep from the goats. But doctrine also binds. John MacArthur writes, 'Disunity in the church comes from doctrinal ignorance and spiritual immaturity. When believers are properly taught…and when the body is thereby built up in spiritual maturity, unity of the faith is an inevitable result. Oneness in fellowship is impossible unless it is built on the foundation of commonly believed truth.'[314]

Grammatically, the phrase 'of the Son of God' belongs to both faith and knowledge. That means that we are to grow in the faith 'of the Son of God.' It is especially essential that Christians understand clearly the person and work of Jesus Christ: his full deity, his spotless life and sacrificial atoning death, his glorious resurrection, ascension into glory, his present intercession, and his soon return to usher in the new heavens and the new earth. It is through the rejection of these doctrines that turmoil and confusion comes upon the church; for us to attain to unity we must become sound in 'the faith of the Son of God.'

The Christian faith does not end, however, in the grasp of sound doctrine. It goes on, as Paul does, to 'the knowledge of the Son of God.' Paul is talking about the deep, personal knowledge that comes from walking with Christ. 'For me to live is Christ,' he said (Phil. 1:21). 'I count everything as loss because of the surpassing worth of knowing Christ Jesus my Lord,' Paul wrote (Phil. 3:8). He gave up his self-righteousness and self-reliance, 'that I may know him and the power of his resurrection, and may share in his suffering, becoming like him in his death, that by any means possible I may attain the resurrection from the dead' (Phil. 3:10–11).

This is the knowledge that Jesus spoke of when he prayed, 'This is eternal life, that they know you the only true God, and Jesus Christ whom you have sent' (John 17:3). James Boice explains this as 'knowledge that goes beyond what can be packed into the head, knowledge that also trickles down into the heart and flows out into the life in obedient and loving service to the Lord.'[315] The best synonym for what Paul means by 'knowledge' is 'love'; to know Christ is to love him because of his great love for us. We grow through our love for Christ and as his love flows through us.

This is Paul's two-fold plan for both unity and maturity: that we should come together in a sound grasp of biblical doctrine and that we should together engage in personal discipleship with Jesus Christ. This happens through the study of God's Word and through prayer, which along with the sacraments are called 'the means of grace.' These lead us to a life of obedience and loving service which elevate us in spiritual stature. This is the only way to Christian maturity. It is simple, though not easy, and it is thoroughly supernatural as we grow up in conformity to Christ through a life shaped by biblical truth and Christian love.

One of my chief pleasures in life is the fellowship of much older Christians, who are especially mature and Christ-like. Truly Christ-like saints are not only stalwart in battle but sweet and kind in person. In mature believers, you hear the Lion's roar and enjoy the gentleness of the Lamb. Believers like this give me hope for myself. I am on the same path that got them where they are: God's Word and prayer, worked out in obedience and in loving service. They remind me that if I just stay on the path I have wonderful things to come. This is what Paul means when he describes maturity in verse 13 as 'the fullness of Christ.' Jesus has glories for us and he fills us with his Spirit, so that we increasingly are able to look and live like him.

A Thirst and Its Remedy

In verse 14, Paul alerts us to a grave and two-fold threat to this process of growth. The first threat is the instability inherent to childhood. Paul writes, 'So that we may no longer be children, tossed to and fro by the waves and carried about by every wind of doctrine.' This describes someone whose beliefs change every time he hears something new, who is moved from his instable perch by every new doctrine that comes along, especially if lots of people are buying into it and it seems like the thing to do. Such people are like rudderless ships tossed back and forth by the churning waves and changing winds.

This danger is greatly compounded by the second threat to our growth, the deceit and cunning of false teachers. Paul adds, 'by human cunning, by craftiness in deceitful schemes.' The Bible teaches that Christians will face the threat of false teachers. These are not merely mistaken but well-intentioned ministers, but wolves in sheep's clothing, whose ambition is to fleece the lambs of God's flock and devour the souls of those who fall prey to their attacks. The fact that someone is a minister and seems well-meaning is not enough: his teaching must be tested according to God's Word. Charles Hodge said, 'Error can never be harmless, nor false teachers innocent.'[316] This means that the immature Christian who chooses a church based on the music and excitement, instead of on the essential matter of its doctrinal faithfulness, is in grave peril. The same is true for those who read purportedly Christian books that are in fact heretical and dangerous to your soul. There will always be men whose chief goal is personal glory, power, and wealth, and they will seldom find it convenient simply to teach God's Word faithfully.

This was something about which Paul specifically warned the elders of the church in Ephesus. Acts 20:30 tells us that in his last meeting with them, Paul said, 'Fierce wolves will come in among you; not sparing the flock; and from among your own selves will arise men speaking twisted things, to draw away the disciples after them.' Jesus warned us that the ultimate source of false and deceitful teaching is none other than the devil, who, after all, used this very tactic to lead Adam and Eve into the first sin, deceiving them with crafty words. Jesus told a parable in which the devil planted weeds in the garden of the Lord. 'The weeds are the sons of the evil one,' Jesus explained (Matt. 13:38).

Let us therefore not be shocked at the idea that there might be deliberately deceitful teachers in the guise of gospel ministers. How do we tell the difference between the true and the false? Paul described a true ministry in 2 Corinthians 4:2: 'We have renounced disgraceful, under-handed ways. We refuse to practice cunning or to tamper with God's Word, but by the open statement of the truth we would commend ourselves to everyone's conscience in the sight of God.' This is the kind of ministry from which you want to learn, one which plainly sets forth God's Word of truth.

It would be hard to find a more accurate description of the evangelical movement in our own time than the one Paul gives in verse 14. It often seems that every novel teaching, even if blatantly opposite to Scripture, immediately acquires a massive, fervent following. Faithful ministers are scorned for not jumping onto a bandwagon that is leading people straight to ruin. The reason for this situation is our generation's determination to avoid maturity at all cost. The sad thing is that we have children who need us to be adults, yet as churches pursue worldly agendas and downplay the teaching of God's Word, there are few genuinely mature believers in our ranks.

What is the remedy? Individually, it is the one given by Peter: 'Like new-born infants, long for the pure spiritual milk, that by it you may grow up to salvation' (1 Pet. 2:2). You need to start growing up, which means getting serious about your knowledge of God's Word. It is always when someone starts going to Sunday School or gets involved in a Bible study, and starts reading his or her own Bible along with quality books on theology and the Christian life, that they start to grow. I know many infant Christians who suffer for their immaturity, but who will not get serious about feeding on God's Word. Until they do, there is little I can do for them apart from prayer.

Corporately, as a church, the remedy is the one Paul writes of in verse 15: 'Rather, speaking the truth in love, we are to grow up in every way into him who is the head, into Christ.' This does not mean that we should all become fascinated with obscure points of theology. Rather, I find that the more mature a believer is the more he or she loves the most basic truths and the plainest doctrines that are central to Christianity. We are to speak these truths lovingly to one another, exhorting those who are going astray, correcting error without arrogance, and explaining the faith from the Bible to lead people to a personal knowledge of and intimate discipleship with Christ.

A more literal rendering of verse 15 would say not, 'Speaking the truth in love,' but 'truthing in love.' Certainly, we have a great need to speak and to hear the truths of God's Word. But they were meant to be lived, and that is their most persuasive form of expression.

Truth and love together are a sure sign of the presence and work of the Holy Spirit. On our own we can often have one or the other: truth without love, which is not Christian truth; or love without truth, which is not Christian love. But when we have truth with love, when we are 'truthing in love,' God is living through us as he grows us into the maturity of conformity to Christ.

Harry Ironside tells of a man who was asked, 'What have you found to be the best translation of the New Testament?' He replied, 'My mother's.' His friend said, 'Your mother's? I didn't know she was a scholar. Did she translate the New Testament?' The man responded, 'My mother was not a scholar, she could not read a word of Greek, but she translated the New Testament into her beautiful life, and that made more of an impression on me than anything else I have ever known.'[317] That is the way we are all to grow in Christ, 'truthing in love.'

Blessed Is the Man

I am reminded by this passage of Psalm 1. It, too, speaks of a path that leads to a glorious vision. But it warns us that there is another path that so many people are taking today. Psalm 1 warns us against 'the counsel of the wicked,' which leads us 'in the way of sinners.' Are you on that path? Have you no interest in the Christian faith and a personal knowledge of Jesus Christ? Psalm 1, along with the whole of God's Word, warns you of where the road of sin and unbelief leads. It says, 'The wicked will not stand in the judgment, nor sinners in the congregation of the righteous... but the way of the wicked will perish' (vv. 5–6). There is a holy God who governs this world, so that sin leads to misery in this life and eternal condemnation in the life to come. But that same God offers the free gift of forgiveness and eternal life through faith in Jesus Christ.

Like our passage, Psalm 1 gives a vision of where the life of truth and love leads. 'Blessed is the man,' it says, '[whose] delight is in the law of the Lord, and on his law he meditates day and night' (vv. 1–2). Why is he blessed? Verse 3 says, 'He is like a tree planted by streams of water that yields its fruit in its season, and its leaf does not wither. In all that he does, he prospers.'

That is a vision of the blessing that comes through Christ-like maturity. Do you believe that it can be true of you? Can you be such a blessed man or woman? Can a person like you be changed so that you are more and more like Christ, and that you become like a mighty oak, standing firm against the changes of weather, your roots fixed deep in the gospel soil and drinking from the waters of eternal life? The Bible says you can and you will, if you commit your way to God and to his Word.

Paul gives us a challenge in verse 15: 'We are to grow up in every way into him who is the head, into Christ.' But if you will turn to Christ in faith and sincerely commit to his plan of spiritual growth, this vision of maturity comes with a great promise, from Philippians 1:6: 'He who began a good work in you will bring it to completion at the day of Jesus Christ' (Phil. 1:6).

48

Growing Up Together

Ephesians 4:15–16

Ephesians 4:15–16 brings us to the end of a major section in Paul's letter. An outline of Ephesians shows its value to any church that is laying a foundation for the future. Ephesians has four main sections: chapter 1 gives praise to God for his grace and includes a prayer that we might come to know his power; chapter 2 presents Paul's doctrine of salvation; Ephesians 3:1–4:16 focuses on the church; and the final chapters give Paul's moral exhortation for Christian living.

As we conclude this section on the church, I would like to look back and summarize Paul's teaching. The reason for this teaching on the church—indeed, the reason for the church itself—is that God's plan for salvation has a corporate dimension. We saw this in chapter 2 at the end of Paul's teaching on salvation. God saves us together as fellow citizens in his kingdom, as family members in his household, and as a temple in which God will dwell by the Spirit (Eph. 2:19–22). God saved us to be his people, and so we have the church.

In chapter 3, Paul expressed concern that the church not be discouraged by his or their suffering. Instead, they should realize that 'through the church'—that is, by saving sinners and preserving them through trials and strengthening them by his grace—God is displaying his 'manifold wisdom…to the rulers and authorities in the heavenly places' (3:10). Meanwhile, together in the church, we believers are coming to know 'the breadth and length and height and depth, and to know the love of Christ that surpasses knowledge' (3:17–19).

In chapter 4, Paul gives his first practical charge, exhorting us all to be 'eager to maintain the unity of the Spirit in the bond of peace' (4:3). This unity contains our diversity of gifts, and as we minister in truth and love we are built up into Christ-like maturity.

If we put all this together, we can ask, 'What, then, is God's purpose for the church?' This is an important question and the answer will make a great difference in our thinking. Some people say the purpose of the church is evangelism. After all, Jesus told the apostles to 'Go and make disciples' (Matt. 28:19). Those who think this look on the church as an army conquering the world through its witness.

Others will answer that the church's purpose is to do ministry in the world. Jesus said, 'I was hungry and you gave me food, I was thirsty and you gave me drink, I was a stranger and you welcomed me, I was naked and you clothed me, I was sick and you visited me, I was in prison and you visited me' (Matt. 25:35–38). Under this view, the church is mainly a giant social service agency.

Still others think the church is to be a safe place where we can escape the damage occurring in our world. Those who think this way look on the church as a fortress and a refuge.[318]

Let me suggest, according to this long teaching on the church in Ephesians, that none of these is the purpose of the church. Certainly, these are things the church is to do. The church must evangelize and minister and protect—but that is not God's purpose for the church itself. We give our children work to do—chores, study, sports activities—but none of them are our child's purpose. According to Paul, the purpose of the church is that we, God's people, should grow so that we finally attain to Christ-like holiness and maturity. Ephesians 4:15 sums it all up: 'Speaking the truth in love, we are to grow up in every way into him who is the head, into Christ.'

God's purpose for us together in the church is Christ-like maturity—individually and as a church. Genesis 1:27 says that 'God created man in his own image.' Together as a church we are to fulfill that purpose by reflecting God's character as we grow into Christ and live out his commands. In a world filled with strife, we are to experience unity; in a world darkened by error we are to embrace truth; and in a world broken by sin we are to enjoy love. Through these means we are to become more like Christ and to know him better.

From Whom? Christ!

In his teaching on the church, Paul has laid out numerous principles, but he reminds us in these final two verses of the most important of all, namely, that the church's health and growth depends utterly on its relationship to Jesus Christ. Every blessing flows to us from Christ through our union with him in faith. This is summed up in the opening two words of verse 16: 'from whom'. That is essential: it is 'from Christ' that we grow and are built up.

This is, of course, the point of the metaphor describing Christ as the head and the church as his body. Paul sees us in verse 15 growing up so that the body becomes proportional to the head. This is to happen 'in every way'—spiritually, emotionally, intellectually, morally—so that the church is a fitting counterpart to Jesus its Lord. The head controls the whole organism. Life and direction and energy come from the head; the purpose of the body is to serve the head and to be at the head's disposal. To serve Christ we need to become mature; we need to take on the character of the head and to possess the stature called for by the glory of our union with Christ.

The head is absolutely necessary to the life of the body. You can lose an arm or a foot and still live; but severed from the head, the body dies. This reminds us of Jesus' teaching in John 15. 'I am the vine,' he said; 'you are the branches. Whoever abides in me and I in him, he it is that bears much fruit, for apart from me you can do nothing' (John 15:5). This is a comprehensive picture of the Christian life—both for us as individuals and as a church. We grow and bear fruit as we are joined to Jesus and as his life flows in us. But when the branch is severed a process of death begins. The branch may look all right for a while, but death is inevitable, because the branch depends on the life of the vine.

I said that this is true of us individually, and it is. The only way for us to maintain our spiritual health and to grow is to be vitally connected to Jesus Christ. This is why each of us must open our minds and hearts daily to God's Word. This is why we must pray. This is why it makes such a difference if we come to church and turn our faces to God and renew our faith in Christ. This is the only way to thrive spiritually, and even to survive in the faith. If you take the strongest, most vibrant Christian and then cut him or her off from the vine—by the cares of life or by work ambitions, or by the allure of sin—a process of decline begins. Why? Because we depend on the spiritual life that comes from Jesus! He is the vine; we are his branches.

The same is true of the church. When a church is fixed on the gospel, when the people are weekly called to put their faith in a crucified and resurrected Savior, when the food of God's Word is regularly served, then there is growth and a process of maturity, because from Christ we gain life. But when the church is diverted by a thirst for worldly acclaim, by a craving for entertainment, by political concerns or social activism—even if these things are themselves worthwhile—a process of death sets in because Christ has been forgotten and we are not abiding in him as our first priority. This is why a faithful gospel ministry, focused on Christ, is not flashy or impressive to the eye—yet it yields the fruit of healthy spiritual growth, because from Christ comes life and power and strength for godly things.

Christ is not only the source of our life and blessing, but he defines the goal to which we are growing in maturity. Verse 15 says, 'We are to grow up in every way into him who is the head, into Christ.' This is what makes the Christian life such a thrill. Do you remember the first time you read the Gospels and your mind was staggered by the beauty and glory of Jesus? Perhaps it has happened recently in your Bible reading. You find yourself lingering over the text, just picturing Jesus. The Beatitudes in the Sermon on the Mount (Matt. 5) and Paul's teaching of the fruit of the Spirit (Gal. 5:22) describe his character. The Song of Solomon was talking about Jesus when it said, 'His mouth is sweetness itself; he is altogether lovely' (S. of S. 5:16).

Here is the point: God intends for us to become like him. In 2 Corinthians 3, Paul speaks about the way Christ works in us by the Spirit. He says that to be a Christian is to be like Moses who stood face-to-face before God so that his face shined with glory, except that our radiance is within. Paul concludes: 'We all, with unveiled face, beholding the glory of the Lord, are being transformed into the same image from one degree of glory to another.' Then, just as he emphasizes in our passage, he writes: 'For this comes from the Lord who is the Spirit.'

This has the most practical implications for the life of a church. People will often speak of a 'church filled with life' when it has a lot of activity going on. But Paul reminds us that it matters very much what kind of activity it is. The only activities that will actually contribute to God's purpose in the church are those that are connecting us with Jesus, that sit us at his feet as his disciples and teach us to trust and follow him like sheep with their Shepherd.

I earlier observed that when a church loses or deviates from its message about Christ that it begins to die. Invariably, when this happens, it will try to stimulate life through activities. It may start a sports league or sponsor a Boy Scout Troop. It may become an arts or cultural center, where people come for childcare or to learn karate or ballet. But none of these activities will actually restore life. The only thing that will restore life is a reconnection of the body to its head, of the branch to the vine. What we must do, then, are those things that lead people into and strengthen their relationship to Jesus Christ. The kind of activities I just mentioned are not bad, but we must ensure that God's Word and prayer are always involved, that they are intentionally used for talking about and learning to trust Jesus Christ, 'from whom,' Paul says, the whole body grows and is built up.

Fitting Together

In these verses, Paul emphasizes the great principle that it is from Christ the head that his body, the church, spiritually grows. As we look at verse 16 we find that this involves both a corporate and an individual dimension. Paul writes, 'From whom the whole body, joined and held together by every joint with which it is equipped, when each part is working properly, makes the body grow so that it builds itself up in love.' This means that to be healthy and grow, the church members must fit together and properly function.

This makes the important point that our individual maturity is shown by our ability to fit in easily with other believers and work harmoniously in the church. There is nothing so incongruous as a Christian who can't get along with people—especially if he or she has a great deal of Bible knowledge and has been in the church for a long time.

In verse 16, Paul uses an anatomical metaphor. He says we are 'joined together.' Martyn Lloyd-Jones, who was a medical doctor before he was a preacher, envisions two bones that fit together like a ball and a socket. He says,

> In the case of a joint in the body there is a kind of cup on one bone and into that cup there fits a kind of ball at the end of another bone. The surfaces of both are smooth so that there is no friction, and everything works easily and harmoniously and in an effective manner…This should be true of the members of the Church.'[319]

Furthermore, we are to be 'held together.' This means that we are to be close-knit in our affections. This is what maturity does for a church as life flows into it from Christ: we work together easily and are close-knit in love. This is what makes a church a joy, and a place where people really can grow.

The earliest Christians experienced this as they were filled with the Holy Spirit (Acts 2:42–46):

> They devoted themselves to the apostles' teaching and fellowship, to the breaking of bread and the prayers. And awe came upon every soul…And all who believed were together and had all things in common…Day by day, attending the temple together and breaking bread in their homes, they received their food with glad and generous hearts, praising God and having favor with all the people.

Paul completes his picture of Christians working together by saying they are 'joined and held together by every joint with which it is equipped.' This is not an easy statement to interpret. What is clear is that the thing that holds us together is also what equips us. If we consider this in the broader context, we see that Paul means Christ's ministry to us through the Holy Spirit, especially as he provides us with spiritual gifts. These are the ligaments that hold the body together. Verse 7 began this section, saying: 'Grace was given to each one of us according to the measure of Christ's gift.' He emphasizes this again in verse 16, talking about every part being equipped, each receiving the proper amount of supply. Christ's Spirit is working in each of us, giving us grace and also binding us together as we are indwelt by the same Holy Spirit.

We should note that it is the ministry of God's Word that especially binds and equips God's people. This is why Paul focused on the teaching gift and offices in verse 11, and why he described maturity in verse 14 in terms of doctrinal stability and soundness. The only unity Paul knows is 'the unity of the faith and of the knowledge of the Son of God' (v. 13). It is especially the sound teaching and believing of God's Word that binds a church and equips its people for ministry. It is, he says, 'speaking the truth in love' that we grow up together.

What You Can Do for the Church

The fact that Paul's teaching focuses on the church working together does not lessen our responsibility as individuals but increases it. It means that we all affect one another and that we all vitally matter. We ask, what kind of church are we going to be? What are people going to experience when they walk into our church? What kind of spiritual life will our children experience as they grow up? Many think this all depends on the minister, but according to the Bible it depends on us all; you personally determine what kind of church we will be.

This, again, is evident from the metaphor of the church as a body. Paul always emphasizes the importance of each part: a body needs more than just a mouth and eyes, but needs hands, feet, caring arms, and listening ears. Christ has given you a gift and a place and a ministry. You don't have to be somebody else. You can just be who God made you, with the gifts Christ has apportioned to the church through you. As you mature and grow so too does the church.

But this works the other way as well. Just as each of us help build the church, we each can harm the church and cause it pain. Anyone who has ever had a splinter in a finger or toe knows how this is. Likewise, anyone in the church who gossips or constantly criticizes, who stirs up trouble or sows division does real and serious harm to Christ's work in the church. Paul said that we must be 'eager to maintain the unity of the Spirit in the bond of peace' (Eph. 4:3). We should be loathe that any of us should cause division in the church or introduce false teaching that harms the church's unity in the truth. We should gladly suffer wrong, gladly lose out, gladly set aside our preference rather than disturb the church's precious unity which is so essential to maturity. Truth, love, and unity—these are essential and cause the church to grow. Everything else is secondary.

This means the most important thing you can do for Christ's church is not giving money, or serving in a ministry, or even sharing the gospel with others. These are all essential, but not the most important thing you can do. The most important thing is that you grow in spiritual maturity. Take a look at Jesus' Beatitudes in Matthew 5, or the fruit of the Spirit in Galatians 5:22. Commit yourself to spiritual growth through God's Word, through worship, and through prayer and ministry. As you mature in Christ, you will help us all to fit together and be close-knit so that Christ's ministry to us will not be impeded and we will all grow and be built up.

The Greatest Thing There Is

It is always good to close a study on the same note with which the biblical writer closes, especially when he is wrapping up an extended doctrinal section. Paul closes verse 16 by speaking of love. All this 'makes the body grow so that it builds itself up in love.'

In 1 Corinthians 13:13 Paul spoke of 'faith, hope, and love,' and says, 'the greatest of these is love.' He obviously still feels that way, because Paul mentions love six times in his teaching on the church. We are to 'bear with one another in love'

(4:2), 'speak the truth in love' (4:15), be built up in love (4:16), and through all this we are to be 'rooted and grounded in love' (3:17) so as together to comprehend 'what is the breadth and length and height and depth' of 'the love of Christ that surpasses knowledge' (3:18–19). Paul says the church is not the church without love. Without love we cannot have unity, and without love we really do not have truth.

In his sermon on this text, James Montgomery Boice set out to prove that love is the most important of all the marks of the church. He did it by looking at each of the other distinguishing marks of the church and noting the importance of love to them all. First, he spoke about joy. 'Subtract love from joy. What do you have? You have the kind of hedonistic reveling found in the secular world, the pursuit of pleasure for its own sake.' Joy without love is ungodly. What about holiness? That is an essential mark of the church. But Boice noted that holiness without love is self-righteousness, 'the kind of thing that distinguished the scribes and Pharisees of Christ's day,' who observed external laws but were so filled with hatred that they crucified Jesus. There is no holiness without love.

What about truth? Boice writes, 'Take love from truth. The result is bitter orthodoxy. Truth remains, but it is proclaimed in such an unpleasant, harsh manner that it fails to win anybody.' The same is true of mission and evangelism. Without love, mission is imperialism and evangelism becomes empire-building, so that 'we work to win people for our denomination or organization, but not for Christ.' What about unity itself? Can there be Christian unity without love? Boice rejects such a thing, saying, 'Take love from unity and you have ecclesiastical tyranny.'[320]

We see why Paul called love the greatest thing, and why he finished his teaching on the church by talking about love. We are called to have unity in the truth and to grow in spiritual stature—this is our calling and purpose together in Christ. But let us never forget that all of this is nothing without love! The whole point is that we would become like Christ in his love and that we would come to know together what his love is like. So while we must foster unity and we must use our gifts and we must stand together on the truth, there is nothing more important than that we do so in love. Boice concludes his treatment by saying this:

> If instead of subtracting love, you express love—for God the Father, the Lord Jesus Christ, the Bible, one another, and the world—what do you have? You have all the other marks of the church, because they naturally follow. Love for God leads to joy; nothing is more joyful than knowing and loving him. Love for the Lord Jesus Christ leads to holiness; as he said, 'If you love me, you will obey what I command' (John 14:15). Love for the Word of God leads to truth; if we love the Bible, we will read it and grow in a knowledge of what the Word contains. Love for the world leads to mission. Love for other believers leads to unity.[321]

No wonder the apostle John wrote, 'God is love, and whoever abides in love abides in God, and God abides in him' (1 John 4:16).

49

Darkened and Lost

Ephesians 4:17–19

The unifying theme to Paul's letter to the Ephesians is the reality and power of the Christian life. This comes through in each of its four sections. Chapter 1 concluded with Paul's prayer that his readers should know 'the power' God has 'toward us who believe' (Eph. 1:18). Chapter 2 begins Paul's teaching on salvation by saying we are all naturally enslaved to sin and to the agenda of the devil. But believers in Christ have undergone a spiritual resurrection, so that we are now 'God's workmanship, created in Christ Jesus for good works' (Eph. 2:10). Paul's section on the church teaches that we are together to 'grow up into Christ' and become spiritually mature (Eph. 4:15). Now, in the last section of the book, Paul insists that our calling demands a holy life, for which we have power through our union with Jesus Christ.

The Two Ways

In presenting this holy Christian life, Paul begins by pointing out what we might refer to as the Bible's doctrine of the 'Two Ways.' According to the Bible there are two humanities co-existing in the world, two ways of living, and two destinations to which they are headed. Psalm 1 spoke of those who walk 'in the counsel of the wicked,' stand 'in the way of sinners,' and sit 'in the seat of scoffers.' They are described as chaff—that is, they lead an empty life and ultimately come under God's judgment: 'The way of the wicked will perish' (v. 6). In contrast is 'the blessed man.' He walks not in that wicked, unbelieving way, but 'his delight is in the law of the Lord.' His life is 'like a tree planted by streams of water that yields its fruit in its season.' The blessed man enjoys favor with God and receives everlasting life.

Jesus similarly spoke of two ways. 'The gate is wide,' he said, 'and the way is easy that leads to destruction, and those who enter by it are many. For the gate is narrow and the way is hard that leads to life, and those who find it are few' (Matt. 7:13–14).

People sometimes claim that Christianity should never be negative, only positive. But it is impossible to do that and be biblically faithful. Christianity always involves both a No and a Yes. There is sin to be rejected and godliness to be embraced. On this Paul insists in Ephesians 4:17: 'Now this I say and testify in the Lord, that you must no longer walk as the Gentiles do.' By 'Gentiles' he is speaking not ethnically—for his readers were Gentiles—but spiritually. They are no longer to live pagan lives. Paul insists, writing,

'I testify in the Lord.' There is always a tendency for people to think they can profess faith in Christ and live the way they did before. But you cannot. To be a Christian is to leave the old life behind and live a new life. We leave darkness for light, hatred for love, selfishness for servanthood, worldliness for holiness, and sin for obedience to God's will.

There are two kinds of people, two ways, and two destinies. You either belong to Jesus Christ and to the heavenly Father, or you belong to the world and to the devil. You are destined for heaven or hell. If you belong to Jesus and are headed to heaven, then you must be on the path of holiness. Isaiah said, 'A highway shall be there, and it shall be called the Way of Holiness; the unclean shall not pass over it' (Isa. 35:8). If you are not seeking to be more godly and Christ-like, if you are unwilling to turn from your sins, then you should wonder if you belong to Jesus and are going to heaven. There are only two ways, and, Paul says, 'You must no longer walk as the Gentiles do,' if you are on the way of Christ.

The True Cause of Immorality

This is how Paul introduces his teaching on the Christian life. It is a sober teaching and an urgent exhortation. We must abandon the sinful, pagan life, and to do this we need to understand it, which is where Paul takes us in these verses. He begins: 'You must no longer walk as the Gentiles do, in the futility of their minds' (Eph. 4:17). The first thing this tells us about the empty, pagan life is its cause: the reason for immorality is godlessness. 'They are darkened in their understanding, alienated from the life of God' (v. 18).

Notice the role of false thinking in this description. Verse 17 speaks of 'the futility of their minds,' coupled with the statement that 'they are darkened in their understanding.' This argues that what we think about God determines the course of our lives. People think they can be indifferent about religious convictions and that this is a peripheral subject, but they are wrong. What we think about God—his existence, his character, his will, his relationship to us—shapes everything else we believe and do. James Boice says of the non-Christian, 'He does not know God; so he cannot think properly. Everything is out of place, and his disordered and sinful conduct reflects his disordered, sinful mind.'[322]

This is what has happened historically in the United States. Early in the twentieth century, the churches began teaching that the Bible is not reliable and that its picture of God is not accurate. Back then they turned away from biblical doctrine but they kept the morality. But it didn't last. By the 1960's, as Judges 2:10 says, 'there arose another generation after them who did not know the Lord.' The result was the moral chaos that has only grown worse year by year.

Some might object, saying, 'Many non-Christian people lead moral lives.' I would agree to that and point to God's common grace. But I would also argue that the more a person or society departs from biblical truth and values, the more immoral they become. I would further argue the record of those atheists who really thought about their rejection of God. What do we find among the philosophers and intellectuals who most forcefully reject God? What we find is a pattern of immorality. Paul Johnson wrote a book called *Intellectuals* that made this point. He chronicled the lives of the leading atheistic intellectuals of the last two hundred years, and in every case they led morally sordid lives characterized by sexual debauchery, dishonesty, and personal cruelty.

Typical among these atheist intellectuals is Jean-Jacques Rousseau, the French intellectual whose arguments for state control not only of education but also of child-raising are back in vogue today. But his argument arose as a self-justification for the fact that Rousseau abandoned his first five children on the very day of their birth, leaving them outside a hospital without even bothering to name them, probably soon to die.[323] Johnson's survey of the lives of Rousseau, Marx, Tolstoy, Hemingway, Bertrand Russell and Jean-Paul Sartre shows that those who most consciously reject God are the most immoral of all people. They betrayed every possible trust, having countless affairs even with the wives of their closest friends, were dishonest in every aspect of life, and callously ruined countless lives.

This is why when Paul speaks of darkness he means more than intellectual darkness. He means a spiritual darkness that penetrates the will and the affections. Jesus said, 'If the light in you is darkness, how great is the darkness' (Matt. 6:23). Sinful man is alienated not merely from the knowledge of God but from the life of God. They know nothing of the spiritual life in fellowship with God, and therefore they are infatuated by things like wealth, fame, sinful pleasures and sordid entertainments. The well of the human nature is polluted by sin, and until we are born again by God's Spirit we are darkened in our whole inner life.

This means that if you have a child or a neighbor or a co-worker who is living immorally, you must realize that the problem is their darkened minds and their alienation from God. The first priority must never be to reform their lives but to lead them to the knowledge of God through his Word. This is why preaching should teach us about God—what God is like, what he has done, what he expects and what he promises to those who trust in him. When they know this, and are born again, as Peter says, 'through the living and abiding word of God' (1 Pet. 1:23), then they will no longer be futile in their thinking, darkened in their understanding, and alienated from the divine life. Hosea 4:6 says, 'My people are destroyed for lack of knowledge,' and so it is when the church stops teaching about God.

The True Cause of Unbelief

If the reason for immorality is unbelief, then we need also to understand the true cause of unbelief, to which Paul turns in the second half of verse 18. Their unbelief is 'because of the ignorance that is in them, due to their hardness of heart.' This assigns unbelief to two sources, first to ignorance and second to moral hardening.

There are a number of reasons why people are ignorant of God. Increasing numbers of people today have never read the Bible. One of the great missionary endeavors that is still going on is translating the Bible into new languages, so people will no longer be ignorant. But according to the Bible, there really is no one who ought to be ignorant of God because he is powerfully revealed in the created world. Paul writes in Romans 1:19-20 that, 'What can be known about God is plain to them [all], because God has shown it to them. For his invisible attributes, namely, his eternal power and divine nature, have been clearly perceived, ever since the creation of the world, in the things that have been made. So they are without excuse.' In other words, though people are ignorant of God they do not have an excuse for such ignorance, since God's creation effectually reveals him to everyone, even without the Bible.

Why, then, are people ignorant? It is in part because of the devil. Second Corinthians 4:4 says, 'The god of this world has blinded the minds of the unbelievers, to keep them from seeing the light of the gospel of the glory of Christ, who is the image of God.' The devil does this in many ways, partly through deception and partly by keeping us so occupied with sinful and worldly things that we never think at all.

But another reason for our ignorance is our sinful nature, inherited from Adam as a result of his sin. First Corinthians 2:14 says, 'The natural person does not accept the things of the Spirit of God, for they are folly to him, and he is not able to understand them because they are spiritually discerned.' They are spiritually blind! Note that Paul says not only that the natural person *does not* accept God but that he *is not able to*. Such is the plight of sinful man. Ignorance is not merely something that is true about them, so that it can be solved simply by providing information; no, the ignorance is 'in them.' Spiritual darkness is characteristic of our sinful nature apart from God's regenerating work by the Holy Spirit.

Martyn Lloyd-Jones tells of two great British politicians, William Wilberforce, a Christian who lead the anti-slavery movement in England, and his close friend the Prime Minister, William Pitt. Wilberforce was constantly talking to Pitt about Christ and encouraging him to come with him to a London church to hear an outstanding and faithful preacher. Finally the Sunday came when Pitt was free to join him and Wilberforce found himself overwhelmed with the power of the gospel as it was preached that day. As Lloyd-Jones describes it, 'He reveled and gloried in the truth, having a feast for his soul, his whole man being moved to its depths; occasionally he wondered what was happening to his friend.' But as they walked out, Pitt turned to him and said, 'You know, Wilberforce, I have not the slightest idea what that man has been talking about.' As Lloyd-Jones points out, Pitt was the greater intellect and the greater man, but he was spiritually blind and deaf. Ignorance was 'in him.'[324]

This leads to the second cause of unbelief, a *moral* cause. Paul says it is due not merely to ignorance but 'due to their hardness of heart.' Literally, Paul speaks here of a 'heart of stone,' one that is rigid and unyielding to God and his truth. Whether they think about it or not, the unbeliever is in moral rebellion against the God they know. Returning to Romans 1, where Paul says the creation reveals God to everyone, he explains, but they 'by their unrighteousness suppress the truth...For although they knew God, they did not honor him as God or give thanks to him, but—*note the connection to our passage*—they became futile in their thinking, and their foolish hearts were darkened' (Rom. 1:18, 20–21). Paul says that sinful men and women suppress their knowledge of God because of their rebellion against him, and as a result their hearts become hard, and they are darkened and lost.

I earlier mentioned Paul Johnson's study of unbelieving intellectuals and their great depravity. Another one of them was Aldous Huxley, one of the leading atheistic thinkers and writers of the twentieth century. In his autobiography Huxley admitted this:

> I had motives for not wanting the world to have a meaning; consequently I assumed that it had none, and was able without any difficulty to find satisfying reasons for this assumption...The philosopher who finds no meaning for this world is not concerned exclusively with the problem of pure metaphysics; he is also concerned to prove that there is no valid reason why he personally should not do as he wants to...For myself...the philosophy of meaningless was essentially an instrument of liberation, sexual and political.[325]

This is something we need to realize about high-minded philosophers and about the man on the street. Cornelius Van Til says of such supposedly objective unbelievers, 'These men are sinners. They have "an axe to grind." They want to suppress the truth in unrighteousness.'[326] A. W. Tozer agreed, writing, 'I do not believe there is anybody that ever rejects Jesus Christ on philosophical grounds. The man who continues in his rejection of Christ has a pet sin somewhere—he's in love with iniquity. He rejects Jesus on moral grounds, and then hides behind false philosophy—philosophical grounds.'[327]

This insight is important for all of us, from ministers to parents to friends. Donald Grey Barnhouse tells of speaking at a college campus, when a young co-ed came up to him angrily denouncing Christianity. She explained that she had grown up in a Christian home, but now that she had gone to college and had her mind opened up and met real people she was set free from religious shackles. Barnhouse wisely asked her to step aside, and then quietly asked her, 'Tell me, what month did you come to this conclusion?' She replied, 'Well, in November.' Barnhouse then kindly said, 'Tell me, what happened in October?' At once the woman broke down in tears, confessing that she had fallen into sexual sin and had only then rejected Christianity. Many of us will likewise meet supposedly intellectual unbelievers who are in fact masking their bondage to sin.

You see in this, therefore, the futility of trying to reach unbelieving people through entertainment or mere human persuasion. They are blind in their ignorance, so we must preach Christ, the light that shines in the darkness, and do so with much prayer. And we must respond to moral rebellion and bondage with spiritual power; Romans 1:16 tells us, 'I am not ashamed of the gospel, for it is the power of God for salvation to everyone who believes.' This cannot be said about anything else. God alone can save the unbelieving sinner, and he does it through our witness of the gospel. This, after all, is how we were saved, 'For,' says Paul, 'God who said, "Let light shine out of darkness," has shone in our hearts to give the light of the knowledge of the glory of God in the face of Jesus Christ' (2 Cor. 4:6).

The Emptiness of an Ungodly Life

In verse 19, Paul describes the emptiness of the godless life, which we are commanded to leave behind: 'They have become callous and have given themselves up to sensuality, greedy to practice every kind of impurity.' The life of sin, without God, is one that goes nowhere except round and round. Indeed, the one direction this spiral moves is downward, until finally the rebel against God sinks into hell for all eternity. It is a futile, empty, and ultimately ruinous life.

Paul speaks of a hardened heart, one that has lost all sensitivity, like feet that are calloused and rough. We noticed how often the intellectual unbelievers fell into sexual sin and this is the very thing Paul describes: 'They have given themselves up to sensuality, greedy to practice every kind of impurity' (v. 19). It is interesting that he puts it that way, for in Romans 1 he says that it is God who gives idolaters over to this as a judgment on their unbelief. Romans 1:24–26 says, 'Therefore God gave them up in the lusts of their hearts to impurity, to the dishonoring of their bodies among themselves, because they exchanged the truth of God for a lie...God gave them up to dishonorable passions.' Paul goes on to describe every kind of impurity and ultimately the very kind of homosexual perversions so rampant in our society today. Indeed, Romans 1:24–26, along with Ephesians 4:19, is a perfect description of our own godless society. Paul says that is God's judgment on unbelief and idolatry. But in our passage he shows that this also is a willing descent into debauchery.

The expression, 'greedy to practice every kind of impurity' indicates the insatiability of perverse sins. The point is, as the *New International Version* puts it, that they sin 'with a continual lust for more.' Sin never satisfies, but a continually hardened heart becomes more and more insensitive so that more and more sin is needed in a desperate and hopeless quest for satisfaction.

Is this how you want to live? Is this how you have been living? If you are partaking of the sensuality of our society today, watching the filthy soap-operas or reading the sensual magazines—men's or women's—or indulging in pornography or adulterous sex, realize where this is leading you. It is not leading to satisfaction but rather to a calloused heart and a life of bondage. It is an empty life, beginning with a willful ignorance of the God who is there, with a heart that is hard to his Word, and a mind that is closed to his truth. Why will you live any longer in such a condition, on such a path that leads to hell—both in this life and in eternity beyond—when God calls you to the grace and mercy he offers you in Jesus Christ.

Good News—No Longer!

I have said that Christians must respond to this situation with the gospel of Jesus Christ. Where is the gospel in a passage like this? I find it in two words, found in verse 17: 'no longer.' Paul writes, 'Now this I say and testify in the Lord, that you must no longer walk as the Gentiles do, in the futility of their minds.' This is what Jesus Christ offers to you: 'No longer' to sin. He says, 'If you abide in my word…you will know the truth, and the truth will set you free' (John 8:32–33). Sin alienates us from the life of God, but through Jesus Christ we receive new life, heavenly life, power from on high for godliness. Jesus says, 'So if the Son sets you free, you will be free indeed' (John 8:36).

If you are a Christian, you need no longer live as you formerly have; indeed, you must not. Turn to the light of God's Word and ask him to cast out the darkness that was formerly in your mind. Turn to the Lord Jesus and ask him to change and sanctify your desires. It was precisely with this in mind that he promised, 'Ask and you shall receive, seek and you will find, knock and the door will be opened' (Luke 11:10). Asking must be combined with seeking—which means acting upon your prayer—and with knocking—which means persevering in faith. But Jesus promises the Holy Spirit with power. He said of the polluted streams of sin and of the world, 'Everyone who drinks of this water will be thirsty again, but whoever drinks of the water that I will give him will never be thirsty forever. The water that I will give him will become in him a spring of water welling up to eternal life' (John 4:13–14).

No longer! That is our gospel. And through Jesus Christ it is the reality to which we are called and empowered by God's grace.

50

In the School of Christ

Ephesians 4:20–29

One of the issues Paul constantly had to address in his ministry was the idea that his teaching of salvation by God's grace alone promoted sinful living. We see this in Romans 6:2, after he has just finished presenting the doctrine of justification through faith alone and apart from good works. Paul has to write, 'What shall we say then? Are we to continue in sin that grace may abound? By no means!'

We find Paul having to address the same problem in our study of Ephesians, which indicates that people often think this way. Paul has just described the pagan life, saying that Christians must no longer live that way. But some at least among his readers did not believe it was important to lead a holy life. So Paul writes in verses 20–21, 'But that is not how you learned Christ!—assuming that you have heard about him and were taught in him, as the truth is in Jesus.' Paul marvels that people who know anything about Jesus could think our Lord tolerates sinful living; no doubt he would wonder even more if he visited many of us today.

Paul says three things about this in verses 20 and 21. First, 'That is not how you learned Christ!' He does not say 'how you learned about Christ,' but 'how you learned Christ.' Christianity is a personal relationship with Jesus. Anyone who is acquainted with Jesus knows about his holiness; his followers must therefore pursue holiness. Paul adds, 'Assuming that you have heard about him and were taught in him.' Literally, Paul says, 'If you have heard him.' He says that a true believer hears the voice of Christ 'and is taught in him,' through the apostolic message in the Bible. Jesus said that his sheep 'shall hear my voice' (John 10:16), which calls us to follow him in the new life he gives.

Paul completes his reproof by saying, 'as the truth is in Jesus.' He means that any attitude or practice we have that does not square with Jesus' life and teaching is not Christian. It is mind-boggling to Paul that there could be any question about the need for holiness among those who are enrolled in Christ's school and follow him.

Christianity—A Transformed Life

The truth that is in Jesus encompasses everything, for Jesus is the Lord of all. But Paul's concern in this section is godly living, so he emphasizes that the Christianity Jesus taught involves a radically transformed life. He reminds us we were taught in Christ 'to put off your old self, which belongs to your former manner of life and is corrupt through deceitful desires, and to be renewed in the spirit of your minds, and to put on the new self, created after the likeness of God in true righteousness and holiness' (Eph. 4:22-24).

This is the very thing we find in Jesus' ministry on this earth. Time and again in the Gospels, Jesus encounters someone who is corrupted in some way or caught in the snare of sin. In every case, faith in Christ leads to a radical transformation. In Luke 5 Jesus meets a leper, whose decrepit body depicts what sin does to us all. The leper fell before Jesus and begged him, 'Lord, if you are willing, you can make me clean!' Jesus touched him, saying, 'I am willing; be clean' (Luke 5:12-13), and the man was totally healed. This saving act of both restoration and cleansing is emblematic of Christ's salvation.

There are many examples. The blind man was made to see. The demon-possessed were freed from Satanic bondage. Greedy tax-collector, Zacchaeus had his heart changed: 'Behold, Lord,' he cried, 'the half of my goods I give to the poor. And if I have defrauded anyone of anything, I restore it fourfold' (Luke 19:8). These examples show that salvation includes renewal and repentance for sin. Repentance is not merely sorrow for egregious and obvious sins, but is a turning away from our whole lifestyle to embrace the new self of Christ-like character and holiness.

Most telling is the raising of Lazarus, recounted in John 11. Lazarus was dead in the tomb, his body decomposing. This is precisely Paul's idea in Ephesians 4:22, when he speaks of our 'former manner of life' that 'is corrupt through deceitful desires.' It is what Paul said in chapter 2, when he taught that apart from Christ we are 'dead in trespasses and sins,' living according to the corrupt 'passions of our flesh' (Eph. 2:1-3). Sin is a living death and Lazarus portrayed it as he lay cold in the tomb. But Jesus came and cried, 'Lazarus, come out' (John 11:43). At the call of the Son of God the dead man rose, and when he emerged through the door of the tomb, Jesus commanded that they take off his grave clothes just as Paul tells us here to 'put off your old self, which belongs to your former manner of life and is corrupt through deceitful desires, and…to put on the new self.'

These transformations all relied on Christ's power, received and responded to by faith. In that same way and by that same power, every Christian is to be transformed, not merely from old habits and practices and often old associations, but from our former nature and life to a new nature and eternal life.

When Paul speaks here of the 'old man,' as the Greek text puts it, he alludes to Adam and the sinful nature we all inherit through original sin. Original sin describes not what Adam did in the Garden but the corrupt state of nature that we all, as his offspring, inherit from that first transgression. The church father Origen wrote, 'It is this "old man," this ancient condition of humanity, that is put off in Christ.'[328] Thus Paul says, 'If anyone is in Christ, he is a new creation. The old has passed away; behold, the new has come' (2 Cor. 5:17). The old man, Adam, and the life of sin is left behind, and the new man, Jesus Christ, lives in us through faith and by the Holy Spirit.

Our transformation involves not only putting off the old, but also putting on the new, just as Christianity is more than salvation from sin but also a new and holy life. We are saved from condemnation and to acceptance with God as his children. We have been saved from judgment and wrath to justification and eternal blessing. We have been saved from the old self to the new self, from Adam to Christ. We have been saved from ignorance to the knowledge of Jesus and his gospel, as Paul emphasizes (v. 20), from hardened hearts of stone to the living hearts that God gives. We have been saved from 'every kind of impurity' (v. 19), and from a former life that is 'corrupt through deceitful desires' (v. 22), to 'the likeness of God in true righteousness and holiness' (v. 24).

Verse 24 contains the statement that our new self is 'created after the likeness of God in true righteousness and holiness.' Do you realize that this is what God intends for you? God said, 'Let us make man in our image, after our likeness' (Gen. 1:26), and this more than anything else defines the image of God: 'true righteousness and holiness.' This is what the human race lost by the Fall, but which Christ came to restore—the image of God in us. It is to this that we are saved. By righteousness, Paul is here talking about our conduct. By holiness, he describes our spiritual attitude, our love for the things of God and our inward purity. Christians are reborn, created in Christ for this—to be like God in 'true righteousness and holiness.' What could be more wonderful or glorious?

This is not a garment we weave by our own efforts, but rather one that we receive as the gift of God through faith in Christ. We are justified—that is, we are forgiven and clothed in the righteousness of Christ—as God's free gift to those who believe. And we are sanctified—made holy in our spirits and righteous in our conduct—also as God's work of grace. We receive this by faith but are called then to put it on, to cultivate it, to wear it, and to live it out in God's power. That is the Christian life and there is no other.

While we will never be perfect in this life, our passage proves that it is both possible and expected that Christians will grow into Christ-like holiness. One of the great ills of the church is that people believe holiness is only for special, high-profile people, Christian leaders and special 'saints'. But Paul says that anyone who has enrolled in the school of Christ is called and empowered to put off the old self and put on the new self, that new self being a holy one in God's own image.

INWARD RENEWAL

How does this actually take place in a person's life? Paul gives the answer in verse 23, where he tells us 'to be renewed in the spirit of your minds.' Our first point was that Christianity involves life transformation, and now we add that transformation requires inward renewal. It is significant that Paul's expressions 'to put on' and 'to put off' are infinitives in the aorist tense—the past tense which shows the definitive nature of this change. But then he says 'to be renewed in the spirit of your minds' in the present tense, indicating a continuous activity. This is Christianity: while our conversion effected a radical, definitive change, we still have to work this renewal into ourselves and to work it out in our experience.

When someone becomes a Christian, it is not that he or she receives a new brain, but rather a new spirit, a new attitude, in his mind and heart. Before, he hated God and rejected every revelation of God. Now, he loves God and loves God's Word and wants to drink it in. This is to be our daily experience as we constantly renew the spirit of our mind. We live in a false world filled with threats and temptations and lies. Moreover, we have been trained to worldly thinking and the old, sinful ways daily press in on us. This is why it matters so much what we put into our minds, and through our minds into our hearts.

What we need is the life-giving Word of God every day—not merely to ingest information but to experience its renewing influence. When you look down from an airplane onto a desert scene and you see a line of green trees you know there is water there. The same is true for us, that God's Word is the living stream that renews our minds and hearts for eternal life. 'For the Word of God is living and active' (Heb. 4:12); 'The Law of the Lord is perfect, reviving the soul…The precepts of the Lord are right, rejoicing the heart' (Ps. 19:7-8).

The particular word Paul uses for 'renewing' is based on the word for 'youth'. That is the kind of 'new' mind we gain from God—a young mind, a freshened inner self, one that is clean and clear. It contrasts with the mind Paul wrote of in verses 17 and 18, the old mind that is 'futile' and 'darkened'. We have 'learned Christ', have heard him and have been taught the truth that is in him. The way to a young and vibrant inner being is to draw near to Jesus. Jesus never did grow old and he never will. To be rejuvenated in the spirit of your mind, you should stay close to him, sit at his feet, spend time with him in prayer, and listen to his voice in God's Word.

One of my favorite of Jesus' miracles is the restoration of the Gadarene demoniac. This is perhaps the most comprehensive portrait of bondage to sin under the devil's reign. This poor man was possessed by a 'legion' of demons (Luke 8:30), living among the tombs, howling at night, and cutting his flesh with stones. But Jesus cast out the demons and renewed the spirit of his mind. Luke tells us that afterwards, the man was found 'sitting at the feet of Jesus, clothed, and in his right mind' (Luke 8:35). The man had been transformed and he knew where to go for further renewal. That is where we need to be, sitting at Jesus' feet with the Bible open on our laps and our hearts open in prayer, clothed in his righteousness as he renews the spirit of our minds day by day.

Practical Change

Third, this transformation *results in practical change*. In verses 25-29 Paul works out some concrete ways our lives must be changed if we have studied in the school of Christ. These are examples of the principle that we are to 'put off' our former lives and 'put on our new lives,' created to be like God. This is how sanctification works, how we grow in godliness, by putting off the old self and putting on the new. But these practical commands are themselves important and necessary for our obedience.

Let me make three general observations about the changes Paul mentions in verses 25-29. First, in each case Paul provides not merely an application but also the reason for it. Second, his reasons all have to do with relationships. We show our love for God by loving others. Third, Paul tells us not merely to put off something sinful but also to put on the corresponding virtue. Indeed, it especially glorifies God when those aspects of our fallen condition that were most obnoxious become the most gracious aspects of our redeemed character. It is the man who once spoke in filthy language who now speaks out in refreshing streams, or the once greedy person who now delights in generosity, who best displays the transforming power of Jesus Christ.

Paul's first example requires us no longer to lie but to speak truthfully: 'Therefore, having put away falsehood, let each one of you speak the truth with his neighbor' (v. 25). Lying and false-hood is always close at hand to the old, depraved life. It was through a lie that the devil tempted our first parents into sin. If we are to live wholesome, godly lives, then we must renounce lying. Jesus said, 'I am…the Truth' (John 14:6), and we must embrace the truth if we are to be like him.

Paul's reason is telling: 'For we are all members of one another.' We remember his illustration of the church as a body; there is no point in the eye lying to the foot, or the ear deceiving the hand. Indeed, this is an essential principle of godly, loving fellowship—that we speak the truth. First John 1:7 says, 'If we walk in the light, as he is in the light, we have fellowship with one another, and the blood of Jesus his Son cleanses us from all sin.' Lying is ever the ally of sin; we lie to cover up and to enable ourselves to keep on sinning. If only we will confess our faults and our sins, then we may be forgiven and Christ's blood can restore our fellowship.

Second, in verses 26–27, Paul writes, 'Be angry and do not sin.' There is a place for anger, the holy anger Jesus showed in response to sin and evil. There is something wrong with us if we are not angered by things that hurt and destroy and offend the heart of God. But how important is what Paul goes on to say—I sometimes think it is one of the most profitable sayings in all the Bible—'Be angry and do not sin.' Our problem is that our anger causes us to sin. So when we are angry—rightly or wrongly—if we put off the old man and put on the new self we will determine not to sin. One way to fulfill this command is to ensure that we only allow ourselves to be made angry at the right things, and not selfishly. One commentator said, 'He that will be angry and not sin, let him be angry at nothing but sin.'[329]

Paul further instructs us, 'Do not let the sun go down on your anger.' This is extremely valuable advice, especially for married couples, who live their lives in such close connection. How often even the most petty spats grow into bitterness because they were not quickly reconciled. William Barclay explains,

> The longer we postpone mending a quarrel, the less likely we are ever to mend it…The longer it is left to flourish, the more bitter it will grow. If we have been in the wrong, we must pray to God to give us grace to admit that it was so; and even if we have been right, we must pray to God to give us the graciousness which will enable us to take the first step to put matters right.[330]

Paul's reason comes in verse 27: 'Give no opportunity to the devil.' It is hard enough loving one another without letting the devil find a foothold between us. With this in mind, we must never cherish anger, but always be eager to put on the mercy and compassion of Christ.

Paul's third example says, 'Let the thief no longer steal, but rather let him labor, doing honest work with his own hands' (Eph. 4:28). One who follows Christ will think about others and respect what belongs to them. This applies broadly to our lives, committing us to the faithful use of our employer's resources and time. The Christian will be eager to work to support his family. When Paul tells us to 'do honest work with his own hands,' he means that we should be productive in wholesome ways, not being a taker but a giver, not skimming through life off other peoples' sweat but digging in and working hard and contributing in useful ways.

This verse also makes an important statement about the Christian motive for work. The greedy person works hard to accumulate more things for him or herself, amassing greater riches to own more homes and take more vacations with little thought of others and the work of the gospel. But the godly person makes money 'so that he may have something to share with anyone in need' (Eph. 4:28). Because God has given so much to us, we are to take a special delight in giving to others, especially those who suffer in need.

Last, Paul highlights our speech: 'Let no corrupting talk come out of your mouths, but only such as is good for building up, as fits the occasion' (Eph. 4:29). How much a part of the old life is corrupt speech! We delight to gossip, tattle, malign, and destroy reputations, people, and even churches over a salad and soda. James 3:6 says, 'The tongue is a fire, a world of unrighteousness… staining the whole body, setting on fire the entire course of life, and set on fire by hell.' How well this describes the tone of much popular discourse today, especially what is pumped out on television, in movies and popular music. But it also describes talk in some of our homes and even in church. We create whole worlds of falsehood and evil just by telling them. It is what we say that largely determines what kind of world we want and the effect we will have on others. Jesus said, 'What comes out of a person is what defiles him…All these evil things come from within' (Mark 7:20, 23). So, Paul says, the transformed Christian will speak to build up, 'as fits the occasion, that it may give grace to those who hear' (v. 29). This should be one of the most distinguishing characteristics of anyone who studies in Christ's school.

Wearing His Coat

It has been said that the clothing makes the man. What we wear tells us about the kind of person we are. A man in a green uniform is a soldier. A judge wears a robe, a bride wears a white gown, and a Christian puts on the new self, 'created after the likeness of God in true righteousness and holiness' (Eph. 4:24). We do not do this to be saved, but because we are saved, because God's Spirit works in us with life-transforming power.

This also makes all the difference to our witness of the gospel. In a book about the spread of the gospel in communist Yugoslavia, Marie Chapian tells of an evangelist named Jakov. One day he arrived in a village and spoke to an old man named Cimmerman about Jesus Christ. Cimmerman rejected him rudely, reminding Jakov of how the official church had acted in that town, plundering, exploiting and even helping the Communists to kill innocent people, including his nephew. 'They wear those elaborate coats and caps and crosses,' he complained, 'but their evil designs and lives I cannot ignore.' Jakov replied that these people did not truly represent Jesus. He compared them to a man who broke into his house, stole his coat and then robbed a bank. He asked, 'What would you say if your coat were stolen and you were accused of bank robbery?' The old man replied, 'I would deny it.' 'Ah, but we saw your coat,' they would say,' retorted Jakov. But before he could go further the man demanded him to leave.

Jakov did not give up on Cimmerman. He came back to the town now and again and looked for ways to encourage the old man and to share Christ's love with him. I can imagine him practicing many of the things Paul mentioned in our passage: lovingly speaking the truth, not allowing anger to make him sin, working hard to give to others, and speaking good words to build up and give grace. One day, Cimmerman finally asked him, 'How does one become a Christian?' and Jakov told him. Cimmerman repented of his sin, trusted in Christ's saving work, and bent his knee on the good soil and surrendered his heart to Jesus. Then, with tears in his eyes, he embraced Jakov, thanked him for his loving ministry, pointed up to heaven and said to him, 'You wear his coat very well.'[331]

Let us do the same thing, putting off the old sinful nature and putting on the new self, the Christ-like character that displays Gods holiness before the world. Then others will see him in us, and renewed through faith in Christ, many will be saved.

51

GRIEVING THE HOLY SPIRIT

Ephesians 4:30

Charles Dicken's famous novel, *Great Expectations*, tells the story of an orphan named Pip who rises in life to become a wealthy gentleman. Pip is working in a blacksmith shop when he learns that a secret benefactor had left him a fortune and arranged for him to be educated in London. He assumes that a rich woman from his hometown is the benefactor, but eventually learns that an escaped convict to whom he once showed kindness and who later came into extraordinary wealth, is the source of his riches.

Christians, too, have a benefactor whose identity is largely a mystery to us. I refer to the Holy Spirit, through whom all the riches of salvation come to us. Were it not for his work in our lives, we would have no faith in which to believe on our Savior Jesus Christ, no power to lead new lives, and no peace or spiritual joy. Yet, we hardly know our benefactor. In *Great Expectations*, the benefactor hid because of his criminal record, but that is not why the Holy Spirit remains so mysterious. He is sometimes called the 'shy' member of the Trinity, because his desire is not to glorify himself but, as J. I. Packer put it, 'to mediate Christ's presence to believers… to give them knowledge of his presence with them as their Savior, Lord, and God.'[332]

THE PERSONHOOD OF THE HOLY SPIRIT

It probably is true that most of us operate with a dualistic rather than a Trinitarian view of God. We may acknowledge three divine Persons—Father, Son, and Holy Spirit—but we only think in relation to the Father and the Son. Partly this is because we can put a face, as it were, on the first two members of the Trinity. I can relate fatherhood to personhood, and God the Son entered into the human race to make himself personally accessible. But relating as a person to the Spirit, whom Jesus compared to the wind, is more difficult, which is why many Christians think of him as an impersonal force.

Ephesians 4:30 is one of many texts that proves the personhood of the Holy Spirit. Paul writes, 'And do not grieve the Holy Spirit of God.' A force does not have emotions and cannot be grieved; only a person can grieve. The Bible consistently speaks of the Spirit in personal terms, possessing personal attributes like knowledge, feelings, and will. He leads (Rom. 8:14), he speaks and teaches (John 16:13), he helps us in prayer (Rom. 8:26), and he can be lied to (Acts 5:3–4). Packer summarizes: 'The Spirit is not just an influence; he, like the Father and the Son, is an individual person.'[333]

This is important because when we think of the Spirit as an impersonal force we tend to think that we control him rather than the other way around. Thinking this way promotes an unhealthy experientialism, as people try to plug into their own brand of spirituality. Instead, biblical spirituality is one of responding to the Spirit as he speaks to us through God's Word and moves our hearts.

When we realize that the Holy Spirit is a person, we also realize how intimate is God's relationship with us. If we can grieve God's Spirit, then he must dwell close to our hearts and love us very much.

All through my youth I studied piano, and during my teenage years I began to blossom as a classical pianist. The main reason was the outstanding teacher I had, an older woman who had studied under the finest masters. She had great aspirations for me as a pianist. But those also were years when things like high school football began competing with piano. Now and again I would show up for my lesson without having practiced, or with bent fingers, and how it grieved her! When I informed her that I was not going to pursue piano in college, I was saddened by how it hurt her. She grieved because of her affection for me, because of the work she had poured into me, and because of her hopes for me. This is the way parents feel for their children, and why a mother's heart breaks when one of them goes astray. The great wonder is that this is how the Creator of the universe feels for every believer. He has plans for our glory and our blessing, he has invested greatly in us, and it grieves his heart when one of us turns astray into sin or folly.

The Motive for Sanctification

Paul makes this statement about grieving the Holy Spirit in the middle of his moral exhortation in Ephesians. He has reminded his readers that Christians are new creatures, 'created after the likeness of God in true righteousness and holiness' (Eph. 4:24). This being the case, we are to put off the old life and put on the new self in Christ, and in verses 25-29 he gives some practical examples: we must not lie, sin in anger, steal, or speak corruptly. He also supplies reasons for godly conduct: we are members of one another, we don't want to give the devil a foothold, and we should be eager to do good. Now in verse 30 Paul rises to a higher level, basing his exhortations on our relationship with God: 'And do not grieve the Holy Spirit of God, by whom you were sealed for the day of redemption.' This is where Christianity differs from mere moralism, with its lists of do's and don't. Christianity bases its ethic in a relationship with God, who loves us and who is holy, who we should want to please and glorify.

There are two main biblical motivations for sanctification, that is, for growth in godliness. One of them we might call the lower motivation, which involves the use of rewards and punishments. Some people say that we should not obey God merely because of the consequences. But since the Bible does use rewards and punishment to motivate obedience, this view is in conflict with the Scriptures. The Bible tells us that as our father God disciplines and chastises his children (Heb. 12:5-11). Moreover, we are told that Christ will reward us for our obedience and our service to his kingdom. Paul says in 2 Corinthians 5:10, 'We must all appear before the judgment seat of Christ, so that each one may receive what is due for what he has done in the body, whether good or evil.' This is not our legal justification; for in Christ there is no condemnation (Rom. 8:1). Believers' sins are all forgiven through the blood of Christ. Rather, Paul is saying that our works of service to Christ will be evaluated and rewarded.

Knowing this, he says, 'We make it our aim to please him' (2 Cor. 5:9).

This is a legitimate and biblical motivation for Christian living, although, as I said, I think it is a lower one. Warfield points out, however, that most people 'are more amenable to appeals addressed to the lower than…to the higher motives.'[334] Nonetheless, there is a higher motivation to which the apostle appeals in our verse. It is higher in the way that older children need a higher motivation to good behavior than small ones. Little children are trained by punishments and rewards. But I remember that as I grew older, what motivated me to do what is right was my love for my parents, and especially my admiration for my father and my desire to please him and make him proud. It is for this reason, by the way, that fathers need to establish a loving connection with each of their children, to get on our knees and play with them when they are little, to laugh and cry with our hearts open, because in later years when rewards and punishments fail to motivate it will be this relationship that moves our children to follow our lead.

This is what Paul is talking about in Ephesians 4:30, and it is a motivation that should grow as we become more mature in the faith. A mature believer obeys God not simply because this works better, but out of a desire to please our loving heavenly Father, who is our glory and is worthy of our obedience. How can I, a mature believer reasons, purchased with the precious blood of Jesus, an heir of eternity in whom the Holy Spirit lives—how can I live like an unbeliever? This is the motive to which Paul appeals when he urges us not to grieve the Holy Spirit by sinning. Martyn Lloyd-Jones writes:

Here is the Christian way, here is the biblical way of looking at this whole matter of sanctification. Not for ourselves, but for His sake! Our sanctification, our life, our conduct, is ever to be the realization and the outcome and the outworking of what He has done for us, and of our sense of His glory and our desire to live to the praise of the glory of His grace.[335]

Grieving the Holy Spirit

How, then, does a Christian grieve the Holy Spirit? The immediate context tells us that we grieve him when we live in the way we formerly did before coming to faith in Christ. For a Christian to lie to fellow believers brings grief to the Holy Spirit (Eph. 4:25). The biblical example is that of Ananias and Sapphira, who boasted about giving more money to the church than they really did. The apostle Peter said they were lying to the Holy Spirit, and the Spirit was not only grieved but struck them dead as an example, after which I presume that Ananias and Sapphira went to heaven since as Christians they had trusted in Christ's blood.

It also grieves the Holy Spirit when we become angry and sin, because this gives an opportunity to the devil (Eph. 4:26–27). Note how Paul puts these together: the old life grieves the Spirit and gives a foothold to the devil, whereas the new life rejoices the Spirit and grieves the devil. This is certainly a potent motive to godliness. The same is true for those who steal or are lazy and thus are not able to support their families or give to those in need (Eph. 4:28). This grieves the Holy Spirit. Especially, unwholesome speech grieves the Spirit, because sinful speech reveals a corrupt heart and the heart is where the Holy Spirit lives in us. John Stott sums up Paul's point: 'Anything incompatible with the purity or unity of the church is incompatible with [the Spirit's] own nature and therefore hurts him.'[336]

Elsewhere in the Bible we find specific occasions when God was said to grieve. Genesis 6:6

says that God destroyed the world with Noah's flood because he saw how great was the wickedness on the earth, 'And the LORD was sorry that he had made man on the earth, and it grieved him to his heart.' Likewise, God grieved in response to the disobedience of Israel's first king, Saul (1 Sam. 15:11).

The most important reference is Isaiah 63:7–14, to which Paul is alluding in this verse. That passage reflects on the events of the exodus, when God delivered Israel from slavery in Egypt and brought them into the Promised Land. Isaiah recalls God's tender love, which he meant to inspire the people to obedience. Isaiah says, 'In his love and in his pity he redeemed them; he lifted them up and carried them all the days of old. But they rebelled and grieved his Holy Spirit.'

Isaiah was referring to Israel's rebellion in the desert, when they complained about having to eat manna and rebelled against Moses. They pined for their former life, even though it involved slavery, because of the fleshly comforts they had left behind (see Numbers 14 and 16).

Is this not exactly the way Christians often respond to the grace and mercy of God? God has delivered us from the guilt and the bondage of sin at such great cost to himself—the precious blood of his only Son. But life in this world is hard; we are not saved immediately into the joys of heaven but are called to live by faith in a hard and trying world. Instead of looking forward with glad hearts to our promised destination in glory, we often think longingly of what it was like before we became Christians, before the Holy Spirit came to live in our hearts. He is holy, and so he takes all the fun out of sin and reminds us to obey God's Word. But instead of gratitude for this vital ministry, we resent him and complain, we think affectionately about sin and our lives start reverting to our former ways. All this grieves the Holy Spirit, who wants our hearts to long for holy things and to respond to God's love with loving obedience.

So what happens when we grieve the Holy Spirit? Isaiah tells us, speaking of the exodus generation: 'But they rebelled and grieved his Holy Spirit; therefore he turned to be their enemy, and himself fought against them' (Isa. 63:10). If you read the Book of Numbers you will see exactly what happened. God had been fighting for Israel, protecting them, and providing for all their needs—Isaiah tells us specifically that it was the Holy Spirit doing all this. But when the people rebelled and their hearts turned back to their former life, their relationship with God became less enjoyable. It is not that God abandoned them or stopped loving them, but that his steadfast love took a new shape. That generation ended up wandering in the desert forty years, until God had chastised them and taught them to obey him from the heart.

This is why so many Christians are unhappy and so spiritually unproductive. Curtis Vaughn explains, 'This fact explains the misery of so many believers, for it is precisely by reason of permitting [sin] that they have lost the joy, peace, and blessedness they once knew.'[337]

One believer who could tell us about this is King David. God made him king because he was 'a man after [God's] own heart' (1 Sam. 13:14). David walked by faith and in the Spirit. That was how he slew mighty Goliath, and, more impressively, how he overcame the fleshly inclination to take revenge on Saul, who had sought his life. It was by faith and through the Spirit that David won his great victories and brought the ark of the covenant into Jerusalem.

David provides us, however, with one of the great cautionary tales in all of Scripture. Success made him self-reliant and proud. David began making provision for the flesh, and sinful desires began to control him. That is how he ended up basking on the roof of his palace while his army was out fighting the Lord's battles. That is how he allowed his eyes to feast upon the sight of beautiful Bathsheba, bathing on a nearby roof, and then sent for her, and then took her, and then manipulated her when she got pregnant, and then murdered her husband to cover up his sin. Do we realize how capable we all are of such things, if we grieve the Spirit by nurturing sinful desires and cause his influence to withdraw, leaving us in the control of the flesh?

David thought he had tidied it all up and that he was going to get away with his sin, but God had seen it all and it angered him (2 Sam. 11:27). When we walk in sin, we may fool others but we always grieve the Holy Spirit, who always knows the truth. So God chastised David; in Psalm 32 David tells us that God's hand was heavy against him (v. 4). Verse 5 tells us what David did, and what we should do when we have grieved the Spirit: 'I acknowledged my sin to you, and I did not cover my iniquity; I said, "I will confess my transgressions to the LORD," and you forgave the iniquity of my sin.' In Psalm 51, written at the same time, David prays, 'Take not your Holy Spirit from me. Restore to me the joy of your salvation, and uphold me with a willing spirit' (vv. 11–12). Of course, the Holy Spirit had never truly left David, or he would have been unable to repent. But it felt that way to David, and when he confessed and cried to the Lord, the joy of the Spirit's presence returned to his heart. Likewise, when we confess our sin and repent, we can be sure of the Holy Spirit's joyful acceptance, just as in Jesus' parable the prodigal son returned home to the forgiving embrace of his loving father.

SEALED FOR THE DAY OF REDEMPTION

Paul concludes this verse by reminding us that the Holy Spirit is the One 'by whom you were sealed for the day of redemption.' He is referring back to what he taught in chapter 1:13–14, that when we heard the gospel and believed on Jesus Christ, we 'were sealed with the promised Holy Spirit, who is the guarantee of our inheritance until we acquire possession of it.' When we believed on Jesus Christ, we were purchased by God from our sin to be his people. But just as it is with many things that we purchase, final delivery does not come until later; in our case, it is not until 'the day of redemption,' that is, the return of Christ to consummate his eternal kingdom. Until then, God sends the Spirit to be his seal—his mark of ownership—on us. The seal guarantees our inheritance and provides us an advance installment of the blessings that await us in the life to come. The Spirit is our guardian and provider, the one who oversees our progress to heaven, provides us the strength we need, and feeds us with sweets from the heavenly banquet where a seat is reserved in our name.

I mentioned Dickens', *Great Expectations*, where the pauper, Pip, learned of a secret benefactor. We are like Pip, in that ours is a rags-to-riches story. We were alienated from God's love, his enemies because of sin, not merely spiritually poor but spiritually dead. But, because of his great and sovereign love for us, God the Spirit has come to us with salvation through faith in Christ. Though we do not see him, his identity is no secret. Hodge says: 'To grieve him, therefore, is to wound him on whom our salvation depends.'[338] Why, then, would we ever want to grieve the Spirit? Why would we cherish sin that will push him away? Why would we turn our hearts back toward our former lives, or go back to our former ways, grieving the Spirit who gives us life and peace, joy and power for a new and holy life?

Ultimately we should never want to grieve the Spirit, not merely because of what it will mean to us, but what it will mean to him. If he has worked so energetically and so lovingly in my life, and if he is in league with our Lord Jesus Christ, who died on the cross for my sins, and if they are doing the will of God the Father in heaven, who set his love on me before the world even came into existence, then as I realize that, surely I will see my highest calling and privilege and joy is to rejoice his heart and glorify his name in this world. Lloyd-Jones argues that we should not grieve the Spirit 'because He is who and what He is. And that ought to be enough! He is the third Person in the blessed, holy Trinity, and He is dwelling as a guest within us, in our very bodies, "a gracious, willing Guest." The very greatness of His Person ought to be enough for us.'[339] Just as we watch our language and behavior in the presence of a very holy or important person, so also when we realize that the Holy Spirit is living in us, and how great is his glory and his love for us, we will never want to offend him, but to please him and cause others to praise him because of our lives.

How does this work out in practice? Paul is telling us in this chapter: put off the old life and put on the new and holy life that is ours in Jesus Christ. He gives examples that were relevant to his Ephesian readers: do not lie, do not sin in anger, do not be lazy or steal, and do not let corrupting speech escape your mouth. Are these things the Spirit is saying to you? Perhaps your case is somewhat different. Perhaps you need an attitude change or to repent of sexual sin, things that Paul will address a bit further on in this letter. Also, look through the Ten Commandments, and study Jesus' Beatitudes in Matthew 5. Read your Bible daily and the Spirit will point things out to you, and when he does do not grieve him but follow his gracious leading. Paul taught this very directly in Galatians 5:16–18, saying, 'Walk by the Spirit, and you will not gratify the desires of the flesh. For the desires of the flesh are against the Spirit, and the desires of the Spirit are against the flesh, for these are opposed to each other.' Paul goes to list obvious sins from which we need to turn: sexual immorality, anger, divisions, envy, drunkenness. Take these off. Then he says to put on the fruit of the Spirit: 'love, joy, peace, patience, kindness, goodness, faithfulness, gentleness, self-control' (vv. 22–23). He concludes in Galatians 5:25 with one of the great statements of the Christian life: 'If we live by the Spirit, let us also walk by the Spirit,' or as one version puts it, 'Let us keep in step with the Spirit' (NIV).

This is why I do not give detailed applications telling people exactly what to do and exactly how to do it. We are all different and our circumstances vary. But the Spirit knows each of us and lives in us, and as God's Word is preached and as you read the Bible and pray, the Spirit will convict you of sins and sinful desires and lead you into a godly life of good works. How should you respond? Do not grieve him, but keep in step with the Spirit. As you respond to his prompting through God's Word, the Holy Spirit will lead you into eternal glory and he will help you to honor our loving God every step along the way.

52

Imitators of God

Ephesians 4:31–5:2

In Ephesians 5:1, the apostle Paul sets before us what William Barclay calls 'the highest standard in the world.'[340] Martyn Lloyd-Jones calls this 'Paul's supreme argument…the highest level of all in doctrine and in practice…the ultimate ideal.'[341] Paul writes, 'Therefore be imitators of God, as beloved children.' Alexander Maclaren says of this, 'To be like God, and to set ourselves to resemble Him, is the sum of all duty; and in the measure in which we approximate thereto, we come to perfection.'[342]

Obviously, this is a matter we should approach seriously and reverently. But we also need to approach it carefully, since many people are led astray by a wrong understanding of the Bible's teaching that we should imitate God or Jesus Christ. This is particularly important in light of the many products people buy today labeled 'WWJD,' for 'What Would Jesus Do?'

Perhaps the first thing we should observe about Paul's statement is where he places it in his letter. When Paul or any of the other Bible writers speak of imitating God, he does not present this as a way of salvation. No one in heaven is ever going to say, 'I got here because I was so much like God.' The first thing we need to know about the imitation of God or of Christ is that in our natural state we are completely unable to do so. This was Paul's point when he wrote in Romans 3, 'None is righteous, no, not one…no one does good, not even one…For all have sinned and fall short of the glory of God' (vv. 9–10, 23). Likewise, in Ephesians 2 Paul begins his teaching on salvation by saying that until God saves us by grace alone, we are imitators not of God but of the devil, 'following the prince of the power of the air, the spirit that is now at work in the sons of disobedience' (Eph. 2:2).

So the first thing we must know about imitating God is that it is not a way of salvation for sinners, since no sinner can ever be godly or Christ-like on his own. Jesus came into the world not first to be a moral example, but to be a Savior by dying on the cross for our sins. If you are wearing a WWJD bracelet, the first thing you must realize is that it condemns you, because you have not done what Jesus did. You need to confess that and trust him as your Savior.

Once we are straight on this, however, we need to avoid another error, and that is failing to embrace Paul's teaching in this passage. Now that we are saved and are empowered by God's indwelling Spirit, we are able to keep God's law and live for him. We are able to follow Jesus' teaching and example, and we should take them seriously, asking 'What did Jesus teach me to do?' Therefore, to those already saved, Paul lays down this highest and greatest of all standards, 'Therefore, be imitators of God, as beloved children.' Children are to imitate their parents, and when their parents love them dearly, as God loves us, this is what children delight to do.

PUTTING AWAY THE BAD

It is undoubtedly instructive to note that when Paul tells us to imitate God, it is in the midst of verses that focus on the inner qualities of Christian character. The Bible talks about behavior and God cares very much what we do. But the Bible's focus is primarily on the state of our heart, since everything flows from it. Lloyd-Jones writes, 'The Apostle is not interested in conduct as such, he is interested in conduct as it is an expression and a reflection of the new life which they had received as the result of their regeneration.'[343] This reminds us that if we want to start honoring God and enjoying the blessings we ought to enjoy as Christians, then the place to start is inside our hearts. If we really want to be practical about our Christianity, then we will get to work on our character. Paul's approach is to tell us to put away the old and the bad and to cultivate the new, the good, and the godly. This is the overall approach to sanctification presented in Ephesians 4:22–24: 'You were taught…to put off your old self, which belongs to your former manner of life and is corrupt through deceitful desires…and to put on the new self, created after the likeness of God in true righteousness and holiness.'

Paul begins, then, with the old and bad qualities that we are to remove from our hearts, starting with bitterness: 'Let all bitterness…be put away from you' (v. 31). Bitterness is the self-pitying reaction to things not going our way, especially when we have been sinned against by others. When we are bitter, we allow everything to be soured by resentment and we nurse all our grievances, forbidding them to die. A bitter person will always find something to complain about and will always see what is worst in any person or thing.

Apart from the misery that bitter people afflict on others, I think the saddest thing is what they do to themselves. I have heard it said that bitterness is an acid that destroys its own container. It is possible for a snake to hold its venom without being affected, but not for a human being.

I have found that bitter people often have what seem like excellent reasons to nurse their grudges. I have known women who resented all men because twenty years earlier their husband betrayed them. I have known people who hated life because their parents showed them no love. I have known Christians who were hostile to their minister because of something a different pastor did to them years before. These may seem like good reasons to stoke the fires of resentment, to prune and nurture the bitter tree in your heart. But I would point out that by so doing, you allow the sin to continue to afflict you. Using my examples, a woman thus allows one man to deprive her whole life of male companionship, a child allows his or her parents to dominate his thinking even as an adult, and a Christian rejects what God gave to be good and uplifting simply because one person used it for evil. How much better would we all be simply to do what Paul says: 'Let all bitterness be put away.'

Next, Paul joins together 'wrath and anger,' saying that these, too, should be put away. We saw back in verse 26 that it is possible to have a holy and wholesome anger, as God does towards sin. But we should never allow even that to make us angry people. For 'wrath', Paul uses a word that means 'burning' and expresses violent outbursts of fury. We should be alarmed if this describes us, since the fruit of the Holy Spirit includes 'gentleness and self-control' (Gal. 5:23). If you are the kind of person who makes your family members and co-workers nervous because of your outbursts, then you should bring your heart to God and put away your violent temper. Do not excuse it any longer. Paul joins to this a word for 'anger' that points to a hostile disposition. To be a disgruntled, angry Christian is to grieve the Holy Spirit. It is a terrible thing to permit your heart to be hard and angry, and it has led many people to sins they would hardly have imagined when they started.

The next term, clamor, is related to and flows from anger. This means shouting and can even be used of brawling. This is something we should all watch for, and whenever we find ourselves arguing with a raised voice or picking fights with people, we should reflect on the conduct of Jesus Christ and repent.

Paul must have verbal outbursts especially in mind, because he goes on to warn against slander. The Greek word is *blasphemia*, which means ill-speech, either against God or man. How common this is in our pagan society; there is no longer any shame towards blaspheming the Lord's name or slandering others. Our whole media is given over to this. But these things ought to be removed from a Christian's life.

I have to say that of all the sins ever committed against me, slander may be the one that has hurt most, because slander harms your reputation. Once you have been slandered, you will never completely remove the impression and lingering doubts will remain. The ninth commandment forbids us from bearing false testimony, and the *Westminster Larger Catechism* rightly says this requires 'the preserving and promoting of…the good name of our neighbour' (Q. 144). This is a sin we all should carefully guard against, because it is so natural and enjoyable to our sinful nature. Jesus said that if we have a grievance against another, we should go personally to them and try to work it out (Matt. 18). If we want to join the devil's attack against the gospel, perhaps the first thing we should do is spread gossip and innuendo about other Christians or about the church.

Paul says that these things—bitterness, wrath, anger, clamor, and slander—must be put away, and then he makes the general summation, 'along with all malice,' a general word for evil intentions. This suggests that Christians will and do struggle with these things and also that our conversion does not automatically remove them. Having been saved, and desiring to honor God, bless others, and enjoy God's blessing ourselves, we must apply ourselves to removing these cursed attitudes. I doubt there is one person who does not have cause to seriously reflect on at least one of these. If we would take these seriously and really repent, it would revolutionize our lives, our families, and our church.

Cultivating the Good

This raises the question, 'How do I put these bad things away?' The answer is found in verse 32: 'Be kind to one another, tenderhearted, forgiving one another, as God in Christ forgave you.'

Before looking at the details, we should make two general observations. The first is that in the Greek text Paul's intention is a bit clearer, because he says not to 'be' these things but to 'become' them. The way for us to remove these bad qualities is to cultivate their opposites. The early church father, John Chrysostom, asked, 'What good it is to weed a garden if we do not plant good seed...To be free from a bad habit does not mean we have formed a good one. We need to take the further step of forming good habits and dispositions.'[344] Jesus warned against sweeping the devils out of the house without bringing in the Holy Spirit, because then 'other spirits more evil' than the ones before will come in and make things worse (Luke 11:24-26). This shows the difference between mere moralism and Christianity and why the former fails. Christianity is not just saying 'No' to evils, and we should never define holiness merely in terms of avoiding certain movies or alcohol or dressing a certain way. There are obvious wrong things that Christians should not do. But true holiness not only says 'No' to sin but also 'Yes' to God, and it displays a beauty of spirit that only God can give.

A second observation is that there is an obvious relationship between the virtues of verse 32 and the vices of verse 31. The order seems to be inverse, so that kindness, which comes first, responds as the corrective to clamor and slander.

Verse 32 begins, 'Be kind to one another.' Kindness is one of the best virtues, and it will keep us from sinning against others. This is one of the best ways to imitate God. Jesus said that God 'is kind to the ungrateful and the evil' (Luke 6:35). That is why the sun shines on our wicked world and why sinners enjoy so many good things—because God is kind. Ephesians 2:7 says it was because of his kindness that God sent Jesus to be our Savior. Kindness is a fruit of the Holy Spirit and a sign of his presence (Gal. 5:23).

Kindness is a desire to do good to others. You see why this is the corrective to a biting tongue. William Hendriksen says, 'When the kind person hears a piece of malicious gossip, he does not run to the telephone to let others in on the delectable tidbit. When someone's faults are pointed out to him, he tries, if he can at all do so in honesty, to offset these failings by pointing out the criticized individual's good qualities.'[345] What a blessed virtue kindness is!

Next, Paul says to become 'tender-hearted.' This is the opposite of having a hard heart that is unaffected by the difficulties and sorrows of others. To be tender-hearted is to feel for others and understand their troubles. We live in a hard world, so what a difference it makes to be compassionate! To show sympathy and offer an encouraging word is one of the best ways we can present Christ to the world. Mark 1:41 tells us that Jesus was 'moved with pity,' and that is why he healed so many people and ultimately took away our sins by dying on the cross. Our unbelieving, secular-humanistic world is marked by its lack of feeling, but Christians are known by a tender heart.

This is the remedy for wrath and anger. The best way to cultivate sympathy is to get to know the difficulties of others. If you do not feel for the poor, then try making ends meet on so little. If you think racism is no big deal, then go someplace where you are a minority. This is one of the benefits of short-term mission trips. If you see firsthand how so many people live and the sufferings they endure, then your heart will become tender towards them and others. This is the very thing Jesus did by coming into the world. Because he has experienced what we go through, even suffering death in our place, Hebrews 4:15 says he is able 'to sympathize with our weaknesses.' That means we should be eager to turn our hearts to him and that we should show his love to the world by cultivating a tender heart.

Paul concludes Ephesians 4, saying, 'Forgiving one another, as God in Christ forgave you.' Here is the antidote that neutralizes the poison of bitterness. It is certainly true that we are the victims of other peoples' sins, in ways small and large. So what is the Christian response to victimhood? It is forgiveness. This is God's command and also his gift. We become free from other peoples' sins by forgiving them. This is how we imitate God, since he forgave us. This is how we best know that Jesus Christ is living in our hearts. Even hanging on the cross, he prayed, 'Father, forgive them' (Luke 23:24).

This begs a question: Have you confessed your sin to God and asked him to forgive you through Jesus Christ? If not, why not? Do you really deny that you have sinned against God and merited his displeasure? If you do, then reckon with his perfect holiness that must judge your sin and condemn you as a sinner. But then realize that Jesus is the Savior of sinners. Paul said, 'While we were still sinners, Christ died for us' (Rom. 5:8). Believe on him, receive him in faith and you will be forgiven and accepted into God's love.

But then, if we are forgiven by God, how can we claim to be his people unless we are willing and even eager to forgive others. We must not think we are forgiven by God because we forgive others—that would make salvation rely on our works and we would never be saved. But at the same time, what Paul says here and what Jesus taught in the Gospels says that if you are unwilling to forgive others you should seriously question whether or not you have received God's forgiveness through faith in Christ. Anyone who knows God's forgiveness cannot help but extend it to others. So take all your bitterness to Jesus, put it away from you, by receiving his grace to forgive as you have been forgiven in Christ by God.

Put verse 32 together and you have a great Christian life. This is what God wants, far more than money, large buildings, and worldly achievements. God wants our hearts, and if we will give him our hearts he will make us kind, tender-hearted, and forgiving. Wouldn't this make all the difference in your life? If you became kind, wouldn't it make a wonderful impact on the lives of other people—your spouse, your children, your neighbors and friends and fellow Christians? If you became tender-hearted, wouldn't this bring beauty and love into your relationships? And if you are ready and eager to forgive, sin will no longer rule you, because of Jesus Christ. What are we waiting for? Our lives are passing by, and God is able and willing to do this miracle of grace in us, if only we will ask.

'The Expulsive Power of a New Affection'

This leads to one last question, which finds its answer in verse 2. The question is, 'Where do I get the strength and motivation to start cultivating these wonderful virtues?' Paul answers, 'Walk in love, as Christ loved us and gave himself up for us, a fragrant offering and sacrifice to God.'

Paul is talking about what Thomas Chalmers called 'the expulsive power of a new affection.' What is it that motivates us really to change? The answer is a new love! We see this all the time, especially in young people. I remember in a former church a college-age man who used to come to church dressed in Army fatigues with unkempt hair, often without shaving. One day he showed up with a new haircut, wearing a suit. I pointed this out to one of the other pastors, who said, 'Well, you see, there is this girl he has met!'

This is what causes us to change—'the expulsive power of a new affection!' Paul is saying to you, 'For a great change like this, you need a great love in your life!' That love is Jesus Christ, because 'Christ loved us and gave himself up for us.' This is why self-help books—even Christian ones—so often fail to do us much good, because they focus us on ourselves when our problem is our self-centeredness. Meanwhile, it is often a book of theology, one that focuses on the attributes of God or the atoning work of Christ that radically motivates us to start living for him. Why? Because what we need is to be shaken by the glory of God, by his love that makes us 'dear children,' and by the love of Jesus that took up the cross for us. The way to love Jesus is not by romanticizing him in a secular way but by believing on his person and work as taught to us in the Bible. This is what so many of our hymns celebrate. Isaac Watts wrote:

> When I survey the wondrous cross
>   on which the Prince of glory died,
> My richest gain I count but loss,
>   and pour contempt on all my pride…
> Were the whole realm of nature mine,
>   that were a present far too small;
> Love so amazing, so divine,
>   demands my soul, my life, my all.

So I ask you, Is your faith centered on the glory of God and on his great love for you and Christ's giving of himself as a fragrant offering in your soul and as a sacrifice to God? If the answer is No, then you will never be an imitator of God, because you will never know yourself to be his beloved child. There will be no affection great enough to expel all the evils that are native to your sinful flesh. You will go on living as you have done before, in bitterness or anger or slander, or in pride or self-righteousness, or some other way of fleshly sin.

I know that many will say, I know that God loves me as his dear child and that Jesus died for my sins and wants to live in my heart. Then I ask you, Are you walking in love? What an expression that is! Walk in love—this summarizes what Paul was talking about in Ephesians 4:32—becoming kind and tender-hearted and forgiving. 'Walk' means 'lifestyle'. So if someone were to characterize your lifestyle—the way you spend your time, what you think about and how you act—would they say this? So many of us are walking in pride or walking in materialism or walking in ambition or in selfish concern—these are the things that drive us. But God wants us, as his dear children, to 'walk in love,' cultivating kindness and a tender, forgiving heart, and in that way offering our own lives 'as a fragrant offering' in Christ's name.

In conclusion, let me say how wonderful it is what Paul says here. Earlier, he told us that we were born again to be like God 'in true righteousness and holiness' (Eph. 4:24). Now he tells us to imitate God as his beloved children, and he sums it all up in terms of love. This is the Bible's ultimate definition of holiness and of godliness—'Walk in love' in the self-giving footsteps of our Savior Jesus Christ. True holiness is always rooted in love and always expresses itself through love. Therefore, what Paul said about himself in 1 Corinthians 13 is true for us as well:

> If I speak in the tongues of men and of angels, but have not love, I am a noisy gong or a clanging cymbal. And if I have prophetic powers, and understand all mysteries and all knowledge, and if I have all faith, so as to remove mountains, but have not love, I am nothing. If I give away all I have, and if I deliver up my body to be burned, but have not love, I gain nothing…So now faith, hope, and love abide, these three; but the greatest of these is love (1 Cor. 13:1–3, 13).

53

Sexual Purity

Ephesians 5:3–7

The apostle Paul lived in a pagan age that wallowed in sexual sin. One scholar writes, 'The moral life of the Graeco-Roman world had sunk so low that…fornication had long come to be regarded as a matter of moral indifference, and was indulged in without shame or scruple, not only by the mass, but by the philosophers and men of distinction who in other respects led exemplary lives.'[346] Sadly, we live in a society that is little different. Western culture has been subjected to a 'sexual revolution' that has transformed our society into very nearly the image of Paul's pagan Roman Empire.

As a result, one of the main criticisms against Christianity today is our view of sex. It is conventional wisdom that Christians hold a revulsion against fun in general and sexual pleasure in particular. It is said, inaccurately, that Christians believe the original sin was the forbidden fruit of sexual love. Everywhere new sexual 'liberties' are discovered and trumpeted against the 'sexual repression' of fundamentalist Christianity.

The truth is, however, that the Bible and the Christian faith have an extremely high view of sex—much higher, I would argue, than the pagans have. We look upon sex as a gift from God to be enjoyed faithfully, reverently, and, yes, passionately. For Christians, love comes from God and is holy and wholesome. The same is true of sex within the designed bonds of marriage; it too is holy and wholesome. This is the difference between the pagan and the Christian view of sexuality. Not that they are liberated and we are prudes. Instead, while the sinful world looks upon sex as its master, Christians look upon sex as the servant of a deeper, more substantial love that mirrors the love of God.

A Call to Sexual Purity

As we work through the final section of Ephesians, we continue Paul's teaching about Christian holiness as a reflection and product of God's saving work in our lives. Paul began by insisting that Christians must no longer live as they did while in spiritual darkness and as pagans still do (Eph. 4:17). He told us to do this by putting off sin and putting on the holiness that is ours in Jesus Christ (Eph. 4:22–24). Paul then worked this out in terms of the attitudes of our hearts, writing that we must no longer live in bitterness, anger, or malice, but instead to forgive with compassion and 'walk in love, as Christ loved us' (5:2).

Paul now turns to sexual purity, which continues his emphasis that Christians must not live as pagans do. The concerns of holiness required Paul to deal with sexuality and the same is true today. His message here is direct: it is pointless for us to claim to be Christians and to hope for salvation if our sexual attitude and behavior is no different from that of the debauched society around us. Jesus emphasized this in his letters to the churches in Revelation. For instance, he praised the church in Pergamum for holding fast to his name, but criticized them because some of them practiced sexual immorality. 'Therefore repent,' he warned. 'If you do not, I will come to you soon and war against them with the sword of my mouth' (Rev. 2:16).

Any sober consideration of the state of Christians in America today, however, must conclude that we are in need of a similar rebuke, as in many ways we resemble our unbelieving neighbors when it comes to sexual sin. We are at ease in the presence of gross indecency—be it on television, in novels, in newspaper articles, or in person. Christians today are more horrified of being seen prudishly blushing than we are of contaminating our hearts and minds with sexual sin. Many Christians think nothing of celebrating adultery in songs that fill their minds or in sitcoms they watch. It is no wonder that surveys show that many Christian teens have sexual practices that are virtually the same as their non-Christian peers, or that stories abound of Christian adults committing adultery—including a shocking number of pastors.

A few years ago, I read of a minister who met with a group of Christian singles who measured their knowledge of sexually-driven movies and television shows against their knowledge of the Bible. He asked, 'Who's the character in Seinfeld with the funny hair?' Everyone screamed, 'Kramer!' 'What time does Friends come on?' A chorus sang out the time and the day and the station. He cited the first half of famous lines from different movies and they could perfectly complete them all. But then he asked them, 'What was the hour of the day that Jesus died on the cross?' There was no answer. Complete the sentence from Proverbs 3, 'Trust in the Lord with all your heart...' No one knew. 'Tell me the difference between justification and sanctification,' he asked, and silence filled the room.[347] That comparison says much about the state of the church today.

Our passage addresses this situation directly. Paul writes in verse 3, 'But sexual immorality and all impurity or covetousness must not even be named among you, as is proper among saints.' In this verse, he condemns sexual sin with three terms. The first is the Greek word *porneia*, from which we get pornography. This did not mean looking at dirty pictures, but sexual intercourse outside of marriage. It is therefore often translated fornication. This statement, along with many others in the Bible, shows that God intends and permits sex only within the marital union.

The second word Paul uses is impurity. This denotes all sexually unclean or indecent behavior. The city of Ephesus was an immoral port city. Their civic religion centered around the worship of Diana, the multi-breasted goddess of fertility, whose temple was filled with ritual prostitutes and where sexual indecency of every kind took place. America and the formerly Christian West is little better. Homosexuality is celebrated. Advertising is pornographic. Popular clothing styles, especially for young women, intentionally draw the eye to parts of the body that will incite lust. The list could go on. Paul says that Christians must turn away from 'all impurity,' which would include a wide range of behavior, including pornography, sexually provocative dress, and sexually charged speech.

Third, Paul speaks of covetousness. This might be translated as greed, but the context suggests a sexual desire for that to which one has no right. The tenth commandment says that we must not covet our neighbor's house or servant or ox or his wife. It is likely the last angle that Paul particularly is taking with this command.

Proper Among Saints

Having defined our terms, let me make four key observations from these verses. First, we may ask, 'Just how sexually pure are Christians expected to be?' We know our society is obsessed with sinful sex, but should we be expected to totally separate from these things?' Paul answers that sexual immorality, impurity, and lustful covetousness 'must not even be named among you.' The point is well made in the *New International Version*, which says, 'There must not even be a hint' of these things among Christians. This is the biblical standard of our calling to sexual purity.

This standard needs to be emphasized because the idea has gotten around that sexual purity involves nothing more than preserving one's technical virginity. But there is a wide range of sexually intimate behavior that is designed for marriage alone, including intense sexual contact and intimate sexual speech. The ancient church scholar, Origen, captures Paul's meaning when he relates this not merely to sexual intercourse, but 'also all the other inventions of sexual licentiousness in all their many and diverse practices.'[348]

Second, when Paul commands us against sexual 'covetousness' he is dealing not merely with our behavior but with our attitude. Jesus taught this in the Sermon on the Mount: 'Every- one who looks at a woman with lustful intent has already committed adultery with her in his heart' (Matt. 5:28). So sexual purity demands pure thoughts. Job was a model of this, providing sound advice for men today: 'I have made a covenant with my eyes,' and therefore he did not permit himself to gaze lustfully on a woman (Job 31:1). It is practically impossible for men to avoid visual stimulation in a society like ours, but if our hearts are determined towards purity we need not sin inwardly. Of course, our sisters in Christ who dress modestly—and this can be done in a way that is still feminine and attractive—are a great help to their brothers in their fight against lust. The point is that instead of asking, 'How much can we get away with?' Christians should be praying, 'Lord give me greater purity of heart.' We should cultivate a positive sexual purity of the heart, of the mind, of our speech and of our bodies.

In verse 4, Paul puts a spotlight on our speech: 'Let there be no filthiness nor foolish talk nor crude joking, which are out of place, but instead let there be thanksgiving.' So our speech is to be free from sexual impurity. Stott says of these descriptions, 'All three refer to a dirty mind expressing itself in dirty conversation.'[349] Curtis Vaughn explains, 'Paul is not condemning lively and sanctified humor. He is not calling upon us to be long-faced, gloomy people who dare not tell anything that evokes innocent laughter. A good, hearty laugh is often medicine for the soul. But there are some things of which Christians should never make jokes—some are too sacred, some too filthy.'[350]

Third, Paul gives us the reason for this high calling to sexual purity, namely that it is 'as is proper among saints.' Some will say, 'Sure, if I were a saint, then maybe I should be sexually pure.' But if you are a Christian, you are a saint. 'Saint' means 'holy one.' This high calling to purity corresponds to our holy calling to be like Jesus and also to our destiny as those who will spend eternity in God's holy presence. Paul reasons this way in 1 Corinthians 6:15, 'Do you not know that your bodies are members of Christ? Shall I then take the members of Christ and make them members of a prostitute? Never!'

The way we dress, the way we talk, and the way we act reveals what we think about ourselves. I hope you would be embarrassed to hear me tell an off-color joke or to make a sexual remark about a woman. I am a pastor and I am supposed to act like one. Likewise, a teacher who respects the dignity of her position will not speak inappropriately around students. A government official disgraces his office when he has an affair or tells a bawdy joke in public. And a Christian who sexually tempts others by his or her dress or demeanor, who tells dirty jokes, and especially who engages in fornication or adultery disgraces Christ before the world. If the way we act shows what we think about ourselves, it also shows what we as Christians think about our Lord, whose name we bear, and who suffered on the cross to make us holy.

Looking at verses 3 and 4 we find our fourth observation, concerning the manner in which we cultivate sexual purity. Paul writes, 'But let there be thanksgiving.' When we are grateful to God we use his good gifts in a reverent and responsible way. Peter O'Brien writes, 'Thanksgiving reflects a Christian attitude to sex that is antithetical to a pagan attitude with its immorality and vulgarity.'[351] When Christians are thankful for our forgiveness through the precious blood of Jesus Christ, then our hearts respond with a desire to please God and to lead a holy lifestyle that glorifies his name.

When sex is received with thanksgiving within the sanctity of marriage, it is one of God's most precious gifts to his people. This is why Hebrews 13:4 says, 'Let the marriage bed be kept pure.' Mike Mason, in his book, *The Mystery of Marriage*, reminds us of the preciousness of God's gift of sex, which we must guard and cherish:

> What can equal the surprise of finding out that the one thing above all others which mankind has been most enterprising and proficient in dragging through the dirt turns out in fact to be the most innocent thing in the world? Is there any other activity at all which an adult man and woman may engage in together (apart from worship) that is actually more childlike, more clean and pure, more natural and wholesome and unequivocally right than is the act of making love? For if worship is the deepest available form of communion with God…then surely sex is the deepest communion that is possible between human beings, and as such is something absolutely essential (in more than a biological way) to our survival.[352]

Be Not Deceived

Having insisted on sexual purity, Paul adds a dire warning that reminds us just how serious this matter is. The warning comes in two parts, the first of which comes in verse 5: 'For you may be sure of this, that everyone who is sexually immoral or impure, or who is covetous (that is, an idolater), has no inheritance in the kingdom of Christ and of God.' Those are sober words we need to take seriously.

We know from the whole teaching of the New Testament that all our sins, and certainly this includes our sexual sins, are forgiven when we trust in Jesus for our salvation. Paul wrote in Ephesians 1:7, 'In him we have redemption through his blood, the forgiveness of our trespasses, according to the riches of his grace.'

So Paul is not saying that sexual sin places us in an unredeemable situation, in which case there would be practically no one in heaven with Jesus. Instead, Paul's point is that habitual, unrepented sexual sin is so incompatible with Christianity that it is impossible that a man or woman willingly and positively immersed in sexual sin possesses a true and living faith in Jesus. If you know someone immersed in sexual promiscuity and the whole debauchery of our society—and we are surrounded by such people—you can be certain that they have no place in that kingdom ruled over by the Lord Jesus Christ and by the holy God, and in which alone forgiveness and eternal life can be found.

I want to emphasize this because of the sexual permissiveness that influences so many of us. We tend to think that sexual sin is no big deal. I had a conversation once with a prominent conservative preacher who was telling me that adultery was a sin, sure, but it wasn't that big a deal. Far worse are sins like pride or malice. I certainly would not downplay those other sins. Moreover, we do not want to so emphasize virginity that it becomes a way of salvation by works. We all have plenty of sins to condemn us, even if we are sexually pure. But I have to notice that when the apostle Paul presents lists of various sins in his different letters, he usually puts sexual sins at the top of the list. An example is Galatians 5:19, where Paul lists the sinful works of the flesh and begins, 'sexual immorality, impurity, sensuality' (see also 1 Cor. 6:9–11). I think the reason is that sexual sin really is serious: it tears apart families and destroys souls. Sexual covetousness is especially bad; Paul calls it 'idolatry,' the worship of a false god. Charles Hodge comments, 'Idolatry, which consists in putting the creature in the place of God, is everywhere in his word denounced as the greatest of all sins in his sight.'[353]

Some years ago, my wife and I were grieved by a young woman we had ministered to who fell away from the church. She came to visit us and we talked about her spiritual situation. She kept telling me how she was no longer a Christian and I kept reminding her about her prior life of faith. Eventually, she informed us that she was involved in an affair with a married man. We urged her to repent, but she said she had not the slightest intention of breaking off the sinful relationship and that she wanted it to continue. At that point, in light of passages like this one, it was my sad duty to inform her that she did not, in fact, have the right to consider herself a Christian or to have a hope of heaven, because those committed to sexual immorality have no place in Christ's kingdom.

Paul adds to this another warning, in verse 6, 'Let no one deceive you with empty words, for because of these things the wrath of God comes upon the sons of disobedience.' Here, Paul warns us about claims regarding sex that are empty of truth but full of lies to deceive us.

Let us consider some deceptions. One lie says that something is wrong with you if you are sexually innocent and pure. But that is not true. Innocence is one of God's great gifts and we should all pursue it instead of the crass insensitivity of our perverse age. Another deception says, especially to young people, that if you remain sexually pure you will lose out. You may indeed lose out on the fellowship of those who are given over to sin. But you will protect your heart from damaging scars and preserve the innocence of sex in your future marriage. You will miss out on a lifetime of shallow, unstable relationships that are built on sexual sin, and you will glorify God in a wonderful way that helps you to know joy.

Another deception says you can get away with toying with sexual sin. You can let your eyes linger and fill your heart with lust; you can start touching one another without going farther; you can safely indulge in pornography. What great lies these are! If a giant of the faith like King David fell hard and fast when he allowed himself to lust after Bathsheba, what will happen to you?

How about this for a mighty deception: 'Why fight it when you can't win?' Here is a lie that many Christians fall for. But in the power of God's Spirit, as those purchased from sin by Christ's blood, you can resist temptation. In verse 8, Paul says, 'At one time you were darkness, but now you are light in the Lord.' You can walk in the light; every Christian has power from on high to turn away from sin.

Those are all dangerous deceptions, but not the one Paul mentions. He says, 'Let no one deceive you with empty words, for because of these things the wrath of God comes upon the sons of disobedience.' Sexual sin is hateful to God and he responds to it with angry wrath—just ask Sodom and Gomorrah. It is idolatry and it is a defiling of what God has made for himself. This bodes very ill for a nation like ours that is self-consciously given over to sexual indulgence of every kind. This is another reason why Christians must be different, why we must be an example to others of sexual purity. It is not a laughing matter; according to the Bible sexual depravity is the harbinger of doom for a people who refuse to repent (see Romans 1:18–32).

When Tempted or When You Fall

So what does a Christian do when tempted by sexual sin? The Bible gives one clear, simple, and consistent answer: Flee! This is what Joseph did when Potiphar's wife sexually lured him: 'He left his garment in her hand and fled and got out of the house' (Gen. 39:12). In 1 Corinthians 6:18, Paul said: 'Flee from sexual immorality.' 1 Corinthians 10:14 elaborates: 'Flee from idolatry.' Writing to the young pastor Timothy, Paul said, 'Flee these things' (1 Tim. 6:11). Again, in 2 Timothy 2:22, Paul wrote, 'So flee youthful passions.' It is in that same spirit that he commands us in verse 7: 'Therefore do not associate with them.' Do not mix with the sexually immoral or partake of their activities.

This means that Christians overcome sexual temptation first by avoiding it. In this regard, the Bible is more realistic than many of us are. The Bible assumes that if you expose yourself to sexual temptation that it is likely to be too strong for you to resist. So do not put yourself in a compromising situation. When you do, it is because you have already decided to toy with the temptation, and so it is no surprise that such situations so frequently result in sin. The choice was made when the temptation was accepted. The biblical way to overcome sexual temptation is to flee it.

Let me apply this in closing to single Christians, to married Christians, and lastly to Christians who have already fallen into sexual sin.

First to singles: the reason so many single Christian adults struggle with sexual sin is that they are not married. Unless you have the gift of singleness that Paul describes in 1 Corinthians 7:7, which amounts to a lack of sex drive, then you should pursue marriage. Some adult Christians today, especially men, want to avoid growing up and so they avoid marriage. But that is gross folly and in many cases it involves sinfully rejecting God's provision for our sexual needs (see 1 Cor. 7:2, 9), and also sinning against single Christian women who have no one to marry as a result. I realize that many Christian singles long to marry, are prayerfully seeking a mate, and that is both challenging and painful.

For this reason, married Christians should be understanding of the challenges that singles face, just as single Christians should be appreciative of the opportunities that singleness provides. Nonetheless, it must be emphasized that the Bible's solution to sexual temptation is marriage. Paul wrote, 'because of the temptation to sexual immorality, each man should have his own wife and each woman her own husband' (1 Cor. 7:2), and gave this rule: 'if they cannot exercise self-control, they should marry. For it is better to marry than to burn with passion' (1 Cor. 7:9). This is not to say that young Christians should marry without careful consideration and sober judgment. But in light of the Bible's teaching, Christians should be generally supportive of marriage early in adult life. Moreover, young adult Christian couples who share a strong love and thus struggle with sexual temptation should consider an earlier marriage than perhaps they had previously planned.

Christians of all ages and generations have found long-term sexual abstinence unnatural, unhealthy, and very difficult. Members of the aesthetic movement of the fourth century AD tried to rid themselves of sexual desire through drastic measures taken against the body. John Chrystostom, the great preacher of that age, once tried to destroy his sex drive by living in a cave for a year in such cramped quarters that he literally could never sleep. After the year, he returned to society, got some sleep, and found that while his health was permanently damaged his sex drive was unharmed. One would like to ask Chrystostom if marriage would not simply be easier!

Those too young or who otherwise are not in a position to be married, but who are old enough to struggle with sexual temptations, must not expose themselves to things that will provoke lust. Today, this includes much that is found in popular music, in movies, on the internet, and in the whole youth culture of debauchery. Paul says in verse 7, 'Do not associate with them.' This is how Christian young people over the centuries have successfully combated sexual temptation, by actively cultivating purity, by avoiding temptation, and by separating themselves from the debauched ways of the world.

Now a word to married Christians. The way for you to be sexually pure is to cultivate an active and joyful sex life with your spouse. The idea that celibacy is a higher form of spirituality is simply wrong. It is opposed to the Bible, and it has tragically subjected countless priests and nuns to a warped life of sexual frustration. We were made as sexual creatures and the Bible tells us to cultivate sex within marriage. Wives must give themselves freely to their husbands, and husbands have a duty of ministering to their wives with their bodies (see 1 Cor. 7:3–5). I realize that in order to have a wonderful sex life in marriage you will have to love one another in other ways. You will need to cultivate emotional intimacy and spiritual unity. But this is what God wants you to do, and why he makes it necessary to a good sex life! So glorify God with the sexual purity of a vibrant and loving sexual relationship within marriage.

Last, what about those who have fallen into sexual sin? Perhaps you are in the grips of long-term sexual failure. It may be pornography or cravings that rule you. It may be an inability to say No. It may be a romantic relationship that already has gone too far sexually. Is there an answer for you, and what is it? Yes, there is an answer, and his name is Jesus. Take your sin to the cross, where the Son of God died to take away all your guilt and to cleanse you body and soul. Enter through him into a renewed relationship with your holy and loving heavenly Father. But you must repent in practical and concrete ways: Jesus said to the woman caught in adultery: 'I forgive you, now go and sin no more.' Devote yourself to him, walk with him, fill your mind with his Word and let prayer flow freely from your heart, and flee sexual temptations. You can always start again with Jesus Christ.

The apostle John wrote words that are valuable in all situations, but especially for those who have fallen into sexual sin: 'if we walk in the light, as he is in the light, we have fellowship with one another, and the blood of Jesus his Son cleanses us from all sin' (1 John 1:7). Let us confess our sin to God and seek his forgiveness. Let us be honest about our temptations. Let us act with integrity, obeying Paul's teaching by pro-actively guarding ourselves and our relationships from sexual sin. Then, knowing that the blood of Christ cleanses us from all our sins, including sexual ones, let us have peace in our hearts and let the power of the Holy Spirit lead us in a new and holy life as we walk with Jesus in a true and obedient faith.

54

Children of Light

Ephesians 5:8–14

At the beginning of Ephesians 5, Paul set forth a great principle for the Christian life. He wrote, 'Be imitators of God, as beloved children.' When we come to faith in Christ, we enter into God's family as God's own dear children, and we are called then to be godly, that is, to be like him. Paul says that we imitate God by the manner of our 'walk.' By 'walk' he means our lifestyle. We are not to have a lifestyle characterized by worldliness, consumer greed, or self-centered leisure. Our lifestyle is to be characterized by godliness.

If we are to imitate God, we need to know what God is like. The Bible has two great descriptions of God, which appear in John's first epistle. First John 4:8 says, 'God is love.' Corresponding to that, Paul says in Ephesians 5:2 that to imitate God we are to 'walk in love.' Paul focused on this loving lifestyle at the end of Ephesians 4. In the place of bitterness and anger and malice, he said, 'Be kind to one another, tenderhearted, forgiving one another, as God in Christ forgave you' (vv. 31–32).

We all like to think about 'God is love,' but 1 John 1:5 gives a second description that we do not remember as often: 'God is light, and in him there is no darkness at all.' This forms the second prong of the godly lifestyle. So Paul writes, 'Walk as children of light' (Eph. 5:8).

Psalm 27:1 says that God is our 'light and… salvation.' God's light warms us and reveals his truth. The apostle John wrote of Jesus, 'In him was life, and the life was the light of men' (John 1:4). So as those redeemed by Christ and adopted as God's own beloved children, it follows that we should 'walk as children of light.' Jesus said, 'Let your light shine before others, so that they may see your good works and give glory to your Father who is in heaven' (Matt. 5:16).

This is Paul's theme in our passage. He presents an instructive summary of the whole Christian life, telling us how to live as God's beloved children of light. The passage unfolds in four points: the qualification for children of light, the characteristics of children of light, God's command to those who would walk in the light, and finally, God's call to children of light who are slumbering in spiritual sloth.

The Qualification

People are drawn to light. The feelings evoked by flickering candles or colored light washing through stained glass makes people want to be religious. But there is a qualification that must first be met if we are to be true children of light. Paul notes it in verse 8: 'For at one time you were darkness, but now you are light in the Lord.'

According to the Bible, Christianity involves a radical and supernatural transformation of the inner life, and this is evident in what Paul says here. He does not say, 'You were in darkness,' or 'You were subjected to darkness.' No! He says, 'You were darkness.' This is what the Bible tells the natural man. You cannot walk in the light. Why? Because you are darkness. You cannot and you will not lead a holy, devout, and godly life. Why? Because you are yourself unholy, profane, and ungodly.

This is, of course, the great offense of Christianity, because it says that you cannot do it unless you are born again by God's saving grace. Christianity says the real problem with people is not the circumstances of their lives, not a lack of education, not bad relationships or dead-end jobs, but their moral bondage and spiritual corruption due to indwelling sin. Paul said in Ephesians 2, 'You were dead in trespasses and sins…following the course of this world, following the prince of the power of the air…by nature children of wrath' (vv. 1–3). Until you are born again, you are not a child of light but a child of darkness and of the devil and of God's wrath.

So how are you saved? To become a Christian is to come to Jesus, confessing your sin and your complete need of his saving grace. It means looking to the cross where Jesus died, saying, 'Lord, let your shed blood pay for my guilty sins.' Faith in Christ then brings us into a new realm, the kingdom of light and of salvation, over which the Son of God is Lord and Savior. Notice that Paul says we become light only 'in the Lord,' that is, through faith in Jesus Christ. He wrote in Colossians 1:13–14, '[God] has delivered us from the domain of darkness and transferred us to the kingdom of his beloved Son, in whom we have redemption, the forgiveness of sins.' This is the qualification for living as children of light. Jesus said of himself, 'Believe in the light, that you may become children of light' (John 12:36).

THE CHARACTERISTICS

How, then, do you know that you have been born again? As we just said, you know it through faith in Jesus Christ. But there are characteristics that will always be evident in the lives of those who have been transformed from children of darkness into children of light. Paul says in verse 9, 'For the fruit of light is found in all that is good and right and true.' These are the characteristics of light, biblically speaking—goodness, righteousness, and truth—and if we are born again into the kingdom of light, these will be seen in us.

The first is goodness. The basic idea here is generosity or benevolence. The word in the Old Testament that this translates was used of a king who had done 'good things' for Israel (Judg. 8:35; 2 Chron. 24:16). In Nehemiah 9:25, it describes the good things God gave to Israel in the Promised Land: 'cisterns already hewn, vineyards, olive orchards and fruit trees in abundance.' If we are children of light and if God's light is living in us, we will be good to others just as God is good to us.

Second, Paul says, 'The fruit of light is found in all that is…right.' We generally speak of righteousness in terms of our standing before God. But here Paul means our faithfulness to people and to obligations. Curtis Vaughn says it is 'regard for the rights of others, giving both to men and to God that which is their due.'[354] God is righteous to us—he fulfills all his promises and is faithful as our God. As he lives in us and as we imitate him as children of light, we will be righteous in all our dealings with others.

Third, Paul speaks of the fruit of 'all that is… true.' Whereas darkness is a place where things hide, light brings all things to view. So to be true is to have integrity and honesty in all things. It is the opposite of hypocrisy, which always wants to give a false impression. According to Leon Morris, 'Believers live their lives on a higher level than do unbelievers. "Truth" is made manifest in both what they do and what they say.'[355]

These are characteristics of those whose lives are filled with God's light. They are good, righteous, and true. So I ask, Does this describe you? Are these things someone living next door to you or working in your office would say about you? Is this what your children would say to their friends who ask about their parents? Or what your parents or friends would say about your children? If the answer is No, then you need soberly to examine your life. This is what matters about us—not money, status, or worldly achievements. Jesus said the tree is known by its fruit, and these are the fruits that grow in his light.

What, then, can you do if you are not good, right, and true? The Bible says you must confess to God, 'Lord, I am not the person you want me to be. I confess my sin and cling to Jesus for salvation, to be forgiven and to have his light shine in me.' This is what Paul was getting at when he said in 1 Corinthians 1:30 that God has made Christ Jesus 'our wisdom and our righteousness and sanctification and redemption.' Alexander Maclaren explained, 'The true way to adorn a life with all things beautiful, solemn, and lovely, is to open the heart to the entrance of Jesus Christ.'[356] This requires effort on our part, and we are to cultivate these characteristics by devoting ourselves to God's Word and by striving in prayer before the Lord. But the goal of all this is what Paul prayed for in Ephesians 3:17, 'That Christ may dwell in your hearts through faith.' Jesus said, 'Apart from me you can do nothing.' But he added, 'Whoever abides in me and I in him, he it is that bears much fruit' (John 15:5).

Corrie ten Boom tells a story about her father in a time of great financial hardship. A wealthy man came into his watchmaking shop and decided to buy the most expensive timepiece available, the sale of which would provide for all their needs. As her father was putting the cash into the box, the man mentioned that he was buying it because a nearby competitor had been unable to fix his previous watch. At this, Corrie's father asked to see the broken watch. After a few minutes of tinkering, he handed it back, fixed. 'There, that was a very little mistake,' he said. 'It will be fine now. Sir, I trust the young watchmaker. Someday he will be just as good as his father…Now I shall give you back your money and return my watch.'

Young Corrie was shocked by her father—by his goodness, righteousness, and truth. But he gently told her,:

> Corrie, what do you think that young man would have said when he heard that one of his good customers had gone to Mr ten Boom? Do you think that the name of the Lord would be honored? As for the money, trust the Lord, Corrie. He owns the cattle on a thousand hills and He will take care of us.[357]

This example reveals the fourth characteristic of the children of light. Paul adds, 'And try to discern what is pleasing to the Lord' (v. 10). This is another way in which we are to grow as God's children: by discerning what is good and pleasing to him. Would we have done what Corrie's father did? Only if we desire above all else to please and honor the Lord before the world.

As we face choices or decisions, we should ask 'Would Jesus like this? Will this bring glory to God?' When about to speak, we should ask, 'If I say this, will Jesus be pleased? Will this advance his kingdom and bear good fruit, or will it tear down and destroy?' This, then, is the standard for Christian conduct: not what men will approve, not what is acceptable according to the shifting morality of our times, not even what our own seared consciences will allow. The standard is this: What is pleasing to the Lord. And when we have gotten to know Jesus and love him, we will realize what a blessing it is to live this way. He said, 'My yoke is easy and my burden is light' (Matt. 11:28). And, as Mr ten Boom said, he owns the cattle on a thousand hills and will take care of us.

To do this, Paul says in Romans 12:2, we must no longer be conformed to the world, but instead must be 'transformed by the renewal of your mind, that by testing you may discern what is the will of God, what is good and acceptable and perfect.' It is only the believer who has learned to think biblically, by the prayerful and believing study of God's Word, who is able to understand and desire those things that please the Lord.

The Command

Having defined the qualifications and the characteristics of children of light, Paul now presents God's command: 'Take no part in the unfruitful works of darkness' (Eph. 5:11).

This is a direct and uncomplicated biblical command. It is something Christians took for granted not long ago, but has lately fallen on deaf ears. Christians have tried to engage the world by becoming worldly; nothing stirs such fears in the heart of an evangelical Christian today as the threat of been called legalistic or narrow-minded. This is especially a challenge as 'tolerance' is now considered the only moral absolute. But Paul asked in 2 Corinthians 6:14, 'What fellowship has light with darkness?' His answer here is none.

Let us be clear on what Paul is not saying. He is not telling us to cut off all contact with non-Christians. We are to be in the world, though not of it. In 1 Corinthians, Paul urged his readers to avoid a brother who had committed gross sexual sin. He told them 'not to associate with sexually immoral people' (5:9). But then he made clear that he was not talking about unbelievers—of course they are sexually immoral. The only way to avoid sexually immoral non-Christians is to leave the world altogether (1 Cor. 5:10). So while Christians are to be separate from the 'unfruitful works of darkness,' neither Paul nor Jesus tells us therefore to associate only with other Christians. How can we reach out to the world if we are cut off from it?

While we are to live in this dark world, Paul insists, 'Take no part in the unfruitful works of darkness' (Eph. 5:11). We are not to participate in things that promote sin and evil. If an activity or an event is spiritually unfruitful, if it represents the values of darkness—if it is not good, right, and true—then Christians are to stay away from it. This touches a broad range of our pagan culture today. But surely it will most significantly restrain us from much that is common fare in the entertainment industry and in matters of sexuality. It will cause us to be careful about business ethics and about interpersonal relations. It will shape what we do in our schools—surely a Christian school will be strikingly different from a secular one and a Christian who attends a public school will be unable to 'fit in' in many significant ways. We are to 'take no part' in the dark works of this godless world.

One reason for this concern is that the deeds of darkness are polluting. It is significant that

Paul says in verse 13, 'It is shameful even to speak of the things that they do in secret.' This probably refers to sexual debauchery, against which Paul spoke in verse 3. Obviously, Paul is willing to talk about this in the way he has done here. What he condemns is dwelling upon it and filling our minds with evil even as we condemn it. This is true with evil in general, not just sexual immorality, that the more we talk about it, it begins to stick to us and leave an indelible impression upon our minds. John MacArthur writes: 'Some things are so vile that they should be discussed in as little detail as possible, because even describing them is morally and spiritually dangerous.'[358]

This is what is wrong with much of the sex education today; it ends up tempting young people as much as instructing them. This is why we should not allow our eyes to be drawn to the newspaper articles that give lurid details of violence or sexual sin, since our fleshly nature will want to drink it in. I have stopped reading novels midway through because the writer was describing sexual encounters or acts of violence that my mind does not need to ingest. Likewise, I have walked out on movies I had mistakenly thought would be tolerable, when it became clear they were unfruitful and dark. This is an important reason for us not to partake in the unfruitful works of darkness. We belong to God and are not to pollute ourselves with sin and evil.

The second reason is found in the second half of verse 11. Instead of taking part in the works of darkness, we are 'to expose them.' This is done mainly by the way we live and the light that shines out from our lives. By seeing us, the children of darkness are to realize what they are missing and see, perhaps for the first time, what is wrong with the things they believe and do. William Hendriksen writes, 'By means of a life of goodness and righteousness and truth [Christians] must reveal what a vast contrast there is between the works of those who walk in the light and the works of those who walk in the darkness.'[359]

Paul wants us to expose sin simply with our lives, but this will inevitably involve speaking out as well. Christians should state the fact that abortion is the sinful taking of human life. We should plainly assert that marriage is between a man and a woman, that adultery is wrong, as is pre-marital sex, and that homosexuality is a sin. We should reprove pornography and point out the obvious evils of institutionalized gambling. We must speak out. But let us make sure that our lives are straight first! The order is essential. We must first live as children of light, then take no part in the works of darkness, and only then will we have the credibility to expose evil in a persuasive manner. It was because the prophets were themselves obedient to God that they could call the people to repent. Before we hold up the Bible before the world, let us first make sure it is the rule of our own lives.

The third reason why we must be separate from darkness is that a true and godly witness will not only expose sin but also serve to lead others into the light. This is Paul's point in saying, 'When anything is exposed by the light, it becomes visible, for anything that becomes visible is light' (vv. 12–13). After all, God saved us from darkness, and in many cases he saved us through the witness of a Christian who was wonderfully different from the darkness we knew. As God's light shines out from us to others he will draw many to himself and cleanse them with the healing light of Jesus Christ.

We see how much is at stake in our obedience to this command: 'Take no part in the unfruitful works of darkness' (Eph. 5:11). Not only is our own purity and blessing bound up in this, but our witness before the world is placed on the line. Alexander Maclaren wrote over a hundred years ago: 'I venture to express the strong and growing conviction that there are few exhortations that the secularized Church of this generation needs more than this commandment of my text: "Have no fellowship with the unfruitful works of darkness."'[360] If that was true in a time of comparative moral virtue, how absolutely vital is it for Christian people today.

The Call

This leaves only verse 14, in which Paul issues God's call to his slumbering children: 'Therefore it says, "Awake, O sleeper, and arise from the dead, and Christ will shine on you."' There is a great deal of debate about the source of this saying. Many commentators take it to be the words of a hymn popular in Paul's day. It is, however, more likely that Paul has a biblical citation in mind, since he writes, 'Therefore it says'. The closest parallel, from which Paul seems to be paraphrasing, is Isaiah 60:1, 'Arise, shine, for your light has come, and the glory of the Lord has risen upon you.'

Whatever Paul's precise reference, his meaning is clear enough. The church tends to fall asleep, its light dim in a world that is perishing in darkness. Looking back on his positive teaching for us to live as children of light and on his negative teaching for us to be separate from darkness, now he concludes, 'Wake up!' The stakes are so very high. The eternal consequences of what we do now are so great and definitive. It is of such importance that we take this to heart, examine ourselves, and arise in faith before the Lord.

It is always the case, without exception, that when God sends a true revival, he begins by first awakening the slumbering church. It is when Christians become serious about goodness, righteousness, and truth, when they begin to gather for fervent prayer, and when they take up a fresh excitement for God's Word and a sense of the glory of Christ's kingdom—it is then that God uses his people to shake the world. Our times and our land are crying out for a revival from God that will cast out this awful darkness and cause the people to see the great light of Jesus Christ. But first God calls to us, 'Awake, O sleeper, and arise from the dead.' Will it really matter if we do? Will such zeal be wasted? Will God respond to our renewed faith with a fresh outpouring of grace?

Jesus assured us that he will. He said, 'I am the light of the world. Whoever follows me will never walk in darkness, but will have the light of life' (John 8:12). Paul concludes our passage by stating this even more succinctly. 'Awake, O sleeper! Arise!' he calls. If we do, he assures us, 'Christ will shine on you.' And then Christ will shine through us, and our lives will have mattered for things of eternal glory and blessing, for the salvation of many who are even now perishing in darkness, and to the everlasting praise of our holy and loving God.

55

REDEEMING THE TIME

Ephesians 5:15–17

In the second half of Ephesians the apostle Paul develops his teaching on Christian holiness. Ephesians is known as one of the great doctrinal letters of the New Testament; but as we study this book I am impressed as well by the thoroughness of Paul's moral exhortations. The way he goes about this is worth noting. Paul does not rely on threats or promised rewards, though he might appeal to either. Instead, he appeals to the mind. This is consistent with his approach elsewhere. Romans 12:2 gives a classic expression of Paul's approach: 'Do not be conformed to this world, but be transformed by the renewal of your mind.' John MacArthur sums up Paul's view:

> Having the knowledge of God's Word control our minds is the key to righteous living. What controls your thoughts will control your behavior. Self-control is a result of mind-control…Knowledge of God's Word will lead to 'all spiritual wisdom and understanding' (Col. 1:9).[361]

In Ephesians chapters 4 and 5, Paul wants us to think biblically about certain key matters. He directs us to a biblical view of the ungodly world (4:17), Jesus and his teaching about holiness (4:21–24), God the Father and his love for us as his children (5:1–2), and ourselves as 'children of light' (5:8). In each case, Paul expects biblical thinking to produce biblical living.

In Ephesians 5:15–17, Paul makes his last point of this kind before moving on to his final instructions. He asks us to think rightly about the times in which we live and biblically to understand this present age. His teaching, in verse 16, is this: 'The days are evil.'

THESE EVIL DAYS

One of the great challenges for Christians today is biblically to assess these times of our lives. There can be little doubt that a worldly view of life exerts an unhealthy influence on Christian thinking today. The world, at least in the affluent West, views life as a playground for the self-focused pursuit of pleasure. In the airport where I once lived was an electronic screen flashing pithy sayings. One of the most frequent read, 'In the end, what life is about is having the most pleasurable experiences.' That sums up the view of our age. But Christians are to think differently.

When Paul says, 'The days are evil,' he is not commending the night-life! By 'the days,' he means this present age in which we live. This is in line with what he wrote to Timothy about the 'last days'. For Paul, the 'last days' are not those few years right before Jesus' return, but this entire age between the first and second comings of Christ, an age that he said is dominated by 'the prince of the power of the air' (Eph. 2:2), that is, the devil. He described it in 2 Timothy 3:2–4:

> For people will be lovers of self, lovers of money, proud, arrogant, abusive, disobedient to their parents, ungrateful, unholy, heartless, unappeasable, slanderous, without self-control, brutal, not loving good, treacherous, reckless, swollen with conceit, lovers of pleasure rather than lovers of God.

Is that not a perfect description of the world in our time? Instead of viewing the world as a giant Disneyland, safe and custom-made for our fun, Paul wants us to see it as it is, a spiritual battlefield where great harm threatens. This is why he concludes this letter with his famous teaching on the armor of God; only as equipped for spiritual warfare can Christians survive and thrive in these evil days.

I particularly appreciate the way the writer of Hebrews deals with this issue in Hebrews 2:1, where he says, 'Therefore we must pay much closer attention to what we have heard, lest we drift away from it.' He uses a nautical term, describing the way a ship at sail might drift off course or a ship in harbor might slip its moorings and be pulled out to sea. The harbor seems safe, but if the boat is not tied securely, it will drift out and be lost in the turblent ocean.

Years ago during a visit to Hawaii, my brother and I went snorkeling in a bay that was breathtaking in its beauty. It was so clear and peaceful and so calm. But the tour guide warned us not to go beyond the reef, lest we be pulled out by the current and have our bodies washed up on a distant island. Likewise, there is a pull to this present evil age, a strong current pulling us and our children into perilous waters. If we do not pay close attention to God's Word, if we relax our guard and become preoccupied with the sights and sounds of these enticing but evil days, we can be swept away forever. James M. Boice writes, 'You are never going to make any true progress in wisdom unless you begin by realizing that this world is hostile to God and opposed to any desires for godliness on the part of God's people.'[362]

Walking Wisely

Paul wants us to think biblically about these present evil days. From this he draws three applications for our lives. First, he says, in verse 15, 'Look carefully then how you walk, not as unwise but as wise.' Wisdom begins, he says, by rightly understanding the days in which we live, and wisdom proceeds by being careful about the manner of our walk, that is, about the kind of lifestyle we lead.

One good way to learn wisdom is to study folly. Paul wants us to do this, telling us to walk 'not as unwise.' So what does it mean, biblically, to be unwise? One place to turn is the Book of Proverbs, which is literally filled with foolishness. Let's look at some examples.

Proverbs 10:8 says, 'The wise of heart will receive commandments, but a babbling fool will come to ruin.' So a fool is one who does not pay attention to God's Word or take seriously God's commands. Proverbs 10:23 says that fools do not take sin seriously: 'Doing wrong is like a joke to a fool.' Proverbs 13:19 says that fools insist on exposing themselves to temptation. Whereas the wise are cautious, the fool is 'reckless and careless' (Prov. 14:16). The wise 'keep aloof from strife,' but 'every fool will be quarreling' (Prov. 19:29).

Lloyd-Jones describes some characteristics of a fool which we should avoid. Fools are governed by their emotions, and cannot give biblical reasons for what they do. Surely this describes much that goes on in churches today, much to our detriment. Likewise, fools are ruled by desires and passions, or by an ungoverned zeal. Fools think only of the present, and do not think through the consequences of what they are doing.[363]

Simply by avoiding these things we will be well on the path to wisdom. If we humble ourselves before God's Word and seek instruction from him, if we will think through our lives and the consequences of what we do, and determine to commit ourselves to God and his way, then we will become wise. Psalm 111:10 says, 'The fear of the LORD is the beginning of wisdom.'

What we want and need, Paul says, is a 'wise walk.' The way to walk wisely is to 'look carefully then how you walk.' Those who lead a wise and godly lifestyle are those who think about their lives, reflect on what they are doing and compare it to the teaching of God's Word, and who make godly corrections by repenting and seeking God's help through his Word and through prayer.

The word translated as 'carefully' (Gk, *akribos*) means 'exactly' or 'accurately.' Not many people think about 'walking exactly' today, except perhaps mountain climbers. On treacherous peaks they note every footstep, lest a slip should send them falling to their deaths. We should do likewise when it comes to our manner of living.

This wise attitude is exemplified in what the Bible says about Noah. In Genesis chapter 6, Noah is told of the great flood that will judge the earth—just as we are told of a coming judgment on our evil days. God gave him detailed instructions for building the ark, including precise measurements. Most people ignored the warning and continued to live loosely; Jesus said that as it was in the days of Noah, when people were devoted to folly and sin while judgment drew near, 'so will be the coming of the Son of Man' (Matt. 24:37). Noah was an example for us; Genesis 7:5 commends him, saying, 'Noah did all that the LORD had commanded him.' This is what it means to walk wisely, to observe and govern our lives so as to walk in careful obedience to God's teaching in the Bible.

Noah was like the Puritans in seventeenth century England. That name was given to them by scoffers because of their care for studying and obeying God's Word in their worship, their teaching, and their lives. Then, as today, people think such reverent attentiveness is narrow religion. They wrongly equate it with the attitude of the Pharisees, who made life difficult not with their biblical obedience but with their man-made traditions. But careful obedience to the Bible—to the moral teaching we have been studying in Ephesians, for instance—does not fetter you or make you narrow. Rather, it liberates you to what is good, true, and wholesome. This is why James wrote of 'the perfect law that gives freedom' (James 1:25). Studying and following through on God's Word will not shrink you but make you grow in wisdom and in life. Yet the path of obedience in this world is a narrow path, one that speaks both yes and no, one that keeps us in the ark and out of the flood, one that makes us ready for death and for Christ's return. It was Jesus who said: 'Wide is the gate and broad is the road that leads to destruction, and many enter through it. But small is the gate and narrow the road that leads to life, and only a few find it' (Matt. 7:13-14).

REASONS TO REDEEM THE TIME

Paul singles out one feature of a wise walk, writing, 'Look carefully then how you walk, not as unwise but as wise, making the best use of the time.' A wise Christian, he says, is one who examines his or her use of time, who treats time as a precious resource, and who makes the most of it. This is often translated as 'redeeming the time,' which better reflects Paul's meaning. He uses a marketplace term, the same one that is used of Jesus Christ redeeming his people at the cost of his blood. So with what do we buy or redeem our time? We buy edifying and godly uses of time by giving up unprofitable and ungodly uses of time. John MacArthur writes, 'Outside of purposeful disobedience of God's Word, the most spiritually foolish thing a Christian can do is to waste time and opportunity, to fritter away his life in trivia and in half-hearted service to the Lord.'[364]

Believers redeem the time by snapping up opportunities to do good and by letting go opportunities to sin or waste our time. Redeeming the time will mean picking up your Bible and turning off your television or walk away from the Internet. It will mean taking time that would otherwise be wasted to pray or to minister to someone in need or to share the gospel. It is no overstatement to say that how we use our time will determine our spiritual health and the usefulness of our lives. Young people should note this carefully, because now is a time when life-habits are formed. But we should also stress this to busy people in the prime of life. We are not redeeming the time if we have devoted our whole schedules to worldly pursuits and have no time for personal spiritual growth or Christian service. We should also emphasize this to more elderly believers. It is a great mistake to retire and stop redeeming the time. Many retired people stop living and begin dying long before their time. They, especially, should devote themselves to personal Bible study, prayer, good works, and service to Christ in the church. Paul says to us all, in Galatians 6:9–10, 'Let us not grow weary of doing good, for in due season we will reap, if we do not give up. So then, as we have opportunity, let us do good to everyone, and especially to those who are of the household of faith.'

I can think of four reasons why we must redeem the time. The first is that opportunities are precious and fleeting. Parents foolishly neglect opportunities to connect with their children and teach them good things. When God sends an opportunity to share the gospel with a loved one we must not waste it. We must have prepared for it in advance and then redeem the time by seizing it for Christ. Every one of us has a finite number of opportunities to do good works in Christ's name, to convey our love to the people in our lives, and to tell perishing sinners about Jesus Christ. Let us, therefore, redeem the time.

A second reason is because of the urgent need of today's evil. 'Redeem the time,' Paul says, 'because the days are evil.' War is not a time to relax. Soldiers in battle busy themselves digging foxholes, sighting weapons, and scouting terrain. Why? Because of the urgency of the matter and the seriousness of the consequences. So it is in these days. The sins that we let into our lives are agents of the enemy, so we must do away with temptations and make no provision for sin. Evil is ruining marriages, families, and children around us. Our whole society is reeling in sin— the prophets used the picture of a drunken man staggering in his stupor to describe a society like ours. So we must be sober and good, serving the causes of love and of truth. What John Calvin said of his time is true of ours as well:

> Since the age is so corrupt, the devil appears to have seized tyrannical power; so that time cannot be dedicated to God without being in some way redeemed. And what shall be the price

of its redemption? To withdraw from the endless allurements which would easily pervert us; to extricate ourselves from the cares and delights of the world; and, in a word, to renounce every hindrance.[365]

Moreover, we must redeem the time because the time is short. Not only is every opportunity precious, but the amount of time we have left to live for Christ is short. Jonathan Edwards pointed out that whenever a commodity is in short supply it has a higher value. Surely this is true of time. Job 9:25 says, 'My days are swifter than a runner; they flee away.' Should we live to an old age we will not look back and say, 'It went so slowly.' No, we will say, 'It went so fast!' And we will want to be glad that we redeemed the time that we had.

Edwards preached a sermon on this text and he argued that most of us need to be reproved for the way we use the short amount of time we have. He observed that many Christians spend 'a great deal of their time in idleness, or in doing nothing that turns to any account…either for their own benefit, or for the benefit of their neighbor.' He asks us to 'consider how much time you have lost already…You ought to mourn and lament over your lost time…you must apply yourselves the more diligently to improve the remaining part,' since time is short and once it is past it is gone forever.[366]

Fourth, we are accountable to God for our use of time, so we must use it wisely. Time is one of the 'talents' our Lord gives us and for which he will ask an accounting. The Bible is very clear that believers will bring their lives before Jesus to be judged by him. Paul says in 2 Corinthians 5:10, 'For we must all appear before the judgment seat of Christ, so that each one may receive what is due for what he has done in the body, whether good or evil.' This is not a judgment that threatens believers with condemnation and hell, because Jesus has removed all our sins on the cross. This is a judgment of accountability and reward. First Corinthians 3:12–15 says:

> Now if anyone builds on the foundation with gold, silver, precious stones, wood, hay, straw—each one's work will become manifest, for the Day will disclose it, because it will be revealed by fire, and the fire will test what sort of work each one has done. If the work that anyone has built on the foundation survives, he will receive a reward. If anyone's work is burned up, he will suffer loss, though he himself will be saved, but only as through fire.

Our use of time now has eternal consequences in terms of the nature of our future reward and calling to service. Jesus says to those who redeem the present time, 'You have been faithful over a little; I will set you over much' (Matt. 25:21). Martyn Lloyd-Jones put it this way:

> The one who came from heaven to earth for us and died on that cruel cross of shame on Calvary's hill; who spared not himself, who endured the contradiction of sinners. He who even bore that agony in the garden and on the cross, He will look at us—and what He will look for is this: how we spent our time in this world after we realized what he had done for us.[367]

The Will of the Lord

Paul sums up with one last application, in verse 17: 'Therefore do not be foolish, but understand what the will of the Lord is.' The ultimate description of a foolish Christian is one who looks on this world without understanding God's purpose. Paul is not talking about God's will for your personal life, or even God's secret and predestined will of what is going to happen. He means that we should understand God's purpose in this time period after the first coming of Christ and before his return to judge the world. As we are made wise by God's Word, we will discern three things about God's will in this present time.

The first is that now is a time to repent and believe. Many people foolishly plan to come to God sometime in the future. Is that you? The problem is that you do not know what your future holds. Jesus may come back tonight, or you may die and stand for judgment this very day. Moreover, you wrongly assume that it will be easy to repent and believe sometime in the future, after you have had your fun. There are three problems with this. First, all your sinning will only further corrupt your character, making it harder to repent. Second, by turning away now from Christ's offer of forgiveness, you harden your heart so that it is more spiritually calloused and less likely to respond. Third, this may be the last chance you ever have to hear and believe on Jesus, and thus to be saved. Paul wrote, 'Behold, now is the favorable time; behold, now is the day of salvation' (2 Cor. 6:2).

Second, this is a time for God's people to live by faith. We are to be growing spiritually. Paul said in Ephesians 1:4 that we were chosen in Christ to be 'holy and blameless before him.' 1 Thessalonians 4:3 says, 'For this is the will of God, your sanctification.' Therefore, we need to 'make the best use of the time, because the days are evil.' This does not mean that we can never relax or enjoy recreation. Christians should partake of the arts and culture; we should work to the glory of God and also play to the glory of God. Only let it be wholesome and not indulgent. 'Take no part in the unfruitful works of darkness,' Paul said in Ephesians 5:11. He adds, in Philippians 4:8, 'Whatever is true, whatever is honorable, whatever is just, whatever is pure, whatever is lovely, whatever is commendable… think about these things.'

Last, this is a time for gospel proclamation. After the resurrection, Jesus' disciples asked what now was to happen. Jesus replied, in Acts 1:8, 'You will receive power when the Holy Spirit has come upon you, and you will be my witnesses in Jerusalem and in all Judea and Samaria, and to the end of the earth.' This, especially, is God's will for these present evil days. When we are witnessing to the gospel, we not only are fulfilling God's will and purpose, but we can be sure of God's power working through us. Therefore, Paul says, in Philippians 2:15–16, 'Be blameless and innocent, children of God without blemish in the midst of a crooked and twisted generation, among whom you shine as light in the world, holding fast to the word of life.' The first Bible most people will ever read is the one they see in our lives. So we must redeem the time by being filled with Christ's light and then by shining that light to a dark and dying world.

If we become wise through God's Word, and thus understand what is God's will for these present days, then we will know what time is for. We will redeem time for every good thing, and especially for prayer, for personal Bible study, for good works, and for witnessing the gospel of Jesus Christ. And when this time has run out, another age will come. There will be a time that is not evil. Daniel 12:3 tells us about it: 'Those who are wise shall shine like the brightness of the sky above; and those who turn many to righteousness, like the stars forever and ever.'

56

True Spirituality

Ephesians 5:18–21

In 1951, Francis Schaeffer went through a spiritual crisis. Having been raised an agnostic, he had come to faith in Christ many years before. He was ordained a minister and served a church for ten years, before moving to Switzerland. Schaeffer was becoming well-known for his brilliant defense of Christian doctrine. But then came this crisis, which he said had two parts. The first was his realization that 'among many of those who held the orthodox position, one saw little reality in the things that the Bible so clearly says should be the result of Christianity.' The second part was worse, because it dawned on Schaeffer that 'my own reality was less than it had been in the early days after I had become a Christian.'[368] In short, though he was a doctrinally correct Christian scholar, his lack of true spirituality caused Schaeffer to doubt the reality of his entire faith.

This is a matter that the apostle Paul would understand. Here at the end of his general exhortation to Christian holiness, he now touches on the issue of spirituality. This is significant, because it warns us against false or counterfeit versions of holiness. It is very possible to do much of what Paul has written about in Ephesians 4 and 5—to be a person who cooperates and is generally loving and moral—without being really holy, indeed, without even being a Christian. Paul's interest is never morality as such; his concern is always that the reality of what God has done for us in Christ—the reality of what we are as born again and beloved children of God—would issue forth in the living fruit of love and purity. It is for this reason, it seems, that Paul ends his general moral teaching with an appeal to true and not false spirituality. In verse 18 he makes this distinction, and then in verses 19-21, he presents three characteristics of the heart that represent true spirituality.

True vs. False Spirituality

In one of the great statements in his earthly ministry, Jesus said, 'I have come that they may have life and have it abundantly' (John 10:10). Jesus said this during his Good Shepherd discourse, and he was talking about his sheep, whom he calls by name, who hear his voice and follow him. Jesus was making a definitive statement about Christianity that we need to hear again today. He says it is an abundant life, not a dreary existence of somberness and gloom. To be sure, Jesus taught that to follow him means to carry a cross, and that his people are the poor in spirit, those who mourn, and those who hunger and thirst for righteousness. But Jesus doesn't leave us that way. Those who hunger and thirst are filled. This is what Paul has in mind here.

It is necessary for us to define what 'spirituality' means. We are living in a supposedly 'spiritual' era. People are turning to spiritual gurus and buying into spiritual quests of all kinds. Popular singers and movie stars become 'spiritual' by taking up Buddhism, the Qabala, or science-fiction fantasy religions. These mystical routs are popular because they make no moral demands on them. You chant words, meditate, burn incense, and perform rituals, and then you are free to go on living any way that you want.

Paul gives us a working definition of false versus true spirituality in verse 18: 'Do not get drunk with wine, for that is debauchery, but be filled with the Spirit.' This tells us that Christians are not to abuse alcohol to get a high. Why? Because it leads to debauchery. John Calvin warned, 'Drunkards soon slip into immodesty and are not restrained by shame…where wine reigns, wantonness will rule.'[369] The Bible does not forbid alcoholic drinks. Jesus turned water into wine at a wedding, so it is hard for Christians biblically to argue against alcohol in general. But the Bible condemns drunkenness. John Chrysostom wrote, 'Wine was given to gladden us, not for intoxication.'[370] Especially in a day like ours where drunkenness is so common and such a plague upon families and our society, Christians should practice careful self-control in this area. Indeed, we should often be willing to forgo alcohol to set a good example for young people and others who may be especially tempted. Drunkenness is specifically listed among the sins of the flesh that God condemns (Gal. 5:21). When Paul wrote, 'Do you not know that the unrighteous will not inherit the kingdom of God?' he specifically mentioned drunkards along with the sexually immoral and the greedy (1 Cor. 6:9–10).

Paul's point in condemning drunkenness has a broader application to the point at hand. Paul is saying that any spirituality that relies on sinful or worldly stimulation is not true spirituality. His point is not restricted merely to alcohol or even to narcotic drugs. It can be applied just as well to music. Music is good, just as wine is; they both gladden the heart. But if in order to free up our spirits and especially to worship God we must first be intoxicated with the throbbing beat and the driving chords of popular music—or for that matter with the soaring elegance of classical music—then ours is not a true spirituality. I have been told, 'I cannot worship until I've first grooved with the beat.' Paul repudiates this utterly, saying, 'Do not get drunk' in order to lift your spirits. Our spirituality must not flow from or depend upon any worldly substance or influence or ritual.

There are addictions of all kinds—alcohol, drugs, music, television, video games, romance, novels, even work. Since what goes in so strongly determines what comes out, we must be self-controlled so as not to get drunk on these things.

'Do not get drunk with wine,' Paul says. 'But be filled with the Spirit.' We are indeed to live 'under the influence,' but that influence is to be the Holy Spirit as he lives and moves within us. This is the promise Jesus gave to all who come to him in faith. Jesus died, rose from the grave, and ascended to the throne of heaven so that we, having been justified through faith, may be filled with the Spirit. He offerred, in John 7:37–38, 'If anyone thirsts, let him come to me and drink. Whoever believes in me, as the Scripture has said, "Out of his heart will flow rivers of living water."'

It is noteworthy that on the day when the

ascended Jesus sent the Spirit onto his church—Pentecost—observers of the apostles thought they were drunk with wine. The onlookers mocked, 'They are filled with new wine' (Acts 2:13). Peter began his great Pentecost sermon by assuring them that they were not drunk but that the Old Testament prophecy had come true. They were filled with the Spirit. This makes the great point that Christians are to be so filled with the Spirit of God and thus to have a quality of life that the unbelieving world cannot make sense of us. Martyn Lloyd-Jones said,

> The Christian is meant to be a joyful person, one who is meant to experience the joy of salvation.... There are certain people, I know, who so react against the false and carnal sort of joy, that they rob themselves of the true joy. But the opposite of carnal and fleshly joy is not to be miserable. It is to have the true joy, the joy of the Lord Jesus Christ himself.[371]

How, then, do we become filled with the Holy Spirit? Some look at Paul's language here, comparing Spirit-filled to wine-filled, and conclude that this requires an intoxicated ecstatic worship experience, perhaps involving speaking in tongues. I find this to be very unlikely. Paul wrote to Timothy about similar matters, saying, 'For God gave us a spirit not of fear but of power and love and self-control' (1 Tim. 1:7). So experiences in which one loses control are not what Paul means by being filled with the Spirit. In 1 Corinthians, he wrote to a church that did speak in tongues that tongues was 'a sign for unbelievers' (1 Cor. 14:22), especially the Jews, and not an expression of outstanding spirituality.

The way to be filled with the Spirit is through the Word of God and prayer so that Jesus is exalted in your heart. Jesus said of the Spirit, 'He will glorify me, for he will take what is mine and declare it to you.' The Spirit is the author of Holy Scriptures, so to be filled with the Spirit is to be filled with the Word. The point of the Scripture is Jesus Christ in his glory as Lord and Savior. So to be filled with the Spirit is to have a present, personal relationship with the living Lord Jesus, to walk with him, to see life through his eyes, and to think with his mind. To be filled with the Spirit is to be filled with Christ. It is to be Christ-like and Christ-infatuated. It is, Paul wrote, 'Christ in you, the hope of glory' (Col. 1:27). This is possible because Jesus died to remove your sins, and rose again so that he might live in you through his Word and by the Holy Spirit if you will only trust in him.

A Heart Filled with Song

I began by mentioning Schaeffer's spiritual crisis. He realized that his Christian faith had begun to consist of little more than answers to questions, without any spiritual life. He took some time off from work and began exploring his relationship with God. As he retraced the steps that had made him a Christian in the first place, Schaeffer regained his confidence in the truth of the gospel. What, then, was his problem? He explains in his book, *True Spirituality*, 'I saw that the problem was that with all the teaching I had received after I was a Christian, I had heard little about what the Bible says about the meaning of the finished work of Christ for our present lives.' His point was that Jesus' death and resurrection relates not merely to our past—by removing our sins—and to our future—by securing us a home in heaven—but also to our present lives as our saving Lord who lives in us by the Holy Spirit.

As Schaeffer sought out the meaning of this in God's Word and in prayer, he says,

Gradually the sun came out and the song came. Interestingly enough, although I had written no poetry for many years, in that time of joy and song I found poetry to flow again—poetry of certainty, an affirmation of life, thanksgiving and praise. Admittedly, as poetry it is very poor, but it expressed a song in my heart which was wonderful to me.[372]

I am not surprised that Schaeffer's rejuvenation resulted in poetry and in song. This is the very thing the apostle Paul turns to next as an overflow of true spirituality: 'Addressing one another in psalms and hymns and spiritual songs, singing and making melody to the Lord with all your heart' (Eph. 5:19).

C. S. Lewis commented that there is no singing in hell. But in heaven, there are songs lifted up to the glory of God. So if we plan to go to heaven, we had best learn how to sing, and singing is ultimately a matter of the heart. So 'be filled with the Spirit,' Paul says, 'making melody to the Lord with all your heart.' Paul mentions three kinds of music, 'psalms and hymns and spiritual songs.' This shows us that there is variety in worship music, including those that come straight from the Bible, those that proclaim Christian truth, and those that express spiritual joy.

This passage tells us what matters most about worship music. In comparison to wine, it should be joyful but not intoxicating. To be filled with the Spirit our songs should be saturated with God's Word and sound doctrine. There may be songs for all kinds of moods and feelings, but there should always be thanksgiving (v. 20) and reverence (v. 21). What matters most is not the harmony produced by our voices—although this verse shows that Christians should learn to sing—but what matters most, Paul says, is 'making melody to the Lord with all your heart.' Kent Hughes writes:

Spirit-filled people overflow in song! This has been attested again and again in times of great spiritual blessing…In the Reformation, Martin Luther brought hymn singing to the Church. During the Wesleyan Revival, Charles Wesley wrote 6,000 hymns…Think of the music…during the spiritual harvest of the late 1960's. There is a sense in which when people are born again, music is 'born again' in their souls. And if they remain full of the Spirit, life brings an ongoing symphony of soul.[373]

A Heart Uplifted with Thanks

Where Christians are filled with the Spirit, they are also filled with thanks. Paul writes about this in verse 20: 'Giving thanks always and for everything to God the Father in the name of our Lord Jesus Christ.' Since being filled with the Spirit means being filled with the glory of Christ and the knowledge of his Word, there is no other response possible than thanks to God the Father. Just as a healthy person, with a good flow of blood, is able to generate his own warmth against the cold, so also is a Christian filled with the Spirit and moved upon by God's grace, able to feel thanksgiving to God. Those who chronically complain and show unwavering discontentment reveal that what they truly lack is the Spirit of God lifting up the heart.

Notice that Paul says that Spirit-filled Christians give 'thanks always and for everything.' If we are filled with the Spirit, our thanksgiving to God will not be dependent on outward circumstances. By faith and through God's Word, Spirit-filled Christians know God's love even when life seems to be against them. They never forget that the Son of God purchased their salvation at the cost of his own precious blood. Remembering that, nothing can take away their thanks to God the Father, who gave his only begotten Son for us.

We should especially give thanks to God when he answers our prayers. Some years ago, one of our nation's space missions was in grave danger and the American people were asked to pray for the safe return of the astronauts. 'When they were safely back on earth, credit was given to the technological achievements and skill of the American space industry. No thanks or credit was publicly given to God.'[374] Sadly, this response is common among Christians, too. When God blesses us or answers our prayers, we seldom take time to thank him. All our prayers should include thanks to God for his abundant blessings and loving care; as we are truly spiritual, 'filled with the Spirit,' we will not have to be reminded of this because our hearts will give thanks 'always and for everything' to God the Father in Christ's name.

A Heart Responding in Submission

As we conclude with verse 21, I have to observe that few of us would have anticipated Paul's third application. If we were to list the marks of true spirituality, submission would not have ranked highly on many lists. This just goes to show how unspiritual we are without the corrective influence of God's Word. Surely, as well, this is one place where Christian spirituality and worldly spirituality most strongly differ. But if we remembered what Jesus taught we would not be so surprised. 'Whoever would be first among you must be your servant,' he said, 'even as the Son of Man came not to be served but to serve, and to give his life as a ransom for many' (Matt. 20:27-28). With this in mind, it is not so surprising that Paul concludes this passage saying that being filled with the Spirit means 'submitting to one another out of reverence for Christ' (Eph. 5:21).

This begins a major theme for the apostle, as he works out the Christian principle of submission in marriage, in the family, and in the workplace. We will spend our next four studies working through those. For now let me just point out that spirituality is not individualistic, but demands a humble attitude of submission and servanthood.

Paul literally says that if we are filled with God's Spirit, we will have 'fear of Christ.' Unbelievers have reason to fear Jesus with dread and loathing. They fear God's justice and wrath and this should bring them to repentance. But for Christ's sheep and God's children, fear of the Lord has a positive quality. Jerry Bridges writes, 'It is the attitude that elicits from our hearts adoration and love, reverence and honor…[like] the awe an ordinary but loyal citizen would feel in the close presence of his earthly king,'[375] only more, since Christ is King of kings and Lord of lords. The apostle John tells us that while he was 'in the Spirit on the Lord's day' (Rev. 1:10), he saw the exalted Lord Jesus in his glory: 'When I saw him, I fell at his feet as though dead' (Rev. 1:17). No one who is filled with the Spirit feels chummy with Christ or casual about worship. True spirituality fears the Lord with awe and, as Psalm 2:11 says, 'rejoices with trembling.'

But notice how fear of God works out in our relationships: 'Submitting to one another out of reverence for Christ.' We will spend more time on this in the passages to come, but suffice it to say that the Spirit-filled Christian does not resent God-given obligations in the church, in marriage, or in the workplace, but out of reverence for Christ freely submits to others for their benefit and God's glory.

My Soul Magnifies the Lord

We should all ask Francis Schaeffer's question: Is there any reality to the life of Christ in me? Do I have a present relationship with Jesus so that he is filling me with his Spirit? We might also ask, Does my heart have a song to sing? Am I thankful always for everything? Am I content to submit and to serve as Jesus did for me? Jesus said, 'I came that they may have life and have it abundantly' (John 10:10). This reminds us that these things can only happen in Christ. Jesus can only live in us if he first died for us, as we receive his salvation through faith. The life that Jesus gives, which makes music in the heart, with thanks and humble reverence to the Lord, comes only through the Holy Spirit he sends to live in us.

When I think of true spirituality, I am reminded of one of my heroes in the faith. It is a sister in Christ who lived long ago, a teenage girl who was filled with the Spirit. Her name was Mariam, although we know her as Mary. She provides as lovely a portrait of true spirituality as any found in the Bible. In a scene of amazing godliness and faith, Mary uttered words that often come to my mind as epitomizing the attitude of reverent submission that God wants from you and from me. Mary was betrothed to be married when an angel of the Lord came to her with astounding news: 'The Holy Spirit will come upon you, and the power of the Most High will overshadow you; therefore the child to be born will be called holy—the Son of God' (Luke 1:35). It did not make sense—since she was a virgin—and the implications must have been terribly frightening for her. But Mary was a believer, she knew she was safe in the hands of her loving God, and she willingly submitted to his will. Humbly, Mary said five words in the Greek text that are six in English, and I can only imagine her kneeling as she said them: 'Behold, the handmaiden of the Lord.'

This is the truest spirituality: our willing, glad, and thankful submission to the will of God as given to us by his Word. Through Mary's submission to God, Jesus Christ came into the world to be her Savior and ours. In an analogous though different way, through our submission to God, and our submission to one another out of reverence for Christ, Jesus comes through us into the lives of other people, for blessing, for salvation and for the glory of God.

Is this all Christianity offers—submission and obedience? By the power of the Holy Spirit, Mary received God's grace not merely for submission, but also for thanksgiving and for joyful song. One of the most beautiful songs in the Bible was written as the music in her heart, a song of thanks to God the Father in the name of her son and his Son. Mary sang the Magnificat: 'My soul magnifies the Lord, and my spirit rejoices in God my Savior' (Luke 1:46–47).

If you are filled not with wine but with the Spirit, with reverent humility and thankfulness to God, your soul, too, will magnify the Lord. And God will give your heart a song to sing. Someday soon you will advance to a heavenly choir that will sing with joy forever, as even now they sing in heaven: 'Hallelujah! For the Lord our God the Almighty reigns. Let us rejoice and exult and give him the glory' (Rev. 19:6–7).

57

WIVES SUBMITTING TO HUSBANDS

Ephesians 5:22–24

One of the great threats to a true and living Christianity is the notion that our religion can be safely compartmentalized into just certain portions of our lives. Nothing so destroys our witness or hinders our spiritual growth as the idea that we can be Christians on Sunday and worldly people on the other six days. Instead, as Martyn Lloyd-Jones observes, 'Christianity has something to say about the whole of life. There is no aspect of life which it does not consider, and which it does not govern.'[376]

This is especially the case when it comes to the various relationships in our lives. Christianity restores us to a right relationship with God and also to a right relationship with other people. If our faith in Christ and the work of the Spirit are to permeate all that we are and all that we do, then this will be seen in every kind of relationship. Beginning in Ephesians 5:22, Paul takes the Christian principle of submission, introduced in verse 21, and works it out in various kinds of relationships. The first of these is marriage, about which Paul writes: 'Wives, submit to your own husbands, as to the Lord. For the husband is the head of the wife even as Christ is the head of the church, his body, and is himself its Savior. Now as the church submits to Christ, so also wives should submit in everything to their husbands' (Eph. 5:22–24).

General Observations

This is a teaching that cuts right across the grain of our society's secular humanistic thinking. It is a teaching that many women, and men, too, find difficult to accept. Furthermore, and I think this is particularly true because it is so controversial, it is a teaching that is often misrepresented and misunderstood. For these reasons, it is best to begin with some general observations.

First, we need to consider the basis of what Paul writes in this passage. Many people who hold a liberal view of Scripture, that is, who will not accept it as God's inerrant Word, write off these remarks as merely representing Paul's personal attitude towards women, which they suppose to be negative. Or, many say, we have to realize how poor was the treatment of women in the ancient world, and assume that Paul reflected or accommodated the culture in which he lived. The fact that Bible-believing Christians continue to advance a teaching like this is considered an outrage in these quarters.

How do we respond to this criticism? Our first response is that the Bible is God's inerrant Word.

What Paul writes as an apostle does not reflect his own attitude but is the revealed Word of God. Paul himself wrote, 'All Scripture is God-breathed' (2 Tim. 3:16). If he was wrong about that, then we should hold every bit of his teaching in suspicion and should evaluate it all against more modern thinking. This is the very thing liberal Christians have done; having found the Bible's teaching unacceptable to their modern ears they have simply set it aside. The result is that they believe very little of what the Bible teaches, whether about wives or homosexuals, or the atonement of Christ and his bodily resurrection. In contrast, we who receive the Bible as God's Word we must receive it all, not picking and choosing according to our own flawed and sinful wisdom.

It was true that the lot of women in the ancient world was very poor. Wives were treated with little respect and they could be easily cast aside by their husbands. The situation in the Israel of Paul's day was so bad that many Jewish girls refused to marry because marriage offered so little security and protection. But far from reflecting or accommodating their world, Jesus and his apostles strongly confronted it. Paul's teaching on marriage is one that gives status, dignity, and security to women. It is no coincidence that in countries where the Bible has had a strong influence the situation of women has improved dramatically, whereas under other religions women are treated as property of their men.[377]

A second observation is that the Bible does not, in fact, single out women for submission. All Christians are called to submit. This is Paul's general theme, which he is now working out in detail: 'Submit to one another in reverence to Christ' (Eph. 5:22). All believers are to submit to Christ, our Lord and King. All of us are called to submit to secular authorities put in place by God (Rom. 13:1-7; 1 Pet. 2:13-17) and to spiritual authority in the church (Heb. 13:17). To be a Christian involves submission and we are all called to it.

This does not mean that there are no distinctions. You will sometime hear it said that Paul teaches 'mutual submission' between husbands and wives. This is not true. Paul has set down the principle of submission (5:21) and he works it out in terms of three relationships: wives submitting to husbands, children submitting to parents, servants submitting to masters. In each case, he also exhorts those who receive submission to provide loving godly leadership. But that is not the same thing as 'mutual submission.' Masters do not submit to slaves, parents do not submit to children, and husbands do not submit to wives.

What the Bible does teach is *mutual servanthood*. When God gave Adam dominion over the earth, it was to servant-lordship. Genesis 2:15 says, 'The LORD God took the man and put him in the garden of Eden to work it and keep it.' Those two verbs might be better translated as 'to nurture' and 'to protect.' This is the Bible's definition of true masculinity: a man who nurtures and protects so that those under his care grow and feel safe. This is servant lordship. Eve was then made as 'a helper fit for him' (Gen. 2:18). The wife is called to be a servant-helper and the husband to be a servant-leader; one submits and one leads, but both minister as servants. John Calvin expressed this well, saying, 'Where love reigns, there is mutual servanthood.'[378]

My last initial observation is that submission, like servanthood, is a mark of redemption in Jesus Christ. God created men and women to live in a harmony of mutual ministry. Sin has changed this, replacing submission and servanthood with an instinct for self-interest and a lust for self-glory. But Jesus said he came 'not to be served but to serve, and to give his life as a ransom for many' (Matt. 20:28). Where he lives and rules, this is always the pattern. He said, 'If anyone would be first, he must be last of all and servant of all.' (Mark 9:35).

Wives Submit

Let's now turn to Paul's actual teaching in this passage. The first question is *what*: what does 'submit' mean? The answer is straightforward. The word Paul uses for 'submit' simply means 'obey'. It means that wives are willingly to accept the authority of their husbands in their God-given role of leading the marriage.

The particular word that Paul uses, *hupotassomai*, tells us important things about the submission of wives. It is used here in the middle mood, which means that it is something that someone does to him or herself. It is thus not husbands who place wives into submission but wives who actively take up this position with respect to their husbands. Moreover, we should note that when Paul goes on to speak of the submission of children to parents and slaves to masters, he uses a different word, *hupakouo*, which speaks of a more drastic subordination. Speaking of the word that Paul applies to wives, while it includes obedience to commands, it has the more general sense of arranging our lives under someone else's direction.

This makes the point that the submission of wives is an active rather than passive calling. Just as a good manager in the workplace is creative and shows initiative, a godly wife does not wait around for detailed orders like some low-level lackey, but she acts assertively in purpose of the goals worked out together with her husband. Daniel Doriani writes: 'A wife can exercise considerable authority in the home and yet be submissive to her husband if she manages their money, property, and time in the ways they have worked out together.'[379] This is exactly what you find in the Bible's great description of a virtuous wife, in Proverbs 31: 'The heart of her husband trusts in her, and he will have no lack of gain. She does him good, and not harm, all the days of her life' (Prov. 31:11–12).

When I was serving as an officer in the United States Army, I learned the difference between an active and willing subordination and a sullen or passive obedience. Soldiers who served under an unpopular commander were quite able to obey the letter of their orders while completely undermining the spirit and intent with which they were given. The submission of wives to their husbands should be a willing subordination working towards shared aims and purposes.

Next, we should note carefully *to whom* wives are to submit, namely, 'their own husbands.' The Bible does not teach that all women are to submit to all men in general, or that sisters are to submit to brothers, or that wives are to submit to other husbands than their own. Paul is writing about the marriage relationship. To be sure, the Bible elsewhere establishes a mandate for male leadership in the church, but it never tells women to submit to men in general in the church; women and men together are to submit to the male spiritual leadership raised up by God to govern his church.

A third question is *how far*: what are the limits of a wife's submission in marriage? Paul says in verse 24, 'Now as the church submits to Christ, so also wives should submit in everything to their husbands.' This means that there is no compartment within the marriage outside of the husband's leadership. If a wife says, 'I will submit to him in some things, but not in our finances, or the raising of our kids, or my career goals,' she is violating God's command. This argues that a Christian woman should be careful about the character and discernment of the man she chooses to marry, because once she has married him God will expect her to submit *in everything*. Likewise, women who doubt the wisdom or godliness of the man they have already married had better pray for their husbands. They should remember that they were given as a helper to the man and get busy giving the help their husbands need.

Does this mean there are no limits to a wife's submission? No, it does not. Husbands have no right to direct their wives to sin. If a non-Christian husband demands that she not attend church, she must refuse, since God is a higher authority (see Acts 4:19). A wife is not her husband's slave. While she is called to minister to her husband's sexual needs, she is not a sex toy. She is not required to endure active abuse, and she has a right to expect her husband to fulfill his biblical obligations to her (see Exod. 21:7–11).

This is part of the value of being members of a biblical church. If a woman is mistreated by her husband or if he breaks covenant with her, she should come to the pastor and elders. A wife does not forfeit her right to pastoral care by virtue of marriage. As church members, she and her husband are called to submit to the same spiritual authority. Having a church which will defend her rights and exercise its authority over her husband as required, the Christian wife is freed and encouraged to submit to him as best she can.

The Motive for Wives' Submission

What, then, should be the wife's motive as she submits to her husband? God always cares about the motives of our hearts as much as our actual actions, and having the right motives will make all the difference for the blessing a wife receives through her submission.

First, let's deal with false and erroneous motives. Does a wife submit because she is inferior? The Bible says, No. The first thing the Bible says about women is that they, like men, are made in the image of God: 'God created man in his own image, in the image of God he created them; male and female he created them' (Gen. 1:27). Women are men's equals before God, which is why Paul wrote, 'There is neither Jew nor Greek, there is neither slave nor free, there is neither male nor female, for you are all one in Christ Jesus' (Gal. 3:27). Paul was not challenging his teaching elsewhere about the differing roles of men and women, but rather was affirming their equal status and worth in God's sight and in the church.

In verse 23, Paul says, 'For the husband is the head of the wife even as Christ is the head of the church, his body, and is himself its Savior.' Does that mean the wife worships her husband as God? Certainly not. A husband is a fellow creature, and therefore is not an object of worship, and he most certainly is not able to be her Savior. Nor does she submit because God has made her his slave, and he her master. A wife is a companion and a helper, not a slave.

How about this: Does a woman submit to her husband when and as he has earned it? Does she submit on the condition that she thinks he will do the right thing? Certainly, it helps for a wife to admire and have confidence in her husband. But this is not the basis of her submission to him, and she has no right in the Lord's eyes to refuse to submit because she doesn't think he deserves it.

Should she submit because it will work out better for her that way? This was the premise of a best-selling book, titled, *The Surrendered Wife*.[380] It taught that women should stop hassling men and give them what they want. Why? Because then they will get along and he will hand over the credit cards. Here is submission as a tactic for manipulation, and it is not a biblical motive.

So what are the motives for a Christian woman to submit to her husband? The place to start is with the order God established in his creation of the human race and marriage, in which the man was called to lead and the woman was called to be his helpmeet. Whenever Paul writes about male-female relationships, in marriage or in the church, he never points to the customs of his day but to God's arrangement in the original creation. This is his point in verse 23, 'For the husband is the head of the wife.'

We see this all through the creation account. Adam was made first and was installed by God as lord over all the creation, under God's higher authority. The woman was made from the man, and God gave her to be his helper (Gen. 2:18). Most significantly, just as Adam named all the creatures of the air and ground and water, he likewise named Eve. Naming is a function of lordship, and God established Adam as her lord and head. This is not erased in our redemption and in the kingdom of Jesus Christ, for redemption has the effect of restoring what God originally intended. Therefore, Paul says, 'The husband is the head of the wife even as Christ is the head of the church, his body, and is himself its Savior.' There is an analogy. A husband takes a wife and becomes one flesh with her and pledges to provide for and protect her, and he is appointed as her leader by God.

But what if the wife is more intelligent or otherwise more able than her husband? In that case, she ought to be an outstanding helpmeet, but not a usurper. This reminds me of an experience early in my military career. Having first served in a terrific unit where I was taught by an exceptional commander, I was promoted to be deputy commander of a tank company whose captain was less sterling. I confess that after just a few weeks I concluded that I was the more competent officer (which was not saying much) and that my captain lacked the ability and character to succeed. But I also realized that it would be wrong for me to usurp his authority or to show him disrespect. To do so would only disgrace me, as his deputy, and would upset all the lines of authority in the unit. So what did I do? I realized that my job was to support him and help him. When he gave bad orders, I tried to dissuade him. When that failed (as it often did), I did my best to implement them in a way that would work out as well as possible. I did not permit the sergeants or men to speak poorly about him in my presence. In all these ways, it was my duty to make him as successful as possible. The same is true of a wife. She is called by God to help her husband—and most of us husbands need quite a lot of help. But she only disgraces both him and herself if she seizes his role or shows disrespect, and she trains their children also to resist authority (including hers). As C. S. Lewis remarked, there is no one who admires a woman who dominates her man, not even other women who might be doing the very same thing.[381]

So the first reason for a wife's submission to her husband is her acceptance of God's design for blessing. But there is a related motive, namely, that her submission is a remedy to the cursed effects of sin in the marriage relationship. When Adam and Eve sinned, God cursed the woman with pain in childbearing, and added: 'Your desire shall be for your husband, and he shall rule over you' (Gen. 3:16). Sin creates striving, and striving brings conflict. The word for 'desire' means both a craving for control and an obsessive desire to possess the man; women abundantly show the effects of this curse even today. In order to remedy this, redeemed wives are called to reject the sinful impulse to seize control and instead to submit. A man who is dominated by his wife has abandoned his calling and is respected by no one; but a woman who submits brings peace and harmony to her home.

The chief motive by which wives should submit to their own husbands is given in verse 22: 'as to the Lord.' This goes along with verse 21, which says we are to submit 'out of reverence for Christ.' Wives are to submit to their husbands not because they are worthy of obedience but because Jesus is. Wives submit to their husbands as part of their living worship to Christ. They look for blessing not merely from their husbands, but also from Christ, who always blesses the obedience of his disciples. Lloyd-Jones writes, 'You are not doing it only for the husband, you are doing it primarily for the Lord…You are doing it for Christ's sake, you are doing it because you know that He exhorts you to do it, because it is well-pleasing in His sight…It is a part of your discipleship.'[382] This is always the true motive for everything Christians do, men and women alike, even as Paul said, 'Whatever you do, do all to the glory of God' (1 Cor. 10:31).

The final motive for a wife's submission is the powerful witness it gives to the gospel. I will go so far as to say that there are few greater opportunities for a Christian witness today than that of a godly woman's submission to her husband. The world's rebellion against God and his way has made an anguishing mess of marriage, with husbands and wives striving against one another and unable to get along. When a Christian woman submits to her husband out of reverence to Christ, she can be sure of ridicule at first, but that ridicule will turn to wonder and marvel at the blessings God gives. Again, Lloyd-Jones puts it well:

> These other people—living as they do, asserting their own rights, and displaying the arrogance which leads to all the chaos that characterizes life—when they look at you will see something so different that they will say, 'What is this? Why do you behave like this?'…And your answer will [be]…'I am behaving like this because it is the will of my Lord.' So you immediately get an opportunity for preaching and stating the Gospel.[383]

If you are an unbeliever here today, and you are listening to this astonishing teaching, and you see women embracing it seriously as their calling in Jesus Christ, realize that you are encountering something the world does not have or even know—power from God for humility and self-abasing love in the name of Jesus Christ. Jesus came to serve us by dying on the cross for our sin, and he now empowers us to redeem our relationships in selfless love. If you will confess your need of him, Jesus will do this for you. He will serve you so that your sins are washed away, and then he will call you to serve others for a life of peace and blessing and joy.

IMPERISHABLE BEAUTY

Let me conclude with a few applications, starting with some words to husbands. First, make sure you read your own mail and do not focus on God's Word to your wife. God does not call husbands to harangue their wives about submission; he calls husbands to love their wives. Second, it is important for husbands to value their wives and the contributions they make to our lives. If God made her to be your helper, then obviously you need help. Seek it and be grateful for it. Listen to your wife when she gives you counsel and, yes, loving criticism. Talk about your life with her, work out your goals together, and cultivate companionship and unity. Third, realize what an obligation comes to you through the submission of your wife. If you love her, your rule will not involve tyranny, and you will never ask her to submit to something harmful or humiliating. Moreover, realize that it is not easy submitting to you. So get serious about your spiritual walk. Start being the man God wants you to be, since your wife and children are relying on you and submitting to you in Christ.

Now let me give just two pieces of advice to wives. Realize the opportunity and influence God gives you as a wife. Your submission has power to inspire your husband to greater godliness, but many wives simply do not give their husbands space to grow because of their controlling demands. You should take special joy watching him grow in Christian stature not merely *as* but also *because of* your submission and ministry of help to him. Second, this means that your speech is especially important. Paul sums up his teaching on marriage in verse 33, saying, 'Let each one of you love his wife as himself, and let the wife see that she respects her husband.' You can destroy your marriage and embitter your husband, through nagging and contemptuous speech. Or you can build him up and fill him with noble desires by speaking to him with respect and affection.

Let me conclude by reminding us that all Christians—men and women alike—are sons of God and brides of Christ. Our 'sonship' speaks to our status as God's heirs. 'Brides' speaks of the purity and beauty we offer to our Lord. We are all called to submit to Jesus, as the bride who offers him her love. But how especially fitting and beautiful it is for Christian women to embrace this calling, finding in it not limitation but opportunity, because of the honor and delight it brings to Jesus.

In his passage on this same theme, Peter wrote, 'This is how the holy women who hoped in God used to adorn themselves, by submitting to their husbands, as Sarah obeyed Abraham, calling him lord. And you are her [daughters], if you do good and do not fear' (1 Pet. 3:5–6). 'Perfect love casts out fear,' says 1 John 4:18. Let Jesus' perfect love for you drive out the fear that keeps you from God's calling. Women who know Christ's love have freedom to adorn themselves with, as Peter wrote, 'the imperishable beauty of a gentle and quiet spirit, which in God's sight is very precious' (1 Pet. 3:4), submitting to their husbands as to the Lord.

58

Husbands Loving Wives
Ephesians 5:25–33

It is not hard to make the argument that marriage is the most important of all human institutions, both in the world and in the church. One way to see this is in Paul's statement in Ephesians 5:32, that marriage is an emblem of the greatest union of all, that between Christ and his church.

Another way to see the importance of marriage is to note that the devil began his assault on God's creation by striking the relationship between Adam and Eve. Steve Farrar, in his book *Point Man,* states accurately that Satan has two main strategies in the culture war: first, 'to effectively alienate and sever a husband's relationship with his wife;' and second, 'to effectively alienate and sever a father's relationship with his children.'[384]

The apostle Paul seems to agree with that assessment. In back-to-back passages he deals with a man's obligations in both relationships. This is especially urgent today as families are dying all over America, on your street and on mine. In most cases the autopsy reveals the same cause of death: the conflict between husbands and wives. An imperative need in our society and in our churches, is for husbands and wives to unite through obedience to God's Word, and for their union to serve as the foundation for a loving, secure, and godly family.

In the previous passage, we noted God's calling for wives to submit to their husbands. This is something everyone in the ancient world would have acknowledged. But Christianity adds the revolutionary idea that husbands also have a duty to their wives and to their children. Such an obligation was unthinkable in Rome, Athens, Persia, or even in the Jewish culture then prevailing in Jerusalem, since women in the ancient world were virtual possessions of their husbands. Paul was making a radical declaration, then, when he wrote: 'The husband is the head of the wife even as Christ is the head of the church.' This kind of headship is one of ministry and responsibility for blessing.

The Bible's approach emphasizes not our privileges but our duties and obligations before God. The world always talks about privileges and rights—so that wives complain about what their husbands owe them and husbands talk about what their wives should be doing. But the Bible directs us to our duties in obedience to God. As John MacArthur puts it, 'God's way to successful marriage focuses on what husbands and wives put into it, not on what they can get out of it.'[385]

How important, then, is the role of Christian men as heads of the home before God. Our society's plague of failed marriages and broken homes must largely be ascribed to the failure of husbands and fathers. Conversely, when Christian men accept their calling to Christ-like leadership in the home, they may confidently look to God for blessing on their marriage and on their children.

A Call to Christ-Like Love

The Bible's commands for marriage have the virtue of simplicity, but they are anything but easy. This is true of the Bible's command that wives submit to their husbands. But how much more difficult is God's command to husbands. Ephesians 5:25 states it plainly: 'Husbands, love your wives, as Christ loved the church.'

You can hardly get more simple than that, but obeying it is possible to sinful men only as Christ lives in them by the power of the Spirit.

This teaching, like Paul's command to wives, serves to remedy the effects of sin in the Fall. Genesis 3:16 says that sin causes wives to usurp their husbands' authority, so the New Testament commands wives to submit. Sin's curse on men, shown in Genesis 3:17–19, works in the opposite direction. 'Cursed is the ground because of you… By the sweat of your face you shall eat your bread.' Thus men tend to neglect their wives to pursue their identity in their work. As a remedy, husbands are specifically told to love their wives.

Men respond, 'But I do love my wife—that's why I married her!' Perhaps, then, we should define our terms. The Bible uses four words for love. First, there is *eros*, which is sexual love. For many men, their love for their wife rises little above this level. Another word is *filia*, friendship love. Here, when a man says he loves his wife, he means that he loves the things she does for him and the fun they have together. Third, is *storge*, which is familial love. People say, 'We're in the same family—we have to love each other!' None of these are the word that Paul uses here. Instead, he uses the highest word for love, agape, which describes God's love. D. A. Carson has ably made the point that the Greek word *agape* does not necessarily mandate a special, divine love, so we should not base this category of love simply on Paul's use of this particular word.[386] Nonetheless, the concept of a God-empowered, giving love is certainly biblical, and it is clearly the intention of Paul in this passage to promote the kind of love generally associated with this word *agape*. Here is a love that is based not on what a man *gets*, but on what he *gives*. It is a love that is not selfish but selfless; it is based not on a wife's worthiness but on what God has done in a man's life to cause him to give his love.

In this light, husbands will not find it so easy to say, 'Sure, I love my wife.' Here is the love modeled by Christ's love for the church, a love that has four features outlined in our passage. It is a *sacrificial love, a redeeming love, a caring love,* and *a committed love.*

Self-Sacrificing Love

How did Christ love the church? Paul says, 'He gave himself up for her' (Eph. 5:25). This, of course, refers to Christ's sacrificial death on the cross. Jesus Christ died so that all who believe in him might be forgiven and live. This is the ultimate definition of love: Jesus said, 'Greater love has no one than this, that someone lays down his life' (John 15:13). This is the *sacrificial love* for their wives to which all husbands are called. The famous theologian Karl Barth was once asked what is the most important word in the Bible. He answered that the most important word in the Bible is *huper*, the little Greek word that means, 'on behalf of.' Here is the heart of the gospel, that Christ lived and died and rose again 'on behalf of' us and for our salvation. This is also to be the heart of a husband's love for his wife as well, to live and to die 'on behalf of' her.

A story from the Greek histories shows what this will do for a marriage. Cyrus the Great was the Persian emperor made famous in the Bible for allowing the Jews to return to Jerusalem after their exile. On one occasion the wife of one of his generals was accused of treason and condemned to die. When her husband learned of this, he rushed into the throne room, threw himself before the king, and cried out, 'Oh, my Lord Cyrus, take my life instead of hers. Let me die in her place.' Cyrus was touched by this display. He replied, 'Love like that must not be spoiled by death,' and he allowed both husband and wife to go free. As they walked away, the relieved husband asked, 'Did you notice how kindly the king looked at us when he gave you the pardon?' But his wife replied, 'I had no eyes for the king. I saw only the man who was willing to die in my place.'[387] If a husband wants to enjoy such affection from his wife, he need only follow this example.

But let me add just one thing. It is easy for men to think of dying dramatically—and bloodily—for our wives in some grand gesture. That strokes our egos. But what Paul specifically has in mind is for husbands to *live* sacrificially for their wives. This means a dying to self-interest to place her needs before your own. It means a willingness to crucify your sins and selfish habits and unworthy character traits. I remember a husband who told me he had always thought that if a man came into the house with a knife to attack his wife, sure, he would be willing to die defending her. 'Then I realized,' he said, 'that emotionally and spiritually, I am that man who assaults my wife and threatens her well-being. What God calls me to do is put my own sinful self to death.' This is the truest understanding of this call to sacrificial love, and it is our duty as Christian husbands.

Redeeming Love

The second feature of Christ-like love is that it is *redeeming love*. Paul expresses this in one of the more remarkable and informative statements about Christ's saving ministry for us: 'He gave himself up for her, that he might sanctify her, having cleansed her by the washing of water with the word, so that he might present the church to himself in splendor, without spot or wrinkle or any such thing, that she might be holy and without blemish' (Eph. 5:25b-27).

If we follow this progression we see the Christian gospel in terms of Christ's preparation of a bride for himself. This is a major theme in the Bible. Revelation 21:2 looks into the future when the church will be presented to Christ, 'coming down out of heaven from God prepared as a bride adorned for her husband.' The gospel is the story of God's Son winning a bride who will bring him glory and joy forever.

Paul says Christ gave himself up 'that he might sanctify her, having cleansed her by the washing of water with the word' (Eph. 5:26). 'Sanctify' means to make holy, especially in terms of 'setting apart' or 'consecrating.' Here, this probably alludes to the ancient bridal bath, in which a young woman prepared for her wedding with a ceremonial bath, signifying the washing away of her former life and the cleansing of her body for marriage. Christ cleansed his bride by 'giving himself up for her,' that is, by dying on the cross for her sins. Paul says he cleansed her 'by the washing of water,' which points to Christian baptism as the emblem of Christ's death. Moreover, Christ accomplishes this 'with the word,' that is, through faith in his gospel.

But this is not the end. He did this 'so that he might present the church to himself in splendor, without spot or wrinkle or any such thing, that she might be holy and without blemish' (Eph. 5:27). Christ's saving work goes beyond merely gaining our forgiveness. He is at work now making us holy and cleansing us from sin. Though our spiritual growth may seem slow and partial, and though Christians in this life never fully attain the Christ-likeness to which we are called, in the age to come we, his bride, will be made glorious in beautiful perfection. This life is like the bridal chamber in which Christians are being cleansed in anticipation of a wedding that is soon to come. Christ adorns us with his own righteousness and in the end he will make us glorious, to sit beside him on his throne and bring praise to his name forever. This is Christ's ultimate goal for us and the destiny of all those who come to Christ in faith. It is something that he does by his power, and therefore it is our sure future. Martyn Lloyd-Jones says of the church: 'She will look young, and in the bloom of youth, with colour in her cheeks, with her skin perfect, without any spots or wrinkles. And she will remain that way forever and ever.'[388]

This is what Christ is doing in our lives, and as we look forward to our wedding day we ought to be filled with thanks and love for him. But what is so remarkable is that Paul points to this as a model for the love Christian men are to have for their wives. As Christ's love redeems us for glory, a husband's love ought to be directed towards the spiritual growth of his wife. Notice, too, that this ministry is associated with a husband's words. The Greek word used here is *thema*, which signifies actual words, rather than the more common *logos*, which speaks of a message in general. This makes the point of how important a husband's words are to his wife. Far from badgering or tearing down his wife with his speech, loving husbands are to remind their wives of God's love and minister for their blessing and increased spiritual beauty. John Stott says of the godly husband:

> His headship will never be used to suppress his wife. He longs to see her liberated from everything which spoils her true feminine identity and growing towards that 'glory', that perfection of fulfilled personhood which will be the final destiny of all those whom Christ redeems. To this end Christ gave himself. To this end too the husband gives himself in love.[389]

CARING LOVE

Third, Christ-like love is *caring love*. Paul explains this in Ephesians 5:28–30: 'In the same way husbands should love their wives as their own bodies. He who loves his wife loves himself. For no one ever hated his own flesh, but nourishes and cherishes it, just as Christ does the church, because we are members of his body.'

One of the tragedies of recent times is the warping of our definition of masculinity. We have been taught that a real man is a self-centered, weather-beaten stoic who is emotionally distant from members of his family. Nothing could be further from God's design. Instead, Paul says a husband's love for his wife should be as intimate and as dedicated as his care for his own body: 'For no one ever hated his own flesh, but nourishes and cherishes it' (Eph. 5:29). Many sincere husbands, however, simply do not know how to care for their wives. Paul gives them direction with two key words: *nourish* and *cherish*.

First, a husband cares for his wife by nourishing her heart. Back in Genesis 2:15 the Bible made its fundamental statement of what a man is called to do: 'The LORD God took the man and put him in the garden of Eden to work it and keep it.' The idea is that of nurture and protection. Adam was a gardener, and a gardener's work is to make things grow. Likewise, a husband is to tend and cultivate the soil of his wife's heart. This requires him to pay attention to her, to talk with her in order to know what her hopes and fears are, what dreams she has for the future, where she feels vulnerable or ugly, and what makes her anxious or gives her joy. The sad fact is that most husbands have no idea of the answers to these questions, for the simple reason that they pay so little attention. First Peter 3:7, an important parallel to Paul's teaching here, says, 'Husbands, live with your wives in an understanding way.' The point is for husbands to live in concert with their wives and get to know them. Every day a husband should know his wife's plans for the day and especially the anxieties and hopes of her heart. This will enable him to pray for her in a meaningful way and encourage her. Most important to her is the simple fellowship of a man who loves her enough to pay attention to her and share her life.

In addition to nourishing, Paul says men care for their wives by cherishing them. The Greek word, *thalpo*, has the specific meaning of *warming*. It is used of a mother who *comforts* a baby by holding it close. The husband is to warm his wife with his affection, which comes through in the way he spends time with her and speaks about her, so that she feels safe and loved in his presence. First Peter 3:7 says that the husband is to 'show honor to the woman,' treating her as a person of great worth to him.

In my experience, a husband's caring love is one of the greatest needs in most marriages. Just as a husband is driven off by a nagging or controlling wife, a wife's heart is dried up by a husband who pays her little attention, takes no interest in her emotional life, and does not connect with her heart. If husbands don't know where to start, they should just ask; their wives will be able to give them plenty of useful advice on how-to, if only they will listen.

The Bible tells us to 'love your neighbor as yourself.' But when it comes to a man's caring love for his wife, it really is love for her and love for himself. This is because marriage is a union of two people into one. Any man who wants happiness, peace, and harmony in his life will wisely pursue it by loving his wife. So seriously does God take a husband's caring ministry for his wife, that our failure to do so may cause God to refuse our prayers (1 Pet. 3:7; Mal. 2:14). A Christian wife is still Daddy's little girl, and husbands are held to account by God for their ministry to the daughters of Zion.

COMMITTED LOVE

The fourth feature of a husband's Christ-like love is that it is a *committed love*. In Ephesians 5:31, Paul cites Genesis 2:24: 'Therefore a man shall leave his father and mother and hold fast to his wife, and the two shall become one flesh.'

Just as Christ is faithful to the church, a husband must be faithful to his wife. He is joined to her so long as they both shall live, and their bond is not to be broken by anything short of death itself. When a man marries, he leaves behind his former life and begins a new life in union with his wife. Commitment expresses itself in a couple becoming 'one flesh,' a statement that refers not merely to sexual union but the sharing of a whole life in the safe bounds of committed love.

One barrier to committed love is when a husband refuses to transfer his allegiance from his parents to his wife. 'A man shall leave his father and mother and hold fast to his wife.' A husband who shares marital secrets with his parents or who cannot break free from his family's control is not able to offer his wife the devotion she needs.

Marriage involves forsaking all others in favor of an exclusive, intimate, and indivisible bond. John MacArthur writes: 'As Christ is one with His church, husbands are one with their wives. Therefore…a husband who violates his marriage violates himself. A husband who destroys his marriage destroys a part of himself.'[390] In Paul's pagan world, as in our own, marriage was undermined by insecurity, as men and women exchanged partners the way they changed clothes. But a Christian husband offers his wife the security of committed love, in which she can blossom emotionally and spiritually.

In all of these ways—in sacrificial love, in redeeming love, in caring love, and especially in that committed love that creates a binding union—Christian marriage is a portrait of Christ's union with the church. 'This mystery is profound, and I am saying that it refers to Christ and the church. (Eph. 5:32). Paul says it is a mystery how Christ can be joined to the church as a husband is joined to his wife, so we are not going to be able to explain it perfectly. But what we do understand is simply wonderful. The Son of God has committed himself to us in love for all eternity. He has promised to complete our redemption from sin until one day we will shine in glory. He cares for our needs, nurturing our spirits and keeping safe our souls for eternal life. Best of all, he promises to receive us as a groom receives his bride with delight, and to give of himself—his treasures, his pleasures, and his glories—forever and ever in unbreakable love.

If marriage is a picture of that—Christ's love-union with the church—then what an incentive everyone has to say, 'I do' to Jesus, by putting their faith in him, and asking him to be their Savior. It also means there is nothing more profound in all this world that the sacred bond of marriage, and no more solemn duty than those owed by a wife to her husband and a husband to his wife. Paul thus concludes, 'Let each one of you love his wife as himself, and let the wife see that she respects her husband' (Eph. 5:33).

BECAUSE GOD LOVED US

In 2 Corinthians 2:16, Paul was writing about the demands of the gospel ministry and he exclaimed, 'Who is sufficient for these things!' No doubt that is how many husbands will feel in light of God's commands to them for marriage. Wives, too, inevitably feel this way about their husbands. But God's call to a wife is not to point out the many ways her husband falls short, but rather to respect and help him. If a wife feels let down by her husband—as most inevitably will—her answer is to look to Christ for her needs and to pray for the Holy Spirit's work in her husband's life. 'No man can love his wife as Christ loved the church unless the Holy Spirit comes into his heart and enables him to do so.'[391] Ultimately, that is the answer to the need of Christian men. Paul said, 'Not that we are sufficient in ourselves…but our sufficiency is from God' (2 Cor. 3:5).

Can we enjoy happy marriages? Worldly wisdom says it happens only if a couple is especially compatible, if their likes and wants are the same. Most of us find out sometime after the honeymoon that we aren't as compatible as we thought, and for so many that spells marital trouble. But the world does not know the love of God, the *agape* love that gives without thought of receiving, and that comes into our lives through faith in Jesus Christ. A Christian couple finds their compatibility through a shared experience of Christ's love and a shared commitment to obey the Word of God. This alone will produce the spiritual resources and the shared vision needed for harmony in marriage. Joel Nederhood rightly says, 'In order to have a good marriage, both partners really need to believe the Bible, love Christ, and have his Spirit in their hearts, and want to live in their marriage the way God tells them to live.'[392] If you want a good marriage, that is what you will do. Christian couples can enjoy the highest blessings in marriage—and it is so important that we do! It is important to our lives, to our children, to our church, and to our Lord. But it will only happen as we walk close to God and devote ourselves to our calling in marriage—wives to submit and husbands to love.

The Bible says, 'We love because God first loved us' (1 John 4:19). Can a man love his wife with Christ's own love? Yes! But only if his life is filled with a knowledge of God's love for him in Christ. Then, filled with God's love—learned in God's Word and cultivated in prayer—he simply shares it with his wife to the praise and the glory and the pleasure of God.

59

IN DISCIPLINE AND INSTRUCTION

Ephesians 6:1-4

One disheartening sign of our times is the family breakdown, including the relationship between children and parents. Several reasons are given for this, such as the stress of modern life or the influence of the media. Some celebrate the breaking of old patterns and look for new arrangements to replace the traditional family.

According to the Bible, however, the breakdown of the family results from a greater breakdown between society and God. Paul argues in Romans, 'Since they did not see fit to acknowledge God, God gave them up to a debased mind to do what ought not to be done' (Rom. 1:28). In his list of depravity, he says they are 'disobedient to parents' (Rom. 1:30). He makes the same argument in 2 Timothy 3:2, where rejection of God's Word leads to a situation that could have been lifted straight out of our newspapers: 'People will be lovers of self, lovers of money, proud, arrogant, abusive, disobedient to their parents.'

The opposite is also true, that spiritual renewal results in a restoration of parent-child relations. In the last passage of the Old Testament, the prophet Malachi looks forward to the coming of the Messiah and the entry of God's kingdom. He says, 'Behold, I will send you Elijah the prophet before the great and awesome day of the Lord comes. And he will turn the hearts of fathers to their children and the hearts of children to their fathers' (Mal. 4:5-6). Paul knew how important this is to the life of God's people, so he continues his teaching on biblical submission, writing, 'Children, obey your parents in the Lord, for this is right' (Eph. 6:1).

The Duty of Children to Parents

When we considered Paul's teaching on marriage, in Ephesians 5:22-33, we noted that the Bible is not afraid to emphasize our duties. We live in a time that cares only for rights and privileges. But the Bible reminds us that there can only be order and blessing when we focus on our duties instead of our rights. In this passage, the apostle points out two duties that children owe their parents.

The first of these duties is for children *to obey* their parents. Here, the apostle clearly places children under the authority of their mother and father. In Colossians 3:20, he amplified this: 'Children, obey your parents in everything, for this pleases the Lord.'

In Roman civil law, a child never came of age and was required to render absolute obedience to his father until death. The Bible does not follow this way of thinking; in Ephesians 5:31 Paul teaches that upon marriage, a man leaves the authority of his parents. But until children leave the home they must obey their father and mother.

The word Paul uses for obedience, *hupakouo*, might be literally translated as 'to hear under.' He depicts child-like obedience as listening to a parents' words and responding obediently. When a parent speaks with words of instruction or command, children are to listen and respond. Obviously, there are limits to this obedience; a parent's authority does not override the higher authority of God. A child should never be forced to sin and should not obey sinful commands.

The second duty children owe to their parents is to *honor*. Paul cites the fifth commandment, which says, 'Honor your father and mother' (Eph. 6:2). Obedience deals with a child's *actions*; honor addresses a child's *attitude* toward his or her parents. Hendriksen explains, 'To honor implies to love, to regard highly, to show the spirit of respect and consideration.'[393] Perhaps this comes through most clearly in the way children speak to their parents. In years past, it was more common to hear children address their parents (and other adults) with respect, calling them 'sir' and 'maam.' Today, some children think nothing of belittling their fathers or mothers; parents should never permit this and Christian children should be countercultural by showing respect to their parents.

Some children will respond that their parents are not easy to honor or admire. The well-known Bible teacher, James Montgomery Boice, admits that this was a problem he had growing up. His father was a busy doctor who was seldom home and did not communicate well when he was. Boice recalls, 'I cannot remember ever having had a meaningful and constructive conversation with my father.' But as he grew into adolescence, Boice's commitment to Jesus Christ challenged him about his attitude. He decided to look for things to admire in his father. He was hardworking and provided well for the family. One reason he was seldom home was his devotion to healing the sick. Furthermore, Boice began to realize that the money his father made provided him with things many other children could not afford, especially a quality education in private schools. He learned that his father was generous and never boasted about his giving. He gave faithfully to the church and charitably to those in need. This helped Boice to appreciate his father, despite his misgivings.[394]

The duty of children to honor their parents extends throughout life. Long after children have grown up and moved away from home, they still are to show this affection and respect. Jesus made clear that this includes the duty to care for our parents in old age; one of his accusations against the hypocrisy of the Pharisees had to do with the sinful neglect of their needy parents (Matt. 15:3–6). There are few more telling indictments of our society than our lack of honor and concern for the elderly in general and parents in particular. We should value the wisdom of older Christians in the church; young parents would do well to get to know some of our older members and look to them for advice. Honoring our parents calls for a mother to send pictures of the grandchildren to her parents and in-laws. It calls for us to move a parent into the guest room, or if they must go into a nursing home to visit them often and pray for them. Honoring our parents may involve sending money to an aged mother or father on a fixed income. It involves giving time for a phone call or a weekend visit.

Paul gives two reasons to go with these two duties. First, he says, 'For this is right.' This is why children are to obey their parents—not because

Dad is bigger and stronger and his punishment is to be feared, for the day will come when none of these may be true—but because this is right.

Obedience to parents is right, simply by the order of nature. This is why nearly every culture emphasizes the submission of children to parents; it is so obvious a duty that only a decadent and warped society—like our own—would question it. It is not wrong for children to be immature and to make mistakes, but it is wrong for them to flagrantly refuse their parents' commands.

It is also right by virtue of God's law: the fifth commandment requires the honoring of parents (Exod. 20:12). It is noteworthy that the ancient Jews placed the fifth commandment in the first tablet of God's law—which teaches our duty to God—instead of the second tablet—which teaches our duty to others. They rightly placed God's command to obey and honor parents under the category of our worship of God. For children, parents represent and mediate God's own authority and love, and their duty to God requires obedience to their parents. This is why Paul tells children to obey 'in the Lord.'

The second reason for children to obey and honor their parents is 'that it may go well with you and that you may live long in the land' (Eph. 6:3). Paul reminds us that the fifth commandment came with a promise of blessing to children, and thus it is for their own good.

It is important for children to learn as early as possible their duty to obey and honor proper authority, beginning with their parents. John MacArthur writes, 'It is the key principle behind all right human relationships in society. A person who grows up with a sense of respect for and obedience to his parents will have the foundation for respecting the authority of other leaders and the rights of other people in general.'[395] A child who cannot even obey and respect his or her parents is going to have a very hard time in life. But obedient children will be protected from physical harm and emotional pain. They may be spared the bad habits and bad friends that can ruin their lives, developing instead godly habits and character. Proverbs 4:10 speaks for all Christian parents, 'Hear, my son, and accept my words, that the years of your life may be many.'

The Duties of Parents to Children

In Paul's Roman world, a father had absolute control over his children without limit. He could punish them savagely, sell them into slavery, or order them to be put to death. But just as God's Word gives both wives and husbands duties in marriage, God also requires duties that parents owe to their children. Parenting is so difficult that a whole industry of how-to books thrives; many of these books are helpful. But in Ephesians 6:4 we have an outline that Christian fathers and mothers should receive as the foundation of their parenting: 'Fathers, do not provoke your children to anger, but bring them up in the discipline and instruction of the Lord.'

Paul highlights the role of fathers because it is the particular duty of the male head to ensure the godly leadership of the home. But this plural masculine term was often used of parents in general, to include mothers. This foundational verse addresses parents with one important warning and three key duties.

First, Paul warns parents against embittering or exasperating their children: 'Fathers, do not provoke your children to anger.' MacArthur writes, 'To provoke…to anger suggests a repeated, ongoing pattern of treatment that gradually builds up a deep-seated anger and resentment that boils over in outward hostility.'[396] This is a much-needed warning today. Parental authority must be calculated to inspire a glad obedience and not to provoke resentment.

Parents may embitter their children in many ways. One is an excessively harsh approach to discipline, especially when the child feels condemned rather than fairly corrected. Luther said, 'Spare the rod and spoil the child—that is true. But beside the rod keep an apple to give him when he has done well.'[397] Children are easily discouraged when they are never praised and when nothing they do ever meets their parents' expectations. MacArthur tells of a young woman he knew who was often in mental and emotional collapse. After she had taken her own life, he remembered what amounted to her epitaph: 'I don't care what it is I do,' she lamented, 'it never satisfies my mother.'[398] Other ways children are embittered and turned to anger include unfairness and arbitrariness in expectations, favoritism of one child over another, constant outbursts of parental anger, and especially abusive treatment—be it physical or verbal or even sexual. God grants parents authority in stewardship to him, for the children's blessing and protection, not to subject them to a parent's rage or abuse.

This warning is followed by three duties that parents owe to children. The first is expressed in the words 'but bring them up.' The expression means *to bring them up with tender care*. Calvin translates it 'let them be kindly cherished.'

The industrial revolution had an effect on the family that changed society. Prior to the twentieth century, most fathers worked at home, whether they were farmers or tradesmen. Children were physically and emotionally close to their parents. There were few social or entertainment opportunities, so the family stayed together. Sons grew to manhood through a direct apprenticeship to their fathers; the same was true for daughters and their mothers. Now, with fathers spending the bulk of their time away from home—and often mothers too—the distance between parents and children has grown. Christian parents must labor to reduce this distance. More important than physical distance is emotional distance, when fathers are physically present but give little time or attention to their children. Psychologists today emphasize this as key to the healthy growth of boys and girls. One writes, 'The psychological or physical absence of fathers from their families is one of the great underestimated tragedies of our times.'[399] God's Word warned against this centuries ago, and directs fathers to be lovingly involved with their children.

Fathers nurture their children by giving them attention, time, and affection. This means getting on our knees to play games with little kids, throwing the ball in the back yard, taking an interest in ballet, reading stories and giving hugs. Mothers are called to nurture, too, especially through kind and encouraging words. As a boy, the famous painter, Benjamin West, was left in charge of his little sister Sally. While playing, he discovered some colored ink. He decided to paint Sally's portrait and in the process spread ink blots everywhere. When his mother returned, she saw a horrific mess, but she also saw the picture. She picked it up and said, 'Why, it's Sally!' and kissed her son. Years later West would say, 'My mother's kiss made me a painter.'[400]

Second, parents are called *to discipline their children with firmness*. Paul says to bring them up 'in the discipline…of the Lord.' This word, *paideia*, means training with the particular idea of punishment for wrong-doing. If children are commanded to obey and respect their parents, parents are responsible to see that they learn to do so. Proverbs 13:24 says, 'Whoever spares the rod hates his son, but he who loves him is diligent to discipline him.' Our permissive society says children should seldom be punished and should not often be told 'No'. But this is the height of folly, says the Bible. Proverbs 29:15 says, 'The rod and reproof give wisdom, but a child left to himself brings shame to his mother.' If this sounds like the Bible endorses spanking, that is correct. Parents should never strike a child in anger or with an intent to harm. But the sensation of pain on a backside that God has kindly padded is one of God's ways of reaching a child's heart. Another form of discipline is the verbal rebuke. Proverbs 15:5 says, 'A fool despises his father's instruction, but whoever heeds reproof is prudent.' It is a mistake for parents to indulge their children, permit disobedience, or fail to erect needed boundaries. Negligent parents think they will win their children's hearts, but instead they more often win their contempt, while failing in an essential duty God gives to parents.

Our discipline of children will not go far unless we provide them a consistent example. If mothers want their children to obey, then submission to their husbands is essential. If fathers want children to grow in the discipline of the Lord, then they themselves must be growing under God's Word and cultivating a godly character.

The parents' third duty is *to instruct their children biblically*. Paul says to bring children up 'in the discipline and instruction of the Lord.' Again, Proverbs sets the ideal: 'Hear, my son, your father's instruction, and forsake not your mother's teaching, for they are a graceful garland for your head and pendants for your neck' (Prov 1:8–9). The Book of Judges records the most godless and chaotic period in the history of God's people. Judges 2:10 tells us how this happened: 'There arose another generation…who did not know the LORD or the work that he had done for Israel.' The most valuable knowledge any parent passes on to his or her children is a biblical knowledge of God and the saving grace of Jesus Christ.

Biblical instruction in the home can take different forms, and parents may adjust to changing family circumstances. I know one godly father who met for a few minutes every morning with his two sons to review a proverb and pray. Others use the breakfast time or dinner; others gather for a Bible reading and prayer after the evening meal. If possible, it is good to sing psalms or hymns together, and prayer should be included with the reading of God's Word.

This is God's program for godly parenting: do not embitter, bring them up tenderly, with firm discipline, and biblical teaching. I suppose some parents will think they have failed by neglecting these duties. If you need to ask God's forgiveness, he will freely give it through Jesus Christ. But do not let the past control the future. Embrace the time that remains and devote yourself to the pattern of a godly home. While your children are still with you, it is not too late. But soon it will be. One father wrote this:

> My family's all grown and the kids are all gone. But if I had to do it all over again, this is what I would do. I would love my wife more in front of my children. I would laugh with my children more—at our mistakes and our joys…I would pray more diligently for my family…I would do more things together with my children. I would encourage them more and bestow more praise. I would pay more attention to little things, like deeds and words of thoughtfulness. And then, finally, if I had to do it all over again, I would share God more intimately with my family; every ordinary thing that happened in every ordinary day I would use to direct them to God.[401]

Children and the Church

Let me make a few observations about the relationship of children to God and to the church. Some Christians believe that until a child makes a profession of faith in Christ, he or she has no relationship to God. These verses refute that. Paul tells Christian children that they have obligations to God; they must obey their parents 'in the Lord.' While they are not saved without a personal faith, 1 Corinthians 7:14 says covenant children are 'holy' in God's sight by virtue of their parents. This is part of the logic behind infant baptism; children receive the mark of God's covenant, with privileges and duties from God. This passage also indicates the presence of children in the worship service. Paul expected his letters to be read in the church; he obviously expects the children to be present and he addresses them with God's Word.

Second, we must remember that our children are sinners by nature. Obedience is not easy for them, and neither is discipline easy for parents. So we must raise our children prayerfully, relying on God's work in their hearts and God's grace to support them in difficult times. This means that we may raise our children tenderly, discipline them firmly, and instruct them biblically, and yet they may go astray. Children are their own people and they have to believe on their own. Faithful Christian parents may confidently look for God to bless their children. But salvation is never automatic and it does not come by heredity. If your children have turned away from Christ, do not abandon hope. God calls many such children to repent at various stages of life. You must continue to love them, to set a godly example for them, and to pray regularly for their souls.

Third, we should remember that the greatest gift a parent can give is the gift of Jesus Christ. He said, 'Let the children come to me' (Mark 10:14). The highest goal of our parenting is not merely that they would learn moral habits, but that they would come to see the beauty of our Lord, learn of his promises to save, and come to the Good Shepherd as lambs for the salvation of their souls.

A Father for You

I want to recognize that many have hearts broken by unloving or unfaithful parents—especially by unloving or abusive fathers. Some, as a result, find it hard to relate to or trust in God.

If you have never had a true and loving father on earth, you can have one in heaven through the salvation Jesus gives. Ryken writes, 'Jesus knows that a father's love is what we have always longed for. He invites us to become God's beloved child. He teaches us to speak to him as our dear Father. That may be difficult at first, but as you learn to pray to God as your Father, you will experience the healing that only a Father's love can bring.'[402]

God will be faithful as only he can be, as he demonstrated at the cross of Jesus Christ. God's Son has already died for you. So you can trust God to forgive your sins, take you into his tender care, discipline you to grow in holiness, instruct you as his child, and enter you into his eternal inheritance of glory. God's love is the model for every parent and his gift to every child through Jesus Christ. 'My son, my daughter, give me your heart,' God says (Prov. 23:26). As you trust him, giving your heart to God, he will give himself back to you in eternal, divine, and fatherly love.

60

Faith at Work

Ephesians 6:5–9

Some of the best compliments ever paid to Jesus were spoken by those who opposed him. Among the things said of him in his trial and on the cross are these: 'I find no guilt in him' (Pilate, John 19:4); 'He saved others; let him save himself' (Jewish rulers, Luke 23:35), 'Hail, King of the Jews' (soldiers, Mark 15:18), and 'He trusts in God; let God deliver him now' (chief priests, Matt. 27:43). All of these statements were true, from the mouth of his enemies.

The same thing happened with the apostle Paul and his friends. Paul and Silas were driven from Thessalonica by a mob whipped up by the Jews. The mob cried, 'these men…have turned the world upside down' (Acts 17:6). What a great description of the kind of people Christians are called to be! In one respect this was untrue, however, as our study of Paul's teaching on the home and the workplace shows. Paul was no social revolutionary, and those who have tried to make him one have always distorted the Scriptures. Paul affirms that wives must submit to husbands and children must obey their parents. In our passage today, Paul teaches slaves to submit to their masters. So Paul was not revolting against the social order. But in another respect, his accusers were right about the Christians turning the world upside down, for where Jesus reigns everything is transformed by his grace and holiness. In Christ, marriage involves mutual ministry and love. In Christ, children are not the possession of their parents but a stewardship of love before God. And in Christ, even slavery can be transformed by grace, peace, and love.

Slavery and Christianity

This is very much what we find when we complete Paul's teaching on the Christian family and home, as the apostle turns to the situation of slaves and their masters. We tend to think of ancient slavery through the lens of 19th century slavery in the American South. Despite obvious similarities, slavery in the ancient world was somewhat different. In the Roman Empire, about half of the population was in slavery to the other half. In cities like Rome, citizens did not work; all the work was done by slaves, much as work is done by machines today. Slavery was not based on race. People of all races became slaves by birth, through conquest, or for economic reasons. By Paul's time important reforms had taken root that reduced a great deal of the cruelty suffered by slaves. Slaves and freemen interacted socially. Slaves held high government positions and operated wealthy businesses. Moreover, slavery was seldom permanent. In Paul's time, almost half the slaves received freedom by the age of thirty.[403]

This is valuable background, both to assess how odious by contrast was slavery in America and also to understand the New Testament's response to slavery. It is not uncommon to read that Christianity failed by condoning or even supporting the practice of slavery. It is true that some Christians have supported slavery over the centuries and that the Bible has been misused to justify slavery. Some of our own theological forebears in the Presbyterian Church argued in support of slavery in the American South, which is why in 2002 the Presbyterian Church in America approved a public statement condemning such teachings and asking the forgiveness of those who suffered through the sins of our church tradition.[404]

It is important, therefore, to understand the Bible's actual stance towards slavery. Some think the apostle Paul sent mixed messages about slavery. After all, he once converted a fugitive slave named Onesimus and then sent him back to Philemon, the master from whom he had run away, with a letter requesting that he be set free. Furthermore, in various of his letters Paul tells slaves to obey their earthly masters (Eph. 6:5, cf. Col. 3:22; 1 Tim. 6:1-2; Titus 2:9-10). So was Paul for slavery or against it?

There can be no question that Paul was against slavery. It is seldom appreciated that he lists 'enslavers' as those who live contrary to Christianity (1 Tim. 1:10). Anyone who owns another human being, Paul says, is unsound in both his life and his doctrine. So why did not Paul attack the institution more vigorously? For one thing, the Christians in Paul's day were politically insignificant. Furthermore, they were not political revolutionaries but evangelists of a spiritual gospel. This is what Jesus meant when he told Pilate, 'My kingdom is not of this world' (John 18:36). The Christians' goal was to live within their evil society in a godly way and to lead others to Jesus. Over the generations, as Christianity spread and gained influence, its presence always subverted tyranny, conflict, and hatred. Philip Ryken explains, 'Christianity eventually did become the single greatest force in history for the eradication of slavery... Wherever Christianity has come to dominate a culture, the institution of slavery has been legally eliminated.'[405]

Paul encouraged slaves to seek their freedom in legitimate ways, just as Christians are always free to move up in society. But when we cannot change our circumstances, the Bible calls on us to conquer them through faith in Christ, seeking the greater liberty that is freedom from sin by his grace (cf 1 Cor. 7:20-24). The Bible's teaching never focuses on what the society is doing wrong but on the good Christians are to do wherever we are found. William Barclay says, '[Paul] does not tell them to rebel; he tells them to be Christians where they are.'[406] This is why Paul's teaching to slaves and masters is directly transferable to our working lives today. Just as in the case of wives and husbands, and children and parents, Paul tells Christians of their duty as slaves and masters, or, in our terms, as employees and employers.

The Christian Servant

The word Paul uses for 'slave' can just as well mean 'servant,' and what he wrote speaks powerfully to Christian employees today. This is important instruction, because there are very few of us who will ever reach the place in life where we do not work for some other person. So much of our work—and thus of our lives and our Christian witness—takes place as servants under the authority of some earthly master or boss.

A Christian servant should first be obedient. As always, Paul directs us to respect those in authority: 'Slaves, obey your earthly masters' (Eph. 6:5). The word for *obey* here is the same one given to children with regard to their parents. It means to 'pay attention to' or to 'follow instructions.' This does not mean that subordinates should not show initiative. But obedient employees are diligently to carry out the tasks given to them and to work towards goals assigned to them. When a boss hires a Christian, he or she should be able to expect an honest day's work for an honest day's pay.

Furthermore, Christians are to show respect to their employers. Paul tells the slaves to obey 'with fear and trembling.' In Colossians 3:22, he tells slaves to obey their masters 'fearing the Lord,' so he probably means for Christians to respect their masters out of reverence to God. At least some of Paul's slave readers would have been owned by cruel, unjust, or inept masters, just as many Christians work for similar people today. Surely Paul is not unaware of this. Furthermore, slaves were usually integral parts of the master's household, so they would have seen him without his socks on, so to speak. The slave would have heard the master's wife nagging and his children complaining and his quarrels with his neighbors, and would have known his affairs inside out. Familiarity breeds contempt, and slaves would be tempted to this. Many would have been better educated, more able, and more moral than their owners. This is why in 1 Timothy 6:1 Paul tells slaves to 'consider their masters worthy of full respect.' Their respect was to be a conscious act, just as soldiers in the Army salute the uniform regardless of the man who wears it. Paul explained why: 'so that the name of God and the teaching may not be reviled' (1 Tim. 6:1). If Christianity was seen to promote revolution and disrespect, then an excuse would be given to suppress or despise its teaching.

The Bible provides excellent examples of obedient, godly servants. Think of Joseph, who worked as a slave in Potiphar's household, and later as a servant to Pharaoh. These were wicked men, but Joseph served them loyally and well. Because of God's blessing on Joseph's work, Potiphar placed all his affairs into his hands. Joseph's service to Pharaoh caused that ruler to show favor to God's people. This should be common among Christians. Daniel served faithfully in the court of the Babylonian king who had destroyed Jerusalem. He reasoned that God had put him in that place and that he represented the Lord. Christians should exercise the same reasoning today, and our work ethic should reflect positively on the Christian faith. When Naaman the Syrian presented himself to the prophet Elisha for healing and blessing, he explained that he learned about the Lord from a slave girl in his household (2 Kings 5:2–3). Likewise, our work as Christian servants should create openings for a receptive hearing of the gospel.

Paul next uses an expression that he may have coined himself, warning Christians not to work 'by way of eye-service, as people-pleasers,' but 'rendering service with a good will as to the Lord and not to man' (Eph. 6:6–7). Christians should not be the kind of employee who loafs until the boss's footsteps are heard, and then doubles his pace of work. Such insincerity is unbecoming a Christian. Our work has the dignity of being offered up to God, who always sees what we are doing.

Paul sums up by reminding us to consider ourselves 'servants of Christ' (Eph. 6:6). This is the dignity that the Christian faith gives to every believer, whether slave or free. When William Carey was asked what his business was, he replied, 'My business is serving the Lord, and I make shoes to pay expenses.'[407] Every housewife should present dinner as if Jesus were sitting at the table; every craftsman should present his work to God for inspection; and every manager should oversee his business as if Christ's money was at stake.

This is why Paul spoke of 'your earthly masters,' or, literally, 'your masters according to the flesh' (v. 5). Christians are to obey such fleshly masters, but really to serve their heavenly Master, Jesus Christ, who loved them and died for them. As such, Christians devote themselves not so much to gaining riches or promotion, but 'doing the will of God from the heart, rendering service with a good will' (Eph. 6:6–7). We are to do good whether or not it will lead to earthly rewards for us. This means that Christians should be the most respected people in the workplace, noted for integrity and self-less service, and never looked upon as those who shirk their duty or climb the company ladder over the backs of their peers.

God's will is summarized in the Ten Commandments, so Christians should never commit character assassination, should never steal money or materials or time, should never lie or covet another's office or bonus or position. But who will reward these ethics? The answer is that the Christian looks to Christ for his or her provision and reward. Christians do not mind pay raises or promotion, but we work for Jesus, 'knowing that whatever good anyone does, this he will receive back from the Lord, whether he is a slave or free' (Eph. 6:8). Karl Marx complained that teaching like this merely pacifies oppressed workers, labeling religion as 'the opiate of the people.' But the Christian sees this as liberation from corrupt systems of human expectations and rewards. It is because God is gracious and good that Paul says, in Galatians 6:9, 'Let us not grow weary of doing good, for in due season we shall reap' our harvest from the Lord.

The Christian Master

In considering Paul's teaching on marriage and the family, we noted that Christ transforms these institutions by insisting on the duties of husbands to wives and of parents to children. The same principle applies when Paul turns to Christian masters. Paul begins by telling them to treat their slaves as they wish to be treated: 'Masters, do the same to them' (Eph. 6:9). R. Kent Hughes calls this the 'Managerial Golden Rule,' to treat employees as you wish to be treated. He writes, 'If you want *respect*, show respect. If you want *sincerity*, be sincere. If you want *conscientiousness*, you be the same. If you want *pleasantness*, model pleasantness.'[408] William Hendriksen summarizes Paul's meaning, 'Promote the welfare of your slaves as you expect them to promote yours. Show the same interest in them and in their affairs as you hope they will show in you and your affairs.'[409]

Whenever we are given authority over others, we tend to think ourselves superior to them. 'Power corrupts,' it is said, and many people become abusive when they are given it. Paul corrects this by reminding Christian masters of their equality before God with their servants: 'He who is both their Master and yours is in heaven.' Every Christian boss should remember that he has a Master in heaven and that his employees have the same Master, who will hold the earthly master to account for the way he treats those under him or her. This is the difference between Christian teaching and the similar advice given today by secular management consultants. Both recognize that enlightened leadership is more effective, but the Bible adds the dimension of divine accountability.

This is why Paul tells Christian masters not to rely on compulsion and bullying: 'Stop your threatening,' he says. Christians can exercise legitimate authority—a Christian will sometime have to employ discipline or fire someone—but their rule should not rely on raw and brutal force. No one who works for a Christian should ever feel dehumanized. Indeed, if you want to see the reality of a Christian's faith, observe how he treats his employees, the check-out clerk, and the people who cut his grass.

Paul reminds us 'there is no partiality with [God].' God is not concerned with human differences; he expects all of us to do what is right according to his will. No luxury office suit, no badges of rank, no stock portfolio, and no dynamic executive persona impresses the Lord of glory. God calls on everyone, high and low, 'to do justice, and to love kindness, and to walk humbly with your God' (Micah 6:8). Indeed, God reserves a particular measure of wrath for cruel and unjust masters. James 5:4 says, 'Behold, the wages of the laborers who mowed your fields, which you kept back by fraud, are crying out against you, and the cries of the harvesters have reached the ears of the Lord of hosts.'

Neither Slave nor Free

No doubt, Paul would prefer for Christian masters to free their slaves. When he sent back the runaway Onesimus, he asked Philemon to receive him 'no longer as a slave but more than a slave, as a beloved brother' (Philemon 16). But more important than the removal of this or any other social injustice is its transformation through the love and the grace of God.

One place to see this is Romans 16, where Paul gives personal greetings from Corinth to various people in the Roman church. At one point, Paul must have taken a breather, for the scribe taking his dictation inserted his own greeting: 'I, Tertius, who wrote this letter, greet you in the Lord' (Rom. 16:22). In the next verse, Paul resumes, 'Gaius, who is host to me and to the whole church, greets you. Erastus, the city treasurer, and our brother Quartus, greet you.'

This little gathering tells us much about the early Christians. Gaius must have been a rich man, since he hosted the apostle and the church met in his home, and since he had at least four slaves. Erastus was a high government official. Archaeologists have found an inscription of his name on a public sidewalk in Corinth. What about Tertius and Quartus? It turns out that slaves in Roman household were named according to their position. The top-ranking slave was Primus (one). Secundus was number two, followed by Tertius (three), Quartus (four), Quintus (five) and so on. This tells us that Tertius and Quartus in Romans 16:22–23 are the number three and number four slaves in Gaius' house. Yet they are not left out by Paul, just as the slaves in Ephesus are not left out of this epistle! In the flesh, they might be master and slave, but in Christ it was 'our brother Quartus'! No wonder Paul could say that in the church, 'There is neither Jew nor Greek, there is neither slave nor free, there is neither male nor female, for you are all one in Christ Jesus' (Gal. 3:28).

Imagine what a difference this would have made in this one household, just as Christ will change our homes and workplaces. Donald Grey Barnhouse imagines an interview with Tertius and Quartus about the difference it made to them. He has them answer this way:

> One day Paul came into the house of our master, Gaius. We saw a great transformation in him. Gaius was transformed. He began to be kind to us. Soon he had Paul tell us about Christ. For two years Paul lived in Corinth, and he came to our house often. We got the bread and the wine ready when the crowd came on Sunday. It made more work for us, but it was delightful. They broke the bread, and we began to eat from the same loaf as our master. They filled a chalice with wine, and our master sipped it and smiled as he handed it to us. Day after day everything was transformed. He put his hand on us and cried as he spoke of the grace of God that had saved us all. He said that he was our master, but he realized that he had a master, Christ. He wanted to treat us the way Christ treated him. Love transformed our lives.[410]

61

Spiritual Warfare

Ephesians 6:10–13

The apostle Paul's ministry in the city of Ephesus involved a violent clash of spiritual powers. Paul considered the city to be of great strategic importance and he invested himself in the work for two years. In 1 Corinthians 16:9, he wrote, 'I will stay in Ephesus until Pentecost, for a wide door for effective work has opened to me, and there are many adversaries.' Ephesus was a great city and the center of occult magic in Asia Minor, as well as the home of one of the chief pagan temples, to the goddess Artemis. Satan and his followers of course opposed Paul, and God responded by supplying Paul with supernatural power, so that he healed many people and cast out demons. His gospel drew large numbers of converts. Many of them had been practitioners of magic, and when they believed on Christ they brought their magic books and burned them publicly.

Given that history, we are not surprised to find that the theme of spiritual power is prominent in the Book of Ephesians. Paul did not write this letter to combat doctrinal error, but to encourage Christians about the power God has for them. In chapter 1, Paul prays that they may know 'what is the immeasurable greatness of his power toward us who believe' (Eph. 1:19), namely, the resurrection power of the Lord Jesus Christ working through the Holy Spirit. In chapter 2, he describes their former condition as having been in slavery to the evil power at work in this world (Eph. 2:2). In chapter 3, he speaks of God's power working through his own ministry (Eph. 3:7). Then he prays that God 'may grant you to be strengthened with power through his Spirit in your inner being' (Eph. 3:16). He praises God for working so mightily in us 'according to the power at work within us' (Eph. 3:20). Ephesians presents a theology of spiritual power, given so that we may overcome the power of evil and live fruitful lives as followers of Christ. If we doubt the importance of the power theme in Paul's message, that doubt is dispelled by this concluding section, which begins, 'Finally, be strong in the Lord and in the strength of his might' (Eph. 6:10).

Our Struggle:
The Reality of Spiritual Warfare

According to Paul, one of the great mistakes Christians make is to forget what kind of world we live in. This is a grave danger to affluent Westerners, with so many enticing comforts. We are told that life is about getting the most toys or having the greatest amount of pleasure. How easy it is to think we live in a big Disneyworld, in which life is about taking as many rides as we can.

According to the Bible, our world is not a pleasure park or a shopping mall but a deadly spiritual battlefield. Paul teaches, 'We do not wrestle against flesh and blood, but against the rulers, against the authorities, against the cosmic powers over this present darkness, against the spiritual forces of evil in the heavenly places' (Eph. 6:12). This means that *spiritual warfare is real*. Paul describes these sinister forces with related terms, so that we are not sure how exactly to distinguish them. First, he names rulers and authorities, which suggests spiritual foes who exercise influence and control. More graphically, Paul then speaks of 'cosmic powers over this present darkness.' This term 'cosmic power' or 'world ruler' was used of the Roman Emperor, and may indicate those spiritual forces involved in government oppression.[411] Last, Paul refers to 'spiritual forces of evil in the heavenly places.' Whatever the precise meaning of these designations, Paul assures us of the reality of an organized spiritual presence that relishes and inspires all that is perverse, harmful and ungodly in this dark world.

It is remarkable that even as Satan's influence on our society has become more overt, with the open spread of the occult and other forms of Satanism and perverse evils widely accepted, people still deny that Satan exists. But the Scriptures present the devil as a real, personal angelic being of great power and consummate evil. Jesus referred to him in a matter of fact way. It is impossible to accept the Bible at face value without accepting its teaching that there is a menacing, evil spiritual power known as the devil.

The devil's agenda is to lead people away from God by any means and in that way to destroy their souls. We live in a society in which that agenda operates in multiple arenas. Our courts present edicts unreasonably skewed against Christianity and godliness. Our entertainment industry glorifies the most destructive immorality through smiling, pretty faces with perfect teeth. Our universities are seedbeds of depravity. Our colleges major in untruths about the created realm through the theory of evolution and then preach the philosophies of despair, in the form of existentialism and nihilism. Our hospitals provide clean, white facilities where unborn babies are savagely murdered, so many that statistically the most dangerous place in America for a child today is in its mother's womb. Paul reminds us that in these things and more, 'We do not wrestle against flesh and blood,' but against Satan and his demons.

Spiritual warfare is not only real, but it is also *certain for believers*. Many Christians make the mistake of thinking that attacks from Satan are only a dim possibility, unaware of the many ways that spiritual warfare impacts us every day. MacArthur is right when he says, 'The true Christian described in Ephesians 1–3 who lives the faithful life described in 4:1–6:9 can be sure that he will be involved in the spiritual warfare described in 6:10–20. The faithful Christian life is a battle; it is warfare on a grand scale—because when God begins to bless, Satan begins to attack.'[412]

This is true of churches as of individuals. Whenever a church commits to doing God's work in God's way, it should not be surprised if all does not go well. To the degree that any church is worldly in its message and methods, then regardless of its apparent success, then Satan has little interest in opposing it. But when a church exalts God's Word and devotes itself to holiness and gospel mission, it can be sure of hardship and difficulty.

Moreover, *spiritual warfare is a deadly struggle*. Paul says we *wrestle* with rulers and authorities, and spiritual powers of darkness. This is hand-to-hand combat, and by his various schemes, the devil wants to lay his hands on us and our families. The smoldering ruins in our society today, which is ultimately his handiwork, should alert us to the very great danger. First Peter 5:8 says, 'Your adversary the devil prowls around like a roaring lion, seeking someone to devour.' Therefore we need to understand spiritual warfare and arm ourselves for the fight.

Our Holy Calling: Strong in the Lord

I mentioned the mistake many secular people make of refusing to believe in Satan or spiritual warfare. But there is an opposite mistake that Christians can make, to become overly fixated on the devil and imagine his direct involvement in every trial or temptation. Mighty as the devil is and numerous as his minions are, they are not omnipresent, as God is. Paul wants us to know about our unseen spiritual enemies, but he does not encourage speculation about what the devil may be doing at any given place or time.

Paul's battle plan for spiritual warfare calls for us to focus not on the devil but on God and his Word. He says, 'Be strong in the Lord and in the strength of his might' (Eph. 6:10). This is the message that redounds throughout Scripture to God's people entering the fray. Before Joshua led the tribes of Israel across the Jordan and into Canaan, God told him, 'Be strong and courageous, being careful to do according to all the law that Moses my servant commanded you. Do not turn from it to the right hand or to the left, that you may have good success wherever you go' (Josh. 1:7). Zechariah 10:12 says, 'I will make them strong in the Lord, and they shall walk in his name.' In 1 Samuel 30:6, we are told how David faced one of his gravest crises: 'David strengthened himself in the Lord his God.'

God is the almighty Creator. Satan may be vastly more powerful than us but he is still a creature before God. Furthermore, Jesus came into this world to overthrow the devil. First John 3:8 says, 'The reason the Son of God appeared was to destroy the works of the devil.' The devil's power works through sin and its condemnation. Jesus broke that power by dying for our sins on the cross, and he continues to break it by sending the Holy Spirit to empower us with God's own might. 'He who is in you is greater than he who is in the world,' John says (1 John 4:4). So Christians face the prospect of spiritual battle by fixing our eyes on Jesus and arming ourselves with the strength that he gives.

Far more than any contests with individual spiritual powers, we contend with *schemes* by which the devil seeks to destroy our souls, and those of our children. Paul uses the Greek word *methodeias,* from which we get the word *method.* He says in Ephesians 2:1–3 that 'the course of this world' follows after the devil's methods. Satan snares mankind through 'the passions of our flesh…the desires of the body and the mind.' The threat facing us is not mainly that some demon will come along and possess us, but that we, 'like the rest of mankind' (Eph. 2:3), will be lured by temptations geared to the mind and the body, falling like mice in the devil's traps. Paul says in 2 Corinthians 2:11, 'We are not ignorant of [Satan's] designs,' and believers today should not be either. It is through his methods and programs that Satan's warfare never relents, so that we live, work, and play amidst the scenery of war; every night we lie down and go to sleep on the battlefield.

The devil is enormously resourceful and has been practicing his schemes for thousands of years. In addition to temptations, he sows doubts, he intimidates and terrorizes, he insinuates lewd thoughts into our minds, and he accuses us of the sins he prompted to draw us away from God. But, like most generals, Satan has a favorite tactic, namely, lying and deceiving. Jesus said of the devil, 'He is a liar and the father of lies' (John 8:44).

This is how the devil led our first parents into sin. He came to Eve in the Garden and deceived her with regard to God's command not to eat from the tree of the knowledge of good and evil. Satan said that God was just holding Adam and Eve back. He said, 'For God knows that when you eat of it your eyes will be opened, and you will be like God, knowing good and evil' (Gen. 3:5). This is a lie the devil uses today: 'Don't listen to God—he's only trying to keep you down. Try the life of sin and don't let rules get in your way—that is the way to reach your potential. If you serve God you will become a small, miserable person; the way to become somebody is to do what you want.' With this lie, in all its variants, the devil has deceived and destroyed countless souls. This is why Revelation 12:9 refers to him as 'that ancient serpent…the deceiver of the whole world.'

This remains the devil's number one strategy. What is the message of television and its advertisements but that sin is the way to be happy? One writer describes 'the amoral and immoral banter of the TV talk shows. The hosts and audiences are…committed to unthinking, doctrinaire relativism, regularly calling good evil and evil good, approving of actions that dogs under full sway of their animal natures would never do!'[413] It all seems so right in the fabricated, manipulative world of television. But it is the devil's deception, telling us how wonderful sin is and causing us to doubt God's goodness.

This is why the Word of God is so important to spiritual warfare. In upcoming studies we will consider the 'armor of God' in detail, but we can note now how much of it centers on apprehending the truth of God's Word. So it has always been. First Samuel 17 tells of the battle between David and Goliath. Goliath was a great giant warrior, the champion of the Philistine army. He cowed the entire Israelite army with his terrifying worldly might, just as Satan's methods reek such havoc in society and in the church today. But David was fortified by the truth about God; he was 'strong in the might of the Lord' (Eph. 6:10). Most inspiring is the speech David made as he stood before the giant: 'You come to me with a sword and with a spear and with a javelin, but I come to you in the name of the Lord of hosts, the God of the armies of Israel, whom you have defied. This day the Lord will deliver you into my hand, and I will strike you down…For the battle is the Lord's and he will give you into our hand' (1 Sam. 17:45–47). David was strengthened in the might of the Lord and he triumphed in spiritual warfare. So can we if we stand in God's mighty Word.

Our Mighty Equipping: The Armor of God

Verse 13 makes the famous statement about how to become strong in the Lord: 'Therefore take up the whole armor of God.' The word for 'armor' means 'panoply,' that is, a complete suit of armor. Paul may have been chained to a Roman soldier during his imprisonment in Rome, perhaps while he wrote this letter, and he probably got the idea for this metaphor from the armor worn by his guards.

We are going to consider the armor of God in detail in subsequent studies, but we can make some general observations now. First, this command proves *our own insufficiency in the flesh*. In Romans 7, Paul describes his attempt to follow Christ in his own power. How easily he was overthrown by sin! He remarked, 'I know that nothing good dwells in me, that is, in my flesh. For I have the desire to do what is right, but not the ability to carry it out' (Rom. 7:18–19). Paul realized that his only hope of survival, much less of victory, was to strengthen himself with the might God gives in Jesus Christ.

This applies to the church as well. We will not make headway against the devil by using worldly methods. I am impressed by an episode that took place just before David went forward to face Goliath. He was just a boy and so was not part of Israel's army. But when he arrived with some food for his brothers, he was shocked to see the Israelites cowering in fear before the giant Philistine. When David tried to exhort the troops, they sent him to King Saul. At first, Saul tried to dismiss David, but when he saw that the young man was in earnest, he offered to let David wear his armor and helmet and sword. This worldly weaponry had not helped Saul in his unbelief, and David realized it would not help him either. He replied, 'I cannot go with these,' and he went forward armed only with a slingshot, five smooth stones from a brook, and faith in God's Word burning in his heart. Likewise, we are tempted to employ all the impressive means the world has to offer—schemes of entertaining worship services, manipulative appeals, and watered-down gospels. But if we want to be dressed in the armor that God gives, we must first set aside the methods of the world. Paul wrote, 'Though we walk in the flesh, we are not waging war according to the flesh. For the weapons of our warfare are not of the flesh but have divine power to destroy strongholds. We destroy arguments and every lofty opinion raised against the knowledge of God, and take every thought captive to obey Christ' (2 Cor. 10:3–5).

Second, it is apparent that *spiritual warfare demands preparation*. We cannot become 'strong in the Lord' in a flash, just when we think the battle is drawing near. The things that Paul speaks of as the armor of God—truth, righteousness, gospel readiness, faith, and biblical knowledge—require cultivation, just as an ancient soldier had to painstakingly equip himself. Any Christian who is too busy to nurture his or her faith and too worldly to devote energy to prayer or ministry, will be vulnerable to spiritual attacks. When such a person falls to temptation or doubt, it is because of their own neglect of the affairs of their soul. Just as many Christian schools have a dress code so that students are orderly and presentable, every Christian is to be dressed for battle in the armor of God. Not one of us is so strong or so safe that we can neglect preparing for the spiritual challenges we can be sure to face. Paul wrote, 'Let anyone who thinks that he stands take heed lest he fall' (1 Cor. 10:12).

Paul remarks that we must take up God's armor 'that you may be able to withstand in the evil day' (Eph. 6:13). It is not obvious what he means by 'the evil day,' but it suggests that there will be times where we are singled out for intense spiritual attack. There may indeed be a particularly strong challenge to your faith somewhere ahead—some trial, temptation, or struggle. You need to prepare now for 'the evil day' by growing in your faith, learning God's Word, ridding yourself of sin, and advancing as far as possible on the path of holiness.

The third observation we should make is that while worldly methods will fail us, *God has provided means of grace* to strengthen us for spiritual battle. Biblically, this term refers to those activities God has promised to bless, namely, God's Word, prayer, and the sacraments. It is through these means that Christians grow stronger and stay safe in a world at war: through personal Bible study and faithful attendance upon the preached Word, through frequent prayer, and through regular worship with God's people, to include the faithful administration of Christ's sacraments. MacArthur writes, 'Dealing with demons in one's Christian life is not a matter of finding the technique to send them away, but of being committed to the spiritual means of grace that purifies the soul, so that there is no unclean place that demons could occupy or by which they might gain advantage.'[414]

James says, 'Resist the devil and he will flee from you' (Jas 4:7). We must resist the devil not by devising our own schemes of battle, but by using the humble, ordinary means of grace that God provides and through which his own power strengthens us with spiritual might.

Our Ultimate Goal: In the End, to Stand

In the end, Christians can be certain that the devil will be destroyed. Romans 16:20 says, 'The God of peace will soon crush Satan under your feet.' This is God's job, not ours. Paul sets down our goal in verse 13: 'Take up the whole armor of God, that you may be able to withstand in the evil day, and having done all, to stand firm.' Our goal is not to root the devil and his minions out of this world—nor can we—although we should take advantage of every opportunity to thwart his influence and rule, especially by proclaiming the gospel. Our ultimate goal as Christians is by all the means of God's appointment simply to stand firm.

Do you realize what a victory it is for you simply to commit yourself to the worship of God and to obeying Jesus Christ? Do you realize what a blow to Satan and his realm is every Bible study and every children's Sunday School class? Every time a mother prays for her children or a father opens the Scriptures on the kitchen table, Satan is cast down. When you refuse to believe the lie that says that sin is good, and when you are inspired to love others sacrificially or to speak the gospel to an unbeliever, thrones and dominions topple in the evil realm. If Christians simply do not give in to the agenda of the world, but hold fast to God's Word, to biblical godliness, and to gospel mission, then Satan cannot win. 'Therefore, my beloved brothers,' Paul wrote to the Corinthians, 'be steadfast, immovable, always abounding in the work of the Lord, knowing that in the Lord your labor is not in vain' (1 Cor. 15:58).

Our goal is this: 'Having done all, to stand firm.' Perhaps in his mind's eye Paul saw that scene so brilliantly depicted in Revelation 7:9–10:

> A great multitude that no one could number, from every nation, from all tribes and peoples and languages, standing before the throne and before the Lamb, clothed in white robes, with palm branches in their hands, and crying out with a loud voice, 'Salvation belongs to our God who sits on the throne, and to the Lamb!'

What does it take to stand in that glorious assembly? The angel told John, 'They have washed their robes and made them white in the blood of the Lamb' (Rev. 7:14). This, ultimately, is the only way anyone will triumph in the battle of this life, through faith in the blood of Jesus Christ to wash away our sins. Have you trusted Christ? If not, you have no hope of standing in God's grace now or in his glory in the age to come. But if you have, and if you will, then you should never serve the devil through sin, but stand against him in the power of the Holy Spirit whom Christ sends, especially when we ask. Then, after all the toil and strife of this battle-scarred world is done, we will stand in the glorious company of God's redeemed, no longer wearing armor but clothed only in white. Then, the battle will be behind us, and we will be safe amidst the glories of God:

They are before the throne of God, and serve him day and night in his temple; and he who sits on the throne will shelter them with his presence. They shall hunger no more, neither thirst anymore; the sun shall not strike them, nor any scorching heat… And God will wipe away every tear from their eyes (Rev. 7:15–17).

That is the day of rest, to which we look forward sometimes with tears. But now is the time of spiritual warfare. So 'be strong in the Lord and in the strength of his might…Take up the whole armor of God, that you may be able to withstand in the evil day, and having done all, to stand' (Eph. 6:10–13).

62

The Armor of God

Ephesians 6:14–15

There are passages of the Bible every Christian should know and understand. This is not to deny the importance of all the Scriptures. But there are some passages that are elementary to the Christian faith and life. Some that come to mind are Psalm 23, which tells of the Lord's shepherding care; John 3, which teaches about spiritual rebirth, faith in Christ, and God's forgiveness for all who believe; Matthew 5–7, the Sermon on the Mount; and Romans 1–3, which explain the doctrine of justification through faith alone. I would not hesitate to include Paul's teaching on the armor of God in that list. There are other passages that clearly present how to become a Christian. But once a person has believed on Christ, what Paul teaches here is absolutely essential to his or her spiritual well-being.

General Observations

In his discussion of spiritual warfare that concludes the Book of Ephesians, Paul uses the metaphor of a suit of armor to depict a believer's spiritual preparedness. In order to rightly understand his overall teaching here and the particular points of detail, we should first make some general observations.

The first involves recapping the point of Ephesians 6:10–13, namely, that a believer's life in this world involves spiritual warfare. Paul said, 'We do not wrestle against flesh and blood, but against the rulers, against the authorities, against the cosmic powers over this present darkness, against the spiritual forces of evil in the heavenly places' (Eph. 6:12). We said in our study of those verses that spiritual warfare is *real*, spiritual warfare is *certain*, and spiritual warfare is a *deadly struggle*. Christianity is not a passive religion; Christians are called upon to fight. Leon Morris is right to say, 'It is important that every Christian be made strong…We are all called upon to resist evil and to fight against the devil…Being righteous involves a conflict with evil, a conflict in which those who use the armor God supplies must emerge victorious. God has provided all that they need, and it only remains for them to use the weapons he has provided for them.'[415]

This points out *the necessity of our spiritual equipping*. When someone comes to faith in Christ, they often wonder, 'What am I to do now that I am a Christian?' Paul answers that Christians must train for spiritual battle—for temptation, trial, opposition, doubt, accusation and for usefulness in Christ's kingdom. Many

Christians act as if Christ has called them to a life of self-indulgent leisure, which is why they are so spiritually weak. But the first requirement of a disciple is to become strong in the Lord.

This teaching on the armor of God is not a suggestion but a command. The main verb of the long sentence, which in the Greek text runs from verses 14 to 20 comes at the beginning: 'Stand therefore' (Eph. 6:14). This verb is in the imperative mood; it is a command. All the participial phrases that follow also have imperatival force. God does not merely provide the belt of truth, the breastplate of righteousness, and all the rest; he commands us to put it on. We are not faithful disciples if we do not so arm ourselves for service in his cause.

Looking again at this leading verb, we should keep in mind *the purpose of our spiritual equipping*. Paul does not tell us to break new ground in the Lord's conquest. He does not tell us to overthrow our foes. He says simply, 'Stand.' The armor of God is mainly defensive, and it is intended to enable us to stand up to spiritual attacks. The reason Christ does not call us to wage a strategic offensive is that he has already conquered the whole field of operations. The Chinese evangelist Watchman Nee explains:

> He warred against Satan in order to gain the victory. Through the Cross he carried that warfare to the very threshold of Hell itself, to lead forth then his captivity captive (4:8,9). Today we war against Satan only to maintain and consolidate the victory which Christ has already gained. By the resurrection God proclaimed his Son victor over the whole realm of darkness, and the ground Christ won he has given to us. We do not need to fight to obtain it. We only need to hold it against all challengers…We do not try to gain ground; we merely stand on the ground which the Lord Jesus has gained for us, and resolutely refuse to be moved from it.[416]

As we turn to specifics, we should examine *Paul's description of our spiritual equipment*. Paul would often have seen Roman soldiers during his captivity in Rome, which may explain how this metaphor of a suit of armor came to his mind. But we should remember that Paul's thought was always shaped by the Old Testament, and Paul's teaching here is mainly drawn from there. For instance, Isaiah 59:17 says that the Lord 'put on righteousness as a breastplate, and a helmet of salvation on his head.' All three of the items we will study in Ephesians 6:14–15 have antecedents in the Book of Isaiah.

The way Paul uses similar metaphors elsewhere, however, tells us not to interpret them with technical precision. In 1 Thessalonians 5:8, he says, 'Put on the breastplate of faith and love, and for a helmet the hope of salvation.' The fact that Paul does not use the same formula there tells us not to take these pieces of armor literally. These are not truly *items* we can simply put on, as we would a helmet or a belt. Rather, they are *graces* we are to receive and *habits* we are to cultivate in our discipleship with Christ.

The Belt of Truth

Armed with these observations, we may now examine the armor of God in detail. Paul presents 6 items, which fall into two categories. The first three are items that were affixed to the body—the belt, the breastplate, and the sandals. The second three were taken up, but not affixed—the shield, the helmet, and the sword. In Ephesians 6:14–15, we will consider the first group. Paul begins, 'Stand therefore, having fastened on the belt of truth' (Eph. 6:14).

In Paul's day people wore long, loose garments, which had to be bound with a belt if one was to engage in strenuous activity. When a soldier was preparing for action, this was the first item of his armor that he put on. With his belt on and his garments gathered, he could move around without fear of tripping.

This is why Paul lists the 'belt of truth' first. In so doing, he reminds us that truth is of the utmost importance to the Christian. Commentators are divided as to whether Paul means truth objectively—as a body of doctrine or truth—or truth subjectively—as a character trait of the Christian. The reality is that we cannot have one without the other. Christians are to equip themselves with truth, and we are to be a truthful people as we wage spiritual warfare.

Sadly, ours is time when the church holds truth lightly. Many Christians think that nothing is worth arguing about and that we should not be too confident about what the Bible teaches. But the example of Jesus says otherwise, as does Paul's whole teaching. It is significant that when Paul last met with the Ephesian elders he warned them to carefully guard the truth he had taught them. He said their great danger was the teaching of false doctrines. 'I am innocent of the blood of all of you,' he said, 'for I did not shrink from declaring to you the whole counsel of God' (Acts 20:27). The elders were to remain alert to the defense of that teaching, as faithful shepherds defending the flock from 'fierce wolves' (Acts 20:29).

No wonder, then, that Paul begins with the belt of truth. James Boice comments, 'This suggests that successful spiritual warfare begins with fixing Christianity's great doctrines firmly in our minds.' To do otherwise is to rush into battle with loose garments tripping up our feet. Americans are a practical people and we never want to study doctrine. But in any serious endeavor we must always apply ourselves to doctrine first and only then to application. None of us would want to be operated on by a doctor who had not devoted himself to the doctrines of anatomy and surgical theory. The same is true in the life-or-death struggle of the Christian life. Boice warns us, 'Without truth, without the doctrines, without the knowledge of who God is, who we are, what we have become in Christ, and what we have been called to do (precisely the kinds of things Paul has been teaching in the earlier chapters of Ephesians)—without this we really do not know what kind of activity in which to engage, and we will be vulnerable to Satan's onslaughts and wiles.'[417]

The whole range of biblical teaching is important. But there are core doctrines that you must affirm to be a Christian, and that we must embrace to grow strong in the faith. First is the doctrine of the Trinity. Christians believe that there is one God in three persons: Father, Son, and Holy Spirit. In Ephesians, Paul has made a great point of stressing the respective roles in our salvation of the three Persons of the Godhead. But an alarming number of so-called evangelical Christians deny this today. If you self-consciously deny the Trinity, you are not a non-Trinitarian Christian; you are a non-Christian. The Trinity is the answer to the question, Who is God?

Other doctrines we must believe and take up are the substitutionary atonement of Christ in his death for our sins and his literal, bodily resurrection. Paul listed these as doctrines 'of first importance' (1 Cor. 15:3). Moreover, in Galatians he insists on the doctrine of justification through faith in Christ alone. Thomas Watson said, 'Justification is the very hinge and pillar of Christianity. An error about justification is dangerous, like a defect in a foundation.'[418] As Paul pointed out, Satan is constantly attacking this doctrine, encouraging us to rely on our good works or our family reputation, or our baptism or church membership, none of which will save us. We must wear justification through faith alone as a belt of truth that keeps us from slipping.

We see why it is so important that a church faithfully teaches biblical doctrine: how else are Christians to put on the belt of truth? People today choose a church for every reason but its soundness in doctrine. What people want from a minister is practically everything except clear, doctrinal preaching. But people who live boldly in the strength of the Lord are always people who are sure of the truth. Why was Martin Luther able to claim, 'Here I stand!' and thus launch the great Protestant Reformation? Because he was girded in his mind with God's truth. What prepared John Wesley to stand almost alone with the gospel before the hostile authorities in England, but that he had memorized almost the entire Greek New Testament. You may not be a Luther or a Wesley, but God wants you to be strong in his might to stand in the evil day. Truth is of first importance to your spiritual well-being and usefulness to Christ, so you should devote yourself to knowing the Bible's teaching and thus becoming strong in the Lord.

The Breastplate of Righteousness

Paul adds to this 'the breastplate of righteousness' (Eph. 6:14). Roman soldiers wore either a tough armored tunic or a bronze breastplate to protect vital organs like the heart from piercing attacks. Paul says that righteousness provides this protection in spiritual warfare. The question here is whether Paul means the righteousness God gives us through faith—Christ's imputed righteousness—or the practical righteousness of godly living.

Let us start with the second, practical righteousness. There is no doubt that Paul affirms the necessity of this, since he devoted Ephesians chapters 4 and 5 to holiness of life. Christians who dabble in sin or simply fail to cultivate godly character and habits invite deadly spiritual attacks. Think of the havoc David's adultery with Bathsheba brought into his life. John MacArthur rightly says, 'Many, if not most, of the emotional and relational problems Christians experience are caused by lack of personal holiness. Many of our disappointments and discouragements do not come from circumstances or from other people but from our own unconfessed and uncleansed sin. And when circumstances and other people do manage to rob us of happiness, it is because we are unprotected by the armor of a holy life.'[419]

We must ready ourselves for spiritual warfare by committing to godliness. Yet none of us will ever be so righteous in ourselves as to be adequately protected from Satan's attacks. This is why Paul also refers to the righteousness we receive from God, the perfect righteousness of Christ imputed to us through faith alone. Paul wrote, 'I have suffered the loss of all things and count them as rubbish, in order that I may gain Christ and be found in him, not having a righteousness of my own that comes from the law, but that which comes through faith in Christ, the righteousness from God that depends on faith' (Phil. 3:8–9). Charles Hodge explains:

> What Paul desired for himself was not to have on his own righteousness, but the righteousness which is of God by faith; and this, doubtless, is the righteousness which he here urges believers to put on as a breast-plate. It is an infinitely perfect righteousness, consisting in the obedience and sufferings of the Son of God, which satisfies all the demands of the divine law and justice, and which

is a sure defense against all assaults whether from within or from without.[420]

We know from Scripture that one of the devil's chief spiritual assaults is to accuse us before God of our unworthiness due to sin, and thereby to make us doubt our salvation and become miserable and weak. This is portrayed in a scene from Zechariah, where Joshua, the high priest of Israel, was standing before the angel of the Lord, with 'Satan standing at his right hand to accuse him' (Zech. 3:1). In one of the great pictures of Christ's gift of righteousness, the Lord rebuked Satan for accusing one of his own. 'Now Joshua was standing before the angel, clothed with filthy garments. And the angel said to those who were standing before him, "Remove the filthy garments from him." And to him he said, "Behold, I have taken your iniquity away from you, and I will clothe you with pure vestments"' (Zech. 3:3–4).

This is how the breastplate of Christ's righteousness protects us from Satan's deadly accusations, and it is worn only by those who have confessed their need of Christ's cleansing blood and the gift of his perfect righteousness. Have you done that? If not, realize that you can be cleansed and made right with God through faith in Jesus Christ. If you have, then put on this breastplate of righteousness, and go on to lead a holy life in service to him.

THE READINESS OF THE GOSPEL OF PEACE

The third piece of armor is designed to provide us sound footwear. Roman soldiers wore short boots, often with nails or studs to provide traction. Ancient battles often involved masses of armored men straining upon each other, so good shoes were a matter of life or death. Likewise, in the spiritual battle of the Christian life we must be fleet of foot, so Paul adds, 'As shoes for your feet, having put on the readiness given by the gospel of peace' (Eph. 6:15).

As before, there is more than one way to take this. One view is that our footwear is the gospel itself, which tells us good news of the peace we have with God. Geoffrey Wilson holds this view: 'As no soldier stands firm in the day of battle unless his morale is high, so believers must be assured of their acceptance with God before they can withstand the assaults of the great adversary of their souls.'[421] Knowing our peace with God gives us good traction in spiritual battle.

In this respect, Paul might have been alluding to the first Passover, where the Israelites were spared from the angel of death because of the blood of the lamb over their doorposts—a picture of the spiritual peace provided by Christ's atoning blood. The instructions for the Passover meal relate closely to Paul's teaching here: 'In this manner you shall eat it: with your belt fastened, your sandals on your feet, and your staff in your hand. And you shall eat it in haste' (Exod. 12:11). In this case, the readiness the gospel provides is the realization that we are being saved out from this world. As pilgrims on the exodus to heaven we are not to attach our hearts to the dying things of this world. That truth does give us readiness in spiritual warfare.

But I think it more likely that Paul had in mind Isaiah 52:7, 'How beautiful upon the mountains are the feet of him who brings good news, who publishes peace, who brings good news of happiness, who publishes salvation, who says to Zion, "Your God reigns."' I think this in part because the other two pieces of our spiritual armor connect back to Isaiah. Isaiah relates our feet to the spreading of the gospel, just as Paul has referred to the gospel in Ephesians as that which brings peace to the world. The point, then, is that a readiness to share the gospel with others gives us a firm footing in spiritual warfare.

There are a number of ways this is so. Those who are sharing the gospel are aware of the falsehoods that keep others from belief. They are alerted to the kinds of deceptions the devil employs, and their minds are exercised in biblical reasoning. People who are sharing the gospel are more likely to see the world for what it is, and to value faith above other things. Furthermore, if you are devoted to helping others to see the riches of a relationship with God in Jesus Christ, you will not likely be cornered in the folly of worldly thinking and your spiritual adversaries will find you an unlikely target for their attacks.

The two approaches to this verse go together. Those who realize the peace they gain through the gospel will always want to share it with others. And those who are always thinking about opportunities to share with others the peace of God we have in Christ will themselves be blessed by that peace. So Christians should always be proclaiming the good news of peace with God through faith in Christ, to others and to themselves. As John Stott points out, 'The devil fears and hates the gospel, because it is God's power to rescue people from his tyranny, both us who have received it and those with whom we share it. So we need to keep our gospel boots strapped on.'[422]

Standing Like a Stone Wall

When I think of spiritual warfare and Paul's command that we should stand, having put on the armor of God, I am reminded of one of the great scenes in American military history. The first great battle of the American Civil War was fought beside the Bull Run creek in Northern Virginia. The Union army under the command of General Irwin McDowell executed a flanking movement against the rebels. McDowell's opponent, General Beauregard, had concentrated almost all the Southern forces on his right, and suddenly one Northern regiment after another poured out from the woods onto the Confederate left. Some of the Southern units threw themselves into the path to buy time for their army, but as reinforcements made their way over the defense was crumbling.

One of the Confederate brigades was commanded by Brigadier General Thomas Jackson. Seeing the chaos before him, he calmly aligned his infantry on a strong position at the crest of a hill across the Northerner's path. Some of the other brigades that had gone into the fight before Jackson's were on the brink of despair and close to the point of breaking. But one of their leaders looked up, saw Jackson's brigade standing firm behind them, and shouted, 'There stands Jackson like a stone wall!' That is where the famous general received his name, Stonewall Jackson. Seeing him, the others took heart. They retreated and took up solid positions beside him, and the Union advance was broken on the stone wall of resolute soldiers.

It makes a similar difference when you stand firm in faith. When you put on the belt of truth, the breastplate of righteousness, and the footwear of the readiness of the gospel of peace, you save not only yourself but God will use you to save and strengthen others. Are there weak, struggling, doubting Christians faltering in the good fight of the faith? Let them see you standing in the armor of God. Let them say, 'There he stands like a stone wall!' What Paul wrote to the young pastor Timothy applies to us as well: 'Take heed to yourself and to the doctrine. Continue in them, for in doing this you will save both yourself and those who hear you.' (1 Tim. 4:16, NKJV).

63

The Weaponry of Our Warfare

Ephesians 6:16–17

One of the greatest Christian books is *Pilgrim's Progress,* by John Bunyan. This allegory tells the story of Christian, who heard the gospel and left his home to seek out the Celestial City. Bunyan leads Christian through a number of trials and challenges that depict the struggles of the Christian life. Early on, Christian visited an armory where he discovered all kinds of equipment provided by the Lord for pilgrims. There was Moses' rod, the jawbone with which Samson killed so many Philistines, and the sling and stone used by David to fell the giant Goliath. Much to Christian's delight, there were items provided for him—just as there are for us—namely, the armor of God spoken of by Paul in Ephesians chapter 6. Christian learned that equipped by what God provides us in Christ, we can be 'strong in the Lord and in the strength of his might' (Eph. 6:10).

The armor of God comes in two groups. The first three items are worn on the body: the belt of truth, the breastplate of righteousness, and gospel shoes. The second three items, which we will consider in this study, are items that we take up for battle: 'the shield of faith…the helmet of salvation, and the sword of the Spirit, which is the word of God' (Eph. 6:16–17). For the first kind of equipment, Paul tells us to stand 'having put on' these items. They are passive items of protection that we wear all the time: truth, righteousness, and gospel readiness. Even when there are lulls in the battle, we keep these items on to avoid exposing ourselves. But the lull ends and a barrage comes in. Then you pick up your active weaponry. You lift up your shield, put on your helmet, and take up your sword. That is Paul's idea in depicting the weaponry of our warfare in Ephesians 6:16–17.

The Shield of Faith

The first item of our active protection is 'the shield of faith, with which you can extinguish all the flaming darts of the evil one' (Eph. 6:16). In ancient warfare, one of the most deadly forms of attack was the barrage of flaming darts. These were sharp arrows or darts soaked or covered in flammable material. They were lit and fired in great numbers at the enemy line. The modern equivalent would be the artillery barrage. The point was to harass, bother, and whittle down the enemy line prior to the main attack.

How does this relate to spiritual warfare? Paul says that 'the evil one,' that is, the devil, launches 'flaming darts' against us. These are spiritual assaults against our minds. Sometimes they take the form of doubts. Some of the greatest Christians have been plagued by terrible doubts and depressions, which came suddenly and powerfully. Elijah suffered this after his victory over the priests of Baal (1 Kings 19:1–4); Charles Spurgeon was also known to suffer this way. Flaming darts may also come as blasphemous thoughts; this, too, is something to which many noble Christians attest. Lloyd-Jones writes,

> Do we not know something of what it is, perhaps, to wake up in the morning and to find that before we have had time to do any thinking, thoughts come to us, evil thoughts, perhaps even blasphemous thoughts?…Have you not found that, when you…are trying to pray, these darts come from all directions at you…you seem filled with all these distracting and evil thoughts and notions and ideas…You can read a newspaper and concentrate on it, but when you start reading your Bible, thoughts and ideas come from all directions and you find it almost impossible to concentrate. Where do they come from? These are 'the fiery darts of the wicked one'.[423]

The devil launches such fiery darts to make us loathe ourselves and discourage us from God's service. This is why it will often be when serving God or worshiping him that such attacks come. It was during the months that Martin Luther was translating the Bible into the German language— probably the most significant achievement of his entire life—that the devil came to him to accuse him of his unworthiness and sin. Luther said that it was his most miserable time of spiritual assault, as Satan called his motives and his abilities into question in his own mind. The devil was trying to stop Luther from spreading the gospel, and through similar mental assaults he wants to take away our confidence so that we will not boldly serve the Lord.

We should also think of 'flaming darts' in terms of trying circumstances. Peter writes, 'Beloved, do not be surprised at the fiery trial when it comes upon you to test you' (1 Pet. 4:12). We think of Daniel and his companions who were the object of such Satanic conspiracies. On one occasion the king ordered everyone to bow down to a gold statue, and on another occasion the king forbade prayer to anyone but himself. The whole purpose of these events was to persecute Daniel and his godly friends and intimidate them into disobeying God.

The devil uses trials to make us doubt God's goodness. He tempted Eve by saying that God had forbidden the tree of the knowledge of good and evil simply to keep her down. He has the same message today, especially when times are hard: God and his commandments are not good for us, so we should avoid him and reject his will.

A great example of this is the book of Job. From the beginning of his story, we know what Job did not know, namely, the source of his great afflictions. His friends blamed his troubles on Job, saying he must have somehow offended God. His wife gave the immortal counsel, 'Curse God and die!' (Job 2:9). Job was tempted to believe it must be God behind his sorrows. 'I loathe my life,' he said, because God 'destroys both the blameless and the wicked' (Job 9:21–22). That is the conclusion many suffering people draw today. But the reader who knows differently wants to shout out, 'Job! Job! It isn't God! It's Satan!' And the very thing the devil wants is for you to turn away from God. This is what Paul wants us to know when Satan fires his flaming darts to cause us to doubt God's goodness and love.

In addition to these attacks, the devil launches

fiery darts to enflame our passions with sinful desires. Satan cannot steal a believer from God, but he tries to ruin our usefulness by leading us into sin. This is what happened to David through his affair with Bathsheba; David never fully recovered his usefulness to God. Just think how many ministers of the gospel today are led into pornography or sexual sin; this is an attack of the devil on our pulpits so as to weaken the church.

What are we to do in response to these flaming darts? Paul says, 'Take up the shield of faith' (Eph. 6:16). When a barrage of flaming arrows poured in, a Roman soldier took up his shield, which was large enough to cover his whole body. The belt, breastplate, and shoes were not enough. Likewise, we must take up the shield of faith to deflect and put out the fiery darts of the evil one.

What does it mean to lift up the shield of faith? It means to hold up the truth about God. This is why we must learn the attributes of God in the Bible. God is faithful, God is wise, God is almighty, God is holy, and God is merciful. So when thoughts come to us to make us doubt or hate God, we must respond with the truth about him. Abraham experienced this in despair over his lack of a child. This was a fiery dart that embarrassed him and made him anxious over the future. But God came to him and said, 'Fear not, Abram, I am your shield' (Gen. 15:1). Paul said that Abraham 'grew strong in his faith as he gave glory to God, fully convinced that God was able to do what he had promised' (Rom. 4:20–21). Knowing who God is, we lift up our faith as a shield, and Satan's attacks are deflected away.

The same is true of God's promises. We need to know the Bible's great promises, which are given for every situation: promises of mercy and compassion, of help, strength, endurance, forgiveness, comfort, guidance, life everlasting, and eternal reward. For each of our needs there is a promise from God that is certain to be kept. We lift our faith in God's promises and they shield us from attack.

Likewise, we must remember God's great saving works: how he faithfully delivered his people, the path he made for Israel through the Red Sea and the safety he provided Daniel in the lion's den. Lift God's works up as a shield of faith! Greatest of all God's works is the sending of his Son to die on the cross for our sins. Paul writes, 'We know that for those who love God all things work together for good' (Rom. 8:28). How do we know this? Because 'he who did not spare his own Son but gave him up for us all, how will he not also with him graciously give us all things?' (Rom. 8:32). Here is a shield of faith: Christ crucified for us.

The Roman shield was designed to interlock with the shields on either side to form an impenetrable barrier. Likewise, our shield of faith works best in company with fellow Christians—whose help we should seek when the fiery darts start flying, and whose faith can cover our weaknesses as ours covers theirs. With our shields lifted up and locked together we are most safe in battle.

The Helmet of Salvation

Paul adds to this 'the helmet of salvation.' After the enemy hurled their flaming darts, they advanced for close combat. To be ready, the Roman soldier put on his thick helmet, which only a heavy sword or axe could penetrate. A more familiar example for us would be a football player putting on his helmet and going into the game. Without his helmet, he is timid and shies away from contact. But with a helmet on his head, he flies into the fight. This is the idea that Paul has for us with the 'helmet of salvation.' By salvation he means our confidence that whatever happens in life, God will save us in the end. With this helmet on, we are able to throw ourselves into the battle.

Since a helmet covers the head, Paul seems to be concerned about our mental clarity. If we question our salvation—if we doubt that God will save us in the end—this will make us timid and weak in spiritual warfare. The devil and the world tell us that Christianity is only for fools, that with the trials and struggles of faith we should just give up or give in, and then all will be well. What good is it to be a Christian? This is the attack and the temptation on our minds.

This must be a real problem, because it is answered in many places in the New Testament. In Matthew 24, Jesus warned the disciples that hard times would come. 'You will hear of wars and rumors of war' (Matt. 24:6). There would be false Christs and tribulations of all kinds. But, Jesus told them, it leads to his return in glory to gather his people for salvation (Matt. 24:29–31). Paul addressed this same issue in the fourth chapter of 2 Corinthians. 'We are afflicted in every way,' he admitted, 'but not crushed; perplexed, but not driven to despair; persecuted, but not forsaken; struck down, but not destroyed' (2 Cor. 4:8–9). 'So we do not lose heart,' he concluded. 'For this slight momentary affliction is preparing for us an eternal weight of glory beyond all comparison' (2 Cor. 4:16–17). The Book of Revelation was written to address this problem of giving in. It tells us to endure to the end and be saved. After all the trials and persecutions it predicts, Revelation ends with a glorious vision of 'a new heaven and a new earth…the holy city, new Jerusalem coming down out of heaven from God' (Rev. 21:1–2). This victory, not defeat, is the future of those who press on in faith in Christ. The helmet of salvation gives us confidence to wage war, knowing that whatever happens we will be saved.

This is how Job prevailed under his extraordinary trials. I mentioned earlier that his friends blamed him and his wife urged him to blame God. But Job continued to hope for salvation. He said of God, 'Though he slay me, I will hope in him' (Job 13:15). Ultimately, he hoped in the resurrection, which no trial in this world can take from us if we continue to trust in the Lord. Job said: 'I know that my Redeemer lives, and at the last he will stand upon the earth. And after my skin has been thus destroyed, yet in my flesh I shall see God' (Job 19:25–27). The Christian who knows this will be bold in battle, wearing 'for a helmet the hope of salvation' (1 Thess. 5:8).

The Sword of the Spirit

This brings us to the sixth and last item of the armor of God: 'And take…the sword of the Spirit, which is the word of God' (Eph. 6:17). This is the one offensive item in our spiritual armory, although it, like the rest, serves a primarily defensive purpose. Paul's overall theme is that we are to 'stand firm' and 'withstand in the evil day.' But a good defense requires some offense, and our offensive weapon is God's Word.

Paul refers to God's Word as a sword because it has offensive power. Hebrews 4:12 says, 'The word of God is living and active, sharper than any two-edged sword, piercing to the division of soul and of spirit, of joints and of marrow.' It is the sword 'of the Spirit' because it is the Spirit who has given it to God's people. The Bible was inspired by the Holy Spirit: 'men spoke from God as they were carried along by the Holy Spirit' (2 Pet. 1:20). Moreover, it is the Holy Spirit who regenerates us so that we can believe the Bible, and who illuminates our minds so that we can understand it. And the Holy Spirit gives the power that makes Scripture so effective in battle. To fight with

God's Word is to fight with the Spirit's power; to fight with the Spirit's power is to fight with the Scriptures. There is no other 'sword of the Spirit' than the Word of God.

The great example of this was provided by our Lord Jesus during his temptations in the desert. Three times Satan tempted him, and each time Jesus replied with God's Word—not merely biblical thoughts but actual texts from the Bible. 'Man shall not live by bread alone,' he said, 'but on every word that comes from the mouth of God' (Matt. 4:4; Deut. 8:3). We are to follow his example, responding to doubts, temptations, or trials with appropriate Scriptures. Satan tried to tempt Jesus to worship him, but Jesus replied, 'It is written, "You shall worship the Lord your God and him only shall you serve"' (Matt. 4:10; Deut. 6:13). When Jesus struck back at the devil with the sword of God's Word, 'the devil left him' (Matt. 4:11). We, too, can drive off Satan with the sword of the Spirit that is God's Word. Indeed, if God's own Son waged warfare with Satan in this way, we who are so infinitely weaker can hardly afford to neglect so potent a weapon.

Bunyan vividly depicted our struggle with Satan in *Pilgrim's Progress*. Shortly after putting on the armor of God, Christian was set upon by Apollyon, the red dragon who represents the devil. Apollyon's fiery darts were met by the shield of faith, so he closed in for close combat. Throwing Christian to the ground, Apollyon readied his killing blow, but Christian grasped his sword. His sword was God's Word. He quoted Micah 7:8, 'Do not rejoice over me, my enemy, when I fall I will rise.' He lashed out again with a deadly thrust: 'Yet in all these things we are more than conquerors through Him who loved us' (Rom. 8:37). With more Scriptures, Bunyan's hero took the offensive, until, he writes, 'Apollyon spread his dragon wings and flew away.'[424]

This is how Martin Luther responded to Satan. The great Reformer described a vision in which the devil appeared with a long list of his sins, reading them one-by-one. All the while Satan mocked Luther's desire to serve God, assuring him that he would end up in hell. Luther says he writhed in spiritual agony until, at last, he jumped up and cried: 'It is all true, Satan, and many more sins which I have committed in my life which are known to God only; but write this at the bottom of your list, "The blood of Jesus Christ, God's Son, cleanseth us from all sin"' (1 John 1:7).[425] With that sword stroke, Luther put Satan to flight.

How, then, can we be ready to use this mighty weapon? First, we must *read* the Bible. It is impossible to prosper spiritually without regularly reading God's Word. If you are struggling in your thoughts and emotions, and especially if Satan has a strong foothold in your life, then I ask, Are you giving time to God's Word? Without filling your mind with Scripture you are neglecting the mightiest of all our weapons and subjecting yourself to defeat. Second, we must *meditate* on and *prayerfully study* God's Word. I say this because we lose the Bible's value if we do not understand its meaning and work it into our minds and hearts. The Bible compares itself to rain falling on the earth; to bring life it must penetrate into the soil. Third, we must *memorize* Scripture. This is what provides us with a ready supply of Bible passages. I noted earlier the importance of memorizing great Bible promises. But if you are subject to a certain kind of spiritual attack—doubt, anger, discouragement, or lust—then you should memorize appropriate verses to use in battle.

Thomas Cranmer led the Reformation in England and was a man of God's Word. In the *Book of Common Prayer* he wrote words that should be embraced by all Christians and prayed by us all:

Blessed Lord, who has caused all Holy Scriptures to be written for our learning: Grant that we may in such wise hear them, read, mark, learn, and inwardly digest them, that by patience and comfort of thy holy Word we may embrace and ever hold fast the blessed hope of everlasting life, which thou hast given us in our Savior Jesus Christ.[426]

Soldiers of Christ

I want to conclude by remembering the simple command that Paul gave at the beginning of his teaching on spiritual warfare: 'Finally, be strong in the Lord and in the strength of his might. Put on the whole armor of God, that you may be able to stand against the schemes of the devil' (Eph. 6:10–11). Are you standing firm? Have you firmly set your feet in the godly life, honoring God, receiving his blessing and serving his people? If not—if you are instead moving back and forth between camps—between Christ's camp and the enemy's camp—then you need to declare your allegiance firmly and take up Christ's cause in earnest. The stakes are the highest: 'The wages of sin is death, but the free gift of God is eternal life in Christ Jesus our Lord' (Rom. 6:23).

How gracious of God to give us this armor in which to fight, not in our own strength but in the strength that God gives. Have you put on this armor? Are you trained in the use of this weaponry of warfare? Do you know how to wield the shield of faith and put on the helmet of salvation? Especially, is your sword sharp? Many people today try to live as Christians with a broken sword—that is, one that has been rendered useless by unbelieving theories and a resulting lack of conviction about the Bible. Others enter into battle with a dull and rusty sword, one that hardly ever comes out of the scabbard. But then there are those whose sword is sharp and whose arms are trained in using it. They are the ones who are mighty for the Lord.

There is a great scene at the end of *Pilgrim's Progress* that describes the kind of soldier we should all aspire to be. After one difficult fight, Mr Great-heart came to Mr Valiant-for-truth:

'Thou has worthily behaved thyself. Let me see thy sword.' So he showed it him. When he had taken it into his hand and looked thereon awhile, he said, 'Ha! It is a right Jerusalem blade.' Then said Mr Valiant-for-Truth, 'It is so. Let a man have one of these blades, with a hand to wield it and skill to use it, and he may venture upon an angel with it. He need not fear its holding if he can but tell how to lay on. Its edges will never blunt; it will cut flesh, and bones, and soul, and spirit, and all.'

What kind of soldier will you be? Will you be a malingerer, the kind who drags others down and relies on those who are fitter for battle? Or will you resolve to start equipping yourself now, confident in God that he will make you strong for the fight? If you want to be a fit, useful, and valiant Christian soldier, then start strengthening your faith, become clear in the matter of your salvation, and take into your hands God's mighty Word, a sword given you by the Spirit of God, and take your stand alongside your fellow Christian warriors. You can be sure, as you do, that Christ's banner will never falter and that to him are the kingdom, the power, and the glory forever.

64

Prayer: Our Secret Weapon

Ephesians 6:18–20

No one ever faced more severe spiritual warfare than Jesus Christ. He perfectly exemplified the kind of holy warrior Paul describes. Jesus possessed all the items in the armor of God: truth, righteousness, gospel readiness, faith and salvation. He wielded the sword of the Spirit, the Word of God, with sovereign authority. Jesus described himself as a strong man fully armed who breaks into Satan's fortress and takes his captives away (Luke 11:21–22).

In addition to the armor of God, Jesus did not neglect the next resource to which Paul directs us in his teaching on spiritual warfare. In order to be strong in the Lord and to stand against the devil, Christians must put on the whole armor of God and we must also pray. How often we read of Jesus in the Gospels that 'rising very early in the morning, while it was still dark, he departed and went out to a desolate place, and there he prayed' (Mark 1:35). Likewise, many of our greatest battles will be fought in the quiet place of prayer, our secret weapon. The Christian warrior fights with his head bowed in supplication to God.

Our Commitment to Prayer

Some commentators identify prayer as the seventh piece in Paul's armor of God. But this is not only mistaken, it is to lessen the place Paul gives to prayer. Paul's injunction, 'praying always', does not place prayer *within* but *alongside* the armor of God. We put on the armor of God and wield our spiritual weaponry in a posture of constant prayer. Charles Hodge writes, 'It is not armor or weapons which makes the warrior. There must be courage and strength, and even then he often needs help.'[427] Therefore Paul urges us to pray. William Cowper, one of the great poets of the Puritan era, put it this way:

> Restraining prayer, we cease to fight;
> Prayer makes the Christian's armour bright;
> And Satan trembles when he sees
> The weakest saint upon his knees.[428]

The medieval ballad the *Song of Roland* tells of a military disaster that could easily have been avoided. Roland, commanding Charlemagne's rearguard, was set upon by Moors in a narrow defile in the Pyrenees. Had he sounded his great horn Oliphant he could have summoned ample help from the main army, but his pride held him back. How many defeats we suffer, if not by pride, by neglecting to sound the horn of prayer to God, whose infinite, sovereign resources are available to the weakest Christian who prays to him.

Paul calls for a commitment to prayer: 'Pray at all times.' He does not mean for us exclusively to devote our time to prayer; neither he nor Jesus did that. There are two ways in which we should take this. First, Paul taught his followers to do everything in an attitude of prayer: 'Pray without ceasing,' he once wrote (1 Thess. 5:17). John Wesley described this by saying that the true Christian's heart

> is ever lifted up to God, at all times and in all places…In retirement or company, in leisure, business, or conversation, his heart is ever with the Lord. Whether he lie down or rise up, God is in all his thoughts; he walks with God continually, having the loving eye of his mind still fixed upon Him, and everywhere 'seeing him that is invisible.'[429]

We can also understand this to mean that we are to pray in all kinds of circumstances and needs. We should pray in every challenge or trial. Paul says to pray 'with all prayer and supplication.' This invites us to make definite requests to God concerning all kinds of needs: for our circumstances, for our spiritual growth, comfort, guidance, faith, grace to obey, and courage to follow. John MacArthur writes:

> When we are tempted, we hold the temptation before God and ask for His help. When we experience something good and beautiful, we immediately thank God for it. When we see evil around us, we pray that God will make it right and be willing to be used of Him to that end. When we meet someone who does not know Christ, we pray for God to draw that person to Himself and to use us to be a faithful witness. When we encounter trouble, we turn to God as our Deliverer.[430]

Most of us need to pray much more than we do. One writer suggests a beginning routine similar to what you would do to get into physical shape. Most doctors agree that if you jog or even walk for 30 to 40 minutes, 3 to 4 times a week, you will get into good shape. That is not a bad goal to set to get your prayer life in gear. In addition to the little prayers that believers should constantly send to God, to prayer at meals, and to prayers at the beginning and end of the day, this discipline of praying 30 to 40 minutes would vastly improve our spiritual fitness.[431]

Our Power in Prayer

Paul adds that our prayer should be 'in the Spirit.' Here, he points to our power in prayer, namely, the mighty help given to us by Christ through the ministry of the Holy Spirit.

There are different views about Paul's meaning. Some insist that Paul is referring to our spirits, so that our prayers should involve passion and inner energy. Our prayers certainly should not be rote, dull exercises, although we are warned by Jesus himself against making public spectacles of our prayers or relying on supposedly spiritual mantras or physical exercises (Matt. 6:5–8). But there is little doubt that Paul is referring here not to our spirit but to the Holy Spirit. Earlier in Ephesians, he emphasized that we come to the Father through the Son by the ministry of the

Holy Spirit (Eph. 2:18). Some therefore conclude that Paul is talking about ecstatic prayers that involve strange tongues. Although people spoke in tongues in Paul's time, it was a gift only for some. But the prayer he is encouraging here is not a matter of a special gift for some but of the Holy Spirit's ministry that is available to us all. Instead of having some ecstatic experience, 'Praying 'in the Spirit' means praying under the Spirit's influence and with his assistance.'[432] Paul explains, 'The Spirit helps us in our weakness. For we do not know what to pray for as we ought, but the Spirit …intercedes for the saints according to the will of God' (Rom. 8:26–27).

How do we pray in the Spirit? The answer is to pray through faith in Christ, who sends the Spirit, in accordance with God's revealed will. Harry Ironside adds, 'If I would pray in the Spirit, I must live in the Spirit, and so I am to watch against anything that would come into my life to grieve the Spirit of God and thus hinder real prayer.'[433]

Our Approach to Prayer

This leads to our approach to prayer. Paul says, 'To that end keep alert with all perseverance.' This is the third 'all' in verse 18: all times, all prayer and supplication, and all perseverance.

First, we are to be alert in prayer. We are reminded of Jesus in the Garden of Gethsemane on the night of his arrest. He told his closest disciples, 'Watch and pray that you may not enter into temptation' (Matt. 26:41). The disciples quickly fell asleep instead of praying, and the danger is that we will do likewise in spiritual warfare. Alertness is one of the essential qualities of a soldier; when standing watch, to fall asleep at one's post is a court-martial offense. The stakes are just as high when our own faithfulness and the needs of others require us to be alert in prayer. Paul wrote to the Corinthians, 'Be watchful, stand firm in the faith, act like men, be strong' (1 Cor. 16:13). This shows us how serious is our delinquency when we fail to pray as we should for ourselves and others in need. Military commanders are trained to scan any new terrain, spying any likely ambushes and identifying likely avenues of attack. We are to be similarly alert in spiritual matters. 'Be watchful,' Peter warned. 'Your adversary the devil prowls around like a roaring lion, seeking someone to devour' (1 Pet. 5:8).

Joined to alertness is one of the most important attitudes in prayer: perseverance. We live in an instant-gratification, quick-fix society. We pray once and wonder why God has not answered. But he calls for us to persevere in prayer. Jesus taught, 'Everyone who asks receives, and the one who seeks finds, and to the one who knocks it will be opened' (Luke 11:10). This is not a recipe for instant prayer answers but rather for perseverance. William Hendriksen writes, 'Seeking is asking plus acting…Knocking is asking plus acting plus persevering. One knocks again and again until the door is opened.'[434]

Many Christians can testify how God answered prayers offered over long years, especially for the salvation of loved ones. Oswald Sanders, a lifelong missionary to China, remarks:

> The very fact that God lays a burden of prayer on our hearts and keeps us praying is *prima facie* evidence that He purposes to grant the answer. When asked if he really believed that two men for whose salvation he had prayed for over fifty years would be converted, George Müller of Bristol replied, 'Do you think God would have kept me praying all these years if He did not intend to save them?' Both men were converted, one shortly before, the other after Müller's death.[435]

God calls for our faith to be persistent because he wants to strengthen our faith and teach us to pray. Many of our prayers need to be tried and refined on the anvil of persistence, and our love for others must often blossom through our ministry of prayer for them.

Our Objects in Prayer

This leads us to the last of Paul's points regarding spiritual warfare and prayer, namely, that our prayers must include supplications for others. This is the fourth 'all' in verse 18, dealing with the objects of our prayer: 'Making supplication for all the saints.'

This does not mean that Christians should not pray fervently for their own needs; of course we should, as any child makes requests of his or her father. And there is something wrong with us if we are not praying for those closest to us: spouses, children, parents, and close friends. But every Christian is part of a great kingdom, with fellow citizens serving in battle on far-flung coasts. We must follow the battle reports and pray. The growth of our circle of prayer because of our love for 'all the saints' is a good indicator of our growth in grace and godliness. Paul is a great model of this. Twice in this letter he has stopped to inform his readers of his prayers for them (Eph. 1:15-23; 3:14-19). Indeed, to read Paul's various letters is to become intimate with his prayer journal; they are one and the same.

The shield of faith was one part of the armor of God that we use best together with other Christians. But this is even more true of the secret weapon that is prayer. John MacArthur rightly says, 'The greatest thing we can do for another believer, or that he can do for us, is to pray. That is the way the Body of Christ grows spiritually as well as in love.'[436] The reason why prayer unites us in love is that to pray effectively we must be involved with others in mind and in heart.

During an all-day prayer meeting in seminary, I was put in a prayer group filled with Korean women. We were to pray for missionaries we knew, and the modest women asked me to pray first. Thinking I was doing a serious work for God, I prayed for What's His Name somewhere in Europe, that God would bless his ministry, and 'that woman whose name I had forgotten' who was serving in Mongolia. Would God provide whatever needs she might happen to have? When I was done, the real praying started. I was deeply humbled by the fervor of the Korean women's prayers for their missionary friends, all of which was by name with detailed knowledge of needs—one had a leaky roof, another had no access to light bulbs, yet another had a harassing neighbor—and of their ministry burdens, to include numerous names of hopeful converts. That kind of heart connection and personal interest is what Paul has in mind and what he models in his letters.

Paul then makes the most wonderful addition. 'Making supplication for all the saints,' he writes, 'and also for me' (Eph. 6:19). This tells us two essential things. First, we must not hesitate to seek prayer for ourselves. Here was one of the greatest Christian men ever, in the prime of spiritual maturity and vigor. When Paul wrote about the armor of God he knew what he was talking about, for who has been mightier in spiritual battle than he, save for Jesus himself? What could get to Paul, whose breastplate of righteousness was battle-tested and whose sword of the Spirit was so deadly sharp? What could he not do in the strength of his faith in Jesus Christ? Yet Paul was unafraid to ask and was even bold to request from the humblest of believers, 'and also for me.' What does this say to us, who do not approach Paul's stature in the faith, but that we should ask for prayers and humbly provide details of our needs so that we might be held up before the Lord in the prayers of our fellow Christians?

This also says something about the prayer needs of anyone engaged in active gospel ministry, and especially in teaching God's Word. Who is a more likely candidate for spiritual attack than a man who preaches the gospel in the church or the missionary who bears Christ's light into the heart of Satan's darkness? Pastors are under spiritual attacks of all kinds: temptations to folly, doubt, error, or sin. Some preachers are led into pride so as to disgrace their labors. But far more are despondent due to opposition, hardship, and lack of evident fruit. Most are wearied by the burdens they bear and their sense of personal inadequacy. Some are tempted by that weariness into sinful comforts that ship-wreck their ministry.

The Bible tells us that Israel succeeded in battle only so long as Moses held his arms aloft. When Moses faltered the battle began to turn against them, so others came alongside God's servant and held his hands in the air for him (Exod. 17:12). Likewise, anyone who teaches God's Word can only prosper long if his hands are held up by the prayers of his faithful church. Harry Ironside said, 'I am sure that those of us who stand on public platforms and preach Christ will never know until we get to Heaven how much we owe to the prayers of God's people.' I would add that few of God's people know what encouragement it brings to those who preach Christ to learn of their prayerful support. Ironside summarizes, 'What is needed is not only the word of the preacher, but that message backed up by the saints in prayer.'[437]

We should note what Paul asks for. He asks for prayer not for his freedom from imprisonment or that he might be personally successful. Instead, he asks 'that words may be given to me in opening my mouth boldly to proclaim the mystery of the gospel, for which I am an ambassador in chains, that I may declare it boldly, as I ought to speak' (Eph. 6:19-20). Paul prays not for success or personal relief, but for faithfulness and boldness. He realized that the gospel is not a topic for debating or a product to sell, but as the mystery of God's salvation it is a matter of God's own revelation, the foolishness of God that is wiser than the wisdom of men (1 Cor. 1:25).

Likewise, preachers today should not pray for eloquence or dynamic oratory—things that commend the messenger more than the message. Instead, preachers should pray for God's message to come from God's own revealed Word. The preacher's goal, for which the church should pray, is the clear presentation of God's Word, faithfully and boldly. This is the freedom that Paul desires, as he put it elsewhere, that 'by the open statement of the truth we would commend ourselves to everyone's conscience in the sight of God' (2 Cor. 4:2). Every preacher should solicit prayer for this liberty—freedom to forget himself, his ambitions, and his fears, and to exalt Christ and the whole counsel of God in holy boldness. Paul realized that he served as an ambassador for Christ, despite his chains. Like any faithful ambassador, he desired to serve his master and king well, presenting the gospel of his Lord 'as I ought to speak.'

We know that God blessed the prayers Paul sought. In Ephesians he writes of the chains that bound him to his Roman guards. He ends Philippians by writing, 'All the saints greet you, especially those of Caesar's household' (Phil. 4:21). This probably includes those very guards, together with others who believed Paul's preaching in accordance with the prayers of the saints. Furthermore, Luke concludes the Book of Acts by telling us that Paul lived in Rome 'two whole years…proclaiming the kingdom of God and teaching about the Lord Jesus Christ with all boldness and without hindrance' (Acts 28:31). Luke's description perfectly matches Paul's request for the prayers of his Ephesian friends. Against their prayers, the principalities and powers, and all the might of Rome, were helpless to hold back the gospel of Christ.

Our Obligation to Prayer

Paul has taught us about our commitment to prayer ('pray at all times'), our power in prayer ('in the Spirit'), our approach to prayer ('alert and persistent'), and our objects in prayer ('for all the saints, and also for me). I want to conclude with one more thought, our obligation for prayer.

Paul knew his obligation. He said, 'I am an ambassador in chains.' He ended the companion letter that he sent with Ephesians, his letter to the Colossians, even more pointedly: 'Remember my chains' (Col. 4:18). Paul says he was the ambassador of Jesus Christ before the Roman Empire. Ambassadors are men of stature, and are normally accorded freedom from restraint or legal action. Yet Paul wore chains. They were symbols of his spiritual warfare, for he served as ambassador to one who is declared an enemy and an outlaw by this world and its powers. Paul's chains spoke of his obligation as an apostle to go and preach to the Gentiles. He asked for prayer to speak boldly, 'as I ought to speak.' In the Greek text, it is more strident; literally, he says, 'as I *must* speak,' or, 'as I am obliged to speak.'

We wear no iron bands, but we are likewise engaged in spiritual warfare on behalf of our Lord and his people, who are despised by this world and opposed by evil powers. We likewise have an obligation, as fellow servants in the kingdom of Jesus Christ: an obligation to pray.

Paul was faithful to stand before Caesar with the gospel. Will we be faithful to order our lives so as to be committed in prayer as we ought—as we *must*? We have the gospel today because Paul and others after him were faithful. Let us remember his chains, and even more the cross that Jesus bore for us, and let us be faithful: 'Praying at all times in the Spirit, with all prayer and supplication… alert with all perseverance, making supplication for all the saints, and also for me.'

65

Grace and Peace Be with You

Ephesians 6:21–24

The Christian faith flows along 'love lines,' traveling not just from page to page but from life to life and heart to heart. The medium by which the gospel spreads is relationships of love. This is how it was with the apostle Paul. He lived and wrote with such passion because of his relationship with the person from whom he received his message, the risen Lord Jesus. He began the letter by stressing this relationship: 'Paul, an apostle of Christ Jesus by the will of God' (Eph. 1:1). Paul's letters contain not only a literary legacy but also a personal legacy. He wrote Ephesians for Christian people he knew and loved, people who preserved it and passed it on until it comes to us through a chain of hearts joining us personally to Paul and to Jesus.

Paul worried that his imprisonment in Rome might discourage the faith of the young churches around Ephesus. 'I ask you not to lose heart over what I am suffering for you' (Eph. 3:13), he said. This is why he wrote in chapter 1 to remind them of the spiritual blessings we have in Christ, and in chapter 2 of the glorious salvation God has given us by his grace. In chapter 3 he showed how God's wisdom is revealed through his care for the church. Instead of being discouraged, the Christians should press on to holiness in the power of God's Spirit, which is the topic of chapters 4–6.

A Warm Recommendation

In the closing verses, Paul says he is sending a messenger to give his personal encouragement and to bring this letter (also delivering Colossians and Philemon). 'So that you also may know how I am and what I am doing,' he says, 'Tychicus the beloved brother and faithful minister in the Lord will tell you everything' (Eph. 6:21).

Who is Tychicus? We first read this name in Acts 20:4, which lists Paul's companions at the end of his third missionary journey. When Paul traveled from Greece back to Jerusalem with the offering for the Jews, he brought representatives from the various Gentile churches. Among them were 'the Asians, Tychicus and Trophimus.' The chief city of Asia was Ephesus, so it is likely that Tychicus was one of Paul's leading converts during his long ministry in that city. He was obviously a valuable colleague and protégé of Paul, since the apostle later writes of his intention to send Tychicus to Crete to replace Titus (Titus 3:12), and since he writes in 2 Timothy 4:12 of sending Tychicus back to help Timothy in Ephesus.

This is all we know about Tychicus, although undoubtedly he led a fascinating and eventful life. But Paul makes two comments about him that serve as a glorious epitaph for any Christian. Two thousand years after he lived, we do not know what Tychicus looked like or much of what he did, but we know this: he was a 'beloved brother and faithful minister.' This is his epitaph, engraved in Holy Scripture. As a brother in the family of God, Tychicus was beloved. Why? In part it must have been because as a minister of God's grace he was faithful. These two words describe the sum of every Christian's calling: to *love* within the family of God, and to minister *faithfully*. The word for *minister* is *diakonos*, from which we derive the title *deacon*, and which means *servant*. Whatever were Tychicus' gifts and abilities, he used them faithfully, loving and being loved in the church.

What words would be written as your epitaph? For what would you be remembered? Would it be for harshness towards people or for kind and sacrificial love? Would it be for always demanding and criticizing the church or for faithful devotion, charity, and godliness? Will you be remembered for thinking mainly of yourself or for giving selflessly to others? When all is said and done, faithfulness to God and love for his people matter far more than much gold. Tychicus is remembered for these two great marks of God's Spirit—love and faithfulness—to which each of us should prayerfully aspire. Tychicus was an ideal emissary for Paul, because he was not merely the bearer of Paul's letter but his life was the bearer of its living message. We must be the same if we are to carry the gospel to the people in our world.

Tychicus was also an ideal messenger because he witnessed the events of Paul's ministry after he departed from Ephesus, and was intimate with Paul's circumstances in Rome. This is why Paul sent him to give an accurate report to his readers. Rumors would have spread about a man like Paul and mischief might be done to the church. John Calvin insightfully explains Paul's likely concern: 'Never has any man of authority, who has edified God's church, been cast into prison or brought to a halt without something or other being spread abroad to disgrace him and bring him, as it were, into disrepute, and all to obscure the things that God has done through him and to overthrow that which he has built.'[438] Tychicus was in a position to speak about Paul's faithfulness to God and God's faithfulness to Paul, and thus to encourage the fledgling Christians who had learned about his trials.

Tychicus appears only briefly on the pages of Scripture, just as we pass only briefly through this world. Because of his godliness, Paul prized him as one who could encourage the church, which in this case was Tychicus' home congregation. He shows us that when we have come to faith in Christ, we often serve him best by returning to our home or our line of work, but doing so as a person who has been transformed and who has a story to tell of God's amazing grace.

Four Blessings in Ephesians

As in all his letters, Paul concludes with a benediction—a 'good word' of blessing—expressing his fondest wishes for his readers. R. Kent Hughes points out, 'There is nothing more revealing about us than what we wish for those we love most.' What do we wish for those we love? That they would go to the best schools, make a great deal of money, or have exciting experiences? Paul shows his heart, conveying as the ambassador of Christ four blessings on his readers. His benediction highlights four words which sum up his gospel: 'Peace be to the brothers, and love with faith, from God the Father and the Lord Jesus Christ. Grace be with all who love our Lord Jesus Christ with love incorruptible' (Eph. 6:23–24). Peace, love, faith, and grace—these are the faces on the Mount Rushmore of Paul's theology. 'They are the greatest blessings we could wish for,' says Hughes, 'and we must learn to wish them for ourselves and for all we love.'[439]

Having studied Paul's thought in this letter, we realize that he places these four items starting with the effects and working back to the cause. First, is peace: 'Peace be to the brothers' (Eph. 6:23).

To Paul, the sum and end of Christian salvation is *peace*. By this, the Bible means more than the mere absence of hostility. It means the blessings of welfare and spiritual prosperity under God's loving care. When the Bible looks forward to the completion of God's great work in history, it depicts a great peace: 'The wolf shall dwell with the lamb, and the leopard shall lie down with the young goat, and the calf and the lion and the fattened calf together, and a little child shall lead them…They shall not hurt or destroy in all my holy mountain; for the earth shall be full of the knowledge of the Lord as the waters cover the sea' (Isa. 11:6–9). A life with peace is what Jesus ultimately offers: 'Peace I leave with you; my peace I give to you' (John 14:27).

God's peace has been one of the main themes of Ephesians. Paul first noted the peace with God that comes through faith in Jesus Christ. 'In him we have redemption through his blood, the forgiveness of our trespasses, according to the riches of [God's] grace' (Eph. 1:7). God remedies the sins and hatred and hostility of this world not by sending an occupying army to enforce a merely outward truce, but by sending his Son to die on the cross and reconcile sinners to heaven. In Christ, we find not only peace *with God*, but also the peace *of God* that unites us as brothers and sisters. The great statement of this peace was made in Ephesians 2:14–17, where Paul was considering the division between Jews and Gentiles. The remedy was that both should come together before God in Jesus Christ:

> For he himself is our peace, who has made us both one and has broken down in his flesh the dividing wall of hostility…that he might create in himself one new man in the place of the two, so making peace, and might reconcile us both to God in one body through the cross.

Christianity offers the peace that comes from being right with God and right with the world, and the living peace of the Holy Spirit as he lives in our hearts.

Because of God's saving blessings, we are called by Ephesians to a life of peace. We are to maintain peace in the church, being 'eager to maintain the unity of the Spirit in the bond of peace' (Eph. 4:3). Paul calls us to order our lives according to God's gracious commands so that we may pursue lives of peace in a world gripped with conflict: wives submitting to husbands and husbands loving wives; children obeying parents and parents nurturing children; slaves giving willing service to masters and masters treating slaves with humanity.

A story is told of a retired couple who feared the threat of nuclear war and global conflict. They studied all the places where they might live in peace, finally settling on an island off the coast of South America. After moving, they sent Christmas cards to all their friends informing them of their new safe haven: the Falkland Islands. Shortly afterwards, of all things, Britain and Argentina went to war over that very island

and their peace was shattered. This proves that the only sure peace in this world is the peace that God gives through Jesus Christ. 'Peace be to the brothers,' Paul writes, and only in the brotherhood of Christ is peace truly found.

Paul adds to this, 'and love with faith, from God the Father and the Lord Jesus Christ' (Eph. 6:23). If the blessing of peace is the end of salvation, its immediate cause is *love*. Paul means not self-love, nor merely love for those things that bring us pleasure, but the giving love for others that comes only from God the Father and Jesus Christ.

This, too, has been an important theme in Ephesians. God's love for us is the motive of our salvation. Ephesians 1:5 says, 'In love he predestined us for adoption through Jesus Christ, according to the purpose of his will.' God sent his Spirit to make us alive with Christ 'because of the great love with which he loved us' (Eph. 2:4). Love begets love, so Paul rejoiced 'because I have heard of your faith in the Lord Jesus and your love toward all the saints' (Eph. 1:15). All through Ephesians, Paul writes of love. We are 'rooted and grounded in…the love of Christ that surpasses knowledge ' (Eph. 3:17-19). Therefore, 'bearing with one another in love,' and 'speaking the truth in love,' we build up the church 'in love' (Eph. 4:2-3, 15-16). As God's 'beloved children,' we must 'walk in love, as Christ loved us and gave himself up for us' (Eph. 5:1-2).

Next comes *faith*, which is the source of both the Christian's love and peace. B.F. Westcott writes, 'Peace and love are God's gifts, and faith is the condition of appropriating them.'[440]

Paul often linked faith and love. Galatians 5:6 says the only thing that really matters is 'faith working through love.' Tychicus was 'beloved' and 'faithful,' and here, Paul speaks of 'love with faith' (Eph. 6:23). These two are joined inseparably in Christians. 'Faith is the recognition and the reception of the divine love into the heart.'[441] Faith responds then with love for God and for those God loves.

Ephesians emphasizes that we are saved through faith in Christ alone: 'For by grace you have been saved through faith. And this is not your own doing; it is the gift of God, not a result of works, so that no one may boast' (Eph. 2:8-9). Faith is God's gift, God's work in us, which is why Paul says that faith comes 'from God the Father and the Lord Jesus Christ' (Eph. 6:23). If we have faith it is because God the Father loved us from eternity and sent God the Son into the world to die for our sins, and together they sent the Holy Spirit to open our hearts to receive his love and believe. It is through the gift of faith that God calls and motivates us to a life of love.

Last, Paul mentions *grace*. He began this letter by saying, 'Grace and peace to you.' He ends with the same idea. 'Peace be to the brothers,' and 'Grace be with all who love our Lord Jesus Christ' (Eph. 6:24). If we had to select one of these four words of benediction as the theme of Ephesians, it would be grace. Grace is God's loving favor to those who deserve his hostility and wrath. Everything we receive in Christ is 'according to the riches of his grace' (Eph. 1:7). How can we inherit eternity with God? How can we be transformed into people of love and peace? The answer to it all is God's grace! The grace that is in God is the only explanation for the wonderful salvation he gives in Christ. That same grace is the power by which God works in us to 'bless us with every spiritual blessing in Christ' (Eph. 1:3).

When we began studying Ephesians I noted that Paul's letter excels in answering one vital question: 'What is a Christian?' At various times we have answered that question during our study of this epistle. As Paul concludes, we may answer it in accordance with the four words of this benediction. A Christian is one who has *peace*—peace with God, peace with self, and peace with the world—because of God's *love* working in us and through us, a love we receive through *faith*—a faith that believes God's Word as it preaches the gospel of Jesus Christ—all because of God's *grace*—his unmerited favor to all who will come, so that his glorious name will be exalted forever in us.

The Final Word

The four words of Paul's benediction, which summarize Ephesians' message of salvation, are not the last word in this epistle. There is one final word apart from which Paul would have no gospel at all: that word is *Jesus*. The very last verse reads, 'Grace be with all who love our Lord Jesus Christ with love incorruptible' (Eph. 6:24).

We have been recalling the great theme words of Ephesians—peace, love, faith, and grace. But there is one expression that always accompanies them. Over and again, Paul has used a phrase to locate the source of all our blessings and the place where our salvation is found and enjoyed. The phrase is 'in Christ.' Our whole salvation is 'in Christ'—in his person and in his saving work. We were chosen 'in Christ' (Eph. 1:4); our hope is 'in Christ' (Eph. 1:12). We are made alive 'in Christ' (Eph. 2:4), and God's kindness is shown to us 'in Christ' (Eph. 2:7). Christ is our peace (Eph. 3:14); ours is 'the surpassing love of Christ' (Eph. 3:19); our confidence to draw near to God comes 'through our faith in [Christ]' (Eph. 3:12); and all of God's grace for us is 'in the Beloved' (Eph. 1:6), that is, 'in Christ.'

Surely, Paul wants everyone to know God's grace and thus to have God's peace. He devoted his whole life to spreading that gospel. But speaking as Christ's apostle and ambassador, he can pronounce his benediction only on those who are 'in Christ'—or, as he puts it, 'all who love our Lord Jesus Christ with love incorruptible' (Eph. 6:24).

We could offer many definitions of Christian faith, but none is better than this: to love Jesus Christ. Saving faith involves far more than mere intellectual assent. R. C. Sproul reminds us that when God opens our hearts through his Word to believe in Christ, this 'involves a change in emotion, disposition, inclination, and volition. We now choose Christ. We embrace Christ. We gladly receive Christ. Indeed we flee to Christ.'[442] Faith sings:

> My Jesus, I love thee, I know thou art mine;
> For thee all the follies of sin I resign.
> My gracious Redeemer, my Savior art thou;
> If ever I loved thee, my Jesus, tis now.
> I love thee because thou hast first loved me,
> And purchased my pardon on Calvary's tree.
> I love thee for wearing the thorns on thy brow;
> If ever I loved thee, my Jesus, 'tis now.[443]

This is what identifies true Christians. Our creeds may differ in minor details, our church polity may vary, different gifts and graces may be more prevalent here than there; yet in this one thing there is an absolute unity: we love Jesus Christ. We adore the beauty of his holy character. We gratefully appreciate the mercy of his saving work. We trust and rely on the sacrifice he willingly made for us, laying down his own life to free us from our sins. And we long to see him at the end of this life or the end of this world, whichever comes first, and to dwell with him in glory forever and ever, we as his people and he as our God. This, above all, is what marks us as Christians.

Paul calls our love for Christ 'incorruptible,' or, 'immortal,' not because our love is so pure and unchanging. Our love is weak and inconstant;

sometimes it is almost imperceptible. But his love for us never ends nor can end, so our love for him can never die.

This, then, is the great question for all our lives: 'Is our love for Jesus alive and growing? Do we love him now more than we did a year ago? Do we realize that this is the true measure of our lives: first, 'to comprehend with all the saints what is the breadth and length and height and depth, and to know the love of Christ that surpasses knowledge' (Eph. 3:18-19), and then to find our love for him growing, so that, Paul says, 'Christ may dwell in our hearts through faith' (Eph. 3:17)?

I might conclude these studies in Ephesians by asking, Do you possess peace? Or, Do you feel love? Do you have faith? Do you know and rely upon God's grace? But all of these can be answered with the one matter Paul brings us to at the end: Do you know and love Jesus Christ? That is the question of questions. If you want to know him and want to grow in your love for him, you do not have to stir up romantic or sentimental feelings. The place to turn is God's Word, where Christ's love for you is written in letters of blood, where his promises are sealed by the Spirit, and where God's grace is as alive today as when Paul first wrote this glorious letter. There is no other question with which to end Ephesians—and everything it has taught us from beginning to end depends upon the answer—'Do you know and love Jesus Christ?' He has loved you, and he invites you by faith into his wonderful grace. 'Grace be with all who love our Lord Jesus Christ with love incorruptible' (Eph. 6:24).

Endnotes

1. Cf. Peter T. O'Brien, *The Letter to the Ephesians* (Grand Rapids, MI: Eerdmans, 1999), 1.
2. Cf. John R.W. Stott, *The Message of Ephesians* (Downers Grove, Ill: Intervarsity, 1979), 15–16.
3. James Montgomery Boice, *Ephesians* (Grand Rapids, MI: Zondervan, 1988), 11.
4. F.F. Bruce, *Paul: Apostle of the Heart Set Free* (Grand Rapids, MI: Eerdmans, 1977), 15–16.
5. Thomas R. Schreiner, *Paul: Apostle of God's Glory in Christ* (Downers Grove, Ill: 2001), 37–8.
6. D. Martyn Lloyd-Jones, *Romans: The Gospel of God, An Exposition of Romans 1* (Edinburgh: Banner of Truth, 1985), 38.
7. O'Brien, *Ephesians*, 84.
8. William Barclay, *The Letters to the Galatians and Ephesians* (Philadelphia: Westminster, 1976), 64.
9. Charles Hodge, *A Commentary on Ephesians* (Edinburgh: Banner of Truth, 1964), xii.
10. For a thorough critique of the argument against Pauline authorship, see O'Brien, 4–46.
11. D. Martyn Lloyd-Jones, *God's Ultimate Purpose: An Exposition of Ephesians 1* (Grand Rapids, MI: Baker, 1978), 36.
12. Leon Morris, *Expository Reflections on the Letter to the Ephesians*, (Grand Rapids, MI: Baker, 1994), 13.
13. Lloyd-Jones, *God's Ultimate Purpose*, 38.
14. cf. Boice, *Ephesians*, 111–112.
15. A.W. Tozer, *The Knowledge of the Holy*, (San Francisco: Harper, 1992), 145–146.
16. John Newton, 'Amazing Grace!' 1779.
17. Cf. John Armstrong, *Five Great Evangelists* (Ross-shire, UK: Christian Focus, 1997), 88–93.
18. Catechism of the Catholic Church (New York: Doubleday, 1995), 828.
19. Ibid. 2683.
20. Ibid. 2156.
21. Ibid. 956.
22. H.A. Ironside, *Letters to a Roman Catholic Priest* (Neptune, NJ: Loizeaux Brothers, 1914), 26.
23. Morris, *Ephesians*, 11.
24. Lloyd-Jones, *God's Ultimate Purpose*, 27.
25. Cf. Ravi Zacharias: *Can Man Live Without God* (Dallas: Word, 1994), 94.
26. John Calvin, *The Mystery of Godliness* (Morgan, PA: Soli Deo Gloria, 1999), 49.
27. Alexander Maclaren, *Expositions of Holy Scripture*, 18 vols, (Grand Rapids, MI: Baker, 1982), 13:9.
28. Morris, *Ephesians*, 13.
29. Benjamin Breckinridge Warfield, *Faith and Life* (Carlisle, PA: Banner of Truth, 1974), 262.
30. Hugh Martin, *Christ for Us* (Carlisle, PA: Banner of Truth, 1998), 210.
31. Ibid, 212–3.
32. Alexander Roberts & James Donaldson, *Ante-Nicene Fathers, Vol. 1: The Apostolic Fathers, Justin Martyr, Irenaeus* (Peabody, MA: Hendrickson,) 163.
33. Ibid., 166.
34. Quoted from A. W. Pink, *The Seven Sayings of the Saviour on the Cross* (Grand Rapids: Baker, 1958), 110.
35. Quoted from James Montgomery Boice, *Psalms*, 3 vols. (Grand Rapids: Baker, 1994), 1:101.
36. Arthur W. Pink: *The Sovereignty of God* (Grand Rapids, MI: Baker, 1918), 218, 219.
37. Lloyd-Jones, *God's Ultimate Purpose*, 103–4.
38. James Montgomery Boice, *Hymns for a Modern Reformation* (Philadelphia: Tenth Presbyterian Church, 2000), 25.
39. George W. Robinson, 'Love with Everlasting Love,' 1890.
40. Arthur W. Pink, *The Sovereignty of God* (Grand Rapids: Baker, 1930, reprint 1993), 143.
41. James Montgomery Boice: *Amazing Grace* (Wheaton, Ill.: Tyndale, 1993), 56.

42. A.W. Tozer, *The Tozer Pulpit*, Bk. 1, *Selection from His Pulpit* Ministry (Camp Hill, PA: Christian Publications, 1994), 89.
43. Boice, *Ephesians*, 25.
44. Eric Alexander, 'My Gracious Lord, Your Love Is Vast,' 2001.
45. John Calvin, *Calvin's New Testament Commentaries*, 12 vols., trans. T.H.L. Parker (Grand Rapids, MI: Eerdmans, 1965), 11:127.
46. Harry A. Ironside, *Ephesians* (Neptune, NJ: Loizeaux Bros., 2000), 33–4.
47. Ibid. 36.
48. John R. W. Stott, *The Message of Ephesians* (Downers Grove, Ill.: InterVarsity, 1979), 39.
49. Ibid. 35.
50. Isaac Watts, 'When I Survey the Wondrous Cross,' 1707.
51. Lloyd-Jones, *God's Ultimate Purpose*, 148.
52. James M. Boice, *Foundations of the Christian Faith* (Downers Grove, Ill.: Intervarsity, 1986), 327.
53. John Murray, *Redemption Accomplished and Applied* (Grand Rapids, MI: Eerdmans, 1955), 47.
54. C. S. Lewis, *The Lion, the Witch, and the Wardrobe* (New York: Collier, 1950, reprint, 1970), 139.
55. Augustus Toplady, 'Rock of Ages, Cleft for Me,' 1776.
56. Charles Colson, *Who Speaks for God?* (Wheaton, Ill.: Crossway, 1985), 76–77.
57. Charles Hodge, *Ephesians*, (London: Banner of Truth, 1964), 17.
58. R. Kent Hughes, *Ephesians: The Mystery of the Body of Christ* (Wheaton, Ill.: Crossway, 1990), 35.
59. Boice, 329–30.
60. Horatius Bonar, 'Not What My Hands Have Done,' 1861.
61. John R. W. Stott, *The Cross of Christ* (Downers Grove, Ill.: InterVarsity, 1986), 19–20.
62. Ibid. 23.
63. Cf. Ibid. 24.
64. Sir Alfred Ayer, cf. Stott, *Ephesians*, 43.
65. Cf. Ibid. 42.
66. J.I. Packer: *Knowing God* (Downers Grove, Ill.: InterVarsity, 1978), 136.
67. William Cowper, 'There Is a Fountain Filled with Blood,' 1771.
68. Nikolaus Ludwig von Zinzendorf, 'Jesus, Thy Blood and Righteousness,' 1739.
69. Charles Wesley, 'And Can It Be That I Should Gain,' 1738.
70. John Shelby Spong, *Why Christianity Must Change or Die* (San Francisco: HarperCollins, 1999), 95.
71. Ibid. 83.
72. Cf. Stott, 43.
73. D. Martyn Lloyd-Jones: *The Heart of the Gospel* (Wheaton, Ill.: Crossway, 1991), 33.
74. William Shakespeare, *Macbeth*, Act 5, Scene 5.
75. Cited from Barclay, *Galatians and Ephesians*, 85.
76. Richard Dawkins, *River Out of Egypt: A Darwinian View of Life* (New York: Basic Books, 1995), 132.
77. O'Brien, *Ephesians*, 111–2.
78. Hodge, *Ephesians*, 27.
79. Andrew T. Lincoln, *Ephesians,* Word Biblical Commentary 42 (Dallas, TX: Word, 1990), 32–34.
80. G. Campbell Morgan, *The Westminster Pulpit*, 10 vols. (Grand Rapids, MI: Baker, 1995), 1:48.
81. D. Martyn Lloyd-Jones, *Saved in Eternity* (Wheaton, Ill.: Crossway, 1988), 48.
82. C.S. Lewis: *The Weight of Glory and Other Addresses* (New York: MacMillen, 1975), 8.
83. Hodge, *Ephesians*, 32–33.
84. Boice, *Ephesians*, 34–35.
85. John Calvin, *Sermons on the Epistle to the Ephesians* (Carlisle, PA: Banner of Truth, 1973), 47.
86. Stott, *Ephesians*, 50.
87. John Bunyan, *The Pilgrim's Progress* (Nashville: Thomas Nelson, 1999), 136.
88. Keith Warrington, *The Message of the Holy Spirit* (Downers Grove, IL: InterVarsity, 2009), 210.
89. Ibid., 211.
90. Morris, *Ephesians*, 26.
91. Hodge, *Ephesians*, 35.
92. Jonathan Edwards, *The Distinguishing Marks of a Work of the Spirit of God* in *Jonathan Edwards on Revival* (Carlisle, PA: Banner of Truth, 1965), 91.
93. Ibid. 115.
94. John Calvin, *Sermons on the Epistle to the Ephesians* (Carlisle, PA: Banner of Truth, 1973), 72.
95. Ibid. 73.
96. Bunyan, *Pilgrim's Progress,* 35–36.
97. James R. White, *The Forgotten Trinity* (Minneapolis, MN: Bethany House, 1998), 16.
98. Ibid. 13.
99. Robert Reymond, *A New Systematic Theology of the Christian Faith* (Nashville, TN: Thomas Nelson, 1998), 763–4.
100. Handley C. G. Moule, *The Person and Work of the Holy Spirit* (Grand Rapids, MI: Kregel, 1977), 11–12.
101. Geoffrey B. Wilson, *Ephesians* (Carlisle, PA: Banner of

Truth, 1978), 32.

102. Donald Grey Barnhouse, *Expositions of Bible Doctrines Taking the Epistle to the Romans as a Point of Departure*, 10 vols. (Grand Rapids, MI: Wm. B. Eerdmans,1959), 4:140.
103. John Grisham, *The Testament* (New York: Doubleday, 1999).
104. John Owen, *Communion with God* (Edinburgh: Banner of Truth, 1991), 186–187.
105. R. Kent Hughes *Ephesians: The Mystery of the Body of Christ* (Wheaton, Ill.: Crossway, 1990), 46.
106. Arthur W. Pink, *The Ability of God: The Prayers of the Apostle Paul* (Chicago: Moody Press, 2000), 13.
107. Jeremiah Burroughs: *Gospel Worship* (Morgan, PA: Soli Deo Gloria, 1990), 55–6.
108. Dietrich Bonhoeffer, *Life Together*, (San Francisco: Harper & Row, 1954), 86.
109. Arthur W. Pink, *The Ability of God: The Prayers of the Apostle Paul* (Chicago: Moody, 2000), 15.
110. D. A. Carson, *A Call to Spiritual Reformation: Priorities from Paul and His Prayers* (Grand Rapids: Baker, 1992), 170.
111. James M. Boice: *Romans*, Vol. 1, *Justification by Faith* (Grand Rapids, MI: Baker, 1991), 76.
112. William Edgar, 'United in Love,' in Philip Ryken, ed., *The Communion of the Saints* (Phillipsburg, NJ: P&R, 2001), 57–8.
113. Richard Sibbes, *Works*, 6 vols. (Edinburgh, Banner of Truth, 1862–64), 3:433.
114. Francis A. Schaeffer, *The Mark of the Christian* (Downers Grove, Ill.: Intervarsity, 1970), 17–18.
115. Boice, *Ephesians*, 41.
116. E. Schuyler English, *H.A. Ironside: Ordained of the Lord* (Neptune, NJ: Loizeaux Brothers, 1976), 94.
117. John Calvin, *Institutes of the Christian Religion*, Trans. Ford Lewis Battles (Philadelphia: Westminster, 1960), I.V.1
118. Carson, *Call to Spiritual Reformation*, 15-16.
119. Charles Haddon Spurgeon: The New Park Street Pulpit, vol. 1, 1855 (Pasadena, Tx: Pilgrim Publications, 1975), 1.
120. Bruce Ware, *God's Lesser Glory: The Diminished God of Open Theism* (Wheaton, Ill.: Crossway, 2002), 21).
121. Ibid. 25–26.
122. F.F. Bruce, *The Epistles to the Colossians, to Philemon and to the Ephesians* (Grand Rapids, MI: Wm. B. Eerdmans, 1984), 269.
123. Augustine, *A Treatise on the Merits and Forgiveness of Sins, and on the Baptism of Infants*, from *A Select Library of the Nicene and Post-Nicene Fathers of the Christian Church*, ed. Philip Schaff, Vol. 5, *Saint Augustin: Anti-Pelagian Writings* (Peabody, MA: Hendrickson, 1999), 29.
124. Charles H. Spurgeon, *Metropolitan Tabernacle Pulpit*, 63 vols. (Pasadena, TX: Pilgrim Publications, 1969), 25:244.
125. Thomas Watson: *A Body of Divinity*, (Carlisle, PA: Banner of Truth, 1958), 296–7.
126. Lloyd-Jones, *God's Ultimate Purpose*, 324.
127. John Chrysostom, *Homilies on Ephesians*, from *Nicene and Post-Nicene Fathers, First Series,* 14 vols., Philip Schaff, ed. (Peabody, MA: Hendrickson, 1999) 13:61.
128. Carson, *Call to Spiritual Reformation,* 177.
129. Morris, *Ephesians*, 33.
130. Benjamin B. Warfield, *The Works of Benjamin B. Warfield,* 10 vols. (Grand Rapids: Baker, 1932, reprint 2000), 9:45.
131. Isaac Watts, 'Marching to Zion,' 1707.
132. Lloyd-Jones, *God's Ultimate Purpose,* 430.
133. Lincoln, *Ephesians,* 75.
134. Hodge, *Ephesians,* 54.
135. John Calvin, *The Epistles of Paul the Apostle to the Galatians, Ephesians, Philippians and Colossians* (Grand Rapids: Eerdmans, 1965), 138
136. Arthur W. Pink, *The Ability of God: The Prayers of the Apostle Paul* (Chicago: Moody Press, 2000), 217.
137. Carson, *Call to Spiritual Reformation,* 179-180.
138. C. Samuel Storms, 'Prayer and Evangelism under God's Sovereignty' in *Still Sovereign: Contemporary Perspectives on Election, Foreknowledge, and Grace,* ed. Thomas R. Schreiner & Bruce A. Ware (Grand Rapids: Baker, 1995), 316.
139. James M. Boice, *Whatever Happened to the Gospel of Grace?* (Wheaton, Ill.: Crossway, 2001), 167. See also p. 178.
140. See Arthur W. Pink, *The Sovereignty of God* (Grand Rapids: Baker, 1993), 168.
141. Cited by Pink, *Sovereignty,* 169.
142. Ibid., 320.
143. Nikolaus Ludwig von Zinzendorf, 'Jesus, Thy Blood and Righteousness,' 1739.
144. Klyne Snodgrass, *Ephesians* (Grand Rapids: Zondervan, 1996), 93
145. Harold S. Kushner, *How Good Do We Have to Be?* (Boston: Little, Brown and Company, 1996), 30–31.
146. D. Martyn Lloyd-Jones, *God's Way of Reconciliation: An*

Exposition of Ephesians 2 (Grand Rapids: Baker, 1972), 19.

147. http://www.ucl.ac.uk/Bentham-Project/who/autoicon.
148. St. Augustine, *City of God* (New York: Doubleday, 1958), 279.
149. Ibid. 313.
150. John Calvin, *Sermons on Ephesians* (Edinburgh: Banner of Truth, 1562, reprint 1993), 37.
151. J.C. Ryle, *Holiness* (Durham, UK: Evangelical Press, 1879, reprint 1979), 3.
152. John MacArthur, *Ephesians* (Chicago: Moody: 1986), 52–53.
153. D. Martyn Lloyd-Jones, *God's Way of Reconciliation: An Exposition of Ephesians 2* (Grand Rapids, MI: Baker, 1972), 15.
154. Morris, *Ephesians*, 42.
155. David McCullough, *John Adams* (New York: Simon & Schuster, 2001), 307.
156. D. Martyn Lloyd-Jones, *Expositions on the Sermon on the Mount*, 2 vols. (Grand Rapids: Eerdmans, 1959), 1:37.
157. James Montgomery Boice, *Ephesians* (Grand Rapids: Baker, 1998), 50.
158. Cf. Barclay, *Galatians and Ephesians*, 100
159. Charles Haddon Spurgeon, 'Satan's Banquet' in *Spurgeon's Sermons*, 10 vols. (Grand Rapids, MI: Baker, 1883), 5:273.
160. Ibid., 5:274.
161. Ibid., 5:275.
162. Ibid., 5:286.
163. Lloyd-Jones, *God's Way of Reconciliation*, 59.
164. D. Martyn Lloyd-Jones, *God's Way, Not Ours* (Grand Rapids: Baker, 1998), 88.
165. Ibid.
166. Ibid.
167. John Owen, *Communion with God* (Edinburgh: Banner of Truth, 1991), 82, 83.
168. Cited from Bryan Chapell, *The Promises of Grace* (Grand Rapids: Baker, 2001), 136–137.
169. James Montgomery Boice, *Ephesians* (Grand Rapids: Baker, 1997), 54.
170. Martyn Lloyd-Jones,*The Life of Peace: An Exposition of Philippians 3 & 4* (Grand Rapids: Baker, 1990), 49–50.
171. Lloyd-Jones, *God's Way of Reconciliation*, 79.
172. James Montgomery Boice, *Romans*, 4 vols. (Grand Rapids: Baker, 1992), 2:678.
173. John R.W. Stott, *Men Made New: An Exposition of Romans 6–8* (Downers Grove, Ill.: InterVarsity, 1994), 48, 49.
174. Hugh Martin, *Christ for Us* (Edinburgh: Banner of Truth, 1998), 50.
175. Cited from James Montgomery Boice, *Ephesians: An Expositional Commentary* (Grand Rapids: Baker, 1998), 59.
176. See the more extensive treatment of our spiritual resurrection in the previous chapter.
177. Lloyd-Jones, *God's Way of Reconciliation,* 89.
178. C. Austin Miles, 'In the Garden,' 1912.
179. Barclay, *Galatians and Ephesians*, 103.
180. Stephen Jay Gould, cited from Ravi Zacharius, *Can Man Live Without God?* (Dallas: Word, 1994), 56.
181. Sinclair B. Ferguson, *Discovering God's Will* (Edinburgh: Banner of Truth, 1989), 16.
182. E.J. Young, *Isaiah*, 3 vols. (Grand Rapids: Eerdmans,), 1:245–246.
183. Hugh Martin, *Christ for Us* (Edinburgh: Banner of Truth, 1998), 213.
184. John Owen, *Communion with God* (Edinburgh: Banner of Truth, 1991), 86.
185. D. Martyn Lloyd-Jones, *God's Way of Reconciliation: An Exposition of Ephesians 2* (Grand Rapids: Baker, 1998), 116.
186. James Montgomery Boice, *Romans*, 4 vols. (Grand Rapids: Baker, 1993), 3:1108–1109.
187. D. Martyn Lloyd-Jones, *Faith on Trial* (Downers Grove, IL: InterVarsity, 1965), 171.
188. A. W. Tozer, *The Knowledge of the Holy* (San Francisco: Harper, 1992), 145-146.
189. Norman Vincent Peale, *The Power of Positive Thinking* (New York: Prentice-Hall, 1952), 99.
190. Charles H. Spurgeon, *Spurgeon's Sermons*, 10 vols. (Grand Rapids, MI: Baker, 1880), 3:260.
191. Arthur W. Pink, *The Life of David* (Grand Rapids: Baker, 1981), 260–261.
192. Adapted from Morris, *Ephesians*, 104.
193. Augustus Toplady, 'Rock of Ages Cleft for Me,' 1776.
194. See for instance, Zane Hodges, *Absolutely Free: A Biblical Reply to Lordship Salvation* (Redencion Viva, 1992) and Charles Ryrie, *So Great Salvation: What It Means to Believe in Jesus Christ* (Chicago: Moody, 1997).
195. Charles H. Spurgeon, *Spurgeon's Sermons*, 10 vols. (Grand Rapids: Baker, 1883), 1:81.
196. G. Campbell Morgan, *The Westminster Pulpit*, 10 vols. (Grand Rapids: Baker, 1995), 1:245.
197. Adapted from R. Kent Hughes, *Ephesians: The Mystery of the Body of Christ* (Wheaton: Crossway, 1990), 82–83.

198. Lloyd-Jones, *God's Way of Reconciliation*, 151.
199. Barclay, *Galatians and Ephesians*, 107.
200. Ibid., 107
201. Lloyd-Jones, *God's Way of Reconciliation*, 169
202. Geoffrey B. Wilson, *Ephesians* (Edinburgh: Banner of Truth Trust, 1978), 53.
203. Lloyd-Jones, 170.
204. Neil Postman, *Amusing Ourselves to Death: Public Discourse in the Age of Show Business* (New York: Penguin, 1986).
205. Cited from Ravi Zacharius, *Can Man Live Without God?* (Dallas: Word, 1994), 58.
206. Ravi Zacharias: *Can Man Live Without God*, p. 51.
207. Theognis, cf. Barclay, 110.
208. Cited in James Montgomery Boice, *The Heart of the Cross* (Wheaton, IL: Crossway, 1999), 13.
209. Cited in J.C. Ryle, *Light from Old Times* (Moscow, ID: Charles Nolan, 2000), 134.
210. Cited in Zacharius, 56.
211. Charles H. Spurgeon, 'A Solemn Deprival' in *Metropolitan Tabernacle Pulipt*, 63 vols. (Pasadena, TX: Pilgrim Publications, 1980), 61:366.
212. Lloyd-Jones, *God's Way of Reconciliation*, 187.
213. H. Maldwyn Hughes, cf. Philip G. Ryken: *The Heart of the Cross* (Wheaton: Crossway, 1999), 148.
214. Tacitus, *Agricola*, 30.
215. James Montgomery Boice, *Ephesians* (Grand Rapids: Baker, 1998), 85.
216. James M. Boice and Philip G. Ryken: *The Heart of the Cross* (Wheaton: Crossway, 1999),148.
217. John Calvin, *Calvin's New Testament Commentaries*, 12 vols. (Grand Rapids: Eerdmans, 1965), 11:150.
218. This is referred to as the *homogeneous unit principle*.
219. D. Martyn Lloyd-Jones,*The Kingdom of God* (Wheaton, Ill.: Crossway, 1992), 82.
220. Philip G. Ryken, *The Prayer of Our Lord* (Wheaton, Ill: Crossway, 2002), 21–21.
221. Lloyd-Jones, *The Kingdom of God*, (Wheaton, IL: Crossway, 1992), 82.
222. William Edgar, 'Disillusioned' in *Finding God at Harvard*, ed. Kelly Monroe (Grand Rapids: Zondervan, 1996), 62.
223. James Montgomery Boice, *Ephesians* (Grand Rapids: Baker, 1998), 90.
224. Lloyd-Jones, *God's Way of Reconciliation*, 328.
225. Hattie E. Buell, 'A Child of the King,' 1743.
226. William Edgar, *Reasons of the Heart* (Grand Rapids: Baker, 1996), 59.
227. Ibid.
228. T.V. Moore, *Haggai, Zechariah and Malachi* (Edinburgh: Banner of Truth, 1979), 141.
229. A.W. Tozer: *Renewed Day by Day: A Daily Devotional* (Camp Hill, PA: Christian Publications, 1980), Feb. 7.
230. 'How Firm a Foundation,' *Rippon's Selection of Hymns*, 1787.
231. Cf. Richard D. Phillips, Philip G. Ryken, and Mark E. Dever, *The Church: One, Holy, Catholic, and Apostolic* (Phillipsburg, NJ: P&R, 2004), 104.
232. Samuel J. Stone, 'The Church's One Foundation.
233. Phillips, Ryken, and Dever, 114–115.
234. D. Martyn Lloyd-Jones, *Romans 1: The Gospel of God* (Edinburgh: Banner of Truth, 1985), 266.
235. From Norman H. Cliff, *Fierce the Conflict* (Dundas, Ontario: Joshua Press, 2001), 63.
236. Ibid., 75–81.
237. Tony Lambert, *Foreward* to Cliff, *Fierce the Conflict*, 12.
238. Martin Luther, cf. Ewarld M. Plass, compiler, *What Luther Says: An Anthology*, vol. 3 (St. Louis: Concordia, 1959), 1359.
239. See James M. Boice, *Genesis*, 3 volumes (Grand Rapids: Baker, 1998), 2:740.
240. J.C. Ryle, *Holiness* (Durham, UK: Evangelical Press, 1979),263.
241. Charles Hodge, *A Commentary on Ephesians* (Edinburgh, Banner of Truth, 1964), 114.
242. John MacArthur, Jr., *Ephesians* (Chicago: Moody, 1986).
243. R.C. Sproul, *The Mystery of the Holy Spirit* (Wheaton, IL: Tyndale, 1990), 110.
244. Stott, *Ephesians*, 121.
245. D. Martyn Lloyd-Jones, *The Unsearchable Riches of Christ: An Exposition of Ephesians 3* (Baker: Grand Rapids, 1980), 81.
246. Boice, *Ephesians*, 98.
247. Ibid.
248. Eric Alexander, 'The Application of Redemption,' in *To Glorify and Enjoy God: A Commemoration of the 350th Anniversary of the Westminster Assembly*, ed. John L. Carson and David W. Hall (Edinburgh: Banner of Truth, 1994), 245.
249. Ibid.
250. Ibid., 245–246.
251. Charles Haddon Spurgeon, *Spurgeon's Sermons*, 10 vols. (Grand Rapids: Baker, 1883, reprint), 1:185.
252. Cited from John MacArthur, Jr., *Ephesians*, (Chicago:

Moody, 1986), 103–104.
253. Morris, *Ephesians*, 103.
254. Robert Boyd Munger, *My Heart Christ's Home* (Downers Grove, IL: InterVarsity, 1986).
255. John McArthur, Jr., *Ephesians* (Chicago: Moody, 1986), 107.
256. Carson, *Call to Spiritual Reformation*, 186.
257. Jean Sophia Pigott, 'Thou Whose Name Is Called Jesus,' 1845–1882.
258. G. Campbell Morgan, *The Westminster Pulpit*, 10 vols. (Grand Rapids: Baker, 1995), 2:277–278.
259. Stott, *Ephesians*, 136.
260. Carson, *Call to Spiritual Reformation*, 196.
261. Ibid., 194.
262. Philip Yancey, *Disappointment with God* (Grand Rapids: Zondervan, 1988), 255.
263. Alexander Maclaren, *Expositions of Holy Scripture*, 17 vols. (Grand Rapids, MI: Baker, 1982), 13:167.
264. Ibid., 169.
265. Harry A. Ironside, *Ephesians* (Neptune, NJ: Loizeaux Bros., 2000), 98.
266. Stott, *Ephesians*, 137.
267. J. I. Packer: *Knowing God*, (Downers Grove, Ill., InterVarsity, 1979), 114.
268. Thomas Watson, *A Body of Divinity* (Edinburgh: Banner of Truth, 1958), 175.
269. Charles Haddon Spurgeon, *Metropolitan Tabernacle Pulpit*, 63 vols. (Pasadena, TX: 1973), 8:337.
270. Susan Hunt, *The True Woman* (Wheaton, Ill.: Crossway, 1997), 92–93.
271. Donald Grey Barnhouse: *Exposition of Bible Doctrines Taking the Epistle to the Romans as a Point of Departure*, vol. 3, *God's Remedy*, pp. 346, 347.
272. Lloyd-Jones, *The Unsearchable Riches of Christ: An Exposition of Ephesians 3* (Baker: Grand Rapids, 1979), 290–291.
273. Issac Newton, 'Come Thy Soul, Thy Suit Prepare' 1779.
274. D. Martyn Lloyd-Jones, *The Unsearchable Riches of Christ: An Exposition of Ephesians 3* (Baker: Grand Rapids, 1979), 314.
275. Alexander Maclaren, *Expositions of Holy Scripture*, 17 vols. (Grand Rapids, MI: Baker, 1982), 13:189.
276. Terry L. Johnson, *When Grace Transforms* (Ross-shire, UK: Christian Focus, 2002), 141.
277. C.S. Lewis: *Mere Christianity* (New York: Collier, 1952), 108.
278. Ibid., 111.
279. James Montgomery Boice, *The Minor Prophets*, 2 vols. (Grand Rapids: Zondervan, 1983), 1:194.
280. Augustus M. Toplady, 'Rock of Ages, Cleft for Me,' 1776.
281. Matthew Henry, *The Quest for Meekness and Quietness of Spirit* (Morgan, PA: Soli Deo Gloria, 1996), 17–18.
282. Cited from R. Kent Hughes, *Ephesians: The Mystery of the Body of Christ* (Wheaton, Ill.: Crossway, 1990), 123.
283. R. C. Sproul, *The Purpose of God: An Exposition of Ephesians* (Ross-Shire, UK: Christian Focus, 2002), 97.
284. Cf. James Montgomery Boice, *Ephesians* (Grand Rapids: Baker,), 124.
285. Harry Ironside, *Ephesians* (Neptune, NJ: Loizeaux,), 105–106.
286. Stott, *Ephesians*, 147.
287. D. Martyn Lloyd-Jones, *Christian Unity: An Exposition of Ephesians 4:1–16* (Grand Rapids: Baker, 1980), 50.
288. Hodge, *Ephesians*, 144.
289. John A. MacArthur, Jr., *Ephesians* (Chicago: Moody, 1986), 129.
290. Cited in Hughes, *Ephesians*, 123.
291. Peter Jones, *Christian Truth and Pagan Lies* (Enumclaw, WA: Winepress, 1999), 7, 39.
292. Cited from Lloyd-Jones, *Christian Unity*, 105.
293. Roger Olsen, 'The Future of Evangelical Theology,' *Christianity Today* Feb 9, 1998 Vol. 42, No. 2, 40.
294. R. C. Sproul, 'One O'er All the Earth,' in *Onw'rd Christian Soldiers: Protestants Affirm the Church*, ed. Don Kistler (Morgan, PA: Soli Deo Gloria, 1999), 92.
295. Boice, *Ephesians*, 131.
296. Peter Jones, *Gospel Truth / Pagan Lies* (Escondido, CA: Main Entry Editions, 1999), 23–24.
297. Stott, *Ephesians*, 151
298. F.F. Bruce, *The Epistles to the Colossians, to Philemon, and to the Ephesians* (Grand Rapids: Wm. B. Eerdmans, 1984), 337.
299. Stott, *Ephesians*, 155.
300. James M. Boice, *Romans: An Expositional Commentary*, 4 vols. (Grand Rapids: Baker, 1991), 4:1582.
301. Derek Kidner, *Psalms 1–72* (Downers Grove, Ill.: InterVarsity, 1973), 242, n.2.
302. John Stott, *The Message of Ephesians* (Downers Grove, Ill.: Intervarsity, 1979), 157.
303. D. Martyn Lloyd-Jones: *Christian Unity: An Exposition of Ephesians 4:1–16* (Grand Rapids: Baker, 1980), 165..
304. Harriet Auber, 'Christ's Resurrection,' 1829.
305. Charles Haddon Spurgeon, *Metropolitan Tabernacle Pulpit*, 63 vols., 17:220–221.

Endnotes

306. Edmund. P. Clowney, *Called to the Ministry* (Phillipsburg, NJ: P&R, 1964), 30–31.
307. Charles Haddon Spurgeon, 'The Ascension of Christ,' in *The Metropolitan Tabernacle Pulpit*, 63 vols., 17:228.
308. Ibid., 229.
309. Philip G. Ryken, *Galatians*, Reformed Expository Commentary (Phillipsburg, NJ: 2005), 175.
310. Stott, 164.
311. Boice, *Ephesians*, 141.
312. Cited in Boice, 143.
313. Stott, 168.
314. John A. McArthur, Jr., *Ephesians*, (Chicago: Moody, 1986), 156.
315. Boice, *Ephesians*, 148.
316. Hodge, *Ephesians*, 171.
317. Harry A. Ironside, *Ephesians* (Neptune, NJ: Loizeaux Bros., 2000), 119.
318. Adapted from James Montgomery Boice, *Ephesians* (Grand Rapids: Baker, 1998), 146–147.
319. Lloyd-Jones, *Christian Unity*, 259.
320. Boice, 151.
321. Ibid., 151–152.
322. Boice, *Ephesians*, 154.
323. Paul Johnson, *Intellectuals* (New York: Harper & Row, 1988), 21–23.
324. Lloyd-Jones, *Darkness and Light*, 49–50.
325. Aldous Huxley, *Ends and Means* (London: Chatto & Windus, 1946), 270–273.
326. Cornelius Van Til: *Christian Apologetics*, p. 50.
327. A.W. Tozer: *The Tozer Pulpit, Book One: Selections from His Pulpit Ministry*, pp. 27, 28.
328. Cited in *Ancient Christian Commentary on Scripture*, New Testament vol. VIII, *Galatians, Ephesians, Philippians*, ed. Mark J. Edwards (Downers Grove, Ill.: Intervarsity, 1999), 172.
329. Quoted from Wilson, *Ephesians*, 99.
330. Barclay, *Galatians and Ephesians*, 157.
331. Cited from Ravi Zacharius, *Can Man Live Without God* (Dallas: Word, 1994), 101–102.
332. J.I. Packer, *Keep in Step With the Spirit* (Grand Rapids: Revell, 1984), 49.
333. Ibid., 62.
334. Benjamin B. Warfield, *Faith and Life* (Edinburgh: Banner of Truth, 1916, reprint 1974), 295.
335. Lloyd-Jones, *Darkness and Light*, 266–267.
336. Stott, *Ephesians*, 189.
337. Curtis Vaughn, *Ephesians* (Cape Coral, FL: Founders Press, 2002), 104.
338. Hodge, *Ephesians*, 199.
339. Lloyd-Jones, 272.
340. Barclay, *Galatians and Ephesians*, 160.
341. Lloyd-Jones, *Darkness and Light*, 291.
342. Alexander Maclaren, *Expositions of Holy Scripture*, 17 vols. (INFO), 13:270–271.
343. Lloyd-Jones, *Darkness and Light*, 278.
344. John Chrysostom, *Homily on Ephesians*, 16.4.31–32.
345. William Hendriksen, *Exposition of Galatians, Ephesians, Philippians, Colossians, and Philemon* (Grand Rapids: Baker, 1967), 223.
346. Kenneth Wuest, *Word Studies in the Greek New Testament*, 4 vols. (Grand Rapids: Eerdmans, 1953), 1:120.
347. Cited from George Grant, http://kingsmeadow.com/blogger.html, entry 8.18.04.
348. Origen, in *Ancient Christian Commentary on Scripture*, vol. 8, *Galatians, Ephesians, Philippians*, Mark J. Edwards, ed. (Downers Grove, Ill.: InterVarsity,), 183.
349. John R.W. Stott, *The Message of Ephesians: God's New Society* (Downers Grove, Ill.: InterVarsity, 1979), 192.
350. Curtis Vaughn, *Ephesians*, 107.
351. O'Brien, *Ephesians*, 361.
352. Mike Mason, *The Mystery of Marriage: As Iron Sharpens Iron* (Portland, OR: Multnomah, 1985), 121.
353. Hodge, *Ephesians*, 207.
354. Curtis Vaughn, *Ephesians* (Cape Coral, FL: Founders Press, 2002), 109.
355. Morris, *Ephesians*, 166.
356. Alexander Maclaren, *Expositions of Holy Scripture*, 18 vols. (Grand Rapids, MI: Baker, 1982), 13:289.
357. Corrie ten Boom, 'Trust the Lord,' *Guideposts* Magazine (Aug. 1976), 7.
358. MacArthur, *Ephesians*, 212.
359. Hendriksen, *Galatians, Ephesians, Philippians, Colossians, and Philemon*, 233–234.
360. Maclaren, 13:284.
361. MacArthur, *Ephesians*, 29–30.
362. James Montgomery Boice, *Romans*, 4 vols. (Grand Rapids: Baker, 1995), 4:1699.
363. Lloyd-Jones, *Darkness and Light*, 428–432.
364. John MacArthur, Jr., *Ephesians*, 222.
365. John Calvin, *Calvin's New Testament Commentaries*, 12 vols., trans. T.H.L. Parker (Grand Rapids, MI: Eerdmans, 1965), 11:202–3.
366. Jonathan Edwards, *The Preciousness of Time*, in *The Works of Jonathan Edwards*, 2 vols. (Peabody, MA:

Hendriksen), 2:234-5.
367. D. Martyn Lloyd-Jones, *Darkness and Light,* 453-454.
368. Francis A. Schaeffer, *True Spirituality,* in *The Complete Works of Francis A. Schaeffer,* 5 vols. (Wheaton: Crossway, 1982), 3:195.
369. John Calvin, *Calvin's New Testament Commentaries,* 12 vols., trans. T.H.L. Parker (Grand Rapids, MI: Eerdmans, 1965), 11:203.
370. Cf. Mark J. Edwards, ed., *Ancient Chrisitan Commentary on Scripture, New Testament,* 12 vols. (Downers Grove, Ill.: Intervarsity, 1999), 8:191.
371. D. Martyn Lloyd-Jones: *Safe in the World,* (Wheaton: Crossway, 1988), 108, 109.
372. Ibid., 196.
373. Hughes, *Ephesians,* 175.
374. Jerry Bridges, *The Discipline of Godliness* (Colorado Springs: NavPress, 1996), 101-102.
375. Ibid., 20.
376. D. Martyn Lloyd-Jones, *Life in the Spirit in Marriage, Home & Work: An Exposition of Ephesians 5:18-6:9* (Grand Rapids: Baker, 1973), 88.
377. See Barclay, *Galatians and Ephesians,* 168-169 for a thorough discussion of the treatment of women in the ancient world.
378. John Calvin, *Calvin's New Testament Commentaries,* 12 vols., trans. T.H.L. Parker (Grand Rapids, MI: Eerdmans, 1965), 11:204.
379. Daniel M. Doriani, *James,* Reformed Expository Commentary (Phillipsburg, NJ: P&R, 2007), 146.
380. Laura Doyle, *The Surrendered Wife* (New York: Fireside, 1999).
381. See his insightful comments in C.S. Lewis, *Mere Christianity,* 102-3.
382. Lloyd-Jones, *Life in the Spirit in Marriage, Home & Work,* 101-102.
383. Ibid., 102.
384. Steve Farrar, *Point Man: How a Man Can Lead his Family* (Sisters, OR: Multnomah, 2003), 25-26.
385. MacArthur, *Ephesians,* 293.
386. D. A. Carson, *Exegetical Fallacies* (Grand Rapids: Baker, 1984), 30
387. Cited from Harry A. Ironside, *Ephesians* (Neptune, NJ: Loizeaux Bros., 2000), 161.
388. D. Martyn Lloyd-Jones, *Life in the Spirit in Marriage, Home, & Work* (Grand Rapids: Baker, 1973), 176.
389. Stott, *Ephesians,* 235.
390. MacArthur, *Ephesians,* 303.
391. Joel Nederhood, *The Forever People* (Phillipsburg, NJ: P&R, 2000), 163.
392. Ibid., 162.
393. Hendriksen, *Galatians, Ephesians, Philippians, Colossians, and Philemon,* 259.
394. Boice, *Ephesians,* 213.
395. MacArthur, *Ephesians,* 312.
396. Ibid., 317.
397. Barclay, *Galatians and Ephesians,* 211-212.
398. MacArthur, *Ephesians,* 317.
399. Samuel Oberson, cited from Steve Farrar, *Point Man* (Sisters, OR: Multnomah, 2003), 48.
400. Barclay, *The Letters to the Galatians and Ephesians,* 178.
401. Cited from MacArthur, *Ephesians,* 318-319.
402. Philip G. Ryken, *When You Pray* (Wheaton: Crossway, 2000), 56.
403. Geoffrey W. Bromily, ed., *The International Standard Bible Encyclopedia,* 4 vols. (Grand Rapids: Eerdmans, 1988), 4:543-544.
404. PCA Position Paper on Racial Reconciliation, 30th General Assembly, 2002, 262-272.
405. Philip G. Ryken, *1 Timothy,* Reformed Expository Commentary (Phillipsburg, NJ: P&R, 2007), 23.
406. Barclay, *Galatians and Ephesians,* 181.
407. Harry A. Ironside, *Ephesians* (Neptune, NJ: Loizeaux Bros., 2000), 169.
408. R. Kent Hughes, *Ephesians: The Mystery of the Body of Christ* (Wheaton, Ill.: Crossway, 1990), 210.
409. Hendriksen, *Galatians, Ephesians, Philipians, Colossians, and Philemon,* 265.
410. Donald Grey Barnhouse, *Expositions of Bible Doctrines Taking the Epistle to the Romans as a Point of Departure,* 10 vols. (Grand Rapids: Eerdmans, 1964) 10:176.
411. Cf. F.F. Bruce, *The Epistles to the Colossians, to Philemon and to the Ephesians* (Grand Rapids, MI: Wm. B. Eerdmans, 1984), 405.
412. MacArthur, *Ephesians,* 331.
413. R. Kent Hughes, *Ephesians: The Mystery of the Body of Christ* (Wheaton, Ill.: Crossway, 1990), 216.
414. MacArthur, *Ephesians,* 341.
415. Morris, *Ephesians,* 200.
416. Watchman Nee: *Sit, Walk, Stand* (Ft, Washington, PA: Christian Literature Crusade, 1977), 55, 78.
417. James Montgomery Boice, *Ephesians* (Grand Rapids: Baker, 1998), 244-245.
418. Thomas Watson: *A Body of Divinity* (Edinburgh: Banner of Truth, 1968), 226.

419. MacArthur, *Ephesians*, 353.
420. Hodge, *Ephesians,* 283.
421. Wilson, *Ephesians,* 133.
422. Stott, *Ephesians,* 280.
423. Lloyd-Jones, *The Christian Soldier,* 301.
424. John Bunyan, *Pilgrim's Progress* (Nashville: Thomas Nelson, 1999), 52.
425. David Baron, *The Visions and Prophecies of Zechariah* (Grand Rapids, MI: Kregel, 1972), 93–94.
426. *Book of Common Prayer*, Proper 28.
427. Hodge, *Ephesians,* 288.
428. William Cowper, 'What Various Hindrances We Meet,' 1779.
429. Cited from R. Kent Hughes, *Ephesians: The Mystery of the Body of Christ,* Preaching the Word (Wheaton, IL: Crossway, 1990), 252.
430. John MacArthur, *Ephesians* (Chicago: Moody, 1986), ?.
431. Steve Farrar, *Point Man: How a Man Can Lead His Family* (Sisters, OR: Multnomah, 1990), 130–134.
432. F. F. Bruce, *The Epistles to the Colossians, to Philemon and to the Ephesians* (Grand Rapids, MI: Wm. B. Eerdmans, 1984), 411.
433. Harry A. Ironside, *Ephesians* (Neptune, NJ: Loizeaux Bros., 2000), 187.
434. William Hendriksen, *Luke* (Grand Rapids, MI: Baker), 612.
435. Cited from R. Kent Hughes, *Ephesians,* 251.
436. John MacArthur, *Ephesians,* 383.
437. Ironside, *Ephesians,* 189.
438. John Calvin, *Sermons on Ephesians* (Edinburgh: Banner of Truth, 1973), 699.
439. Hughes, *Ephesians,* 264.
440. B.F. Westcott, *St. Paul's Epistle to the Ephesians* (Eugene, OR: Wipf and Stock, 1998), 100.
441. Alexander Maclaren, *Expositions of Holy Scripture*, 18 vols, (Grand Rapids, MI: Baker, 1982), 13:387.
442. R. C. Sproul, *Faith Alone* (Grand Rapids: Baker, 1995), 87.
443. William R. Featherstone, 'My Jesus, I Love Thee,' 1864.

Subject Index

Abel 59, 182, 204
Abraham 13, 62, 65, 70-1, 72, 108, 147, 148, 151, 152, 194, 253, 254, 266, 303, 312, 445
active obedience 55
Adam 45, 59, 62, 132, 134, 148-9, 204, 205, 207, 211, 343, 358, 402, 405, 409, 413, 432
Adams, Abigail 141
adoption as sons 33-4
agape love 285, 311-12, 410, 414
Alexander, Eric 35, 270-1
Amazing Grace (hymn) 6, 7
'Amen' 306
Amusing Ourselves to Death (book) 195
anakephalaioo 62, 63
Ananias 259, 365
angels 266-7, 268
anger 361, 370-1
anticlericalism 337
ark of the covenant 328
Arminius, Jacob 132
armor of God 432-4, 435, 437-42, 443-8, 449
Armstrong, Neil 39
arrabon 85, 86, 89
Artemis 193
assurance of salvation 27-8, 78-9, 215
atheism 147, 148, 352-5
atonement 54, 55, 56, 324
Augustine 24, 133, 134, 142

authorship of book 2-3
baptism 325, 411-12, 422
Barclay, William 3, 168, 361, 369, 424
Barnhouse, Donald Grey 86, 93, 174, 295, 355, 427-8
Barth, Karl 410-11
Bathsheba 147, 367, 380
Beatitudes 309, 340, 347
Beauregard, General 442
belief/assent 12, 179
'belt of truth' 438-40
Bentham, Jeremy 133
bitterness/ resentment 370
boasting in God 182-3
Boice, James Montgomery 1, 28, 32-3, 45, 49, 71, 94, 96, 109, 125, 143, 153, 156-7, 176, 189, 205, 228, 269, 270, 310, 325, 342, 350, 352, 390, 418, 439
Bonar, Horatius 49
'bond of peace' 320, 326, 345, 349, 457
Bonhoeffer, Dietrich 93
Book of Common Prayer 447-8
breadth of Christ's love 289
'breastplate of righteousness' 440-1
Brown, Harold O.J. 225
Bruce, F. F. 1, 103, 109
Bunyan, John 15, 75, 81, 84, 107, 443, 447

471

Burroughs, Jeremiah   92
'But God'   148, 149-50, 151-3

Caesar, Augustus   203
Cain   59, 182, 204
calling, minister's   257-9
Calvin, John   13, 24, 72, 79, 92, 95, 109, 133, 134, 207, 292, 392-3, 396, 402, 420, 456
Cana, wedding at   144, 145
Carey, William   302-3, 426
caring love   412-13, 414
'carnal Christians'   140-1
Carson, D. A.   94, 100, 109, 111, 121, 283, 288, 290, 410
celebrity, cult of   171
Cephas   12, 324
Chalmers, Thomas   373
Chamberlain, Neville   203
Chapian, Marie   362
children of God   229-30
children of light   383-8
Chrisitanity Today (magazine)   323
Christianity
   and access to God   220-1
   and ascension of Christ   331-2
   atheist critiques of   147, 148
   and calling of God   108-9, 431-2
   'carnal Christians'   140-1
   and children of light   383-8
   and Christian 'walk'   307-8
   and Christian life   151-3, 307-13, 351-3, 355-6, 357-62, 368, 401-7, 409-15, 417-22
   and Christian masters   426-7
   and 'Christian perfectionism'   340
   and citizenship of God's kingdom   226-8, 230-1
   and 'conformity with the world'   140-1
   and cultivating the good   371-3
   definitions of Christians   9-15, 121-2, 219, 459
   and division   192-4
   and 'evil days'   389-90
   and four vital graces   308-12
   and fullness of God   297-8
   God of   150-1
   'held together' in Christ   348-9
   historical nature of   60-2
   historical perspective of   64-5
   historical purpose of   62-4
   and 'holy temple in the Lord'   233, 236-9
   and hope   108-9
   and imitating God and Jesus   369-70, 372-3, 374
   and indwelling of Christ   281-3, 284
   and inheritance of God   69, 87-8, 110
   and inward renewal   359-60
   and knowledge of God   99-100, 104-5
   and love   95-6, 287-8, 455, 456
   and marriage   207, 208, 284-5, 361, 377, 378, 381, 401-7, 409-15
   and meaning/purpose of life   171, 175-6
   message of   148-50
   and ministry of the gospel   257, 261, 262-3
   and mystery of Christ   254-5
   and new humanity   214-16
   and parent-child relationships   417-22
   and peace of Christ   208
   and plan/purpose of God   68, 393-4
   and power of God   111-12
   and practical change   360-2
   and prayer   91, 92-5, 104-5, 124-6, 269-70, 273, 276-9, 399, 449-54
   and preeminence of church   119-20
   and prisoners for Christ   243, 244-5, 246-7
   and purpose of the church   345-6
   and putting away the bad   370-1
   and reconciliation to God   202
   and redeeming time   391-3
   and remembering   191, 196
   and return of Christ   117

and righteousness   440-1
and servanthood   424-6
and seven 'ones'   316-20, 321-6
and sexual purity   375-82
and slavery   423-4, 426
and spiritual equipment   437-42, 443-8
and spiritual gifts   327-8, 331-2, 333-4, 338, 348
and spiritual maturity   293, 294, 295, 297, 298-9, 339-44
and spiritual resurrection   155-61
and spiritual unity   315-20, 321-6, 350
and spiritual warfare   429-35, 437-42, 443-8, 449-54
and submission   399
and symbolism of the cross   51-2, 56, 57
and teaching gifts   335-7
and technical theological terms   53-4
and transformed life   357-9
and Trinity   83, 84
and true spirituality   395-400
and 'two ways' of life   351-2
and union with Christ   13-14, 96, 117-18, 163-8, 346-7
and walking wisely   390-1
and wisdom of God   269-71
Chrysostom, John   109, 110, 372, 381, 396
Cicero   51, 196
circumcision   192
citizenship of God's kingdom   226-8, 230-1
clamor   371
Clark, G. N.   62
clericalism   337
Coleridge, Samuel Taylor   1
Colson, Charles   46
committed love   413-14
conflict   204-5, 208-9
Confucius   245
Copernicus   95
cornerstones   237

corrupt speech   361-2, 368
Cortez, Hernando   158
covenant of redemption   24
covetousness   377
Cranmer, Thomas   447-8
cravings   135, 165
cross, symbolism of   51-2, 56, 57, 244-5
Cyrus the Great   411

Daniel   92, 425, 444
darkness   386-8
David   14, 45, 92, 100, 134, 147, 148, 151, 188, 234, 331, 366-7, 380, 431, 432, 433, 440, 443, 445
Dawkins, Richard   62-3
depth of Christ's love   289
Diana   193, 376
Dickens, Charles   363, 367
discipline   420-1, 422
divine accountability   426
divine adoption   33-5
division   191-4
doctrine   307, 439-40
doctrine of election   23-8, 30-1
Doriani, Daniel   403
doubt   301-3
doxologies   301, 306
drunkenness   396-7
dunamis   111
duty   417-21

Edgar, William   95, 225, 230-1
Edison, Thomas   39
Edwards, Jonathan   77-8, 92, 393
Elijah   105, 417, 444
Elizabeth I, Queen   21
energeis   111
energeo   142
Erastus   427
Esau   24, 32, 206

Esther   92, 128-9
eternal covenant   24, 266
eternal death   135-6
Eve   59, 62, 132, 134, 148-9, 204, 205, 207, 211, 343, 402, 405, 409, 432
'evil days'   389-90, 392-3
exodus   366
expiation   54, 55, 56
Ezra   92, 235

fairness   32-3
faith
  and definitions of a Christian   11-13
  and God's plan   71-2
  in Jesus Christ   11-13, 21, 39, 71-2, 81, 94, 95-6, 179-80, 181-3, 224, 238, 285-6, 323-4, 346-7, 384, 451, 457
  salvation through   179-83, 185, 238
  and spiritual unity   323-5, 341
false spirituality   396-7
Farrar, Steve   409
'federal headship'   164
Ferguson, Sinclair   171
Finding God at Harvard (book)   225
firm foundations of the church   236-7
First Apology (Justin Martyr)   21
firstfruits   87
flesh   143-4, 165
fools/foolishness   390-1, 393-4
Ford, Henry   39
forebearance   311-12
Forsyth, P. T.   56
four vital graces   308-12
Franklin, Benjamin   39

Gadarene demoniac   360
Gaius   427-8
Gates, Bill   38
Gentiles
  alienation from God   193-4, 195, 196, 198, 199, 211, 226
  and division   192
  and mystery of Christ   253
  and peace of Christ   219
  and prisoners for Christ   243, 246
  reconciliation to God   70-1, 72, 202, 211-12, 212-13
  and 'two ways' of life   351-2
Ghandi   52
'glorious grace'   37-40, 41-2, 88, 113
Gnosticism   116
God
  access to   220-4
  and 'Amen'   306
  armor of   432-4, 435, 437-42, 443-8, 449
  and assurance of salvation   78-9
  attributes of   100-102, 294
  authority of   84
  being 'without'   194-6, 197-9, 225, 226
  blessings of   17-22, 174, 178
  boasting in   182-3
  brought near to   199-202
  calling of   108-9, 242, 257-9, 312, 388, 431-2
  children of   229-30, 383
  choosing of   23-8, 30-1
  of Christianity   150-1
  and citizenship of God's kingdom   226-8, 230-1
  committing to   179-80
  communicable attributes   294
  and divine adoption   33-5
  and doctrine of election   23-8, 30-1
  doubting   301-3
  dwelling place for   233
  and exaltation of Christ   115-16, 118, 127-8
  and faithfulness   11, 12, 94-5, 179-83, 443-5, 458
  as Father   274, 422
  fear of   221-2, 399
  feast of   144, 145
  finished work of   84
  forgiveness of   46, 166-7, 373
  fullness of   293-9
  in future ages   173-4
  gift of   177, 180-2, 458
  'glorious grace' of   37-40, 41-2, 88, 113

glory of   28, 37-40, 41-2, 68, 69-70, 88-9, 171-6, 235, 269-70, 275-6, 279, 304-6
grace of   3-4, 6-7, 32-3, 37-42, 47, 57, 71, 88-9, 159-60, 168, 174-5, 176, 177-9, 180-3, 249-51, 254, 259, 278, 328, 398, 455, 456, 457-60
grieving of   365-6
and historical nature of salvation   60-2, 63
and 'holy temple in the Lord'   233-9
and hope   108-9, 194-6
household of   226, 228-30
identity through   29, 33
image of   102, 135, 148-9, 193, 200, 204, 297, 305, 306, 331, 354, 359, 404
imitators of   369-74
incommunicable attributes   294
and indwelling of Christ   281-2, 283, 285-6
inheritance of   69-70, 85-8, 109-11
insight of   47-8
judgment of   79-80, 258, 266, 393, 394
and justice   32, 150, 178-9, 267
justification from   55, 56, 57, 358-9
knowledge of   88, 99-105, 179, 261
law of   131-2, 149, 188, 204, 213, 310, 329, 419
light of   383-8
love of   18-19, 30-1, 34-5, 38-9, 150-1, 221-2, 223-4, 267, 275-6, 292, 296, 312, 374, 415, 458-9
mercy of   32, 38-9, 150-1, 267, 275-6
and message of Christianity   148-50
and ministry of the gospel   257-63
mystery of   61, 62, 64, 65, 251-5, 265
and 'Open Theism'   101-2
peace from   3-5, 191-2, 205-9, 211-12, 216, 219-21, 224, 441-2, 457-9
plan/purpose of   67-73, 190, 249-50, 251, 268, 304, 326, 345-6, 347, 393-4
as potter   67, 72-3
power of   6, 84, 87, 111-12, 116, 158-9, 245, 259-61, 276-9, 301-4, 429
praise of   18, 37, 41-2, 88-9, 94
and prayer   92, 93-5, 96-7, 273-6, 452-4
and predestination   29-34, 67-8, 188
reality of   171

rebellion against   4-5, 366
reconciliation to   199-202, 205, 211-13, 224
and redemption in Christ   44-5, 46-8, 367
rejection of   352-3
revelation of   61, 102-3, 252-3, 254-5, 265-7, 271
riches of   109-11, 172, 174-5, 275-6, 277
sacrifices to   53, 54
and saints/sainthood   10-11
and salvation through Christ   18, 27, 41-2, 64-5, 71-2, 136-7, 168-9
seal of   75-81
seated with Christ   166-8, 169
security through   29, 33, 79
seeking   297-9
and servanthood   402
and sin   131-7, 147-51, 174, 267
sovereignty of   2, 25-6, 30-2, 61, 67-8, 72-3, 84, 121, 123-9, 150, 174, 273, 326
and spiritual resurrection   156, 157-9, 161
and spiritual unity   316-17, 319, 321-2, 323-4, 325-6
and spiritual warfare   431-4, 437-42 , 443-8, 449-54
strength from   431-2
and teaching gifts   334-5, 337-8
thankfulness to   398-9
and transformed life   358-9
and Trinity *see* Trinity
trust in   28, 179-80, 182, 338
truth of   440
and unbelief   353-4
way of salvation   6
will of   2, 29-31, 61, 62, 65, 126, 275, 393-4
wisdom of 47-8, 265-71, 345
Word of   3, 24, 87-8, 93, 97, 103-4, 105, 112, 113, 156, 157, 175, 187, 194, 242, 243, 246, 251-3, 254, 260-1, 286, 288, 290-1, 295-6, 334-6, 337-8, 343-4, 348-9, 359-60, 390-1, 394, 401-2, 446-8, 453
workmanship of   186-7, 189-90, 261
wrath of 54, 55, 57, 80, 134, 148, 149, 150, 204, 258, 267

Goliath   366, 432, 433, 443
Gomer   38, 48-9
Gould, Stephen Jay   171
Great Expectations (novel)   363, 367
grieving the Holy Spirit   363-4, 365-8
Grisham, John   86, 88

Hagar   152
Haman   128
Hannah   151
Havergal, Frances   296
heavenly places   20-1
height of Christ's love   289
'helmet of salvation'   445-6
Hendriksen, William   372, 387, 426
Henry, Matthew   311
Henry, Philip   110
Hezekiah   92
Higgins, Jack   196
Hitler, Adolf   203
Hobbes, Thomas   195
Hodge, Charles   3, 47, 63, 70, 76-7, 109, 120, 254, 343, 367, 379, 440-1, 449
Holy Spirit
    age of   84-5
    and assurance of salvation   78-9
    and blessings of God   19-20, 22
    and Christ's church   118
    distinguishing marks of   77-8
    as foretaste   86-8
    and God's plan   304
    grieving   363-4, 365-8
    as guarantee   85-6
    and 'holy temple in the Lord'   237, 238
    and indwelling of Christ   282, 283-4, 286
    and inheritance of God   69
    and judgement   79-80
    and knowledge of God   103-4
    and Pentecost   211
    and perseverance   79
    personhood of   363-4
    power of   276-7
    and power of God   111-12, 260
    and praise of God   88-9
    and redemption in Christ   367
    and revelation of God's Word   252, 254
    as seal of God   75-80
    and sovereignty of God   125-6, 127
    and spiritual gifts   329, 330
    and spiritual unity   317, 318-19, 321
    'sword' of   446-7
    and Trinity *see* Trinity
'holy temple in the Lord'   233-9
honor   418, 419
Hosea   38, 48-9
household of God   226, 228-30
Houston, Sam   191
Hughes, R. Kent   47, 87, 398, 426, 457
human responsibility   31-2
humanism   132, 193, 401
humility   25-6, 309, 310, 312, 322-3
Huxley, Aldous   354

identity/self   29, 33, 357-60, 362
idolatry   379, 380
immorality   352-3, 376, 379, 386-7
inheritance of God   69-70, 85-8, 109-11
insight   47-8
Intellectuals (book)   352, 354
Ironside, Harry   10, 40-1, 96-7, 315, 344, 453
Isaac   152
Isaiah   60, 64, 101, 109, 124, 149, 178, 224, 261, 366
Israel
    God's election of   25, 30
    and God's Law   329
    and historical nature of salvation   62
    and power of God   278, 302
    and prayer   453
    rebellion against God   366
    and remembering   191
    and revelation of God   102
    and wisdom of God   266
isxuos   111

Jackson, Brigadier General Thomas   442
Jacob   24, 32, 147, 148, 151, 205-6

James 135, 204, 285
Jeremiah 67, 76, 84, 175, 235
Jesus Christ
   and access to God 220-3, 224
   and age of Holy Spirit 84-5
   and 'Amen' 306
   and armor of God 449
   ascension of 115-17, 118, 165, 328, 329-32
   and assurance of salvation 78-9
   as 'Beloved' 40-1
   betrayal of 31
   and blessings of God 17-22
   blood of 52-3, 54-7, 145, 161, 197, 200-202, 216, 221, 222, 224, 233, 261
   calling of 108, 312-13
   church of 117-21, 214-16, 238, 304-6, 333-8, 341-2, 346-50, 401, 403-4, 405, 409, 410-14
   and citizenship of God's kingdom 230-1
   and conversion of Paul 243-4
   as 'cornerstone' 237
   'crucified with' 163, 164, 245
   crucifixion of 51-2, 56, 57, 139, 161, 202, 330, 331
   death of 12, 35, 45, 51-3, 54-6, 72, 115-16, 118, 200-202, 212, 214, 267-8, 324, 330, 331, 410-11
   deity of 323-5, 331, 341
   and divine adoption 33-5
   and doctrine of election 23-4, 25, 27
   as 'door' of church 238-9
   exaltation of 115-17, 118-22, 127-8
   exalted dignity of 115-16
   exalted dominion of 116-17
   faith in 11-13, 21, 39, 71-2, 81, 94, 95-6, 179-80, 181-3, 224, 238, 285-6, 323-4, 346-7, 384, 451, 457
   fear of 399
   feast of 145
   forgiveness of 283-4, 373
   'fullness' of 120-1
   and fullness of God 296, 297-8, 299
   and Gadarene demoniac 360
   and glory of God 172-3, 175-6
   and God's plan 70-3, 394
   and God's workmanship 187, 190
   and grace of God 6, 7, 39-41, 168, 175, 459
   and 'Great Confession' of 333
   and heavenly places 20-1
   and historical nature of salvation 60-2
   holiness of 357
   and 'holy temple in the Lord' 233, 234, 237-9
   humility of 309, 322-3
   imitating 369-70, 383
   being 'in Christ Jesus' 13-15, 23, 80, 121-2, 199
   indwelling of 281-6
   and judgment of God 80
   knowledge of 341-2
   and knowledge of God 100, 102-3, 104
   as Lamb of God 23, 35, 53
   and Last Supper 167
   and Lazarus 148, 156, 358
   light of 388
   love of 220, 284-5, 287-92, 296, 298, 350, 373-4, 383, 410-15, 459-60
   'made alive together with' 164-5
   meekness of 310-11
   and ministry of the gospel 257-63
   mystery of 251-4, 265
   and new humanity 214-17
   and Nicodemus 104, 157, 159-61
   and parable of the prodigal son 229
   and parable of the talents 250, 332
   and Paul's apostleship 1-2
   peace of 3-4, 191-2, 203, 206-9, 212-13, 214-16, 219-21, 224
   and Pentecost 211, 277, 329, 397
   plan for growth 341-2, 346
   power of 118-19
   and power of God 111, 277, 278, 279
   and prayer 92, 275, 279, 451, 452-4
   and predestination 29-30, 31
   and preeminence of church 119-20
   prisoners for 243-7
   'raised up with' 165-6
   and reconciliation to God 70-1, 72, 199-202, 205, 211-12, 224

and redeeming time   393
redemption in   43-9, 55-6, 85-6, 367, 392, 411-12
resurrection of   72, 115, 214, 324
return of   117
and revelation of God   102-3
righteousness of   440-1
sacrifice of   53, 54, 410-11
salvation through   18, 27, 42, 43-4, 64-5, 71-2, 136-7, 168-9, 214, 238, 459
and seal of God   75, 76, 77-8, 80-1
'seated with'   166-8, 169
and Sermon on the Mount   19, 227, 309, 310, 340, 347, 377, 437
and servanthood   402-3, 426
soldiers of   448
as solution to sin   136-7, 139, 143, 145, 150
and sovereignty of God   124-5, 127-8, 129
spiritual gifts of   327-30, 332, 333-4, 338, 348
and spiritual maturity   294, 295, 297, 339-44
and spiritual resurrection   156, 157-8, 159-61
and spiritual unity   316-17, 319, 320, 321-5, 326
and stewardship of God   250
supremacy to the angels   116-17
and teaching gifts   336-8
temptation of   447
and transformed life   357-9
trial of   423
and Trinity *see* Trinity
and true spirituality   395-6, 397, 400
trust in   27, 338
truth of   360-1
and 'two ways' of life   351-2
'unsearchable riches' of   261-2, 263
and wedding at Cana   144, 145
and wisdom of God   267-8, 269
being 'without'   192-6
Jews/Judaism   70-1, 72, 192, 212-13, 219, 253
Job   377, 444
John   139, 141, 159, 166, 168, 202, 276, 277, 305, 324, 340
John the Baptist   53, 76, 131, 209

Johnson, Paul   352, 354
Johnson, Terry   309
Jonah   148, 253
Jones, Peter   321, 325-6
Joseph   32, 118, 380, 425
Joseph of Arimathea   161
Joshua   116-17, 441
Judas Iscariot   2, 31
justification   55, 56, 57, 358-9

katoikeo   282
Kidner, Derek   329
kindness   372, 373, 383
King, Martin Luther   335
Knox, John   92
kratos   111
Kushner, Harold   132

Lamech   204
Last Supper   167
Lazarus   148, 156, 358
length of Christ's love   289
Lewis, C. S.   45, 69-70, 309-10, 398, 405
Life (magazine)   195
Lincoln, Abraham   128
Lincoln, Andrew   63, 109, 120
Lloyd-Jones, Martyn   2, 3, 4, 11, 26, 44, 56, 68, 109, 110, 119, 133, 148-9, 155, 156, 165, 176, 177, 190, 194, 197-8, 222, 224, 229, 244, 266, 298, 305, 317, 330, 348, 354, 365, 368, 369, 370, 391, 393, 397, 401, 406, 412, 444
'lower regions'   329
Luke   24, 48
Luther, Martin   92, 127, 252, 276, 420, 440, 444, 447
Lydia   180

MacArthur, John   135, 259, 282, 320, 341, 387, 389, 392, 409, 419, 420, 434, 440, 450, 452
Macbeth (play)   59-60
'machine view' of the church   317
Mackay, John   1
Maclaren, Alexander   289, 305-6, 369, 385, 388
Malachi   417

Subject Index

Mark 48
marriage 207, 208, 284-5, 361, 377, 378, 381, 401-7, 409-15
Martin, Hugh 18, 19, 163, 173
Martinez, Jose 195
Martyr, Justin 21
Marx, Karl 426
Mary 267, 328
Mary Magdalene 13, 102-3
Mason, Mike 378
materialism 26, 140-1, 166, 195, 374
Matheson, George 168
Matthias 2
McCullough, David 141
McDowell, General Irwin 442
meekness/gentleness 310-11, 312
message, minister's 261-2
Micah 206-7
Miles, C. Austin 167
ministry of the gospel 257-63
mission, minister's 262-3
Moore, T. V. 235
moralism 77, 364, 372
Moravians 323
Mordecai 128
Morgan, G. Campbell 67, 189, 283
Morris, Leon 4, 11, 76, 111, 140, 265, 276-7, 385, 437
Moses 25, 30, 32, 53, 62, 69, 92, 102, 147, 148, 151, 173, 191, 192, 266, 302, 303, 310, 329, 366, 453
Moule, Handley 84-5
Munger, Robert 282
Murray, John 45
music 396
'mutual servanthood' 402
'mutual submission' 402
My Heart Christ's Home (booklet) 282
Myconius, Friedrich 276
'mystery' 61, 62, 64, 65, 251-5, 265

Naaman 425
Naomi 14, 193
Napoleon 195, 289
Nebuchadnezzar 107, 309
Nederhood, Joel 415
Nee, Watchman 5, 245, 246, 438
Nehemiah 92
Nero, Emperor 21, 243
new humanity 212, 214-17
Newton, Isaac 303
Newton, John 6-7
Nicodemus 104, 157, 159-61, 268
Nietzsche 51
Noah 100, 266, 391

O'Brien, Peter 2, 109, 378
obedience/disobedience 417-20, 421, 422, 425
'one baptism' 325
'one body' 317-18
'one faith' 323-5
'one God' 325-6
'one hope' 319-20
'one Lord' 321-3
'one Spirit' 318-19
Onesimus 424
'Open Theism' 101-2
Origen 358
original sin 134, 310, 358, 375
Owen, John 150, 174

Packer, J. I. 54, 363
paganism 116, 325-6, 375-6
Palm Sunday 53
pantheism 293
parent-child relationships 417-22
passive obedience 55
Passover 53, 79-80, 441
pastor/teachers 334-5, 336
patience 311, 312
Paul (apostle)
   as apostle of Jesus Christ 1-2
   and authorship of book 2-3
   conversion of 2, 119, 237, 243-4, 259-60
   as man of prayer 91-3, 274-9
   as minister of the gospel 257-9, 262

persecution of Christians   243-4
  as prisoner for Christ   243-7
  as prisoner for gentiles   246
  sin of   172
  stewardship of   249-51
peace
  'bond of'   320, 326, 345, 349, 457
  from God   3-5, 191-2, 205-9, 211-12, 216, 219-21, 224, 441-2, 457-9
  of Jesus Christ   3-4, 191-2, 203, 206-9, 212-13, 214-16, 219-21, 224
  need for   203
  and salvation   457-8
  song of   208-9
Peale, Norman Vincent   179
Pentecost   76, 326, 329, 397
Pentecost, J. Dwight   321
perseverance, spirit of   79
personal commitment   12
Peter   11, 23, 35, 76, 79, 103, 124, 156, 201, 207, 211, 233, 252, 267, 277, 295, 324, 329, 331, 333, 334, 336, 343, 365, 397, 407
Pharaoh   152, 173, 266, 302, 310, 425
Pharisees   159
philanthropy   38
Pilate   20, 161, 423, 424
Pilgrim's Progress (allegory)   15, 75, 81, 84, 107, 443, 447, 448
Pink, Arthur   25-6, 31, 91-2, 93, 121, 163, 180
Pitt, William   354
Point Man (book)   409
pornography   135, 356, 376-7, 380, 381, 387, 445
Postman, Neil   195
Potiphar   425
power, minister's   259-61
practical change   360-2
prayer
  and access to God   223-4
  approach to   451-2
  commitment to   449-50
  encouragement to   127-8
  and faithfulness   94-5
  and knowledge of God   104-5
  lack of   273
  and love   94-6
  necessity of   93-4
  need for   125-7
  objects in   452-4
  obligation to   454
  and Paul   91-3, 274-9
  power in   450-1
  and power of God   276-7, 278-9
  reason for   124-5
  secret of   96-7
  and sovereignty of God   123-9, 273
  and spiritual warfare   449-54
  and strength from God   277-8
  and thankfulness to God   399
  why pray?   123-4, 128-9
  and wisdom of God   269-70
predestination   29-34, 67-8, 188
Prentiss, Elizabeth   291
presumption   27
pride   25-6, 309-10, 312
privileges of sonship   33-4
prodigal son   229
propitiation   54, 55, 56

Quartus   427-8

Rebecca   32
reconciliation   56, 70-1
redeeming love   411-12, 414
redeeming time   391-3
redemption in Christ   43-9, 55-6, 85-6, 367-8
remembering   191, 196
Reymond, Robert   84
Rock of Ages (hymn)   13, 46
Rockefeller, John D.   47
Roman Catholicism   10, 117, 185, 236, 325, 337
Rousseau, Jean-Jacques   352-3
Ruth   14, 193-4
Ryken, Philip   205, 224, 334-5, 422, 424
Ryle, J. C.   134

sacrifice   53, 54, 410-11
saints   10-11, 377-8

salvation
  assurance of   27-8, 78-9, 215
  bringing peace   205-6
  through Christ   18, 27, 42, 43-4, 64-5, 71-2, 136-7, 168-9, 214, 238, 459
  descriptions of   131
  and exaltation of Christ   118
  through faith   179-83, 185, 238
  and glory of God   68, 171-4
  and God's plan/purpose   71, 304, 345
  by grace   168-9, 177-9, 180-3, 455, 457
  'helmet' of   445-6
  historical nature of   60-2, 63
  and peace   457-8
  and reconciliation to God   199, 201-2
  and sin   131, 136-7, 172, 174
  and sovereignty of God   125
  and Trinity   83-4, 281
  through works   185-90
sanctification   340, 364-5, 411
Sanders, Oswald   451
Sapphira   365
Sarah   152
Satan
  banquet of   144-5
  domination of   141-3, 144-5
  and Fall of man   132, 343
  and fullness of God   295
  and Gadarene demoniac   360
  and marriage   409
  and redemption in Christ   45-6
  and spiritual gifts   330
  and spiritual warfare   429, 430-2, 433-4, 437-8, 439-40, 441, 442, 443-5
  and temptation of Christ   447
  and Tower of Babel   211
  and unbelief   354
  and wisdom of God   268-9
Saul, King   366, 433
Saulk, Jonas   39
Schaeffer, Francis   96, 225, 395, 397-8, 399
seal of God   75-81
secularism   193-5, 198, 213, 266, 401

security   29, 33
self-justification   182
self-sacrificing love   410-11, 414
Sermon on the Mount   19, 227, 309, 310, 340, 347, 377, 437
servanthood   402-3, 424-6
seven 'ones'   316-20, 321-6
sexual purity   375-82
Shakespeare, William   59-60
'shield of faith'   443-5
Sibbes, Richard   96
Silas   269, 277, 423
Simeon, Charles   311
sin
  of 'all'   133-5
  and anger   361
  and atheist critiques of Christianity   147, 148
  and conflict   204-5, 208-9
  and 'conformity with the world'   140-1
  and cravings   135
  and death   132-6, 157-9
  defining   131-2, 139
  and domination of the devil   141-3, 144-5
  and flesh   143-4
  forgiveness of   19, 46-7, 57
  and fullness of God   295, 296
  and God's blessings   178
  God's wrath against   54, 55, 57
  and grace of God   6-7
  and holy life   357, 358
  and justification   55
  life in   140-5
  and message of Christianity   148-50
  and peace from God   4-5
  and predestination   32
  and reconciliation to God   200-202
  and redemption in Christ   44-5, 46-9
  and sacrifice of Christ   54
  and salvation   43-4, 131, 136-7, 172, 174, 182
  and sexual impurity   375, 376, 377, 378-82, 386-7
  and slander   371
  and spiritual gifts   330

481

and spiritual resurrection　157-9
　　and spiritual unity　322
　　and spiritual warfare　432
　　and Tower of Babel　211
　　and tragedy　59-60, 64
　　and unbelief　354
　　and ungodly life　355-6
　　and wisdom of God　267
singing/song　398, 400
slander　371
slavery　44-5, 48, 423-8
Snodgrass, Klyne　131
Sodom and Gomorrah　380
soldiers of Christ　448
Solomon, King　92, 234, 235
Song of Roland (ballad)　449-50
Speer, Albert　46
spiritual blessings　17-22, 174
spiritual equipment　437-42, 443-8
spiritual gifts　327-30, 332, 333-8, 348
spiritual maturity　293, 294, 295-9, , 339-44
spiritual power　429
spiritual resurrection　155-61
spiritual unity　315-20, 321-6, 350
spiritual warfare　429-35, 437-42, 443-8, 449-54
Spong, John Shelby　56
Sproul, R. C.　259, 311, 323, 459
Spurgeon, Charles　100-101, 108, 109, 144-5, 180, 186, 196, 259, 260, 274, 290, 331, 334, 444
status　29
Stephen　277, 296
stewardship　249-51, 254
Storms, C. Samuel　124, 127
Stott, John　42, 51, 72-3, 109, 157-8, 262, 315, 326, 329, 327, 335, 337, 377, 412, 442
submission　399, 401-7, 421
'sword of the Spirit'　446-8
symbols/symbolism　51-2, 56, 57

tabernacle　278
Tacitus　203
talents, parable of　250, 332
Taylor, Rowland　195

teaching gifts　333-8
Temple of Jerusalem　198, 200, 234-5
ten Boom, Corrie　385, 386
Ten Commandments　188, 204, 213, 303, 310, 329, 426
tender-heartedness　372, 373, 383
Tertius　427-8
The Cross of Christ (book)　51
The Diminished God of Open Theism (book)　101-2
The Distinguishing Marks of a Work of the Spirit of God (book)　77-8
'The Holy Club'　9
The Lion, the Witch, and the Wardrobe (novel)　45
The Mystery of Marriage (book)　378
The Power of Positive Thinking (book)　179
The Return of the King (novel)　167
The Surrendered Wife (book)　404
The Testament (novel)　86, 88
The Weight of Glory (essay)　69-70
The Wizard of Oz (film)　223
Thomas　180, 221
three 'whats'　107-13
Timothy　92, 336
Tolkien, J. R. R.　167
Toplady, Augustus　46, 150, 182
'total depravity'　133
Tower of Babel　59, 204, 211, 266
Tozer, A. W.　6, 32, 178, 235, 355
tragedy　59-60, 63-5
transformed life　357-9
Trinity
　　and access to God　220-1, 222-4
　　and doctrine　439
　　and knowledge of God　103-4
　　and salvation　83-4, 281
　　and spiritual unity　317, 324, 325
　　working together of　17
True Spirituality (book)　397
true spirituality　395-400
'two ways' of life　351-2
Tychicus　455-6

unbelief   353-5
'uncircumcision'   192
ungodly life   355-6
'unity of the faith'   341
'unsearchable riches' of Christ   261-2, 263
Usher, Dr.   40-1, 42

Van Til, Cornelius   355
Vaughn, Curtis   366, 377, 384
virtues   372-3
vision   339-41, 344
Voltaire   21, 195

'walk' of Christian life   307-8
walking wisely   390-1
Wallace, Lew   33
war   4, 5, 203, 204
Ware, Bruce   101-2
Warfield, Benjamin   17-18, 111, 365
Warhol, Andy   171
Warrington, Keith   76
Watson, Thomas   110, 439
Watts, Isaac   113, 374
weaponry of warfare   443-8
Wesley, Charles   268
Wesley, John   9, 450

West, Benjamin   420
Westcott, B.F.   458
Westminster Confession of Faith   83, 171, 180, 227, 270, 371
White, James R.   83
Whitefield, George   334
Why Christianity Must Change or Die (book)   56
Whyte, Alexander   151
Wilberforce, William   335, 354
Wilde, Oscar   143-4
Wilson, Geoffrey   194, 441
wisdom   47-8, 265-71
World Parliament of Religions   321, 325
'world', conformity with   140-1, 165-6
worthy life   307-13
WWJD (What Would Jesus Do?) bracelets   369

Yancey, Philip   288
Young, E. J.   172

Zacchaeus   180, 358
Zacharias, Ravi   195, 260
Zechariah   209, 234-5
Zedekiah   107, 113
Zinzendorff, Count   129, 323

Scripture Index

Old Testament

Genesis
1:2   156
1:26   359
1:27   346, 404
2:15   402, 412-13
2:16-17   148
2:18   402, 405
2:24   413
2:25   205
3:4-5   132
3:5   432
3:8   204
3:12   205
3:15   62, 204, 212, 330
3:16   204, 405, 410
3:17   204
3:17-19   410
3:18-19   59
3:21   149
4:23   204
6:6   365-6
7:5   391
11:1, 4   211
11:7-8   326
11:9   211
12:2-3   70
12:3   253
12:17   152
15:1   108, 445
15:2   303
17:1   312
18:22   275
22:11-12   152
32:26   206
39:12   380
50:20   32, 153

Exodus
6:6-7   44
12:11   441
15:2   173
17:12   453
20:12   419
20:12-17   204
21:7-11   404
34:6   151

Leviticus
16:10   54
17:11   52
25:25-28   44

Numbers
6:24-26   205
12:3   151

Deuteronomy
4:9   191
4:20   69
6:13   447
7:7-8   25, 30
8:3   447
10:9   69
21:23   51
32:9   69

Joshua
1:7   431
10:24   117
24:2   108
24:15   31

Judges
8:35   384
2:10   102, 352, 421

Ruth
1:16   14, 193

1 Samuel
2:2   151
13:14   366
15:11   366
17:45-47   432
30:6   431

2 Samuel
7:12-13   234
11:27   367

1 Kings
8:10-11   234
19:1-4   444
19:11-12   105

2 Kings
5:2-3   425

2 Chronicles
24:16   384

Nehemiah
9:25   384

Esther
4:11   128
5:2-3   128-9

Job
2:9   444
9:21-22   444
9:25   393
13:15   446
19:25-27   446
19:27   88
31:1   377
38:7   266

Psalms
2:11   399
16:5-6   145
16:11   145
19:1   100, 172, 189
19:7-8   360
19:8   336
19:18   188
27   195
27:1   109, 383
29:11   207
32   367
33:12   109
34:14   209
41:9   31
46:4-5   227

485

Psalms (cont'd)
51:1   151
51:5   45, 134
62:2   196
68:18   329
68:20   331
73:26   153
103:12   46, 289
110:1   116
111:10   391
113:5-8   151
119:11   188
119:105   336
139:7-8   149
149:4   313

Proverbs
1:8-9   421
4:10   419
8:18   110
10:8   390
10:23   390
13:19   390
13:24   420-1
14:16   390
15:5   421
15:6   20
15:25   309
16:18   309
19:29   390
23:7   296
23:26   422
29:15   421
31:11-12   403
31:25   65

Ecclesiastes
4:12   83

Song of Songs
2:4   57
5:16   347

Isaiah
9:6-7   206
11:6   60, 62
11:6-9   39, 217, 457
11:9   64
35:8   352
40:31   109
46:9-10   25, 124
46:11   126
52:7   224, 441
53:6   149, 310
55:9   48
55:10   261
55:12   89
57:15   310
57:21   204
59:17   438
60:1   388
63:7-14   366
63:10   366
64:6   178
64:8   67

Jeremiah
6:14   4, 203
9:23-24   235
17:9   310
18:2   67
18:4   67
18:6   67
29:11   18, 68, 69
29:12   126
31:31-34   227
31:33-34   100
31:34   84
32:11   76

Ezekiel
3:12   235

9:4   80
36:26   181

Daniel
4:28-33   309
6:1   275
7:13-14   116
12:3   110, 173-4, 338, 394

Hosea
2:19   38
3:2-3   49
4:6   353

Joel
2:28-32   76

Jonah
2:9   148

Micah
5:2   206
5:4-5   206-7
6:8   427
7:8   447
7:18   151

Zechariah
2:5   235
3:1   441
3:3-4   441
3:4   81
10:12   431
11:12-13   31

Malachi
2:14   413
4:5-6   417

NEW TESTAMENT

Matthew
1:21   43, 139
3:17   13
4:4   340, 447
4:10   447
4:11   447
5:3   309
5:3-6   298
5:4   64
5:5   310
5:9   209
5:14, 16   263
5:16   175-6, 383
5:17   213
5:28   377
5:45   22
6:5-8   450
6:9   279
6:9-10   296
6:10   340
6:21   166
6:23   185, 353
6:24   166
6:25-32   19
7:8   229
7:11   229
7:13-14   351, 391
7:23   78
9:9   108, 312
10:32   80
11:27   102
11:28   168, 386
11:29   311
12:50   214
13:38   343
13:43   40, 305

13:44   175
15:3-6   418
16:15-18   324
16:16   238, 333
16:18   333
16:23   333
18:4   322
18:15   208
19:26   6
20:27-28   399
20:28   43, 45, 313, 340, 403
24:6   446
24:29-31   446
24:37   391
25:15   250
25:21   250, 338, 393
25:34   80, 110
25:35-38   346
26:24   31
26:41   451
26:53-54   267
27:43   115, 331, 423
27:46   57
27:51   200, 207
28:6   268
28:18   117
28:18-20   224
28:19   345
28:20   291

Mark
1:35   449
1:38   295, 336

1:41   372
2:5   81
4:39   208
5:5   48
7:20, 23   362
9:35   322, 403
10:14 422
11:25 275
15:18 423

Luke
1:35   267, 400
1:46-47   400
2:14   172, 206
2:78-79   209
5:10   312
5:12-13   358
6:35   372
8:26-9   48
8:30   360
8:35   48, 360
9:23   245
11:10 356, 451
11:13 112, 319
11:21-22   449
11:24-26   372
12:20 166
15:10 268
15:20-24   229
18:10-13   201
18:11, 13   275
19:8   180, 358
19:10 57, 291
19:14 180, 332
19:17 332

19:20 332
19:27 332
21:27-28   85
22:20 14
22:31-32   124
22:34 124
22:41 275
23:24 373
23:34 290
23:35 423
23:43 202
24:27 251

John
1:4   383
1:12   103, 199
1:12-13   229
1:29   53
2:5-6   186
2:10   144, 145
3:1   159
3:2   159
3:3   104, 107, 157, 159
3:6-7   157
3:8   64, 77, 161, 163
3:14-15   160
3:15   289
3:16   18, 57, 140, 177, 178, 221
3:36   22
4:7   213
4:13-14   298, 356
4:14   338
4:23   213
4:42   213
5:24   137
5:25   156

6:35, 40   298
6:37-39   25
6:38   296
6:65   25
7:37-38   396
7:38   292
8:12   261, 312, 388
8:23   329
8:24   182
8:31-32   137
8:32-33   356
8:34   45
8:36   356
8:44   432
10:9   238
10:10 395, 400
10:16 357
11:25-26   137
11:43 156, 358
12:31 142
12:36 384
13:12-14   323
13:34-35   96
14:6   12, 22, 221, 261, 360
14:15 296, 350
14:16-18   87
14:19 121
14:23 282
14:27 203, 208, 216, 457
15:5   117, 346, 385
15:8   186
15:9-10   284, 290

15:9, 12   296
15:13 284, 289, 410
15:16 25, 108
15:18-19   244
15:20 80
15:26 77
16:7   331
16:13 363
16:13-14   237
16:14 77, 283
16:33 119, 330
17:1   172
17:3   100, 261, 342
17:4   18, 24, 221
17:9   25
17:17 87, 104, 286, 336
17:23 316
18:18 20
18:36 424
18:36-37   227
19:4   423
19:30 53, 164
19:38-39   161, 163
20:17 13, 103
20:28 180
20:31 324

Acts
1:8   2, 118, 220, 237, 277, 394
1:21-22   236
1:22   2
2:7-12   211
2:13   397
2:19   329

2:23   31
2:33   329
2:42   237
2:42-46   348
2:42-47   277
4:19   404
4:29   277
4:31   279
5:3-4   363
5:41   277
6:2, 4   336
7:60   275, 296
8:3   244
9:4   244
9:13-16   259
9:16   244
12:7   110
13:48 24
14:23 337
16:25 269
16:25-26   277
16:30-31   95, 277
16:31 260
17:6   423
17:26 123, 124
19:1-6   131
19:6   76
20:4   455
20:17 337
20:27 439
20:29 439
20:30 343
26:16 237
26:16-18   249
28:31 454

Romans
1:1   258
1:16   258, 260, 355

Romans (cont'd)
1:18   204
1:18, 20-21   354
1:18-32   380
1:19-20   353
1:24-26   355-6
1:28   417
1:30   417
3:4   295-6
3:10   310
3:12   185, 200
3:20   55
3:21   55
3:23   32, 55, 132, 178, 202, 310
3:23-25   201
3:24-25   54, 55
4:4   178
4:5   147
4:16   71, 181
4:20-21   445
4:25   52
5:1   205
5:2   319
5:3   311
5:4   311
5:5   292
5:6-8   233
5:8   18, 38, 57, 150, 163, 373
5:10   52, 128, 205
5:12   132
5:20   172
6:1-2   78, 185
6:1-4   157
6:2   357
6:8-10   111-12
6:11   158
6:12-14   143, 158
6:14   167
6:23   44, 137, 182, 285, 448
7:18-19   432-3
8:1   55, 364
8:2   168
8:4   308
8:7   4
8:14   363
8:15   78
8:16-17   19, 110
8:17   69, 230, 247, 289
8:18   174
8:19   89
8:19-21   63, 64
8:26   224, 363
8:26-27   451
8:27   224
8:28   73, 101, 445
8:29   30, 294, 340
8:30   27
8:32   101, 445
8:33-35   168
8:34   163
8:37   87, 168, 291, 447
8:39   101, 118
9:10   24
9:11   24
9:11-13   32
9:14-15   32
9:16   32, 133
10:9   72
10:13   254
10:14-15   72
10:17   95, 260
11:1   70
11:29   108
11:32   41, 174
11:33   301
11:33-6   268
11:34   126
11:36   28, 37, 68, 69, 172, 174
12:1-2   235
12:2   126, 140, 176, 242, 244, 286, 295, 338, 386, 389
12:2-3   48
12:5   328
12:18   209, 216
12:21   209
13:1-7   402
13:9   62
14:17   22, 292, 299
16:20   434
16:22   427
16:22-23   427

1 Corinthians
1:18   52
1:22-24   52
1:25   47, 453
1:26   233
1:27-29   153
1:30   385
2:9   303
2:9-10   87, 153
2:12   252
2:14   104, 125, 298, 354
3:12-15   393
4:2   250
4:20   158-9
5:10   386
6:9-10   141, 396
6:9-11   379
6:15   378
6:18   380
6:20   233
7:2   381
7:2, 9   380
7:3-5   381
7:7   380
7:9   381
7:14   422
7:31   64
9:4-14   337
9:16   250, 259
10:12   433
10:13   153
10:14   380
10:31   406
11:26   52
12:13   317
12:14-17   317
13:1-3, 13   374
13:2   296
13:4-5   112
13:13   349
14:22   317, 397
15:1-2   11-12
15:1-11   324
15:3   439
15:3-4   72
15:3-6   324
15:20   87
15:32   63, 64
15:53   86
15:58   434

16:13   451
16:9   429

2 Corinthians
1:20   70
1:22   85
2:11   431
2:15   258
2:16   414
3   347
3:5   414
3:18   14, 73, 87, 112, 331
4:2   343, 453
4:4   142, 353-4
4:4-6   295
4:6   102, 165, 261, 355
4:7   153
4:8-9   446
4:16-17   446
4:16-18   22, 65
4:17   228
5:1   86
5:5   86
5:7   308
5:9   365
5:10   364, 393
5:15   163
5:17   155, 190, 214, 358
5:18-21   56, 205
5:19   200
5:19-20   224
5:20   213
5:20-21   200
5:21   41, 163

6:2 394
6:14 286, 386
8:9 38
9:8 186
10:3-5 433
10:4 260
10:5 94
11:28 92
12:8 278
12:9 80-1, 119, 158, 312
12:10 278

Galatians
1:1 2
1:4 140
1:8 324-5
2:1-10 2
2:16 324
2:19 163
2:19-20 164, 245
2:20 14, 112, 187, 281, 290, 292
3:6, 9 72
3:13 46, 163
3:23-29 212
3:24-28 212
3:27 404
3:28 427
5:6 95, 458
5:16-18 368
5:19 379
5:19-21 143
5:21 396
5:22 294, 340, 347, 349
5:23 371, 372

5:25 285, 368
6:9 426
6:9-10 392
6:14 57
6:15 192

Philippians
1:3 92
1:6 79, 190, 344
1:12-14 246
1:21 21, 155, 323, 342
1:29 245
2:3-8 309
2:4-5 112
2:8-10 331
2:10-11 88-9
2:12-13 71, 187, 285-6, 308
2:15-16 394
3:7-10 159-60
3:8 342
3:8-9 440
3:10 245
3:10-11 342
3:12-13 276
3:12-14 308
3:12 340
3:18-21 165
3:20 227
4–5 94
4:6-7 126, 208
4:7, 19 223
4:8 394
4:13 158, 190
4:19 275
4:21 453
4:22 246

Colossians
1:3-4 94
1:9 389
1:12 109
1:13-14 64-5, 384
1:15 102
1:27 187, 281, 397
2:6 180
2:13 46
2:14 46
3:1 37
3:1-2 331
3:14 320
3:15 209
3:15-16 216
3:16 216
3:20 417
3:22 425
4:8 247
4:18 454

1 Thessalonians
4:3 26, 394
5:8 438, 446
5:17 92, 450

2 Thessalonians
1:3 94-5
1:8-9 136
2:13 124

1 Timothy
1:7 397
1:10 424
1:15 262
2:5 10
3:1-13 337
4:16 442

5:6 134
5:17 337
6:1 425
6:11 380
6:15-16 301
6:16 102

2 Timothy
1:3 92
1:7 159
1:11-12 244
2:9 246
2:10 167
2:19 14
2:22 380
3:2 417
3:2-4 390
3:12 244
3:16 249, 402
3:16-17 187, 254, 336
4:1-2 336
4:6 21
4:7-8 21
4:12 455

Titus
1:5-9 337
2:14 186
3:5 26, 30
3:5-6 160
3:12 455

Hebrews
1:3 102, 115-16
2:1 390
2:14 46, 330
2:14-15 330
4:12 360, 446

4:15 372
4:15-16 127-8
6:1 293
6:19 108
7:25 221-2
8:8-12 227
8:10 69
8:10-11 200
8:12 46, 168
9:13-14 53
9:26-28 53
10:11 116
10:19-22 54-5
11:10 320
12:5-11 364
12:6 26
12:10 26
12:11 292
12:14 209
12:23 110
13:4 378
13:5-6 81
13:17 402
13:20 24

James
1:17 18
1:25 391
2:18-26 250
2:19 179
3:6 362
3:8 158
4:1-2 135, 204, 285
4:2 279, 285, 303
4:3 302
4:10 136, 179, 310
5:4 427

1 Peter
1:1   25
1:5   79
1:12   39, 267
1:16   294
1:18-19   201, 233
1:19-20   23
1:23   156, 336, 353
2:2   343
2:4-5   234
2:9   69
2:10   11
2:13-17   402
2:21-23   207
3:4   407
3:5-6   407
3:7   413
3:18   35, 73, 139
3:19-20   328
4:12   444
5:2-3   334
5:3   337
5:8   431, 451

2 Peter
1:10   25
1:20   252, 446
1:21   103

1 John
1:5   383
1:7   46, 80, 206, 260, 308, 361, 382, 447
1:8   340
1:9   54, 221
2:1   139
2:15-16   140, 166
2:17   141, 168, 228, 299, 305
2:22   324
3:2   86, 110, 340
3:8   211, 431
4:1   77
4:4   431
4:7   286
4:8   18, 151, 383
4:10-11, 19   292
4:11-12   95
4:16   291, 350
4:18   407
4:19   415
5:4   94
5:14   276

2 John
1:4   308

3 John
1:3, 4   308

Revelation
1:10   399
1:17   399
2:5   117
2:16   376
3:3   191
4:5   316
7:9-10   255, 434
7:11-12   88
7:14   434
7:15-17   435
11:15   64
12:9   432
13:8   23, 35
13:16   80
14:9-10   80
14:13   189
19:6-7   400
21:1-2   446
21:2   89, 411
21:3-4   200
21:11   40, 235-6
21:22-23   202
22:3-5   86
22:4   80
22:14   202
22:17   202

Further books of interest from

Christian Focus Publications

1, 2, 3 JOHN

A MENTOR EXPOSITORY COMMENTARY

TERRY JOHNSTON

ISBN 978-1-78191-747-3

1, 2, 3 John

A Mentor Expository Commentary

Terry L. Johnson

Terry L. Johnson takes a Christ-centred approach to the exposition of 1-3 John, the personal, pastoral, and passionate pleas from the apostle John for the church to remain united and strong in the face of persecution.

The Mentor Expository Series holds to an inerrant view of Scripture. This is a resource for pastors and Bible teachers who want to draw on Christ-centered expository teaching and for the lay reader who wants to delve more deeply into the riches of the Word of God.

> ... Terry Johnson's work on these Epistles to be one of the very best and most accurate expositions of the meaning of these letters. He is a careful exegete, knows well the original text, and the Christian tradition of interaction with it, and is especially helpful in taking us down the roots of the matter, and nowhere have I seen a more vivid pastoral application of these truths to the spiritual life, especially in light of the relativistic culture we all inhabit. I wish I had had this volume when I last preached through I John some five years ago!
>
> Douglas F. Kelly,
> Richard Jordan Professor of Theology, Reformed Theological Seminary
> Charlotte, North Carolina

Terry L. Johnson is Senior Pastor of the Independent Presbyterian Church in Savannah, Georgia.

GALATIANS

A MENTOR EXPOSITORY COMMENTARY

TERRY L. JOHNSON

ISBN 978-1-84550-689-6

Galatians

A Mentor Expository Commentary

Terry L. Johnson

'What must I do to be saved?'
This is the message that the book of Galatians seeks to answers. It tells us that there is a gospel message to preach even 2000 years on from when these words were first penned. It presents for us the truth of the gospel, unearthing the central message that righteousness can only be obtained through justification by faith. We are told in no uncertain terms that we cannot have this on our own merit. It considers the original context that there would have been questions as to what of the Jewish custom should be adopted if any as Gentiles joined the church. There were issues that could divide them but above all they needed to preach the gospel and to live lives that were bearing the fruit of God's word in them. Terry L. Johnson skilfully exposits 22 chapters which look at the theological aspect of Galatians then 18 chapters looking at the practical outworking of the letter. It contains a wealth of material for helping us to live Christian lives; to walk by the Spirit.

> Johnson clearly explains some of the most difficult passages in Scripture, stalwartly defends evangelical doctrines such "justification by faith alone.
>
> Greg Gilbert
> Senior Pastor, Third Avenue Baptist Church, Author of *What is the Gospel?*
> Louisville, Kentucky,

REVELATION
A MENTOR EXPOSITORY COMMENTARY
DOUGLAS F. KELLY

ISBN 978-1-85792-688-9

Revelation

A Mentor Expository Commentary
Douglas F. Kelly

A compelling presentation of Paul's theology enriched There is so much in the past, present and future that we do not understand. The book of Revelation helps us understand who is in full and sovereign There is so much in the past, present and future that we do not understand. The book of Revelation helps us understand who is in full and sovereign control, the victorious lamb on his throne. And what a great unveiling of the glorious saviour is revealed in this apocalyptic book! In 65 expositional chapters, Douglas Kelly draws our attention to the central theme of this profound book; the Lord Jesus Christ himself.

> Written from a semi-preterist point of view, Dr. Kelly provides both theological and pastoral insights of great consequence to John's apocalyptic vision that often puzzles its readers. Highly recommended.
>
> Derek Thomas,
> Senior Minister of Preaching and Teaching,
> First Presbyterian Church, Columbia, South Carolina

> The Church, including the Western church and the global South in the global Eastern Church, need to read the book of Revelation now more than ever. Let Douglas Kelly be your guide.
>
> Michael A. Milton,
> President and Senior Fellow at D. James Kennedy Institute for Christianity and Culture

Douglas F Kelly is the Richard Jordan Professor of Theology, Reformed Theological Seminary, Charlotte, North Carolina.

ISBN 978-1-84550-264-5

Ephesians

Encouragement and Joy in Christ

Paul Gardner

Ephesians is a letter to a church very like yours. Paul is obviously commended that this young church gets its foundations right. It is intriguing that later, when writing to Timothy, he says that there are some there promoting 'false doctrines'. The leadership was in revolt! Yet in the Revelation given to John, Jesus commends the Ephesian church that they have thrown out the false teachers and are a congregation who have staying power despite their setbacks.So a church that had been through the mill but back out the other side! What was their secret? You will find out as you explore this letter to the church, ably expounded by Paul Gardner. Paul Gardner is also the author of *1&2 Peter and Jude* (ISBN 978-1-78191-129-7) and *Revelation: Compassion and protection of Christ* (ISBN 978-1-84550-344-4) in the Focus on the Bible commentary series.

Dr. Paul Gardner was previously a lecturer in New Testament at Oak Hill Theological College in London and a Rural Dean in the Church of England. In 2005, after serving as Archdeacon of Exeter for three years, Dr. Gardner moved to the United States and now serves as the Senior Minister at Christ Church Presbyterian, Atlanta, Georgia.

ISBN 978-1-84550-684-1

Teaching Ephesians

From text to message

Simon Austen

Who are we to be in this materialistic age? Our identity, Ephesians tells us, can only be found in Christ. The spiritual blessings that we receive can only be found in him. We are chosen and raised in him. We form together to be the church in him. Ephesians paints for us a glorious picture of who we are and what the church is meant to be as we seek to teach others with these timeless truths.

"a closely argued, warmly applied letter from the heart of the Apostle to the Gentiles, reflected in Simon's careful analysis for the Bible preacher or teacher. His love of the book and understanding of its relevance for today comes through clearly in this important contribution to the Teaching the Bible series."

David Jackman & Adrian Reynolds, series editors

This useful resource, alongside the others in this growing Teaching the Bible Series, are for those who have the privilege and the joy of teaching or preaching a particular book or theme from the Bible. Whether you are a small group leader, preacher or a youth worker, it will help you to communicate the message from Ephesians. This book will provide a useful launching pad for a biblical exposition with background, structure, key points and application.

Simon Austen has degrees in Science and Theology. A previous chaplain of Stowe School, he is now Rector at St Leonard's in Exeter in England.

Christian Focus Publications

Our mission statement –

STAYING FAITHFUL

In dependence upon God we seek to impact the world through literature faithful to His infallible Word, the Bible. Our aim is to ensure that the Lord Jesus Christ is presented as the only hope to obtain forgiveness of sin, live a useful life and look forward to heaven with Him.

Our books are published in four imprints:

CHRISTIAN FOCUS

Popular works including biographies, commentaries, basic doctrine and Christian living.

CHRISTIAN HERITAGE

Books representing some of the best material from the rich heritage of the church.

MENTOR

Books written at a level suitable for Bible College and seminary students, pastors, and other serious readers. The imprint includes commentaries, doctrinal studies, examination of current issues and church history.

CF4·K

Children's books for quality Bible teaching and for all age groups: Sunday school curriculum, puzzle and activity books; personal and family devotional titles, biographies and inspirational stories – because you are never too young to know Jesus!

Christian Focus Publications Ltd,
Geanies House, Fearn, Ross-shire,
IV20 1TW, Scotland, United Kingdom.
www.christianfocus.com